Sir William MacGregor

Sir William MacGregor

R. B. JOYCE

MELBOURNE
OXFORD UNIVERSITY PRESS
LONDON   WELLINGTON   NEW YORK
1971

*Oxford University Press, Ely House, London, W.*1

GLASGOW   NEW YORK   TORONTO   MELBOURNE   WELLINGTON
CAPE TOWN   IBADAN   NAIROBI   DAR ES SALAAM   LUSAKA   ADDIS ABABA
DELHI   BOMBAY   CALCUTTA   MADRAS   KARACHI   LAHORE   DACCA
KUALA LUMPUR   SINGAPORE   HONG KONG   TOKYO

Oxford University Press, 7 Bowen Crescent, Melbourne

ⓒ *Oxford University Press*

ISBN 0 19 550367 8

Registered in Australia for transmission by post as a book
PRINTED IN AUSTRALIA BY BROWN PRIOR ANDERSON PTY LTD

Contents

		Page
INTRODUCTION		ix
1 From Croft to Colony 1846-72		1
2 Enthusiasm in the Seychelles 1872-5		12
3 Fiji: A Doctor's Dilemma 1875-88		22
4 Fiji: Finance and Frustration 1875-88		39
5 Fiji: Labour and Development 1875-88		67
6 New Guinea: The Limits of Power 1888-98		95
7 New Guinea: The Limits of Control 1888-98		120
8 New Guinea: The Nature of his Rule 1888-98		144
9 New Guinea: The Quality of his Rule 1888-98		181
10 Lagos: The Fear of Death 1899-1904		219
11 Lagos: African Rights 1899-1904		240
12 Lagos: An Independent Hinterland 1899-1904		258
13 Lagos: Progress as a Colony 1899-1904		278
14 Newfoundland: A Fossilised Colony? 1904-9		300
15 Newfoundland: Fish and the United States 1904-9		315
16 Newfoundland: External Policies 1904-9		332
17 Queensland: Limited Responsibility 1909-14		341
18 Queensland: The Problems of Education 1909-14		361
19 Retirement: 1914-19		372
NOTES		390
BIBLIOGRAPHY		450
INDEX		467

List of Illustrations

Facing page

1 Knowehead (or Knowhead), the farm of the Thomson
   family   16
   (Reproduced with permission from Mr John MacGregor, London)

2 A copy of Mary Thomson's (MacGregor's) death certificate   16
   (Reproduced with permission from the Registrar-General, Fiji)

3 A lime spatula and gourd from the Trobriand Islands
   thought to have been collected by MacGregor before
   August 1894   17
   (Reproduced with permission from the Queensland Museum)

4 Two pages from MacGregor's Diary, 21 March 1892   17
   *(Reproduced with permission from The National Library of
   Australia)*

5 Government House, Lagos   32
   *(Reproduced with permission from the Foreign and Commonwealth
   Office Library, London)*

6 Some Lagos chiefs, including in centre front Gbadebo,
   the Alake of Abeokuta   32
   *(Reproduced with permission from the Foreign and Commonwealth
   Office Library, London)*

7 MacGregor's coat of arms   33

8 MacGregor visiting the Aboriginals at Barambah,
   Queensland   370
   *(Reproduced with permission from the Foreign and Commonwealth
   Office Library, London)*

9 MacGregor with a local family in the Beenleigh area,
   Queensland   370
   *(Photograph by W. J. Stark, reproduced with permission from the
   Oxley Memorial Library, Brisbane)*

10 MacGregor in his robes as Chancellor of the University
   of Queensland   371
   *(From a painting in the Darnell Art Gallery in the University of
   Queensland, photograph by courtesy of the Photography Department, University of Queensland and reproduced with permission
   from the University of Queensland Press)*

Facing page

11 MacGregor with Bryce and Griffith   386
   *(Photograph by Lady King-Hall, reproduced with permission from
   the Oxley Memorial Library, Brisbane)*

12 Chapel-on-Leader bought by MacGregor for his retirement   387
   (Reproduced with permission from Mr John MacGregor, London)

13 The tombstone at Towie, Aberdeenshire   387

14 A detail of the inscription   387
   (Reproduced with permission from Mr John MacGregor, London)

Maps

Page

1 MacGregor's Scotland   5
2 The Seychelles and Mauritius   15
3 Fiji   69
4 New Guinea   131
5 Lagos   241
6 Newfoundland   335
7 Queensland   363

Acknowledgements

The author wishes to record his thanks to the librarians and archivists whose collections made this biography possible, and to the relatives and friends of Sir William MacGregor (whose names appear in the bibliography at page 450) for their willing co-operation. I have already personally thanked those who read the whole or parts of the manuscript. The opinions expressed are mine but the improvements my readers suggested have undoubtedly improved the text. My gratitude is also due to Miss Joyce Wood, the cartographer, and the careful staff work of the Oxford University Press whose editing has assisted considerably. For the translation of my often indecipherable scrawl I owe much to a succession of typists at the Department of History, University of Queensland. Finally my research would not have been possible without research grants from the University of Queensland, the Social Sciences Research Council of Australia and the Australian Research Grants Commission.

Introduction

William MacGregor* lived from 1846 to 1919, a period which matched the zenith of the second British Empire from the pomp of the 1851 London exhibition to the demise of rival German imperialism. His role in the assertion of the power of this mighty empire was as a doctor, an administrator and eventually as a governor. He served the British Colonial Office for forty-two years—in the Seychelles (1872-75), in Fiji (1875-88), in British New Guinea (1888-98), in Lagos (1899-1904), in Newfoundland (1904-9) and in Queensland (1909-14). These colonies typified the extent and variety of the British Empire, in that not only were they far-flung across the seas, but also their governments and peoples were at varying stages of development. Accordingly, MacGregor's role varied from that of being almost an autocrat in New Guinea to having to accept the limited power of a governor dominated by his ministers in Queensland. Further, he had to adjust to Africans who were far more conscious of political rights than the Papuans. The unifying theme of the colonial problems facing him was the imperial philosophy of rule—a philosophy which was continually developing and causing the machinery of rule to change with it. In the 1860s a dominant British attitude was to regard the colonies as 'millstones round our neck'. Gradually these same colonies became symbols of national prestige, as British rivalry increased, particularly with Germany, France and the United States of America. Within the British Empire the Colonial Conferences of 1887, 1902 and 1907 considered the possibilities of devoluting responsibility from London; and the greater part of the colonial possessions achieved dominion status soon after MacGregor's death.

The history of William MacGregor would not seem to vary so much from that of any other administrator of his period if it were not for the fact that he started life as the son of an impoverished Scottish crofter. It is a truism to say that the reasons for a man's success in life can usually be found in his family

---

* Although his name was originally spelt 'McGregor', he adopted the form 'MacGregor' while in New Guinea. The second style has been used throughout the text except in quotations which used the earlier spelling.

xi

background, or in the opportunities of his early years. In this case, however, neither of these factors applies; for the MacGregor family do not seem to have had any educational aspirations, nor do they appear to have encouraged William in his search for knowledge. So the normal opportunities to acquire a higher education must have seemed almost unattainable to this boy who expected to work for hard, long hours as a farm labourer helping to support his parents.

It is, therefore, necessary to look for fortuitous circumstances to explain the progress of the crofter's son to the position of colonial governor, and to his retirement as the owner of a splendid estate in one of the most agreeable parts of the Scottish border country. Most important among these considerations was the fact that MacGregor was born in Scotland, a country where the duty of providing means of instruction had been regarded as a national obligation since the time of the Reformation. As well between 1410 and 1583 Scotland founded four universities—St Andrews, Glasgow, Aberdeen and Edinburgh—and in 1796 another relevant to MacGregor's career, Anderson's in Glasgow. This small, poor and sparsely populated country maintained universities of a high academic standard which produced a large number of well-educated people who covered a wide social span. They were by no means, as in England, members of the aristocracy, the landed gentry or the rich merchant class. Many of them became the encumbents of parish schools and churches, with the result that the sons of farm labourers and village artisans were taught by academics of the highest calibre, who in other countries might well have held the positions of university dons. These men would in turn inspire their more intelligent pupils to study for academic careers or for the professions.

In this respect fortune again aided MacGregor, for the parish minister, the doctor and the schoolmaster all recognized his ability, and helped his progress from the parish school to the grammar school and the university. Religious instruction, an integral part of the school education, was still based on the Book of Discipline of 1560, which stipulated that it was the duty of a Christian to teach, to preach and to heal the sick, This must be taken into account when considering MacGregor's obvious sense of vocation in his medical work, notably with native people in underdeveloped countries.

His original intention seems to have been to enter the church and so he studied the classics, both at school and for one year at

Aberdeen University. These studies no doubt contributed to his ability to write in his own language with a clarity that makes his dispatches and private papers of great value to the historian. Although most of his diaries and many of his letters have not been located, those that remain make clear that his ambition to succeed in his colonial career, which he had begun almost by chance, had been influenced by his early struggles against poverty. Also the democratic nature of the Scottish education system had left its mark in so far as he expected to judge men by their efforts rather than by their social standing. He should himself be judged against this background which helps to explain his constant insecurity and touchiness towards the Colonial Office composed chiefly of members of the English establishment who did not, in MacGregor's view, accept him for his worth or fully appreciate him for his ability as a doctor and an administrator. MacGregor never fully mastered the idea that he was an outsider amidst an *élite*, despite his long and close friendship with Arthur Gordon, who became Lord Stanmore, and he seems to have exaggerated his sharing of confidences with Edward VII and George V, nominal heads of the English establishment, his accounts carrying a flavour of self-enhancement.

MacGregor was always geographically remote from Whitehall yet he was entirely dependent for the acceptance of his plans on the interests of British politicians and on the decisions reached within the Colonial Office. Even when he and his own local officials were in full accord, the opinions of the successive colonial secretaries at Whitehall had to be taken into account, as well as those of prime ministers and foreign secretaries. His was also the problem of the interrelation between all his masters, and the general tenor of the British electors, whose opinions on colonial matters varied greatly over the years. It is difficult to assess, within the scope of a biography of MacGregor, his individual responsibility for the policies that were adopted. A full-scale history of British foreign and colonial policy would, in fact, be needed to appreciate the changing support given from London to his endeavours as a governor.

MacGregor was to become increasingly critical of the growth of an aggressive imperial ethos. Yet he remained in the colonial service. His ambition and his constant search for financial security partly explain his persistence. More positively, the strongest motivation came from his personal support of a philosophy of peaceful rule. Like other servants of the second Empire, he persisted in his humanitarian concern for the people and problems of the colonies he governed.

In several ways MacGregor seems in retrospect to have been ahead of many of his contemporaries, notably in his scientific approach to problems and his understanding of native people, whose languages he learned so that he could communicate with them. He had a genuine rapport with people of most other races (but not with the Indians in Fiji), which was certainly out of tune with the xenophobic tendencies of his era. This rapport was demonstrated in the genuine friendship accorded him by the African chiefs of Lagos, and by his own statement that while talking to a black man he was never aware of the difference in colour. This was a more modern approach than that of the Colonial Office at the turn of the century, which was that the governor must maintain British prestige and so should not treat the chiefs as his friends, but rather as inferiors. There are many other instances of the compatibility of MacGregor's ideas with modern thinking. Two cases could be mentioned in particular. The first, his anger when he heard that the Esquimaux of Labrador were being put on show in Chicago as a curiosity; the second, his horror at the squalor in which the Aboriginals were living in government establishments in Queensland.

He won his greatest tribute as 'a model of what a Colonial Governor should be' from his diplomatic handling of the Newfoundland fishing dispute. His most important contributions, however, were during the twenty-three years that he served in Fiji and New Guinea, where many of his policies were to have far-reaching effects. He was certainly in the vanguard in Fiji when he planned the training of native medical assistants and founded the Central Medical School at Suva. As Receiver-General (Treasurer) he suggested to the Colonial Office that the Government should set up a Savings Bank for the Fijians, which would be backed by the Government in the event of Fijian securities being inadequate. In the *laissez-faire* society of the day this suggestion greatly shocked the Colonial Office. Referring to this Bank, MacGregor's remark that 'The Government is already in debt, and probably will remain so for all time, like other civilized governments', caused many eyebrows to rise that now would remain unmoved. More importantly he tried to keep faith with Gordon's attempts to protect the Fijians, although aware of increasing difficulties and the need for constant review of all policies, especially the controversial taxation scheme.

For ten years MacGregor administered New Guinea, and during that time he had only sixty-four officers to help him to introduce British civilization to a million people spread over a vast and mountainous terrain. The fact that he attempted it on foot, by canoe and by launch shows the man's dogged determination; the fact that he achieved anything is little short of a miracle. But in spite of the commendation of the Colonial Office, he derived little satisfaction from his time in New Guinea. He feared that he might be transplanting too much of British culture too rapidly, and that he might be opening the country for the benefit of the 'sons of English gentlemen'. Eventually he came to prefer Australian to British control of the Papuans. No matter which country was in control he still sincerely believed that the government should 'never spoil a native tribe to make way for any other person'. Yet MacGregor had become increasingly aware of the dilemma of developing countries especially from his years in Lagos, where he had clashed with the educated Africans. He must have perceived that there could be no happy conclusions to the problems raised by colonial rule.

MacGregor was disappointed, too, in his personal life. He found few who shared the variety of his interests in medicine, sciences and the classics. Most of his friendships had to be maintained by letters rather than by personal contact. After Gordon left Fiji he rarely saw him, nor did he spend much time with Sir Charles Mackellar, with whom he had studied medicine at Glasgow University. He spent a little more time with Sir Samuel Griffith, the Queensland parliamentarian and Italian scholar who became Chief Justice of Australia; but was infrequently with his other close friends, Ronald Ross, famed for his malarial research, Fenwick Reeve, a fellow civil servant in Fiji, and John Marnoch, the Professor of Surgery at Aberdeen University. For MacGregor's biographer most of these friendships are evanescent, for almost all his letters except for those to Gordon and Griffith have vanished.

His friends seem to have held him in the highest regard, but he could find solace only in their letters and he remained a lonely man. His seclusion as a 'hermit' in Fiji, his escape to Greek classics from the everyday reality of New Guinea, his studious reserve in Queensland, his retreat to books in his retirement in Scotland—all reflect his sense of insecurity which was more basic than his external reputation as a man of action, as the energetic doctor in Fijian campaigns, the curious traveller among the

Esquimaux of Labrador, the tireless climber of mountains in New Guinea, or the probing wanderer in Queensland. Yet in his actions he was often seeking self-aggrandizement, conquering the Owen Stanley Range or going hundreds of miles up the Fly River to surpass earlier explorers.

The same ambivalence was discernible in his appearance. His penetrating eyes and his heavy frame—he weighed sixteen and a half stone in his prime—suggested a sense of power which led one subordinate to compare him with Napoleon and a friend to call him 'a great block of rough, unhewn granite'. Yet this impression was belied by his soft voice, which was difficult to hear even in a normal-sized room, and by his characteristic reticence.

His family life was not one to lift him out of his insecurity or depression. As was so often the case with colonial administrators, he was forced to suffer long separations. These separations allied with his insecure obstinacy caused a complete rift between MacGregor and the children of his first wife, who had died in Fiji. He had some family life in the kinder climates of his later appointments, but the year before he died he was cruelly hurt by the death of his favourite daughter by his second marriage.

His opinionated stubbornness often led him to resent criticism. He had many clashes with his colleagues and subordinates in the colonial service. His lack of trust in the officers under him in Fiji caused him to exclaim 'I certainly do drive about the weakest team ever harnessed to the colonial coach'. A combination of remarks like this and evidence of ill-considered judgements led Joseph Chamberlain, the Colonial Secretary, to write, 'I suppose Sir William MacGregor, with all his good points, is a bad manager of men'.

In his letters there are many comments that reveal the embittered, frustrated man that MacGregor often was—the man who constantly felt that he had been overlooked for promotion, that his salary was inadequate or that he had been unfairly treated by the Colonial Office in some other way. But this mood was brought on, too, by bigger issues than self-aggrandizement for this was a man in a frenzy of concern about so many things. He knew what might be achieved in the colonies where he served, but he was constantly thwarted by the difficulties of colonial rule and the lack of means at his disposal to carry out his plans. The legacies of his rule, however, despite the pervading mood of despair in his life, save his history from being dominantly tragic.

I

From Croft to Colony 1846-72

He could not afford to hand it [a thesis] in like the rest, bound with
green ribbon and written on superfine paper.

The chances that the son of a poor Scottish farm labourer will
become a governor must still be remote. The odds against were
far greater in the middle of the nineteenth century, when there
was little social fluidity in the United Kingdom; when the prejudices of Englishmen generally against Scotsmen were so strong;
and when opportunities for education were so limited. Yet
William MacGregor, born on 20 October 1846, the eldest son of
a poor Scottish crofter, did become a colonial governor before
the end of the century. A study of his life needs to show how far
the attainment of this office was due to his ambition directed
towards a colonial career, how far a result of other factors over
which he could have no control, as well as how far chance influenced his actions.

There seems little at first sight in the history of his close relatives to suggest any driving ambition or complete dissatisfaction
with Scottish life. The influence of the MacGregor clan history,
however, with its examples of restless ambition and strong pride,
cannot be entirely disregarded. William was intensely proud of
this background, mythical or not.[1] He wore the MacGregor kilt,
adopted their motto of 'E'en do and spair nocht' when he took
out arms, and developed a lively curiosity about his predecessors.[2]

Yet it needed more than clan inheritance for William to become a governor. His father, John, as much a MacGregor as
William, was never able to escape from a life of labour, whether
breaking stones on the roads, or working as a crofter or farm
labourer. There are hints that he resented William's efforts to
leave this kind of existence. It is alleged, for example, that he tried
to squander the money that William had acquired for his education.[3] William inherited his father's stubbornness and his strong

1

identification with Donside—which must have acted against his leaving Scotland.

Furthermore, the known facts of his mother's life seem unlikely to have aroused ambition in William. Agnes Smith was working as an agricultural labourer on a farm by the age of eighteen, married John MacGregor about the age of twenty, bore his nine children during the next twenty-one years and brought them all up in abject poverty—though well-grounded in a knowledge of the Bible.[4]

His brothers and sisters appear to have remained satisfied with their achievements in Scotland. Indeed, when William later lent some of them money to start afresh in America they proved unsuccessful as emigrants. Their failure and return to Scotland suggests that they shared William's patriotism—and his pride, in so far as they resented his patronizing interference with their lives. He may have aroused the same reaction when he sent money for the education of some of his nephews and nieces.[5] Nevertheless, even if William had lacked ambition and had been influenced by the acceptance of this existence by his relatives, the extreme poverty of his life in Scotland may have been sufficient to arouse his desire for a change.

William spent his first twenty-two years in the Donside area working mainly as an agricultural labourer. So restricted were his horizons that not until he was sixteen was he to travel the forty miles to Aberdeen.[6] The lot of a poor agricultural labourer in Scotland was by most standards pitiable. Although there had been an agricultural 'revolution' in Scotland from about 1760, which made the description 'deplorably primitive' no longer applicable to Scottish agriculture as a whole, at the bottom levels methods were still archaic, living conditions poor and monetary returns abysmal.[7]

The known facts about the life of the MacGregors illustrate the continuing poverty of agricultural workers in Scotland. John MacGregor's frequent changes from one job and home to another,[8] the low standard of all of these and his acceptance of poor relief all reflect economic instability. He is usually described as a 'crofter', a term derived from the word 'croft', which could be used to describe both a habitation and a holding. The habitation was usually of stone, generally of only one or two rooms with no flooring and possibly a gap for a window, and this thatch-roofed dwelling was often shared with the family's livestock. One of the MacGregor crofts, Claverhouse, was classified in the 1861 census as having 'two rooms with one or more windows'. While there John kept a cow, grew turnips, corn and potatoes for his farm, as well as assisting on the farm on which the croft stood and labouring on other farms.

The MacGregors' constant moving reflects the instability and insecurity of John's occupations—or even lack of employment, as parochial records for poor relief indicate. John's name was only removed from the roll of paupers in 1869, when he was fifty-four, as his children were then considered old enough to support him.[9] But he often accepted money from William from 1873 until his death in 1890.

Obviously John's children had to work from an early age. In every census the children up to the age of eight were registered as being home as 'scholars' but most went to work soon after. Ann, the first-born, at the age of eighteen was a 'mill-worker'; William was a 'servant cattleman' on a farm at Knowhead by the age of fourteen; Catherine was registered as a 'domestic servant' at fifteen, and George, fourteen, and John, twelve, worked as farm hands away from home, suffering the long hours and hard physical work which this job entailed.

Perhaps the early age of commencing work would seem adequate to prevent ambition arising in any member of the Mac-Gregor family. On the other hand, some in the same position as the MacGregors retained hopes for a less impoverished life and there was a high rate of assisted emigration from Scotland in this period. It is always necessary to distinguish between lack of ambition and lack of opportunity and there is no objective way of proving the point made by one of William's nieces that her father 'could have got further if he'd had the education'.[10] William's background of poverty, instability and insecurity, however, was probably very important in fostering in him an ambition to escape from his environment. He also made the most of his limited opportunities.

Outside factors were important in nurturing William's early promise, particularly the influence of the Church of Scotland with its emphasis on education, and, in comparison with England, the less rigid class barriers of Scotland. The Church of Scotland's prestige was reinforced by its social activities and by the fact that most schools were run by it or by clerical institutions. In Aberdeenshire, where in 1875 a Royal Commission found that eight-five per cent of the teachers held Masters of Arts degrees, there was a tradition of young graduates, often waiting a call to a parish, beginning their careers in small schools. The enthusiasm of these clerical schoolmasters was reflected in the encouragement they gave to any child, regardless of his family's financial position, to make the most of his intellect.

In William's case, the influence of the church was first represented by the Reverend John Watt of Towie parish church. An M.A. from Aberdeen University,[11] his concern in education was typical of those Scottish clerics. He was deeply impressed by William's talents and aroused his desire for wider knowledge in studying the Bible, Homer and Livy, and encouraging further work both in the classics and mathematics. After William's departure from Scotland in 1873 their relationship developed into a personal friendship which endured till Watt's death fifteen years later.

One of William's teachers, James Kennedy, also recognized his potential,[12] as did the local doctor, Robb, who helped to awaken William's interest in medicine and scientific subjects and like Watt became a personal friend.[13] It is clear that William was fortunate that his talents were recognized early in his life by these men representing Church, School and Science. Their influence developed his promise by fostering in him a habit of study which lasted throughout his life.

Yet this did not necessarily mean that William would be able to use his learning to change his social class. An English farm labourer at that time could have had little chance of education or of being accepted as an equal even by the middle class, let alone have had any hope of attaining the position of colonial governor, which seemed reserved for a favoured few chosen from the ranks of a narrow group in the upper classes. In Scotland, however, class divisions were less rigid (influenced by the more democratic nature of the Scottish church and other Scottish institutions) and considerable changes of class position were possible. Moreover, there was little prejudice about a man because of his social upbringing. For example, although there were some instances of inverse snobbery towards William by some of his relatives, William was never ashamed of his relatives (though understandably they had little in common), tried to help them and sincerely wished to return to Donside and finally to be buried there.

William's early Donside years left clear marks on his character, helping to shape his contempt for any sign of laziness, his endurance of harsh conditions, his distaste for frivolities and his

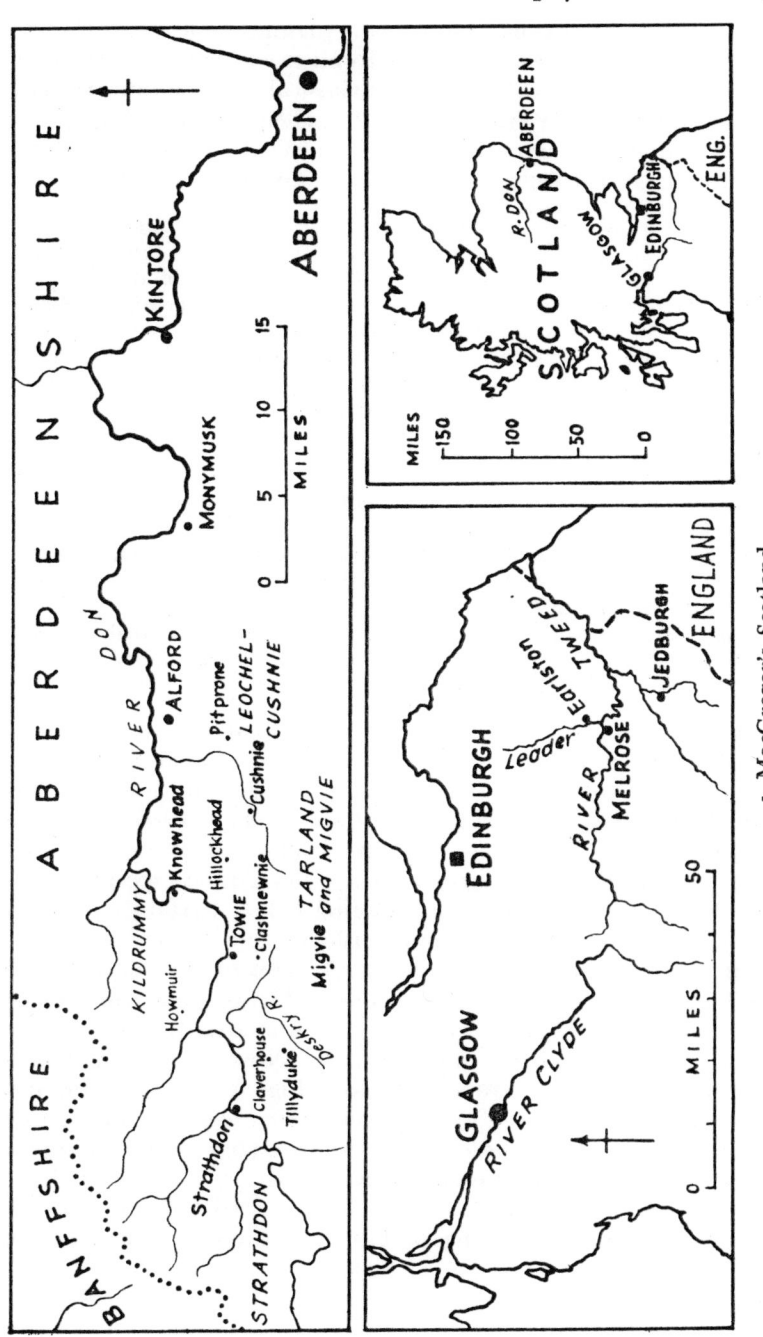

1 MacGregor's Scotland

dedication to hard work and logically planned endeavour. He had worked with Watt, Kennedy and Robb from his tenth year, dabbled in various areas of study, both classical and scientific, worked under difficulties in croft and field, and apparently throughout faced his father's opposition. He had acted as assistant school teacher at Tillyduke[14] and a contemporary of his wrote:

> . . . he showed a great thirst for knowledge, and found time to carry on studies, in which, by his perseverance, he made considerable progress. . . . It is related that a respected farmer in the Alford district, in engaging him for farm labour, asked a relative . . . what sort of lad he was, and received for answer that he was a good worker, and would give no trouble if he had his books. A considerable library of the higher school-book type was brought to the farm, its contents being devoured when working hours were over.[15]

Another anecdote records that

> . . . on one occasion an eminent botanist came to the district to work through it, and, happening to see the lad, asked casually if he could tell him anything of certain plants. To his amazement the youngster reeled off the botany of the place like a book. In the evening he told his friends of the astonishing discovery, only to find they were amused. They knew their McGregor, and tried to get off a joke upon the botanist by telling him that all the lads thereabout were similarly equipped.[16]

William was nineteen and much older than most of his fellow students when he first went to Aberdeen Grammar School. His choice of Aberdeen Grammar must have been influenced by his friends and it is probable that Watt and Robb assisted him financially. He later claimed to have 'paid for his education entirely out of his earnings as a farm servant'[17] but this was special pleading for an advance from the Colonial Office. Certainly no help could have come from his impoverished father, who was on poor relief for most of these years and who seems to have understandably resented the aid given to William. He was first admitted to the school on 17 April 1866, at least a term after the bulk of the class, which had been enrolled on 7 November 1865. On 8 August 1866 he was transferred to a higher class but did not enrol for the next year until 9 April 1867, whereas the normal date for the rest of the class was 6 November 1866.[18] Thus in both school years he missed the winter terms, during which he worked on various farms. Presumably his need for money necessitated his working during part of the school year and as the school examinations were held in summer, he chose to work on farms in the winter.

He proved a good scholar whose results justified his mentors' faith in him. After doing well in the school grading test[19] he was immediately enrolled in the fourth class and consistently won prizes in Latin and Greek.[20] His reputation at school was that of a 'grinder' who gained his results mainly by the amount of work he did. He would work till after midnight and be awakened by his landlady's son before 6 a.m.[21] This is partly an undeserved reputation, since he must have missed so much in his months away from school and he was hardly likely to waste his time in secondary school, reached at so late an age and after so much effort. Yet 'grinding' was to prove characteristic of his thorough approach to most subjects.

His results in the 1867 Aberdeen University Bursary examination[22] (in which he came second) brought him £20 a year and entry to Aberdeen University and in October 1867 he enrolled as an Arts student in English, Latin and Greek, apparently intending to follow Watt's example and join the Church. He had a great and constant interest in these subjects and later, after he had begun Medicine at the University of Glasgow, this student of science was found to be just as good at Greek. A fellow student remarked that:

> He would sit at the head of the table of the students' symposium, and while the rest were laughing or drinking or arguing, he would recite Homer in the original 'by the yard'.[23]

In later life he retained enough Greek and Latin to read the classics and to write part of his diary in these languages.

Nevertheless, this first university year was to prove almost fatal for all his plans. In the annual examinations he failed in English, came sixteenth of twenty-seven in Latin and twenty-fifth of thirty-two in Greek.[24] A familiar cause, a woman in his life, seems the simple explanation of his poor results. When the university session ended in April 1868 William returned to Donside to work on a farm and about the same time Mary Thomson, the daughter of a farmer for whom William had once worked, became pregnant. William accepted the responsibility, married Mary,[25] and in October gave up his plans for a clerical career and enrolled for Medicine. The marriage, perhaps partly because of its enforced beginning, was not happy.

A Scottish medical course at the end of the 1860s had an extremely high reputation and part of MacGregor's success in his colonial career can be attributed to his training as a doctor in Scotland. Like many other Scottish students he was trained in more than one school: Anderson's University in Glasgow,[26] at which he began mainly because its fees were much lower than those of any other United Kingdom university; Glasgow University,[27] which he attended for part of his second and all his third year; and Aberdeen University,[28] where he completed his fourth academic year.[29] Much of the reputation of these Scottish schools depended on their receptiveness to new ideas and techniques. He was fortunate also in that parliament was concerned in improving medical education.[30]

William gained his Degree of Medicine in less than four years and achieved far better results[31] throughout his course than he had previously—perhaps because of his more settled life now that he was married and perhaps because studying Medicine suited his talents better than studying languages, despite his grammar school results and his professed interests. He achieved these results in Medicine despite—and perhaps because of—considerable poverty. A fellow student recorded years later that:

> his purchase of a microscope in those days is reminiscent of Charles Lamb's self-denial to buy a much desired volume of old plays, foregoing much needed meals and leisure to obtain the prize, and spending anxious moments day by day going backward and forward to see whether it was still available at the second-hand shop.[32]

Another anecdote also makes the point that his lecturers had no prejudice against poverty:

> he could not afford to hand it [a thesis] in like the rest, bound with green ribbon and written on superfine paper. 'Is it an exhibition of calligraphy?' he asked indignantly, when remonstrated with by the other students. Whether or no, the thesis was so good that it obtained the gold medal at Glasgow.[33]

Two of his professors later gave him fine references based on the result of his four years' work. Even when they are assessed with all necessary caution they are indicative of William's success as a student. One of them, Professor Macrobin, the Professor of Medicine and Dean of the Medical Faculty at Aberdeen University, wrote:

> It affords me much pleasure to express the high opinion I entertain of the professional qualities of Dr William McGregor, a graduate of this University. Dr McGregor has had a very complete medical education, is possessed of excellent talents, and has had unusually good opportunities of acquiring a practical acquaintance with the

various departments of the profession.[34] He has shown much devotion and skill in the pursuit of pathology and morbid anatomy—in proof of which I may mention that for his Thesis . . . which consisted of a valuable and extensive series of microscopical preparations illustrative of a variety of Diseases—he received a high mark of commendation from the Medical Faculty and University Examiners.[35] I feel assured that Dr McGregor is, in an especial manner qualified . . . by reason of his professional acquirements—his natural abilities—and his great industry, and devotion to scientific research.[36]

Perhaps the greatest tribute to his education was that throughout his life William retained an insatiable interest in research and a scientific inquiring approach to all questions.

William had thus successfully faced the challenge of academic training and justified the trust and money of his supporters. He was duly registered under the 1858 Act on 9 May 1872 with the qualifications of a Licentiate of the Faculty of Physicians and Surgeons of Glasgow (L.F.P.S.), Licentiate of the Royal College of Physicians of Edinburgh (L.R.C.P.) and a Bachelor of Medicine of the University of Aberdeen (M.B.).[37]

At the age of twenty-six William was employed as a medical assistant at the Royal Lunatic Asylum, Aberdeen. He was married, with one son, and was earning £40 a year. The horizons of Donside had been replaced by interests in scientific research and in medical practice. The evidence shows him as a successful and conscientious student and one likely to succeed as a doctor.

There is no indication that at graduation he contemplated a career in the colonies. The only stimuli would have been, first, the numbers of overseas students reading Medicine in the Scottish universities he attended, and secondly, the number of doctors like David Livingstone[38] who had gone from Scotland to the colonies. Yet before the end of 1872 MacGregor had accepted a post as an assistant medical officer in the Seychelles. The reason for his decision can be partly attributed to his ambition—always to be significant in his career—with all its concomitant factors, varying from adventurousness or restlessness and youthful dreams, to the need for more money to support his wife and son. There is no indication at this stage of any 'indoctrination with Britain's imperial mission'.[39]

It was chance that took him to the Seychelles. The governor there, Sir Arthur Gordon, another Scot from Aberdeen, had found in the previous year, 1871, an urgent need for a doctor who would also be expected to act as a magistrate 'in trifling cases'.[40] When the Colonial Office was slow in acting on his despatch, Gordon, with a rather typical disregard for the formal procedure for applicants laid down by the Colonial Office, wrote to a schoolmaster friend of his asking him to find a suitable doctor. Finally Professor Dickie of Aberdeen University was contacted and he recommended MacGregor—

> ... the only man known to me at present likely to fulfil expectations in the Seychelles—if considered qualified he is prepared to go at once. He is able bodied and energetic, and willing to make himself useful in science, his professional qualifications being also excellent.[41]

It is likely that when MacGregor graduated in 1872 he spoke or wrote to Professor Dickie asking generally about jobs, but there is no evidence that he was seeking a position in the colonies: medicine and scientific research were his prime interests.

It was to be claimed that MacGregor wanted to go to the colonies because he suffered from 'chest weakness',[42] but this is unlikely considering Dickie's reference and his later active life, although one might expect weariness immediately after his exhaustive medical course, his long hours, his poor diet (mainly oatmeal) and living quarters.[43]

The limited opportunities in Aberdeen for an ambitious young doctor, combined with his low salary, seem sufficient to explain his desire for any other position offering more opportunities and better pay. In any case his dealings with the Colonial Officer before he decided to accept the Seychelles post offered at £250 a year, fully dispel any idea of a strong keenness to go to the colonies, let alone any feeling of accepting a colonial mission. The emphasis was on the possibilities of salary increases and paid private practice, whether he was to have sufficient extra money for scientific research and whether medicines were to be supplied, rather than he himself having to 'expend the half of his salary on medicines'. His final acceptance of the position he made conditional on his being supplied with all medicines by the government and his wife's fare to the Seychelles being paid. He also requested and obtained an advance of three months' salary to pay for 'a good microscope, a small dredging apparatus, and some other instruments requisite for scientific pursuits'.[44]

The evidence thus suggests that MacGregor began his life in the colonies cautiously, that he went out mainly as a doctor with an added interest in general scientific research and that he was keenly aware in the best Scottish tradition—in his case reflecting his poverty-ridden background—of the importance of money.

Whether MacGregor was in any way typical of others joining the Colonial Service is a far more difficult question to answer. A review of the outlines of the careers of all colonial governors of the period in fact indicates that when MacGregor attained that level he was in various ways unique. There was no other crofter's son or the equivalent who became a governor, nor indeed in Mac-Gregor's lifetime did any other doctor.

In 1870 the Secretary of State for the Colonies, Kimberley, had agreed with an inter-office minute which claimed that

> to obtain . . . [a colonial] appointment it is necessary to be known to the Secretary of State, or to someone of position, or to furnish such testimonials as will show the applicant to be fit for the post sought.[45]

and the Minute certainly carried the suggestion that the first two were more important qualifications than the third. 'Fitness for the post' did include ability and some physical and psychological aptitude, but it was a long time after MacGregor's appointment in 1872, not indeed until near the end of the century, that there were set forms for all applicants and forms for references and testimonials which seemed to give equal weight to both education and experience. Indeed for most colonial appointments throughout MacGregor's colonial career either knowing the Secretary of State, or someone else influential, was more important than fitness for the job.[46]

Nevertheless, MacGregor's career in some ways counters his own charge that talent was disregarded. Without privilege of birth this impoverished doctor with no colonial mission was to rise to the position of governor, to receive the usual series of colonial honours and to retire a wealthy man. An analysis of his career provides a judgement on the Colonial Office. How far does his career provide an example of the Colonial Office recognizing the value of good administration? How far does his career show the role of conservative English prejudices in favour of breeding and patronage, in keeping this obscure Scot from ever attaining the top level of administrators?

By 1872 MacGregor had come a long way from the croft. With hard work, assistance from friends and an environment permitting opportunity for talent, he had qualified as a doctor. It remained to be seen whether he could continue to rise in his new life which, almost by chance, was then to begin in the colonies.

2

Enthusiasm in The Seychelles 1873-75

An unshakeable determination that their responsibilities extended to primitive peoples.

What were the thoughts of this young Scottish doctor as he left his home country? He must have been conscious of his inexperience, for he had practised for only a few months after graduation; he was insecure, for in speech and manner he was still the agricultural worker whose acquired professional status had yet to be accepted; he was ambitious, for having come so far in the last crowded seven years he had realized where hard work might lead him. Furthermore, he was probably not particularly happy, for his relationship with his wife was not mentally satisfying and their son—then almost four—had had to be left in Scotland with so much else. He was certainly not about to embark on a career for which he had planned.

In his four years in the Seychelles and Mauritius, MacGregor was never to attain a position where he had much influence in policy decisions. He was, however, to become involved in many of the problems of these islands, particularly in his capacity as assistant medical officer. He accepted other administrative responsibilities which involved a measure of decision-making, for example, as an Inspector of Schools and Liberated Africans and as a Sub-Collector of Dues and Taxes. Besides these administrative responsibilities he became a friend of the governor, Gordon, whose policies and attitudes, including a decision to leave Mauritius for Fiji, proved to be important factors in shaping MacGregor's approach to colonial administration, both in the Seychelles and elsewhere.

Mauritius[1] had become a British colony in 1810, when it was acquired from the French. Its main produce was sugar, grown on plantations whose wealthy owners (mainly French) tried to dominate political as well as economic power. They had acquired a

12

majority on the Legislative Council, where it became clear that their opposition to British colonial rule involved both their national and personal pride. Gordon, in his years there, tried to increase the power of the governor and consequently of British colonial rule. He found planter and French feeling so strong that in an 1871 letter to Gladstone he suggested exchanging Mauritius for some of the French possessions in India[2] and a year later to a friend admitted his personal dislike of the planters: 'I don't like the people—that is, the swells . . . they don't like me, for they resent my efforts to improve the condition of the coolies'.[3]

The system of sending indentured Indian labour to Mauritius had begun soon after the abolition of slavery in the British Empire in 1833. Gordon was in favour of Indian labour because of the prosperity it brought to the colonies, but he attacked the shocking abuses of the system, which he hoped to reform so as to protect the interests of the Indian labourers.[4] A Royal Commission in 1872-73, set up at his instigation, did lead to important reforms. MacGregor was to share Gordon's criticisms of the French planters and to support his efforts to improve the lot of the Indian and African labourers, probably his most important work of this period.

Besides Gordon's disputes with the French planters, especially over the labour question, he was dissatisfied with the quality of the British administration, which he found inefficient due to a 'ludicrously excessive number of useless officials'.[5] Generally his experience in Mauritius helped to make him 'more and more convinced that the present system of colonial appointments is radically wrong'.[6] His criticisms extended to previous governors; to Colonial Office control; and to government finances, which he tried to improve by reforming the taxation system, in which the planters were undertaxed and the lower classes overtaxed. It is significant that 1,215 Indians and Creoles wanted to follow him to Fiji. At a lower level of administration MacGregor also experienced examples of inefficiency, and he inherited Gordon's general criticism of British administration.

Even if eventually achieving some success, Gordon was never happy in Mauritius, complaining almost from the day he reached the island. It was a dismal colony, pervaded by malaria (40,000 of a population of some 300,000 had died in the 1867 epidemic), and regarded as so unhealthy that the tradition of officers from India taking holidays in Mauritius to recuperate had broken down. During his short time in Mauritius MacGregor was concerned with its health problems, but he does not seem to have developed enough affection for the island to remain to solve them.

Gordon's reaction to the Seychelles group of islands was different. He found these islands,[7] separated by over a thousand miles of Indian Ocean from their parent colony of Mauritius, far healthier than Mauritius, and their problems less trying; indeed, he found it 'rather interesting work, the organization of these pretty and now very progressive little islands'.[8] MacGregor had been appointed to the Seychelles and spent most of his time in these remote but attractive and thriving islands.

One particularly important problem of the Seychelles concerned the supply and treatment of labourers for its plantations. The few administrative officers and planters (mainly French) were vastly outnumbered by African residents, who made up over ninety per cent of the 1871 population of about 11,000. These Africans were either working on the plantations, usually serving five-year indentures, or were ex-labourers who had occupied small areas of land. Some of these Africans were descendents of the slaves of the French. Others had been captured from Arab slave dhows and 'liberated by the Court at Zanzibar'.[9]

Shortly before Gordon arrived, the importation of Africans had been suspended and the planters, wanting more cheap labour, asked him to recommence this traffic. The Colonial Office, probably after pressure from humanitarians in Britain, asked for information

> as to the ability and willingness of these islands to provide for the maintenance and treatment of such among the Africans so introduced as might fall sick or become destitute from inability to work.[10]

Thus Gordon approved a sanitary rate which would enable hospital accommodation and treatment to be provided for both African workers and the other Seychelles residents and, after a visit to the Seychelles, he urged the expansion of their medical establishments and wrote the despatch which was to take MacGregor to those islands. Gordon pointed out that the Seychelles consisted of two groups of islands, one centred round Mahé, with a few islands near by; the other of the more numerous but smaller islands, with a population of two or three thousand, in the neighbourhood of the comparatively large island of Praslin. At that time there was no doctor at Praslin and it was not convenient for the busy Mahé doctors to visit the island. Thus illness in the

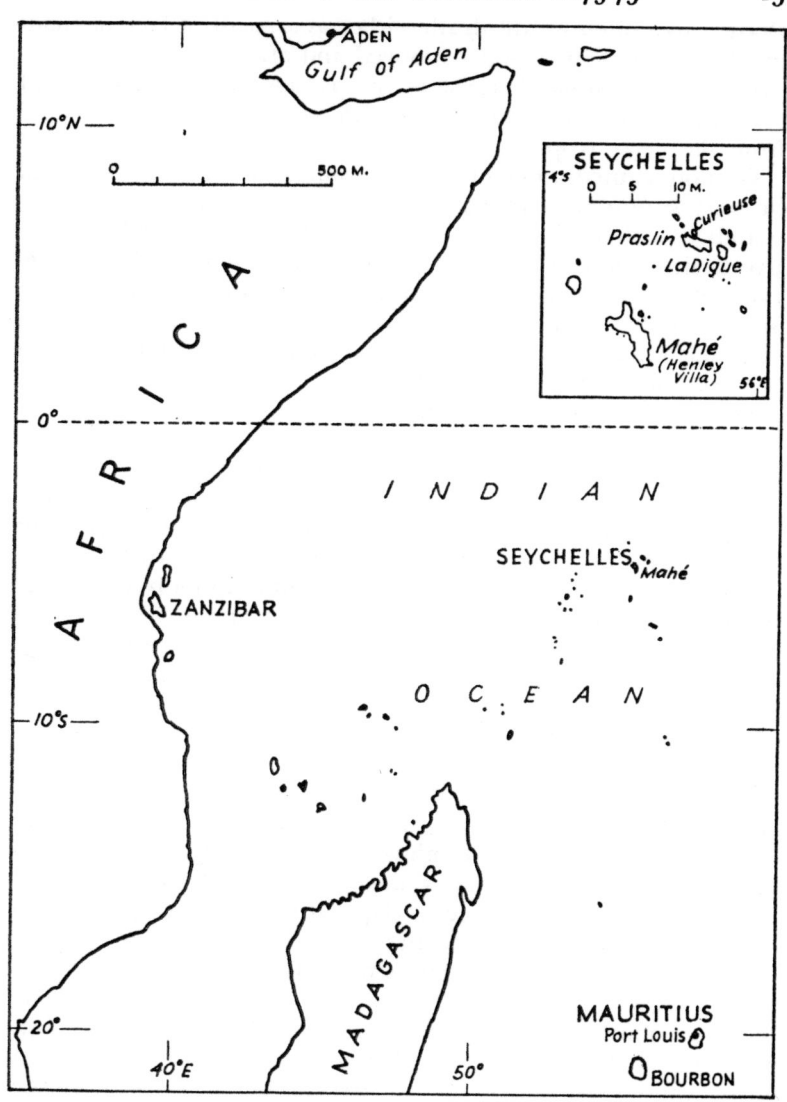

2 The Seychelles and Mauritius

Praslin area often meant death, either as a result of lack of treatment or, if patients could be moved and attempts were made to bring them to Mahé, because of the passage of many hours, and sometimes more than a day's duration, in open boats unsheltered from the fierce tropical sun, and equally fierce tropical rains'.[11]

Gordon wanted a doctor to be stationed at Praslin, who could in every season and almost any weather reach most of the other islands in a short time. The doctor was to undertake administrative duties and also to be empowered to act as a magistrate, because of the isolation which prevented appeals to the Mahé Court: 'so cases unless of a very serious nature are generally abandoned . . . and much petty lawlessness prevails'. Colonial Office action on Gordon's suggestion was not rapid, so Gordon began the particular chain of correspondence which led to the choice of MacGregor.

MacGregor and his wife arrived in the Seychelles on 10 February 1873 and first lived at Henley Villa on Mahé island. After visiting most islands in the Praslin group he decided to move to Praslin about the beginning of March, settling into a house in 'a convenient and central position . . . in a bay opposite the Government Leper Establishment at Curieuse',[12] of which MacGregor was in charge. Some time in the next year they moved across to Curieuse, so that he could better superintend the leprosarium and more closely study leprosy. It was on this 'solitary island inhabited by lepers',[13] that his first daughter, Helen, was born on 25 February 1874.

Contrary to expections, MacGregor found only a limited amount of medical work awaiting him and he was very willing to accept the additional administrative tasks suggested by Gordon, especially if extra money was authorized. A fortnight after his arrival MacGregor wrote to Captain W. H. Franklyn—who as Chief Civil Commissioner was in charge of the Seychelles —hoping to expedite his formal appointment as Justice of the Peace and as an Officer of the Civil Status for Praslin and La Digue.[14] It was nine months, however, before MacGregor was finally appointed a Civil Status Officer[15] and he never became a J.P., other than on paper in 1874[16]—these details stressing Gordon's point of the inefficiency and slowness of the Mauritius administration and the Colonial Office.

Franklyn may well have expected delays in these civil appointments, for he suggested to MacGregor that he should apply for another position that had been approved. This was the conjoint

1 Knowehead (or Knowhead), the farm of the Thomson family

1st SCHEDULE.—(Form No. 2.)
(CAP. 117—FIJI)

REGISTER OF DEATH.

Nº 1987

1877.
of Mary Thomson nee McGregor.

DEATH .... Registered by Horace Emberson *District Registrar, Registrar-General*

Date of death Friday, 6am. February, 9th Where it occurred at Levuka.

DESCRIPTION—
Name and Surname, rank and profession ...... MARY THOMSON nee McGREGOR ----------

Sex Female Age 29. Where born Aberdeen, Scotland How long in Fiji ----------

Cause of Death DYSENTRY ----------

Duration of last illness 6 days duration ----------

Medical attendant by whom certified Hernickrhaum ----------

When he last saw deceased 6th February. ----------

Christian and Surname of father Peter Thomson. ----------

Rank or profession Farmer ----------

Christian and maiden Surname of mother Helen Ritchie ----------

BURIAL—
When buried 9th February. ----- and where Nautotu. ----------

Name and religion of Minister, or names of witness of burial Rev. Wm. Floyd.
Church of England. G.L.Griffiths, Mathew Wilson. ----------

IF DECEASED WAS MARRIED—
Where at Aberdeen, Scotland ---------- At what age 20. ------

To whom Wm. McGregor. ----------

Issue in order of birth, their names and ages James R.McGregor 7. ----------

Helen McGregor 3. ----------

Signature, description and residence of informant and witness Wm. McGregor, Doctor of
Medicine. Seychelles, Mauritius, Scotland. (now) Levuka. ----------

Date and where registered. ----------

I hereby certify that the above is a true copy of an entry in a Register of Deaths kept at the Registrar-
General's Office, Suva, Fiji, and extracted this 21st day of July, 19 61.

Registrar-General.

R.G 1/1877.

2 A copy of Mary Thomson's (MacGregor's) death certificate

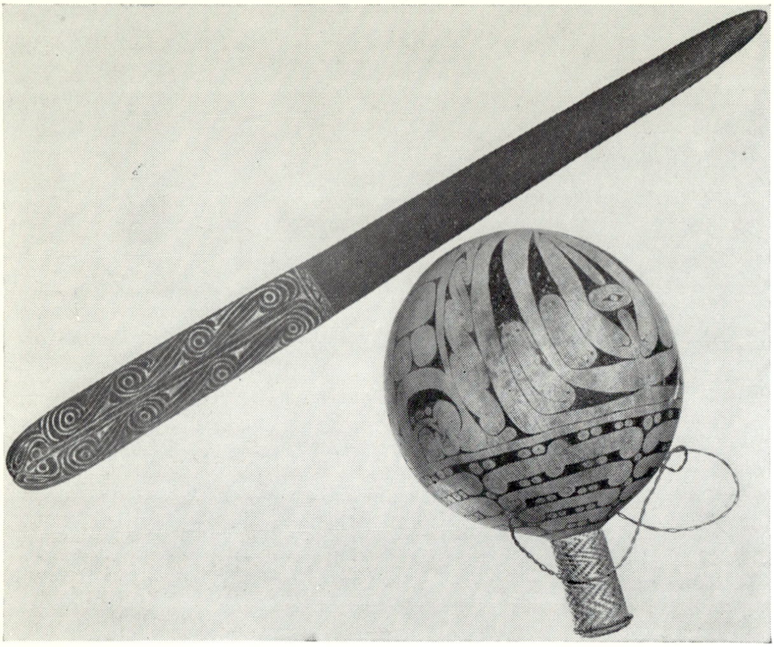

3 A lime spatula and gourd from the Trobriand Islands thought to have been collected by MacGregor before August 1894

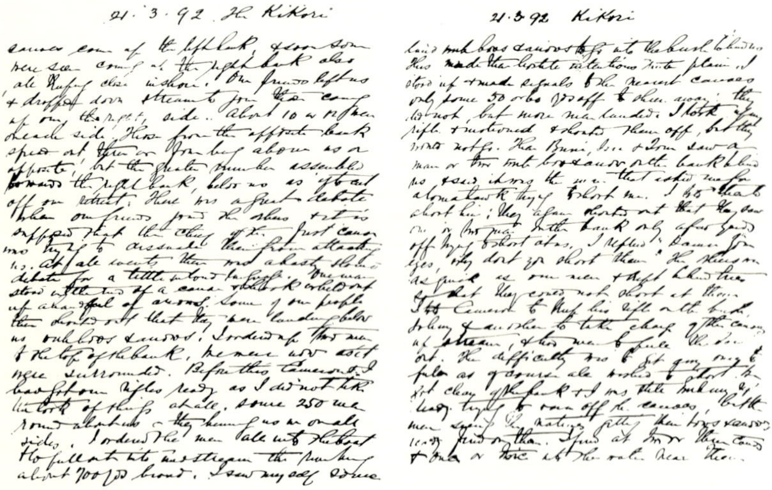

21 · 3 · 92 The Kikori

21 · 3 · 92 Kikori

4 Two pages from MacGregor's diary, 21 March 1892

office of Inspectorship of Schools and of Liberated Africans, and MacGregor agreed to this 'provided always that the salary . . . shall not be less than the sum you [Franklyn] then suggested, viz £150 per annum'.[17] This gained local approval but then began a wrangle with the Colonial Office which stated that £150 was 'an excessive addition' and finally decided to reduce it to £100.[18]

Meanwhile MacGregor had enthusiastically thrown himself into his new duties with the Africans. H. M. Stanley's[19] charges in England that Africans were being taken to Mauritius and the Seychelles to be sold as slaves aroused the Colonial Office's desire for an inquiry and MacGregor was empowered

> to enter and inspect any asylum, hospital, school, camp of labourers, or other establishment of any kind in which liberated Africans are received and any estate or premises except private dwelling houses in which any liberated African is employed or located.[20]

He could also request that any liberated African be brought before him and could inspect every written record on any plantation. MacGregor went beyond the letter of his instructions to a very personal and devoted concern for these people as individuals. Behind this attitude was his background of poverty, which inclined him to sympathize with the underprivileged. Partly from it—and partly from the example of other humanitarians such as Gordon—stemmed his concept of a duty toward 'primitive' peoples. It seems probable, however, that his immediate motive in accepting the additional position was financial, for there is no previous evidence of his interest in any colonial mission.

Thus MacGregor complained about the reduction in his salary for the inspectorship, since the office was a most unpleasant and

> laborious one involving a great deal of very hard walking under a tropical sun, and necessitating my being absent from home very frequently. It is thus calculated to lead to very considerable travelling expenses.[21]

His financial concern is obvious, though the comment also suggests how thoroughly he was carrying out his duties.

Franklyn supported MacGregor, making this latter point clearer,[22] as did Gordon, and Gordon's support finally convinced the Colonial Office. If MacGregor were paid £150 Gordon felt he would make only a small profit, perhaps £50, a small compensation for

> the sacrifice of time involved, the unpleasant nature of the duties, and I may add the serious amount of danger to which those duties constantly expose him . . . not only is there certainly no-one else in

c

these islands so well fitted for the discharge of its duties, but I may almost say that there is no-one else here who is fitted to perform them at all. Dr McGregor's suitability for the post is conspicuous. He is firm, cautious, and thoroughly impartial . . . since his arrival he has not only made himself acquainted with the Creole French commonly spoken here, but has also learned the Swahili language, in which he is now able to converse with the Africans. He is, I believe, the only white man here at all able to do so.

He has already effected much good as Inspector. The treatment of the Liberated Africans by their employers has on the whole been satisfactory, but there were exceptions and Dr McGregor has secured the detection and punishment of two or three large proprietors who habitually cheated their labourers of a large proportion of their pay and rations. The result has . . . been most beneficial to the labourers generally and has caused a more rigid adherence throughout all the islands of the group to the law and regulations on the subject.[23]

Gordon was convinced by MacGregor that 'the feelings and traditions of slavery still subsist among the colonists'[24] and made certain that any planter who failed to observe the regulations was prosecuted. This extended even to one of the unofficial members of the Board of Civil Commissioners. Undoubtedly the conditions of the Africans were improved by these actions spurred by MacGregor's inspections.

Gordon's verdict and others[25] assert the point that MacGregor had carried out his duty in a way that went well beyond the reasonable requirements of his position. He had learnt the local languages so he could converse with both employer and employee; he had risked danger and his own health had suffered; he had to leave his wife for long periods while on arduous tours; and he had succeeded in improving conditions.

Gordon was obviously greatly impressed by MacGregor, as was MacGregor by Gordon, and this was the beginning of a long and firm friendship which ended only with Gordon's death in 1912. Gordon's support for MacGregor was not only based on an objective assessment of his qualities but influenced by a subjective assessment of a fellow Scot. Despite their vastly different social backgrounds* they had the bonds of nationality and of shared interests in the classics and history. Undoubtedly the lack of other

---

* Gordon was the son of Lord Aberdeen, the prominent Peelite and a British Prime Minister in the 1850s; he had a secluded and leisured youth in London, Scotland and Cambridge before entering the colonial service at the top, as Governor of New Brunswick, then of Trinidad and Mauritius.

congenial colleagues helped MacGregor to gain Gordon's confidence, and MacGregor's efficiency, already expected by Gordon because of the references he had read, must have impressed him. The gap of seventeen years between Gordon, then forty-four, and MacGregor, then twenty-seven, helped to make Gordon dominant throughout the relationship, as did Gordon's capacity for leadership and his ability to select and direct men.

But the affection which developed between the two can be explained by more fundamental similarities of character. In their outward behaviour both tended to be reticent and retiring, but inwardly and in their writing both were stubborn, opinionated and assured of their rightness against almost any criticism. This last trait was most important for their colonial careers, especially beginning with this case of the Liberated Africans both shared an unshakeable determination that their responsibilities extended to primitive peoples.

MacGregor had far less to do in his other position as Inspector of Schools because there were so few schools. The dependency had no government schools, relying on Anglican and Roman Catholic mission schools which 'were starved for money and consequently were bad'.[26] Gordon tried to improve and expand the activities of these schools, especially for the children of the Liberated Africans. Eventually, in 1874, some government aid was given to the Roman Catholics but not to the Anglicans because they refused to adopt a conscience clause. It can be presumed from the general praise of MacGregor's work that he contributed to the exposure of the weaknesses of these schools and henceforward regarded the expansion and regular inspection of schools as part of his colonial responsibility.

In December 1873 he was appointed Officer of the Civil Status and Sub-Collector of Dues and Taxes at Praslin and for a few months held concurrently five positions—although there is little evidence that the last two offices added anything substantial to his tasks.

MacGregor was to spend very little more time in the Seychelles, for on 22 April 1874 a summons issued by the district judge of the Seychelles ordered him to proceed to Mauritius to give evidence in a murder trial.[27] He remained in Mauritius until December 1874, the length of his stay being only partly due to the long delay before the trial reached the courts and apparently far more the result of Gordon's personal desire for him to be in Mauritius.[28] MacGregor was given several official positions including that of Acting Resident Medical Officer at the Civil Hospital, and there were complaints from the Seychelles that 'no complete or satisfactory inspection of the Liberated Africans took place during the year 1874'[29] and that another officer had to inspect the schools.

There were attempts, probably welcomed by MacGregor, to keep him in Mauritius rather than letting him return to the Seychelles. The Chief Medical Officer, Dr Reid, suggested that MacGregor take up the vacant position of Resident Superintendent of the Lunatic Asylum, as he was most impressed by Mac-Gregor's qualities and was

> extremely desirous, as indeed he [MacGregor] is himself, that he should be promoted from the isolated appointment he holds where there is scarcely any occasion for the practice of his profession, to the Medical Staff of this Colony.[30]

The appointment did not eventuate, as the Colonial Office made alternative recommendations and MacGregor returned for a short period to the Seychelles.[31] Reid's statement that Mac-Gregor desired to stay in Mauritius illustrates a constant conflict of his career. In favour of Mauritius was his ambition for higher status and pay, combined with his insecurity and his fear of being left in isolation in a remote part of the colony. In favour of the Seychelles was his conscientiousness in whatever task he undertook, reinforced by his acceptance of a duty, in this case his care of the Liberated Africans. This particular conflict was resolved when he returned to the Seychelles, but meanwhile a similar clash had developed between the claims of Fiji and of his present colony. He had to choose whether to build on his growing reputation in the Seychelles and Mauritius, or to follow Gordon, who wanted him to go with him to Fiji. His decision was soon made. When he received the offer of the position of Chief Medical Officer and Health Officer in Fiji at £350 a year, he accepted without delay and left the Seychelles in March 1875.

His two years in the Seychelles and Mauritius gave him confidence as a doctor as a result of his variety of medical opportunities and the trust placed in him. He found the security of the support and friendship of his governor. His ambition led him to undertake as many responsibilities as possible and in the end made him choose to go to Fiji. He found some happiness in the fulfilment of his work and in the gratitude of the Africans and others whom he served so tirelessly, if little in his family life. It seems certain that his attitudes towards the planters in Fiji and their use of Indian labour were affected by his experience on Mauritius. Finally, after these two successful years, combined with his acceptance of the Fijian appointment, his future seemed inevitably bound to a colonial career. He had started to fulfil the obligations of a responsibility to colonial peoples.

3

Fiji : A Doctor's Dilemma 1875-88

I am . . . torn in opposite directions by my duty to myself and my
duty to the service.

The fourteen years spent by William MacGregor in Fiji were
vastly different from his time in the Seychelles and Mauritius.
From the first he was at the centre of policy-making; he discussed
Fijian problems with Sir Arthur Gordon before they even saw
the islands; as Chief Medical Officer his medical decisions affected general policies, though within a few years he was doing far
more administrative than medical tasks. His acceptance within
two years of the position of Receiver-General (Treasurer) and consequent membership of the executive and legislative councils,
was followed by his rise to the position of Colonial Secretary
and he was to act as Governor within ten years of his arrival. The
obscure assistant doctor from the Seychelles would seem to have
made the most of his opportunities.

But although one might expect this meteoric rise to have satisfied the ambitions of an agricultural labourer's son, it in fact hid
constant frustrations, both in his official and private life. He felt
at forty that his official life was a failure and that the Colonial
Office had refused to recognize his talents. His personal life was
not happy; his first wife died twenty months after their arrival
and for about six years he lived almost as a recluse, lonely and
harbouring grievances against his fellow officials. After his second
marriage in 1883 these clashes continued, especially with John
Thurston. Indeed, after Gordon left in 1880, MacGregor had no
close personal friend among the officials in Fiji. Neither of the
governors who succeeded Gordon, Sir George des Voeux (1880-86)
or Sir Charles Mitchell (1887), inspired his confidence. But he did
not leave Fiji or the colonial service to return to medical practice
as he so often threatened to do. Instead he was elevated in 1888
by the Colonial Office to take charge of the new colony of British

New Guinea, and the official comments on his career throughout his Fijian years would suggest that many of his fears of being overlooked were either imaginary or exaggerated. There must have been thousands of similarly placed colonial officials in obscure corners of the British Empire magnifying their personal problems because of the restrictions of their horizons while in London the harassed Colonial Office staff tried within its own limitations to do justice to them all.

The history of the reluctant acceptance of the islands of Fiji into the British Empire (mainly the result of pressure from the Australian colonial governments, traders, planters and missionaries) is one relevant reason why all British colonial servants in that colony could consider themselves of less importance than their fellows in other colonies which were longer established or more important to British interests. Whatever overall interpretation is placed on British policy in the Pacific up to 1874 it is clear that this area was never at the centre of British concern.[1]

Gordon left Mauritius after July 1874 and was in England in October when the cession of Fiji was accepted. In the same month he was asked by Lord Carnarvon, Disraeli's Colonial Secretary, whether he would accept its governorship. Carnarvon later wrote that it would have been false economy to commit the control of Fiji to 'weak or inexperienced hands'[2] and intended to entrust Gordon with more discretionary powers than were usually given to colonial governors. Gordon, however, strained the patience of the Colonial Office from the beginning and his inharmonious relationship with the British Government weakened support for his policies. The clashes began over the choice of officers to aid him in Fiji. Carnarvon wrote that

> the officers who with [the Governor] will administer the new colony must I think be comparatively few but all of them as strong men in their several posts as I can secure—instead of being as in ordinary cases very subordinate to the Governor. I do not mean of course to have any divided authority . . . but I think that I see that I *may* be able to secure the services of one or two men who from past positions and services could hardly be expected to take office unless the case were an exceptional one.[3]

Gordon, however, while agreeing with the idea of having strong men with him, felt that he must choose his subordinates. Carnarvon and R. G. W. Herbert, the Permanent Under-Secretary of State for the Colonies, objected on the grounds that persons entirely unknown to them could not be appointed and, if Gordon's stay in Fiji were short, the men he had chosen might not be equally liked by his successor; his government might be too personal.[4]

Gordon had only given Carnarvon a conditional acceptance of the offer and was undecided for weeks whether to go to Fiji or not. The dispute between them, however, was finally patched up before the end of December and Gordon formally accepted 'the mission to Fiji', somewhat solaced by the fixing of his salary at the high figure of £4,000 a year.[5] He was, however,

> not very sanguine of success, for the problem of reconciling the claims of European settlers and of natives has failed to be solved by abler heads than mine, but I do not think success impossible, and it is worth trying for.[6]

His friend, Gladstone, then leader of the Opposition, was also pessimistic and warned Gordon of the danger that he might 'do all that is possible and yet be blamed because [he had] not achieved the impossible',[7] a common problem for colonial administrators.

MacGregor went to Fiji because of Gordon's insistence on choosing some of his own subordinates, and accepted Gordon's offer to become Chief Medical Officer at a salary of £350 a year. As he was being paid at least £400 a year in the Seychelles and as he claimed to have been offered £800[8] to stay in Mauritius it seems likely that Gordon had offered him other inducements besides the personal satisfaction of working under him—possibly the right of private practice and a promise of other remunerative administrative positions. On 10 March 1875, with his wife and daughter, MacGregor sailed from the Seychelles.[9]

Immediately on his arrival in June MacGregor took up his duties as Chief Medical Officer and Health Officer at Levuka[10] and he was to hold this position practically throughout his time in Fiji. Although he was to become primarily an adminstrator, his approach to men and their problems was always that of a doctor. Furthermore, his concern with problems of health went well beyond the scope of his official duties and his humanitarianism embraced not only medical treatment but an attempt to eradicate the economic cause of maladies.

MacGregor was aware of the extent of the problems facing him in Fiji, writing soon after his arrival that

> at present nine-tenths of the natives are allowed to die without medical attendance, scores of them lose their eyesight for want of proper treatment, whilst hideous, raw, uncovered fly-eaten

ulcers may be seen in every town. Dysentery and diseases of the chest, by no means rare, are allowed to take their own fatal way. Such a state of affairs will I hope not long exist.[11]

He also soon realized the difficulties of fulfilling his hopes. The major problem was that there were never enough Government doctors; in 1875 there were four, in 1882 seven, in 1883 eight, and in 1884 at one stage ten, but during the year this dropped to four (of whom one was on leave). These doctors had to serve a population of more than 10,000 Fijians and some 2,000 Europeans, as well as Polynesians and Indians,[12] scattered over about 700,000 square miles on more than 300 islands. Furthermore, their quality and that of the few private doctors often fell below the standards MacGregor desired. He insisted on introducing and enforcing an ordinance in 1876, revised in 1881, to ensure registration of only qualified medical practitioners, dentists and apothecaries. There are records of doctors, traditional in stories about the Pacific islands, who had failed everywhere else and come to the Pacific as their last resort. In 1887 a Government doctor, when accused by the Chief Medical Officer of insobriety, scrawled a reply with an unsteady hand:

> I was drunk both in Suva and here. I hate writing to you as I cannot help feeling that I am writing to a 'Rabbit'. I have shot many thousands. I await your instructions and will hand over my duties and my position to anybody but a mother-in-law.[13]

When a doctor applied from Ceylon as a medical officer MacGregor could find nothing in his certificates to show that he held any medical qualifications and even 'if there were I could not recommend the appointment of a man of the applicant's inferior education'.[14]

Not surprisingly, doctors from Scotland received preference from MacGregor and in 1883 he devised a scheme for attracting medical students at Scottish universities to the colony. Des Voeux supported these doctors in a tribute that can be applied to MacGregor himself:

> Whatever be the cause, I have not the least doubt that the Scottish doctors sent to this colony have, speaking generally, proved more valuable officers than others, not merely in their medical and surgical qualifications, but in their capability of withstanding the climate and of adapting themselves to the conditions which present themselves here.[15]

The urgent need for medical care was emphasized by the drastic decline of the Fijian population. In 1875 the introduced disease of measles killed about 40,000 of the estimated population of 150,000, and the 1886 population of 110,335 represented a decline of 4,413 since 1881.[16]

J. Blyth, the Native Commissioner, in 1887 attributed the decline not only to introduced diseases, poor sanitary conditions and lack of medical care, but also to changing social relationships, particularly the changing status of women. The premature destruction of polygamy could lead, he warned, to 'the decline, possibly the extermination of the people'.[17]

MacGregor was more cautious in diagnosing the decline, although agreeing with most of Blyth's suggestions. He tried to enforce sanitary precautions and improve medical care,[18] well realizing that their adequacy depended on a knowledge of local diseases. Thus he began medical research and within three months of his arrival he had set up a laboratory for 'such chemical analyses and other scientific investigations as may be undertaken in connection with the Medical Department'.[19] In December 1875 he reported at length on the prevalent local disease called 'Coko' (possibly yaws)[20] and soon had studied others such as Tokelau ringworm.[21] By 1877 he was ready to have his researches on local endemic diseases published and wanted the Government to pay for publication. An interesting exchange followed: Gordon asked for an approximate cost, but MacGregor, wanting full coverage of actual costs, would not give a figure. Gordon then played MacGregor the Acting Receiver-General off against MacGregor the Chief Medical Officer by minuting 'were such a proposal submitted to the Acting Receiver-General that officer would undoubtedly and very properly advise His Excellency to exercise caution before pledging himself to such expenditure'.[22] Gordon finally agreed to grant £50 for publication of MacGregor's 'useful work'.[23]

MacGregor was disappointed in his efforts to investigate diseases new to him; the sheer immensity of the problems was sufficient to prevent much advance in the limited time he could spare from his official medical and administrative duties. He recorded in 1876 that his official duties alone 'if properly performed would completely occupy my time',[24] and as it was he did post-mortems and his chemical analyses on 'Sundays and at night'.[25]

A more basic reason for inadequate research was the lack of funds for this aspect of colonial welfare. For example, when MacGregor, in February 1876, urged the appointment of at least four more doctors, funds were so short that Gordon could not approve this proposal, nor send it on for Colonial Office action, until 1877. Although the Colonial Office then agreed that 'no better employment of £2,000 a year could be found than the payment of four more medical men',[26] its sanction was conditional on the availability of finance and a warning was added about the dangers of increased expenditure. Des Voeux, when Acting Governor, also argued for more doctors, in October 1878,

> with a view to the solution of the most difficult and at the same time the most important of all the problems we have to face here: I mean the preservation of the native population.[27]

A Minute written by Lord Kimberley, Gladstone's Colonial Secretary, when there were renewed requests in 1881 for more medical staff, showed how far apart views in Fiji and London could become:

> The sooner Mr des Voeux and all others concerned with Fiji know that the islands must rely on their own resources the better. As to saving the natives from extermination by the natural decay of the race, it is an interesting experiment and should be fairly tried. I wish I could believe in the probability of success.[28]

In fact there were never enough doctors so that the limits of possible policies were quickly realized in medical as in other administrative fields. MacGregor, however, tried to compensate for the lack of doctors by using, in some cases, Wesleyan mission teachers as his medical assistants from 1876 onwards.

MacGregor was personally responsible for drawing up and implementing laws such as the Public Health Ordinance of 1875, and others dealing with quarantine, vaccination and venereal disease, and for controlling the hospital at Levuka. He also travelled widely to study diseases and the sanitary conditions of native villages. One protracted tour lasted from May to August 1876, during the so-called 'little war'[29] against the Fijians in Viti Levu, when MacGregor, as Medical Officer, accompanied the force led by Captain L. F. Knollys, and reported on the health problems of the Colo district and their relationship to its topography and climate. His conclusions, based on his study of 1,076 individuals from twenty-four towns, stressed the dangers that could arise from the interchange of diseases between Fijians and foreign labourers and the particular need to begin vaccination against smallpox.[30]

A vital aspect of MacGregor's medical work was facing the problems of newly introduced diseases, of which measles had the worst effects. The severe epidemic of 1875, which killed about a quarter of the Fijian population,[31] was enough to drive home every lesson: the need for preventive medicine, for more staff, for more education of the Fijians, for strictly controlled quarantine and widespread vaccination. The disease was introduced five months before MacGregor's arrival in June 1875 by H.M.S. *Dido*, which brought the powerful native chief Cakobau back from a visit to Sydney, and was ironically spread throughout the islands by the Fijians who had come to Bau to welcome him.

By September 1875 MacGregor was urging that vaccination be made compulsory and eventually in 1877 an ordinance was passed to this effect. MacGregor estimated in 1880 that only about 15,000 to 20,000 Fijians remained unvaccinated, to which had to be added the annual births (between 3,500 and 4,000). He felt that by spending less than £500 a year the 'population of Fiji could be maintained in an efficient state as to vaccination'.[32] Yet he remained uneasy, writing the next year,

> I am very nervous about smallpox. It is some little comfort to me that so many have been vaccinated; but I doubt not that the epidemic would cause many deaths here.[33]

MacGregor's insistence on full observation of strict quarantine often aroused the anger of more careless or less far-seeing officials.[34] Herbert's comment in London that many Europeans in the South Seas 'for a few shillings profit would readily risk the extermination of thousands by disease'[35] supports MacGregor's stand, as do the melancholy facts of the over-all effects of diseases introduced into the Pacific islands.

One of the scourges of these islands was venereal disease. When MacGregor reached Fiji he was surprised at its infrequency, having seen in his first three months only two Fijians affected, besides several cases among the 'foreign labour girls'. But three years later, in December 1878, he was convinced of the need for urgent action as gonorrhoea was increasing, and although syphilis had not been present until 1877, in 1878 there were about ten cases in Levuka alone and probably others in the provinces. Thus he suggested an ordinance providing *inter alia* for the compulsory examination of any woman suspected as a carrier. He well realized, in dealing with this 'question of the greatest delicacy', the difficulties of enforcing any effective measures, even in countries where respect for law was far more widespread than it was in Fiji. The Rokos, Fijian provincial chiefs, gave in their council strong support to the idea of preventive measures.[36]

One particular cause of the spread of venereal disease among the Fijians appeared to be the conditions on labour ships bringing Polynesian women from the New Hebrides and the Solomons. MacGregor wrote in 1879 that

> speaking generally, all women imported into this colony from those islands are seduced or violated during the passage, if I am to believe what is told me by the women themselves, everyone of whom I have for some time past submitted to a speculum examination.

He was shocked and, fearing publicity aimed at attacking the government, he urged immediate measures to end 'a disgraceful and abominable practice'.[37] A relevant comment was made by another official, however, that some Polynesian women 'are of remarkably easy virtue' and that 'male patients suffering from venereal disease may be only one degree less dangerous than female patients'.[38] But whatever the cause, the result was the spread of unchecked venereal disease.

The 'delicacy' of the question was clarified when an ordinance[39] was sent for Colonial Office approval, since strong differences of opinion existed in England. The grounds of concern centred on the question of enforcing the examination of women suspected of venereal disease. In a January 1881 report supporting the proposed ordinance, MacGregor reiterated the urgent need for action to prevent the disease spreading and assured the Colonial Office that both the Wesleyan missionaries and the native chiefs fully approved his government's action. On the particular point of examination, he did not think Polynesian women would be sensitive; 'once a Fijian woman becomes a prostitute she appears destitute of sentiment on the subject';[40] and he did not believe there were any white prostitutes in Fiji. The Colonial Office, however, wanted more evidence before risking attack in the British Parliament, in the form of written approval from the Wesleyan ministers; details of any discussions with native chiefs; certain specified changes in the ordinance and, if possible, a separate women's hospital.

Both a majority of Wesleyan ministers and native chiefs reiterated their support, though one fear of the Fijians was that white police officers might be given powers to interfere with their women. The Colonial Office again delayed sanctioning the ordinance by asking in February 1882 for more safeguards to cover this point.[41]

An ordinance embodying the amendments, forwarded to the Colonial Office in September 1882, was received in November and finally sanctioned. MacGregor's urgent request for action in December 1878 had taken four years to gain official approval.[42] Even then, in 1887, there were attempts from England to repeal the ordinance; but Governor Mitchell, presumably briefed by MacGregor, insisted that it remain in force.[43] This whole case is a good example of the restrictions on the powers of administrators in colonies.

Fijian health problems were always personal to MacGregor and they became even more so when his wife died on 9 February 1877 from dysentery.[44] Mary could not have seen much of William in Fiji as he was a tireless worker and frequently absent from home. Even if her interests had not widened as much as his she had given him one form of security. She was only twenty-nine, but her death after only six days of illness was typical of so many in Fiji, both European and Fijian. After her death William became almost a hermit, working up to twenty hours a day. His family life was ended, for his only child in Fiji, Helen, then three, was cared for at first by Lady Gordon and afterwards by Mrs des Voeux.[45]

As a doctor MacGregor won an excellent reputation[46] which was to maintain his popularity with the local planters and press when all other government officers were being reviled for their native policy. 'He is one of the very few whose presence is really appreciated, out of the many officials who have come and seen and—gone',[47] wrote one journalist, whose praise was typical of other comments:

> during the earlier part of his career in Fiji he practised [his profession] regularly. His credit for skill in this soon became great among his patients, especially as he very materially reduced the high rate of fees. . . . Possessing but few of the attributes of what is technically known as 'a lady's doctor'—his manner partaking rather of the unpolished roughness of an Abernethy than of the sauve demeanour of a Parker Pepps [sic]*, he yet was a favourite in domestic circles and secured the regard of the matronage of Fiji.[48]

His reputation as early as 1876 was sufficiently high to surmount press criticism of the 'little war' and, indeed, enhanced ideas of his skill as a surgeon. His account of an amputation of a native's leg was quoted as truth (when so much else of the official

---

* Doctor Parker Peps was 'one of the Court Physicians and a man of immense reputation for assisting at the increase of great families'. (Charles Dickens, *Dombey and Son*, Chapter 1). For surgeon John Abernethy's (1764-1831) 'masterly roughness' see *D.N.B.*

accounts was disbelieved), for his 'reputation gives sufficient assurance for its veracity'. MacGregor reported finding that his white assistant was drunk and likely to kill his native patient if allowed to act as anaesthetist. Consequently, MacGregor was forced to attempt the operation alone:

> I must confess I found the holding the end of a catch-forceps between one's teeth, when tying the vessels held by it, with a half a dozen small arteries projecting as many streams of hot blood into one's face, is not the most pleasant position in the world, especially if surrounded by two or three hundred spectators quite capable of believing that one was drinking the blood of one's patient, and dividing his body for the purpose of the larder.[49]

The native survived.

The greatest legacy of MacGregor's work as chief medical officer was his plan to train Fijians as medical assistants and the beginning of the Central Medical School at Suva, which has been responsible for much improvement of health throughout the Pacific.

MacGregor first suggested such a scheme in 1879, because of the difficulty in the forseeable future of providing enough European doctors 'to give anything like adequate attention to sufferers in many parts of the colony'. (He referred specifically to an outbreak of dysentery at Kadavu where over sixty had died with no treatment.) He suggested training Fijians who had finished their mission training at Navuloa, as an insurance against 'abuse of the power and knowledge that an acquaintance with medicine would give'. The medical course would aim at teaching them to recognize and treat 'ordinary cases of sickness' and he intended personally to superintend a purely practical course at Levuka Hospital. Although 'quite aware that such an education would be defective', he was

> equally sure that such a course of teaching carried out for even one or two years would fit some of those men for treating such cases as dysentery, bronchitis, worms, wounds, burns, erysipelas, ophthalmia and a few other maladies of frequent occurrence here. Of course these diseases would not be thus so well treated as by thoroughly educated men, but unquestionably these medical missionaries would be able to relieve a great amount of pain and I doubt not in such diseases as dysentery save many lives every year.

It was a practical way of alleviating an immense problem.

The subject lapsed till 1883, when Governor des Voeux gave his official support. MacGregor believed that in the meantime the suggestion had been 'raised at one time or another by . . . every officer connected with the Native Office'.[50] In addition, both the Wesleyan Mission and the Fijian chiefs approved. The scheme was successfully launched when the first students began their course in 1885. Three years later ten trainees were ready to face tests by MacGregor and his successor as chief medical officer, Dr Corney, and regulations were prepared to give legal recognition to these medical assistants. Fears were expressed, however, by Governor Mitchell that they might relapse 'into the slothful life of petty chiefs' and a balance was sought between giving them their deserved 'well-defined high positions . . . bearing in mind how easy it is to upset the equilibrium of a Fijian's mind by rapid promotion above his fellows'[51] and keeping them in due subjection to their chiefs. MacGregor seemed less concerned with such problems. He was glad, after eight years, to see his 'original idea and intentions with regard to these native students' reach fulfilment at last and was sure that they had 'a consciousness of professional importance and are willing to work'.[52] The experiment was successful and, years later in retirement, MacGregor urged its extension throughout the islands of the Pacific.[53]

Two other problems related to MacGregor's medical position in Fiji need consideration: first, whether he was successful as a departmental head, for this was the first time he had to control men and determine policies; and secondly, the strength of his desires to end all his non-medical functions and live as a doctor by medical practice and research.

As chief medical officer he was very efficient; he insisted on full knowledge of what his subordinates were doing and was critical of any lapses. He wanted control in his own hands and supported an 1884 ordinance making him, rather than a committee, 'the authority responsible for the control and management of Public Hospitals'.[54] Nor did he hesitate to emphasize this control.[55]

In 1875 a dispute developed between MacGregor and one of his subordinates, Dr Mayo, the medical officer for Vanua Levu and the eastern islands. There were allegations on both sides of insulting and contemptuous behaviour, centring round the formal way each should be addressed. Papers were returned unopened and complaints were made to outside officials. MacGregor found evidence that Mayo was not fulfilling his duties, that he was not complying with full quarantine regulations and criticized him as an 'errant functionary' who had deserted his post at Kadavu—an

5 Government House, Lagos

6 Some Lagos chiefs, including, in centre front, Gbadebo, the
Alake of Abeokuta

7 MacGregor's coat of arms

action 'worthy of the highest censure, [which] deserves to be visited by the severest disciplinary measures'. Mayo claimed, on his side, that MacGregor had no right to be placed over him and he wished, in October 1876, 'to withdraw from a service the conditions of which are so unfavourable, and in which all my previous experience is only a disadvantage'. Gordon backed MacGregor and, in April 1877, advised Mayo that if he desired 'to "shorten his time of servitude" the Colony will be prepared to release him from it'.

Mayo then became ill, so MacGregor advised as an absolute necessity his speedy departure to a more congenial climate. Mayo boarded the *Ly-ee-moon* but died thirty days out of Levuka on 15 July 1877. The captain of the ship complained that he had been put aboard 'in a dying state' and without 'a single person to see to him'. MacGregor denied both points, claiming that 'it was in the belief that the sea voyage might afford him more chance of recovery that I advised his removal on board the vessel'.[56]

The significance of this dispute with its tragic end was not only that Fiji lost an experienced doctor at a time when more doctors were needed, but also that this sort of personal clash was to occur frequently in MacGregor's colonial career. These disputes went beyond the jealousies and incompatibilities which are almost inevitable in a small group isolated in remote colonies. MacGregor never suffered opposition gladly. He was an obstinate and strongly opinionated person, who refused to compromise even for the eventual benefit of the service. In fairness to him, however, this was the only major clash of his fourteen years in the Fijian Medical Department. In addition, he had good working relationships, despite some differences of opinion, with other doctors and especially Dr Corney, which help to balance the Dr Mayo case. One sequel of Mayo's death, reinforced by the deaths of other doctors, was MacGregor's insistence to the Colonial Office that any doctors sent out to Fiji must be physically strong and in good health.

MacGregor found his duties as chief medical officer onerous; thus he objected to visits to the sick outside his official hours. Gordon agreed with him but suggested that he should set apart special hours at the dispensary for giving free advice to poor patients.[57] Although MacGregor was not satisfied with this and requested more precise instructions as to the limits of his professional duties,[58] attempts at definition of these were unavailing because he often had to undertake medical tasks beyond his

D

strictly official duties, due to the shortage of staff. Furthermore, MacGregor's case for limiting his responsibilities was weakened as he continued to practise as a private doctor, a right that could clash with his official tasks. His employers rarely questioned this right, though Gordon refused to grant him the £21 compensation he claimed for private cases allegedly missed while he was out of Levuka for a fortnight on official duties.[59]

MacGregor insisted that the Health Department be run, if possible, at a profit. In certain issues his functions as treasurer clashed with his humanitarian feelings and, knowing how restricted finance was, he realistically came to accept some limitations on possible medical action. In 1886, for example, when the reduction of patients' fees at Suva Hospital was suggested, MacGregor pointed out that

> the rate for Europeans, 10/- a day [was] the average charge for residence in second class hotels, and consequently [could not] be considered to be exorbitant for maintenance and medical treatment

and that voluntary contributions were too low to overcome the loss on most patients, so that 'the greater the number of people that go to hospital the greater the loss'.[60]

Another example of conflict in MacGregor's mind is seen in two of his Minutes on a petition from a sugar company's manager for establishing a hospital in the Rewa district. In October 1884 MacGregor, as chief medical officer, supported the building of a hospital as 'the welfare of the labourers is the paramount consideration in the matter of hospitals'. In January 1885, however, as treasurer, he had to advise des Voeux that 'there will . . . be no possibility of obtaining any funds from current revenue for this purpose during the present year'[61]—so the project lapsed.

His frustrations with official finance often found expression in his desire to go back to full-time private medical practice or research. His defences of the medical profession showed the strength of his loyalty to it. In 1884 des Voeux made a strong criticism of doctors on government service in Fiji who 'are in the habit of charging fees in their private practice on such a large scale that people cannot avail themselves of their services' and complained that this habit was so pronounced as to be rapidly becoming a serious public scandal.[62]

MacGregor took considerable umbrage at this slur, defending doctors both generally and in Fiji by an impassioned eighteen-page departmental Minute:

It may be said that by universal acknowledgement, no . . . class of men in civilized communities is more unselfish than medical men, that no other incurs equal risks for so small rewards, and that none are more ready to bestow help in distress, not merely in giving their services and in incurring danger for no pecuniary return whatever, but even in giving away their own means.

He itemized his takings and those of the doctor who had been the cause of des Voeux' censure and claimed that

the private practice of Levuka is worth in cash about £200 a year, that of Suva not more than £250, [and] that the earnings of doctors in Fiji do not exceed those of the average medical practitioner in England.

He gave examples of the difficulties he had faced in enforcing the payment of accounts (one relative refused to pay £4 as an 'excessive charge', although it covered twenty-five professional visits, a post-mortem and an ophthalmoscopic examination; another refused to pay because MacGregor was 'paid by the Government'). He made a suggestion that a fixed 'tariff of fees' should be introduced:

I have not known of such a tariff in any other country, but I think it may be good in depriving those that complain of the power of making such complaints in the future, and it will probably induce many people to pay medical accounts that have hitherto taken no notice of such documents.[63]

Des Voeux agreed with this idea and a tariff was drawn up by Dr Corney and approved by MacGregor as 'fair and reasonable'.[64]

MacGregor's desire to return to full-time private medical practice fluctuated in accordance with his feelings of frustration or achievement in Fiji. A clash with Thurston, difficulties with des Voeux, a failure to enforce quarantine or vaccination regulations or the continuing unhealthiness of Fijian finances, would all accentuate his feelings, never far below the surface, that he was wasting his time as an administrator.[65] It was his dissatisfaction with the progress of vaccination and his belief that he would be blamed, particularly by des Voeux, and 'left in the end without support' that led to his plaint:

I am . . . torn in opposite directions by my duty to myself and my duty to the service. I have been too long cut off from communication with other students, and deprived of books[66] and instruments, and must therefore gradually retrograde into deeper intellectual darkness.[67]

In April 1882 des Voeux reported that MacGregor's health was

> really beginning to suffer, . . . [he] imperatively requires change and
> relaxation, [because of] the remarkable amount of physical and
> mental labour which . . . [he] every day [undergoes] not only in the
> performance of his public duties but in answering the many pri-
> vate calls for medical help during an unusually sickly season.[68]

Urgent telegrams persuaded the Colonial Office to send another
doctor to Fiji and MacGregor was able to go on leave between
July 1882 and August 1883. He went to Berlin, apparently to
study medicine, as well as to Scotland where he visited university
medical schools, both to recruit more staff for Fiji and to acquaint
himself with progress in medical science.

A letter sent to the Colonial Office from Berlin made it quite
clear that he felt underpaid for his official duties in Fiji, so that
he would have to continue private practice on his return.

> For the last few years I have avoided private practice and devoted
> all my time day and night to my official duties. . . . I must either
> contract debts, which I certainly shall not do, or I must accept
> private practice.

Furthermore, he was going to ensure that his private patients
were 'those . . . in the best position to pay for medical attention'.[69]

Des Voeux asked the Colonial Office in 1883 to increase the
salaries of Thurston and MacGregor. He also wanted to separate
MacGregor's two major offices, of Receiver-General and Chief
Medical Officer, for they were 'in many ways incongruous; and
indeed it was only the exceptional energy and versatility of Doctor
McGregor which rendered the two at all compatible'. Des Voeux
thought there was a strong case for raising MacGregor's salary,
especially as

> his exceptional ability in his profession is now well known out here,
> and he would therefore without any question secure in the Aus-
> tralian colonies a much larger income than he obtains in Fiji.

Although one Colonial Office clerk summed up the gist of des
Voeux' request as giving 'more pay and less work to Dr M. and
to Mr T. and showed that the proportions of the salaries of the
Colonial Secretary and Receiver-General to revenue were higher
in Fiji than in comparable colonies, he was still sympathetic.[70]
The stringencies of Fijian finances, however, prevented any rise
at this time.

In May 1884 MacGregor, feeling financially unrewarded and
passed over for promotion, wrote 'I am really beginning to think

seriously of leaving the service to practise in Australia'.[71] Mac-
Gregor's unhappiness was apparent to des Voeux who therefore,
in July 1884, urged the Colonial Office either to grant to both
MacGregor and Thurston promotion in the colonial service or
to increase both their salaries to £1,000, a figure which he had
suggested in 1883. A personal friend of MacGregor, Dr Mackellar,
who was the Chief Medical Officer of New South Wales and also
ran a lucrative private practice, had told des Voeux that he

> had been for some time endeavouring to persuade McGregor to
> settle there and that his surgical and medical knowledge was so
> well recognised in the profession and would thus become so quickly
> known to the public, that he would be sure to obtain a large
> income at once and would within a year or two be in receipt of
> from £4,000 to £6,000 a year.

Mackellar also wanted MacGregor to attend a conference aimed
at establishing a federal quarantine, as his ' "strength" and knowledge of the subject would enable him to lead the older medical
delegates and would thus be all important for success'.

Des Voeux feared that the service might lose MacGregor
although he believed that MacGregor had 'an ambition to rise in
the service to a higher position than he would be likely to attain
in the practice of the medical profession' and consequently would
prefer to retain the Receiver-Generalship. One Colonial Office
clerk, however, denigrated des Voeux' arguments in favour of
MacGregor as 'the usual vague menaces of retirement' and the
device of 'a brother Scot . . . giving [him] a push' and claimed
that MacGregor and Thurston had 'looked after themselves remarkably well'. But this was not typical of general Colonial Office
feeling, which was far more flattering, especially that of the influential Herbert, who wrote:

> Both are men of greater ability and better service than almost any
> colonial officers (I put it strongly after consideration) and if we
> cannot pay them adequately in Fiji they should be promoted
> when practicable.

The official reply to des Voeux stressed appreciation of the 'value
of the services' of the two men but refused salary increases because of the low revenue of Fiji and the proportionate rate of
remuneration of similar officials in other colonies.[72]

MacGregor did stay in the colonial service and he did take on
more and more administrative responsibilities, thus justifying
the attitude of his critics who said he was bluffing for more pay or
for promotion. But the weight of evidence of MacGregor's con-

stant insecurity suggests that he was genuinely undecided. Certainly he was unhappy and dissatisfied in Fiji. His despondency emerges in a letter to Gordon in 1887, when MacGregor was forty-one and unwell, when his financial position was depressed and when he felt that he had been passed over for promotion:

> I have lost a good deal of money in Fiji . . . I could not possibly sell my place at present; and worst of all, my health is not good. If I went home, I should certainly receive no other appointment from the Colonial Office; and I am not able to go up and down stairs as I should have to do in private practice.* I could not now obtain medical teaching after being so long abroad and having my attention taken away so much from professional work and study.[73]

The editor of the *Fiji Times* was puzzled even at the end of MacGregor's Fijian career:

> Why a personage like Dr McGregor, who could make an income in the colonies of from £4,000-£5,000 per annum (as a doctor) should prefer an official position, even though that be the governorship of a colony, and that colony New Guinea is one of those mysteries for which a solution is sought in vain . . . the mind of man is inscrutable.[74]

There is enough evidence to argue that MacGregor, throughout his Fijian career, maintained ideas of an alternative life as a doctor and that the frustrations of his existence were sufficient to make this possibility more than a pipe-dream. But these ideas did not prevent his conscientious application to his duty as a doctor within the colonial service, where his achievements were considerable.

---

* This is the same MacGregor who a few years later climbed the highest peaks of the Owen Stanley Mountains in New Guinea.

4

Fiji: Finance and Frustration 1875-88

The Government is already in debt and probably will remain so
for all time . . .

The clash between MacGregor's work as a doctor and as an administrator began almost as soon as he reached Fiji, and was
intensified as he accepted increasing responsibilities. It was not
unusual in those days for an officer in the colonial service to act
in a number of capacities in the same colony during his term of
duty, because the necessities of leave, sickness and sudden post-
ings often made it necessary for positions to be filled by whoever
was available in the colony at the time. Thus MacGregor acted
as Agent-General for Immigration for three months between
December 1879 and March 1880 while the holder of the office,
William Seed,[1] was on sick leave. It is clear from the number of
important posts[2] MacGregor held that he had considerable
influence and authority in Fiji.

The second main office held by MacGregor in Fiji after that
of Chief Medical Officer was that of Receiver-General or Treasurer. Within five months of his arrival he was appointed to the
Native Debts Commission (set up to inquire into debts incurred
by the Cakobau Government before British annexation) with
two others, one the Receiver-General, A. Maudsley. A year later,
when Maudsley went on leave to England, MacGregor took over
his position in an acting capacity. This became one of his permanent appointments, being confirmed two years later, and
MacGregor, except when Colonial Secretary or Administrator,
held this office for all his years in Fiji. A cognate appointment
he held from 1883 was that of Commissioner of Stamps. He held
the leading position in the civil service, the Colonial Secretaryship, for most of his second term in Fiji after his return from leave
in August 1883, and was in charge of the colony as Acting Administrator from 23 January to 8 August 1885, and from 21
December 1887 to 26 February 1888.

MacGregor was also one of Gordon's confidants during his governorship from 1875 to 1880, and was known to be one of his trusted informants while he held the momentous right of supervision over Fiji from New Zealand, from 1880 to 1882. When Gordon was succeeded by des Voeux in 1880 his influence, and thus MacGregor's, persisted, especially since des Voeux proved weak and indecisive. Even when Mitchell, a stronger personality, was appointed in 1887, he still had to rely partly on the by then long experience of MacGregor and his chief rival, Thurston.[3]

MacGregor showed his ambition in this rivalry, which sometimes seemed measurable only in terms of status or of financial reward. It is, however, as misleading an interpretation of the man to overemphasize these factors as it would be to ignore them. While MacGregor was always aware of his position and salary, this never implied that the only motive for his efforts was to improve his status or pay. He was, however, disappointed in the preference given to Thurston, and in the fluctuations of his pay.

He initially came to Fiji as Chief Medical Officer on £350, but this amount could be supplemented by private medical fees. He was pleased to receive a gratuity of £200 for his service in the 'little war' of 1875.[4] When he took the position of Acting Receiver-General in 1877 his salary rose to £600 a year and to £950 in 1879 when this appointment was confirmed (£350 as Chief Medical Officer, £500 as Receiver-General and £100 for his hospital duties). It dropped after his leave to £850, when the hospital allowance was withdrawn, and he lost his right of private practice in 1884 when he became Colonial Secretary. The acceptance of this office did not increase his emoluments, however; indeed in August 1885 he was receiving only £600, the salary of this new office. In 1887 as Medical Officer and Receiver-General or Colonial Secretary his salary had risen to £765 (Receiver-General or Colonial Secretary £600 and 'personal allowance' £250, less ten per cent),[5] but in July 1887 this was reduced to £680. His acceptance of New Guinea at £1,500 a year more than doubled his income.

In the period up to 1882 while Gordon was in Fiji, or in charge from New Zealand, his ideas, supported by MacGregor, dominated the colony. Gordon, realizing how important was the problem of reconciling the claims of European settlers and of natives made strenuous efforts to satisfy both groups. He encouraged European plantations producing copra, coffee, fruit and sugar, hoping to end the dependence of the colony on British financial aid. He tried to ensure adequate labour for these plantations by importing Polynesian and Indian labourers. This importation of labour was related to his 'native' policy, in which his dominant motive was to protect Fijian society by disturbing it as little as possible. He feared that indigenous economic enterprises would be disrupted if Fijians had to work on European plantations, and he also hoped that these Fijian enterprises would expand and contribute to the Fijian economy. He sought to achieve the latter aim and to obtain increased revenue by imposing on the Fijians a produce tax, which he believed to be fairer than any levied previously. Another important facet of his policy was his attempt to rule through the existing political structure by delegating some responsibility to Fijian chiefs.

MacGregor's second term in Fiji, which coincided with the end of Gordon's direct influence, can be seen as a period of trial for these policies. MacGregor's faith in Gordon's ideas was severely tested by the continuous crises. The colony's economic position was never encouraging. The initial reliance on direct British aid, always opposed by the British Treasury, was not replaced by healthy returns from any crop. Instead, the slow expansion of the Fijian economy was retarded by the world depression of the 1880s, resulting in severe financial restrictions. The price of copra was never stable—it dropped from £15 10s per ton in 1879 to £8 10s in 1881, for example; sugar was not yet a major export crop and faced competition from Australian production and German beet sugar; the extension of coffee-growing was checked by a leaf disease; no other industry was established. Attempts to aid the Fijian economy by tying it closer to the Australasian colonies proved unsuccessful. The tax system, although continued, had obvious defects and did not contribute as much as had been hoped. Moreover, these financial problems were accentuated by political and social problems: planter dissatisfaction with the emphasis on the protection of the Fijians; missionary suspicion of the exercise of power by Fijian chiefs; the beginnings of Fijian individualism challenging the traditional dominance of the chiefs; and conflicts between Indians, Polynesians, Fijians and Europeans.

It was invaluable experience for MacGregor, as a highly placed and influencial official in this latter period, to face so many problems, solutions to which were so difficult to find. His Fijian apprenticeship well prepared him for the frustrations of administering colonies on the periphery of the British Empire.

The immediate reason for MacGregor's initial appointment as Receiver-General was the chronic shortage of staff in Fiji. Gordon also wanted somebody he could trust in this crucial position, however. On MacGregor's part the extra salary involved must have been an important consideration. Yet he stood to lose fees if he had to reduce his private practice as a doctor and he must have realized that his new responsibilities would make inroads into his already overloaded time.

His lack of formal training in accountancy practice, let alone in economic theory, and lack of experience in any similar position, should not be given too much weight. The British colonial service was still largely an organisation of amateurs, and except for established professions such as law (although few Attorneys-General were legally trained) or medicine, all positions were open to all men. Where patronage had not produced favoured candidates, choices were based on general education or length of colonial experience. Even if MacGregor denied it, Fiji was not alone in having 'a Treasurer that did not understand his business'.[6]

MacGregor's concern with the accumulation of money and his allied dislike of any waste, his meticulousness and strict attention to detail, were qualities that were fully utilized in his new position. Just as his medical reports depended so much on careful observation of facts before any deductions were made, so did all his financial reports rely on painstaking accuracy down to the last penny, with cautious recommendations based on these exact figures.

His major financial reports which suggest these qualities were the annual reports on revenue and expenditure, and on foreign trade; an exhaustive Report on the 'Commercial Statistics of Fiji for its first Six Years as a British colony (1875-81)'; in 1879 report on Tongan finances;[7] the Customs Ordinance which he drafted in 1881 with a fifty-four page explanation of its provisions; his 1878 report on the pre-cession financial claims of the Bank of New Zealand and of G. A. Woods;[8] and his 1885-86 reports on possible reciprocity treaties with Victoria and New Zealand. But these were only his major reports. An examination of Treasury files in the Fijian archives reveals the full details of his meticulous Minutes on all aspects of his financial duties.

When MacGregor became Receiver-General he had to reorganize completely office procedure in the Treasury, for accounts were as much as two years in arrears. He had an extremely difficult job to do but did it painstakingly. The judgements already quoted on his work as Chief Medical Officer from the Colonial Office, or from the governors under whom he served, included implicit reference to his work as Treasurer. More specific praise came for some of his major financial reports. He had, wrote des Voeux, 'bestowed much pains on the [Customs] Ordinance and has shown with reference to it his wonted ability and discretion'.[9] J. B. Thurston called his report on G. A. Woods 'a most elaborate and well written report of a most vext and costly claim'.[10] Non-official press opinion also praised MacGregor in all his activities, including his financial work:

> a highly educated and thoroughly erudite man, he has ungrudgingly given the benefit of the results of anxious and honest study and enlightenment, to those with whom he has identified himself in their earnestness to do the best in their power for the advancement of the colony. Every movement which had this object in view has received his kindly, his sympathetic assistance. While shrinking from the glare of publicity, Dr McGregor has done his best, according to his lights, to advance the material prosperity of the colony.[11]

He tried to insist on efficiency and justice, based on equality, in the working of his department. As he wrote in 1881:

> I have never ceased to inculcate on the several officers that the utmost care is to be observed that all persons whatever their social and official position are to be treated alike, with a strict courtesy, but with a strict construction of what the law requires.[12]

Portia's dictum, however, that 'it is a good divine that follows his own instructions' can be applied to criticize MacGregor's own application of the principle of equality. He allowed personal considerations to affect his actions, insisting on his pound of flesh and the full application of often petty regulations when he was opposed. He was quick to defend himself against censure, often with a ponderous sarcasm that did not hide his obstinate conviction that his actions could always be justified. For example, when a stipendiary magistrate queried the running of the Suva Powder Magazine he wrote:

> apparently he, like certain others, is quite unaware that only a very limited expenditure can be incurred under any one department, and that every officer ought to keep down that expenditure to the lowest possible amount short of absolute inefficiency. Neither weighty wisdom nor powerful penetration would be neces-

sary to frame a hostile criticism of several of the makeshifts adopted in connection with Suva by the Colonial Secretary, Mr Berry [the Crown Surveyor], and myself; but time can be better employed than in interpreting their meaning and justifying their existence to those that do not understand their necessity.[13]

Above all else MacGregor's holding of the Receiver-Generalship led to his thorough and realistic appreciation of the restrictions placed on any policy by the shortage of available finance. He took office on 1 January 1877, and in sending on the Estimates for 1877 probably concurred with Gordon's optimistic belief that Fiji was 'in a sounder, more truly prosperous and more progressive condition' than ever before. In contrast, Carnarvon, the British Secretary of State, was pessimistic:

> Sir Arthur Gordon must be told in the plainest—though of course in very civil—terms that he must carry out all the proposed reductions . . . under present circumstances it seems to me very dangerous to speculate, and our financial policy in Fiji for the next twelve months cannot be too cautious.[14]

If the Minute is read with fourteen years substituted for twelve months it can serve as a text for British financial policy in the colony in this period.

A basic British attitude was that colonies must live within their incomes. The opinions behind this belief have been well expressed by Professor Legge:

> it was consistent with an age when enlightened thought deprecated any State interference with the 'natural' laws of economics, when the pursuit of self-interest was held to produce the greatest happiness of the greatest number, and when self-help was the remedy offered for the encouragement of those who fell by the wayside, that any contribution to colonial revenues from the Treasury of the mother country should savour of pauperization. Individual failure in the economic struggle was a sign of lack of effort, and was therefore blameworthy. Charity was no remedy for poverty as it would only encourage such moral shortcomings. By analogy, charity was bad for a colony too.[15]

If this basic assumption were accepted, then Fiji was an economic failure. The bald figures were enough to confirm Carnarvon's continued pessimism, for in each year from 1875 to 1888 expenditure exceeded revenue. Gordon, however, hampered by the limitations imposed on his policy by the lack of finance, queried the revenue principles involved, especially when he feared that the interests of the Fijian people might suffer.[16] One question to be asked about MacGregor is how far as Receiver-

General in Fiji, and later as governor of other colonies, he accepted these restrictions.

An early case of Colonial Office disagreement with MacGregor's financial approach concerned his 1880 drafting of an ordinance to set up a government-controlled bank for Fijians. MacGregor proposed that this bank should hold the proceeds of natives' land sales and should pay them interest on these deposits. A dispute developed between MacGregor and the Colonial Office as to the security of such a bank and whether the government should interfere in banking. A consultant of the Colonial Office maintained that the three basic principles for a Savings Bank were, firstly, that it should be self-supporting; secondly, that its investments should be in sound securities, little affected by market fluctuations; and thirdly, that there should be constant supervision over its managing officers.

The important point is the first. The consultant quoted Gladstone's explanation, made as Chancellor of the Exchequer, of why the British Post Office Savings Bank Act of 1861 had insisted on the Bank being self-supporting. If it was not, the poor would become a charge on the Treasury, so making

the working class pensioners on the Exchequer, . . . a principle [to which] we should be altogether opposed. . . . [It is the] duty of Parliament to check and limit its operation so as effectually to obviate so enormous an evil.

A further application of Gladstone's remarks to the Fijian bank was the warning text that

the proceeds of general taxation should not be used for the purpose of providing interest on the deposits of those particular tax payers who may desire to invest their money in Savings Banks.

One point queried by the Colonial Office was whether it could be guaranteed that the bank's holdings could be invested to provide a return sufficient to cover the proposed interest payments to the Fijian depositors. MacGregor was not overconcerned with this point, however, quoting the analogy of the Fijian Government which was paying seven and a half per cent on an overdraft received from the Bank of New Zealand: 'The Government is already in debt and probably will remain so for all time, like other civilized governments' (a shocked Colonial Office clerk wrote an exclamation mark next to this flagrantly unorthodox remark).

The acceptability of Fijian securities also came into dispute. MacGregor argued that they should be considered acceptable, since this would avoid the costs of exchange involved with either Australian, New Zealand or British securities. The Colonial Office claimed that 'investments should be made rather with a view to safety than with the view of getting a high rate of interest' and that Fijian securities did not offer this safety. It was, for example, pointed out 'that in case of a run on the Bank such securities would probably be simultaneously depreciated'.

Another issue involved was whether a government was justified in interfering in banking, which to *laissez-faire* ideas was the exclusive province of private enterprise. Fiji's desperate circumstances, the Colonial Office admitted, however, might justify such interference.[17]

It seems fair to deduce from the whole dispute that MacGregor gave priority to Fiji in both his aims of ensuring a return to the Fijian depositors, and of aiding Fijian development by reinvesting the deposits in Fijian securities. The Colonial Office, on the other hand, gave first thought to the necessity for economy and their principle that the prime necessity of any bank was to be self-supporting. This particular disagreement can be widened to apply to the total question of Fijian governmental finance: the local administrators beginning with Fijian interests; the Colonial Office, influenced by the British Treasury, with balanced budgets. Although this banking ordinance was finally passed, as in most issues the Colonial Office insisted on amendments.

In Fiji some exceptions were of necessity made to the Colonial Office idea that budgets had to be balanced and that no finance outside of the annual Imperial grant for government expenses would be available. For example, when the British Government agreed that as an act of grace the colony should meet some of the claims for debts incurred by the Cakobau government, loans were raised in London. MacGregor became responsible for paying these claims and spent much time dealing with the details of late and disputed claims. In July 1881 he listed £101,558 14s as the total sum due. The main outstanding disputed claim was that of the Bank of New Zealand and MacGregor's long report of 21 March 1882 gave strong reasons (which the Colonial Office hoped would be 'considered conclusive') why this bank's claim for £1,229 10s (including interest since 1874) should not be met.[18] The Crown Agents initially raised £100,000 specifically to cover most other claims.

Other objects for which special finance was raised included the cost of returning time-expired labourers from the plantations, aid towards the introduction of Indian labourers and funds to meet anticipated budget deficiencies for public works, such as roadmaking and the erection of public buildings. In sum there were three Imperial loans of £100,000, £10,000 and £150,000, a special loan of £10,000 for Suva works and a working overdraft on the Bank of New Zealand, the limit of which was eventually raised to £50,000. Fiji thus received £320,000 in this way, which, although pitiably ineffective for real needs, helped the colony to survive.

Until Gordon left Fiji at the end of 1880 the control of financial policy remained largely in his hands. MacGregor wrote important reports and made recommendations but it is difficult to determine the extent of his final decisions. He faced most responsibility in the difficult years after 1880, when the instability of Fiji was constantly stressed in Britain. Concern was expressed in the Colonial Office in 1882 when it was faced with a deficiency between general receipts and expenditure of about £7,000, together with a deficiency on immigration of about £3,000. MacGregor had met this latter deficiency by using money from one of the special Imperial grants. A leading official, J. Bramston, condemned this as 'ingenious' for both relevant accounts were in debit, and stated that 'it is a pity that it is unsound—for it would be very useful in private life'. The Colonial Office became worried about MacGregor's work, for it was believed that he was 'breaking down lately from overwork and want of repose'. But most censure was directed against Governor des Voeux, because of considerable scepticism about his 'financial abilities',[19] scepticism which was justified.

MacGregor was as bitterly disappointed as anyone else in the slow improvement each year in Fijian finances. When final 1884 figures showed a deficit of over £7,000, although the budget had estimated a surplus of about £4,000, he stressed how 'very unsatisfactory'[20] was the result. The prevailing low prices for sugar and copra, and the losses following the smallpox epidemic and consequent quarantine which led to cuts in shipping, could not inspire either London or Suva with confidence in Fiji's future.

MacGregor's 1885 report analysing financial prospects was as optimistic as possible. He could find 'no reason to suppose that there are any difficulties impending in the financial condition of the colony that cannot be met by care and foresight'. The Colonial Office, however, remained pessimistic, and criticized the mistakes made, particularly by des Voeux, in controlling expenditure. It alleged that £10,000, requested specifically for labourers for the coconut plantations, had been expended instead on labourers for the sugar industry (which, admittedly, was in 'a desperate state'); that more labourers had been imported than had been applied for; and overall that MacGregor's report 'shows how fortunate it was that the Secretary of State disallowed the wild proposal [made during the year] for a loan of £75,000'.[21]

The continued close relationship between the economy of Fiji and of the Australian colonies gave rise to suggestions that one way of recovering from Fiji's dismal position was to make these bonds even closer. MacGregor was involved in the 1880s with specific plans for arrangements with Victoria and New Zealand.

The question in its wider implications was concerned with the economic links between Britain and the Australian colonies and the bitterness of Australian inter-colonial rivalry. Henry Parkes's vigorous support of free trade as compared to Victoria's advocacy of protection and the rise of political parties in New South Wales in the 1880s based on protection and free trade were as relevant as the fact that so many of the interests involved in Fiji were centred in New South Wales. Most of the Fijian planters came from Australia (including the Colonial Sugar Refining Company based in Sydney) as did most of the shipping and trading firms. Most trade was with Australasia; 1884 figures showed that of total trade figures of £879,866, the three main components were New South Wales (£400,000), New Zealand (£110,000) and Victoria £105,000).

Fijian support in 1884 for a reciprocity treaty with Victoria was taken up by the Chamber of Commerce and backed by the *Fiji Times*. The idea gained government support after des Voeux read of the tariff agreement between Victoria and Tasmania, and while on leave in Australia he raised the suggestion with 'certain influential members of the Victorian Government', who were not unfavourable. MacGregor as Acting Administrator in 1885 became involved when des Voeux passed this suggestion on to him in a private letter written in February. Soon after, MacGregor wrote to the Victorian Government and the Colonial Office suggesting a reciprocity treaty with Victoria as the

> only means . . . I can see at the present moment that offers any hope of rendering it possible for several employers of labourers to continue their operations unless . . . the price of produce becomes better during this year.

MacGregor said he had chosen Victoria since 'Mr. Service [its premier] had given more attention than any other statesman in those colonies to the subject of intercolonial politics', and because a reciprocity treaty had 'been concluded between Victoria and Tasmania'. Further, as Victoria was the most populous of the Australian colonies, it was 'probably in a position to consume at least as much of our products as any other Colony could do'. If Fijian products could enter Victoria free of customs dues, the immediate saving to Fiji would be some £4,000 (based on 1884 figures for customs duties paid on Fijian goods entering Victoria). In Victoria's favour he suggested admitting free into Fiji certain specified Victorian products which were now dutiable, rejecting as unwise an alternative proposal to impose a discriminatory tariff on 'articles now imported into Fiji that are products of and directly shipped from New South Wales or New Zealand', because of the risk of retaliatory tariffs.

The Colonial Office was critical both of MacGregor's procedure and of the looseness of his ideas.

> Considering that MacGregor is only administrating as a 'stop-gap' I don't think he acted with his usual judgement in writing to Victoria on the subject before consulting the Secretary of State.

The substantive objections were based on a realistic appraisal of the sugar industry. In fact the value of exports of sugar varied inversely to the rate of duty: £153,673 (5s per cwt) to Sydney, £17,085 (4s 8d per cwt) to Auckland, £4,008 (3s per cwt) to Melbourne. The greater part of the capital invested in the sugar industry came from New South Wales, so that 'business connections would still draw a large portion of the sugar to that colony'; all the profit from remission of duty would not go to the Fijian growers—'owing to the competition with Queensland, the Victorian public would probably get the lion's share'; the Colonial Sugar Refining Company based in Sydney was trying hard to establish a monopoly at which it would probably succeed—'it will have the planters under its thumb; and they will be compelled to sell their cane at the Company's terms'. In addition, the rising green fruit market (mainly in bananas) would probably be injuriously affected. If these could only be sold in Victoria, the Australian Steam Navigation Company, whose headquarters were in New South Wales, would probably claim that it would no longer pay to run fruit steamers.

The Colonial Office also felt that MacGregor had too closely followed a suggestion from Fijian commercial interests and that

E

he had not devoted enough time to considering the implications of his proposal.[22] It appears that he became convinced that in the emergency, the highly critical position of Fiji's economy, the proposal might lead to improvements. It was not till later when des Voeux was in London that he told the Colonial Office of his part in the scheme. The suggestion temporarily lapsed in 1885, when Thurston took over from MacGregor as Acting Administrator.

In 1885 another suggestion to redeem the critical position of Fiji's economy was that a closer relationship with New Zealand should be established, either by a reciprocity treaty or by annexation. MacGregor passed on the suggestion without expressing either personal support or opposition.[23] But he had opposed it in the Legislative Council, where he had spoken of the difficulties and dangers if the existing form of native government were ended, and he distrusted New Zealand's capacity to rule native peoples.

In February 1886 Thurston reported that the general feeling of the colony was decidely against any annexation to New Zealand, but in May he (Thurston) asked for instructions, after correspondence with New Zealand and a petition from Fijian traders again requesting a reciprocity treaty. MacGregor, then Colonial Secretary, showed his opposition by advising that the specific suggestions made by Sir Julius Vogel, the New Zealand Treasurer, were unacceptable, especially because they insisted on preference for New Zealand against Australian goods when in fact Fiji did five times as much trade with Australia as with New Zealand. MacGregor, however, suggested limited proposals which he felt could aid the economy, involving Fiji's letting certain New Zealand goods in free, such as dairy produce and fish, in return for similar concessions by New Zealand.[24]

The renewed suggestions followed the growing crisis in the Fijian economy. The financial figures for 1885 told their own tale: excess of expenditure over revenue was more than £11,000; and the destruction in March 1886 caused by a severe hurricane, intensified the effects of fever, drought, measles, quarantine and the depressed condition of the sugar and copra industries.

Thurston analysed the melancholy outlook in May 1886 and suggested another possible economy measure: either a reduction in civil salaries or a further reduction in establishments. Generally the Colonial Office praised him for 'trying to struggle through without clamouring for a further grant in aid—which we should try to avoid by every means in our power',[25] and at this time it debated how to provide a small loan to tide Fiji over the emergency (perhaps the Crown Agents[26] would lend £10,000 from funds in hand from other colonies); the last thing wanted was 'an application to Parliament for a grant in aid'.[27] Indeed it was hoped that either the end of the commercial crisis or an increased overdraft might solve the problem, especially as Fiji was already saddled with so much indebtedness. In October the British Treasury condemned Fijian finances and emphasized that there could be no expectation, on any terms, of a further grant from Parliament; that the overdraft must be reduced to at least £16,500; and that

> 'great as [the] reduction [in expenditure] is, as compared with 1885 . . . it will be absolutely necessary to reduce the expenditure still further, by a temporary abatement from salaries and the postponement of Public Works, and Indian Immigration until the low standard of the years 1876-8 has been reached, at least, *and the revenue balances the expenditure*'.*

The Colonial Office pointed out that part of this argument was illogical, one clerk writing that 'to postpone immigration as a remedy for commercial depression seems to me to savour of insanity'.[28] This, however, was the only part of the Treasury's advice that was not accepted. Salaries were to be cut (five per cent on those earning between £200 and £350, ten per cent on £350 and over; the Governor's salary was excepted at first, but the Treasury later insisted that it should be cut), public works were to be postponed, and it was reaffirmed that no more Imperial help could be expected.

In October 1886 Thurston, as Acting Administrator, pressed by petitions from the Planters Association and the Levuka Chamber of Commerce, and supported again by MacGregor as Colonial Secretary, suggested reciprocity with Victoria. A new factor was the arrival of samples of German beet-sugar in Australian markets, leading to fears that, aided by bounties from the German Government and cheap freights on the subsidized German shipping lines, this sugar could mean 'the speedy ruin of sugar estates in Queensland and Fiji'.[29] Following negotiations between Victoria and Queensland, and Victoria and Fiji, Thurston asked the Imperial Government if it would concede to the Fijian Government the right of entering treaties of commercial reciprocity. A Commision, which included MacGregor, was set up

* Author's underlining

in Fiji to investigate the whole question of reciprocity and Mac-Gregor was praised for its detailed forty-four page report.[30] The argument of the report that 'none of the schemes hitherto put forward would work satisfactorily in practice or conduce to the general interests of the colony' and that the best hope for Fiji was an 'extended development of the many latent resources of the Colony' was accepted.[31] As was usual, the Colonial Office refused to discuss the principles involved (of protection as against free trade or of the right of the colonies to sign reciprocity treaties) as these became purely theoretical if no practicable scheme existed.

In the last eighteen months spent by MacGregor in Fiji its unhappy financial position showed no improvement. The figures for 1886, which showed a gap of £14,000 between expenditure and revenue, emphasized the need for urgent measures by the new Governor, Sir Charles Mitchell, who arrived in Fiji on 2 January 1887. By 17 January he had been 'engaged for some days in going through, with Mr Thurston and Dr McGregor, the details of Establishments and Services with a view to seeing what further retrenchments can be effected'.[32] Finding that few further cuts were possible he urged the need for a loan of £10,000 from the Imperial Government. The Colonial Office commented cryptically, 'Fiji cannot afford a highly organized government; it must be content with what it can pay for'.[33] Efficiency of government, let alone expansion of services or welfare expenditure, was irreconcilable with such ideas.

Mitchell renewed requests for a reciprocity treaty with Victoria and hoped a similar treaty with New South Wales could also be negotiated. The Colonial Office agreed that discussions should be allowed to continue. Early in 1887 the question of annexation to New Zealand was again raised. Herbert wrote

> if New Zealand is still willing to take over Fiji that consideration is now within a reasonable distance; tho' Sir A. Gordon and the Aborigines Protection Society would strongly object; and so, apparently, may Fiji itself.[34]

This suggestion, however, like the previous ones, lapsed without doing anything to solve Fijian problems.

MacGregor's long report on the revenue for 1886 revealed no easy solution, but stressed that a lack of finance could result in the curtailment of measures for the benefit of the Fijians.[35] In July 1887 Mitchell had to dismiss more officials and reduce salaries even further (five were dismissed; salaries less than £100 were not cut, but those from £100 to £300 were cut by ten per cent, those of £300 to £500 by fifteen per cent, and those of £500 and over by twenty per cent). Mitchell implied some criticism of MacGregor and some lack of sympathy with continuing efficient government when he wrote that

> the Administrators of the government during the years 1885 and 1886, partly from a dislike to make radical changes during their temporary administrations, and partly from a belief that the trade depression was only temporary, and that the Colony would yet fulfil the prophecies that had been made of its prosperity, allowed the amount of the floating debt to gradually increase, until it had attained the large sum which I found existing on my arrival.[36]

The effects of Colonial Office, and Treasury, insistence on balancing the budget were well expressed by Mitchell in November 1887:

> I hope that this endeavour to bring the cost of governing Fiji within its means will meet with your approval. The task has not only been an unpleasant, but it has been a painful, one. I have been compelled since I have been in Fiji to deprive 34 out of 125 European officers of their positions, with what at best must be considered a very inadequate sum on which to start a new life. I have had to lay a heavy burden of taxation on each of the remaining officers, with many of whom life has been a continual struggle during past years now intensified by the large reduction of their narrow incomes. The utter stoppage of the flow of promotion and almost all prospect of advancement for years to come will have a deadening effect on energies already fully taxed by an enervating climate [even if] for a time I have no doubt their high sense of duty to overcome the depressing effect of the line of action I have felt compelled to take.[37]

As could be expected in these conditions various officials, including MacGregor (as well as Blyth, H. Anson and B. H. Thomson), left Fiji. The same depressed feelings induced 520 colonists in August to urge that Fiji be annexed by Victoria.[38]

Treasury attitudes hardened, showing no sympathy for Fijian officials:

> would it not be possible in the case of colonies with a very fluctuating revenue dependent on uncertain crops and markets, to make it a rule that all increases [in salaries] granted in view of growing prosperity should be conditional on the continuance of that prosperity and withdrawable whenever expedient without compensation.

Anderson, of the Colonial Office, wrote indignantly,

> the observation . . . is perfectly absurd. How wd. the Treasury
> clerks like their increments to depend on the Revenue. . . . We
> fix salaries according to the duties and responsibilities attached
> to the office.

He continued that the precedent of a 'special tax on public servants' was a very bad one, 'contrary not only to all the accepted
principles of taxation, but to the most elementary notions of justice, and ought never to be repeated'.[39] The Colonial Office, however, made no official criticism of the Treasury, and instead reaffirmed British policy by writing to Fiji in September 1887 that,
while admitting the truth of the argument

> that all possible reductions have already been made, and that if
> the development of the colony is to be assisted still further services
> should be provided . . . the amount of Revenue paid into the
> Colonial Treasury must be the sole measure of the expenditure; and,
> until better times, the Colony must be content to dispense with
> expenditure that in other circumstances would be not merely
> desirable but even essential for the welfare of the community.[40]

There was no relief for Fiji during Mitchell's brief year as
governor. His rule was terminated mainly as an economy measure; to save payment of his salary he was promoted to the Lee-
wards and the salary of his successor in Fiji, Thurston, was reduced.[41] Nor could MacGregor have seen much hope in his last
six months in Fiji. He was in charge of the government from 20
December till 27 February, until the return of Thurston from
leave. MacGregor continued expedients, such as the temporary
transfer of credit from the Indian Immigrants Return Fund to
public funds, but realized that there must be more permanent
and fundamental improvement. There was a need for confidence
in Fiji's future since the

> very serious commercial depression is still existing in the Colony,
> and a long course of disappointment has done much to make its
> inhabitants lose heart and courage for the renewal of further
> efforts.[42]

Thurston amalgamated senior posts to save finance, adding more
work to his top harassed officials. This directly affected Mac-
Gregor who in March was given the work of Native Commissioner to add to his duties as Colonial Secretary.

The Colonial Office almost reached the *reductio ad absurdum*
of their financial arguments in discussing the proposed amalgamation of the duties of the Agent-General for Immigration with
the Receiver-General. As it was feared that this would result in

inadequate supervision of Indians, E. Wingfield, an Assistant Under-Secretary, suggested that 'we should inform the India Office that Fiji can no longer afford to maintain the necessary staff to look after Indian immigrants and that therefore Lord Knutsford does not propose to allow any more Indian immigrants to be introduced for the present'. Some officials realized, however, that such a step 'would complete the ruin of the place',[43] so this suggestion was not carried out and Thurston was told that Indian immigration must, somehow, be supervised adequately.

At last, in 1888, Treasury officials gave recognition to the efforts of the Fijian administrators to reach solvency, recording that they could 'not recall any instance of more vigorous and prompt economy on the part of a whole body of Colonial Officials'. But the efforts in Fiji were taken as support for the Treasury arguments, as proving the 'success with which circumstances of great depression can be met by resolute self-denial and a spirit of determined independence'.[44] MacGregor and other Fijian officials could well have countered the Treasury by pointing out that the self-denial and enforced efforts to achieve independence by balancing immediate budgets had in many ways prevented any chance of development in Fiji in that period.

In a significant internal Colonial Office debate in July 1887 on the estimates for the coming year some of the basic problems of the Fijian economy had been faced realistically. One clerk, Fiddes, argued that he supposed there was no chance of Imperial aid, but he could

> scarcely imagine a case in which there would be a stronger claim on the Treasury seeing that (1) it is by the continuous policy of successive Imperial governments that Fiji has been restrained from any attempt at development on the ordinary lines of a British colony (2) there has been no gross wastefulness or mismanagement (3) the present depression is due to exceptional circumstances which are (I think) passing away, and there is some prospect of improvement.

He therefore suggested borrowing £25,000 from the Crown Agents, realizing that to write an official letter to the Treasury would be a waste of energy, though a direct approach by the Secretary of State (Holland) to the Chancellor of the Exchequer might assist. Most opinion, however, in the Colonial Office was against Fiddes's view. No one expected any aid from the Treasury and the Under-Secretary, Herbert, stated that consequently Britain 'must give up . . . the idea of maintaining as good a government as was originally contemplated',[45] so renouncing after thirteen years the plans of Carnarvon and Gordon. Treasury attitudes had triumphed.

Herbert's minute was written on 4 August, three days after MacGregor accepted an offer of the governorship of British New Guinea. He was soon to face similar frustrating financial limitations in that colony, without ever having the opportunity of forming as good a government as had been begun in Fiji. Moreover, the Colonial Office, under constant Treasury pressure, became increasingly less sympathetic with governments that did not pay their own way, or which did not develop 'on the ordinary lines of a British colony'.

One assumption of the Treasury's attitude was that Fiji could have been developed on these 'ordinary lines': that is, rapid economic development could have followed if private European capital had been fully encouraged to invest in the colony and had been allowed to use indigenous labour. Instead, Gordon's policy, at first backed with few reservations by the Colonial Office, gave priority to protecting Fijian indigenous society and restricted the use of Fijian labour, even though this resulted in a slower rate of European private investment. Gordon's native policy did not imply that European development should not also be encouraged, however, and he endeavoured to aid the expansion of industries, particularly that of sugar, by importing labour. Further, he intended that Fijians should contribute to colonial economic development by supplying exportable surpluses after paying taxes by part of their produce. The crisis of the Fijian economy was partly due to the limitations of his policy in practice and particularly the difficulties experienced with native taxation and immigration.

MacGregor was involved in both these issues in his official capacities. As Receiver-General he dealt with the collection of taxes; as Chief Medical Officer he was concerned with the health of the immigrants. Further, he briefly acted as Agent-General for Immigration, for three months between December 1879 and March 1880. Naturally as Colonial Secretary, or as Acting Governor, he was concerned with all policy decisions, and in his private capacity he was consulted by Gordon, des Voeux, Mitchell and Thurston on these issues during all his years in Fiji.

Gordon's scheme for obtaining contributions from the Fijians towards the costs of administration was to impose a tax to be paid in their produce rather than cash. As such a tax was not unique even in British colonies, it is largely fruitless to try to decide who first thought of imposing such a system in Fiji. Mac-Gregor, who was always a defender of Gordon and usually critical of Thurston, is a biased witness when he gives all the credit to Gordon. He claimed Gordon had discussed the idea with him in Sydney in June 1875,[46] following Gordon's reading of a book published in 1861, J. W. B. Money's *Java; or, How to manage a Colony,* which described the Dutch produce taxation system. Gordon himself acknowledged his indebtedness to others for the actual plan adopted: he used a memorandum on the subject by Thurston, as well as papers written by David Wilkinson, W. S. Carew and others.[47]

The tax was to be based on annual assessments, estimated in money, by the Legislative Council of the amount to be paid by each province. These assessments were to take account of the population, soil and 'degree of civilization' of each province.

Once the assessment was decided the government was to invite tenders for the purchase of certain articles of exportable local produce (copra, cotton, candle-nuts, tobacco and maize were originally listed, and beche-de-mer later accepted) at fixed prices. The government guaranteed to have the produce needed to discharge the amount of the tax delivered to the highest tenderer for each article.

The assessment and tender prices were then passed down the chain of Fijian councils for determining the shares needed to be produced by each district and village. 'The individual share of produce to be contributed or work done by each family in each village' was to be decided 'by the town chief, aided by the elders of the township', as Gordon tried to base his system on the Fijian 'primitive' community system.

Tax-collectors were to take the produce to the tenderers who paid the government in money. Provision was made for refunds when any area (village, district or province) supplied more produce than was required to meet its assessment. The surplus products remained the property of the taxpayers, to whom the government had to refund their value.[48]

Although a vital part of the system was that it was a produce tax, certain exemptions were to be made. Fijians employed for money—plantation labourers, religious or school teachers—could contract out by money payments, and Gordon realized that 'paradoxical as it may seem, it is nevertheless strictly true that the reception by the government of produce in payment of taxes has

been an important step towards the introduction of cash transactions in the dealings between the traders and the natives' because they were gaining an understanding of the changing monetary values of products. Gordon regarded the scheme as experimental and said that it should be reviewed after two or three
years. If it had then failed it should be abandoned. But if it had
raised an abundant revenue and had stimulated 'the industry and
doubled the produce of the colony', as well as helping to keep
the people content and prosperous, it should be continued.[49]

Some historians have argued that this scheme was a success.
G. K. Roth, for example, in 1953 claimed that it had 'promoted
the integration of Fijian village society by making use of Fijian
lands according to customary practices, a policy on which much
of the welfare and good government of the Fijians has since depended'[50] and Morrell in 1960 wrote that the system had 'certainly achieved its financial object'.[51] Chapman in 1964 went
even further, concluding that 'the produce tax conferred positive
and even dramatic social and economic benefits upon the
Fijians'.[52] Although it is beyond the scope of this study to assess
the effects of this system up to the present day, a consideration
of its operation up to 1888, when MacGregor left the colony,
casts grave doubts upon the validity of these judgements.

The system was certainly preferable to the earlier methods of
taxation used in Fiji. A poll tax of £1 per man and 4s per woman
had been introduced by the Cakobau Government in 1871, with
its sanction of hard labour on European plantations for those
defaulting in payments; and a tax on labour had been introduced by Sir Hercules Robinson in 1874, which involved twenty
days labour a year on public works in the Fijian's own province,
convertible to a money payment varying from ten to five shillings.
Neither of these forms could have satisfied Gordon's objective of
keeping most Fijians working communally as agriculturalists in
their traditional areas, encouraging the expansion of their production and avoiding the introduction of money payments, and
of using part of the increase in production as a tax to assist in
meeting the costs of administration.

The attacks on the system included much special pleading by
its opponents. Traders were concerned because the system with
its competitive tenders prevented sharp practices whereby they
could obtain native products in exchange for goods worth far
less. Those involved in European industries were almost obliged
to attack, since it could deprive them of labour and prevent the

development of their industries. (One European's request to fish shore reefs for beche-de-mer, for example, was criticized by Mac-Gregor because 'the effect produced on the natives, some of whom would be deprived of the means of paying their taxes . . . would be very bad'.)[53] English critics, such as Sir Charles Dilke and others, drew an erroneous analogy between this system and the Dutch culture system in Java and therefore spoke as if it had introduced industrial servitude or slavery. Gordon's defence of his system stressed that the produce raised, out of which taxes were paid, remained the property of the producer so that he could gain the advantages of competitive sales or rising prices, whereas in the Dutch system the whole produce was considered as the property of the Government which would take it without competition at the price originally agreed on.[54]

But a strong case can be made against the way the system worked. Its objectives were throughout misunderstood. Wilkinson referred to a misconception by some Fijians that they were working on 'Government Gardens' when villages combined to grow enough produce to cover the tax in one plantation, but Gordon backed by MacGregor stressed that such plantations and their produce remained the property of the Fijians.[55] MacGregor's reply to a request for commutation of tax for twenty Fijians, who had been engaged to work for a European, suggests another difficulty:

> if the district has paid its assessment and there is a refund to be made, cases like that quoted would be recompensed in the refund; but if there is no refund to be made I do not see very well how such cases can have fair play so long as the tax is regarded as a communal and not as a poll tax.[56]

The difficulty was to make assessments of produce required and work to be done which were just to all, if some were subsequently allowed to leave the village. In another case MacGregor argued that native craft should not be used to bring in native tax produce, apparently on the ground that such voyaging could act against the principle of non-interference with native activities and would not keep the Fijians in their provinces.[57] This aim of keeping Fijians in their own provinces and villages had limited success, for some Fijians went to the towns, at first to deliver produce, then permanently. Thus another official, Blyth, in December 1884 claimed that sixty men from Ra and Ba were in Suva, without the permission of their chiefs. He wanted to use a native regulation which made it an offence to be absent for more than three months without permission to send these men back to their provinces.[58] Action was similarly requested against the Fijians who had come to Levuka, and official fears were expressed that 'unless some . . . example is made the evil will grow beyond all control'.[59]

There were examples of irregularities in the collection of the tax. In 1885 the Buli Saivo appropriated 4,000 leaves of the tax tobacco presumably to sell on his own account,[60] and MacGregor's comments in a private letter to Gordon in 1888 that there had been the 'usual cases of chiefs misappropriating tax copra, provincial moneys etc.'[61] suggests that such abuses had come to be accepted as inevitable.

Many Fijians apparently resented the necessity of producing for the tax. Thus MacGregor in February 1887 criticized the Bau people for being so 'far behind other people in the cultivation of their tax cane', although, as Mitchell pointed out, they 'should be the most advanced of all in intelligent cultivation of the ground', Thurston's defence that the 'past year had been one of exceptional hard work and difficulty'[62] is only part explanation for the opposition to the collection of tax. The resentment is also indicated by a revealing suggestion by MacGregor that when tax refunds were made the tax collectors should accompany the Native Commissioners, for the present system was 'very unfair . . . as it puts them [the tax collectors] before the people only as taskmasters, while the Native Commissioner comes forward as an openhanded benefactor'.[63]

There were considerable lags in tax payments. When Bega taxes were much overdue in August 1887, the Native Tax Inspector wrote:

> 17 months ago these people agreed to pay their 1886 account in beche-de-mer, yet the amount for 1886 not paid up in full. This year to pay in copra . . . unless they are hurried up it will very likely be about the end of next year before I can close their account.[64]

Odd ways of paying taxes, some of which threatened to break down the system, were spreading. For example, MacGregor objected to the Cakaudrove natives purchasing copra from Europeans at £10 to £11 per ton to make up their tax payments.

> The natives should not be allowed to purchase copra from Europeans at such rates as those quoted [since] they lose £2-£3 a ton. The practice is therefore worthy of condemnation on financial considerations, but it is equally objectionable on political grounds.

It would be far better to accept taxes in money, but that I am not prepared to recommend.[65]

The same point appeared when the Namata natives in 1887 offered their tax payments in cash. MacGregor wrote:

> If money is accepted from a single district on Tai Levu there will soon be an end of native taxes. I see no hardship whatever in their fishing for beche-de-mer and growing cane as well: they will not be asked to pay tax in beche-de-mer and then to pay over again out of cane, but will have the latter as refund if they pay their taxes in the former.

The governor, Mitchell, affirmed that 'under no circumstances will money be accepted'.[66] When later in 1887, however, Namosi Fijians asked whether money for bananas sold locally could be accepted for their taxes, there is evidence of weakening opposition by government officials. MacGregor minuted 'this was done without authority, was disapproved by the Governor, and was not to be repeated', but another officer, Emberson, asked 'may not "our poverty" be again pleaded for the adoption of this proposal,' and it seems that, eventually, the money was accepted.[67]

'Our poverty' is the clue to another criticism of the system, for the returns of early years were not maintained to 1888. Legge, in his praise of the tax scheme, stresses the best of the early figures.[68] Gordon's preliminary estimate, that £22,000 could be raised in 1876, was found to be too optimistic and it took time before the scheme was working. In 1877 of an estimate of £19,300, £15,103 was raised. In 1878 the estimate was £20,000 and £18,178 was raised; in the best year, 1879, the estimate was £19,800 and £19,885 was raised, but this was the only year the assessment was reached. In 1881 the assessment was £18,000 and £12,800 was the net produce; in 1882, £18,000 and £14,711; in 1883, £19,675 and £17,171; in 1884, £18,000 and £17,700. After the hurricane of 1886 estimates were dropped to around £10,000, but this was raised again to £17,700 in 1887. Native taxation did not produce enough revenue to make Fijian administration buoyant and it had not proved possible to increase the assessments. Instead, depressed prices in the late 1880s meant that the natives had to produce more to reach their quotas.

These defects in the working of the taxation system suggest reasons for doubting its alleged success. MacGregor, who had given wholehearted support to the tax when it was introduced by Gordon, was to make no secret of his uneasiness with the scheme both in his private letters to Gordon and in his public reports. In 1879 his criticisms centred on two points—the degree of interference with native production and the standing of the tax collector. He suggested to Gordon, who was on leave away from Fiji, that it was unwise to receive all the natives' produce; instead some should be left to them 'to sell as they liked [which] would deprive the commercial part of the community of what will no doubt be considered by many as a real grievance'. He thought Gordon might think it

> foolish to advance such an argument in what may be called the hour of victory, for from here [Levuka] at least you seem to have carried everything before you: but it is at such a time that concessions can best be made; and it should not be forgotten that with the exception of about three or four officials every white person in the colony is opposed to the scheme [MacGregor probably exaggerated] and will not cease to attack it so long as they can find a weak point in it. Another defect is the anomalous way it is conducted. Surely the time has now come when those employed in this work should be put on the same footing as other officials in the Government service. So long as the thing remains as an 'experiment' it courts attack and invites criticism and opposition much of which would cease were this branch of the service put on a permanent and regular footing.[69]

In April 1881 MacGregor reverted to his criticism of the way the taxation system was run. He thought that it was not in a healthy condition, and never would be 'until managed quite differently'. A refund owing to the Kadavuan people for 1879 was still held in the office; no refund had yet been paid to anyone for 1880 and the amount received by the Treasury was only a little over £15,000. A remedy would be to appoint better collectors. He suggested two men for the whole colony who would

> enter into the feelings of the natives, that will aid them, not bully them; that will be looked to with respect and not be regarded as enemies . . . I have several times warned you [Gordon] that the thing was not on a sound footing, and I do trust that you will endeavour to rectify the greatest defects. . . . Up to the present time the scheme has been managed by the Tax Collector. Its conception embraces more laudable aims, which it misses, however, by the plan of working. What crop of a permanent character has been put in for the future benefit of the natives? What improvement has been made on his soil? I have looked in vain for these on the places I have visited lately. These things must be considered, and acted on too, as well as how to raise revenue, otherwise the natives will not have fair play.[70]

In June 1881 he again stressed defects in management rather than

any inherent weakness in the system itself. The refund has proved a failure. Properly managed it should have given a strong incentive to extend cultivation on account of the high price secured for crop, but anything received from a district over the assessment has disappeared from the vision of the owners, and no result been visible for a year or more. Hence for last year there is no refund; planting is either limited to the amount required by assessment or falls short, sometimes far short of it. How could it possibly be otherwise in the nature of things? The Colonial Secretary [Thurston] is a hard man, destitute of imagination and deficient in sympathy, well adapted for putting on the screw and for making the scheme temporarily a success, or something near it, financially, because he looks only to the book result at the end of the year. You have put the matter entirely in his hands, and although he has not yet brought to it irretrievable ruin, it has fallen much short of what it was capable of becoming under the control of a man so constituted as to gain the confidence, respect the habits of thought, and enter into the feelings of the natives. If the scheme is not to die out the future *must* be looked to: as soon as a district, and for this purpose districts should be small, has paid its assessment, let each man, or each town, or each family, or each mataqali,* as maybe best, on delivering produce receive the contract price for it there and then, and I believe cultivation will at once receive an impetus. Nothing pleases a native like prompt payment. Under the present arrangements his energy is crippled, because he looks on the sale of produce to traders as something bordering on the illicit, on account of the restrictions in his way, and he has no other means of obtaining ready money to buy a loaf for his children or a sulu for his wife.

MacGregor felt he could not raise these suggestions, because of the uncomfortable power relationships between himself, Thurston and Governor des Voeux:

I am of course powerless to introduce the modifications I suggest. I should only incur the resentment of the Colonial Secretary [Thurston] if I meddled with the matter; if I gave my reasons and proposed my remedy to the Governor he would probably write a minute to the Colonial Secretary on the spur of the moment directing that my proposal should have an immediate trial. Even if I am right, I therefore cannot move.[71]

In July 1882, however, in a financial review, MacGregor made official suggestions to improve tax collections. He claimed that

* Sub-groups of the *yavusa*, descendants of a group of brothers; each *mataqali* consisting of the descendants of one brother.

the present system of making assessments (in November), then
calling tenders for the purchase of the produce (in December),
was wrong.

> The tenders should be opened first, the assessment should be
> based on the tenders accepted . . . if this is not done the assessment
> should perhaps be one in produce and not one in money.

A money assessment would be better for the Treasury, 'but the
assessment in money in a year when prices were low must tell
with severe effect on the people'.[72] So much produce would be
required that they would be left with little to meet the ordinary
wants of life, and they could receive little for the smaller quantity which they could divert to their own use.

The Colonial Office became increasingly critical of the system,
going even beyond MacGregor's uneasiness. By 1882, six years
after its introduction, the Colonial Office thought the Fijians
were being 'worked to the highest point, consistent with safety,
to produce articles of constantly less commercial value'. It was
also recognized that 'natives, with native overseers and native
methods of cultivation, will be less than able to stand against
European enterprise'. Perhaps if the natives produced an article
of 'greater value and less liable to fluctuation in price than
copra' the position might be relieved. The tax system has been

> an experiment from the first, and though it has answered fairly
> well hitherto, some other arrangement may no doubt be accepted
> as soon as the Governor sees his way to proposing it.

Yet it was realized how hard it would be for the governor to
admit that the 'native scheme [was] moribund'.[73]

The Fijian administration throughout MacGregor's period was
committed to Gordon's system and resisted all pressures for
change. Thurston raised traditional arguments in 1884 when he
defended the produce tax following a petition of European
colonists for a change in policy. He opposed a suggested head
tax of £1, claiming that its real object was to make the Fijians
agricultural labourers for the planters.[74] MacGregor, also, at this
time supported Gordon's ideas, attacking only the working
of the system.

In June 1884 des Voeux seemed unfavourable to the tax and
considered the substitution of some other scheme. MacGregor
again defended the principle of a communal produce tax as
against an individual money tax and criticized Fijians who
argued for the latter. He thought these Fijians were the very

ones who were breaking down the old communal system. For example, he could not approve of the Fijians of such districts as Tai Levu, who earned large sums of money by clearing ground under contract and then wanted to pay taxes in money, rather than working in the fields for their produce tax, in order to have more freedom and a greater amount of time to themselves. He also attacked the chiefs of such people, the 'foremost in asking why they should not pay in money', since they reaped the greatest profit from the contracts and were beginning 'to think more of themselves than of their people'.[75]

His criticism of the scheme's administration remained unabated. When he became directly responsible for native taxation in 1884 another reason appeared. MacGregor found difficulty in ascertaining details because the previous director (D. J. Chisholm) had become 'a kind of alcoholic sponge. He objects to my taking over as he says he has looked after [taxes] for years and others have had all the credit'.[76]

The declining figures for produce, combined with the growing gap between these figures and the annual assessments, persuaded the Colonial Office in November 1884 to suggest the appointment of an investigator, independent of the government, and to hope for frank discussions with Thurston when he reached London on leave.[77] There was growing suspicion about the success of Gordon's policies: Herbert admitted he was

> becoming very doubtful whether the policy, right in its original intention, of teaching the Fijians to govern themselves and tax themselves on tribal principles is not being injudiciously carried to a point at which it oppresses the natives more than the opposite policy would do.

Another London official agreed that the system had

> degenerated into a control by the chiefs over the services and earnings of the inferior natives. Now that there is growing up in Fiji a regular and recognised demand for hired labour this system must not only be liable to become unjust but must hamper greatly those who require paid labour.[78]

Herbert and the Secretary of State, Derby, felt that a compromise, which would mean more government control over the chiefs, as in the Java system, might be the best solution to Fiji's growing problems. Thurston, however, persuaded the Colonial Office to make no changes.

MacGregor's criticisms still did not go as far as some of the Colonial Office suggestions, for, when he was acting as governor,

F

he still hoped to make Gordon's plan work. He was, however, at this time persuaded that the natives were being overtaxed and that some better method of refund should be devised. Objections had been made that if there were an excess of produce over a group's share of tax, and the surplus were refunded, it often was not distributed but seized by the chief for himself. MacGregor put it this way to Gordon in April 1885:

> a conviction is gaining ground on me that the natives, what with reduction of their numbers, what with the low prices of produce, are overtaxed. The total amount should be reduced at once to £15,000, the principal relief being required for Ra, Nadroga and Macuata.

He believed it then took the same amount of labour to produce £15,000 as it formerly had to produce £20,000. He felt the method of refund should be put on a different footing for it had proved a failure. He suggested that after the tax assessment had been met in produce 'each mataqali should be able to take its produce to the contractor [and] receive payment for it on the spot'.[79] He was, however, doubtful about advocating even this change, presumably because it would mean that money would be controlled by the *mataqali*, so further breaking down the traditional Fijian economic system.

By 1886 MacGregor had reduced his estimates of the amount that should be derived from taxes to £10,000. This followed the hurricane of March, which made it appear probable that the natives would be 'incapable of paying taxes in kind for some years', so that it seemed that 'the Native Taxation scheme, elaborated with so much pains, [would] die a natural death, at least for a time'.[80] In 1887 MacGregor said the taxes had 'so far been the left hand of the government and must not be overdriven or evil will come of it'.[81]

In the dire financial straits of Fiji from 1886 to 1888 every possible way of gaining more revenue was canvassed (including a money payment, or hut tax or a poll tax), but the native taxation system with all its displayed faults was maintained. MacGregor, like other officials, had kept faith with Gordon's ideas.

Until the workings of the taxation system in every province, especially after 1880, are adequately analysed, it is not possible to evaluate this contemporary debate. Even then speculation will be needed to consider the effects of alternative systems. Perhaps the most important result for MacGregor was increased suspicion of any theory or system of colonial rule, which he realised must depend on constant review.

5

Fiji: Labour and Development 1875-88

The more the officers of any government associate with the people, the more fully cognisant must that government be of the wishes and wants of the country.

One of the aims of the native taxation system was to keep the Fijians on their lands and to prevent their exploitation as labourers for the planters. Gordon was not opposed to European expansion, however, and supported the introduction of labourers from outside Fiji to satisfy the planters' needs. Before he arrived the planters had already found difficulties in obtaining enough Fijians and from 1864 had been recruiting workers from other Pacific islands. These labourers, called Polynesians, were usually brought in on three-year contracts and came mainly from the New Hebrides, the Solomon, Gilbert, Kingsmill and Tokelau islands. This labour traffic, and the simultaneous introduction of islanders into other Pacific islands and Queensland, was closely watched by the Imperial and Australian governments under pressure from humanitarians and missionaries. In 1872 the British Pacific Islanders Protection Act had been passed, giving some control over the recruitment and transportation of labour. It left the problem of control over the labourers on the plantations to local governments, whether in Queensland or Fiji.

From the 1860s there had been suggestions that Indian labourers should also be used in Fiji. Gordon suspected that there might be a decrease in the supply of Polynesians, due to better regulation of recruiting, depopulation and increased competition from Queensland, Samoa and New Caledonia, so that an alternative source of labour might be needed. Consequently, in his first speech[1] to the Fijian colonists he proposed the introduction of Indians, and the first arrived in 1879.

Although the Polynesian and Indian labourers were brought to Fiji to assist the planters, ironically these planters provided the

67

main opposition to all Gordon's immigration policies. The reason was his protection of Fijian labour and insistence on strictly regulated immigration and control of all labour.[2] Gillion succinctly sums up the planters' attitudes to Indian labour:

> Most of them had small estates (200 to 1,000 acres), were in debt, and could not afford the large initial payments needed for Indian immigrants, or the elaborate hospital requirements in the draft Indian Immigration Ordinance. Unlike Fijians and Islanders, Indian labourers were an unknown quantity except to a few coffee planters who had come from Ceylon and thought that Tamils should be introduced.[3]

MacGregor's concern in immigration in his early years in Fiji arose mainly from his position as Chief Medical Officer. Although he was increasingly concerned in general policy decisions affecting immigrants as he rose in the service, he was only actually in charge of immigration for a few months.

The health of the Polynesians and Indians gave him considerable trouble. Although the number of these immigrants was never greater than the Fijians, whose health problems were so immense, he knew that the Indian and British governments, and humanitarian opinion overseas, were concerned with their treatment. Consequently he devoted a disproportionate amount of time and effort to them.

As soon as Indian immigration was mooted MacGregor as usual insisted on strict quarantine and other rules. He clearly expected difficulties:

> after a considerable amount of experience extending over some thousands of cases of sickness among Indian Immigrants [in the Seychelles] I came to the conclusion that as a class they are the most delicate people I have ever had to deal with professionally. Exposed to cold and wet they have an extreme susceptibility to diseases of the chest, Bronchitis, Pneumonia, and Pulmonary Consumption, to Diarrhoea and Dysentery, and to attacks of malarial fever arising from the renewed activity of fever poison formerly dormant in their systems.[4]

He wanted a large quarantine site to be chosen, assurance that Indian food would be available, a new ward for the hospital and, of course, more doctors.

His fears were reinforced by the arrival in May 1879 of the first Indian migrant ship, the *Leonidas*, on which among the 464 labourers there were people with cholera, of whom eleven died, and smallpox and dysentery, of whom six died. Elaborate quarantine precautions were taken, particularly against small-

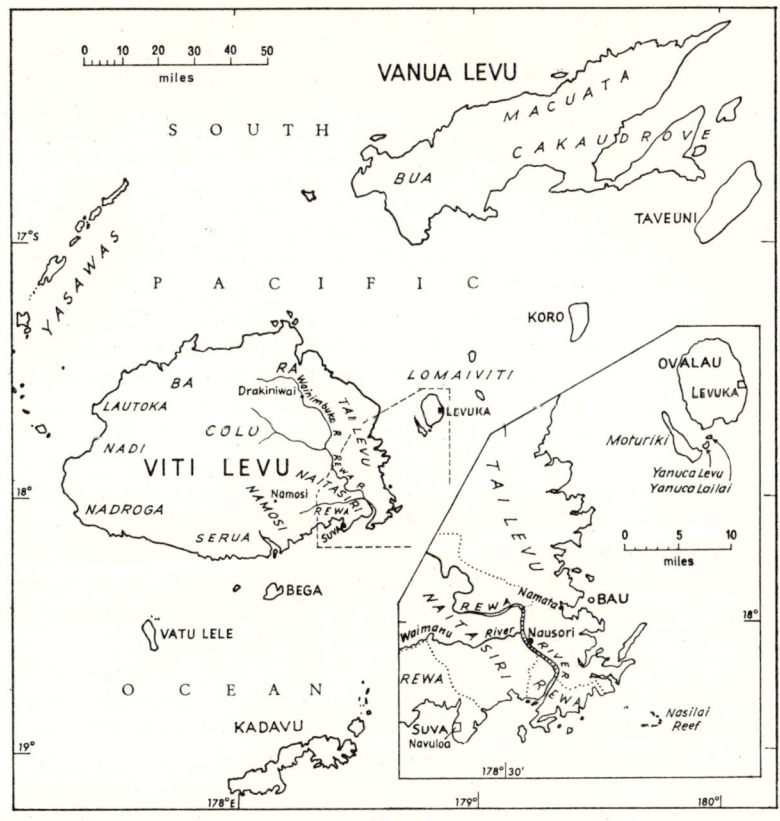

3 Fiji

pox as one case had been diagnosed only five days before they reached Fiji. MacGregor's determination to prevent the spread of disease was shown by his instructions to guards on the Fijian coast 'to fire on any boat or any person from any boat attempting to land or to approach the shore'[5] elsewhere than at the new quarantine depot of Yanuca Lailai, a small islet near Levuka. MacGregor overruled the doctor on board by insisting that 'so long as there appears to me *the slightest chance* of danger I must deprecate the liberation of the coolies'.[6] They were quarantined for ninety days, during which another fifteen of the total of 464 died.

Morrell's account of the arrival of the *Leonidas,* while pictures-

que, is misleading for the emergency was not 'a triumph of im-
provisation'[7] but rather the reflection of the wisdom of precautions taken by experienced men. Vaccination was begun by 1876;[8]
MacGregor had discussed quarantine arrangements and inspected Yanuca Lailai and Yanuca Levu in April 1876, which were
almost ready for use in March 1877.[9]

As a result of the *Leonidas* voyage MacGregor increased the
scale of medicines required for future migrant ships[10] and in
January 1880 advised the erection of an isolation ward for sick
Indian immigrants on one of the unoccupied islands in Suva
harbour.[11] In May 1882 Nukulau was chosen.[12] As Receiver-
General, he had to decide the rates of duty for Indian foodstuffs.
The rate on rice was 'intentionally made low in view of the
prospective introduction of Indian immigrants',[13] and later special
low rates were fixed for cymbal, ghee, tamarinds, chillies, must-
ard seed, turmeric, coriander seed and black pepper.[14] A more
important problem which concerned MacGregor as treasurer
was how to pay for Indian immigration. One cheerful feature
however, was a surplus (over £4,000 in 1888) in the funds provided
for the return of Indian immigrants, from which he was able
to borrow to meet other debts.[15] These funds had not been used
because so many Indians preferred to stay in Fiji.

Fortunately MacGregor's early fears about Indian health
proved misleading, especially in comparison with the Polynesians,
for labour vessels after the *Leonidas* had few major health problems and Indians in Fiji were fairly healthy. A return for plantation labour in June 1882 showed that the average annual mortality for Indians was twenty per 1,000 as compared with the
shocking figure of 540 per 1,000 for the Polynesians. MacGregor
argued that the 'cunning, exacting, complaining Indian' was
far more able to look after himself than the average Polynesian,
who was 'more passive, greatly more ignorant and far less able
to protect himself'. Other advantages, he thought, were that the
Indian often worked on piece rates and so had

> the choice of avoiding exposure to the worst heat of the sun, or
> the heaviest rain, besides which he could feed himself and had
> showed a talent for cooking and for making himself comfortable.

Thurston agreed that MacGregor had given 'a concise and exact
statement of the facts'.[16]

MacGregor's analysis of Indian character reflected his growing
lack of sympathy with them, and this was made quite clear by
some of his Minutes. For example, he wrote in September 1883,

when scavengers were wanted for Suva Hospital, 'if Fijians or Polynesians of any kind are procurable they are preferable to coolies who are eternally pilfering about the hospital, and are, moreover incorrigibly filthy in their habits'.[17] Or, as he wrote in 1887:

the evil behaviour of the Indian prisoners is not . . . to be put down to want of supervision, but to the natural viciousness of the Indians and to the fact that the majority of them are there because they will not work on their plantations.[18]

The alleged statistical support for MacGregor's opposition on this racial ground of 'natural viciousness' was an 1884 report which showed for each 'race' (European, Fijian, Polynesian and Indian) the relationship between convictions for offences against the laws and total numbers. The Indian percentage of 33.28% was far higher than the European 9.49%, Polynesian 4.23%, or Fijian 0.76%.[19] The figures are, of course, questionable because of the nature of the laws, particularly those concerning labour, and also because the numbers of charges reflect the prejudices of officials and planters.

These prejudices were clearly expressed after several Indians had bought land and proposed settling in Suva. A group of property owners protested in November 1883 that such a colony would 'very seriously deteriorate the value of our properties . . . taking into consideration the objectionable habits and mode of life of this race of people'. MacGregor minuted:

no doubt it is undesirable to have coolie neighbours because the latter pilfer, are dirty in their habits, congregate together and overcrowd their settlements, breed goats and are nothing short of being a nuisance to near neighbours. It would probably have been better for the Indians themselves to settle in a more secluded neighbourhood; but I am afraid nothing can be done now in the matter as the Indian will doubtless stick to his rights, and part with the land only at a profit.

Thurston agreed that the purchases could not be overturned, but recommended future sales by auction to prevent such results from silent sales.[20]

MacGregor made no secret of his attitudes, which were fairly generally shared. For example, in his farewell speech after praising the Fijians—'no other [race] on the face of the earth so interesting'—and the Polynesians—who 'commanded admiration'—he stated that the best he could say for the Indians was that 'they are necessary evils'. The press report recorded 'applause and laughter' at this point.[21]

Happily, however, some officials tried to appreciate the Indian viewpoint, the magistrate Walter Carew, for example, who urged concessions for Indian customs.[22] Nor did MacGregor allow his prejudices to smother his humanitarian feelings completely. He unhesitatingly risked his life to save Indians endangered by the wreck of a migrant ship.

As she neared Suva at 8.45 p.m. on Sunday 11 May 1884 the *Syria,* carrying 448 Indian immigrants from Calcutta, struck Nasilai reef four miles off shore in heavy surf. Much of the equipment was smashed, but the mate and four others left for help in the one remaining lifeboat. Ironically these men were taken into quarantine at Levuka and were unable to persuade anyone of the urgent need for help. By daylight the ship was beginning to break up, yet it was not until Tuesday that most people were saved. Even so, fifty-six died in the disaster.[23]

MacGregor arrived off the reef on Tuesday and with John Fowler was mainly responsible for organizing the rescue operations. His personal bravery undoubtedly saved many lives. His own description written a month later to Gordon was vivid and emotional:

> I hardly like to mention the matter because the press and people have spoken of myself in connection therewith in a way that makes me ashamed, and that I tell you honestly hurts me very keenly. . . . The scene was simply indescribable, and pictures of it haunt me still like a horrid dream. . . . People falling, fainting, drowning all around one; the cries for instant help, uttered in an unknown tongue, but emphasised by looks of agony and the horror of impending death, depicted on dark faces rendered ashy grey by terror; then again the thundering, irresistible wave breaking on the riven ship, still containing human beings, some crushed to death in the debris, and others wounded and imprisoned therein; and all to be saved then or never. . . . [Some sacrificed their lives to save others; some, such as the strong lascar crew] thought only of themselves, and rushed into the boats surrounded by dying women and children. One of these lascar seamen I took out of the wreck paralysed with terror; afterwards by brute force I threw him twice out of a boat to make room for drowning children . . . in spite of everything that could be done the loss of life was fearful. At 2 p.m. I was almost faint with despair, I did not then think that more than a hundred or so could be saved. As I had somehow got to have charge of the whole concern, you can imagine the crushing weight of the responsibility I felt, and you will, I am sure believe me when

I tell you that I do not feel the same man since. I fear you may think it strange that 56 people should be killed and drowned and I, whose duty it was to see that assistance was given in the worst cases, came off with only a few bruises and slight wounds that were healed in a week. I can only say that I did the best I could. I did not ask any of those with me to risk their lives in going into the wreck with myself, save the four Fijians, whom I have recommended for the medal of the Royal Humane Society: and I could not know each time, for I went many times, whether I could return alive, especially as I am no swimmer of any use—although in the breakers there swimming was not of much avail. I feel it almost ludicrous to offer, as it were an apology for being alive: but I *am* sure you can understand the feeling that I entertain, half fearful lest you should think that because I *am* alive I did not do all that might have been done.[24]

Outside observers were certain that he had done all that was possible, and he was rewarded from England with the Albert Medal and from Australia with the Clarke Gold Medal[25] for his bravery. Fowler received a Clarke Silver Medal, and the four Fijians were also rewarded. A typical press report said

foremost of all stands Dr McGregor who took a leader's place and kept it by his tireless energy, and the cool daring with which he exposed his life repeatedly in his successful attempts to succour and save the drowning.[26]

A more dramatic account described how he had

rescued the emigrants, clambering along a broken mast and carrying them one by one to safety on his back. One of the women had fallen overboard and with the captain of the ship and a police officer who had gone to her help was being swept out to sea. The doctor, who was a man of tremendous physical strength, slid down a rope, and with the woman's hair in his teeth and a man in each hand dragged them back to safety.[27]

Despite this instance of his bravery in saving the Indians, in everyday affairs MacGregor showed far more sympathy to Polynesian immigrants than to Indians. Before Gordon had arrived a Fijian Government proclamation of 14 October 1874 had adopted the Queensland Act governing the introduction and treatment of Polynesian labourers. Gordon replaced this Act by an 1876 Ordinance which provided that only licensed British vessels could trade. Their licences could be cancelled at the discretion of the Agent-General for Immigration and a bond of £500 was required from their masters. The type of vessel, the amount of accommodation for each immigrant and the rations and medicines to be provided were set out. A government agent was to accompany and supervise each vessel and had to make certain that the prospective recruits understood the nature of the contract, the conditions of work and were willing to be engaged. On arrival in Fiji the Polynesians were to be inspected and allotted to employers by the Agent-General for Immigration. MacGregor probably assisted in framing all sections of this 1876 ordinance and was certainly the author of its medical requirements.[28]

He was also partly responsible for the drafting of the ordinance of 1877 which controlled the conditions of employment in Fiji. By this law planters had to apply for labourers,[29] who were assigned to them on contract for periods up to five years. Regulations covered housing, food and medicine and power was given to the Agent-General for Immigration to inspect plantations. If there were more than fifty labourers on a plantation a hospital building had to be provided. The working day was fixed at nine hours per week day and five on Saturdays, and pay was to be a minimum of £3 per annum, payable every six months into the Colonial Treasury on behalf of the labourers.

Few Polynesians were introduced into the colony during the first few years that these regulations were in force, however. The return of time-expired labourers whom previous governments had lacked finance to move was the main initial task of the Immigration Department. The numbers of Polynesians in Fiji fell from 3,835 in 1875 to 1,697 at the end of 1877. About 1,500 were obtained in 1878 and 1,428 in 1879, in which year 3,200 Polynesians were indentured by employers.[30]

Having drawn up the health provisions of both ordinances, MacGregor insisted on their fulfilment. The high death-rate on labour vessels worried him; for example, twenty-four out of fifty-three immigrants died on the *Daphne* in 1878, and fifty-seven out of 153 on the *Stanley* in December 1879.[31] As Chief Medical Officer, and following his work as acting Agent-General for Immigration, on 13 September 1880 MacGregor presented a long report on immigration. This incorporated suggestions he had made in May 1879 and dealt with every stage of immigration from recruiting to work on the plantations.[32]

This report showed that, especially since the *Stanley* tragedy, improvements had been made. Recruiting vessels were checked for cleanliness, for carrying capacity (the old scale of three adults to two registered tons had been reduced to not more than one for each ton), for the medicines carried on board and for the food provided for the Polynesians (to the basic six lb yams per day or its equivalent in vegetable food, a reserve store had to be carried, including special provisions for the sick and all had to have a daily dose of lime juice). To ensure that only the most healthy islanders were recruited, payment was made not on the basis of the numbers *recruited* in good health but on numbers *landed* in Fiji in good health. MacGregor had made the government agents more useful, for while he was in charge of the Immigration Department he had given 'employment successively to nearly all [of them] as warders for a short time in Levuka Hospital' where they could study the treatment of common diseases. He suggested that they should become permanent government officials, instead of being picked up casually for a trip or two, as was so often the case. He maintained that an absolute rule should be imposed 'that no labour vessel should be out of port from the middle of December to the beginning of April', the hot, wet hurricane period. He thought that permanent recruiting stations in various Pacific islands might be a way of avoiding some of the worst aspects of indiscriminate recruiting.

Changes had been made to ensure the health of Polynesians after their arrival in Fiji also. If unhealthy they were to be kept in the depot to be medically examined and, if possible, vaccinated. The last requirement was an ideal hard to attain owing to the lack of trained vaccinators. In July 1880 MacGregor admitted that the revenues of the country were not in a position to warrant keeping Polynesians in the depot, and as the government was liable for their pay after thirty days they would have to be released whether vaccinated or not. He trusted that his 1877 regulations would give adequate protection on the plantations.[33]

This was one issue on which the Colonial Office seemed prepared, partly because of humanitarian pressures, to question the limitations of expense: 'We must not attend too much to the financial side of the question in a matter of life or death'. But typically it added: 'If the importers can't afford to pay for doctors they must not import immigrants during the season when medical aid is indispensable'.[34]

In 1881 MacGregor drafted another ordinance providing for regular visits of doctors to immigrants on plantations. This idea had been under discussion from at least 1878 and followed complaints by some planters of lack of governmental inspections. The money to be paid to the doctors for these visits was to be provided by the employers, on the basis of the number of their employees. MacGregor claimed that the 'ordinance . . . secures medical attention and treatment to every coloured labourer in each medical district'.[35]

The necessity for such an ordinance was emphasized by the high mortality, especially among Polynesian labourers. The death-rate in Viti Levu in 1880 was forty per 1,000, and dropped the next year to 31.25 per 1,000, an improvement which Dr Corney attributed not to any medical inspections but 'to the weakly ones having already died out and the survivors becoming acclimatized'.[36] In May 1882 MacGregor made a careful personal inspection of eight Viti Levu plantations. As a result of his discussions with the managers and the Agent-General for Immigration he drew up detailed suggestions for protecting the health of these labourers. He blamed the high Polynesian death-rate on the change from a 'lazy and indolent life' to one of 'continuous and hard work fed on food of inferior quality, and exposed to all kinds of bad weather'. He set out requirements for housing and sleeping accommodation, food (he supported the use of manioc or kassava as 'it is largely used by planters in Seychelles and is there a healthy and nutritious diet'), water, and care of the sick. He again contrasted the passive Polynesian and the cunning Indian labourer to make the point that 'if this comparison of the two races is a fair one . . .the law should provide greater protection for the Polynesian than for the Indian'. Realistically he concluded that 'the mere passing of a law will not per se supply the remedy . . . efficient inspection of estates is the only safeguard against the abuse of the Polynesians'.[37] While MacGregor was in Fiji inspections were ensured and his supervision undoubtedly aided the Polynesians. He was easily aroused by any possible abuse of these labourers. In 1885, for example, as Acting Administrator he refused permission to the Macarthurs (European planters) to take some Polynesian labourers to Samoa. When Derby, as British Colonial Secretary, overruled him, MacGregor wrote: 'What suffering he will cause thereby! the proposal deserves condemnation on the ground of humanity and for fiscal reasons'.[38]

The depressed conditions in Fiji meant that planters found it difficult to afford labourers and MacGregor, as Colonial Secretary, in 1885 had to devise some methods of using the Polynesians in the depot and the 1,200 Indians who had been demanded. He suggested allotting the Polynesians to planters at a lower rate (£15 a year) and using many of the Indians on governmental works. Polynesians, like Indians, were drifting to the towns in those years and there were complaints of their 'mekes' (noisy, long-lasting celebrations) in the Suva suburb of Toorak.[39] As conditions seemed to improve more Polynesians were absorbed by the planters and the task of supervision again became important. Outbreaks of dysentery and some cases of cerebro-spinal meningitis stressed the need for constant care.

The cost of both Indian and Polynesian labour, however, was felt by the government to be higher than the economy could afford. Therefore, in part contrast to Gordon's policy, an ordinance was passed in 1886, permitting Fijians to work on task or time work. Minimum wages of 8d per task or per day were fixed; a quarter was payable weekly and the other three quarters at the end of the contract. Thurston felt that this ordinance gave 'much satisfaction'. Wilkinson wanted the inducement of cash payments as most Fijians were 'far too well off and contented . . . to voluntarily leave their homes to go and work for hire'.[40]

This change was only in part contrast to Gordon's policy since it was not intended to disturb village life. A condition which was intended to be strictly enforced was that a Fijian accepting such work was to be paid off in the district in which he was engaged. It was feared that if paid off elsewhere he would soon be relieved of his wage, or of the goods purchased by it.

> Under such circumstances the man is ashamed to return to his family and village and either vagabondises about the country a nuisance to everyone or he engages with the same or another employer for a second term of service and in many cases keeps away from his family for years.[41]

MacGregor sincerely desired to protect the Polynesian labourers and his plea in February 1888 was a typical one:

> I deem it an imperative duty on the governor here to never lose an opportunity of making it plain to employers of Polynesians that these labourers must not be beaten . . . such things will not be tolerated.[42]

A bitter Colonial Office comment of 1888 on the whole traffic is apt: 'In view of the frightful mortality among these Polynesians, it is a good thing that this importation is so very small. It should be discouraged as much as possible'.[43] These unfortunate men were exploited by their employers and by the Government of Fiji; it was only due to officials such as MacGregor that the exploitation did not become intolerable.

It should not be deduced from MacGregor's medical and humanitarian concern with Indian and Polynesian labour that he was indifferent to planter interests. These labourers had been introduced to assist European development and, as in the Seychelles, MacGregor tried to appreciate the viewpoint of the planter as well as that of the labourer. His attitude has been unfairly contrasted[44] with that of Henry Anson, the Agent-General for Immigration (1882-88), who sympathized markedly more with the labourers, particularly the Indians, and insisted on inspection of labour conditions. MacGregor also did his utmost to safeguard the labourers by regulations and inspections, but the comparison is justified in so far as he was unsympathetic to the Indians and perhaps in so far as he was vitally concerned, as Treasurer, with the contributions of the planters to the Fijian economy.

His interest in the coffee industry exemplifies this concern. In May 1879 a disease attacked the leaves of the trees. It was first observed in the Great Amalgam Estate, on the Waimanu, a branch of the Rewa River. There was no government botanist so MacGregor, using techniques and knowledge acquired in his one brilliant university year of botany, undertook an investigation to identify the disease and find a cure. As with any task he undertook, he did not spare himself. Despite other pressing duties he found time to visit the plantations and to carry out intensive research which led to very detailed reports, a map of affected and unaffected areas and clear recommendations.[45] He was then given the job of attempting his suggested cure: destruction of the whole plantation in which any tree had the disease. Aided by some of the first Indian migrants who had not been allotted and ignoring obstinate planters and the first denials by London experts of his identification of the disease as hemileia vastratrix, MacGregor began this destruction. He also faced acting Governor des Voeux' lack of enthusiasm. Gordon, when he returned, however, backed MacGregor and was critical of des Voeux, whose hesitation was explained by his fear that the government would not be able afford compensation for the planters.[46]

Eventually MacGregor's drastic methods were approved, as were his later attempts to apply treatment with lime, sulphur and hyposulphate of soda. His reports gained adulation from London and his untiring work brought admiration in Fiji, despite the severe blow to the economy. But MacGregor became dispirited and wrote to Gordon from Kasava:

the mental worry that I suffer from fighting against an enemy that must in all probability conquer affects me very much more than all the fatigue and exposure I have to undergo in connection with it. Of course I act precisely as if I entertained no doubt of success, although that is hard to do with failure and discredit ahead.[47]

Publicly he showed no signs of any lack of confidence in his work, and clung to his opinions in his debate with the experts of Kew Gardens.

It would doubtless be great presumption on my part to express an opinion . . . at variance with the views of Sir Joseph Hooker, one of the greatest, if not the greatest, authority on such subjects. I however have no doubt whatever that the disease prevalent in Fiji is Hemileia Vastratrix.

Nor did he hesitate to press the case for more scientific aid for himself.

Fiji is outside the scientific world, . . . I am cut off from intercourse with scientific men and have to provide out of my salary of £350 a year all scientific instruments and appliances I require as Chief Medical Officer of this colony.

But he did go beyond his own interests to more general Fijian development in his argument for the appointment of a full-time government botanist 'better qualified than myself to continue the struggle and with more time at his command'.[48]

The highest praise for MacGregor came eventually from Kew Gardens.

Sir Joseph Hooker is of opinion that Fiji is very fortunate in possessing in Dr. McGregor an officer of sound scientific views and excellent powers of observation and resource. Some assistance should certainly be given him both to relieve his private means of any expenses attendant on work of this kind and also to allow him leisure to attend to this and similar matters which Sir Joseph Hooker thinks from the perusal of the papers could not well be in more competent hands. Nothing seems to have been left undone on Dr. McGregor's part and it is much to be lamented that the result has not been attended with greater success.[49]

MacGregor's support for the major plantation productions in Fiji, copra and sugar, was as wholehearted as his efforts for coffee. In addition, both Gordon and he became landowners.[50] MacGregor looked after Gordon's financial investments in plantations, even going to the lengths of a conspiratorial, secret midnight meeting to sign a Bill of Sale.[51]

MacGregor argued that only outside investment and continued

planter enterprise could keep any form of government going in Fiji. Thus, as Gillion has shown, he sympathized with the interests of the Colonial Sugar Refining Company, especially in the depressed years in Fiji,[52] and stated that 'were the affairs of the Colonial Sugar Refining Company to become crooked, the colony would utterly collapse'.[53] He thus also criticized undue interference with the planters:

> I am much grieved by the 'morbid spirit' that inspires our immigration office. The ruling idea is that the employer of a black or brown man is a cheat and a conspirator. Anson cannot see that men are under a contract, and that there are reciprocal obligations. Men are persecuted, worried by inquiries, irritated by interference, and that too all over such trifles. A genuine case of bad treatment is far from common here. I would not myself be a manager, overseer or planter in this colony for any inducement. I have said that the condition is a morbid one; it is being carried out too in a moribund colony.

> The General Manager of the Colonial Sugar Refinery Co. has been fined £3 because he does not daily sign the Ration Book. It is utterly impossible that he can be every night at Nausori to sign the book . . . I . . . consider it very foolish and very unjust. These proceedings annoy me so at times that I wish I could go and leave the country for ever. I have taken a stand against them, and I am sure that His Excellency will soon see that he must recognise that the employer is also entitled to justice. Could you not offer Anson something that would tempt him to Ceylon before he bursts up Fiji?

In the same twenty-five page letter MacGregor claimed to be 'nearly blind' from detailed financial work necessary to save the colony from complete collapse.[54] In such a desperate economic situation he obviously had to be concerned with the planters' interests—even though his prime concern, which he did not regard as incompatible, remained the protection of the Fijian people. His attitude to native health and taxation clearly indicated this, as did his attitude to Fijian native government.

MacGregor supported Gordon's policy of trying to prevent the disintegration of Fijian society, and thus upholding as far as possible the authority of the chiefs. The 'good government, prosperity and advance in civilization',[55] of the Fijians was to Gordon the principal aim of the new British administration. It is clear now that his methods can be criticized. The authority held by the chiefs in 1874 did not represent an ideal fixed condition: the disturbed history before that date of the struggles for power should have made this apparent to British rulers. Gordon's aim of advancing Fijian civilization of necessity clashed with his aim of maintaining the chiefs' authority, since certain customs, although supported by the chiefs and part of the fabric of Fijian culture, were judged by Gordon to be uncivilized. Thus murder, cannibalism and the marriage of women against their will were made criminal acts. Other institutions, such as the chief's right of *lala* (the services, as distinct from freewill offerings, customarily rendered by commoners to their chiefs) were to be limited. The authority of the chiefs had already been curtailed by their act of cession to Great Britain, and was likely to become increasingly diminished as British responsibilities increased. Anthropologists have shown how the breakdown of the bases of Fijian customs must have been accelerated by some of Gordon's measures ironically aimed at their very protection: Gordon was by choice stultifying the growth of Fijian individualism.

All these criticisms are in a way unfair and anachronistic, however. The emphasis should be on the alternative colonial policies that might have been introduced in the 1870s. If the planters had been allowed full use of Fijian labour, the breakdown of Fijian culture must have been much more rapid and destructive. If British or Australian exploitation of Fiji for profit had been the main aim of the policy, the interests of the Fijians would have been given far less consideration.

The most valid criticisms are those which suggest that Gordon's guiding principles became over-rigid and dogmatic, and that, consequently, changes needed to do justice to Fijians were not made. Such censures centre particularly around the misuse of authority by Fijian chiefs, especially in the later 1880s, a period when MacGregor's influence in the government was considerable.

Gordon continued British recognition of Cakobau as the leading chief in Fiji and to mark the unity of the colony introduced a new council of chiefs, the Bose vaka Turaga. This council, consisting of the provincial chiefs, a few district chiefs and Fijian stipendiary magistrates, was to meet annually in each of the twelve provinces—Lau, Cakaudrove, Tai Levu and Maitasiri, Lomaiviti, Macuata, Bua, Rewa, Kadavu, Nadroga, Ra, Ba and Yasawas, and Namosi. The mountain areas of Viti Levu were later added as this council was to be the medium through which Gordon and following governors passed on major policy decisions and suggestions. The Bose vaka Turaga was also placed above the previously existing provincial (Bose vaka Yasana) and district (Bosi

G

ni Tikina) Fijian councils, whose functions were to be maintained. These minor councils consisted of existing rulers: twelve provincial (Rokos) and eighty district (Bulis) rulers as recognized in 1874 by Sir Hercules Robinson, the Governor of New South Wales.

This three-level structure of councils was confirmed by ordinance and was to be supported by the continuance of Fijian district and provincial courts, which were to enforce native regulations. Despite the opposition of his Chief Justice, Sir William Hackett, Gordon had decided to introduce 'a native code, in addition to the general law and subsidiary to it'.[56]

In this system much depended on the characters of the chiefs. In cases of oppression, the sanctions were complaints to the annual meetings, or protests to British officials, missionaries or traders. In upholding the authority of the Rokos, Gordon found difficulties at both extremes. If he accepted as likely and thus carefully investigated all protests against the Rokos he might undermine their authority. If he trusted them completely he might confirm actual oppression. Thus he tried to steer a middle course, based on as wide an acquaintance and influence with the chiefs as possible. To be successful, the Gordon system had to be based on a high degree of intimacy and trust. It was flexible in so far as there was now power above the chiefs (the Bose vaka Turaga) to check abuses that might be subsequently discovered in Fijian customs. The choice made to confirm the power of the chiefs, and to rule through established institutions, implied a preference for the communal as against the individual rights of the Fijians. However, Gordon's encouragement of Fijians to work as individuals on plantations, or to be trained as individuals, either as missionaries or medical attendants, could work against communal institutions.

There are many instances which show that MacGregor understood and accepted Gordon's ideas. He realized that they were counter to the prevailing ideas of the time and that they needed personal supervision and the continued empathy of the administrators with the Fijians for success. He told Gordon,

> No man, or animal, more readily discovers the presence or absence of sympathy than a Fijian. Therein alone lies the whole secret of your own success and influence among them.[57]

He became convinced that although this was not an ideal system, it was the best under the circumstances and could not be changed, despite the inevitable opposition.[58]

MacGregor's acceptance of the broad principles followed by Gordon in ruling the Fijians was important when as governor he had to shape policies in British New Guinea and in Lagos. His realization in Fiji that such a system could only work well if there was deep sympathy and intimacy with the indigenous people was applied in his later governorships. There was another side to MacGregor's experiences in Fiji, however, for his later years in the colony provided many examples of failures in the operation of Gordon's system.

By 1884 MacGregor thought European control was degenerating, because the necessary intimate knowledge of the Fijians was not being maintained.

> In the turmoil of contentious minutes the Governor [des Voeux] has not been able to visit any Fijian towns, has seldom seen any of them, and there has consequently been a lack of government by personal influence on the natives during the last year or two. One result has been the development of a certain amount of lawlessness or more properly disrespect for the law, amongst both chiefs and people . . . no doubt several chiefs, notably your [Gordon's] old, spoiled friend, Roko Tui Ba, require to be brought sharply to book for their peccadilloes.[59]

The main danger to the system was this abuse of authority by the chiefs.[60] In July 1884 MacGregor stated that the 'punishment of chiefs should be swift: then it could be lighter', and went on to generalize from the actions of the 'thoroughly unprincipled' Ratu Lala:

> I hold that one chief cannot to the exclusion of others be suffered to appropriate land and work plantations on his own account; and the moment that all chiefs are allowed to do so native government becomes impossible. Separate the interest of the chief from the interest of the community, and the first time the chief sulks he retires to his plantation and becomes a white man.[61]

Such an end seemed quite clearly to MacGregor to mean a breakdown of Fijian communal life and thus to be contrary to Gordon's ideas. Thurston, however, was reported by MacGregor in an 1884 letter to Gordon to believe

> that in a short time all native government must be carried on by white men, the Magistrates, as was done by the old government. He says you [Gordon] wished the chiefs to have their own private property and their own plantations, that you approved of this special one for Lala, that it is entirely in accordance with your policy and to prevent Lala and others from establishing private plantations would be a great wrong.

MacGregor continued by giving a significant outline of his views about Fiji's future and the end-aims of Gordon's native policy.

> Probably he [Thurston] and I agree to a considerable extent, but we differ completely as to the time when all this should have a commencement. If you approve of private plantations for native chiefs *now* I can only say that I have completely misunderstood your system and policy. The Czar of Russia might as well make all his provincial governors independent sovereigns and then expect them to execute his decrees, or a school-master allow his pupils to determine the duration and frequency of holidays. I see nothing very difficult in carrying on native government here on its present lines for at least one generation. I see a multitude of evils in the establishment of government by white commissioners, the first of which is the degradation of the race as such; the second the breaking up of towns and the scattering of the people; the third the alienation of their land; the last the disappearance of all trace of your hard work here. If my conception of your policy here is correct or nearly correct, it would be a profound mistake to allow anything to interfere with the communal system, the antithesis of individual interest. Then again I am sure that if it were a mistake to adopt my view and prevent or prohibit private ownership by chiefs and to forbid them to become 'planters', it would be a mistake easy of rectification at any time, whereas a start in the opposite direction admits of no return.[62]

This discussion clearly indicated the existence of problems. Some chiefs were wanting to go beyond the traditional Fijian economic structure: decisions allowing them to do so would help to break down the communal system. On the other hand, decisions preventing them would mean that European rule was obstructing developments desired by some Fijians. On the whole there was a considerable degree of European interference, justified by claims that the European administration knew which values were right for the Fijians to adopt. This paternalistic attitude seems to have been maintained in a manner which stifled the Fijians and was applied first to the chiefs, then to other Fijians.

A letter written by MacGregor to Gordon in 1888 typifies this paternalism. It has the tone of the report of a headmaster who is going to insist on disciplinary measures to maintain the traditions of his school. He referred to the 'usual cases of chiefs misappropriating tax copra, provincial moneys etc', then continued to particularize about the 'delinquent' Roko Tui Bua, and Ratu Marika, who as Roko Tui Lomai Viti gives a good deal of trouble, squabbling with Bau about contributions from Lomai Viti and quarrelling about Namata-Bau borderlands. In some respects he is not a bad Roko,

because he had sufficient ability, an established social position and was dependent on the government and so was amenable to control, but 'he is a coward and covetous'. Marika was needed for Rewa since it would be impossible to continue with Roko Tui Drekiti as 'his sons are troublesome blackguards'.

Ratu Peni is still impelled by white men and money along the road to ruin. [Nevertheless] he has more originality of ideas than any chief I have met in Council lately, and he has a certain amount of sturdy independence of mind. . . . Roko Tui Tai Levu is deeply in debt [£1,000], so much so that it will cause serious embarrassment to him and the Government . . . [Luki of Nadroga was] getting along quietly, so is the fool of Namosi whose province is always in a deplorable condition. They stop warrants, never clear roads, seldom build or repair houses, and are behind with taxes. Making that man a Roko was one of your mistakes.

Neimani at Ba was giving satisfaction since he had been rebuked for 'glorifying himself by cutting and giving away sandalwood wholesale'. He had ability but was 'honestest when watched'. The weak and lazy man of Lau 'continues to misappropriate money and drink yaqona, but he does little else'. However, there was no one to take his place.

MacGregor's letter[63] covered most of the twelve provincial chiefs and the amount of space given to them, in comparison with the rest of the Fijian people, accurately represents his idea that it was by judging the nature of the chiefs that the quality of rule should be tested. Nor was he alone in criticizing the chiefs' exercise of their powers. The missionaries had long been suspicious of them, and most planters disliked entrusting any authority to them. The debate came to a head in the case of Zephania, which became a *cause célèbre* in 1886-87. In 1885 this Fijian, a commoner of Drakiniwai and a member of the Wesleyan Methodist Church, was flogged at the orders of his district chief, the Buli Bituvatu of Sawakasa, in Tai Levu province.

The chain of reasons for the flogging was traced as far back as 1866, when a raiding party from Sawakasa had been persuaded to spare certain villages including Drakiniwai from destruction. In June 1885, however, a group of Fijians from Sawakasa, on their way to visit a neighbouring chief, pillaged the gardens of

Zephania and others in Drakiniwai, taking away and wantonly destroying produce. This pillaging was supposedly related to *solevu*, a Fijian custom entitling chiefs to demand food from their commoners.

Zephania defied native custom by writing a letter of complaint to the provincial council of chiefs (though he was said to have admitted in 1887 that 'it was an insolent letter . . . and quite improper for a man of my standing to write'). The Buli Bituvatu objected to this complaint and ordered the flogging of Zephania in the presence of over a thousand Fijians. His justification for ordering the flogging was that he would not be interfered with by his inferiors, and that he was entitled to do as he liked with those who owed *solevu* to him.[64] Zephania received three strokes with a stout vine from a chief, three more with part of the stem of a coconut leaf from a sergeant of police and then was flogged by another of his neighbours.

This occurred in 1885 and for a year nothing was done; neither complaint nor report was made to the European administration, nor to any other European. Then the Reverend Frederick Langham of the Wesleyan Methodist Mission heard about the flogging and on 6 July 1886 he reported it, in Zephania's presence, to the native commissioner, Blyth, who was astonished that he had not heard of the case. Blyth wrote next day to the Colonial Secretary reporting the case. MacGregor minuted on this report:

> It would appear . . . that Sefania has been very ill used, and unquestionably full inquiry should be made and punishment inflicted if this story, which has been received ex parte is true, but it certainly appears to me at first sight as if there existed a disposition to make the most of Sefania's wrongs.

Thurston, who was Acting-Governor, decided because the case was stale, and because Zephania was an intelligent man 'quite capable of taking his own part if he really desires to do', not to direct any prosecution. He checked that Zephania's story was substantially correct and directed the Buli Bure through the Roko to compensate Zephania for the injury done to his garden. The Buli Bituvatu was to be reprimanded by his provincial chief in Council and his pay was to be temporarily stopped.[65]

There the matter could again have ended. Injustice had been done by a despotic minor chief, the administration had shown that it was not aware of every case of such injustice, the governor had belatedly tried to redress the wrong and he had judged that it was not a major issue.

Langham, however, was not satisfied with Blyth's assurance that the governor had dealt with the case and his promise to let Langham know what action followed. When Langham heard no more from Blyth during the next two and a half months, he wrote to the Aborigines' Protection Society in London urging pressure in support of his complaints. The Colonial Office had its first report of the case from the Society in November 1886 and asked the Fijian Administration for a report of the case (although reprimanding Langham for not forwarding his complaints through the governor).[66]

A detailed investigation was begun in February and a long report was forwarded to the Colonial Office by Governor Mitchell on 12 March 1887. This included MacGregor's medical evidence, based on an examination of Zephania twenty-one months after the flogging, that there were no cicatrices which seemed to have any relation to flogging. A 'frightful wale', that Langham had said was caused by the flogging and which Zephania would 'carry to the grave with him', was a badly healed blister which Zephania admitted had been caused by his 'girdle' catching fire when he was a boy! There seems no reason to doubt the sincerity of MacGregor's medical report, which was backed by two other doctors;[67] after all, MacGregor had agreed that Zephania had been 'very ill used', and it would have needed remarkably severe blows to leave scars after such a long period.

When Mitchell brought the case before the Council of Chiefs in May 1887, the chiefs showed 'considerable irritation' at what they considered to be 'an instance of misdirected missionary zeal'.[68] Moreover, the March report of the Fijian Administration seemed to satisfy the secretary of the Aborigines' Protection Society, who said in September 1887 that he believed 'both Sir J. B. Thurston and Mr Langham equally desire to promote the well being of the native population, and to establish a just administration of affairs in Fiji'.[69]

Langham, probably backed by other Fijian missionary opinion, was far from satisfied, however, and in October 1887 in the Fijian Supreme Court Zephania took out a writ against Bituvatu for assault, in which damages of £200 were claimed. At some stage Zephania refused to accept an apology according to Fijian custom—an offering of whales' teeth presented in a public meeting by the Buli. His refusal was said to have been instigated at the 'command of his ecclesiastical superior'.[70]

MacGregor again made his position quite clear on 2 November

when he asked: 'Is this chief, who was no doubt quite in the wrong according to European ideas, to be defended by the Attorney-General, that is by the Government?' This embarrassment, however, was partly overcome, since the chiefs retained the Attorney-General in his private capacity. MacGregor, of course, realized that the whole business had been exaggerated and that 'there is another finger than Zephania's in all this'.[71] He wrote to Gordon in June: 'So far as I can judge at present the native administration is quite safe', because he thought that the attack was less against the system than against Thurston.[72]

Langham and Thurston had clashed since the pre-cession government. In September 1875 Langham had written: 'Brother Thurston is put into a position where he can do no harm. . . . The members and toadies of the old government are nowhere (Here I sing the Doxology)'.[73] In March 1887, in the midst of the Zephania case, he impliedly contrasted Thurston and Mitchell:

I have given Thurston some harder nuts to crack since those you saw. The governor is one of the right sort. *He will do justice* and that is all we want.[74]

MacGregor was largely exempt from Langham's attacks (significantly he later recommended Langham for a Doctorate of Divinity at the University of Glasgow). The issue involved more than personalities, however. Langham was an influential missionary, the Chairman of the Wesleyan Fiji District from 1869 to 1894, and was expressing Christian ideas which emphasized freedom of choice for the individual. He and his fellow missionaries had often argued against the power of the chiefs and expressed misgivings about the trust placed by the government in them. Thus Langham wrote on 31 December 1886:

I *have* been writing some harsh words . . . for I am on the war path . . . over the treatment the Fijians are receiving at the hands of the government. I fancy I have stirred the folks at home and I have now sent a dose to the colonies—and I am preparing a bolus for Mr. Thurston and Co. here.

It is about time the Fijians got a little relief from the oppression some of them are subjected to.[75]

A clear statement had been made eight years earlier by another senior misionary in Fiji, the Reverend Lorimer Fison (who, it should be pointed out, had quarrelled with Gordon):

We do not approve of his [Gordon's] policy, because we know that it is an exaltation of the chiefs and a grinding of the faces of the poor; but we have not used our influence with the natives to oppose it.

He does not know, and no one could make him believe, that the people are grieviously, scandalously oppressed under his rule. He hears only what the chiefs say, and he will hear nothing else. We hear the groans of the people, for they come to us in their griefs. It is useless for us to tell him what we hear. We have done so, and he has inquired from the accused chief as to the accusation against him, and has accepted his version without further investigation. And besides, the oppressed themselves dare not openly complain of their oppressors lest a worse fate befall them. They tell us of their troubles, but if we were to bring them face to face with their lords, they durst not repeat in their presence what they tell us as their pastors.

Fison went on to report that Langham favoured sending a joint letter to the Chief Justice, pointing out that they had chosen not to make these facts public

> . . . because we do not wish to embarrass the Government, yet . . . we are prepared to prove, whenever it may be necessary so to do, that the natives are bitterly oppressed under the present regime.[76]

In this sense Zephania's case was the sequel to ten years of waiting and it brought to the surface an interesting array of grievances.

In the Supreme Court judgment was given in June 1888 in favour of Zephania, though he had to pay the costs of the action. The result was not a wholesale condemnation of native policy—not only because of the technical point that by the nature of British law the judge could hardly go beyond the issues of the particular case, but also because there had been sufficient delay to cast doubt on the extent of Zephania's sincerity, and the government had never denied its belief that the Buli had acted unjustly. MacGregor reflected the government's desire to minimize such attacks on native policy when he wrote to Gordon some months before the trial:

> Winter's defence will be that Zephania condoned; that matter was disposed of; that question was brought forward at instance of third parties for purposes of agitation. I trust that it will not come before Berkeley, who is a fool hunting popularity with his hat in his hand like a cowboy after a cabbage butterfly. It is to my mind a serious oversight in our legislation here that it is possible to bring such a case into the Supreme Court as a Civil Action. However if decided against the Buli, advantage should be taken of the occurrence to make some provision for such cases while closing the door

of the Supreme Court against them. I have much confidence in Winter whom it is a great comfort to have as advocate for the Buli.[77]

Efforts to prevent any more Fijian disputes reaching the Supreme Court were instigated by Mitchell in a confidential despatch to the Colonial Office in November 1887. The main arguments used were that all the anti-government forces would use legal actions to show the shortcomings of the present system, and that the village or district councils should not be replaced by the Supreme Court, for such a development would be a 'fertile source of disintegration and a wide field for the interference of those pests of primitive countries, the petty lawyers'. Another reason was raised by MacGregor—the undermining of the authority of the governor as 'Head Chief'. As Colonial Secretary he had the difficult task of explaining to the chiefs involved why this court action could begin after the issue had been decided by the governor.[78]

The Colonial Office was not overimpressed by these rather authoritarian arguments, however, nor by the additional point, made by Thurston in April 1888, that

so long as the Fijian retains his present social status (and many years will pass before he grows out of it and is fitted for that of his European fellow subjects) so long will civil actions against him be barren of normal results.

The logic behind this claim was that as individual Fijians had little personal property, any substantial fine imposed would fall on the community, which would hardly be just. Imprisonment of a Fijian by a European court was also regarded as objectionable and an embarrassment to existing relations between whites and Fijians. The Secretary of State, Knutsford, summed up Colonial Office views: 'I do not like this proposal. The interference of the Governor—that is of the Executive—with the administration of justice is not lightly to be allowed'; consequently any legislation should be deferred 'until either we are pressed by the native chiefs to undertake it, or are forced to do so by the actual increase of litigiousness'.[79] The Colonial Office, arguing from the example of India, agreed with the Fijian Administration that there were dangers in the over-encouragement of law suits. Action was taken to refer the question to the Council of Chiefs for their view. A bill drafted by the Fijian Government in August 1888 to empower the Government to decide whether writs could be heard in the Supreme Court was allowed to lapse.[80]

Generally the Colonial Office supported the existing native policy of ruling through the chiefs, although refusing to make the system more limited by closing the door of the Supreme Court to individual Fijians. The Zephania case did not then lead to any change in the main lines of existing policy, but it certainly emphasized the existence of opposition to Gordon's ideas of trusting the chiefs.

The Zephania case was by no means isolated. There were other cases of oppression, such as that of Pita and Anasa in 1886, in which a Fijian was tied up and questioned for four days; or the 1887 case of Iveri Boi who was tied up for some forty hours and then, because of the pain he suffered, confessed to a murder which it was later proved he did not commit. MacGregor examined the wrists of this man two months after he was tied up and, as with Zephania, found no material evidence beyond a 'mere abrasion of the outer skin' to support the allegations of cruelty.[81] He was, however, concerned in the practice and supported its reference, in the spirit of indirect rule, to the Council of Chiefs. They admitted that this custom was 'old and common among us', and that it was also bad and should be stopped. Mitchell called it 'revolting to the civilized mind' and insisted on the introduction in 1887 of a native regulation forbidding the examination of supposed criminals in this way.[82]

Gaps in certain records suggest the difficulties in documenting cases of Fijians being mistreated by their chiefs. It was revealed in 1888 that charges brought before the Council of Chiefs against whites for ill-treating Fijians were not always recorded in the Minutes of their meetings. For example, a charge that a European had 'tied one end of a rope to a Fijian and the other to his saddle and galloped the man . . . to prison' had not been recorded. MacGregor was indignant:

I may say frankly that this matter shakes my faith in the Bose reports. If they are to be purged of such complaints the Council loses at once one of its most useful functions.[83]

MacGregor's view of the 'useful functions' of the Council indicates that his attitude would be that if full supervision were exercised by this and other councils working properly, then rule through the chiefs would be just. It is difficult to give a simple judgement on this debate between chief and communal rights on the one hand, and individual rights on the other. In the long term it is clear that the former rights would be diminished; it is

probable that they were bound to decline once European contact had begun. But this was common ground: Gordon, Thurston, MacGregor, Langham and Fison all agreed. The question
at issue mainly involved the timing and method of change. The
Fijian Government following Gordon tried to slow down change
which might undermine the stability of existing Fijian society
by working through the existing authority of the chiefs; the
missionaries wanted to hasten change towards a Christian society
by gaining recognition for the rights of the individual Fijians.
From the lack of records it is impossible to gauge how much
oppression of the Zephania type did exist; it would be difficult
to prove that in the circumstances (lacking finance for a much
larger European staff for more direct rule, or for troops to enforce justice) that there would not have been just as much oppression of individuals if the rule of the chiefs had been abruptly
ended in 1874. While it is clear that there was a growth of individualism among the Fijians and increasing dissatisfaction
with the rule of the chiefs, this does not necessarily lead to a
condemnation of Gordon's system as interpreted by Thurston
and MacGregor.

Like most practical administrators MacGregor often had to
make decisions without having had the chance to fully consider
their theoretical implications. But he worked very hard to
ensure that Gordon's native policy was carried out satisfactorily
and that no one suffered unjustly. Throughout these years he was
bedevilled by the strains of overwork, frustration and unhappiness in his personal life. After his wife's death he absorbed himself even more in his work and was close to breakdown before
he took his leave on 15 July 1882, his first leave since joining
the Colonial Service over nine years before. In a farewell speech
he regretted having led

> a life of comparative seclusion, and [being] debarred from mixing
> among my fellow-citizens and fellow-colonists, as much as I other-
> wise should and ought to have done [for] the more the officers of any
> government associate with the people, the more fully cognisant
> must that government be of the wishes and wants of the country.[84]

He had not been completly a recluse before his leave, however,
as he had been quietly courting Mary Jane Cocks, the daughter
of Captain Cocks, a trader and harbour-master at Suva.[85] Besides
his intensive reading and attempts to master the Fijian language[86] he may also have found another solace for his loneliness in the hope of eternal rewards from his Christianity, which

he applied to his official life, holding that ' "God's work" consists in doing one's duty'.[87] MacGregor once described his views as 'advanced Presbyterianism',[88] though this did not prevent his sincere support of the Wesleyan missionaries[89] and regular attendance at the Wesleyan Church at Levuka.[90] The Cocks family also attended this church.

Perhaps the difficulty of affording another fare postponed MacGregor's second marriage till after his leave. Then it was delayed after his return on 1 August 1883 until he went into his own home. On 3 November they were married at Navuloa by the Wesleyan minister.[91] There are no Minutes written by MacGregor between 2 and 8 November—his conscience allowed him five days break.

This marriage brought him considerable happiness. A close bond developed between the two and their two daughters, Alpina Viti (named after the island) and Mary,[92] who were idolized by their parents. They partly compensated William for his increasing disappointment with the two children of his first marriage. James made one visit to Fiji but later events show that he and his father were never close. Helen, who was nine when MacGregor remarried, was never as favoured as the daughters of his second marriage. This family happiness was brief, however, for on 22 June 1887 Mary took the three girls back 'home' for their health and education.[93] William thus had only just over five years of real married life during his thirteen years in Fiji.

His private life gave him brief and insufficient relaxation from the crowded hours of his official life, leading to his increasing frustration and bitterness. This largely explains his frequent irritation with his fellow officials and his serious thoughts about leaving Fiji for a better administrative job, or of turning to private medical practice.

Even his receipt of high honours, when he was awarded the C.M.G. in 1881, failed to raise him from his overall despondency:

I completely forgot to thank you [Gordon] for your recommendation on my behalf in the matter of the C.M.G. . . . Probably few people could less value, for itself, such a matter; but not many could more appreciate such a favour if looked on as a mark of approval of one's honest endeavour to do one's duty, than I can. Appreciation of the second kind is, however, in my case not heightened by the fact that my name was not on the original list for the 24th May and was only added on the urgent advocacy of 'my claim' by Mr.

Pender,* Mr. Herbert objecting as the list was completed and could not be augmented. I am of course deeply indebted to Mr. P. for interesting himself on my behalf, but I cannot esteem H.M.s grace and favour procured for me by a stranger in the same way I could, and unquestionably would, if obtained for me only by the chiefs I have served. Therein lies the secret of my silence and my forgetfulness.[94]

Perhaps his disappointment with the Colonial Office, an institution of the English Establishment, led him to emphasize his Scottish origins by taking out arms in Edinburgh in October 1884.[95]

From 1884 his despondency and sense of failure increased and was particularly evident in 1885, mainly because both the Colonial Office and Gordon had disapproved of some of his actions while he was acting as governor, such as his suggesting a reciprocity treaty with Victoria by writing directly to the colony without consulting the Colonial Office, and supporting Fijians as volunteers to the Sudan.[96]

In 1887, partly because he was recovering from dengue fever and since he had now passed his fortieth birthday, he thought any other job

better than to stay stagnant here much longer. What I should like would be the Administration of some small place, like British Honduras or one of the places even on the west coast of Africa. I would be prepared to go to the Falkland Islands [the lowest paid British administrator] to even get a move before I come to be regarded as a 'fixture' in Fiji.[97]

It was at this time that he most clearly expressed this theme of failure.

I am simply like an old boat run high and dry with so many ribs stove in. My pay is £760 a year, £40 less than I was offered by Newton to stay in Mauritius in 1874, less than it has ever been in Fiji except during the first few months [here]. My work is hard enough, too. I start regularly at 7 a.m. to visit the Hospital, prison, and Lunatic Asylum, and to teach the native medical students. I get to my office about ten and work there until between four and five, and not infrequently have to take work home with me. I wish I could say I have the same heart to work and the same interest in the place that I used to have. It would have been well for me now had I been less zealous in what I deemed to be the discharge of my duty, and taken better care of myself. . . . I cannot but look on my failure to get to Ceylon as the turning point in my career, as the commencement of a facilis descensus.[98]

* From later letters it appears that Sir John Pender was des Voeux' father-in-law who, presumably, was the source of this backstairs gossip. MacGregor, because of this intervention, later said 'he hated the trinket'.

6

New Guinea: The Limits of Power 1888-98

As alternatives I trusted that it would be better to make Sir Henry lay foundation stones in Queensland than to capsize my edifice in British New Guinea; or that he held inspections of hospitals and asylums instead of driving me into one of them.

William MacGregor's reputation was established in British New Guinea. Indeed his achievements in ten years in charge of this new British colony have been described as 'little short of miraculous'.[1] This was his first long-term responsibility and his first opportunity to make major innovations for which he had had neither the time nor the power in Fiji. He now discovered how wide was the gap between being the head of a department and becoming the administrator and his qualities as a leader were thoroughly tested amidst the strains imposed by a small group of officials living in a tropical climate. He also experienced success, being lionized in Britain in 1894-95, facing the glare of publicity, especially from the Australian press, and being paid lip service by distinguished visitors and writers. Above all he found a greater degree of satisfaction in his achievements, since he felt he was fulfilling a useful function, and that he could satisfy his concept of a duty towards the peoples of New Guinea.

On the other hand, the extent of his frustrations and the conviction, felt so strongly during his thirteen years in Fiji, that his career was a failure, had left their mark on him. He was forty-one when he was appointed to New Guinea and much of the enthusiasm of his youth had been spent on the road to his new position. He found the limitations on his powers as a colonial administrator as gruelling as service under an inefficient governor, and had the special burdens of an ill-defined responsibility to some of the Australian colonies added to the normal supervision by the Colonial Office. Lack of manpower, finance, interest or the sheer immensity of the problems facing him frequently made the achievement of his goals impossible. But perhaps this suggests the true measure of the man, since he persistently strove towards greater achievements and refused to accept as binding the limitations on colonial administrators.

A British Protectorate over part of the islands of New Guinea was first proclaimed in 1884. The development of interests in this island area was in many ways a continuation of the process that had finally persuaded Britain to accept the cession of Fiji in 1874. Further, a direct link between the two groups of islands had been established in 1877 when Gordon in Fiji became the High Commissioner for the Western Pacific, a lordly title that gave him a shadow of power over vast areas including New Guinea. Deputy Commissioners had been sent to Port Moresby, again with powers that were far more impressive on paper than in practice.[2] These official links between Fiji and New Guinea were strengthened by the fact that Gordon was often consulted privately on New Guinea's future by statesmen in London. It is not surprising that there was much conjecture in Suva as to who might be put in charge if a British colony were to be established in New Guinea. The leading candidates were Thurston and MacGregor, both promised promotion by the Colonial Office, both underpaid for their experience and service and both supported by Gordon.

When MacGregor was on leave in London in 1882-83, he discussed his future with Herbert and with Gordon, who was about to take up the governorship of Ceylon, where he promised to try to obtain a position for MacGregor. After he returned to Suva MacGregor explained his position:

> I fear there are many obstacles between me and Ceylon . . . Sir Robert Herbert . . . is very decided that both Mr. Thurston and myself should not leave Fiji at the same time. Now, surely my colleague will receive substantial promotion and that soon: unless, indeed, it is meant that he [be] the next Governor of Fiji, a position which, however, he has assured me that he would not accept. I am expecting that he will be sent to New Guinea to make a start there. Sir Robert Herbert certainly led me to understand that such an appointment was a very probable one. If that comes off I do not expect to be removed from Fiji for some time.[3]

Herbert praised both these officers highly:

> both are men of greater ability and better service than almost any Colonial officers (I put it strongly after consideration) and if we cannot pay them adequately in Fiji, they should be promoted when practicable.[4]

This Minute was written on 9 October 1884 at a time when New Guinea's future was being decided, and on 23 October (mistakenly) and on 6 November (officially) the British Protectorate was proclaimed.[5]

Instead of either Thurston or MacGregor being promoted to take charge, however, Major-General P. H. Scratchley was chosen. He was an engineer who was well known in Australia because of his years of service advising on Australian defence, and being acceptable to Australians probably gave him an advantage over candidates in Fiji or elsewhere. It is known, for instance, that H. H. Romilly (who had served as a Deputy Commissioner in New Guinea) was considered but rejected, largely because of his opposition to the Queensland labour traffic.[6] Australians, already strongly aroused against the Colonial Office by the disavowal of the purported 'annexation' by Queensland's premier, Sir Thomas McIlwraith, in July 1883, would hardly have greeted the appointment from London of anyone not well known to them.

If Scratchley had lived he would almost certainly have continued as administrator till 1888 when British sovereignty was later proclaimed. He caught malaria, however, after only a few months in New Guinea and died on 2 December 1885. Thurston offered his services by a telegram to the Colonial Office, but in January Scratchley was replaced by the 'most experienced man on the spot', John Douglas. He was then resident at Thursday Island and was a former Premier of Queensland. He was told by the Colonial Office that his appointment was only 'a temporary measure'.[7]

Meanwhile, after Scratchley was appointed to New Guinea, MacGregor wrote a private letter to Herbert asking for the treasurership of Ceylon which Gordon had offered him. He was not overly optimistic, telling Gordon:

> I should think that for such an office there would at any time be many candidates, but at present probably a host. If one can depend on Herbert's professions I should however stand a good chance.[8]

MacGregor was in Melbourne in January 1886 when Douglas was appointed to New Guinea. MacGregor did not regard this as a temporary appointment and believed that as a consequence Thurston would remain in Fiji for a long time and his own chance of promotion to Ceylon would be improved.[9]

In December 1885 MacGregor was appointed to go to Australia to represent Fiji at the annual meeting of the Federal

H

Council in Hobart. This visit was very fortunate as it was most significant in his appointment to New Guinea. Originally the Colonial Office chose Thurston to attend, notifying him by telegram, but he preferred not to go. Instead he asked MacGregor to replace him and MacGregor left on 1 January 1886. Meanwhile in London the Colonial Office believed that Thurston could not have received their telegram before MacGregor left. Pressure on the Colonial Office to have Thurston appointed continued from Murray Smith, the Victorian Agent-General. The Colonial Office then decided, without depreciating MacGregor's 'great ability and experience', that Thurston's 'special knowledge' might be required at the Federal Council meeting. So by a telegram of 7 January they authorized Thurston to replace MacGregor—an instruction Thurston ignored.[10]

At the Federal Council meeting MacGregor showed his interest in New Guinea by a speech pleading for consideration of the rights of the Papuans[11] and discussed the future of the Protectorate with the Australian delegates, particularly with Sir Samuel Walker Griffith of Queensland. From this meeting a friendship developed between MacGregor and Griffith, which rivalled the intimacy that MacGregor already had with Gordon and Mackellar.

Griffith, aged forty, was the son of a Welsh Congregational Minister. He had taken a law degree and besides practising this profession had spent much of his career in Queensland politics as a middle class liberal. The two men both had university training and political experience and were in agreement on certain specific issues. Griffith had been McIlwraith's leading opponent against the use of Kanaka (Polynesian in Fijian terms) labour on Queensland sugar plantations, and had a deep sympathy for native peoples which corresponded with MacGregor's sympathy. Another very different but nevertheless important bond was their common interest in Italian language and literature. MacGregor became one of the main critics of Griffith's translation of Dante. Whatever the reasons for this lasting friendship, the fact that Griffith was deeply impressed by MacGregor at this meeting was very fortunate, for it was Griffith who recommended MacGregor for the governorship of New Guinea.

The two men must have openly discussed New Guinea as is shown in MacGregor's letter to Gordon, written on his way back to Fiji:

Thurston we see is appointed Governor of Fiji, and Douglas to

New Guinea. The appointment of the latter is only a temporary arrangement [he must have learnt this from Griffith]. New Guinea has been offered to Queensland on condition that they govern it without expense to the Home Government. Griffith does not want if for Queensland, and he will not have Thurston there [it is a fair surmise that MacGregor influenced Griffith in this decision]; nor is he satisfied with Douglas. I would accept it if offered, but I will not ask for it. I believe Queensland, Victoria, New Zealand, and Tasmania would offer no objection to my having it; but I do not suppose there is any likelihood of the Colonial Office offering it to me.[12]

On 28 May 1886 he wrote to Griffith, continuing their discussions begun at the Federal Council:

. . . during the last few days I have been very undecided whether I should offer you my services in New Guinea. I have thought that I might be able to carry out your policy there as well as perhaps almost any one else, because I believe your views on the matter are those that I consider right. If Douglas does not wish to have the permanent appointment, I shall be glad to go and assist you there to the best of my ability.

I have made no application for the appointment, nor even hinted at it, to any other person [MacGregor ignores his letter to Gordon!] If you have any one in your eye, good and well, if you have not, and think I could do any good in New Guinea, I have some reason to think the Colonial Office would favourably consider the matter if you submitted my name as a candidate. Stout, Agnew, some of the Victorians, and some of the Sydney people, McKellar and Sir John Robertson, would probably be favourable. Sir Arthur Gordon's voice would also have some influence.[13] But I leave the matter entirely to you, and shall make no application myself to the Colonial Office. Thurston would not of course accept the appointment at the salary fixed [MacGregor gave a different version in his letter to Gordon].[14]

Griffith must have replied giving his support to MacGregor, for MacGregor wrote to Gordon on 5 June:

Mr. Griffith, Premier of Queensland, has told me by this mail that when this scheme [for the administration of New Guinea] was agreed on at Sydney he mentioned my name as the fittest person he knew for the post.

MacGregor showed little hesitation in making his choice between the two ways of escaping from Fiji. The reasons he gave Gordon for wanting to go to New Guinea rather than Ceylon are important in understanding his colonial philosophy:

I have long looked forward to joining you in Ceylon and taking a share in your work there, however humble my part might be. Personally nothing could be more agreeable to me than to go to Ceylon. I am aware that my duties in New Guinea would be attended by many and very serious inconveniences, yet, in face of all this I would prefer the New Guinea appointment. The lessons I have learned from you are I feel lessons that fit me better for administration, especially of the particular kind required in New Guinea, than for anything else. There I could put into practice many of the principles which I believe are founded on a high sense of justice, although in many quarters they are not appreciated, not fashionable. It might be that in New Guinea I might do more good, or better prevent the doing of evil, than a man that has had fewer opportunities of studying the government of native races than I have had the good luck to meet with. It seems to me therefore that my duty would be to plant your school in New Guinea if I can obtain that appointment. The remuneration is not attractive, but the work to me most inviting, especially as you would be so near to give me advice, counsel and encouragement. . . . I would therefore ask you to assist me in obtaining not the appointment that would by far be the most agreeable and the most profitable to me, but that where it seems to me duty leads me. It is time that some of the young men of your school, who think they understand it, who certainly believe in it, got into the lines of administration.[15]

Despite MacGregor's plea to Gordon to help him, it was Griffith's support that was more important at this stage. The British Government had never had major interests in New Guinea and they were trying hard during the few years of the Protectorate to make certain that the Australian colonies would accept financial responsibility for it as well as a measure of administrative control. Any appointment to take charge of the colony thus had to be approved or suggested from Australia.

MacGregor soon became impatient,[16] hoping for rapid action and not realizing that delays were caused by the reluctance of the Australian colonies to guarantee finance for future government. In a letter dated 9 August, Gordon told him that he had submitted his name for the treasurership of Ceylon, which led MacGregor to write to Griffith on 17 September urging that

if you have not yet put me up as a candidate for New Guinea I would ask you to do so now . . . the truth is I should be very much disappointed were I sent to Ceylon and not to New Guinea.[17]

In February 1887 he wrote to Sir Graham Berry, of Victoria, asking for his support. He knew that his friend Dr Mackellar, who was going to England in March, would 'do anything for me that he can', though his hopes centred on Griffith's influence at the 1887 London Colonial Conference.

MacGregor was frequently pessimistic during the early months of 1887, fearing that he had missed promotion to either Ceylon or New Guinea and that he did not have enough influence 'at home' in the Colonial Office to secure this.[18] In July rumours led him to despairing speculation when writing to Gordon.

> I am told Sir John [Thurston] or I goes to New Guinea as Administrator. Had my competitor been any other I might have had some chance, but against him I have none. He has long stood between the sun and my tub, and will of course remain my evil genius until the end of the chapter. I am the Australian nominee. Thurston is backed by Sir Robert Herbert, and the latter is nearer the ear of the Secretary of State than the Australians. Of course Thurston would have to be promoted first, Herbert declines to send him elsewhere, hence the block. You are unreasonable to me in saying I look at Sir John through a yellow medium. Have I not been the Ona man, the maid of all work, for this colony for years, and annually been going down hill whilst my fortunate colleague has as steadily been rising? It is distance now, and not a distorting machine, that gives me an imperfect view. But let that pass, I do not envy him; he has worked hard and well, and has been as honest as could have been expected. Most men can be when it is made worth their while.[19]

Unwittingly MacGregor was being unnecessarily bitter, for his selection had been virtually finalized in May 1887 during the London Colonial Conference,[20] at which Griffith's proposals for the administration of New Guinea were accepted by those present, subject to ratification later by the British and colonial parliaments. His proposals provided amongst other things for an administrator to be paid £1,500 a year, and on 25 March 1887 Griffith recommended MacGregor for this position in a conversation with Sir Henry Holland, the Secretary of State for the Colonies. This suggestion was put in writing on 12 May and then debated within the Colonial Office. The choice lay between MacGregor and Thurston. A clerk, Fuller, wrote that MacGregor had

> a very good record here, and I believe a very good constitution— an important thing for a Papuan Governor. (In a private letter some months ago he spoke to me in a way that showed he had been sounded and would probably accept the appointment if offered him.)

Holland supported MacGregor as 'Sir Samuel Griffith spoke in the highest terms of Dr McGregor and it will be a good thing to get an administrator persona grata to Queensland'. Herbert, the Under-Secretary, amplified the reasons why MacGregor was eventually preferred:

> Mr. Thurston will no doubt be disappointed at not being selected for this post: and probably he would have been if he had had the advantage, as Dr. McGregor had, of attending the Federal Council and so making the Australian Governments aware of his capabilities. I told Sir Samuel Griffith that Mr. Thurston is at least as strong a man as Dr. McGregor, and Sir Samuel Griffith said that might probably be so, but he did not happen to know anything of him personally.
>
> It is of great importance to appoint a specially able and trustworthy man whom the colonies happen to prefer and as soon as we are in a position to do so I think Dr. McGregor should be offered the post by telegraph.[21]

Thus two months later, on 11 July 1887, MacGregor was offered the governorship of New Guinea 'subject to approval of Queensland [and] after declaration of sovereignty'.[22] As there was no Pacific cable, telegrams had to be carried by ship, usually from Auckland, on the last stage to Fiji, so that it was 1 August before MacGregor's telegraphic acceptance left Fiji and 15 August before this reached London.[23]

As Herbert anticipated, Thurston was grievously disappointed. When in England in October 1887 he urged his claims for promotion, and complained at being passed over for MacGregor. He stressed that his objections were not personal, for MacGregor 'is an active and able man and will I believe discharge his new duties with credit to himself and advantage to the public service', but were based mainly on his seniority to MacGregor. Thurston pointed out that he was Colonial Secretary when MacGregor first reached Fiji. As a result of MacGregor's appointment he felt that his 'official status [was] comparatively lowered and that [his] mental embarrassment and pain . . . [was] but natural'. He did, however, admit that he 'had no wish for transfer to New Guinea unless the Administration of its Government was directly and exclusively under the control of the Colonial Office'. In the circumstances, clearly because he did not wish to face MacGregor, he hoped it would not be necessary to order his immediate return to Fiji.[24]

This problem was solved by the transfer of Governor Mitchell and Thurston's promotion to Governor combined with the

Colonial Secretaryship of Fiji. It would have been awkward had this solution not been possible; Fiji in 1888 with neither Thurston nor MacGregor would have been in an even sorrier position than it was.

MacGregor, meanwhile, heard nothing in Fiji from the Colonial Office after 11 July, and he must have begun to believe that Queensland had not approved of his appointment or that sovereignty was not to be declared. He again became despondent and his sentiments to Gordon on New Year's Day 1888 were familiar ones.

> Time is an old deceiver: how he saddens and sobers the aspirations of the young and vigorous. No one endowed with the spirit of prophecy could have convinced me that the year of grace 1888 would see me on a total income of £56 a month. Of course I was infinitely better off as Assistant Medical Officer in the Seychelles. There is a certain disease of the human eye that attacks the circumference of vision, and gradually eating into it symmetrically, makes the patient see as if looking through a decreasing series of round tubes. Such is the history for the last seven years of the mental view of my future. Well it is a long road that has no turning; perhaps the New Year may lead me to better luck.[25]

Six months later, still not having heard final confirmation of his appointment, he applied to Thurston for leave—three months vacation on full pay and three months ordinary on half pay. It was anticipated in the colony that this could be his final departure and in his public farewells his appointment to New Guinea was clearly in the minds of some of the speakers.[26] Thurston arranged that his pay from Fiji would cease if the appointment to New Guinea were confirmed in the next six months.[27] So MacGregor left Fiji on 6 June for Sydney, still in the employment of that colony. Herbert was not pleased at this development. He minuted on 19 June:

> Dr. McGregor has made a mistake in proceeding to leave Fiji without orders. It may be months before he is required in New Guinea. Sir T. McIlwraith [then Queensland's Premier, having defeated Griffith in the elections in May] may even raise objections to his appointment.[28]

It was felt, however, that protests would be wasted, and in any case MacGregor could always be sent back to Fiji.

The delays in 1888 were caused not only by the Colonial Office's fear that some Queensland politicians might make objections (which in fact never happened openly) but by an unsettled

dispute between the Governor of Queensland, Anthony Musgrave, and the British Government. Musgrave wanted an exact
statement of how far he, or his government, could intervene
in the future administration of British New Guinea.[29] Nevertheless, MacGregor began discussions with the Australian colonies
on policies desirable for the new government. On 4 September
he reached Port Moresby and, having formally proclaimed British sovereignty over the colony of British New Guinea, was
sworn in as Administrator.

These long drawn-out negotiations, with their alternating
raising and dashing of MacGregor's hopes, were caused by factors
which had considerable significance for the future of the colony.
The disputes between the British Government and the Australian
colonial governments over the limitations of their administrative
and financial responsibilities led to a division of powers and
severely limited finances which made MacGregor's position even
more difficult than that of other colonial governors. Just as the
final ratification of his appointment might have depended on
the result of a Queensland election, so the future whims of a
Queensland governor or of a Victorian premier, as well as the
usual complex pressures from London, affected his policies. The
limits of the possible in British New Guinea seemed weighted
against the independence of its first Administrator. It was within
these restrictions that he had to try to 'put into practice many of
the principles' which he believed were 'founded on a high sense
of justice'.[30]

Besides the choice of MacGregor other significant arrangements
followed decisions made at the 1887 Colonial Conference. British New Guinea formally became a Crown colony, with an un-
certain and anomalous power of supervision given to Queensland. In addition the other colonies contributing substantially
to the cost of New Guinea—New South Wales and Victoria—
were given the right to intervene in any matter which went
beyond ordinary administration. The Australian colonies guaranteed to provide £15,000 annually for ten years, while Britain
was to supply a steamship for administrative purposes and pay
for its maintenance. The supervisory powers of the colonies were
subject to British control, through the Colonial Office, as were
all MacGregor's actions. Moreover, the British Government's
powers of reservation applied to any ordinance involving dealings with the indigenous people; the purchase of land from them;
their deportation; or any trading with them in arms, ammuni-

tion, explosives, intoxicating liquors or opium. Besides these provisions specifically designed to protect primitive people, there were provisions general to most colonies for the reservation of ordinances affecting other parts of the Empire, or believed to be repugnant to English law, or inconsistent with treaty obligations.[31]

Although Governor Musgrave did not think the complicated system could work the Colonial Office thought it could and advised MacGregor to report to the Governor of Queensland 'as fully as the Governor of a Crown Colony is in the habit of doing to the Secretary of State', and to consult him on all important matters. Copies of all despatches, except those on minor details of administration involving no question of principle, were to be sent to the Colonial Office; and the Queensland Governor was to send to London, with his observations, copies of his replies to MacGregor. The arrangements were primarily meant to ensure that the Colonial Office would be kept fully informed and would be able to intervene in any important question. As replies from London to MacGregor were to be sent through Brisbane except on 'special occasions', the Governor of Queensland was also to be kept aware of all developments.[32]

Not surprisingly throughout the ten years of his governorship MacGregor felt over-restricted and on three occasions—in 1890, 1893 and 1894—threatened to resign after quarrels with Sir Henry Norman, the Governor of Queensland (1889-96). Some of his plans, such as allowing a British company, the British New Guinea Syndicate, to invest heavily in the island in 1898, were thwarted by the intervention of the Australian colonies and others by the Colonial Office, such as a suggested 1897 Ordinance concerning native marriages.

He could have been restricted far more, however, had public opinion in the Australian colonies and Great Britain been more concerned with New Guinea. If the intense feelings engendered in Australia by Britain's disavowal of McIlwraith's annexation in 1883, and the subsequent recognition of German claims in 1884, had been maintained, all his policies would have had to endure the tests of public popularity. Instead there was a lessening of interest, specially as other Australian questions—ranging from the depression of the late eighties and early nineties and the great strikes to moves towards a federation of the divided colonies—claimed more public attention. New Guinea news was still given regular columns in the newspapers of all capital cities;

MacGregor was always interviewed when he visited Australia; dramatic stories of exploration or startling items on native customs could always claim space. Yet mundane administrative details, or MacGregor's attempts to cushion the impact of white civilization on the New Guinea peoples, were rarely debated. Public interest in New Guinea had never had as its starting point the future welfare of its indigenous people. It had stemmed rather from a consideration of the importance of the colony to Australia: the question of the strategic importance to Australia if these islands were in the hands of another power, or the exploitation of the supposed wealth of the islands by Australians. There were some individuals and groups who had more lasting interests in New Guinea—the missionaries, for example, whose concern began long before any governmental intervention; the planters, or the seekers for gold; or the trading firms such as Burns Philp. Whenever MacGregor's policies affected them, they tried to arouse the public or the government, but the majority of Australians remained indifferent.

While Australian public opinion concerning New Guinea was limited and decreasing in these ten years, British public opinion was hardly aroused. New Guinea, like Fiji, was such a remote, unimportant, small part of a vast British Empire that it could not arouse much concern. As in Australia the bizarre, the odd, the striking event might stir the press and sometimes its readers; much of the interest in MacGregor when he was in Britain in 1894-95 was of this ephemeral nature. Though missionaries could rouse humanitarian feelings New Guinea questions always seemed far less important than Indian or African problems.

Most opposition to, or even interest in, MacGregor's policies came from government sources. Queensland's relationship with MacGregor was made difficult by the attitudes taken by three successive administrators: Sir Anthony Musgrave (November 1883-October 1888) Sir Arthur Palmer (October 1888-May 1889) and Sir Henry Norman—particularly the latter, and Premier McIlwraith.

Musgrave believed that power of supervision of New Guinea was given to the governor not to the governor-in-council. Thus he argued that he need not consult his cabinet and a crisis developed. Fortunately Musgrave's death on 9 October 1888 ended this difficult situation. MacGregor reported to Gordon—probably from information obtained from Griffith—that

a dreadful storm was brewing and a very warlike minute prepared

by his cabinet at the moment Sir Anthony died; this document was
to show that he was acting contrary to the letter and spirit of the
constitution, in advising me without consulting his cabinet. I have
no doubt he was wrong, and would not, could not have been supported by the Secretary of State.

MacGregor, however, personally found Musgrave 'very friendly
. . . and [he] meant to not interfere at all with my work'.[33]

Palmer, who acted as Administrator after Musgrave died, had a
different criticism of the situation. He argued, probably reflecting the attitude of his premier, McIlwraith,[34] that Queensland
should have almost sole control of New Guinea. MacGregor, on
the other hand, never welcomed Queensland's intervention in
New Guinea policies, partly because of Queensland's attitudes
to Aborigines, but mainly because of its use of kanakas on sugar
plantations. Queensland had a bad reputation at the Colonial
Office[35] and among administrators such as Gordon and Mac-
Gregor because of its attitudes to natives.[36] Admittedly these
outsiders did not always appreciate the divisions within Queensland about native labour. Generally the sugar planters, who
wanted cheap labour, had made their voices politically heard
through the Nationalists led by McIlwraith, whilst humanitarian
and working-class opposition to this labour had been politically
represented through the Liberals, led by Griffith.[37] Native labour
was a factor in the decision of the British Government not to support McIlwraith's proposed annexation of New Guinea in 1883.
It was believed by many at the time, including Gordon, Mac-
Gregor, Griffith, the Aborigines' Protection Society, the explorer
Baron Mikluho Maclay and the missionary the Reverend James
Chalmers (who were both residing in New Guinea), that
McIlwraith's main motive was the desire to control a field for
recruiting black labour.[38] MacGregor's belief was made public
when he challenged McIlwraith on this point in his address to
the Royal Colonial Institute in London in 1895:

> more than half a score of years ago . . . Sir Thomas McIlwraith
> declared at a meeting of the Royal Geographical Society that the
> desire for the annexation of British New Guinea did not spring
> from the wish to possess more land or to get natives to work on the
> sugar plantations in Queensland, as it was known that the natives
> of New Guinea were not fitted for that work, but it arose simply
> for the purpose of preventing undesirable neighbours from coming
> near them. A week before Sir Thomas McIlwraith made this state-
> ment, two recruiting vessels arrived in Queensland with 233 lab-
> ourers from New Guinea. They were followed by others, so

that by the end of November of the same year, 1884, some 625 of them had been landed in Queensland—a number large enough to demonstrate the unfitness ascribed to them by Sir Thomas McIlwraith.[39]

McIlwraith, as MacGregor said, always denied the charge, and the balance of evidence (despite the coincidence of the beginning of recruiting in New Britain) seems to be on McIlwraith's side. One exchange in the Queensland Legislative Assembly suggests that both the principal leaders knew that the charge was false: when McIlwraith said 'the fact is that we never did bring black men from New Guinea into the colony', Griffith's revealing response was 'the fact is you never thought of it'.[40]

Even if it is true that McIlwraith did not have this motive in 1883, this does not mean that if New Guinea had been fully controlled by Queensland, labourers would not have been introduced. During most of MacGregor's time in New Guinea reports continued that McIlwraith was planning to use New Guinea natives on the Queensland plantations, and when MacGregor visited Brisbane in July 1894 and discussed this question he found that the government had indeed been considering this.[41] He strongly opposed it and argued at the Royal Colonial Institute in 1895 that it would be an outrage to force natives to go; it would mean the end of chances for the future development of New Guinea if its labour supply were lost; and it would be a 'deadly blow' at the chances of teaching the natives to be useful producers on their own account.[42] In fact no British New Guinea native was allowed by MacGregor to work on the Queensland plantations.

Native labour had been very much an issue of the May 1888 election in which McIlwraith defeated Griffith, and the Colonial Office had thought that McIlwraith's victory might result in disapproval of MacGregor as Administrator. MacGregor made his uneasiness with the Queensland Government with which he knew he had to work quite clear:

> in Queensland Griffith is a safe, able and enlightened man, but he has been turned out solely and simply because he has been called an Imperialist: and McIlwraith who is an able bully, with a face like a dugong and a temper like a buffalo, has come into power because he has dubbed himself a Nationalist . . . such things . . . [have] a special bearing on British New Guinea. The Possession is a thing of some intrinsic importance but not of such value as to induce the Imperial Government at any time to support a policy

here which would be contrary to the wishes of the Queensland Cabinet, or which would at all events evoke from them active opposition. I am thus quite conscious that in any dispute with the Queensland Government I should have to give in, and therefore I have to be careful to avoid contention. I have no doubt that by working with them loyally I shall obtain much more of my own way than if I were to attempt to ignore them, which would be flying in the face of my Instructions.[43]

The main difficulties MacGregor faced with the Queensland ministers occurred in his first months in Brisbane in 1888. These difficulties centred around the attitudes and positions of McIlwraith and Griffith, as MacGregor's comments to the latter make clear:

I find my position very embarrassing. No one is so well able to advise in such matters as yourself, but I have much reluctance to ask you to study these matters, because on the one hand you are under no official obligation to consider them, and because I am not sure how far it would be loyal on my part to the present Government to consult the Leader of the Opposition . . . I have to feel my way with—I need not say the Ministry—the Premier.[44]

Four months later he wrote:

I estimate that I had to bear more insolence from Sir Thomas McIlwraith than I have had to tolerate in the sum total of my previous existence; but somehow I had come to the conclusion that he wished to provoke a quarrel and I made up my mind that I should put up with anything rather than fail to obtain a start.[45]

MacGregor expected that the new Governor of Queensland, Sir Henry Norman, who arrived in May 1889 would work closely with the Queensland cabinet and affect him little.

He will doubtless convey my despatches to his cabinet and advise me as he is advised by them. It is difficult therefore for me to divine beforehand in any given case what may be approved or disapproved, and as communication is very irregular with Brisbane, I have of course to act in every case on my own judgement.[46]

MacGregor was mistaken, however. Norman interfered directly with him, expressing soon after his arrival his strong disapproval of MacGregor's omission to send copies of all despatches to Brisbane. He then introduced new rules for the conduct of correspondence which were intended to make Queensland's and his control more effective. Not only was every despatch from MacGregor to go to Brisbane and be seen by the Queensland Governor, but there were rules as to which despatches should be sent to London. Those which were merely formal, or of local detail, or which formed part of an incomplete correspondence, were not to be sent. The Colonial Office agreed to Norman's suggestions, provided they received a schedule of all despatches sent from MacGregor to Queensland.[47]

One result of this revised system was to increase the time period before MacGregor's suggestions were considered in Brisbane and London. The minimum time that a ship took to sail from Port Moresby to Brisbane (about 1,200 miles) was four days. But because ships were infrequent and because MacGregor did so much travelling, his despatches were often delayed before they left New Guinea. Norman reported periods of nine to eleven weeks during which no despatches were received from MacGregor and that a despatch sent from Brisbane two months before had not been acknowledged. These delays caused frustrations in both Brisbane and New Guinea.[48]

The time elapsing before despatches reached London was of course much greater. It took about eight weeks for a ship to go from Brisbane to London, so that the minimum time for a despatch to reach the Colonial Office from New Guinea, allowing a fortnight for getting to Brisbane and being considered there, was ten weeks. This time was increased when Norman began holding despatches for longer periods, either because he had no clerk to help him with all this extra correspondence, or, more importantly, because he wanted to make criticisms. A reply from the Colonial Office to a request from MacGregor could then hardly be expected in less than six months and could take up to ten months. Urgent questions could be dealt with by cable, but because of the poor financial position of the colony, the expense always limited their use.

Clearly MacGregor gained a measure of independence in his policy because of these delays. At the same time the difficulty in gaining rapid approval for his decisions could, and did, lead to a conservative tendency in policy.

Relationships between MacGregor and Norman worsened rapidly. Norman insisted on enforcing his interpretation of the powers given to Queensland; in particular he argued that the functions of the Queensland governor were more than advisory. MacGregor insisted that Queensland's role was only advisory and that he would accept directions only from the Colonial Office. The clash on principle was accompanied and intensified by the clash between the personalities of the two men. Norman, after thirty-five years military and administrative experience in India (1844-59, 1861-65 and 1867-82),[49] was not disposed in his sixties to accept the arguments of a mere Scotsman in his first gubernatorial appointment. MacGregor, with his natural obstinacy and conviction that his arguments must be right, never found compromise easy, let alone with a representative of the class of military governors that he so disliked.

When Norman quite reasonably objected to the legal looseness of MacGregor's proposed regulations for a Native Regulation Board—a project for which MacGregor had high hopes—MacGregor told Gordon of

the great and profound disappointment Sir H. Norman had inflicted on me. . . . My heart was full of grief before and this fairly cracked it. Never probably will the psychical moment return that was thus lost by the blind unnecessary interference of Sir H. Norman. He does not know, never can appreciate, the evil he has done. . . . I have told him to suppose an artist on fashioning a statue [having] to stand by and see a Commissioner of Police come and smash it up with a sledge hammer because it is not on academic lines, and I have told him that may give some idea of my disappointment. . . . I have offered to accept undivided responsibility for what I do or propose, but I decline to accept save under duress any responsibility for time and opportunity lost.

He cannot help it. He has always been fully occupied, and now he cannot keep out of the St. Vitus dance of affairs. He has had 70 years of motion and now he thinks it should be perpetual. He dare not attempt to cook the Queensland cabbage so he turns his restless hands to my Kail pot. Had he consistently refused sanction I could have respected his position, but he refuses to sanction in September on arguments which grow stronger with time and then sanctions in October. I have torn his arguments and returned them to him in tatters. I fear I am an enthusiast and he an idle, ignorant, unimaginative, unsympathetic busybody. I shall probably be removed or turned out of the service; but not with impunity, for the Government have steadily supported me and given effect to all my proposals in a way that is really very surprising. I have reminded Morehead, the Premier of Queensland, that Honorius and Lord Augustus Loftus had chickens with distinction when they could not govern and were thus kept out of mischief: and I did not forget Louis XVI and his locks.[50] As alternatives I trusted that it would be better to make Sir Henry lay foundation stones in Queensland than to capsize my edifice in British New Guinea; or that he held inspections of hospitals and asylums instead of driving me into one of them. You, knowing how intensely one can devote oneself to such work as I have here, can understand how it tears and muti-

lates one's soul to have this moulded clay pot dashed out of one's
hand by an unthinking philistine. All this and much more I have
said to Sir H. Norman,[51] so you need not be surprised if I am
promptly retired.[52]

Although this particular dispute was won by MacGregor, for
the Ordinance creating the Native Regulation Board was passed
on 15 November 1889,[53] the possibilities of clash remained, as
MacGregor's tone in April 1890 makes only too clear:

> I have had my way with Sir H. Norman as regards my draft Ordin-
> ance, and I do not think my bile will be stirred on that point again.
> In short I had by much the best of it. But he has not forgiven and
> never will forgive me. He has driven me into a protracted wrangle
> over a subject in which he is right in the matter of form, which
> I admit, while claiming I was right under the circumstances.[54]

MacGregor had spent about £900 in buying a launch and al-
tering the government steamship, the *Merrie England,* with the
concurrence of the Queensland ministers and then had asked
for Norman's sanction; MacGregor later alleged Norman had
known of and acquiesced in this expenditure, but he said

> I shall be severely handled over this, and then let down when the
> matter finally reaches the Secretary of State, as it must do even-
> tually. . . . He [Norman] does not in controversial correspondence
> come square to his fences. He likes writing; I like acting. And so
> long as I can act I let him write, until like a Leyden jar I become
> overcharged and transmit a shock as brief as provocative. In my
> work he has been kept at bay so well that he has done no harm
> save as regards the Native Regulations Ordinance. He assures
> me that he is as willing to assist me as were Sir A. Musgrave, and Sir
> A. Palmer. Well, I suppose every swan sings his own song; but I am
> too dense to comprehend his bird language, and, Scotch like, judge
> him by results. I have accepted his protestations of friendship, but
> have said—if so and so, then I like the Prince of Denmark, have
> shot mine arrow o'er the house and hurt my brother. . . . One
> . . . fray we had over the trifle of 'semi-official correspondence'. I
> firmly declined to recognise it or to carry it on, stating my
> reasons. Oddly enough he remarked in the course of it: 'it is
> strange that when I was in Ceylon Sir Arthur Gordon told
> me he disapproved of semi-official corespondence'. So there you
> [Gordon] are held responsible for my doings in a way you would
> hardly have expected. It is said he is going home soon. It really
> will not make much difference to me. So long as the Government
> of Queensland support my action Sir H. Norman cannot suspend
> me, whatever his instructions are.[55]

He protested again in June 1890 especially over Norman's

delaying of matters; another quarrel had begun also, over the procedure for sanctioning repairs to the *Merrie England*. In September 1890 MacGregor devoted eleven of thirty-two pages of a letter to reviling Norman and in other letters he accused him of not understanding men and affairs, trouble making, interfering and 'nibbling at power', and thinking 'nothing of a coloured man.[56] I fear it is so with many old India men'.

The Colonial Office rebuked MacGregor over the tone of his protests against Norman and his procedure in maintaining the *Merrie England,* once saying that he had been 'guilty of a grave error of judgment [which] might . . . have caused serious trouble between Sir Henry Norman and his Ministers'. MacGregor wrote long defences of his positions ('I am not going to be condemned quietly on a garbled ex parte statement') and felt sure the Secretary of State would 'modify his opinion when he has heard the other side of the story'. In fact the Colonial Office expected MacGregor 'would not like [being rebuked and] would have a good deal to say', but after receiving MacGregor's answer saw no reason for withdrawing their censure.

There could be no winner in disputes like these: rather both were losers, and so was New Guinea. The attention given by both governors to the formal rightness or wrongness of their actions could have been devoted to more useful ends. The Colonial Office wisely stated in July 1890 that it was 'most desirable' that the correspondence cease.[57]

MacGregor feared the result of Norman's intervention would be to increase Queensland's power. Thus when told by the Queensland Premier that 'everything must be initiated' by him or his ministers, MacGregor thought this would be most undesirable

> with a man say of the type of McIlwraith as Dictator and an Administrator not selected by Australia but appointed by the Colonial Office. In such a combination the shortsighted fussy action of Sir H. Norman will bear thorny fruit.[58]

He was slightly more cheerful on 24 March 1892 (just after he had been visited in New Guinea by Griffith) about the prospects of intervention by Queensland politicians. He thought that Griffith,

> Morehead, Sir A. Palmer, Sir Charles Lilley[59] and most of the leading men of Queensland are quite sound on New Guinea. McIlwraith would sacrifice it without any compunction, but he is not likely to ever be Premier again, though nothing is more risky than political

J

prognostication in Australia. I do not think there is the least likelihood of any unfair treatment of the place as long as I remain
here. I have had to gain over these men, to lay down a course, and
to start the vessel on it. Surely my successors can keep her going,
once under way.[60]

His forecasts were accurate and there was little further intervention until the final year of his governorship. He again disagreed with Norman, however, at the end of 1893, in an argument
which seemed likely to end MacGregor's association with the
colony. Early in November 1893 MacGregor, deciding that he
would not continue in New Guinea, advised the Queensland
Government that he wanted to leave in June 1894. Privately
he wrote to Griffith, doubting if he could even last until June:

> I am getting used up, and have had some sharp attacks of fever
> lately. Great exposure and much anxiety are telling on me, and
> if I do not leave before long I shall stay here for ever.

He went on to repeat the sort of ideas he had expressed so often
before in Fiji:

> My plans for the future then are simple. If I get no appointment
> I care to have, I shall give some time to European hospitals and
> come to practise medicine somewhere in Australia. That I should
> prefer to a small West Indian colony. I am no favourite with Lord
> Ripon [the British Secretary of State]. . . . I have therefore not
> much to expect from him . . . I feel much the having to leave this
> work but I have no option; the usual period is nearly up, and I
> require a thorough change.[61]

MacGregor wrote formally to the Queensland governor on 23
November 1893 asking for permission to leave in June 1894. In
his reply of 15 December Norman questioned whether Mac-
Gregor's term of office was limited to six years but promised Mac-
Gregor that leave of absence would be given at any time as the
value of his services was well recognized.[62] MacGregor took considerable umbrage at this and said flatly that after his leave he
would never return to New Guinea. He regarded six years as the
normal term of office for a governor and was 'surprised and . . .
deeply disappointed' that Norman had queried this point. He
did not feel that the existence of a ten-year agreement justified
the extension of his term for another four years: such an agreement gave him 'no additional physical strength', nor did it
'reduce the effects of exposure to sun and rain, or lighten the
load of my anxiety in dealing with new, strange, savage tribes'.
On the other hand he felt there were special circumstances in his

favour. He had undertaken far more extra-ordinary duties than officers in similar situations: he had, for instance, been a leader in dangerous situations, a lexicographer, a geodetic surveyor, a cartographer, an apothecary, a medical officer. As well he had hardly seen his family for six years and had endured many dangerous risks to health, such as malaria.[63]

Besides the official correspondence between MacGregor and Norman there were also 'semi-official' (according to Norman) or 'private' (according to MacGregor) communications passing between the two men. These became increasingly bitter as the dispute continued. Eventually Norman sent these letters on to the Colonial Office, whose officials regretted he had not kept them to himself.[64]

A letter written by MacGregor in March 1894 gives a clear indication of his weariness and irritation:

> I feel like one of Hobson's horses, tired and jaded, drawing a four-wheeled vehicle, but within sight of home, having nearly finished the longest stage [over] hills, ruts, mires and stones. [The comfortable party in the vehicle wish to drive beyond the changing station to enjoy the landscape. The horse] will, if not relieved . . . slip his head out of the collar rather than be driven past by those that think not of his painful joints and quivering muscles . . . they may give the beast a viciously bad character, but they will certainly have to change him or stop.[65]

He repeated these feelings in a private letter to Griffith. MacGregor had been astonished that the Queensland governor and ministers had doubted the length of term of his office.

> This is likely to be a most serious matter for me. I can not stay after June. I shall not return here after that unless brought back in irons. If they get the Secretary of State to adopt their view, it means I must resign . . . If I lose everything in the world I will not longer sacrifice my family life and my own health.

He claimed that the whole issue reflected Norman's spite after their previous clashes:

> Your intervention put official matters on a footing the Governor did not like; now I am being paid out for that.[66]

MacGregor knew that Griffith had disregarded Norman, since in his diary he recorded that Griffith

> chuckled over the way that he has put Sir H. Norman out of the government of British New Guinea. Sir H. N. still sends him papers in which he says 'I propose to do'; or 'If you see no objection'; or 'I

intend'. Griffith always sends the same answer, never taking any notice of these positions, 'I advise so and so'.[67]

Despite all these protestations, in May 1894 MacGregor decided to return for a second term to New Guinea. This change of heart obviously surprised those who had read his protests. It was predicted in the Colonial Office at the time that this decision 'may be a good thing for the Possession, but I should have thought hardly desirable for himself'.[68] In later years MacGregor came to the same conclusion: 'I certainly ruined my career by remaining [in British New Guinea] a second term, and thus losing a step in promotion. I was younger then and more hopeful'. He constantly repeated this assertion over the years, for example in 1903, referring to it as a 'fatal mistake' and in 1904:

> my taking a second term of office . . . was the turning point in my official career. I was simple enough to believe that it would count for and not against my future promotion in the hierarchy of the service . . .

and in 1907:

> taking a second term in New Guinea was ruin to my official career, and I took it only on the urgent request of Lord Ripon and of the three colonies.[69]

How true is the assertion that he was almost forced to accept this second term? The first intimation of MacGregor's desire to leave New Guinea reached London in January 1894. The disputed point, the length of MacGregor's service, was discussed without any authoritative decision being reached. As no time was mentioned in the formal documents the question seemed open: he held his post under a commission 'during the Queen's pleasure', but also he was serving 'virtually . . . under the Queensland Government'. The Colonial Office felt they could not prevent him retiring but believed it 'desirable, if possible, that he should continue in the post till 1898, when the present arrangement with the contributing colonies comes to an end'.[70] A confidential despatch of 10 February 1894 under the signature of Lord Ripon said that there was no agreed limit but that it would be appreciated if MacGregor returned.[71] This was the extent of the 'urgent request' that MacGregor spoke of years later.

The Colonial Office was surprised when MacGregor changed his mind.[72] It had been thought that MacGregor's decision not to return was irrevocable and discussion had begun in London about his future career: 'It will be considered whether he should not get something in a better climate. He has earned promotion'.[73] Premier Nelson said in April 1894 that the Queensland Government, although greatly regretting the loss, had no intention of raising any barrier to MacGregor's retirement. In London a financial motive was suspected, as MacGregor's wife had come to the Colonial Office in April or May 1894 and interviewed Sir Robert Meade about the payment of MacGregor's passage back to England. MacGregor had written to Mary asking her to confirm that such a payment would be made, undoubtedly fearing that it would be stopped if he resigned from New Guinea. Meade, however, assured Mary that it would be paid.[74]

The decisive pressure which persuaded MacGregor to change his mind may have come from Griffith. MacGregor told Griffith this on 16 May 1894: 'Guided largely by your advice I have proposed to continue here'.[75] MacGregor may have been mistaken in attributing this advice to Griffith for as early as 30 November 1892 Griffith had urged the Colonial Office to start considering a successor for MacGregor who 'can not be expected to continue indefinitely the laborious duties which he has now discharged for some four years'.[76] Griffith may well, however, have been persuaded by 1894 that it would be best for New Guinea if Mac-Gregor stayed there. MacGregor, in a letter written to Norman on the same day as he told Griffith he had accepted his advice to return, had said it was his 'duty to regard the clearly expressed wish of the Secretary of State [in the despatch of 10 February 1894] that I should continue the Administration of the Possession'. Perhaps his decision reflected an ambitious calculation that he would gain credit from the Colonial Office if he returned. Clearly MacGregor had forgotten his giving credit to Griffith when he complained so often to him about this 'fatal mistake'.

MacGregor made his decision to return to New Guinea conditional on the granting of four concessions to him.[77] He wanted his wife to be able to stay with him and live in comfort, so he wanted improvements both at Government House and on the *Merrie England* (he estimated that suitable alterations could be carried out at a cost of £150). His separation from his family was a constant source of dissatisfaction, though Mary visited Australia quite frequently during these years, sometimes bringing her two daughters.[78] Helen was left at school in Edinburgh and James also remained in Scotland. MacGregor was disturbed and shamed by reports of his son's conduct at Glasgow University, for he was evidently going to the bad there too as fast as possible. His clothes and watch have been pledged I do not know how often. Unfortunately I know from a note from Principal Laird that that gentleman knows he is my son.[79]

The division between father and son is obvious from this comment, which does not show MacGregor in a particularly favourable light: his concern for his own reputation is more obvious than his concern for James. Although he desired the stability, security and affection that having his family with him would bring, one sometimes wonders how much he was capable of giving in return and how much time he could have spared from his official duties and varied pursuits for the responsibilities of being husband and father.

The second condition was that he was to have six months leave on full pay and an additional three months, if necessary, on half pay. His argument was that while on leave in Europe, when obtaining instruments and stores, he would be on official business. He justifiably maintained that his salary of £1,500 a year was not a large one and that he had to maintain establishments for himself in New Guinea and his family in Britain.

Thirdly, he wanted the Imperial Government to confirm that the *Merrie England* would definitely be retained for ten years. He also required a launch and a more complete surveying outfit. This request followed a long dispute, in which Norman as well as the governments of the contributing colonies and Britain had been involved, about the future maintenance of the *Merrie England*. It was essential for any form of government that MacGregor had efficient means of transport always available.

Finally he wanted his official designation changed from Administrator to Lieutenant-Governor. This was frankly a point of prestige, a product of his ambitions and his insecurity. He felt he must always be improving his position and this renaming would at least be a symbolic rise. He also claimed that the new title would be more apt as he was already known by the natives as governor.

Even while making these conditions MacGregor was still bitter over Norman's attitude, so he frankly told Griffith 'I really hope your Government will find that my proposals are not acceptable'.[80] The Queensland Government, however, agreed immediately to the grant of leave and to the improvements in his quarters and referred the other two points to the Colonial Office for their decision.

The concession of a change of title had been discussed early in 1893. At that time the Colonial Office had not been enthusiastic because of one likely interpretation of this change of title:

> the real objection . . . is one which we can't offer publicly . . . the popular idea of a Lieutenant-Governor would . . . be someone subordinate to a Governor, and although for purposes of administrative convenience MacGregor is practically controlled by the Queensland Governor, there is nothing in his Letters Patent giving Norman any legal authority over him. People outside are jealously watching our action with regard to New Guinea, and if they see this change made they will assume it to be part of a deep-laid plot to hand over the natives to the care of Queensland planters.[81]

In 1894, however, this objection was felt to be less important than keeping MacGregor in New Guinea. The change was formally possible under the existing Letters Patent and no new objection was raised. It was felt that MacGregor's 'good services in New Guinea render him eminently fitted to receive this mark of Her Majesty's favour'.[82] But it was considered that the contributing colonies should be asked their opinion of the change. In July all three colonies gave their approval.[83]

The final point, the continuation of the Imperial grant for the *Merrie England,* proved the most difficult to promise for it involved the consent of the Treasury. The Colonial Office considered that they would need a stronger case than MacGregor's threatened resignation to justify a continuance of the grant after its expiry at the close of the agreement.

MacGregor did agree to come back nevertheless and, after taking leave from July 1894 to June 1895, spent another three years in New Guinea. These negotiations over MacGregor's conditional acceptance show the importance of the three contributing colonies and the Colonial Office to policies in New Guinea. MacGregor was working within limits of which he was constantly aware. It took a skilful administrator to frame all his policies in such a way as to satisfy Australia and Britain.

7

New Guinea: The Limits of Control 1888-98

That the paternal form [of justice] is the most suitable for a native population in the act of stepping out of savagery and barbarism into civilisation, I entertain no manner of doubt.

Throughout his two terms in New Guinea MacGregor found the limits set by an allowance of £15,000 a year almost crippling. The bounds of what was possible were rapidly reached. As Treasurer in Fiji he had faced similar restrictions, but in New Guinea there were more sources of criticism and opposition to his policies. His annual estimate of revenue and expenditure had to be sent to the Queensland Governor-in-Council for approval and could also be questioned by the Colonial Office. If his appropriation exceeded £15,000, agreement for the extra grant had to be obtained from the three colonies as well as the Colonial Office and British Treasury, all of which gave low priority to New Guinea affairs.

MacGregor had the added difficulty of being able to find few ways of supplementing this allowance. He was handed over a credit balance of only £1,500 from the Protectorate and receipts from revenue were never high. For the first nine months (to June 1889) a total of £2,680 was received; for the following year (to June 1890), £3,016. Despite decreases in some years, by 1896 they had slowly risen to £6,548 and exceeded £10,000 for each of MacGregor's last two years. Customs dues provided the only substantial receipts, making up eighty-four per cent of total revenue. Others such as those from the goldfields, fines imposed and costs of licences (mainly for fishing), increased but not sufficiently to give a significant boost to the revenue. Returns from the alienation of land were not high.[1]

The maximum that MacGregor had, therefore, in any one year was just over £25,000. It was difficult to maintain minimal policies in these stringent circumstances, let alone implement any expansive ideas. In every year except one, however, he managed to frame his appropriation ordinance within the set limits of £15,000 and his efforts to economize and make do with little were appreciated in the Colonial Office, a typical judgement being that he was 'evidently still exerting his ingenuity to make every penny he can get hold of available in some shape for discharging some service or other incidental to the general administration'.[2]

By the 1887 agreement the British share towards the expenses of the first ten years of New Guinea, apart from the yearly grant, was fixed at a maximum of £29,000. This sum was to be devoted to the purchase of a steam yacht for the Administrator, to cost no more than £18,500, and its maintenance for three years at £3,500 a year. The cost of the *Merrie England,* including purchase, refitting, the voyage out and repairs, was £15,132—thus less than the fixed maximum.[3] In the first year, however, the figure for maintenance and repairs was seen to be inadequate. The estimates had been framed on West African experience and so made no allowance for Australian union regulations which did not allow white seamen and firemen to work with coloured men.[4] MacGregor also found that he needed a better launch, particularly for river exploration.

The Colonial Office realized that MacGregor's requests for additional funds amounted to a good deal more than the Treasury was likely to grant and some members argued against increasing or even continuing the grant.[5] There were doubts

whether the maintenance of a steam yacht for the Administrator at a cost approaching £7,000 per annum is not a charge out of all proportion both to the importance of the settlement and to the benefit derived from the use of the vessel.[6]

In 1893 the British government went so far as to say 'we have done more than we contracted to do at the Conference and the interest in New Guinea is purely Australian'.[7]

The arguments in the Colonial Office in support of MacGregor's demands proved stronger, however, and it was decided to back him against the Treasury. Reasons given included that

in the present temper . . . of Australia, and particularly of Queensland, it is particularly desirable to give a little more, rather than anything less, than the total £29,000. And it is very important that nothing contrary to what the Colony or Colonies will consider just should be decided without the question being fully understood by Her Majesty's Government outside the Treasury.[8]

Another reason, showing a wide appreciation of the issue, was that

> it is partly due to the policy insisted upon by Her Majesty's Government of closing New Guinea to anything but the most resistricted exploitation by Europeans that the revenue remains so small, and while the colonies loyally carry out that policy they have a moral claim on Her Majesty's Government to assist them in bearing the burden thereby thrown upon them.[9]

MacGregor also used powerful arguments to persuade the British government to continue its payments for the *Merrie England*. These included an implied threat in 1891 to sell the vessel and so cripple his administration,[10] and a suggestion in 1892 that the Solomons and New Hebrides be added to his responsibility (partly to control labour recruiting), in which case he would have even greater need for the *Merrie England*.[11] His main argument, however, was that his initial task was to spread knowledge of the government throughout the island—an impossibility without the steamer—and this finally prevailed.

Thus the total expenditure on the steamer during his term of office was £76,000—a very high sum in comparison with the total of £153,000 for all other administrative purposes and one which could well be expected to provoke criticism and opposition. The British government was persuaded to provide £50,000 of this cost over the ten years of the agreement, and the guaranteeing colonies agreed that the £26,000 deficit should be made up from the accumulated revenue fund which, by the original agreement, was to have been shared among the colonies. Although the British government had provided for the steamer the same amount as each of the three contributing colonies had paid for all other administrative purposes, it could not convince colonial opinion of its generosity and a comparison was often made with the Imperial grant of £100,000 to start the Fijian government.[12]

The whole question of MacGregor's requests for additional finance was further complicated by his prolonged dispute with Governor Norman over responsibility for expenditure. Finally the Colonial Office ruled that

> MacGregor should . . . be regarded as subordinate to the Queensland Ministry in the matter of expenditure from Colonial funds and as subordinate to the Secretary of State through the Governor in the expenditure of Imperial monies.[13]

After Norman's departure in 1895, however, MacGregor experienced comparatively little interference from the Australian colonies except for one outstanding example. Almost at the end of his second term the plans of a British company, the British New Guinea Syndicate, involving private investment in New Guinea seemed to offer a solution to the need for finance. But despite MacGregor's support, these plans were frustrated by effective interference by Australia and Britain.[14]

In 1897 the British New Guinea Syndicate was formed in London to acquire land in New Guinea on which to grow rubber and other tropical products. The scheme had originated in 1896 during the visit to Australia of one of its backers, a British M.P., J. Lowles, on behalf of the United Empire Trade League. The Syndicate submitted its plan to the Colonial Office in May 1897. A meeting followed in London in June between the promoters (Lowles, Sir Somers Vine and Sir C. M. Kennedy) and the Queensland ministers who were attending Queen Victoria's Jubilee celebrations (Sir Hugh Nelson and T. J. Byrnes). Nelson told the Colonial Office that he was in favour of the Syndicate, but Byrnes made no comment. MacGregor was told of the scheme, approved it in December 1897, and on his orders an Ordinance was drafted to allow for a grant of 250,000 acres to the Syndicate. He approved because the colony needed revenue and because his Fijian experience had convinced him that private investment was necessary for economic development and could be compatible with a protective policy towards the indigenous people. In his first few years of rule in New Guinea he had been mainly concerned with the initial problems of contact between Europeans and natives and therefore wished to restrict the number of Europeans in the colony, but by 1898 was prepared to encourage European investment.

In March 1898 the Ordinance was passed in New Guinea and forwarded to Queensland. It was approved there and sent to the Colonial Office for Imperial sanction. The Colonial Office asked for minor amendments, which were accepted by New Guinea, Queensland and the Syndicate, then told the Syndicate it could proceed. At this stage the other two contributing colonies had not been consulted. In April Victoria and New South Wales were officially informed of the Ordinance and in May the premier of Victoria, Sir George Turner, attacked the scheme. His protests were supported by the New South Wales premier, G. H. Reid, and by Queensland's premier, Byrnes, who asked the Colonial Office not to sanction the Ordinance. Although the Colonial Office was not a strong supporter of the Syndicate, however, it refused to disallow the Ordinance, on the grounds that it would be 'shameless' at such a late stage.[15] MacGregor and Queensland's governor, Lamington, continued to support the scheme, but the opposition of the three colonial governments in the existing power structure of British New Guinea meant there could only be one result—the scheme was not approved. The Colonial Office could only insist that compensation be paid to the Syndicate.

The governments of New South Wales and Victoria opposed the scheme mainly because of pressure on them by Australian companies which wished to invest in New Guinea or which were already established in New Guinea.[16] Public opinion, as in the days of the annexation of New Guinea, was again aroused against what seemed to be British indifference to Australian rights.[17] Yet the representatives both of New South Wales and of Victoria wanted to avoid making any more payments for New Guinea after 1898. Reid said Britain should take over New Guinea as a Crown Colony—at times arguing oddly as if he hoped for Australian political control with Imperial finance. Turner said he had continued contributions only because Queensland and New South Wales had and he now hoped that the impending federation of the Australian colonies would take the matter out of the hands of the Victorian Government. MacGregor rightly regarded such arguments as irrelevant for he believed the Syndicate would bring considerable financial advantages to New Guinea and thus very soon ease the burden on the Australian colonies.

The external pressures upon the governments seem to have been most important since there is clear evidence that the premiers of both New South Wales and Victoria knew of the Syndicate well before they made their protests. They had many chances of gaining unofficial knowledge—from discussions in London at the time of the Jubilee; from semi-official advice passed on by their Agents-General in London; from Australian sources ranging from public discussions to newspaper accounts, or the January 1898 meeting in Melbourne at which MacGregor met Nelson, Reid and Turner to discuss the future of New Guinea.[18] At the official level Nelson reported that both Turner and Reid were sent a letter of 28 May 1897, from the Colonial Office to Queensland, which advised that the Syndicate had applied for land.

For ten years these two southern governments had shown virtually no concern in New Guinea policies; they had merely rubber-stamped Queensland's supervision over MacGregor. Now, because of interest groups and aroused public opinion, they insisted on intervening, utilizing their right to be consulted in all matters other than 'ordinary administration'.

In Queensland there were conflicting interests. Australian firms were constantly pressing the government to oppose the Syndicate. Nelson, the Premier until 13 April 1898, had been one of the strongest advocates of the scheme because he hoped it would help solve the financial problems of the colony. His successor, Byrnes, on the other hand, argued that the Syndicate was a danger to Queensland sugar and to Australian national rights. He thought the Syndicate would grow sugar and with lower labour costs, undercut Queensland sugar. A personal motive, the slight to him at the Jubilee (he was not allowed to ride in the procession), was also suspected at the Colonial Office[19] as a reason for his opposition to a scheme which he identified largely with Great Britain.

In any case the result was a defeat for a policy strongly supported by MacGregor. When Australian interests were involved Australian governments had to intervene in his policies. He had insufficient power to resist these pressures, especially when the three colonies were united against him. Nevertheless, he was so convinced of the necessity of the Syndicate, or something like it, that when he was in Brisbane in October 1898 he tried to persuade the Queensland government, led by Dickson after the death of Byrnes, to change its views. After he reached London in December he interviewed the Under-Secretary of State at the Colonial Office and reported that the Colonial Office's

> interest in British New Guinea is confined to the Syndicate question. . . . I have urged on [the C.O. officials] to clear the road by deciding one way or the other. There are now two other companies ready to enter on negotiations as soon as they can be dealt with.[20]

Thus, he did not regard the defeat of his policy as a permanent one. In fact it can be argued that the degree of interest aroused in New Guinea eventually aided the island. The glare of publicity, unwelcome as it was at the time, led to a strictly defined land policy which was aimed at encouraging large-scale grants for Australian companies some of which were inspired by the activities and near-approval of the British New Guinea Syndicate to become interested in the island. Finally, the doubts over the provision of finance after the end of the ten-year agreement seemed resolved since the southern colonies now found it politically unwise to wash their hands of all concern.[21] These results prompted MacGregor's eventual adoption of an impartial attitude to the question. He thought other aspects of his policy were more important, as is suggested by his implied regret that the interest of the Colonial Office was 'confined to the Syndicate question'.

Whatever the extent of interference by outside governments in New Guinea, MacGregor well realized that for the indigenous people the clearest symbol of 'government' was himself as governor. Thus he tried to make his existence known to as many of them as possible. One of the reasons why he had insisted on his designation being changed from Administrator to Lieutenant-Governor was to aid this identification of himself as governor. In 1896 he objected to a suggested visit of the Queensland Governor to New Guinea:

> I will have no 'bigger fellow Governor' here in my day. If he ever comes he must come as an ordinary individual and not to put in the shade your humble servant. My prestige and authority has been built on so much labour that I could not complacently see it cracked by the rays of a greater sun.[22]

During his attempt to establish a personal relationship with the Fijians, Gordon had become known as the 'great chief', and MacGregor was similarly recognized in New Guinea. Thus a missionary wrote of him in 1890:

> his whole life is spent in studying the natives and endeavouring to understand their peculiarities. Already he has gained a marvellous influence over them and they recognize him as the 'Big Chief of New Guinea'.[23]

MacGregor's desire to spread knowledge of government gave strength to his debates with the Imperial Government about the *Merrie England*. He wanted his own vessel always available since he was anxious to intervene whenever there were major disturbances, such as large-scale native wars or the murder of a white man. His 'visits of inspection', which took up so much of his time, were vital in these initial contacts with the natives.

By the time of his arrival in New Guinea there had been several centuries of contact between Papuans and white men. Explorers, traders, missionaries, gold-seekers and planters had lived in the island and every contact had given the Papuans more knowledge of white culture, whether of larger sea-craft, or of different religious ideas. The missions, particularly the London Missionary Society, were the best organized groups and in some areas where they had placed white missionaries or native teachers their influence had been widespread. But overall these contacts had been sporadic and uncontrolled, with often unexpected effects. Very little systematic control had been imposed during the few years of the Protectorate (1884-88). In theory the officers of the Protectorate had no jurisdiction over natives; in practice some of them were accepted as advisers. In this capacity they helped to prepare the way for MacGregor. The Protectorate years, however, left an unfortunate legacy for him in so far as the Royal Navy had been responsible for enforcing justice and white rule had been equated with naval justice. This 'justice' had proved inequitable, sporadic and ineffective. Often the only action possible for the unfortunate captains was to order the shelling of the village where the suspected criminals lived; often no ship was available for months; often the strong words used by Protectorate officials had no effect when no action followed.

MacGregor naturally wanted to substitute effective government action and justice for this deplorable state of affairs. He was particularly concerned by the reputation of his colony for murders, both of visiting Europeans and of other Papuans. One of his first impressions supported this reputation:

> They fight among each other and periodically murder members of the neighbouring villages—the people for protection, presumably, all live in villages. To lie in wait for and to kill an old woman seems to give as good a title to a young brave to assume and wear the beak of the Hornbill as if he had overcome a Brennus in single combat.[24]

After little over a year in the colony MacGregor was optimistic about his success in increasing government influence, despite the fact that he had difficulty in finding men who could stand the work.

> I firmly hope and believe that the place will be transformed in a few years. Murders are still of fearful frequency; but they are not a tittle of what they were; and over a large area they [the people] begin to look to the Government to suppress them.

His next comments throw an interesting light on the man and his work:

> For some reason or other Lord Knutsford seems to think I am doing too much. . . . [He] puts it on the ground that he is afraid of my health and safety; but these are not likely to be of much concern to a Secretary of State. It may be the doing of Sir H. Norman.

But if I continue in good health I shall continue at work until the government is known over the whole Possession.[25]

His suspicion that Norman was troublemaking again was met with characteristic defiance when his sense of duty was involved.

He hoped in the next twelve months to see new Christian missions begin work and to introduce a constabulary and specific native regulations (see Chapter 8). 'Of course I hope at the same time to extend our influence and authority. My hand has been forced hitherto in the matter of inspection.' In September 1888 he had planned to travel inland from Port Moresby but instead had been forced to go to the eastern islands first because of the influx of gold-miners and then by the murder of a trader; his visit to the west end had been forced as 'people from Queensland were coming daily into contact with our natives there'; the north-east had demanded attention because the trepang traders were working there and because of the need to establish the Anglican mission in that area; he had had to go to the St Joseph district originally to settle land claims involving the Marist mission. But once in an area he felt bound to see the local tribes completely pacified and the authority of the government recognized. He continued:

Lord Knutsford thinks I am too much away from Port Moresby, but at Port Moresby I can do little beyond replying to useless correspondence from Sir H. Norman. Port Moresby from a native or future development point of view is comparatively unimportant; it is in fact insignificant compared for example, to the St. Joseph district.[26]

Every patrol was also a voyage of discovery for MacGregor. His letters from New Guinea, his diaries and reports all reveal his keen powers of observation. Small details caught his eye and were enriched with his knowledge of native lore and his humanity. On his first trip he mentions

the prettiest thing . . . a child of about five or six months, of a rich bronze colour, laid on the floor in a small net made of twine with a mesh about half an inch square, and put into the position into which certain people bury, or buried, their dead, with the knees bent so that they could spring into activity to enter a new phase, and then the whole lifted up and the bag suspended from a hook on the roof-tree. Nothing could be more natural than the pose of the baby, nothing more funny than the whole picture.

He made notes on diseases and on flora. Rossel Island was botanically the richest place he had seen; he found a beautiful new pure white orchid there and assessed economic possibilities: he found taro, yams, bananas, papaya and sugar cane, but 'no representative of the orange family, no tomato, no earth nut, no corn, no bean, no tapioca in any of all these islands'. He obtained information on his predecessors' quirks: for example, he met the infamous Nicolas Minister, a Greek trader in the east end, who told him how he was instructed during the Protectorate to produce 'outward evidence' of punishment inflicted on natives—whereupon Minister cut off an old chief's head and took it on board to an official who photographed it. (On 27 June 1891 on Pannaet Island MacGregor had the head buried as 'an end to that piece of disgrace'.) [27] He was already the collector, amassing artefacts which he later left to museums as far apart as Aberdeen and Brisbane—'it is not easy even already to get specimens of stone axes [at St Aignan]'. He was the tourist, watching the bitter lake of Fergusson Island with its boiling, ploppering mud, water-holes and springs and 'smell that would do credit to the place of future punishment'.[28]

Many of his patrols, however, left scant time for such civilized, peaceful pursuits, for they led to or followed warlike incidents. That precipitated by 'the Ansell case' was a prime example.

On 29 October 1888 a trading schooner was attacked in Chads Bay, the captain, Ansell, killed, the crew disabled and the schooner stripped and burnt. MacGregor in his first months in New Guinea was forced to decide what policy he would adopt in such a case. He 'determined to make an example of the perpetrators if possible, acting in the belief that severity would under, the circumstances be mercy'.[29] The two aspects of his policy were to meet force with force in order to show the Papuans that the power of the government was the stronger; but, at the same time, to begin the gradual introduction of the concept of the guilty individual bearing responsibility for his actions rather than a group or village.

MacGregor found the Ansell case peculiarly difficult. He considered it not a case of murder by one or a few, but 'a long hatched and carefully prepared conspiracy', originating far from the place of attack, and involving altogether a population of at least ten thousand people from the southern side of Milne Bay to Tauputa, north of Chads Bay, thus of many villages. MacGregor met resistance from the time he first reached the area, for one village on Chads Bay proved

rabidly hostile and boasted of having two of those most deeply

K

incriminated in their midst, and expressed a determined desire to remain on the beach to fight me, in short it was such open defiance that it could not be overlooked without involving complete loss of consideration among all the natives in that part of the Possession.

During that case, which lasted almost two months and inspired comparison with Gordon's 'little war' in Fiji, he wrote:

I live . . . at present in a state of great anxiety. I must stay at Samarai until I build a prison, and I must send the schooner to Port Moresby to bring down Winter, who is Chief Judicial Officer, to try these men. When I sent parties out before there was bloodshed and nothing accomplished; and I fear that finding I am gone the fugitives will combine and attack our friends when off their guard and probably kill a number of people. The feeling of responsibility under which I have daily bidden into the bush a number of men, whose duty it certainly was not to perform such work, to hunt these savages has been great in proportion to the risk incurred. Most fortunately I have had no casualty; but almost everyone save myself has had fever; and I, partly through severe physical exercise, but more from anxiety and bad fare, have gone down from near 15 stone to 13½ and I am as thin as a lath.

Finally four Papuans were arrested and hanged.

Dr Mair and Lewis Lett have deduced from this patrol and others where Papuans were killed, that MacGregor 'believed in the punitive expedition'[30] and approved its use of force and the execution of Papuan offenders against European laws. Such assertions, already queried by Professor Morrell,[31] need close consideration. There is nothing in MacGregor's background up to 1888 which could lead one to expect him to believe in the value of such punishments to establish his control. He had, while a medical officer in Gordon's 'little war', shot a Fijian, but this man was threatening his life:[32] all that could be deduced from this incident and from the support he gave to Gordon's war was that he was not a pacifist.[33] His attitude towards the native people of the Seychelles and Fiji was sympathetic, humanitarian and paternalistic.

Nevertheless it could be argued that he did not have the responsibility of deciding what policy to adopt until he reached New Guinea. The evidence that he supported a punitive policy arises from his orders to fire on natives both in the Ansell case and in subsequent expeditions. He never ordered a punitive expedition, however, which was instructed to wreak vengeance on a tribe or group of villages. From the beginning, as the Ansell case makes clear, he tried to introduce the idea of individual

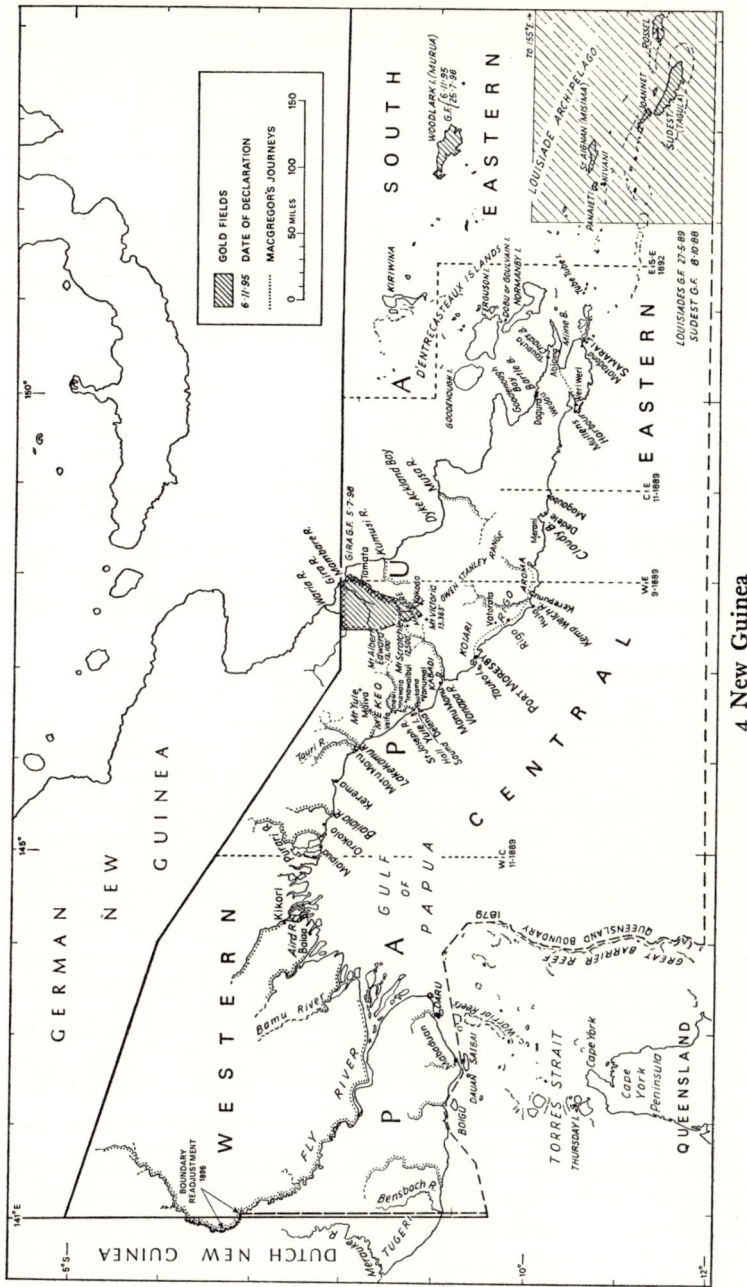

4 New Guinea

responsibility and adopted group punishment only as a last resort. Most of his patrols were intended to be peaceful, even if some of them included instructions to arrest individuals for punishment. Only if peaceful methods failed would the threat of force be used: only if this threat failed would shooting be ordered. More importantly, MacGregor always had hesitations about the use of force.

The truth of these assertions can best be tested by resort to his diary entries and letters, written within a day or so of the events. Even these, however, cannot be thoroughly relied on, as every man tries to justify his own behaviour.

After the four Papuans in the Ansell case had been sentenced to death, Winter, the Chief Justice, advised in the Executive Council that all these sentences should be commuted. His arguments were that this was a first trial, that all the people of the district were implicated and that mercy would be a better way of encouraging future submission to the law. MacGregor disagreed and decided to hang the four,[34] in the district where the uprising had taken place.[35] Thus one was hanged at Samarai, one at Abioma on Milne Bay and two at Chads Bay, the scene of the murder. In a frank letter to Gordon MacGregor wrote:

> I looked on it as my first duty to impress on the natives that white men are not to be robbed and murdered and I was determined to teach them by an awful lesson that killing is murder and the punishment for it death . . . the natives at each place assembled to see the sentence carried out, and their behaviour was all that could have been desired. The impression produced on the natives by the captures, the trials, and the executions, has been profound.

So far his tone was objective and his arguments those which have become classic for the supporters of capital punishment. But he continued:

> It was with the greatest reluctance that I signed the warrant of execution for the Chief Murderer. He was by far the finest specimen of a coloured man I ever met; so perfectly truthful, frank, unselfish, certainly one of the best mannered men I have ever met. He tried to take the whole guilt on himself at the trial at Samarai so that the others should not be convicted. He left a message for his people 'to never kill any more white men, but to live at peace with them'. When brought to the scaffold he was as calm and collected as John Huss or Dido, and said 'Farewell my pickanninies; farewell my place' but he would not say adieu to his wife who had already found solace in another's breast. Poor old Totini Wai! I doubt that

he has left his equal in British New Guinea. Only the stern com-
mands of duty could make one send such a man to the scaffold.
I confess I would have given a year's salary to be able to commute that man's sentence. In all the years I have been near you I
never heard you once say 'how will this or that affect me', and
partly from this training, partly from entertaining so earnest a
desire to do what I feel to be my duty, I never think of the result
to myself personally.[36]

It might be argued that this shows only personal sympathy
for Totini Wai, but this was not an isolated case. In May 1891
MacGregor was faced with a similar conflict:

I had to order no less than three executions all cases in which
white men had been murdered without provocation, in two instances
for the sake of plunder. In these I have to stand alone; my advisors
favoured the commuting of the capital sentences.[37] It was however
clear that it was necessary in the interests of the natives that punishments should be condign, if I let my head conquer the heart, although in doing so the punishment was nearly as great to me as to
the natives.[38]

And in another case:

These miserable executions have been a great grief to me.[39]
Fortunately, all our arrangements being very carefully made, the
two men were killed instantaneously. I am so glad it is all over.[40]

Nevertheless, after only five months in New Guinea he stated
why he believed the use of force would be necessary:

we have already got a start in gaining some ascendancy. It does not
come from any commanding, subduing power in the eye of the
Administrator, nor from moral suasion exercised by his subordinates,
but is the result of meeting them in open fight. These natives, probably all natives in a certain stage of mental development are alike,
respect first of all physical force. Those that have made peace with
me have said 'we cannot fight you'; when one tribe has authorised
another to submit it has been 'you know you cannot fight the white-
men'. Had we been defeated once, we were doomed ourselves, and
it would have taken a military expedition to establish authority.
But now being successful the Government is becoming known and
what is more is being obeyed.[41]

He expressed the same ideas again, though tempered by regret,
early in his governorship in 1889:

I have just returned from Cloudy Bay, where we have had a regular
pitched battle with savage tribes of whom even I had never heard
until they murdered in a most treacherous manner two adventurous
prospectors. Brave fellows these savages were, and showed splendid

pluck and skill, trying to surround us and cut us off from our camp. It caused me extreme grief to deal with them as they are a superior race. All hostilities were declined by me until a crushing defeat could be inflicted which would settle the matter once and for all. This led to an affair in which I faced the two tribes with 14 rifles or shot guns. Eleven natives fell, and they say ten are dead, I can vouch for six killed. The humiliation of these and all tribes in that part of the country was completed;[42] and now Cloudy Bay is quiet and safe.[43]

Soon after this he lamented that 'these dreadful murders I cannot stop; and these occasional bloody encounters we have make my life as stormy as that of the Lord Geist in Faust'.[44]

Diary entries suggest the consistency of his ideas: he was trying to end 'wars' and spread government authority and peace; he preferred talk to taking prisoners and taking prisoners to shooting natives. But the threat of force was behind any of these alternatives.[45] Towards the end of his governorship in 1897 he was applying the same policies he had begun with:

my present plan . . . is to go straight inland from Port Moresby to the main range, to fight the troublesome tribes if they wish to try conclusions, at any rate to subdue them and destroy their prestige, if possible to make full peace.[46]

When his own life, or the lives of those with him, were threatened he had few compunctions about shooting. This is well illustrated by an incident in March 1892. MacGregor was making a visit of inspection to the 'last corner of unknown coast in British New Guinea', the area between the Fly and Aird rivers. He went up the Aird with a steam launch towing his whaleboat. The launch broke down and he went on in the whaleboat accompanied by one European, two Solomon Islanders and six Papuans. Near Kikori this party of ten, five of whom were armed, went ashore for lunch. A dozen or so canoes approached.

I ordered up two men to the top of the bank. We were now as it were surrounded. Before this Cameron and I had got our rifles ready as I did not like the look of things at all. Some 250 men round about us and they hemming us in on all sides. I ordered the men all into the boat and to pull out into midstream the river being about 700 yards broad. I saw myself some land with bows and arrows to go into the bush behind us. This made their hostile intentions quite plain. I stood up and made signals to the nearest canoes only 50 or 60 yards off to sheer away: they did not, but more men landed. I took up my rifle and motioned and shouted them off, but they would not go. Then Buni, Issi and Tom saw a man

or two with bow and arrow on the bank behind us and said . . .
[one was] trying to shoot me. I told them to shoot him: they again
shouted out that they saw one or two men on the bank only a few
yards off trying to shoot at us. I replied 'Damn your eyes, why don't
you shoot them'. The others were as quick as our men and kept
behind trees so that they could not shoot at them. I told Cameron
to keep his rifle on the bush, Johnny and another to take charge of
the canoes up stream, and two men to pull the boat out. The
difficulty was to get any one to pull as of course all wished to
shoot. We got clear of the bank and I was still making rifle ready[47]
trying to warn off the canoes, but the men seeing the natives getting their bows and arrows ready fired on them. I fired at two or
three canoes and once or twice into the water near them.[48]

Three days later, when he wrote to Gordon, his emphasis had
changed from the necessity of saving European lives to concern
at possible deaths of Papuans:

It is not improbable that some natives perished. I myself fired at
the canoes and found that quite enough to make the occupants
jump out . . . but I do not think that all the party were so merciful.[49]

On the same trip at Baiaa he was threatened by men in forty-
five canoes and his reactions were similar:

Most of them were behind us as we got opposite the lower end of
the village, when several of my boys called my attention to two or
three men who were getting their bows ready to shoot. I could not
see them at first, but on my being warned a second time I saw a
man about 80 yards distant bend his bow. When I lifted my rifle
he laid it [down], but immediately after when he thought I was
not looking he drew it again and aimed in our direction: he had
the bow almost fully bent but could not for a moment shoot for
a man that stood in front of him, for the same reason I could not
shoot at him but I planted a bullet near him that made him and
several others jump overboard. . . . They only know that a rifle
can make a splash in the water and a noise, and they have no idea
of its offensive properties, which they may I fear have to be taught
yet.[50]

Another criticism of MacGregor's 'visits of inspection' was that
they became 'visits of exploration', unconcerned with making
contact with any Papuans. This is a type of criticism that had
been made of many governors—Captain Ross's sneers at Governor
Phillip's 'parties of pleasure',[51] for example. MacGregor denied
that any of his numerous journeys were made only for geographical exploration and this is true in so far as on all of them he met
Papuans and when he went to new country he did not know

whether it was inhabited or not. Obviously for a government to be effective it had to know how many people it was ruling and where they lived, and MacGregor's concept of a personal government meant that his name should be known throughout his colony. Also, the economic potential of a country could hardly be known until that country had been thoroughly explored.

Certain limitations on such a defence of MacGregor's explorations arise from these same points, however. It cannot be denied that he derived personal satisfaction from reaching new areas. He went as far as he could up the Fly River and to the peaks of the Owen Stanleys for reasons other than contacting Papuans. As for government not being effective unless population details were known, more than fifty years after MacGregor had left New Guinea all its people had not been contacted by the government, let alone brought under its control. MacGregor well knew that he could not hope to exercise effective control over many of the people he contacted: in other words his patrols went well beyond the limits of his ability to govern. He used his explorations to demonstrate the availability of unused vacant land, but during his governorship little of this land was taken up by Europeans.

The balance of judgement on these points can favour MacGregor, however. Even if some of his journeys were unjustified in the time of his governorship, they were all attempting tasks that would have had to be done at some time. His preference for governmental over private exploration can be defended because of his justifiable suspicion of the attitudes towards native peoples adopted by many private explorers. If these explorers came to blows with native tribes the government had to be called in and MacGregor feared the upsetting of his overall plan of peaceful penetration. Even before he reached New Guinea he laid down as his policy that it would not be

> advisable to encourage exploration of any kind, unless it is conducted by men that can be trusted, who are fitted out in an adequate manner, and who can be held responsible for their treatment of natives[52]

and that he preferred all parties to be under government supervision.

Whatever his motives, MacGregor covered vast areas on these explorations and regarded this as an integral part of his duty. Thus he said in 1895:

> A large part of the Colony has now by degrees been examined,

including the whole of its coastline from boundary to boundary, and most of its great rivers have been inspected as far as a steam launch can penetrate, and the majority of them further. There remain, however, large tracts in the interior of the mainland that have not been reached. Authority has gradually been extended from the Government stations, and the different areas under control are beginning already to meet, so that before very long there will be no part of the whole coastline where the Queen's warrant cannot run, and where the individual cannot be punished for his own crime.[53]

MacGregor's exploration also helped to delineate the boundaries of his control with those of Germany, Holland[54] and Queensland and he occasionally suggested changes to make administration more satisfactory. In 1893, for example, he suggested moving the border with Queensland south, to bring under New Guinea's control 'the inhabitants of Boigu, Dauan, Saibai and Warrior islands [who] have intimate intercourse with the New Guinea tribes, and [who] obtain much of their food from the Possession.[55] When this idea was rejected he carried out more careful surveying work

> with a number of astronomical observations, to prove that the present boundary line puts on the Queensland side many, if not most, of our western tribal fishing grounds. . . . I am afraid my hard work on those muddy reefs may not be too acceptable to your [Griffith's] government but it will be found that a case is made out that cannot easily be set aside without a change of boundary in our favour. It was my duty to do this to protect the rights of those that cannot protect themselves. Let us hope Queensland may be just.[56]

It has, however, proved impossible even after MacGregor's departure for the two governments to reach agreement.[57]

A reading of his comments on his expeditions shows that although he was interested in the novel and the strange for their own sake, he was always concerned with the administrative significance of his journeyings. Thus after his 600 miles expedition up the Fly River, when he went 200 miles farther than the Italian explorer D'Albertis, he wrote to Gordon:

> More than my usual luck attended me in the West. After we were attacked on first ascending the Fly, we never fired a shot at or to frighten a native. We did not shed a drop of human blood in the west, although we searched both the North, the German boundary, as well as the Dutch boundary on the coast. From close to d'Albertis' furthest every shovelful of sand and shingle gives 'colours' of

gold: and many stones contain interesting organic remains in silica or lime. It will not be necessary to do anything administrative more than 200 miles up the Fly. Above that the people are wanderers; the country does not look as if it were of much account, too low and wet.[58]

His trip to the summit of Mt Victoria (13,363 feet) within six months of his arrival in New Guinea was motivated not only by the sheer excitement and challenge of this epic climb through thick and mist-shrouded jungle to the bare mountain tops but by a desire to stop clashes between private exploratory parties and the Papuans in the area and to see how many people were there. Perhaps also the conquering of mountains symbolized his own efforts to rise in the world for this insecure but ambitious man.

> The feeling of loneliness was increased by the trees; roots, trunks and branches were wrapped up in thick coverings of moss, even the leaves were not free from it. Everything was soaking wet, and the fog, especially when the clouds lifted a little from the ravines or broke on the rugged spurs, made the crags and ridges look much more formidable and inaccessible than they really were, and forced me to think that one would never be able to continue the upward march the next day.[59]

Certainly his attempts to explore farther than his predecessors seems partially motivated by ambition and a desire to boost his prestige and confidence. When in 1891 he followed the left bank of the Fly Estuary around the corner of the Gulf of Papua, he boasted 'we went some 60 miles up the river [the Bamu] entered by Jukes and Captain Blackwood in 1846, since which, so far as I know, that part has not been visited by any European'.[60]

His criticisms of other exploratory trips probably betray the same motive. He took an expedition of the Victorian Royal Geographical Society to the foot of the Yule Range in November 1890, then reported 'they brought back very little, and the work will have to be done over again. They saw several villages, but carefully avoided them!'[61] Yet his basic insecurity paradoxically led him at times to belittle his own remarkable achievements. After he had ended both his Fly trip and his ascent of Mt Victoria, he wrote to Gordon that he would have 'literally nothing to say' before the Royal Geographical Society.[62] His strenuous patrols continued to open up new areas and locate more Papuans, but by 1897 he was beginning to doubt his capacity to explore, telling the Australian premiers that they wanted 'a younger man'. 'I have just passed my 50th year—and after a man has passed 50 he is not fit to go over those mountains. I think I am becoming physically unfit for it.'[63]

One special problem which arose because MacGregor's 'visits of inspection' were so extensive concerned the Tugeri, natives who lived in Dutch territory but raided villages on the British side of the border in the south-west corner. These raids were noticed in the days of the Protectorate by John Strachan, a private explorer.[64] MacGregor investigated the area early in 1890 and regretted that these people did not live in British territory 'for they are active, powerful, daring, enterprising spirits, the men from among whom a police force, teachers etc. could be procured'.[65] At first he hoped to work through the missions in pacifying them. The Reverend James Chalmers, of the London Missionary Society, who had accompanied him in 1890, was optimistic and hoped with the aid of 'a couple of good Samoan or Raratongan teachers' to turn them to Christ and obtain 'a splendid supply of teachers for the future'.[66]

These hopes for a peaceful conversion of the Tugeri proved vain. MacGregor sought Dutch co-operation because these people lived in Dutch territory, but the Dutch took no action. The result of diplomatic correspondence in 1891 convinced the Colonial Office that the Dutch government 'probably know no more of Dutch New Guinea than they can help'.[67]

MacGregor contacted the Tugeri again in 1891 and was soon forced to consider the alternative of group punishment if peaceful methods proved unavailing. He commented in May 1891 that

Nothing can exceed their ferocity, hunted as they have been and accustomed to regard every newcomer as a mortal enemy. They are by no means contemptible as foes, as they are good marksmen up to 200 yards.[68]

MacGregor renewed his requests for action from the Dutch, basing his arguments on 'considerations of humanity . . . [for] to cause the slaughter of a large number of these people is repugnant to my mind'.[69] Late in 1891 the Dutch Minister for Foreign Affairs requested the Resident at Ternate to investigate the Tugeri and subsequently it was established that their villages were indeed in Dutch territory. In October 1892 a Dutch warship was sent out to make further investigations and in 1893 a Dutch party met with Tugeri opposition and was forced to withdraw with eleven casualties. Despite this rebuff the Dutch claimed that they would attempt 'gentle and friendly means'[70] in obtaining control inside their territory, but took no further action until 1900. On the British side any report of the Tugeri caused alarm at Daru station, the nearest to the border, and the resident officer, Hely, was forced to defend the area when they attacked.[71] It was decided at the February 1893 meeting with the Dutch representatives that MacGregor would be justified in meeting with force further invasions of British territory by the Tugeri, so that they were now to be treated as aggressive invaders who were to be counter-attacked as an operation of war.

In June 1896 MacGregor intercepted and defeated the Tugeri: forty-eight canoes were captured; and many of the Tugeri were killed or wounded, the remainder retreating over the boundary which MacGregor scrupulously refused to cross.[72]

The change in MacGregor's policy towards the Tugeri is compatible with his motives on other 'visits of inspection'. In both cases he first used peaceful methods and in both cases if these failed he was prepared to use force. The object of the 1896 action was 'not simply to drive them out of the district, but to do that while inflicting on them such punishment as would prevent them from returning, and impress them with the superior strength of this government'.[73] James Chalmers was still unconvinced of the necessity for such a policy:

> through our Boigou teachers we were making friends [with the Tugeri] and I hear Saibai and Boigou natives had been to visit them. . . . I fancy Sir William McGregor's nerves must be weakened and he fears meeting natives. Formerly he would meet armed crowds and without firing a shot would make capital friends with them.[74]

His criticism of MacGregor ignored the governor's sincere efforts to implement an alternative peaceful policy and his hopes of using the Dutch as pacifiers. Moreover, Chalmers's hopes for gradual development of peaceful relations through missionary teachers and neighbouring tribes were disappointed by the continued aggressiveness of the Tugeri, who in 1900 and 1902 again invaded British territory. Control was not established over these people until after a Dutch station was set up on the Merauke River.

MacGregor's efforts to control the Tugeri were typical in another way, in so far as they proved how limited his control of the colony was. All his visits of inspection or patrols covered far more territory and involved contact with far more natives than it was possible with his limited staff and limited money to control effectively. MacGregor's main justifications for executions after murders, for patrols that used force, or for exploratory journeys that were not immediately necessary, was the effect of his actions on the future. He argued that the end for which he was aiming—the introduction of civilization—justified the means, however distasteful these means were to his own ideas. His belief in European civilization implied its superiority to Papuan culture; thus after his ten years in New Guinea he stated

> that the paternal form [of justice] is the most suitable for a native population in the act of stepping out of savagery and barbarism into civilization, I entertain no manner of doubt.[75]

Moreover, the positive steps he introduced to spread his concept of civilization (which will be examined later) were more important than his moves to establish authority, since they could have more far-reaching effects. MacGregor himself anticipated criticisms later made by anthropologists about his policies, since he realized that actions such as ending the custom of war, or giving the authority of government to men regardless of the traditions of the group, attacked the bases of native society. However, he took it as axiomatic—and this point is implicit in all his writings on spreading the authority of government—that his duty was to eliminate what he regarded as the evils of savagery and barbarism. He was a Victorian in his almost unquestioning acceptance of the superior values of European civilization, but, like Gordon, he did have an innate sympathy with some aspects of native culture. MacGregor's approach, however, was certainly not the detached objective anthropological approach that seeks complete understanding of the complicated workings of an existing society. Indeed it would be hard to deny that such an anthropological approach can lead to a far deeper sympathy with primitive societies than was ever felt by MacGregor. At the same time such anthropological criticisms can go too far. In the light of the possible courses actually adopted in the nineteenth century MacGregor was far more sympathetic towards the native people than were most other colonial governors.

Thus even while he was deliberately destroying some parts of New Guinea culture, he decried English policy in Africa for its extreme lack of sympathy with African cultures.

> It seems to an onlooker, who is at such a distance that he might as well be in Mercury, that at no previous period has cant and hypocrisy ever been higher in the ascendant than they are now in Great Britain and Germany. The Teutonic tentacles are waving and

thrashing about everywhere; the Britisher is roaming the world open-mouthed and why? The newspapers and periodicals tell one that on the one hand it is to graciously and mercifully extend the Deutsche Kultur to the benighted of mankind; the sole object is unselfish and humanitarian: the Britisher is disinterested, and he wishes to spread the gospel of charity. They make of it in old Africa a headlong steeplechase through human blood, killing when they do not stop to civilise; and under the cloak of Christianity thrusting themselves on people who have not time to set their house in order to receive them, robbing and plundering like so many condottieri. Of course we shall have a set of new Crown colonies to take the place of those sufficiently matured to be planted out from the nursery. But where is the Sir Arthur Gordon of the service now to go and put the crooked straight in these new dominions?[76]

He urged Gordon to become a director of

one of the great African companies [because to] me, in the wilderness, it has seemed a disgrace to the nation and the century how Christian England has trafficked in African matters. I am afraid were I to write the history of the last ten years I should say the god of England was gold. I have not yet decided which to me is most hatefully contemptible, the religious cupidity of the old invading Spaniards, or the selfish, hypocritical dealings of our own country on the African continent. I should be glad to see you join one of these companies. You cannot annihilate them by keeping aloof; but by joining them you may do infinite good by giving a direction to actions which you cannot prevent. I fear the rule over these people on commercial lines. You would require an extremely strong directorate at home, and men out there with very uncommon qualifications, if you were to insist on anything like a just rule. You remember the wise and humane Ordinances of Ferdinand and Isabella.[77] They will compare with your native legislation in Fiji, yet they were of no profit to the weak. But although England goes hysterically 'daft' now and then in such questionable matters as this African business, she always falls back into a reflective mood; and, when the reaction is at high tide, she will do penance. I hope therefore that in the end the right and best thing may be done, that is that government under the Crown may be established, and that before the misrule of Dividends has done for the owners of the country.[78]

It is relevant to see the consistency of MacGregor's thinking on this question. Thirteen years later, after he had governed for four years in a West African colony, he felt the same way. He defended his policy of attempting to do what he had written of as the 'right and best thing' in the interests of the 'owners of the country'. He was convinced that he had followed such a policy in Fiji and New Guinea and that he had attempted it in Lagos. He wrote to Griffith in 1904:

> I am not able to return to West Africa. I have given a new trend to government there, and I met with great, almost virulent, opposition to my peace policy. Lagos is the only British colony we possess there that has had no war since I went out. I alone can travel without a great military escort to the most remote corner of the territory. West Africa is the arena for ribbons, and crosses, and medals. A man of peace is not wanted nor liked there. Those that at first opposed me bitterly, now ask the Colonial Office that my methods may be maintained. I have not shed a drop of blood in Africa. This is considered phenomenal but is it not a sad and woeful commentary on British rule? The policy of smash in West Africa is I fear an outcome of military imperialism. Why can they not adopt and practise elsewhere the peaceful imperial idea that you so successfully carried out in Australasia? It grieves me now that all the little special knowledge and experience I possess should be utterly useless.[79]

Thus MacGregor believed that the authority of the government had to become recognized before civilization could be introduced and he came to believe that force was necessary for this purpose, although he never welcomed it. He did not want to maintain native society as he found it and his measures (beginning with the ending of the custom of war) did much to break down the existing structure of society. He could have shown far more sympathy and understanding toward native society, as some early anthropologists were doing at the time, such as Seligmann with the Torres Strait Islanders in the 1890s. On the other hand, MacGregor had far greater respect for native society, particularly for native rights to their land, than most of his contemporary colonial administrators, and his comparison of his policy with some British policies in West Africa is amply justifiable. Above all this comparison draws attention to the limitations of his control in British New Guinea. His adoption of the 'peaceful imperial idea' implied less interference with Papuans than might have occurred with a policy of 'military imperialism'. The German New Guinea Company in the north interfered far more directly with village culture.[80] MacGregor's self-imposed restraint was a further restriction added to the limitations created by the supervision of the Colonial Office and of the Australian governments, and by the failure of these authorities or private enterprise to provide adequate finance for expansive policies.

8

New Guinea: The Nature of his Rule 1888-98

All government officers must be prepared to do anything they can to further the public service. The question as to whether a given duty comes within the scope of an officer's special duty is one that is seldom given a hearing to. The man that does all he can is sure to find advancement when an opportunity offers.

The limitations on MacGregor's power, both self-imposed and created by authorities outside New Guinea which he was unable to control, always restricted his policies. Within the colony he faced further difficulties: he had to work within the formal framework of advisory councils and had to rely on an inadequate staff, Papuans and missionaries to apply his policies.

His powers as Administrator were formally limited in so far as generally he could not act without the advice of his Executive and Legislative Councils, unless he deemed it 'right to do so'.[1] If he overruled either council he had to report his reasons to the governor of Queensland. In fact neither council offered significant opposition to his policies. MacGregor in ten years called 118 meetings of the all-official Executive Council which discussed most important aspects of policy. The discussions were dominated by the chief officers of the colony, particularly by the Administrator (MacGregor attended eighty-nine of the 118 meetings), the Chief Judicial Officer and the Government Secretary. Government officers resident at Port Moresby also frequently attended. Many of the council's functions were hardly executive, however. Much of its time was spent as a land office, minutely scrutinizing every claim, even though several principles of land policy were evolved in this way; the control, movements, leave and pay of government officials were all approved in council; and it had to confirm death sentences (MacGregor's power over it is indicated, for example, by the instances in which he overruled its decisions when he favoured carrying out these sentences).

All the members of the Legislative Council were officials also, until September 1892 when the local manager of the trading firm of Burns Philp was appointed. MacGregor called fifty-eight meetings of this council in his ten years and attended forty-six. The most regular attenders were the same as at the Executive Council. Theoretical discussions in 1888 and later of how far legislative power should be delegated to this council were largely irrelevant for, although all legislation was brought before it, the minutes show that its considerations amounted to little more than a rubber-stamping. The ideas behind most ordinances came from MacGregor; their general provisions were drawn up by him, or under his close supervision; the drafting was completed before they reached the council. In only a few cases did the council even change clauses, let alone criticize the substance of a law. Every measure was passed unanimously except for one when the unofficial member had his opposition vote recorded against an ordinance restricting the immigration of Chinese.[2]

Thus, with both councils as advisory bodies whose decisions almost invariably reflected his views, MacGregor regarded the contributing colonies and the Colonial Office as the only 'opposition' to his policies. In formal terms there was neither responsible nor representative government in New Guinea. MacGregor's powers were greater even than those of Governor Darling in Australia in the 1820s, for example. Although both their councils were dominated by official members and ruled over a population the majority of which were politically inarticulate, MacGregor was not confronted by divisions in the minority of society, nor by an opposition such as that organized by Wentworth, nor by an independent press.[3]

In governing, MacGregor relied greatly on personal supervision and efforts, as his leadership of expeditions shows, largely because he lacked trust in the officers under him. He had exclaimed when he was acting as Administrator in Fiji that 'I certainly do drive about the weakest team ever harnessed to a colonial coach',[4] but in New Guinea the team was even weaker. The complete roll of European government officials in MacGregor's ten years only totalled sixty-four; at any one time he was assisted by only about twenty men. With this diminutive staff he had the nominal task of ruling about a million Papuans scattered over ninety thousand square miles.

The organization of native affairs was based on control from Port Moresby of geographical areas called divisions, each to be

L

controlled by a resident magistrate. MacGregor's plan was to have sub-districts within these divisions controlled by government agents.

> Gradually I hope to connect . . . [the divisional centres] by stations for government agents, who will be magistrates for native matters, but without the powers of a stipendiary or police magistrate, which could be given only to a better class of men than we can afford to pay.[5]

MacGregor first divided the colony into two divisions—western and eastern, with headquarters at Mabudauan and Samarai. In addition two government agents were appointed to the districts of Mekeo and Rigo, both in the western division. Changes were made as government control extended, as more men became available, and to supervise mining expansion. In November 1889 the western division was reduced in size when a new central division, with headquarters at Port Moresby, was proclaimed. Mekeo and Rigo were then included in the central division. In 1892 the eastern division was reduced in size when the Louisiades were made a separate south-eastern division with headquarters at Nivani. Previously in this area governmental officers on the gold-fields had been given limited jurisdiction. In 1893 the head-quarters of the western division was moved to Daru. Government agents were appointed at Cloudy Bay for short periods in 1889-90 and 1894-95, and in the same area a temporary travelling agent was installed between 1896 and 1898, mainly to assist the miners in the ranges of the central division. The gold-rush to the Mambare led to the appointment of a government agent in the north at the end of 1895.[6] Not until after MacGregor left, were separate northern and north-eastern divisions proclaimed.

The main task of the few officers in these areas, as of Mac-Gregor's expeditions, was to spread knowledge of the existence and intentions of the new government to the Papuans. Surviving documents, particularly station records but also annual reports, show how limited the extent and effectiveness of control over Papuans was during MacGregor's governorship. As Mac-Gregor admitted, large areas of the divisions and districts were under no control at all. Even near station headquarters contact was often rudimentary and the indolence, illness or inefficiency of an officer could hold up all developments in his area.

The magistrate of the eastern division was frank about the limitations of his control in August 1890:

> As it is at present I am perfectly unable to act in any case where

force is likely to be required as the risk of failure is too imminent with only native boys. In the event of disturbances occurring even in the immediate vicinity which would require arrests being made if the natives chose to resist I could do nothing, and the whole prestige of the Government would be destroyed before assistance could arrive from Port Moresby considering the very irregular postal communications.[7]

The position was not substantially changed throughout Mac-Gregor's period.

The western station was always isolated and the magistrate's acknowledgements of letters show how irregular the contact was with Port Moresby. MacGregor's letters took an average of six weeks and a maximum of twenty-one to reach him. B. Hely, the magistrate from 1892, was justifiably criticized by MacGregor for his inefficiency, but his reply is indicative of some of the problems involved:

What with non-fulfilment of my requisitions—the mail contractors acting as they think fit as regards calling here—a new station to be erected without any assistance in the way of labour or material, and the want for the past year of adequate means of transport within the district, the efficient working of my Division is almost an impossibility.[8]

Control was restricted even close to MacGregor's headquarters, Port Moresby, which was also the base for the central division. Both magistrates there, F. E. Lawes and his successor Dr J. A. Blayney, tried conscientiously to fulfil their tasks. Lawes, the son of the veteran London Missionary Society missionary, was accepted and trusted by Papuans, and Blayney, a doctor whom Mac-Gregor had recruited from Scotland in 1894, like MacGregor was devoted to a mixture of medical and native work.[9] Nevertheless, Lawes' statement in July 1892 could still have been applied to some villages in the division in 1898: 'This is the first visit to these tribes by any foreigner'.[10]

In parts of the south-eastern division the government officers had to persuade Papuans that their intentions were different from those of previous traders, gold-seekers or missionaries. There were far more Europeans in this area than in others so government officials were less concerned with making initial contacts with the natives than with European development or relationships between Europeans and natives.

The resident magistrate wrote in October 1897 that

it is very gratifying to learn that the tribes on Misima are so peaceable and well-conducted, not a single offence, beyond a little loud talk to the village constable at Enauta, which meant nothing, having been reported to me.

No doubt the influence exercised by the teachers stationed on the island has, in some measure, to do with this satisfactory state of affairs, but I think that the chief cause is due to the fact that the natives now thoroughly understand the intentions of the government, and recognize in it a superior power, which alone makes an impression on the native mind, but more so, when that power acts as their protector, not only from the unlawful actions of unscrupulous Europeans, but also from violence by their own countrymen.[11]

MacGregor made constant appeals for more officers from as early as 1888.[12] An analysis of the careers of his sixty-four officers shows some of the limitations of their assistance. Only thirty-eight of them stayed long enough and were sufficiently trusted to be appointed to the important office of magistrate. Of these thirty-eight, half died or resigned while holding office. Most resignations were caused by bad health. Sickness was frequent, especially malaria, which could incapacitate a man for weeks and often make recuperative leave to the mainland essential. As MacGregor stated, 'Here if one does obtain a man of the right stuff he probably breaks down with fever before he has learned his duties'.[13] A minority left because of dissatisfaction with the service, or for better opportunities. Some who did stay were discontented and constantly applied to the British Colonial Office for transfer or promotion.

A mere skeleton staff filled positions below the level of magistrate, whether on government ships, or as surveyors or clerks, and MacGregor was forced to use men outside government service. But such expedients could not overcome the limitations arising from inadequate staff.

The shortage meant that every official was overworked; each one held a variety of posts and had to be prepared to turn to any job whether involving physical labour or routine clerical skill. R. J. Kennedy, for example, was appointed to eight positions in November 1895: five general offices (Resident Magistrate for the Possession, European Officer of the Armed Constabulary, an officer authorized to issue timber licences and act as timber inspector, Warden for the Possession, and Magistrate for Native Matters for the Possession) and three specific offices (Resident Magistrate, Postmaster and Warden of the Goldfields for the Louisiades, or south-east, division).[14] These formal titles also covered a multitude of functions and there could be difficulties when a resident magistrate had to act as prosecutor, counsel for the defence and judge in the same case.

From his Seychelles and Fijian experience MacGregor was familiar with this accumulation and diversity of tasks and had little sympathy with officials who complained.

> All government officers must be prepared to do anything they can to further the public service. The question as to whether a given duty comes within the scope of an officer's special duty is one that is seldom given a hearing to. The man that does all he can is sure to find advancement when an opportunity offers.[15]

This shortage of men meant that to fulfil his aims MacGregor had himself to undertake more responsibility than he anticipated, and the poor quality of his few subordinates meant time spent on supervision of their work.

MacGregor constantly hoped that the attractions of service in New Guinea, which came to mean so much to him, would overcome its disadvantages to potential new staff. He hoped that the opportunities for an adventurous life, especially when combined with a sense of fulfilling an obligation to the Papuans, would attract suitable men. Also his own achievements and qualities might have been expected to add to these appeals. The scarcity of recruits and the calibre of those who did serve in New Guinea suggests, however, that the possible attractions of its government service were outweighed by the disadvantages; the poor salaries and living conditions, limited opportunities for promotion, the unhealthiness of the island and dangers, especially in initial contacts with the Papuans.

Yet another grave disadvantage was that no New Guinea appointment offered security because of doubts whether these public servants were members of the British colonial service, or were, anomalously, members of a new Australian (or Queensland) colonial service. All officers were appointed 'temporarily and provisionally' by the Administrator after the Queensland Governor-in-Council had concurred in the suggested appointment. Then the Secretary of State had to confirm the appointment. Every appointment was apparently subject to renewal at the end of the ten years agreement between Britain and the Australian colonies. Dismissals also needed Colonial Office confirmation. All applications for transfer or promotion were in practice referred to London, partly because the appointments had been confirmed in London and partly because some of the officers had previously held positions in the British colonial service. Applications for leave were left to the Administrator-in-Council in New Guinea, subject to approval by the Queensland Governor. The Colonial Office refused to consider applications for leave when any were made directly to it.[16]

Thus MacGregor was never satisfied with his staff, complaining typically in January 1889:

> I have no man I can depend on to do a thing 'thoroughly', and I have no man I can depend on to execute a task promptly. How I should like to have Allardyce here, but I see no probability of getting him. And I badly want the useful man, the Woodruff of Seychelles or the Heffernan of Fiji. I have got to do too much myself and when I break down the whole machine will be at a standstill.[17]

MacGregor tried to bring some trusted friends with him to New Guinea, just as Gordon had insisted on choosing his own staff for Fiji. He succeeded after 'some difficulty'[18] in obtaining F. J. Winter as Chief Judicial Officer and B. H. Thomson, who became his private secretary. He also attracted two others from Fiji to become magistrates in New Guinea, J. Meredith and A. M. Campbell.[19]

Winter, MacGregor's 'colleague and subordinate' in Fiji, then a middle-aged bachelor, was a Queensland-trained lawyer who, MacGregor claimed, had obtained from his Fijian experience a good knowledge 'in such laws and regulations as are suitable for the government of native races'.[20] He became MacGregor's main support and acted as Administrator while MacGregor was on leave. He disagreed with MacGregor's policy in some ways; for example, in showing a greater readiness to commute death sentences. But they complemented each other in so far as the lawyer was better suited for paper work that for making the initial contacts with Papuans which MacGregor so enjoyed. MacGregor gave him unstinted praise: 'Winter is of the greatest use to me; calm, quiet, thoughtful, with a good head and fair to natives. He is my right hand here in everything'.[21] In 1891 MacGregor recommended him for the C.M.G.[22]

Thomson, on the other hand, disappointed MacGregor. After acting as secretary to his father, the Archbishop of York, Thomson went to Fiji in 1883, as one of the cadets recommended by Gordon. From this cadet scheme Gordon had hoped to find men to deal 'temperately and judiciously' with the Fijians, and whose promotion would depend on proficiency in Fijian languages.

Although MacGregor was sceptical about the scheme, believing that most of those appointed were uneducated friends of clerks in the Colonial Office, he specifically excepted Thomson from this criticism.[23]

Thomson proved the brightest of these cadets, becoming proficient in Fijian and Tongan languages, and succeeding in native and magisterial work in which he showed 'aptitude, interest and the requisite degree of firmness'.[24] At the end of 1887, however, his father wrote to the Colonial Office, asking for Basil's employment in another colony with a better climate, where he would have more 'scope' than in depressed Fiji[25] and soon afterwards Thomson conditionally accepted the position of secretary to MacGregor in New Guinea.

He was at first of considerable assistance, particularly in the tedious clerical work of preparing duplicates of despatches for the outside governments. But he left after only a few months. MacGregor told Gordon

> he suffered a good deal from fever; and I was sending him to Australia to recoup; but I was 'concussed' when he told me he would not return. He said he was afraid of the fever, engaged to be married; his people were alarmed at his being here; and he frankly admitted he thought first of all of himself. You have had desertions and can sympathise with me; I confess I was always doubtful that he came here for more than a 'sara-sara', Thurston always said he only made a convenience of the public service, but he certainly did suffer a great deal from fever. . . .[26]

W. Telfer Campbell, who attained magisterial rank in 1890, proved little more satisfactory and MacGregor criticized his work as slow and peremptory; he was accused of cutting down Papuans' coconut trees and burning their houses as a punishment.[27] He was always dissatisfied with conditions in New Guinea ('not a house to his ideas nor constables of sufficient training and education')[28] and MacGregor was not unhappy when Campbell left in 1895.

MacGregor thought he was 'not fortunate' with the staff he inherited from the Protectorate. The most important was Anthony Musgrave who had come to New Guinea in 1885 and was Government Secretary. MacGregor wrote of him that

> he is hard working, and never happy save when writing; but he has a penchant for going on leave. He has been three years here and does not know a score of words of the language of the Motu people among whom he lives . . . I believe he means and desires to be very loyal; but his wish to be so is so intense it leads him into blunders.[29]

One example MacGregor gave of Musgrave's loyalty to him concerned the London Missionary Society, to which Musgrave had been persistently hostile. When he realized that MacGregor's policy favoured the mission Musgrave loyally changed his official attitude, but at the same time made his private hostility quite obvious.

Much of MacGregor's lack of sympathy with Musgrave arose over native policy, for he felt that Musgrave regarded 'a native as an unclean thing'.[30] He had other doubts about Musgrave's value also, and when Musgrave wrote to say that the strains of the last two and a half years had been undermining his health MacGregor noted: 'Frankly I fear that the idle times of the Protectorate unfitted him for any steady work or application'.[31] Musgrave became increasingly discontented, mainly because of lack of promotion, and worried the Colonial Office repeatedly for consideration of his services. MacGregor supported these applications, for, as in the case of Thomson, he did not allow his disappointment to develop into personal opposition. Though perhaps one might also suspect a desire to be rid of the man, officers were precious and later events suggest MacGregor's genuine concern for Musgrave: Musgrave stayed in New Guinea for over twenty years until his retirement in 1908, and when MacGregor became Governor of Queensland he employed Musgrave as his private secretary, and aided him financially until his death on 13 June 1912.[32]

Another officer whom MacGregor inherited in 1888 from the Protectorate was Bingham Hely, the Resident Magistrate at Samarai, who had been a clerk in the Queensland Audit Office. MacGregor was well aware of Hely's failings: like Musgrave, although he had spent three years in New Guinea, he did 'not know any native language'.[33] As well 'Hely has many men and large resources at his command but he is not doing so much as I should expect'[34] because he was 'so lazy and so flatulent'.[35] One illustration of Hely's indolence given by MacGregor was that while MacGregor went ashore and visited villages needing to be resettled after the Ansell murders, and walked 'across the mountain range from Milne Bay to Chads Bay'[36]—all in Hely's district—Hely had stayed aboard the government vessel.

MacGregor did not entirely disapprove of Hely, however, and freely granted that he was just to the Papuans and showed interest in their customs. For example, he wrote sympathetically about *puri-puri* sorcery:

it is curious that people should be so dominated by superstition although, after all, it is not a great while since people of our own race had a firm belief in things as preposterous as those in which the Papuans believe now,[37]

and later wrote that he had been

engaged most of the day in procuring information from Gauria, Gume and Genii, concerning religious customs, demonology, futurity etc. This has been the happiest day I have ever experienced in New Guinea.[38]

Nor was Hely out of sympathy with his environment, writing that the country was 'swarming with bird life—toucans, parrots, white blue and Goura pigeons and whistling ducks', which he felt made up for the defects caused by mosquitoes and sandflies.[39] Hely stayed throughout MacGregor's term of office and his health, 'undermined' by 1897, was the reason for his final resignation from the service in 1900.

MacGregor found faults, too, with the Swede, E. G. Edelfelt, who had been the Protectorate's government agent at Motu Motu. He first judged Edelfelt as being 'not of remarkable talent, but very zealous'[40] but later found him unreliable. When MacGregor sent one of the Ansell murderers to him for custody, 'this outlaw was allowed . . . to walk about Samarai without irons, without guards, and could have swum easily to the next island'. Edelfelt also bungled the mails and MacGregor reported that he had 'suffered great inconvenience and the service much loss'.[41] Edelfelt resigned from the service in July 1889.

The Hunter brothers were also found wanting by MacGregor, who had been warned by his predecessor, John Douglas, of their failings. MacGregor kept Robert Hunter as a special constable for a few days only, as he found him 'quite unfit to be employed', but in July 1889 decided to keep George Hunter, the government agent at Rigo, in the service, for he had shown 'no grave dereliction of duty',[42] although he 'drinks, lives with a native woman, bullies those that offend him' and was alleged to have accused a native of murder who was his rival for the favours of another native woman.[43] MacGregor judged both brothers as 'active, seasoned [and] dashing, even if 'not truthful, . . . intemperate, quite uneducated, destitute of patience, harsh and domineering with natives, and revengeful'.[44] When George Hunter was murdered by natives in May 1890 because of his ill treatment of his latest Papuan mistress, MacGregor regretted the loss of 'his best government agent, who was not quite trustworthy'[45]—

a remarkable paradox which illustrates how hard-pressed for men he was.

MacGregor's main objection to all these officers was that their attitude to Papuans was inefficiently sympathetic. In 1889 Mac-Gregor thought there was

> no 'native' man in the service unless perhaps young Lawes, and he is in Musgrave's black list and of course as Collector of Customs his time is now much taken up with work not native . . . not one of my officers except young Lawes knows anything at all of the Motuan [language] even.[46]

Thus MacGregor entrusted Lawes with an increasing amount of native work. Lawes was Resident Magistrate for the central division from 1890, and after his death in 1894 MacGregor concluded an address before the Royal Colonial Institute in London with a strong public tribute:

> the service has lost a most valuable, loyal, intelligent, and highly qualified officer, possessed of much special knowledge of the country and people.

> In him the Administrator has lost an intimate friend and a faithful follower; and the natives have lost one who knew them and sympathised with them, one who can hardly ever be replaced.[47]

MacGregor's praise of Lawes was exceptional for the officers he inherited from the Protectorate. A clue was given in 1897 to the number of valuable supporters he was able to recruit subsequently when he only added two other names to that of Lawes for praise: 'the deaths of Kowald, Lawes and Gleeson[48] greatly weakens my hands. They were my most devoted followers'.[49] MacGregor did in fact occasionally praise other officers and he was eager to recognize valuable service. Moreover, it would be unfair to suggest that he praised so few officers because he withheld praise until after death. One plausible alternative explanation of the preponderance of obituary tributes is that his better officers were killed because they were more active in native affairs.

Charles Kowald was one of MacGregor's most useful officers. He was in charge of the Mekeo district, and surviving station records show that from the day he took up his appointment he had appreciated the need to understand the Papuans, writing 'I am a good deal hampered, as yet, in not understanding the language properly, and having also no reliable interpreter',[50] and how his patience combined with firmness gradually won their confidence.

His attempts to deal fairly with the local people are illustrated by his actions in 1891, when he arrested one man for stealing and killing a pig and another for burning the thief's house down in revenge. The natives were disturbed by these arrests and Kowald, threatened by five hundred men who followed him to the station and 'kept howling', warned that 'an attempt to fight or rescue the prisoners would only result in some of their number being shoot.' He made the trials, in the presence of at least two thousand natives, 'as imposing as possible' before sentencing one for theft to twelve hours in irons and the replacement of the pig, and the other for arson to twenty-four hours in irons. Kowald hoped that his actions would end thefts 'as all seemed greatly frightened by the sight of the two men chained up'.[51]

In 1893 MacGregor praised 'his pluck and perseverance under extremely difficult circumstances' and by that date Kowald was able to record a definite change in the Inawa area as a result of his efforts: 'it is satisfactory to see the natives of the surrounding villages reporting thefts etc. . . . and also assisting to catch the culprit'.[52] In November he reported that

16 Maiva men passed through the station on a visit to the other villages for trading purposes, this is the first time Maiva natives going up the river trading on their own account, without taking arms or other warlike weapons with them, I am encouraging this interchange and visit between the coast and inland people in every way.[53]

In July 1895 he reported from Inawi that

In all the villages about here I am glad to state the people come now to the government station direct for redress, in former times they often went first to the fathers[54] with their complaints . . . I have fairly succeeded in making the natives understand that the government will not be influenced by anybody, and can therefore be trusted by them in all matters concerning their peace and welfare.[55]

Economic progress also impressed him, thus he reported that for collecting sandalwood natives were being

fairly paid in useful articles such as blankets, shirts [and even a dinghy] . . . no complaints have come, either from natives or traders connected with this trade. And as far as I am able to observe [this trading] tends much to civilize and brings a desire for the possession of European articles.[56]

Once a degree of control was established in an area MacGregor introduced a system of regular inspection of villages. Each magistrate had to complete forms, with columns for the names of the villages visited, the names of their chiefs (this heading reflected MacGregor's Fijian experience), the number of houses, the estimated populations, the dates visited and any remarks. The extent of Kowald's task can be suggested by his return for January-March 1892 when he visited over forty villages with an estimated population of over 7,500—even though most visits were short and inadequate for effective control.[57]

MacGregor tried to maintain his personal influence through his representatives. Thus when Kowald in February 1892 wrote reporting that the wife of a chief had died, MacGregor asked him to extend his, MacGregor's, sympathy.[58] MacGregor also insisted on as complete and as rapid information as possible from all out-stations. He showed his annoyance when station diaries did not reach him promptly and always asked for explanations. In Kowald's case these explanations were comprehensive—and qualified.

> I must point out to you that I have to entrust my letters to natives in Delena village for forwarding to Port, and in that case I never know, how they are send, by canoe, boat or cutter, or wheater they are ever send or reach port.[59]

If they went through the Roman Catholic mission station on Yule Island they were usually promptly forwarded through Thursday Island, though he once found his letters written two months earlier still awaiting a boat. MacGregor had hoped a boat, the *Alice Meade,* could run regularly between Hall Sound and Port Moresby, but communications remained irregular.

Experiences at Mekeo showed how personal government influence was and also how easily it could degenerate. When Kowald was away on leave in Europe for eight months until March 1895 W. E. Armit acted as Resident Magistrate for some months and then left a convict, Tom Manila, in charge. The Roman Catholic missionaries of the Sacred Heart Mission complained in February 1895 of a 'pretty mess' at the station, goods being squandered and Tom interfering with the wife of a corporal. When Kowald returned on 4 March, he found the station much neglected.

> Tom Manila . . . who for some to me inexplicable reason was put in charge, was lying in the grass, smoking a pipe, while some of the police and prisoners were doing likewise.

The station was dirty; private and trade stores had been broken open; a prismatic compass and carpenters' tools had disappeared.

It is very clear that the government has lost most of its former prestige and confidence with the natives, it cannot be otherwise, when a number of savages in policeman's clothes with rifles and ammunition left without controll for months, to levy blackmail, falsely imprison natives and afterwards receiving payment for their liberation.[60]

Unfortunately Kowald was killed in November 1896 while showing a Papuan how to use dynamite. Although he had succeeded admirably in helping to pacify the populous and turbulent district, the problems which had arisen suggest some of the difficulties facing MacGregor, even when he had an officer on whom he could rely.

Another officer MacGregor singled out for praise was John Green who was appointed as Government Agent on the northeast coast in 1895 and was killed in 1897. Green, aged twenty-nine in 1895, was healthy, unmarried, temperate, active and intelligent. After three years in New Guinea, he knew some of the language of Kabadi and Moresby districts, and had much knowledge of natives.[61] MacGregor recognized his good qualities but reserved his highest praise until after Green was murdered on the Mambare: 'the best man I had; the most intelligent, the most persevering, and the most in sympathy with native work'.[62]

The problem of attracting suitable staff remained unsolved and MacGregor complained after Green's murder that he had no one

> fit to succeed Mr. Green: English has become demoralised by Green's death: I have no Commandant: Moreton's legs are useless:[63] Hely's health is undermined. etc. etc. It is not an easy matter to see how to make the best of the present situation.[64]

Criticism of his officers was, however, far more usual for MacGregor than praise. When his commandant, A. W. Butterworth, was on leave in Brisbane and did not hasten back to New Guinea, MacGregor wrote that Butterworth

> was delighted to be out of it. Had he been a zealous [officer] I should certainly have looked for him back by the 'Merrie England' but I know the calibre of Mr. Butterworth too well to expect him back in whatever difficulty the service might be placed. Had he come back then I should have considered him worthy of promotion. He lost his opportunity, and has caused the service an infinity of inconvenience.[65]

There seems to be no recorded tribute to J. B. Cameron, although this surveyor was so often MacGregor's companion on patrols. He was especially critical after Cameron became a magistrate, stating on one occasion that he was 'a failure', condemning him of fearing 'the leaden sword of the Thursday Island press' and of cutting down some coconut trees and burning several houses as a punishment.[66]

Of his private secretary, T. Hatton-Richards, he wrote:

> He and his uncle want to work out that he is a victim to climate, hardship and overwork here. All of which is interested exaggeration. He is a good officer, but rather 'girlish' in disposition, and cannot get over being jilted. His indisposition is more nervous than climatic and I advise them to take for him anything he can get worth £150 a year, *and society*.[67]

Clearly MacGregor felt that he was never able to delegate full authority. None of the men who served under him in New Guinea were able to win his confidence to that extent, which partly explains why his successor was George Le Hunte, a fellow official in Fiji, instead of one of his senior officers. MacGregor was largely justified, for his subordinates were not inspiring men, yet one also suspects a reluctance to share his power. In so far as this existed MacGregor can be criticized as a leader. Moreover his refusal to delegate authority partly stemmed from his failure to appreciate the qualities of those who differed from him. Just as he had quarrelled in Fiji with Thurston, so was he always liable to be intolerant of any difference of opinion.

Nevertheless for those who endorsed or were convinced by his ideas he was an inspiring leader. The much-criticized Hatton-Richards wrote:

> No better person could have been found for such arduous work as New Guinea supplies. As a leader of men, as a friend to his officers, Sir William MacGregor inspires mixed feelings of gratitude and confidence. To the dark men he is an object of daring courage and firm, but silent will. . . . I shall never be able to forget his conscientiousness in duty, and his earnest desire to lay the foundation of a good government. . . . I shall ever look back with pride to . . . those days when we stood side by side in long hours of danger, when my knowledge of his character was my best support.[68]

C. A. W. Monckton, who shared some of his qualities and who certainly proved an energetic resident magistrate, was also deeply impressed by MacGregor as a leader:

> Short, square, slightly bald, speaking with a strong Scotch accent, showing signs of overwork and the ravages of malaria, there was nothing in the first appearance of the man to stamp him as being

out of the ordinary, but I had not been three minutes in his cabin before I realised that I was in the presence of a master of men— a Cromwell, a Drake, a Caesar, or Napoleon—his keen grey eyes looking clean through me, and knew that I was being summed and weighed. Once, and only once in my life, have I felt that a man was my master in every way, a person to be blindly obeyed and one who must be right and infallible, and that was when I met Sir William MacGregor.[69]

Another brief tribute titled MacGregor the 'iron governor'.[70]

Despite MacGregor's general dissatisfaction with his staff, they were responsible for the major part of routine native work. Mac- Gregor exercised a paper supervision over them from Port Moresby, aided by his visits of inspection—which were often feared, as Monckton's tribute suggests. He dismissed incom- petent officers, or tried to move those unsuitable for native work into Port Moresby. Throughout he endeavoured to convert men to his ideas. But his overall verdicts on his staff show how in- adequate he felt that his efforts had been.

MacGregor recruited Papuans to help spread the influence of government, partly because he was unable to obtain as large a European staff as he needed, but mainly because of his conviction that much in native society should be maintained. He was pre- disposed from his Fijian experience to work through native institutions and he hoped to find the equivalent of the chiefs in Fiji.

This hope was disappointed, however, by the nature of Papuan societies. MacGregor soon realized that effective European rule would require far more interference with existing societies than had been found necessary in Fiji. After five months in Papua he wrote that

the Government is becoming known, and what is more is being obeyed. But now comes the great trouble, no chiefs to take respon- sibility. I of course am trying to give certain authority to certain men, but that is a slow process, I have submitted draft laws for creating an Armed Constabulary that will also be our only police . . .[71]

and in 1890 he wrote:

I have hopes of being able to use some of the chiefs . . . in such a way that before long they may assume some of the functions of government. Unfortunately they soon relapse after I leave a dis- trict.[72]

MacGregor's idea of using Papuans as village authorities was not new. General Scratchley had argued that as the chaos of native authorities which he observed in 1885 could not be continued under British rule, there should be created in each district a 'tribal chief' who would be a British official and trustee for lands and who would be responsible for the conduct of the inhabitants of his district.[73] At the declaration of the Protectorate in 1884 staffs of office had been given to various 'so-called chiefs', usually selected by missionaries though sometimes by the villagers themselves. MacGregor showed himself to be well aware of the fallacies of this system, however, when in his first letter to Gordon from New Guinea he wrote that the natives of the Port Moresby district had

> sufficient cunning to carry out the policy of the old Elector of Köln, in respect of the Holy Roman Emperor, when invited by the Protectorate government to elect a chief, to put forward a nonentity who 'reigns but does not govern'.[74]

Similarly MacGregor's idea of recruiting a native police force was not new. Gordon as long ago as 1878 had suggested a Fijian police force for New Guinea.[75] Scratchley favoured the formation of a native police force, as had Douglas, who had suggested obtaining

> some trained men from Fiji, and with a force of 12 men, 6 afloat and 6 ashore, I can guarantee that order shall be maintained and inter-tribal atrocities prevented for at least 60 miles along the coast.[76]

Later Douglas foresaw that Papuans would eventually replace imported natives. Rear-Admiral Fairfax had put the British naval arguments in favour of a native police force (whether from Fiji or the New Hebrides), because

> they are from their habits, and colour, and capacity for standing heat and climate, able to cope with the New Guinea natives far more effectively than landing parties from Her Majesty's ships

and because this would mean the end of the crude practice of naval justice: the shelling of villages, burning of houses and destruction of canoes were common forms of punishment and 'this method of dealing though effectual usually, is not satisfactory; the employment is hardly worthy of our Service'.[77] The Colonial Office, which had noted all these suggestions from its Commissioners and the Navy, supported the idea of a native police force so long as its members were British (so excluding New Hebrides natives), and specifically advocated 'a little force of Fijians if among that mild and lazy race 30 enterprising young men could be found to volunteer for the service'.[78]

MacGregor brought these discussions closer to reality when he formulated draft laws for establishing an armed contabulary within his first few months in New Guinea. The Armed Constabulary Ordinance was not passed for over a year, however, as MacGregor had 'not much felt the want of the force' at first. Nor did he plan to depute the responsibility of arresting natives in new districts to any subordinate officer, though he was prepared to devolve this duty 'over a large area of country in which the Government is known, and where the arrest of murderers is recognised as the usual and proper course'. Another reason for delay was his attempt to use the crew of the *Merrie England* as police. This had failed, particularly because of their incompetent and inaccurate rifle shooting.[79]

When he appointed a police commandant he hoped for assistance in his visits of inspection to new areas. The first commandant, D. A. McNeill, soon proved unsuitable, for

> he has given way to fever and hysteria, and leaves by first chance for safer quarters. It really does not matter very much for if serious work is undertaken I must direct it myself. But . . . work is needed everywhere over 90,000 square miles and I can be only at one place at once.[80]

McNeill's successors, especially G. Wriford[81] and Butterworth, proved somewhat more reliable.

MacGregor wanted the nucleus of the constabulary to come from outside New Guinea because he had doubts about the suitability and courage of Papuans, so he asked Thurston to recruit 'ten time-expired Solomon Islanders, Guadalcanal men being preferred'.[82] Twelve men were signed on for three years on 25 August 1890, and before September had arrived in New Guinea from Fiji. The sergeant and corporal were Fijians and the ten constables were from Malayata, in the Solomons, as there were no Guadalcanal men available. Thurston claimed that the Malayata men had 'the reputation of being the best fighting men in the Solomon Islands and of being loyal to their leaders'.[83]

The Armed Constabulary Ordinance provided that all fit New Guinea natives (if unmarried and between fifteen and forty) could be compulsorily recruited for at least a year for the force. The Queensland government made no objection to this provision; indeed Griffith defended it because such service would lead the natives 'to understand . . . [their] duty, when required, to assist

M

in the maintenance of order'.[84] The Colonial Office, however, saw dangers in the compulsory recruiting of 'such untutored savages'.[85] In fact compulsory recruiting was never introduced for the constabulary, but an argument similar to that of Griffith was later used to justify the compulsory service of Papuans as carriers for the government.

MacGregor, having overcome his initial doubts, decided to use Papuans as constables and asked his officers to look out for suitable men. In the first year eight volunteers were enlisted; by May 1891 the total strength of the constabulary was twenty-four: two Fijians, twelve Solomon Islanders, nine Papuans and one Malay, and by 22 December 1892 it had reached fifty, including ten recruited in Fiji and forty Papuans. By 1898 their numbers had increased to one hundred and ten, all of whom were Papuans, including one of the rank of sergeant. The patrolling detachment had grown from fifteen to twenty-five and the station numbers had all increased proportionately. The annual number of recruits had risen from eight to about one hundred in eight years, which MacGregor explained by the lure of the uniform, the carrying of arms (otherwise strictly forbidden, except in other special service with Europeans) and the regular supply of food.[86]

The constables had all the 'duties and functions of police constables in Queensland'[87] though their tasks varied according to the extent of government control over the Papuans with whom they were working and the consequent degree to which native regulations were being enforced. Penalties were provided for most possible abuses but in MacGregor's years there were not many, only thirty-four proceedings against the constables reaching the higher courts.

Their most important work was undertaken on patrols, especially those which went into previously unpenetrated areas. MacGregor stressed that his constables were police and not soldiers and the distinction led him to boast that he had used no troops in New Guinea. The armed constabulary were always to operate defensively, never offensively as MacGregor's instructions to his officers made clear—'on no account whatever is a shot ever to be fired at a native by the constabulary save only in self-defence'.[88] Nevertheless, as he claimed that knowledge of government implied respect for its power they needed to be armed and with weapons that were far superior to any held by the Papuans, though these were not to be used except as a last resort. Practice rather than precept is more important when such fine distinctions are made. As far as MacGregor's patrols were concerned the evidence indicates that he maintained these principles, to the extent of risking his own life. Nevertheless, some of his officers gave orders to fire more readily, while some of those appointed as constables completely misunderstood MacGregor's methods.

The events at Cloudy Bay in 1893-94 showed some of the difficulties faced by MacGregor because of his officers' use of the armed constabulary. In 1893 Moreton and W. E. Armit were leading a patrol and some Papuans were killed. MacGregor was disturbed:

> I do not at all like the appearance of these reports. It looks as if some innocent people have been shot. I do not see how shots came to be fired at all. . . .
>
> I cannot allow the police out of my own sight again until I am satisfied on this matter.[89]

Moreton claimed that he had given clear instructions to Armit:

> The police must be made to understand that they must be very careful how they shoot as the police will be on three sides of the village. Also they must not shoot unless forced and in defence of their lives, any natives breaking through the cordon and running away must not be fired on . . . do let us get through this if possible without loss of life and in a friendly spirit.[90]

The armed constabulary was unsatisfactory in various other ways also. There were desertions[91] and the standard of its drill and discipline, MacGregor admitted, was not high. The need for constables was at first greater than the number enlisting, thus a Minute in 1892 reads:

> see that the six men engaged for Mr. English receive as much drill as possible while in Port, as they will be sent to Rigo in a few days. One man will have to be appointed a lance-corporal and explained his duties as well as time will permit.[92]

During one patrol Armit protested at the

> utter uselessness of the majority of his men. . . . It is impossible to achieve success with a body of men whose leading characteristic is an entire want of discipline, a cowardly desire to avoid meeting natives, and an entire disregard of the responsibilities vested in them when guarding the lives of their comrades at night.[93]

MacGregor answered petulantly:

> Inform Armit that it is of no use to complain of the constabulary. They are easy to train and to order if one is patient with them. He has plenty of time to train them. . . and should address himself to

that . . . he must like others do the best he can with the material at his command until he improves it.[94]

There were social problems. MacGregor insisted in 1892 that 'the rule must be strictly enforced that only women married to the men are to be allowed in camp'. Wriford minuted in reply: 'His Honour cannot think that I want my camp to be a brothel'.[95] In 1898 the marriage of a member of the armed constabulary was approved, but the general question whether constables could marry was not answered. An inquiry by C. A. W. Monckton in 1898 into charges of misconduct with native women by the constabulary at Goodenough underlined another aspect of this problem (as old as the first army) when a witness gave evidence that

the police then said . . . don't take them on board give them to us . . . we never have a woman, all the time when we go bush if we find a woman we do not take her in but have her in the bush and then let her go.

He also stated that

the whole of the police and two Siai boys had connection with the two women. I gave the women three sticks of tobacco each and told them to run away.[96]

MacGregor insisted, in the case of all European officers, that 'intercourse with native women will be regarded in itself as sufficient ground for dismissal from the service'.[97]

Officially MacGregor praised the courage of the constabulary. He had never seen one 'flinch before opposition', and in 'dealing with refractory, wild or hostile tribes they have on many occasions shown an amount of forbearance that was simply astonishing'.[98] He especially praised Corporal Sedu, who could have escaped when John Green was murdered, but returned and died with him; and good conduct medals were recommended for two other non-commissioned officers. MacGregor's official verdict hid, as he well knew, earlier difficulties with some of the constabulary.

The constables were important to MacGregor both while serving in the force and as individuals after their discharge, for ex-constables could be significant in their villages as ambassadors in promulgating the peaceful intentions of government. The armed constabulary were not the only Papuans on whom MacGregor relied, however. From his first contacts with the villages he continued the practice of the Protectorate of recognizing men of authority and of trying to influence the rest of the village through these men. This practice was systematized by regulations

in December 1892 providing for village constables. By that time
there were 'nearly a score . . . and as a rule they are doing good,
some of them excellent, service'.[99] Kowald advised MacGregor
against making appointments in areas where there had been few
contacts:

> You also suggested, if it was possible to form a volunteer police
> force, this I think at present to soon as the natives, do not troughly
> understand all the meaning of Government yet, and a little more
> time will have to elapse, before this can be undertaken, as their
> sympathys are at pressent to strong yet, with the thief or otherwise
> evildoer, unless they have a particular enmity against him, to help
> in bringing him to justice.[100]

The village constables were paid 10s a year[101] and received
a suitable uniform, and their numbers increased to 202 by 1898.
By the regulation the men appointed were placed under the control of the European officers and all had to promise to be 'true
to the government'. They were given the power to arrest natives
who committed 'forbidden acts' (under other native regulations)
and to take offenders to the magistrates; all 'good' men of the
village were exhorted to help these constables against offenders.[102]
It depended on the individual government officer how much
use was made of these village police, so that the numbers appointed in each division need not accurately reflect the extent
of control in that area. By 1898 there were eighty-three in the
central division, sixty-three in the western division, but only
thirty-six in the well-settled eastern division and only twenty in
the south-eastern division. Central control was exercised over
these constables through the divisional officers who had to
provide monthly returns of the village constables, giving their
names, villages, dates of appointment, pay in trade for the year
(money values), special allowances, advances and amounts due,
and any appropriate remarks. MacGregor regarded these constables as 'the best substitute that can be created in the place
of the tribal chiefs that do not exist in British New Guinea'.[103]

Nevertheless there were fallacies in this system also. Some of
the village constables were misusing their authority for their
own profit and other natives had been pretending to be in the
service of the government. Thus in 1895 a new regulation was
introduced against extortion, though there were very few proceedings under this regulation during the three years it was
in force while MacGregor was still in office—only eight cases
before the native magistrates' courts.[104]

One unique development introduced by MacGregor was the appointment of Papuans whom his government had imprisoned, either as members of the armed constabulary or as village constables. He admitted to the Royal Colonial Institute in 1895 that another

> favourite Government measure is to enlist a few young men into the constabulary from a new or hostile tribe . . . [for instance] the powerful Aroma tribe was subjected . . . by moral pressure alone; six of them were at once enrolled. . . . These are hostages, they receive training and will go back to their own tribe as village police.[105]

The concept behind such appointments was that Papuans who had been imprisoned or subdued would be the ones most likely to be weaned from the features of native culture of which Mac-Gregor disapproved—such 'barbarous' customs as the waging of war, ritual murder or belief in sorcery. MacGregor hoped that while they were being trained these Papuans would acquire knowledge of and sympathy with European ideas and thus would help in the civilizing of their fellow Papuans.

One problem arising from MacGregor's attitudes to and use of Papuans, either as armed constables or as village police, is whether this foreshadowed ruling indirectly through the indigenes. As has been shown, particularly by Dr Mair,[103] it is the spirit of indirect rule, rather than the form of the institutions, that is most indicative. MacGregor hoped to rule indirectly in so far as he wanted to use native institutions and his dismay at finding no recognizable authority structure is clear evidence of this. He did not, however, intend to rule indirectly in so far as he was convinced that certain aspects of native society had to be eliminated, even if his interference destroyed the structure of that society.

When he imposed Papuans who had no authority within the reciprocal structure of the village or kin group, he was manifestly not ruling in an indirect spirit. Rather this was a direct contravention of the structure of native society. In the cases where he did use existing 'chiefs' (for there were some in the south-eastern division that approached this title) or men who had authority given by their kin, he could be said to have been ruling in the spirit of indirect rule, for some of the changes advocated, for example, the ending of wars, could be accepted by consent of the kin groups and therefore introduced without a direct interference in native polity.

MacGregor generalized wrongly in many ways in saying that

The Papuan elder has never at any period of his life rendered obedience, never acknowledged an established authority, and there are few or none that have been able to rule, save on narrow and precarious tenure.[107]

But in so far as he believed this he was consciously creating a new society for the Papuans. Certainly the concept of government, like the concept of a unified British New Guinea, had to be imposed on Papuans, whose concepts did not often go beyond the extended kin group usually living in a single small area. As in the case of Fiji, the dangers of anachronistic thought exist in such arguments. Historically it is probably more significant to realize the alternative to MacGregor's paternalistic encouragement of the Papuans' acceptance of what he regarded as the benefits of civilization. A policy which showed no sympathy for native society, which regarded the Papuans simply as a labour force, or their lands simply as sites for European plantations, would have destroyed native society far more rapidly and painfully than the 'slow process' envisaged by MacGregor.

Another way in which MacGregor attempted to counter his shortage of staff was by using missionaries. Besides using the two established missions, the largely Congregational London Missionary Society and the Roman Catholic Sacred Heart Society, he also successfully encouraged the Wesleyans and the Anglicans to begin work in New Guinea. It was a marriage of convenience on his part, with a realization before the ceremony had been celebrated that the interests of the two contracting parties were divergent and that judicial separation if not divorce was almost inevitable in the future.

Among the earliest missionaries in New Guinea were the French Marists on Woodlark Island from 1847-52, who left some memories, although forced to abandon their work: a chief thirty years later recalled them, and MacGregor found natives nearly forty years later saying something that he interpreted as the French words 'travaillez comme ça'.[108] They were succeeded by Italian priests, who were later killed by the natives as were the crew and passengers of a ship taking supplies to them in 1855. Clearly neither of these two missionary bodies had achieved their desired object of leading converts to Christianity. Nor had they done much to accustom the islanders to accepting European interlopers.

In 1881 a Roman Catholic Vicariate Apostolic of Melanesia and Micronesia was established with Louis André Navarre as vicar. In 1884 work was begun in the British New Guinea area and in 1885 the Reverend Stanislas Henri Verjus was working at Yule Island. In 1887 Navarre was given formal permission by Douglas as Special Commissioner to establish a mission on Yule Island.

The London Missionary Society had first planned to work in New Guinea in 1867 and Dr Samuel McFarlane placed the first teachers at Manu Manu in 1873. When this station proved too unhealthy the mission moved to Port Moresby in November. This beginning was not successful and a new start was made after the arrival of the two most outstanding men that the London Missionary Society sent to New Guinea: the steady, bookish Reverend William G. Lawes, who in December 1874 went to Port Moresby and who was joined in October 1877 by the adventurous, restless Reverend James Chalmers, in some ways a New Guinea equivalent of Dr Livingstone.

By 1884 there were some twenty mission stations, worked mainly by Pacific island teachers. No one realized better than the English missionaries how slow their task of conversion would be. Chalmers was very frank in 1884:

> What awful nonsense to suppose any savage tribe seeks to have teachers simply that they may be taught the Gospel. I have never met one and I do not believe there ever has been one. . . .[109]

More important for the government than conversion to Christianity was the fact that these missionaries had accustomed some Papuans to having foreigners living with them and had created desires for the white man's goods. If there were sincere converts an even firmer basis for white control was established, inasmuch as these Christian Papuans broke away from their own society.

The missionaries' aim was to convert all natives to Christianity and many did not develop their ideas beyond this. Although they showed far more respect for the Papuans than did most other Europeans who were trading or settling they destroyed elements of native culture that seemed to them irreconcilable with the Christian religion. Their letters and reports condemn many customs, such as sorcery, war, cannibalism, homosexuality, dancing and nudity. The perceptive missionaries realized the extent of this destruction of native society, but argued that the positive doctrines of Christianity would more than adequately replace the losses.

Generally the London Missionary Society distinguished its ends from those of the administration and tried to be indifferent to government. But clashes developed during the Protectorate and Lawes reported in 1886 that

> The attitude of the Govt. here towards us is harrassing and annoying. The Spec. Comm. Mr. Douglas is in sympathy with us, but his Deputy who is resident here, Mr. A. Musgrave Jnr. treats us with suspicion and distrust. A big sneer best represents his attitude towards us.[110]

The clash was partly based on differing beliefs, but also reflected the government's concern at the high death-rate of London Missionary Society teachers. Between 1873 and 1887 104 of the 202 teachers died, and the government felt that the mission was partly to blame because of inadequate supervision. Part of this charge seems justified for deaths were due not only to the unaccustomed climate and food but also to shortages of food and lack of medical care. The Mission's desire for expansion to fulfil its spiritual duty went beyond its material resources and its available European manpower to carry out any regular inspections. There was much questioning within the mission; for example, Lawes wrote to the Secretary in London in 1886:

> I can't ask you to send any more young men now. I can't take any responsibility for bringing out young men to die here. I don't believe God asks for all this sacrifice of life.[111]

After his arrival in 1888 MacGregor queried the contribution of some members of the London Missionary Society. But he praised Lawes, who had devoted much time to amassing and printing Papuan vocabularies, as 'a splendid philologist; there is no one else here I can trust to write one word correctly; but that may be less their fault than my hypercriticism',[112] the last comment being an unusual piece of self-perception for MacGregor. When Lawes went to England MacGregor wrote to Glasgow University asking if an honorary degree could be conferred. One of his tributes to Lawes in a letter to Griffith also reveals much of his attitude to missionary work generally:

> Lawes is a very superior man; kind-hearted, unselfish, devoted to his work, who never thinks of his own glory, but works honestly, assiduously, faithfully in propagating the gospel. But all the great islands in the East End are without missionaries of any kind, and it may be doubted that the London Missionary Society can overtake the work. The truth is that their organization is defective. There is a great want of proper inspection and supervision. It is of course my plain duty to assist them, and I do so. Many towns have promised me to build churches and to receive the missionary

in this [eastern] end of the mainland and I shall keep them to their word; but I fear Chalmers may think I am encroaching on his domain.

I have heard a great deal of the influence Chalmers has with natives: I have not seen its manifestation: but plainly it is not exercised to make them go to church or to receive the missionary. Of course what I tell you is quite confidential in regard to mission work, and I have not told any other person that I am stirring up the missionaries by doing inspections which should be done otherwise: they may not like it: for that I shall be sorry; they may have all the credit, provided the work is done somehow. I am sorry to say I regard the Christian veneer of the natives here as painfully thin. I should like to see the Wesleyans in the East End.[113]

MacGregor was prepared to allow missionaries of every denomination to assist government work. He used the London Missionary Society, supporting Lawes both as translator of the various Papuan languages and as a missionary. He worked with Chalmers in the west and utilized his considerable knowledge of the local peoples. He later spoke of him as 'courageous, indefatigible, ever-active and fearless'.[114] His temporary opposition to Chalmers was based on a dispute about the Ansell murders, which Chalmers said were a result of the methods of labour recruiting used by a recruiting ship the *Hopeful,* and excusable, but MacGregor regarded Chalmers' words as seditious.[115]

Despite this rather acrimonious personal quarrel MacGregor disapproved of verbal attacks by his officers upon missions. Thus he persuaded Musgrave, so long a critic of the London Missionary Society, that the missions 'should be assisted whenever possible'.[116] He wrote to the Society's Secretary in London pleading for the continuance of their work since

I depend upon your people for loyal assistance in the attempt to establish law and order. . . . The savage dispositions of many tribes have through missionary effort been greatly influenced for good.[117]

The result for the Papuans was often a confusion of government and missionary, as MacGregor admitted a few months later:

So actively and persistently have I advocated mission work in the east end that the natives will insist in regarding me as being, amongst other things, the Master Missionary. I have made them build churches at many places: I have stood by again and again and made old savages cut down the human skulls suspended

on their houses as trophies and bury them before me. There
are scores of towns now in the east end without a native skull in
them.[118]

Efforts were made to distinguish the function of missionary and
government and to prevent the missions using threats of government in enforcing religious observance. Hely complained to Mac-
Gregor about mission attempts in his western division to enforce
the observance of Sunday as a day of rest. In one case a policeman,
at the instigation of the London Missionary Society teacher, had
tied up a native for getting coconuts on Sunday. Hely objected
and told the policeman that there was no law against a man
doing as he pleased on Sunday and 'that the chiefs and village
police were not to interfere on behalf of the mission teachers
in such matters'. MacGregor tried to compromise, advising Hely
to tell Chalmers that

> the government will try to support them in introducing the ob-
> servance in any way short of using compulsion but the teachers
> should not ask the policemen to arrest for it.[119]

Hely complained again in 1894:

> I have never known *one case* here since the institution of the
> government in 1888, teachers of the London Missionary Society
> have not bolstered up what little powers and influence they may
> have had by threats of 'government'—in the East End, this, to-
> gether with foolish statements and remarks made to natives by the
> white missionaries concerning the relative positions of mission and
> government, retarded the advancement of the district, from one
> point of view, by six months out of every twelve . . . as people
> look upon the government as an oppression in some ways.[120]

The *reductio ad absurdum* of missionaries asking for government aid was reached in a case at Kiriwina in March 1895. The
Wesleyan minister, Mr Fellows, complained to government officers that the natives were not attending his church. So Commandant Butterworth promised 'to stay in camp the following
Sunday and to persuade if possible all the natives to come to
church'. Next Sunday Butterworth

> marched the men to church, about 600 natives also attended ser-
> vice—at the afternoon service about 500 women, children and men
> were preached to by Mr. Fellows, he was delighted, that so many
> of the local natives had come to church, and thanked Kennedy
> and self for asking the natives to attend divine service. [At Port
> Moresby someone, probably MacGregor, marked this entry '!!'.][121]

In August 1895 MacGregor disapproved when Butterworth

reported that he had borrowed a mission boat to carry the constabulary to make an arrest:

> with the 'Siai' [the government boat] at his disposal the Commandant should have borrowed no one's boat; but last of all a mission boat for such a purpose. I am sure I said to the Commandant at Dobu when he thoughtlessly asked Mr. Bromilow for a mission official to assist him to arrest a thief, that I objected to mixing up missions with such work.[122]

MacGregor encouraged measures which improved the efficiency of the missions and tried to assist them financially so that they could continue to supplement his policy. In 1889 he sought exemption from tariffs for mission stores on the ground that missions were charitable bodies. After both the governor of Queensland and the Colonial Office had approved, the Queensland government intervened to reject the proposal, apparently partly for sectarian reasons.[123] MacGregor wrote:

> Lawes . . . told me he was afraid the present Government of Queensland were unfriendly to the Mission [the London Missionary Society], that the Griffith Cabinet would, he believed, have assisted them in every way, but McIlwraith had a dislike to them. This I know is so as regards McIlwraith.[124]

MacGregor sought an alternative way of aiding the missionaries, arguing that

> it will not be creditable to Queensland, New South Wales and Victoria to make a few pounds per mensem out of these bodies. If the dues are collected for the maintenance of the principle, which I declare to be sound, that there should be no exemptions in matters of taxes, the amount paid by them should be given to them as an educational grant.

He intended to argue this case with Premier Morehead of Queensland and although he anticipated opposition from the 'Irish element in the Queensland Cabinet' he thought that the mission could make a strong case that would

> appeal to the sentiments of a great many people of the better sort, make a vigorous newspaper diversion, and the Government may be forced to yield what it might well concede gracefully.[125]

The question lost its urgency, however, when general rates of customs were lowered.[126]

The London Missionary Society Foreign Secretary, R. Wardlaw Thompson, visited New Guinea in 1897 and promised expansion, including opening two new stations and an industrial mission settlement. He complained that in land matters 'the common testimony of our missionaries is that the spirit of your views on this subject is not apparent in the action of the Divisional officers of your government'.[127] MacGregor's reply requested specific instances when London Missionary Society claims had been disregarded. He thought he had aided the expansion of the mission, which by 1898 claimed 1,600 church members and 10,000 native adherents served by nine English missionaries and 103 ordained native agents.[128] One way in which MacGregor had hoped to improve the efficiency of the London Missionary Society was by reducing the area for which it had accepted responsibility. This aim fitted in with his expressed desire, inspired by his observation of the success of the Wesleyan missionaries in Fiji, to see the Wesleyans at work in New Guinea. By April 1890 the Wesleyans had agreed to be responsible for the Louisiades and D'Entrecasteaux group and at the same time MacGregor hoped that the Anglicans would accept the north-east coast as their area. At a meeting in Port Moresby on 17 June 1890 between MacGregor and representatives of each of the three Protestant missions,[129] fields of influence were defined. The agreement was to be backed by government policy that in any one native village only one grant of land would be given to a mission by the government. MacGregor was optimistic after this meeting, believing it would benefit both the missions and the Papuans. The Sacred Heart Mission refused to ratify the agreement, however, being suspicious of a Protestant government and for reasons well expressed by a later Bishop:

> because the Catholic Church is unflinching in her conviction of being the true Church of God, she never will agree to any scheme of spheres of influence that would divest her of her right to teach all men.[130]

Following the meeting MacGregor took the 'large-hearted brave veteran' the Reverend George Brown[131] of the Wesleyans, (who had been working in Samoa since 1860 and in New Britain since 1875) and the Reverend Albert Maclaren of the Anglicans (of whom he recorded 'I have known few more lovable men') [132] to their respective areas. He wrote in June 1890:

> I may be able to see our long line of savagery attacked simultaneously by the four missions. I am looking forward to this and many other important developments next year which I hope will see . . . the Government more widely and better known.[133]

In September 1890 he reported that Brown was well pleased with the islands as a field for mission work, with their estimated population of fifty to sixty thousand, and that the mission's head station was planned for Goulvain Island. Maclaren went with MacGregor north to the German boundary, contacting many tribes who had never seen whites before and selecting five sites for Anglican mission stations from which all coastal villages could be reached. Maclaren planned to go to England to try and raise the necessary men and money for this new mission field.[134]

MacGregor regularly praised the progress of the Roman Catholic mission. By the end of 1897 the mission claimed that there were 2,020 Papuan Catholics and even more catechumens; eighteen stations were occupied and two others visited by their mission staff of over sixty. Father Dupeyrat's history of the mission shows how expansion was consistent (except for setbacks in 1892) from the establishment of the mission on the mainland (1889-90) till 1900.[135]

MacGregor was very impressed by the work of the Wesleyans after their first missionaries arrived in May 1891. Typical entries in his diary read: 'there is tremendous earnestness in these Wesleyans', their South Sea teachers 'are better taught than the London Missionary Society men and . . . they throw themselves more completely into their work' and it is 'really most affecting . . . to brave the unknown dangers of this new country of evil character and its actual hardships and dangers all for Christ's sake'.[136] By 1898 in their four circuits (Dobu, Panaieti, Tubetube and Kiriwina) the Church claimed 314 native members of this church, a further 162 'on trial', and 299 catechumens, a small proportion of the 11,509 listed as attending public worship. The leader of the mission, the Reverend W. E. Bromilow, was convinced that converts would increase and he, George Brown and MacGregor claimed that 'a new spirit was taking possession of the life of the people generally'.[137]

The Anglicans began work in 1891 but achieved very little during MacGregor's governorship. Maclaren died of malaria after less than a year in the field and although MacGregor pleaded with the Bishop of Brisbane for 'the speedy and vigorous prosecution of the work'[138] there was only a skeleton staff under the Reverend Copland King, a 'sturdy Evangelist', who occupied the area for the next six years. In 1897 MacGregor wrote to the Anglican authorities in Australia, requesting more Anglican missionaries. He wanted to consolidate the spread of peace after the defeat of the Mambare tribes and said, 'a missionary settling

there . . . could at once obtain a hold on the natives', and warned
that if the Anglicans could not come the Wesleyans would
rapidly set up a mission.

> It is clearly my duty to do all I can to have a Christian catechism
> brought at the earliest possible date to the knowledge of these
> tribes, and it is incumbent on me to draw attention to the fact
> that adequate measures have not been taken by the Anglican mis-
> sion to do this for the septs on the north-east coast.[139]

In 1897 the Reverend Canon Stone-wigg of Brisbane was con-
secrated as Bishop of New Guinea, but in 1898 the total Anglican
Mission staff was fourteen and only seventeen Papuans were
baptized that year.

MacGregor officially asserted that

> all Christian churches are exactly alike, and that which does the
> best work will be the most appreciated . . . so that the natives may
> derive from them the greatest possible benefit.[140]

Publicly he praised all denominations and their leaders, including Bishop Verjus, 'a well-educated man, broad-minded and an
excellent missionary',[141] though he was not personally sympathetic to the Roman Catholic Church and his diaries reveal his
Protestant prejudices. After a visit to a Roman Catholic station
near Mekeo he wrote 'I went into the house of the sisters, at
present, in their absence, occupied by the bloodless brothers';
he saw pictures which he described as being 'of the rather
repulsive crucifixion type'; he smelt 'in the men's quarters that
musty smell which is almost peculiar to lunatic asylums'.[142] Yule
Island Mission records show that MacGregor's prejudices were
reciprocated and Navarre wrote in 1889:

> Toutes les autorités et presque tous les commerçants et capitaines
> sont écossais, presbytériens et franc-maçons du vite écossais qui
> est le plus acharné contre l'église . . . je ne serai pas étonné qu'ils
> nous persécutent par tous les moyens. . . . Le gouverneur de Nlle
> Guineé qui est lui-même écossais presbytérien et franc-maçon comme
> aussi les ministres protestants de la société de Londres, parle déjà
> de nous faire payer des droits de douane sur le pied du Queensland.
> Et le vin qui nous fions venir de l'Australie nous coutera d'entrée
> pour plus de deux fois de sa valeur. Et cependant il nous en faut
> pour les malades.[143]

When the two men met, however, they found more in common
than Navarre's statement might suggest, and more importantly
Navarre realized that MacGregor was not as opposed to his
church as he anticipated.[144] Bishop Verjus was also much im-

pressed by MacGregor, especially by his encouragement to this Mission to expand in the St Joseph district, and he wrote: '*Le Gouverneur a été charmant, et cependant Mgr Navarre me dit de m'en défier. Mon Dieu! je suis donc bien nigaud que je ne vois rien de bout ce que l'on m'annonce! que ferais-je donc si j'étais seul? Mon Dieu, Mon Dieu, je vous en conjure! faites-moi mourir avant Mgr Navarre!!!*'[145]

The Sacred Heart Mission, however, quarrelled bitterly with the London Missionary Society about its operations in the Mekeo district. Besides general Catholic-Protestant differences this was particularly based on the alleged corruption of London Missionary Society native teachers which the Catholic missionaries claimed was well known by the British administrators but was ignored because the London Missionary Society was

> *toute puissante au gouvernement. Elle a rendu et rend encore en bien des endroits sous le rapport politique et des interêts nationaux bien des services à l'Angleterre. Ou le gouvernement redoute cette société ou on lui conseille de fermer les yeux.*[146]

The quarrel was intensified by sectarian pressures in the Queensland and British governments. MacGregor wrote to Griffith

> We have let the Sacred Heart mission have 155 acres and a good frontage. They are sapping and mining in Queensland to get more. I have adhered to the principle we agreed upon, to let them have a liberal allowance, and then to take a firm stand. I have now done with it. They will certainly appeal. I believe they have already been at Lord Ripon on the subject.[147]

MacGregor clashed with the Roman Catholic leaders on this issue. Navarre complained to MacGregor in 1896, alleging preferential treatment of the London Missionary Society. MacGregor in reply stressed that Australian public opinion, which could not be ignored, supported the division of the island into religious spheres, and therefore

> the government recognises the mission districts and will no doubt continue to support them so long as the missions do their duty in occupying with reasonable speed the fields assigned to them. . . . I make no distinction between the different missions. I am most anxious to see a Christian catechism brought to every tribe in this colony. To what sect that catechism may belong is to me, as far as religious teaching is concerned, a matter of complete indifference.[148]

A review of the various disputes between the London Missionary Society and the Sacred Heart Mission over land grants suggests that, despite private prejudices against the Sacred Heart Mission, official attitudes were unbiased.[149] Attempts were made to do justice irrespective of religious beliefs.

MacGregor tried consistently after the 1890 meeting to insist on the principle that only one mission would work in one village and sought ratification of this policy by the Australian colonies and the Colonial Office in 1896. His argument was that the government had to intervene as any clash, whether physical or spiritual, could disturb the peace of 'a large population only half a dozen years out of the stone age'. He admitted that spiritual conflicts were unlikely as

> so few Papuans set any value on religious teaching that it is very doubtful that any serious disturbance could arise between native communities merely on account of sectarian difficulties; but there is no want of innumerable other old causes of quarrel that could be stirred up to set the different tribes by their ears in the name of conflicting faiths if missions were to be rival candidates for a few villages near the coasts, instead of directing their efforts to the hundreds or thousands that are neglected towards the interior.[150]

The Queensland government and the British Secretary of State for the Colonies, Joseph Chamberlain, endorsed Mac-Gregor's policy, but the Catholic Archbishop of Westminster, Cardinal Vaughan, argued that the State should not have intervened and that a Protestant governor must inevitably favour a Protestant mission. The Colonial Office, however, discounted Roman Catholic objections, basing their views on MacGregor's defence of his policy and his counter-attack on the Sacred Heart mission claiming that there were far more unoccupied Sacred Heart stations than London Missionary Society stations. Further he claimed that

> the London Missionary Society complies with the law and makes its applications before it occupies; the Sacred Heart sometimes does so also, at other times it disregards the law and occupies first.[151]

MacGregor's objections to the Sacred Heart Mission went beyond personal and religious convictions and included national motives. Thus in a confidential despatch to Admiral Bridge he objected when there was a possibility of a French warship visiting the Yule Island mission station. Such visits, he said,

> are apt to assume objectionable forms, apparently with the object of impressing on natives and others that the mission is under their

N

protection. The head of the Roman Catholic Mission here [Navarre] is a Frenchman of the type that dislikes everything English so cordially as to avoid all knowledge of their language and institutions.

A later despatch stated that

the Archbishop wishes to pose as the friend of the natives and to protect them from the English. This will enable [you] . . . to understand clearly what advantages the Archbishop—a Frenchman of the ultra anti-English type—would try to derive from the visit here of a French ship of war.[152]

The possibility, however remote, of a French coup in New Guinea in 1897 added to MacGregor's private opposition to the Sacred Heart Mission, which in his official capacity he tried his hardest to conceal.[153]

MacGregor was always prodding all four Christian missions to do more work and was disappointed in their failure to travel far inland or to occupy the north-eastern coast. How far Christianity was accepted by the natives is difficult to ascertain. Most missions were very well aware of this difficulty and knew that even after twenty years (as in the case of the London Missionary Society) true converts could not be expected to be numerous. But MacGregor, in assessing the value of missionaries to the government, emphasized their value as a civilizing agency:

on fair play, on mission teaching, and on the example of decent lives in the presence of the native race, is built that intangible fabric of moral force by which alone we hold our footing in this colony . . . years ago I pronounced mission teaching to be indispensable to the progress and settlement of a country such as this is. Experience only confirms this opinion. We can have no better colleagues than the members of a loyal mission . . . the coloured teacher with all his human failings has been to us a most important ally.[154]

Father Dupeyrat has criticized MacGregor for what seemed, to him, a narrow approach to religion: *'Il avait l'étroitesse d'esprit de ne considérer le religion que comme une forme de gendarmerie nécessaire à la police d'un pays'*.[155] This judgement, based particularly on MacGregor's statement of indifference as to which Christian sect worked in which tribe, does less than justice to MacGregor's own Christian—admittedly Protestant—beliefs and to his attitudes to the missions in New Guinea.

Besides their moral assistance to the government, the missions were responsible for what little was done in the colony in the way of education. MacGregor's £15,000 could not extend to any expenditure for beginning government schools, so that the only schools were those run by the missions.

Only a small percentage of Papuan children attended any school in these ten years. In 1898 there were about 6,000 students in the schools: 3,600 at eighty schools run by the London Missionary Society; 1,100 at over twenty schools of the Sacred Heart Mission; 1,176 at twenty-three schools of the Australian Wesleyan Society; and about 200 in seven Anglican schools.[156]

The education provided was very limited and usually not adapted in any way for Papuans. As the missionaries realized that their greatest hope of obtaining true converts was by working through the children, much time was spent on teaching religious doctrine. Few of the missionaries were trained teachers, with some exceptions, particularly among the Roman Catholics. MacGregor seemed impressed with the belated commencement of the Anglican school, St Marks, at Wedau. After his inspection on 14 July 1898 he testified that the writing and arithmetic of the younger children 'appeared to me up to the level of European children of the same ages'. Altogether he was

> satisfied that a substantial educational foundation has already been well begun, and I look forward to the time when the fruits of it will become manifest on the whole of the north east coast . . . I wish that some of those that question the utility of mission work could or would come here and judge for themselves.[157]

But there were only 200 children in Anglican mission schools.

The native colleges set up by the missions to train future evangelists represented the only form of institutionalized education beyond the primary stage. Even there the education was limited.[158]

Trade schools, such as were set up by a London Missionary Society missionary at Matadona, teaching carpentry and joinery to the boys, washing, ironing and sewing to the girls, could have value in giving these children the opportunity of employment by Europeans.[159] The majority, however, probably never used their acquired skills after they left these schools. MacGregor gave encouragement to the London Missionary Society's suggested similar new industrial settlement, particularly because it would teach 'our people that labour is honorable'.[160]

MacGregor, concerned by the slowness of educational progress, decided in 1897 to institute a native regulation making school attendance compulsory on three days a week for all children between the ages of five and thirteen. The sanction was a small fine on the parents of defaulters. MacGregor had consulted all four missions and some of their suggestions were incorporated in the regulation. The London Missionary Society objected to the principle of compulsion, but wanted the government officials to bring about the same result by inducement. They also suggested that a qualified officer be appointed to protect and defend defaulting parents and children. MacGregor said he would leave it open for individual members of each mission to decide whether the regulation would be enforced in their schools.

The regulation insisting on compulsory school attendance was not questioned by the Queensland government. It was, however, criticized in the Colonial Office as 'practically a measure for compulsory conversion', since all the schools were missionary schools. The Secretary of State, Chamberlain, overruled this objection, agreeing with MacGregor's practical justifications for the regulation, for there was no other method of giving any immediate impulse to education as the colony could not afford to establish state schools.[161]

As MacGregor left British New Guinea in 1898 there could by then have been little result from a regulation introduced only in 1897. It would be unfair to criticize him for not introducing the measure earlier, as it would have been hard to introduce any effective educational measure before government rule had been established.

9

New Guinea: The Quality of His Rule 1888-98

The modest record of a wonderful ten years work.

It remains to consider what changes MacGregor's policies made in the lives of the Papuans. As has been seen, the first effect of his extension of government control could be described as destructive, as he tried to eliminate those aspects of native culture which were incompatible with 'civilization'. Nevertheless, he wanted to preserve much in native society and tradition and to ensure that change was gradual:

> It is impossible to civilise such people hurriedly . . . if we proceed too rapidly and try to do too much, if we pursue a destructive policy, I fear a very great evil will ensue.[1]

Did MacGregor ever envisage how European and Papuan cultures could be reconciled? He realized his measures were changing native lives,[2] but overwhelmed by day-to-day affairs he probably regarded this reconciliation as a future problem, to be dealt with by his successors, sympathetically following the guide-lines he had established.

His first concern was to establish control and to enforce order and respect for the individual by law. MacGregor had accepted the British veneration for the rule of law, though he understood that Papuan society could be based on commonly accepted unwritten principles, such as reciprocity. In 1894 Winter presented an analysis of the importance of justice in Papuan communities, which, even though open to much criticism in the light of later anthropological analysis, shows that he, like MacGregor, sought to understand native society rather than simply to condemn Papuans as barbaric savages.

> The Papuan has undoubtedly a keen, though a perverted, sense of justice. His whole system of ethics has for foundation the principle of compensation. Compensation for a crime may be given in blood or property. Only time and experience can convince him that it is

safer for himself to leave the State to extort the 'payment' for a crime. He is quite clear that 'payment' must be had in some form or other.[3]

Written law was traditional in British colonial rule and was administratively far easier to enforce than any reliance on unwritten conventions, especially since MacGregor realized that he was imposing a new unity on the great variety of Papuan cultures by passing regulations common to all British New Guinea. The laws, however, allowed considerable latitude in the imposition of penalties and government officials were given discretion in enforcing them.[4]

The laws of British New Guinea were a combination of those operative in other British colonies (especially Queensland), ordinances specially drafted for the colony, and simplified native regulations. The Colonial Office had instructed MacGregor to introduce a judicial system that was, 'as far as . . . possible, summary in its operation and free from technicalities of procedure'. The codes of other British colonies, such as Bechuanaland and Zululand, were suggested as models.[5]

When British New Guinea became a British colony all British law suitable, enforceable and not inconsistent with the acts forming the colony was in theory introduced. MacGregor had then to decide which laws should be copied. Governor Musgrave opposed copying Queensland laws as

> altogether premature and inapplicable to the present condition of the territory where the great mass of the inhabitants are native savages, and those of European extraction do not number as many as 30,[6]

but MacGregor, supported by Griffith and by Winter, decided to introduce them as a temporary expedient. These laws were made applicable to all natives, who became by the declaration of sovereignty British subjects, although MacGregor passed legislation which could exempt the natives of any defined district from the operation of any law.

In addition the Colonial Office insisted, from British experience of the nature of contracts between Europeans and natives, that strict regulations be enacted prohibiting the supply of firearms, ammunition, explosives, intoxicating liquors or opium to the natives. As has been stated, these essential concomitants of European civilization were judged to be unsuitable for Papuans.

MacGregor introduced a Central Court, presided over by a single judge, to hear indictable charges, whether against whites or natives. Below this he set up Courts of Petty Sessions, presided over by resident magistrates, who were given jurisdiction, covering both summary charges and committal proceedings in indictable charges, equivalent to police magistrates in Queensland. In 1889 special Native Magistrates Courts and Native District Courts, presided over by magistrates for native matters, were given jurisdiction in cases which would arise from the native regulations. Though MacGregor intended that the magistrates for native matters would eventually be Papuans, no Papuan was appointed during his governorship.

MacGregor rejected trial by jury as 'of course inapplicable',[7] since there were very few Europeans in the territory and the Papuans could not be expected to understand such a system. Procedural rules were made simple, to the extent that the judge could act as counsel for the defence.

Appeals, available to Papuans, could be made from the Central Court to the Supreme Court of Queensland in criminal cases when a sentence of over three months was imposed, or in civil matters involving property valued at more than £100. MacGregor suggested in 1891 that this right should be eliminated for Papuans because of the consequent delay in carrying out the sentence and the time expended by government officials in travelling to Brisbane. Griffith, however, insisted that all residents of British New Guinea should retain this safeguard of their rights.[8] In MacGregor's decade no Papuan exercised the right of appeal.

When death sentences were imposed the Administrator-in-Council had the power of review and the Administrator had the right to overrule the advice of his council. As the judge of the Central Court sat in the Executive Council, he had an opportunity to reconsider his judicial decisions on equitable and humanitarian grounds. Winter often advocated that death sentences he had imposed as a judge should not be carried out.

The 1889 introduction of native courts was accompanied by the appointment of a Native Regulation Board consisting of the Administrator, at least two other legislative councillors and such others as MacGregor appointed, to consider 'questions relating to the good government and well-being of the native population'.[9] Besides this consultative function, the board was empowered to draw up regulations for natives, which had to be approved by the Administrator-in-Council and the Legislative Council and reviewed in Queensland and London. These regulations, covering both civil and criminal matters, were framed in simple language so that they could easily be explained to Papuans. The chief object of the 1890 civil claims regulation was 'to appease quarrels and disputes about property and rights, real or imaginary'. Such claims covered arguments about the exclusive right to the use of land, water or reefs, or claims to the produce of land or trees. In 1893 a civil regulation was introduced to control the disposal of the estates of deceased natives.[10]

The criminal regulations forbade acts which were regarded as incompatible with civilization and which interfered with the spreading of British control. The main ones were stealing (1890), adultery (1891), assault (1890), sorcery (1893), certain burial customs (1890), spreading of lying reports or using threatening language (1891), destruction of coconut trees (1894) and the destruction of any valuable tree (1895).

An examination of the offences which led to most actions in the various courts is the best way to illustrate how MacGregor applied the new laws to bring about the desired changes, though the fact that they were enforced differently in different areas, depending on the degree of government control established, must be taken into account.

The most serious charge against Papuans was that of murder, which was heard in the central court under the Queensland Crimes Act.

> If I can only put a check on the abominations committed here constantly in laying in wait for and murdering women and children I shall feel I have not come here in vain. The natives of this country put some value on human life as something that it gives them pleasure to destroy, but in no other sense is it valued or respected.[11]

MacGregor hoped by imposing punishment to change existing custom:

> the payment of blood money is the established usage of the country and it cannot be put down until the penalty of our law for the commital of murder has been inflicted on a number of native murderers,[12]

and was opposed to the

> sentimental and doctrinaire propaganda of those that would teach that the native murderer should be dealt with leniently, because it has been customary for the Papuans to treacherously butcher each other.[13]

During MacGregor's ten years of office 418 Papuans were charged with murder and about two-thirds of these cases were brought to trial.[14] A verdict of guilty was returned in 138 cases, for all of which the death sentence was imposed. In only eleven cases was the death sentence carried out, however, all for murders committed before June 1894. MacGregor's argument that he wanted to enforce death sentences only as a warning and as an example of the power of the government gains support from these figures and from the increasing commutation of sentences. The carrying out of capital punishment was approved in every case both by Queensland—most of whose politicians had far less concern for Papuans than had MacGregor—and by the Colonial Office, despite its realization, from bitter experience in many other colonies, of the dangers involved in applying British laws in cases where native customs were so important.

The motives for these murders—inter-tribal warfare, sorcery, revenge for stealing, sexual offences—indicated to MacGregor the customs which he would need to eradicate in order to reform native society. It could be argued that action against the customs causing the murders should have preceded action against murderers, but MacGregor's reply would partly depend on administrative realism. He felt it was impossible to impose control over the people when murders were so frequent and that if he could stop the murders this might change the customs. Thus he attempted to 'educate the natives out of murder'[15] by the publicity given to the arrests and subsequent trials and punishment. His European and Papuan officers were all instructed to do their best to persuade the Papuans not to kill. He also, of course, proceeded against many of the customs by the native regulations. The total effect of this 'education' campaign is hard to assess, however, for even if in villages under control the number of murders decreased, the possible traumatic effects on related customs and the balance of native society cannot be measured.

One special category of murders was the thirty cases where non-natives were killed by Papuans; in sixteen of these the death sentence was passed and ten Papuans were executed. The Papuans could well have argued that British law had operated in a way that closely resembled revenge, for of the total of eleven executions for murder, all but one were for the murder of whites and the one exception was for the murder of a government official, a native of the armed constabulary.

Obviously MacGregor's decision to carry out the death penalty in these cases involved a motive additional to his desire to enforce respect for the sanctity of individual life. These executions were part of his policy of showing the power of the government, just as official patrols followed any murder of a white man. Papuans had to be shown that they could not kill any representative of the government with impunity and this was soon applied to all white residents, for MacGregor realized that government officials, missionaries and traders were often lumped together by Papuans. Even if there were apparent justification for the murder in the conduct of the white victim this would not be considered a defence.

The clearest illustration of this was the murder of government agent George Hunter, provoked by his ill-treatment of his latest native mistress. Several Papuans conspired to kill him; all were tried; six were sentenced to death and two were executed. Had Hunter been a Papuan almost certainly all sentences would have been commuted to imprisonment.

A relevant factor in determining the punishment in most cases of murder was the degree of contact experienced between the government and the natives responsible. Where there had been little contact the natives could not be expected to realize that murder was forbidden, thus treatment would be more lenient. But this could be ignored in cases where the victim was white, as was shown in the case of Ansell, when MacGregor decided that severe punishment was necessary to enforce the power of government, and was further illustrated by the murder of a trader, Albert Kickbusch, at Woodlark Island. MacGregor overruled the Executive Council's recommendation for commutation, one of his grounds being that the question was not essentially

> affected by the point that the natives had no previous practical acquaintance with the Government. Had there been none in the country they would have been punished by the High Commission [of the Western Pacific] an authority of whom they had no knowledge whatever.[16]

MacGregor's decision was also influenced by his awareness of the long history of contact with missionaries and traders on Woodlark Island.

Despite the conflict between his humanitarian feelings and his principles MacGregor had to be realistic about these executions: in a situation where so few whites had nominal control over so many Papuans and individual life was regarded as so unimportant by the Papuans he had to take strong measures. Cases of violence that did not lead to death were proceeded against for the same reasons. The large number of these cases adds to an appreciation of the extent of MacGregor's problem of controlling violence.

Larceny, one of the motives which was seen as an important cause of murders, produced the greatest number of proceedings in all courts. MacGregor, who was always trying to encourage native planting, frequently met the excuse that any crops planted were sure to be stolen. There were several additional problems involved in the concept of larceny, however, for some Papuans— individuals, kin groups or even wider groups—had proprietary rights in various goods and some did not recognize individual ownership. Further, as exchanges with whites increased, new standards of values were imposed and goods previously worthless to the natives became well worth owning. In every case Mac-Gregor insisted on imprisonment, rather than imposing a fine or other form of compensation, to try to replace the native custom of resolving differences by payment or exaction.

Adultery led to a large number of proceedings (435) in the native courts. After debate both in New Guinea and Queensland it was decided that not only an adulterer but also an adultress should be punished, and MacGregor pressed for the enforcement of this regulation when it was introduced.[17] This regulation is particularly open to criticism, for conduct regarded as marital irregularities by British law could well be the accepted custom of Papuan groups. Again MacGregor's justification would be the relationship between adultery and cases of violence.

In 1893 a native regulation forbade the practice or pretence of sorcery, threatening any person with sorcery, or procuring another to practise sorcery. MacGregor argued that this was necessary because most Papuans believed that death was caused by sorcery rather than by natural causes and this belief led to a large number of murders or acts of violence following deaths, in revenge against sorcerers. MacGregor realized that

> it may be objected . . . that in passing a law for the suppression of the practice of sorcery a reasonable inference is being supplied to the native that the white man believes that there is such a thing; and that thus ignorance and error are being perpetuated while they should be left to education and teaching.

His solution lay in precedents in English, Fijian and West Indies laws whereby the 'pretence' of holding such powers was made an offence. He realized that it would take generations to extinguish the oppression of men practising sorcery and the belief in them, and that 'the utmost patience and caution is necessary. . . . Each measure has to be begun tentatively and delicately'.[18]

MacGregor admittedly did not fully realize the important functions of sorcery in native culture, but he did have to face the problem of violence and thus was acting in what he felt to be the natives' interest. Sorcery would have been better combated by an attempt to achieve a complete change in native beliefs, but this of course was beyond MacGregor's power. Moreover, later anthropological studies suggest that the effect of MacGregor's regulations was far less than he hoped as the belief in sorcery was little diminished. Indeed it has been suggested that sorcery accusations increased as control widened as a symptom of native reactions to bewildering white values and institutions.[19]

The spreading of lying reports, forbidden in 1891, was a typical reaction to white rule which emphasizes how bewildering the presence of Europeans was to the Papuans. These reactions have been classified as manifestations of what is now called the cargo cult. The underlying idea is a belief by some Papuans that they are the rightful owners of all goods used by the whites, often associated with a conviction that a ship would bring these goods as a cargo to them, and that all whites would finally be killed, enslaved or removed from New Guinea. Prophecies of this type appeared at an early stage in the history of New Guinea. Thirty-six cases of 'spreading lying reports' were heard in the courts up to 1898, some of which were almost certainly associated with manifestations of this cult.[20]

An indication of how far MacGregor was prepared to go in changing native society is shown by his marriage ordinance of 1897. This regulation was opposed by the Colonial Office and was never put into operation. MacGregor's approach was particularly conditioned once again by the number of cases involving violence and death that had been caused by breaches of custom concerning marital relationships. He wanted to introduce the western concept that marriages should follow the free choice of two individuals. Thus he planned to end marriages which were forced on unwilling spouses, criticized the bride-price system, the limitations placed on the choice of partners by kin group or totemic restrictions and the restriction that widowers and widows should not remarry.

He wanted to retain some limitations on freedom of choice,

however, including restrictions because of consanguinity, which followed those accepted by Christian countries: he used European kinship terms in the ordinance, such as grandchild, nephew, stepson and half-brother, which must have been unintelligible to many New Guinea groups. He included restrictions providing that no boy under fourteen or girl under twelve could be married, while marriages between the minimum ages and sixteen needed special consideration of the welfare of the parties and the views and wishes of their parents. He hoped that this ordinance, in combination with other government regulations, would help in the creation of unity from the diversity of New Guinea cultures.

Temporarily a choice was to be given between this new way of defining and celebrating marriages between Papuans, and prevailing marriage customs, and he wanted the new system to be introduced gradually, for 'violent change is to be avoided so as to spare native susceptibility'. Nevertheless he believed that native customs, such as totemic restrictions on marriage, were losing their force as white ideas spread:

> The provision as to 'totem' relationship is applicable to the northeast coast, the islands, and as far west as Mairu, beyond that point I have not been able as yet to identify 'totemism'. The totem is losing its force already, and it will soon become feebler but will probably not become extinct for many years yet.

He revealed his firm belief in the inevitability of change and the superiority of Western to native forms of marriage: 'what is at fault . . . is the condition of native society, change it for the better and the system will die out'.

MacGregor sought the advice of all four mission bodies before introducing this ordinance. Many objections were made, with most of which MacGregor disagreed. He did not think it was necessary, for example, to introduce a divorce ordinance at the same time as a marriage ordinance; he did not agree that brideprice was so important to native culture that it should be retained; he refused to accept the evidence that totem marriages were not declining; he denied that the administration lacked the power to enforce this ordinance.

The Colonial Office, however, gave more heed to mission objections, as well as doubting on other wide grounds the wisdom of introducing such an ordinance at this particular stage of New Guinea's development. Some support was given to MacGregor, however. It was suggested that certain native customs should be condemned, such as the bride-price and the ban on widows and widowers remarrying, based on the 'principle . . . [of] the gradual substitution of a more perfect form of marriage contract for old native customs'.

Doubts about the timing of the ordinance arose from a consideration by a senior clerk, Anderson, of British colonial experience:

> In Natal where we have the most perfect form of native administration in the world worked out by the Shepstone family[21] the marriage of natives by Christian rites is only allowed when the natives are Christians and further have been formally exempted from the operation of native law.

As the Papuans had far less knowledge of Christian marriage status than Natal Zulus, the ordinance should be deferred and

> the proper policy would seem to be to discourage rather than to encourage natives from entering on a marriage involving a status of which they can have but a very imperfect conception, and probably conflicting at every turn with all those ideas which are part of their mental framework. . . . Sir William McGregor's long outburst about the evils of the purchase system shows how completely at variance native and European ideas are. The native pays for his wife because he thereby acquires a useful chattel. . . . It is no doubt desirable to change all that but if, as Sir William MacGregor advocates, we are to 'avoid violent change' and 'spare native susceptibility' this is scarcely the way to do it.

Chamberlain, the Secretary of State, accepted this advice against the ordinance:

> We must certainly shelve this question. I cannot understand what has prompted Sir William McGregor's zeal, or why he could not 'let it alone'. New legislation must be confined to the strict minimum that is necessary to meet any proved or urgent grievance.

MacGregor's feelings that there were existing grievances that could be met by this ordinance were therefore overruled and he was advised that it exceeded 'the present requirements of the Possession'.[22]

MacGregor realized that he was destroying much of the Papuan culture by these criminal regulations, even if he did not appreciate the extent of mental confusion caused by his administration. He seemed to believe that somehow the resultant gaps in native belief could be filled by the basic tenets of humanitarianism and of Christianity: his native regulations could be interpreted as an application of the ten commandments.

In contrast to these 'thou shalt not' type of regulations were those like the 1894 law, which compelled each village to 'make and keep clear the roads on its land or near the village'.[23] Government officials worked through Papuan authorities in enforcing this regulation—the village authority decided which work was to be done by each Papuan. If the share was not done and the task allotted was judged to be reasonable, offenders could be imprisoned for seven days. In the next year a further roads regulation provided that Papuans had to consult government officials before they blocked any path. Permission would be granted only if an alternative way was first made.[24]

In 1897 a carriers regulation was passed making it compulsory for villages when requested to supply carriers to the government. MacGregor had found difficulties in obtaining Papuan assistance on some of his patrols. His opinion that such a regulation could be enforced shows how control was increasing.[25] All prosecutions were in the more controlled Central District.

From his concern with the health of the Papuans arose a regulation in 1890 which forbade keeping bodies unburied or burying them within occupied villages. The regulation was enforced with caution since MacGregor realized the significance of burial rites to native society. The punishment was almost nominal—a maximum of only three days imprisonment. No legal proceedings were to be taken against offenders until a burial ground had been chosen outside a village, and magistrates were given a discretionary power as to whether or not to prosecute. Some of the Roman Catholic missionaries opposed the introduction of this regulation, as interfering overmuch with native custom, but its enforcement was gradually increased as control spread.[26] There were few proceedings until after 1896, when it was utilized particularly by Dr Blayney in the Central District.

The shortage of government finance, which had always hampered adequate action in Fiji, proved even more restrictive in New Guinea. MacGregor introduced the Queensland Health Acts, but could not adequately enforce them. His despatches and letters repeatedly show examples of his awareness of the tremendous medical problems both of the Europeans—he and almost all his officers suffered regularly from malaria—and of the Papuans. A diary entry reads:

I do not know that I ever saw so many sickly people in a native village as there are at Wereweri [on Mullens Harbour]. Two lepers, one eruption, a woman of 30 suffering from Coko, a great many

with lipoid sores and ulcerations. The houses are all falling into
decay and are really very bad.[27]

After only three months in New Guinea he spoke on its diseases
to the Second Session of the Intercolonial Medical Congress of
Australasia. He admitted that he had not devoted much time to
medical subjects, so that his paper was little more than 'rough
notes', but these prove his awareness of the problems, and of the
urgent need to check the spread of diseases. For example, he
said of tinea desquamans that it was his misfortune to have to
witness in some areas the further distribution of this loathsome
malady and anticipated that 'it was only a question of time,
when it will be distributed over the whole of New Guinea'. He
reported that Papuans thought that yaws, which he had only
seen in a mild form, had always been present in the New Guinea
islands, 'but they think nothing of it'. Leprosy was rare, as in
the rest of Polynesia, and did not occur in the malign and
tubercular form to which he had become accustomed in the
Seychelles. Elephantiasis was also rare, and he had not found
any cases of dysentery, 'the scourge of the tropics'. Ophthalmia
and venereal disease he had also not seen, though he felt that
both would probably soon come. Fever was the bugbear of New
Guinea, especially for Europeans. His conclusion was optimistic,
however, for he thought the Papuans were generally 'a healthy
race',[28] and it is true that at no time in his ten years were there
to be the tremendous decimations of population that there were
in Fiji, caused by widespread outbreaks of dysentery or measles.

He repeated some of his optimistic verdicts about health in an
1895 address[29] which amplified some of the points he had made
in 1889: 'in all probability . . . the day will come when British
New Guinea will be regarded as one of the healthiest of the
tropical Colonies of the Empire'. Scarlet fever, smallpox,
chickenpox, measles and whooping cough were unknown. Dysentery was all but unknown, and the

> deadly, multiform, contagious dysentery that has devastated the
> South Sea Islands and has produced at times such deplorable and
> ruinous mortality among the South Sea labourers in Fiji and
> Queensland, is quite unknown.

Leprosy occurred only in its milder forms, yellow and typhoid
fevers were unknown, rheumatism rare, croup unknown and
diphtheria had not yet been introduced. No case of cancer had
come under his notice ('but lupus is common, frequently des-

troying the nose, cheeks and eyes of natives'). Tuberculosis was rare; tapeworm was unknown.

His main theme, however, was one of warning on the need for careful enforcement of health regulations:

> The four diseases that have been devastating the Pacific are first and before all others, dysentery; then hooping cough, measles, and venereal disease. Civilisation will introduce and distribute these in New Guinea; can it, or rather will it, control them? It has not done so, but it has not fairly tried to do so, in the majority of the Pacific Islands.

A few cases of venereal disease had since 1889 been introduced from Australia and he realized how difficult it would be to prevent this disease from spreading.

On his theme of warning he stressed again the prevalence of malaria, the 'great bugaboo of British New Guinea'. This was before the mosquito theory had been evolved and he listed as predisposing causes

> long exposure to the full glare of the sun, severe fatigue, cold produced by wet, but above all else a cold wind playing on the body, or even on a part of it, producing sudden cessation of transpiration from the skin.[30]

Prophylactic measures included doses of five-grain tabloids of quinine and antifebrine and he claimed that 'when anyone, native or European, perceives the approach of fever he makes application for two or three tabloids, and in nine cases out of ten nothing more is heard of it'.

Besides malaria he again stressed the importance of skin diseases such as tinea, yaws and scrub itch which were 'unfortunately too common' and were likely to spread over the whole colony. At least 'it was not civilisation that introduced this pest [tinea desquamans] into British New Guinea, though it will, it is to be feared, greatly facilitate its spread'.

The comparative lack of development of medical remedies among the Papuans had the result that:

> Although they are very suspicious of strangers, they do not hesitate to take the white man's remedies. Their favourite medicines are Epsom Salts, quinine and bluestone, but many of them have come to know the beneficial results of speedily applying permanganate of potash to snake bite, and will hurry to a missionary or government officer to have this tried.

Magical measures were usually regarded as more efficacious, however, and MacGregor gave limited praise to native methods of

o

treatment. On one occasion he suffered an attack of fever on a path between two villages separated by a swamp, which he did not want to wade through until he recovered.

> Swift messengers, sent spontaneously by the natives, speedily brought six women from the nearer village. They carried a mat on which they deposited the patient, and in half an hour they, aided by two grains of quinine, squeezed the fever out of him. But it would be hard to say which was the greater relief, to be free from the burning fever, or to be delivered from the kneading of the dozen hard and wiry hands of these active and industrious manipulators.[31]

In MacGregor's last few years in New Guinea he tried to take measures to improve health conditions, yet he never went as far as he had in Fiji or attempted to introduce a similar scheme for giving some natives elementary medical training. As late as January 1898 a magistrate in the South-Eastern Division commented that:

> It seems a matter for regret that the native teachers do not undergo a slight training in medicine before being sent, as they often are, to places where it is not possible to obtain advice from Europeans and many simple complaints become, through inability to treat them, very serious complications.[32]

There was one fairly serious epidemic of dysentery in 1897 in the Kerepunu district. Dr Blayney reported ninety-eight deaths, and had ordered the London Missionary Society clergyman Pearse at his services 'to instruct natives re epidemic and [to tell them] that medicine would be given to all sick'. Belated attempts were made to enforce sanitary advice: 'Inspected water holes, found them in a disgusting state, pigs, dogs etc. allowed to use them', Blayney wrote,[33] and a native was given seven days imprisonment for throwing the body of his son into the river.

MacGregor's most positive steps were taken in 1898 with the introduction of ordinances providing for the compulsory vaccination of all Papuans, and for the establishment and maintenance of public hospitals.[34] After cases of smallpox were reported in German New Guinea MacGregor insisted that all officials, European and Papuan, be vaccinated. The Reverend Copland King also vaccinated some Papuans on the north-east coast. The Colonial Office refused to give immediate sanction to the vaccination ordinance, however, and left it for reconsideration by MacGregor's successor, the reason for delay being that vaccination by force might lead to agitation against the ordinance;

and that the provision for isolating a village where there were smallpox cases might lead to the extermination of the whole population because of the lack of medical staff.[35]

This 1898 dilemma of lack of staff preventing action that could save many lives was the constant bugbear of MacGregor's health programme. Lack of money also explained why legislation for public hospitals was only passed in his last year. Malaria and skin diseases continued little checked; many Papuans still died at a very young age and were by 1898 subject to far more of the diseases of 'civilization' than they had been in 1888.

MacGregor hoped to make all his laws effective by punishing Papuan offenders, as well as by the deterrent effect of these punishments. He also introduced a peculiar application of the reformatory theory of punishment. He attempted to 'educate' Papuan prisoners to accept some of the values of white civilization: the prisons were to be the adult 'schools' of the colony.

MacGregor's ideas of punishment are shown more in the practical administration of the prisons than in the ordinances governing them, which followed closely the form of the Queensland Act applying penal theory. The prison rules, however, were based on MacGregor's Fijian experience, applying Gordon's methods,[36] including an instruction to gaolers to treat prisoners with 'kindness, humanity and impartiality'.[37] The beliefs of white civilization were not inculcated by any formal schooling (which MacGregor regretted) but by insisting on 'obedience, regular habits, and the inflexibility of government orders'.[38] This discipline was based on compulsion and stressed, like the visits of inspection, the power of government. The sanctions for disobedience were not heavy and there was no corporal punishment: 'No adult prisoner has been flogged, and it is to some extent owing to this that our prisons have been perhaps the best educational establishment in the country'.[39] Physical labour was the main occupation and many government works were carried out by this labour force.

At first his system did not work, for 'prisoners fretted, lost courage, pined, sickened and died',[40] but he persisted and the prisoners' resistance against his methods gradually lessened. The change in native reactions was probably largely due to the conversion of a few long-term prisoners who realized the futility of resistance and perhaps the advantages they could derive from more co-operation with their gaolers. It is extremely doubtful,

however, despite MacGregor's claims, whether they fully understood the system or that they accepted white values.

Nevertheless all prisoners were inculcated to a certain extent
with an awareness of the government. Even if this did not go
beyond knowledge of its superior power it was important,
especially when these prisoners returned to their home villages.
Having been imprisoned by the government did not necessarily
affect their status in their home villages. On the other hand, their
position could well have been enhanced. Often a returned
prisoner was given authority from the government, as Mac-
Gregor chose many of his village constables from ex-prisoners,
while other ex-prisoners joined the armed constabulary.

MacGregor derived many of his colonial ideas from his
experience in Fiji, thus he tried to apply to the Papuans the
tenets that their land should be secured to them; their lives
should be as little disturbed by government or other whites as
possible; they should follow the traditional, usually agricultural
economies and they should not be forced to supply labour for
white planters. Each one of these tenets was revised during his
governorship better to suit what MacGregor felt were the needs
of the Papuans and New Guinea.

Because of his conviction that the Papuans should not be
deprived of the ownership of their land he was ready to disregard part of the Colonial Office instructions which, in accordance with their ideas of the normal development of a British
colony, provided for the purchase of land from the natives.

> While it will be your duty to take care that the natives are not
> deprived of land which they are clearly not desirous of parting
> with, yet when a proposal respecting land is brought under your
> notice, and you are satisfied that it is fair in itself, and that its effect
> is really understood by the natives, there is no reason why you
> should not give effect to such proposals by purchasing the land
> for the Government, in accordance with the law, and subsequently
> transferring it.[41]

He was also instructed that he could regard uninhabited and
unclaimed land as Crown Land.

During his first few years in New Guinea MacGregor reverted
to a very literal interpretation of Commander Erskine's promise
to the Papuans in 1884 that their lands would be secured to
them, so that no European acquisition of land would be
recognized. In so doing MacGregor varied the policy of his
immediate predecessor, Douglas, who had supported European

settlement with a number of compulsory land purchases from Papuans and favoured large land concessions to Europeans. MacGregor's reasons were similar to those held in 1883 by the Fijian governor, des Voeux:

> even for the purely economical interests of Australasia, and apart altogether from higher considerations on the score of humanity, the best policy to be pursued in Polynesia [here intended to include New Guinea] would be to discourage planting there except such as could be carried on in each island by the natives indigenous to it, there being no other apparent means of putting an end to the depopulation now going on, and of thus preserving the only secure foundation for commerce in the future.[42]

MacGregor's predisposition in favour of the Papuans was reinforced by the knowledge he gained of the companies and individuals who were seeking land in New Guinea, for he doubted whether they were sufficiently concerned with the welfare of the Papuans. Thus when asked in 1890 to give his views on a proposal for ' "opening up" the country for the benefit of the younger sons of English gentlemen' MacGregor replied, 'I should never spoil a native tribe to make room for any other person'.[43]

Moreover, his early patrols convinced him that until the Papuans had some idea of the government's intentions it would be unwise to alienate land, especially as 'Papuans are agriculturalists . . . [who] are almost entirely dependent on their gardens for the means of existence . . . [with] fixed proprietary rights in the soil'.[44] Another reason stemmed from his belief that hard physical work by whites in the tropics was inadvisable, so that white plantations would need to use Papuans as labourers. As he wished to protect Papuans by keeping them working in their own villages and as he doubted whether a surplus of labourers existed, he did not at first advocate such plantation labour and thus discouraged would-be white plantation owners.

A very strong reason for his opposition to unchecked white occupation of the land arose from his desire to encourage native efforts. In March 1891 he told Griffith that 'the more I see of this west country confirms my first impression that we must teach these natives to build boats and fish and trade on their own account'.[45] Thus in 1890 he began a government coconut plantation at Tauko (Fisherman) Island near Port Moresby, hoping to encourage similar work by Papuans, and in 1894 introduced a native regulation[46] making it compulsory for some natives to plant coconuts. He regarded this as the culmination of one of the main points of his policy, for this regulation had

> directly to do with the industrial, economic and commercial future of the native race of this colony.
>
> If the natives do not become producers on their own account, if they cannot greatly increase present exports and create new ones, they cannot exist long as a race. . . .
>
> In consequence of the gigantic strides that have been made in settling so many of these savage tribes, it is liable to be forgotten what a heavy task lay before the government five years ago to prepare any place whatever for . . . such a Regulation . . . it may be thought that this modest beginning could easily have been commenced long ago, and without any laborious preparation. Much . . . patience has however been required to clear the way even so far as this . . . there are many hundreds of tribes to which it is, and will for long remain, inapplicable; but there are scores that can now be made to plant under it. . . .
>
> Clearly in the face of my views as to the future of the country such a Regulation should be introduced as soon as it is thought it can be enforced . . . I believe that under wise perseverance with it the export of the produce of the coconut tree can be enormously increased here, and the position of the natives be greatly improved by the same means.[47]

The limited area of the colony under government control, MacGregor's restricted finance to pay for experimental plantations to ascertain which crops could be economically produced, the few staff available to supervise and encourage the Papuans, were some of the reasons why his plans were only partially successful.

Macgregor used government finance to experiment with possible crops, both for native producers and later increasingly for white producers. A botanical garden was begun near Port Moresby; aid was given to those settlers who were prepared to experiment; bananas and coffee were introduced from Jamaica, through Kew Gardens. He tried to exploit local plants, such as the wild fig for possible rubber, but with little success. He also discussed the economic possibilities of a mallow *(hibiscus ecultentus)*, pigeon pea and West Indies ginger. Most of the tropical crops tried did not succeed either in production or in finding markets, however, though one of the few exceptions was india-rubber,[48] which became a significant export for a few years after 1897.

The main agricultural product during most of MacGregor's administration was copra. Except for using more of the coconuts on already planted trees, the only way to increase production was by new plantings. As it took about five years before new trees bore there was an inevitably prolonged introductory stage of low production.

Timber production had declined since the Protectorate days, when there had been a considerable trade especially in cedar. A brief sandalwood boom after 1892 led to MacGregor's introduction of a regulation to prevent Papuans destroying young trees.[49] Sea products were always of considerable value, and *bêche-de-mer,* fisheries and pearling provided important exports. Gold was the most important mineral found in the colony, although hopes were held for coal production.[50] But in all these industries the Papuans contributed little. Most of their production remained on a primitive level of agriculture for their own subsistence. Only as labourers did they significantly contribute in production for export. MacGregor's optimistic hopes of 1893 for their economic future proved dupes throughout his governorship.

Ever since Europeans had arrived in New Guinea they had used Papuans as labourers. Papuans were paid less than Europeans, but there was no apparent shortage of volunteers. Thus on the mission stations natives built houses, helped in the gardens and did domestic work. Papuans collected *bêche-de-mer,* or attended to the smoke houses which cured them. One trader claimed in 1887 to employ about 1,000 natives.[51] Other Papuans collected coconuts, or helped in the maintenance of plantations. Payment varied, but was usually in kind, such as hoop-iron, foodstuffs, tomahawks, beads, salt and half-axes. Eventually tobacco became the accepted means of payment in most parts of Papua.

Some Papuans from the Louisiade Archipelago had been taken to work on the Queensland sugar plantations between 1881 and 1884, which led to the clash between Griffith and McIlwraith discussed earlier.[52] Partly because of the abuses of the labour traffic it was a fundamental provision of the acts creating British New Guinea that Papuans could not leave the colony for any purpose. MacGregor was fully in agreement with this, particularly because his experience in the Seychelles and Fiji with Indians and Polynesians had taught him so much about the difficulties of imported labour. The use of Papuans was advocated in Queensland several times, specific proposals in 1892, 1895 and 1898 being defeated mainly by MacGregor's firm opposition.[53]

MacGregor allowed some exceptions to the ban on Papuans leaving the colony, however. The most significant concerned those who worked for Torres Straits fishermen. As these Papuans had traditionally worked in this area MacGregor was loath to interfere, though it was against the law. He obtained a list of Papuans engaged by the Thursday Island fishermen and in 1891 proposed concurrent jurisdiction by Queensland and British New Guinea, suggesting that Griffith should pass a labour law similar to that of British New Guinea. MacGregor was confident

> that if you [Griffith] could find the time you could arrange the means whereby your magistrate and ours could each have jurisdiction in the Straits. Once that is done I can advise greater elasticity in regard to the employment of our natives in the Straits.[54]

By an 1892 labour ordinance Papuans were allowed to be employed in the Torres Straits fisheries, if their employer lived or had a business in New Guinea and if his boats were stationed in New Guinea waters.[55]

MacGregor wanted to extend his jurisdiction to include the control of recruiting in the Solomon Islands and the New Hebrides and obtained Griffith's support for his attempts. He was opposed by the High Commissioner for the Western Pacific and by Queensland's Governor Norman, however, and the Colonial Office never approved of the scheme.[56]

Another way partially to solve the problem was to adjust the border between New Guinea and Queensland, extending New Guinea's jurisdiction southwards. Some Papuans went farther south to the islands just off the Australian mainland, however, which Queensland would never sacrifice.[57]

Another exception to removing Papuans from the colony was made by the provision allowing missionaries to take Papuans for education and instruction as far as 10° South.[58] This exception was based on a London Missionary Society plan to place the centre of their western district on Dauan, an island within Queensland territory. In 1893 this mission exception was extended beyond 10½° South to allow the Sacred Heart Mission to take Papuans to Thursday Island.[59]

Two other exceptions were made in 1898. Papuans could be engaged as seamen for one voyage to and from Australia or to other parts of New Guinea, on a ship whose owner lived or had his place of business in British New Guinea. European missionaries were permitted to take natives to Australia for the special purpose of aiding translation of religious books. Both exceptions had to be covered by adequate guarantees.[60]

Inside British New Guinea the use of labour was also controlled. By an ordinance of 1888[61] no Papuan could be employed more than ten miles from his home, except with his consent and that of his 'tribe or family'. Government service and employment on coastal boats for periods up to six months were also exceptions. All employment was safeguarded by guarantees of fair pay, fair treatment, return of labourers to their homes after discharge, and by insistence on records being kept and regular government inspections being made.

Because he hoped to encourage the Papuans to become 'useful producers' by stimulating increased production of their traditional agricultural crops, MacGregor was not opposed in principle to the mobility of Papuan labour to aid Papuan industries needing more workers. He saw no objection to using Western Division Papuans in aiding coconut plantations in the Central Division, for example. As Papuan industry did not develop as much as he hoped he became more interested in encouraging European enterprises. Nor did he object to Europeans using Papuan labour, so long as it was duly safeguarded, and his increasing support of European enterprises meant that he also supported a gradually extended use of Papuan labour.

MacGregor stated in 1889 that he regarded the internal restrictions on the mobility of labour as temporary since he hoped to break down the 'domestic exclusiveness of the different coterminous communities' to make a unified colony. Increasing mobility would also follow his policy of gaining control over the Papuans, which would make it safe 'to allow natives to be freely removed for employment to or from any place within the boundaries of the possession'.[62] In March 1889 he divided the colony into two 'native districts' (each side of 148°), so ending the ten mile restriction, for Papuans could then be employed anywhere in the district in which they lived. In these districts the regulation of labour contracts was left to the discretion of the resident magistrates.[63] The result was that the services of the Papuans were not as closely supervised as their rights to land. Every claim to land was reviewed by the Executive Council, but this would have been far too time-consuming a procedure for the signing-on of labourers.

The *bêche-de-mer* fisheries were regulated by a series of special ordinances in 1891, 1894 and 1897,[64] which included some clauses dealing with labour. The names of all labourers engaged for over a month were required to be entered in a written agreement and the master of the ship was responsible for paying for the return home of his labourers. From 1894 wages had to be paid at least every three months, in the presence of a government officer and without deductions for money advanced or goods supplied.

In November 1891, after more than three years in the colony, MacGregor decided that the government had gained sufficient control to relax restrictions on the employment of Papuans. He argued that 'the removal of natives from one district to another can not only be permitted without danger, but would be a positive advantage to all concerned'.[65] A new ordinance was passed in 1892[66] in line with his 1889 hopes to allow the free employment of Papuans anywhere in the colony. More freedom of contract would help to solve the language problem, teach the Papuans habits of industry and new forms of cultivation and would aid employers by giving them more Papuans to choose from.

The ordinance provided that all private (as distinct from government) employment of Papuans, which was to last for over a month, or which involved the Papuan moving more than twenty-five miles from his home, was to be regulated by contract. These contracts were to be drawn up before government officers and the term of employment was to be limited to a year. The ordinance tried to ensure that the labourers were willing recruits and that they were protected during their employment: conditions of work, amount of pay and methods of treatment were all defined and made subject to government inspection. MacGregor's experience in Fiji was reflected in his insistence on adequate diet, the observance of sanitation rules (for shelter, sleeping quarters and bedding) and provision of medicines. If these obligations were neglected by the employer the Papuan could be returned home by the government at the employer's expense. It was an offence for an employer to hinder or refuse to answer any inquiry affecting the welfare of his labourers. The maximum punishment for all offences was £50 or three months imprisonment.

The employer was protected from fulfilling his obligations if the labourer died, deserted, refused to return home or leave his place of employment, or was committed for an indictable offence or imprisoned.

Dr Mair has praised this labour ordinance as being 'a long way in advance of the legislation of its time', particularly because of the lack of a penalty for labourers breaking their contracts and because of the restricted term of one year for employment.[67] MacGregor's concern to protect the Papuans is shown clearly both by the ordinance and by its operation in the following six years. During 1893 eleven officers were appointed to carry out the recruiting and inspection provisions of the ordinance. These included government officers, a missionary (the Wesleyan Reverend William Bromilow at Dobu) and private settlers (T. Anderson of Dedele and R. E. Guise of Hula). Three more officers were appointed in the following years, including another settler, E. C. Lobb of Woodlark Island. The shortage of staff necessitated such extra-governmental appointments, but they also reflected MacGregor's trust in the missionaries and some settlers.

The increasing permissiveness of MacGregor's attitudes to the employment of Papuans was shown in March 1893:

> In my opinion it is desirable for the general common weal, as well as for the native race itself that restrictions on the employment of the latter should gradually be removed as the natives become prepared to fight their way in the world, until their labour is made as free as that of a white man.

> But the removal of restrictions is a matter that requires time as it demands some previous education. If planting does not prosper sufficiently in other parts of the Possession to furnish employment for these western tribes, who, now that war is no longer a profession for them, have time on their hands, it will become an urgent matter to find marine employment for them.[68]

Another way in which he sought to remove restrictions was by encouraging the development of individual, rather than mass, employment of Papuans. He introduced an ordinance in 1893 'to facilitate and encourage fair and equitable job contracts and other dealings between natives and others'. These contracts had to be in writing if the job was to be done more than twenty-five miles from the Papuan's home, if it was to take longer than six months, or if the pay was to be greater than £5. Inspectors were to be appointed to approve the contracts. Examples of the 'other dealings' which would be governed by this ordinance were the sale or purchase of boats. MacGregor wanted to protect the Papuans from being given old, rotten, worthless boats or from attempting tasks which were beyond their means and power in order to get a boat. As was noted in the Colonial Office these were 'tentative steps towards encouraging natives to enter into civilized transactions', in so far as MacGregor was treating the Papuans as individuals with rights and trying to enlarge their horizons.[69]

In 1893 MacGregor found it necessary to introduce an amendment to the 1892 labour ordinance[70] which seemed to conflict with his earlier policy. The amendment provided for a penalty for natives who deserted from, or neglected to enter into, agreed labour contracts. Thus one facet of Dr Mair's praise of the ordinance is justified only for the first five months of its operation. Yet a case can be made for the consistency of MacGregor's motives. At all times he was more concerned with the clause protecting willing workers being abused by unscrupulous employers. He believed that Papuans who undertook regular employment for Europeans would be improved by these services and he probably omitted penal clauses in the original ordinance because of an optimistic trust that the virtues of undertaking paid tasks would become obvious to the Papuans. When, however, cases of desertion occurred, he realized that further 'education' was necessary before the Papuan could reach the 'civilised' state of accepting the need for work. The penalty imposed was to be a month's imprisonment and loss of wages. MacGregor realized that compulsion might be necessary to convince the men of the value of agricultural work, so much of which was traditionally done by Papuan women. It is not coincidence that six months after he made this change in the labour ordinance he introduced the regulation making it compulsory for certain Papuans to plant coconuts. A further motive behind this amendment was his increasing realization that if there was to be any economic hope for New Guinea he must encourage white development, and thus the supply of Papuan labour.

Between 1893 and 1898 both private and government employment of Papuans increased. In 1898 twenty per cent of government expenditure was for native services. Besides the armed constabulary and village police, all boat crews were Papuans. The labour provided for under the coconut, road and carrier regulations all increased the numbers of Papuans engaged in non-traditional tasks.

The emphasis of MacGregor's labour policy swung farther towards limiting the restrictions on employers, as was shown by an 1897 ordinance[71] which allowed areas to be declared 'settled labour districts'. The south coast was immediately declared settled. In this district labour contracts did not need to be in writing unless the labourer was working sixty miles from his home (instead of twenty-five as previously) and any qualified officer could engage labour, not only a resident magistrate. In addition, a clause provided for punishment (fourteen days with optional loss of wages) for a labourer refusing to work without reasonable cause. Other changes in favour of the employers came later in 1897,[72] when it was provided that deserters could be handed back to the employers by the Court and that anybody inducing or assisting a deserter was liable to punishment. MacGregor declared in his final report of 1898 that the next step he envisaged was an increase in the period of contract, as well as declaring more areas as 'settled labour districts'.[73]

His policy was a logical extension of his ideas of 1893, as his underlying motives had been strengthened in the five intervening years. From the experience of plantations he had found more need to educate Papuans about the value of work; he had become more conscious of the failure of his plans to make the Papuans independent producers. Thus he wrote despondently that 'natives are not likely alone to ever add much to the exports of the colony'.[74] His encouragement of white development had culminated in his plans for large-scale enterprises, notably the British New Guinea Syndicate and his sympathy for the employer was growing. At the same time as dominant groups in Australia—after the 1890s strikes which involved the issue of the open shop against unionism—had concluded that organized labour could not be trusted, MacGregor had decided that the Papuans needed to be persuaded to work.

An outline of the development of gold-mining, the major European industry, suggests the extent of the support MacGregor was prepared to give to European expansion. Specific legislation, visits of inspection, the appointment of special staff and of prisoners to assist, could all be justified by MacGregor if he felt that increased production would follow.

Gold obtained in the Possession was the most valuable export recorded, almost every year, and in aggregate was far ahead of any other product, comprising about sixty per cent of exports. In addition, gold-mining attracted the majority of whites who came to New Guinea. As an excess of exports over imports was interpreted as meaning that the colony was self-supporting, every encouragement was given to greater production. Direct revenue to the Possession was comparatively small, coming at first from miners' rights and later from mining leases and dredging claims. Indirectly, revenue came from the increased white population because of increased customs revenue from greater imports of foodstuffs and other goods. The total value of all gold exported from 1888 to 1898 was only £103,592, however, and thus insufficient to aid MacGregor to any appreciable extent. But these figures for gold exceeded the total value of the other four major exports: pearlshell (£27,972), *bêche-de-mer* (£25,005), sandalwood (£21,232) and copra (£19,858).

The control and regulation of the miners was one of MacGregor's constant concerns, beginning with the problems of a gold-rush to Sudest Island in the month he arrived. At first MacGregor was inclined to regret the number of miners (in 1888 there were 700 to 800 on Sudest and St Aignan) because he wished to give priority to the work of establishing control over the Papuans. He did not, however, oppose gold-mining and in 1895, when a measure of control over the Papuans had been established, he suggested greater inducements to prospectors and gave as much governmental support as he could to those already in the colony. Nevertheless in 1897, in an article published in the Australian and British press,[75] he warned prospective gold-seekers of the limited aid he could give them, as well as stressing the difficulties of the country and the need for each miner to have some capital.

The Queensland mining laws, which were adopted in 1888, provided for the declaration of certain areas as gold-fields. There were four areas so declared in the following decade: Sudest on 8 October 1888; Louisiades and Misima on 27 May 1889; Woodlark on 6 November 1895; and Gira (on the north coast) on 5 July 1898. The Queensland laws provided for Gold-Wardens with their own courts and jurisdiction in these areas. Their powers did not exclude those of the resident magistrate of the particular division. Nor did they prevent other enterprises, fishing or agricultural, from being carried on in a gold-fields area.

The land rights of Papuans were nominally preserved in these gold-fields as in other areas of the colony, but apparently not as carefully as claims by Europeans for lands used by Papuans for agriculture or fishing, especially when rich finds of gold were involved. For instance, although MacGregor reported that the Sudest operations had not touched native plantations, because the miners were only working in the creeks and watercourses, these waterways were probably essential to the plantations. Similarly the Saganai gold-field settlement on St Aignan was built on the site of a native village, the houses of which had been sold to the storekeepers for tobacco. The justification for not interfering with this alienation (which was not even considered by the Executive Council) was that the village was never more than a fishing village for Papuans who lived in other parts of the island.[76]

Each of the gold-fields presented special problems for Mac-Gregor. On Sudest the initial rush was embarrassing because of his unpreparedness and his lack of staff, though it was not sustained, and by 1890 the numbers on the field had dropped to 150 and by 1891 to seventy. MacGregor tried to encourage one company which had introduced quartz-crushing machinery, by allowing it to use prison labour, in the hope that quartz-mining would become a stable industry and induce further settlement. The venture failed, however.[77]

The Misima field, later called the Louisiades, never prospered. There were 500 miners there in 1889, 150 in 1890, but after that never more than fifty. All prospecting on various islands—on Joannet in 1888, on Rossel in 1888 and 1893, on Normanby in 1889 and 1895 and on Fergusson in 1895—proved unrewarding.

The Woodlark field, proclaimed in 1895, was more profitable. Within a year there were 190 mining there, in 1897 400, though numbers fell to 160 in 1898. On a visit to this field in July 1896 MacGregor appointed the local storekeeper as a justice of the peace and postmaster. There was no Gold Warden as MacGregor had not enough staff, so that the warden on the Louisiades field was given jurisdiction over this field. Petitions from the miners for government officers increased after some minor clashes with the Papuans.

On the mainland such clashes were more frequent, for the miners often penetrated new areas in their search for gold. Mac-Gregor reported his own finds whenever he saw possible gold-bearing rocks on any of his visits of inspection, and he encouraged miners in 1895 by increasing the area of the claims given as rewards for new discoveries. Searches behind Bartle Bay in 1894 and 1895 were fruitless and the leader of one party was murdered by Papuans who had not previously been contacted by the government. Prospecting above Goodenough Bay also failed to find any gold. Then in 1895 a party under an experienced Queensland miner named Clarke, moved to the Mambare River where the natives had never seen Europeans except for infrequent government patrols. Disagreements between the natives and miners led to the murder of Clarke and retaliation by the miners, who, MacGregor charged, 'illegally set about inflicting punishment after their own fashion by breaking canoes, shooting pigs and burning houses'.[78] He maintained that they should have defended themselves and left punishment to the government.

Papuan hostility was the main problem on these northern gold-fields, for

> Whereas in other parts of the Possession it has been found feasible to gradually bring tribe by tribe under Government influence, using a nearer tribe to prepare and instruct another more remote, this method in the present instance was rendered impossible by the sudden rush of miners into the interior immediately after the discovery of the goldfield,

and the natives were 'unusually aggressive and difficult to bring under restraint'.[79]

Developments on these gold-fields forced government action. In 1895 a patrol of twenty-three men was sent to investigate the murder of Clarke and a government agent was left at a new station at the junction of the Mambare River and Tamata Creek. About twenty-five prospectors kept searching in this difficult country, in the headwaters of the Mambare and in the mountains behind. MacGregor praised one of their journeys, led by William Simpson, as 'by far the most arduous undertaking ever performed by any private exploring party in the colony'.[80] The murder of government agent, John Green, in 1897 resulted in more government patrols, one led by Moreton and one by MacGregor, to placate these natives who MacGregor said were 'more warlike, pugnacious and cunning than we have had to deal with hitherto'.[81] Eventually the area was pacified and the prospectors who had remained were assisted by the Papuans. The proclamation of the Gira gold-field in July 1898 was a sign that control had been established.

Thus except for the first few years of his rule MacGregor saw no major conflict between supporting this industry and Papuan rights. The same can be said for his land policy. He respected the Papuans' rights to their land and in his first few years tried to prevent whites unsympathetic to native rights from coming to New Guinea. In the whole decade he granted less than 14,000 acres to non-Papuans, and declared only about 700,000 acres as vacant Crown Land. As there were claims by large firms in 1888 for areas from 250,000 to 1,000,000 acres, the limiting effects of his policy were clear. If an alternative policy had been adopted he would have been far less able to cushion the impact of Europeans on the Papuans.

In 1897-98, however, he supported the British New Guinea Syndicate's claim for 250,000 acres and said there was plenty of land available to meet such claims.[82] His increasing concern with encouraging white settlers was not a complete *volte-face,* for even before he reached New Guinea he had considered the problem of land alienation, and much of his time was later spent on deciding the validity of claims to land obtained by various means prior to the declaration of sovereignty in 1888. Although he did not formally decide any of these claims until 1891, in the intervening thirty months he did not exclude missionaries, traders, fishermen and settlers who were using land for their various purposes.

He seemed to grant these individuals a kind of semi-official permission to remain; thus a coffee planter wanting 250 acres asserted in 1889 that

> no natives claimed the land in question; but, nevertheless, we had to obtain the consent of the Administrator at Port Moresby before we could commence operations. His consent was readily given.

The formal claim for the land was made later, in 1891, and granted.[83] Similarly, MacGregor supported increased land grants to the missionaries, to aid their expansion.

All land legislation before 1890, MacGregor stressed, only provided the machinery for granting land and in no way committed the government to any particular line of action. MacGregor's instructions empowered the Administrator-in-Council to make grants and other dispositions of land in accordance with some future ordinance. An 1888 law[84] declared all previous dealings in native lands null and void, affirmed that only the government could purchase land from the natives and said that land would be able to be transferred to others by methods to be designated in a later law. An 1889 law[85] provided for the purchase of land from the natives as Crown Land; another law in the same year[86] adopted the Torrens system for regulating future titles; a third law[87] to regulate future Crown grants, subject to the discretion of

P

the Administrator-in-Council, allowed grants to persons who had acquired their land before 4 September 1888 and had since enjoyed peaceable possession.

The Crown Lands Ordinance of November 1890[88] was the first land legislation under which action was taken. Private claims were divided according to whether they originated before 1884 or during the Protectorate (1884-88). Grants could be made depending on proof of purchase and lack of disturbance of native rights. Government purchases and leases were similarly legalized and land could be acquired as waste and vacant if it was neither used nor reasonably likely to be used by natives. The control of future sales and leases of Crown Lands was the main object of the ordinance. The colony was now open for settlement.

MacGregor's policy at this stage was not in favour of large-scale settlement for he had not yet found enough vacant land. Nor did he feel that the government had sufficient control over the Papuans to allow for any development of an *imperium in imperio* which would follow if a company were given a large area to exploit. He did, however, want to encourage small-scale settlers, who could be controlled by the government and whose relationships with the Papuans could be strictly supervised. He still hoped that Papuans would be the main producers, with their efforts supplemented by European settlement. These aims could conflict with each other and were the cause of his writing some contradictory reports. For instance he wrote that 'any plan for the systematic settlement of an agricultural population of Europeans . . . is inadmissable', yet in the same report he wrote, 'the agricultural settler who is prepared to turn the land to use is the only land purchaser for whom there is any opening'. An even more positive welcome for some settlers was also included: 'areas of good land of a few hundred acres each are procurable at very many places in the Possession suitable for almost any form of tropical cultivation'. So there was a good field for 'industrious men with small capital' who could inspire the natives to systematic cultivation for export.[89] The distinction he made between 'selectors' and 'speculators' shows his problem:

> I want people to come and settle upon the land. . . . We have received several applications for land, but they have been mostly for large areas, such as half a million or a million acres. Of course I could not entertain any such application, as the granting of them would mean serious interference with the native tribes. . . . A few hundred acres is quite sufficient for the bona-fide selector, and as

for speculators—well, we simply don't want them, and we will not have them![90]

MacGregor was worried because the value of imports was so far above that of exports—the difference in each of the three years to June 1891 was £5,000, £10,000 and £7,000. He was influenced, too, by the fact that the grant for the maintenance of the colony was so small and he could see no crop or mineral becoming a staple for the islands. The situation worsened after 1891.

Consequently MacGregor increasingly encouraged white settlement. From the contradictory statements and opposition to speculators in 1891, he changed by the end of 1892 to a hope that on the rivers flowing into the Gulf of Papua he might find lands suitable for sugar growing and so 'induce one of the large sugar companies to take up land and start operations there'.[91] He found in the Gulf area in January 1893 'a large quantity of [unoccupied] fine land fit for settlement . . . well adapted for growing sugar-cane, corn, tea and coffee'.[92]

By 1894 he was convinced that Europeans could do hard manual labour despite the climate. While on leave in England in 1894-95 he encouraged potential settlers and capitalists to become interested in a variety of tropical products, saying they would find cheap and good land, a supply of local labour and a fairly healthy and agreeable climate undisturbed by hurricanes.[93] At the same time in London he had an interview with 'the head of a great firm established in Sydney' and negotiations dragged on until the end of 1897. He approached two other Sydney firms, to one of which repeated offers were made. MacGregor reported that the main object of all these companies was to start a sugar industry in New Guinea.[94] By 1896 he could claim that the 'most discouraging element' in the colony was that no European planting on 'a scale of any importance' had been started.[95] In 1897-98 he strongly supported the grant of land and rights to the British New Guinea Syndicate.

An analysis of the land claims[96] in New Guinea shows Mac-Gregor's increasing concern in white development. Claims, including all from the earliest settlement, were first decided at the end of February 1891. In the six years to 1896 some five hundred were considered: 235 private claims, in addition to 234 mission claims and thirty-seven dealing with the acquisition of Crown Lands. In the next two years, however, there were over two hundred claims: 135 private claims, seventy-two mission claims and a few dealing with Crown Lands. As all these were discussed in the Executive Council an increasing amount of time was being spent by MacGregor and his leading officials on matters relating to European expansion. The detailed work done by the Council indicates not only MacGregor's lack of trust in his staff at lower levels of administration, but also the import-ance he placed on land alienation.

Council Minutes show that the interests of the natives were consistently given full consideration. Certain principles were insisted on: land must not be too close to a native village; crops or trees on the land must be purchased separately; native water holes must be reserved; every purchase must have the full con-sent of natives; full details of all transactions must be approved. These principles led to considerable delay—sometimes up to ten years—yet only about thirty claims were eventually disallowed. In purchasing land for the government consideration always had to be given to economizing, so that if natives' demands were considered too high, the land was not purchased.

At no time was there a rush of prospective settlers to New Guinea. The delay in settling land claims and the belief that priority was given to native rights must have discouraged some. MacGregor's later attempts to attract Europeans could only partly overcome these considerations, especially when they were reinforced by such constant factors as the continued slow expan-sion of most crops, the disadvantages of the climate, reports of the savagery of the natives and the better opportunities (despite the economic crises of the period) in near-by Australia. In fact much of the land was taken up in a few hands. The greatest landowner was the shipping and trading company of Burns Philp, which owned land in over thirty parts of the colony, ranging from a plantation of 1,280 acres (the largest single grant to 1896) to various small trading stations of one acre each. Until 1896 there were only about twenty holdings of over fifty acres, including two owned by Burns Philp. The majority of holdings were small, either town allotments (of which there were fifty) in Port Moresby (Ela, or Granville West, and Granville East), Poukama (Hall Sound), Samarai and Daru, or trading stations (of which there were about forty).

After 1896 when the emphasis of MacGregor's land policy was known to be changing, seventeen applications for large areas, averaging 300 acres each, were lodged: five of these came from government employees and seven from established settlers; only five were from outside New Guinea. Following the British New Guinea Syndicate claim, another seventeen applications were lodged, mainly from outside the colony. These included a claim for 250,000 acres by the Adelaide and New Guinea Rubber Planting Syndicate, and one individual application for 10,000 acres to plant rubber.

Clearly between 1888 and 1898 there had been a change of emphasis. In the early years there was a tendency to disallow or delay claims if there was the slightest doubt that native rights were being neglected, but by 1898 the initial tendency was to seek for available land. At the end of his term in New Guinea MacGregor claimed that his policy had always been dominated by support for European development:

> from beginning to end the goal of the Government of the Posses-
> sion, acting entirely under control from Queensland, and with the
> full and uninterrupted concurrence of that colony, has been to
> convert the country into a British colony. The officers of the Pos-
> session have not worked there day and night for the past ten years
> simply to put down inter-tribal warfare and to reduce the natives
> to control. They have been trained to treat natives justly and
> fairly, and to see that they are so dealt with by others; to fit them
> for a useful place in developing the resources of the Possession;
> but above all to prepare the country for development by Euro-
> peans. There is not, and there has not been, any other policy.[97]

As an analysis of the whole of his governorship this is correct, although it plays down his constant efforts to protect the Papuans and obscures his discouragement of large-scale settle-ment in his early years in New Guinea. (This claim was also made at a time when MacGregor was seeking to lull opposition to the British New Guinea Syndicate scheme.)

Such general statements are important in bringing together the various facets of his policy. MacGregor was a governor of a British colony and as such was expected to develop it. Every step he took in the interests of the Papuans had to be compatible with such an end. In arriving at a verdict on his administration this point must be kept clearly in mind. He was not an indepen-dent leader with freedom to choose his own policies; he had neither adequate funds nor sufficient staff to carry out the policies he desired; and he did not have the benefit of anthro-pological analyses of New Guinea's many cultures, nor even the opportunity to obtain much insight into their ideas—he was restricted by the nineteenth-century boundaries of knowledge and by the fact that his own time was overcrowded.

The Colonial Office was unstinting in its praise at the end of his rule in British New Guinea and in 1897 supported his recognition as Companion of the Order of the Bath.[98] His final report, which reviewed much of what he had attempted, was said to be a

> modest record of a wonderful ten years work . . . if McGregor had not inspired those serving under him with some of his own indomitable patience, perseverance and courage there would have been less praise to give and less result to show. It is one thing to possess those qualities and another thing to inspire them in others.[99]

In the framework of the limitations on his policy verdicts such as 'little short of miraculous'[100] have been applied to his work.

MacGregor, however, found only a limited degree of satisfaction in his achievements in New Guinea, because he knew better than anyone else how much more was needed. The restrictions placed on his policies by Queensland and the Colonial Office drove him almost to despair on occasion.

A similar lack of satisfaction can be discerned in his personal life. He was unable to make a home for his family; the various visits of his wife to Australia hardly compensated for this deprivation. He left all his family in Lausanne, Switzerland, after his 1894-95 leave. Apart from these five months of his leave he missed the childhood of his two favourite daughters: he saw practically nothing of Viti between her third and fifteenth years, nor of Mary between her first and thirteenth years. He had already lost all effective contact with his only son, James, and his first daughter, Helen.

He had always been ambitious and his realization of the unimportance of New Guinea must have irked him. He was torn by conflict between his duty to New Guinea and his personal ambition. He had despondently passed his fortieth birthday before he came to New Guinea and was to pass his fiftieth before he left. Six months before he was fifty he wrote:

> My time here is slowly but surely drawing to a close and my sinews cannot remain forever elastic. I have therefore to get over as much work and ground as I can while I am able to do so.[101]

His heartfelt cry that 'after a man has passed 50 he is not fit to go over those mountains. I think I am becoming physically unfit for it'[102] could be applied to his governorship as a whole, for it demanded a younger body to face its incessant problems.

His experiences on leave in England and on the continent in 1894-95 did not completely make up for his despair of 1893. Gordon reported that 'MacGregor is now here and a bit of a

lion',[103] but MacGregor was never one to attach much importance to social success. He found more satisfaction in the distinguished audiences at meetings of the Royal Colonial Institute,
and of the Manchester and Aberdeen Geographical Societies, all
of whom listened to his analyses of the problems of New Guinea
and praised his work. He felt even more rewarded by the receipt
of an honorary doctorate of laws from Aberdeen University and
an honorary doctorate of science from Cambridge University.[104]
But he received only limited promises of any more money or
other aid from the British government.

Another cause of frustration was the contrast between the
importance of the issues he met in his wide reading and the
triviality of many of his daily problems. Also, as his correspondence shows, he often felt isolated from major happenings
in the outside world. He found relief from the monotony, tedium
and triviality of many of his tasks in his books. Most of his
reading seems to have been of serious works. He seems to have
had no time for novels, although he read and enjoyed poetry,
and he maintained his interest in classical language and literature. He 'read most of the *Iliad*, scores of times',[105] including
when he was on patrols, and he praised Gladstone because he
knew and understood 'the *Iliad* far better than any other man
that has ever read that work'.[106] MacGregor also read Latin and
he asked Griffith to obtain some old Latin hymns for him.[107]

He enjoyed studying modern languages. He kept up his French
and German and in May 1891 he told Gordon he was learning
Italian to enable him to read Dante and the new Italian criminal
code which came into force in January 1890.[108] He wanted to
read the latter because of its possible significance for New
Guinea, for instance, in defining adultery as a crime, 'but I have
only a German treatise on the Italian code and hence the necessity for my learning Italian at once'.[109] When on leave in
Brisbane in 1894 he sent Griffith a copy of *Il Codice Penale* and
a small Italian dictionary. 'The latter will only do till you
procure a better. Millhouse's seems to be the best English-
Italian and Italian-English'.[110] Back from Europe he assured
Griffith he need not return the Italian code for

> when in Italy I obtained a complete set of all the Italian codes. The
> Italian is in my opinion the best criminal code, and next to it comes
> the German one. I doubt that any person, except yourself, would
> have a code converted into law in a British colony; and I fear
> you may have great difficulty in getting it put through.[111]

In 1899 Griffith's Crimes Act of Queensland, the first codified criminal law in Australia, was enacted.

This shared interest in the Italian language became a constant link between Griffith and MacGregor. The latter became Griffith's confidant and critic about his work on Dante. MacGregor received as a parting gift from Griffith in 1898 a dedicated copy of his translation of *Stories from Dante*. MacGregor thanked Griffith from Switzerland:

> several of my fellow passengers were much interested in them. Unfortunately my trunk in which they are has not yet reached Lausanne, but I have promised copies to several people like Principal Sir William Geddes and to some Italians. I hope you will not rest on your laurels, but continue until you have done the whole *Divina Commedia*.[112]

MacGregor's main interest in modern works was in biography and history. He applied his knowledge of modern languages, particularly of French and German, in reading books and periodicals in these subjects.

> I wish you [Griffith] would take in *La Nouvelle Revue*. I subscribe to *La Revue des Deux Mondes* and we could then exchange when anything interesting turned up in them, they are both excellent periodicals.[113]

In April 1890 he advised Gordon that

> perhaps the best periodical I get, next to the *Revue des Deux Mondes*[114] is the *Deutsche Rundschau*, which I can strongly recommend to you if you do not take it in.[115]

Some indication of his reading and his critical ability comes from comments in his letters. He had old favourites, like Schiller's *Geschichte*, which he read on alternate nights to the *Iliad* on one patrol, as 'they were the two smallest books he possessed'.[116] B.D.S. Baden-Powell remembers MacGregor 'sitting beneath a palm-tree, gun in hand, reading Goethe in German, or a French edition of the *History of the Ottoman Empire*'.[117]

But he also seemed to keep up well with new publications, despite his isolation. In January 1889, for example, after a long description of New Guinea matters and a discussion of the possibility of Australia leaving the Empire, he wrote:

> Now let all those weary subjects rest. Have you copies of Von Beust's *Memoirs*—or of volumes published by Duke Ernst of Saxe-Coburg? If either, let me have the book . . . I should prefer to have them in the original if you have got them in that form for I know you learned German. I find these memoirs much more instruc-

tive than any ordinary history. I have seen a review of the Duke's memoirs in the *Revue des Deux Mondes* and fancy they must be extremely interesting.[118]

Nine months later he received some of these from both Gordon and his bookseller,[119] and had just finished reading the third volume of Duke Ernst's *Memoirs*, in which there were many allusions to Gordon's father. He advised Gordon, who was writing a biography of Lord Aberdeen, to see these memoirs

> in original before you complete your work, as his acts and policy are several times disapproved of by the Duke, although generally he speaks of him favourably. We are reading Walpole and Lecky just now, with Pierson's *Preussen*. I shall get Bismarck's memoirs from Lucas Graefe as they come out. I have got Gustav Freytag's *Frederick*. I do not care for Lecky. His history is a series of essays. I am reading also Michelet's *Revolution*, the state centenary edition, which I recommend if it is still procurable. I cannot find in Australia a copy of the *Lex Salica*, and have to send to London for it.[120]

In other letters he reported reading 'the life of Dupleix by a Frenchman, and Frankish Institutions by F. de Coulanges [which] I found very interesting' and 'Kugler's Life of William the I, the finest combination of the mild and firm the world has seen'.[121] Or, from another letter in October 1890:

> I have just got through the life of Lord John Russell. I am disappointed with it. It is patchy somehow, and is not quite well woven. It seems to contain but little that is new. It shows next to nothing of the internal working of the state machine. It is in this way far behind the Duke of Saxe-Coburg's memoirs. Still it has left me with a feeling that Russell was honest and honourable and nearly a very great man. His Reform became a God: and he showed badly in the American dispute. In fact, only two of our statesmen have ever shewn well in dealing with the United States. Walpole shows the Court to have been often fussy and sometimes intriguing.[122]

His reading could not overcome the feelings of frustration which were so much a part of MacGregor, however, and a familiar melancholic strain appears again and again in his private correspondence.

In 1889, writing to Gordon, he began by explaining why he had in an earlier letter reproached him.

> You are by far the best and most consistent friend I ever have had or likely to have as this world is constituted; but you have been to me much more than a friend: you have been my teacher, and

have served me as a type which it has been my ambition to copy
. . . I presume that at the time I made the reproach you complained
of I was labouring under a feeling of injustice and despondency,
for certainly I had some reason to think I was not fairly treated
by the Colonial Office: and I fear I may have used words not well
chosen and which may have appeared to mean more than to express how much I required sympathy from the quarter whence
it would be most welcome.[123]

Next year this feeling persisted:

It *is* rather a trial to start back to the dark domain of savagery;
often weeks without a letter, and up to ten months on tinned
meats, to say nothing of the delirious nights of fever; and then
the Colonial Office.[124]

A clear statement of his uncertainty appeared in another
letter to Gordon in the same month after Gordon had suggested
he return to England:

My place is the jungle not the drawing room. I cannot say in fact
that I wish my work to be known. . . . My work is well worth doing
on its own account; it is not, so far as my efforts are concerned, worth
talking about. I shall probably not be offered any other appointment, but I do not think I should regard that with much sorrow.
Another thing, I cannot afford to go to England at present. It is
therefore all out of the question. I have no doubt you are right.
You know England, and you are well acquainted with the world.
But I am not wordly wise nor much aware of the world. Society
would be to me a desert. I must therefore take my chance, and if
nothing comes my way I cannot help it. I am of course not in
exuberant spirits at present. It is even difficult at times to completely repress the feeling of going back to the bush 'at a sacrifice'.
I am well provided with classic authors, old and new, the tinned
meat of society.[125]

These classical authors, modern biographers and historians,
represented civilization to him, but they could not completely
overcome his frustration. Sincere as were his feelings for
Papuans their values were far removed from his 'civilization' and
he found it always hard to turn back to his duty, like a 'bushman
relapsing into the condition of the cave-man' as he turned back
to the 'humdrum of the bush and the swamp'.[126]

Lagos: The Fear of Death 1899-1904

I have an invincible, selfish, irrational objection to being buried in
these swamps.

MacGregor never felt proud of being Governor of Lagos. Long
before he was sent to this African colony, which was described
at the time as an 'insalubrious and comparatively unimportant
Dependency',[1] he had expressed strong opposition to the policies
of Britain in Africa, and he claimed, after he left the colony, that
it was the unwillingness of the Colonial Office and of commercial interests to accept his 'peaceful imperial idea'[2] that led to
his demotion. Yet, in spite of his disappointment, his constant
necessity to economize in his projects and lack of rapport with
many of the men with whom he worked, MacGregor threw himself wholeheartedly into the problems of administration and
health in Lagos. On many occasions it was the health of the
colony that was uppermost in his mind, and the ability with
which he tackled this problem, particularly in the field of
malaria, makes it tempting to contemplate the heights to which
MacGregor might have reached had he chosen academic medicine as his career, rather than colonial administration.

During his five years in Lagos he felt, even more than in his
other governorships, the limitations on the freedom of a British
colonial governor. In policies towards the Africans, neither Mac-
Gregor nor the Colonial Office could avoid in Lagos some of
the problems concerning the ends of colonialism which were to
become increasingly significant in the twentieth century. In Fiji
and New Guinea policies without clear aims could be applied
without much criticism; the future was not so urgent when there
was little desire for self-rule. The difficulties arising from attempts to preserve parts of a cultural whole were not so obvious;
native leaders whose rule was already being challenged within
the society could be propped up temporarily by the alien British

without too many stresses appearing. But this was less so in Lagos where definition of policies for the future, and even of eventual targets, was more urgent, where stresses in native society were obvious, and where the educated Africans were already foreseeing eventual independence.

As in Fiji and New Guinea, European intervention in West Africa forms a minute part of its history. Centuries before the European arrived complex African societies had flourished, creating traditions which were proudly maintained, and which were to be partly appreciated by MacGregor. The African people with whom he was to be concerned included Bini and Hausa but dominant were the sovereign states and peoples of Yoruba.[3] A mixture of motives led to British concern in Africa. The most important was trading, and dated back in parts of West Africa to the fifteenth century. The main interest was in palm oil, but other goods were exported, including pepper, elephants' tusks, local cloth, brass work, wood and ivory carvings. Most goods were exchanged through ports such as Lagos for Lancashire cotton products. The slave trade provided Britain with another incentive for intervention—firstly for profit, and then, paradoxically, in the nineteenth century, for its abolition. In addition missionaries resident in Africa increased British responsibilities. A further motive which had become very important by the time of MacGregor's governorship was imperial rivalry, mainly between Britain and France but also with Germany. Although Britain had been interested in Africa since the fifteenth century, her official intervention in Lagos could be dated from the appointment of a vice-consul following the 1852 treaty with Akitoye, the 'King (or Oba) of Lagos'.[4] And it was not until 1861 that formal sovereignty was transferred by Docemo, Akitoye's successor, to Britain.

There were 33,000 people packed in the new colony, the islands of Lagos and Iddo and the near-by mainland, and as a result of a series of peace treaties Britain made with Yoruba states, one and a half million more in the hinterland were brought under some form of British protection.[5] 'The heterogeneous mass' that was the population of Lagos under this régime included British administrators, traders, missionaries, thousands of ex-slaves who had returned mainly from Brazil, as well as Yoruba Africans. Many of the educated Africans who held senior positions in the civil service were not Yoruba but were from the Gold Coast or Sierra Leone. Some of them were 'black Englishmen' who had trained in England as doctors, clergy, teachers, journalists and in other professions, while others had commercial links with the midlands and the north of England. Both these groups tended to send their children to school in England, and saw the future of Lagos in terms of its becoming more like England.[6]

From 1874 to 1886 Lagos had been joined for administrative purposes to the Gold Coast, and in that period a series of bitter and involved Yoruba wars developed in the hinterland. These wars, mainly struggles for power among the Yoruba kingdoms which were to end Ibadan's predominance, were complicated by British concern in trade, and consequent efforts to keep open the trade routes, either by river or road. The British government was neither prepared to end the wars by direct intervention nor to guarantee treaties of peace with separate towns and states. Eventually in 1886, when Lagos was again separated from the Gold Coast, the Governor of Lagos, Sir C. A. Moloney, sent delegations of peace to the interior. A form of peace was reached in the same year, and in 1888 a treaty was signed with the Alafin of Oyo (whom MacGregor was to describe as 'traditionally and theoretically the greatest chief of the Yorubas')[7] nominally placing all of Yorubaland under British protection. From that date until MacGregor's arrival in 1899 was a period in which a chain of treaties linked Yorubaland with Great Britain, in a way reuniting Yoruba under Lagos. This extension of British control was related to the moves of other nations: Germany had annexed the Cameroons in 1884; the French were active in various parts of Africa; and the tenor of the Berlin Conference of 1884-85 favoured increasing European responsibilities.

The series of treaties that Moloney (1886-91) and his successors as governors, Sir G. T. Carter (1891-97) and Sir H. E. McCallum (1897-99), signed in Yorubaland were deliberately vague. The Colonial Office did not want any precise definition of British jurisdiction for it wished to minimize its responsibilities, but at the same time to ensure its influence as against other European powers. There were two types of treaties: one offering peace, friendship and commerce; the other protection. Both included clauses designed to maintain British interest in Yorubaland. All were content to allow much internal sovereignty to the protected states—so long as this sovereignty admitted British control. More specifically an Order-in-Council of 29 December

1887 provided that the British laws of Lagos could be applied to these hinterland states.

Under Moloney and his two successors most of the agents of British influence (whose aims were so often discordant) were at least united. The expansionist view was supported by traders —organized particularly under the Liverpool and Manchester Chambers of Commerce—and by most missionaries, to aid respectively the expansion of British commerce and the promotion of Christianity. In addition, many of the educated Africans supported British expansion in so far as their livelihood depended on the expansion of Lagos as an *entrepôt,* a centre for the trade of the interior. As long as the treaties apparently maintained the independence of the Yoruba kingdoms the traditional loyalty—often still strong—of these Lagos Africans to their states could be satisfied.

The period of Governor Carter's administration (1891-97) was notable for his insistence on keeping open the interior trade routes, and for this purpose he felt justified in using force when necessary. Dr A. A. B. Aderibigbe has described him as a typical 'pacificator'.[8] Carter was encouraged in his policy by the British merchants, but fell foul of the Aborigines' Protection Society and most, though not all, the educated natives of Lagos. His war with the Ijebu in 1892 persuaded the Egba, whose centre was the city of Abeokuta, to reopen their trade routes and led to a treaty in January 1893, by which the Egba among other concessions promised that no roads should be closed in future without the consent of the Lagos governor in return for the important British assurance that there would be no annexation of Egba territory.[9] Treaties were also signed with Oyo and at Ibadan, whose leaders agreed to accept a British resident commissioner. In these arrangements there was little evidence of the Colonial Office's alleged 'principle', however vague, of non-intervention. Instead a form of indirect rule had been instituted, with representatives of the Lagos governor consulting with rulers of these states. Aderibigbe argues persuasively that by the end of Governor Carter's period the educated natives of Lagos favoured more systematic indirect rule. At the same time they consciously resisted attempts to 'Europeanize' Africans and supported any moves that promised eventual African self-rule.[10] Their incipient nationalism was marked by the preparation in the 1890s of three histories of the Yoruba, by J. A. Otonda Payne, J. O. George and the Reverend Samuel Johnson.[11]

MacGregor's immediate predecessor as governor, Colonel H. E. McCallum (1897-98), applied his Malayan experience in attempting to include Africans in the administration by setting up indigenous councils both at the centre of government and at the provincial level. A Native Advisory Board was set up in 1897 in Lagos, where meetings of some of the Yoruba Obas and other chiefs were held. In the same year the first provincial council was summoned by Resident Commissioner Fuller of Ibadan, followed in 1898 by an Oyo council. McCallum wanted to go farther and have Britain claim all Yorubaland as a British protectorate, 'over the whole of which British laws shall be held to apply'.[12] In this he seems to have been concerned to prevent French encroachment in this area, rather than to provide more efficient government of the Yorubas. The Colonial Office considered, however, that such a policy might well weaken rather than strengthen its case over any territory that was disputed, for the French could well argue if a protectorate were declared that previous treaties must not have sufficiently secured British rights. For such reasons Chamberlain decided to take no immediate action. In May 1898 McCallum had a serious illness and was forced to resign from the governorship. During Denton's interregnum before MacGregor arrived British jurisdiction was extended in Egba territories. In 1899 Britain leased a strip of land for railway construction, and an Order-in-Council of 4 April 1899 applied the laws of Lagos to this part of the Egba nation. Although the *Colonial Office List,* its unofficial publication, subsequently claimed that Britain now controlled 'the whole of the Yoruba country'[13] this was to discourage other nations, for the actual extent of power depended on the terms of the various treaties with the Yoruba states.

This was the involved situation into which MacGregor arrived in May 1899—a melee of conflicting interests. There were traders with their eyes on the markets and produce of the interior, Christian missionaries seeking to convert Africans, chiefs who wanted to hold a tight rein on their people and lands, educated Africans who distrusted both British interference and the authority of the chiefs, French and German neighbours who might encroach on British spheres of influence. Above all, and most difficult, was the insistence of the Colonial Office on retaining its influence in Africa without giving any precise definition of British jurisdiction. Part of the tragic failure of

MacGregor in Lagos was his refusal to follow the subtle legalistic arguments of the Colonial Office.

MacGregor had arrived in England from New Guinea in December 1898, had been consulted by the Colonial Office on New Guinea questions, had fully briefed Le Hunte, his successor in New Guinea, and then gone to Switzerland to his family. His salary ceased on 7 December and he felt forgotten:

> the Colonial Office has not offered or promised me anything. They merely said that they had nothing to offer me at the present time. So here we are in the most modest and cheapest quarters we can procure.[14]

It would seem, therefore, that one reason for MacGregor's appointment to Lagos must have been his availability: here was an experienced governor who had been commended for his work in British New Guinea and who needed employment. How far his experience in dealing with native people in Fiji and British New Guinea was considered as a qualification for the job is unknown. Certainly no analysis seems to have been made of the differences between Pacific and African policies or stages of development. It is tempting for a biographer to argue that Mac-Gregor's appointment was a recognition of his success in British New Guinea, and that the Colonial Office appreciated a relationship between the aims of his policy there and Chamberlain's acceptance of positive goals in West Africa.[15] But there is scant evidence in favour of this interpretation.

MacGregor was dissatisfied with the offer of Lagos and protested to Griffith, who tried, through the Australian premiers, to persuade the Secretary of State to give MacGregor a better appointment.[16] But nothing came of this attempted pressure on London. He had, however, some consolation in that his salary at Lagos of £2,500 together with £100 duty allowance was £1,000 more than he had received in New Guinea, and that he was

> installed in a house that is at least twice or three times as large as Government House in Brisbane. It is not old, cost £25,000, has four bedrooms, no library and no bath! I am allowed 52 lbs. of ice daily, a steward, ten servants, gardeners, electric light, a palatial steamer, a horse, carriers, three launches, and so on.[17]

The appointment was announced on 24 January 1899. A columnist in the *Lagos Standard* took the fact that in Lagos very little was known about MacGregor as a text to make some valid criticisms of the system of appointing governors.

The sentiment that England regards her colonies as rich fields for rewarding her deserving sons is never so well illustrated as in the choice of her Governors. A man is brought from the opposite end of the globe and placed among a strange people, whose ways and customs are quite new to him; no sooner does he begin to gain some experience that would be useful to him, than he is promoted to some other post. . . . We have no choice in the selection of our rulers . . . we know nothing, of course, about Sir William personally, and Lagos stands ready to give him a hearty welcome, devoutly hoping that he may prove the right man in the right place.[18]

This lack of continuity, for which MacGregor was later to be attacked in Lagos, was also criticized by Mary Kingsley in her *West African Studies,* published in January 1899. She wrote of administrators

armed with absolutely no definite policy, subsisting on official and non-expert opinion, . . . [drifting] along, with some nebulous sort of notion in their heads about 'elevating the African in the plane of civilisation'.[19]

MacGregor was the fourth new governor in Lagos in a decade, and he and his three predecessors (Moloney, Carter and McCallum) all had different emphases in their policies. Mary Kingsley seems justified in criticizing the resultant adminstration as 'a coma accompanied by fits',[20] especially as Colonial Office ideas were also clearly changing. MacGregor's administration initially fitted into Mary Kingsley's criticism of a lack of definite policy in so far as he had no prior experience of Africa and in so far as he anticipated that he would be able to achieve nothing. But it was not long before he developed policies and he was able to achieve some of his aims.

As in previous colonies one of his first moves, and one which was often to be his dominant concern, was to improve the standards of health. The death-rate of Europeans in Lagos (in the town and adjacent islands) was high: in 1899 it was 71.12 per thousand, in 1900, 87.64 per thousand. The total deaths in the same area, including Africans, exceeded 2,200 of a population of over 33,000 in each of those years, about half of whom were children. More dramatically MacGregor said that between 1892 and 1900, forty-five out of every 100 children died in their first year.[21]

His letters from Lagos show a horror at this appalling death-rate that reflected his personal fear of death and his shame that nothing had been done to try to prevent the spread of malaria. Two days after he arrived he told Griffith,

Q

The fatal malaria is everywhere. The less one thinks of that perhaps so much the better . . . I think it very doubtful that I can hold out here. If I do get ill I suppose I must remain, for ever.[22]

After surviving seven months he wrote:

I am very solitary, tristissimo, alone. My wife and daughter came out and were here for about three months, but the risk was too great, and I felt immense relief when I got them both away alive. They left nearly a month ago, and I have heard nothing of them since, so that I am not yet quite free of anxiety for our fever frequently kills between Lagos and Liverpool. It is, I find, quite impossible to maintain a connected administration here, what with death, invalidings, and the endless going on leave. I can sympathise with officers, for I could not affirm that I had ever been quite well a day and a night in West Africa . . . for weeks at a time my head is so light that I dare not try to turn around quickly.[23]

After surviving nine months, MacGregor told Gordon that

What you wrote to me I find to be perfectly true: that one may be cut off in a few hours at any time. It has several times happened that I have heard someone had been taken to the Lagos hospital ill, and I have gone to see the patient, to learn that his corpse had just been removed. Fever comes on with great suddenness sometimes. Two weeks ago I went to the opening of a great new church, I sat down perfectly well, and in less than five minutes was seized with fever. [On another occasion] I was sitting in the door of my tent reading, felt my right thumb become cold, and was immediately overwhelmed with an ague that lasted for two hours and would have shaken me an inch shorter had I not been case-hardened. . . . The climate is unhealthy, and I, already run down, do not stand it well. And I have an invincible, selfish, irrational objection to being buried in these swamps.[24]

But in spite of illness and depression he never stopped working to rid the country of disease. He was quick to realize the importance of the new railway as a means of bringing improvements to the hinterland, and within a fortnight of his arrival he reported that the hospital for railway employees was not fit for fever patients. Although he understood that the medical department of the railway was beyond the scope of his duties he suggested that he should take over ultimate control. After he had been in the colony just over a month he prepared the draft of a comprehensive Public Health Ordinance. He stressed the immediate need for action in Lagos town. 'The necessity for . . . an active, intelligent and competent Sanitary Engineer for Lagos is very great'.[25] He made proposals for the replacement of the

existing inefficient engineer and for the appointment of a surveyor from Queensland, one reason for this being that he had
become acutely aware of the necessity for filling in the swamps
of Lagos. He wanted to turn them into eucalyptus parks, for, as
he said, 'It does not matter whether mosquitos produce fever or
not: the swamps produce mosquitos, and fever, and therefore
have to be filled up'.[26] Chamberlain, as the Secretary of State for
the Colonies, approved these schemes, and wrote:

> I am prepared to back Sir William MacGregor thoroughly in every
> recommendation for improving the sanitary conditions of the
> colony. Expense should not stand in the way of this even if it leads
> to a deficit—and I will allow no Treasury interference in this
> question.[27]

MacGregor subsequently made his first principle in drawing up
the estimates in November 1899, 'to provide to the best of our
ability for improving the sanitary condition of the country in
every attainable way'.[28]

In a private letter to Gordon in February 1900 he indicated
his criticisms of the efforts of his predecessors, of the apathy he
encountered in Lagos, and of the delay in obtaining assistance
from England. 'I am trying to fill in the Lagos swamps. Had
the prisoners been employed at that for the last twenty years it
would be finished now, and Lagos would have been healthier . . .
I am now about, I hope, to start the prisoners on to this work.'
He was also critical of the Colonial Office and the Crown Agents:

> I have great difficulty . . . in obtaining anything from home.
> We have no medical instruments yet, I asked for them eight
> months ago. We are totally ignorant of the quality of the water
> of our wells. We have no knowledge of the temperature or rain-
> fall of the interior, though eight months ago I asked for meteoro-
> logical instruments. There is not a microscope in the colony yet,
> except a private one belonging to the Chief Medical Officer and
> though we have 14 medical officers.[29]

He did not hesitate to make the same complaints to the Colonial
Office. Thus he said that the health department's laboratory

> for enabling the department to prevent sickness, to detect and to
> investigate disease, . . . [was] clearly the worst provided I have seen
> in an experience of thirty-one years, since I began to study medi-
> cine. . . . The Chief Medical Officer will, no doubt, wish to explain
> to you why these matters have not previously received his atten-
> tion.[30]

Five months later, in December 1899, he again complained that the hospital still had not medical instruments—not a single workable microscope nor any test tube. The Crown Agents' defence rested on their difficulties in revising the list to suit MacGregor, in supplying some of the items which were not kept in stock, and on their desire to save freight 'by sending the whole supply in one consignment'.[31]

His interest in hospitals was not confined to the town of Lagos, and on visiting the hinterland he completely altered the proposed plans for a new hospital in Ibadan.[32] He also intensified the vaccination campaign and, acting on his experience in Fiji, paid the vaccinators only for successful inoculations. Owing to the lack of knowledge about hygiene, he felt it necessary to set up a Board of Health to represent different sections of the community and to educate the Africans in the more obvious principles of sanitation.[33]

The condition of the wells also came within the orbit of Mac-Gregor's concern, and he was scathing in his condemnation of the experiments on the Ikoyi water plan by the Consulting Engineer for the Crown Agents, Mr Chadwick, who had spent some seven thousand pounds on them. MacGregor was sure that stored water could be used because 'since the 29th June 1875 I have practically lived on rain water collected and stored "near a dwelling" and have seen thousands of others do the same, without any evil result'.[34] More impartially he wondered why there had been no analysis of well water, nor any topographical survey.

Despite Chamberlain's promise that health would be aided without consideration of costs, the financial position of Lagos very soon led to the expression of familiar Colonial Office and Treasury insistence on economy. Thus after five months the Assistant Under-Secretary of the Colonial Office, Sir Reginald Antrobus, minuted: 'nothing will be done so long as Sir William MacGregor keeps on hurling one scheme after another at us without considering the question of ways and means'.[35] MacGregor was soon, as in every colony in which he had served, to be very conscious of the financial limitations on his efforts. He knew that his interests in health were in line with general Colonial Office policy, but he had to justify every particular expense. There was always the conflict between his dreams for the future, and what was financially possible at the moment; this contrast can be illustrated by his support in 1899 for the establishment of a School of Tropical Medicine in England.

The step taken is, so far as my lengthy experience enables me to judge, in the right direction, and should do much good if supplemented by what is of still greater importance, the proper equipment of medical officers with the means of detecting, investigating, preventing and curing diseases that are peculiar to the tropics.[36]

He related his support, however, to his particular policy in Lagos, where by 1900 he had been forced to retrench and adopt strict economy:

Instructing medical officers in tropical diseases by special courses and equipping expensive and costly commissions of experts to investigate malaria, must all be to a large extent lost for a place like Lagos so long as such a noisome place as this swamp now is remains on the windward side of the town.[37]

As far as Lagos was concerned he preferred a particular goal, and in an interview with Chamberlain in 1900 he won support for the rapid completion of the filling of the swamp.

In 1897 Dr Patrick Manson was appointed to be the first medical adviser to the Colonial Office; he had previously carried out research in China on filarial worms in elephantiasis, and had argued that the worms were conveyed by a biting mosquito. He gave public lectures in London and it was one of his students, Ronald Ross, who, in August 1897, after research in India, first propounded the theory that malaria was related to the bites of the anopheles mosquito. In the next few years schools of tropical medicine were set up in Liverpool (May 1899), where Ross worked, and in London (October 1899), and then introduced as part of the medical courses at Cambridge, Edinburgh, Aberdeen and Belfast. And the rivalry between these schools stimulated results. The Liverpool school had been set up following plans inaugurated by a local committee headed by Sir Alfred Jones of the commercial firm, Elder Dempster, which had large interests in Africa, including Lagos. Jones once said in a conference with MacGregor:

No question [was] so dear to the African merchants as that of trying to improve the state of health in Africa, for they felt it was a duty which had been thrown upon them, and they were exceedingly anxious to carry it out.[38]

Duty apart, it would clearly be to the advantage of both traders and government to reduce the toll of disease in the colonies, and Chamberlain probably had both thoughts in mind when he approached Lord Lister in 1898 and sought the co-operation of the Royal Society, which subsequently set up first a malaria committee and then a permanent tropical diseases committee. The Liverpool school organized further expeditions by Ross to test his malaria theory. His visit to West Africa was largely financed by Jones, not by the Colonial Office, although Chamberlain instructed the British governors to give Ross every assistance.[39]

MacGregor needed no convincing of the significance of malaria, especially after his ten years in New Guinea, and his first thirteen months in Lagos had convinced him of the essential need both for immediate measures and long-term research. He tried to keep up in his reading with advances in medicine and was aware of the controversy since 1897 over Ross's claims. His letter to Gordon of February 1900 suggests he was aware of, but still not convinced about, the new theory: 'It does not matter whether mosquitos produce fever or not. The swamps produce mosquitos, and fever, and therefore have to be filled up'.[40] His Chief Medical Officer, the West Indian Dr Strachan, was an early convert to Ross's mosquito theory. Subsequently Strachan corresponded with Ross[41] and the mounting evidence was sufficient to convince MacGregor before he went on leave later in 1900 of the theory's validity. MacGregor realized that basic research was needed if the health of the Lagos population was to be improved, a lesson reinforced by his personal health which had certainly been affected by his first term in Africa:

> I saw the *Bulletin* said I had returned from Africa looking more than 200 years old, I really hardly recognize myself in the glass, so haggard and washed out did I look.[42]

During his leave in 1900 MacGregor lectured at the new Liverpool School of Tropical Medicine about which he wryly commented: 'An address on medical matters by a minor Governor is so rare a production that it has been translated into German and Italian!'[43] This visit to the school began his close contact with Ross. MacGregor spent over a month at a Hydropathic in Scotland trying to shake off his malaria. He then went to Italy, still not recovered, to discuss research on the disease:

> I suffered from fever till I got to Florence five weeks ago, since which I have been decidedly on the mend. My body corporate is nearly ready to receive a new crop of the parasite of malarial fever. I went to Rome to see the great Grassi and the celebrated Celli, and I studied the Italian fever parasite in the Eternal City. . . . I hope to perhaps do some good in . . . sanitary matters

next year in Lagos. . . . We are hopelessly backward on the West
Coast, and I fear immovable.[44]

On his return to Lagos he claimed to be 'chiefly occupied in
fighting death and disease',[45] one important measure being to
make all the sleeping quarters of the European officials and
the railway staff mosquito-proof. He also set up a Commission of
Enquiry into infantile mortality, which found[46] that only one
per cent of the many children dying under the age of one had
any medical attendance during fatal illness. Various remedies
were proposed: for example, an improved system of registration
of births and deaths and free medical attendance on the poor.
MacGregor pointed out that more than mere attendance was
needed, since most European doctors were ignorant of the
languages, prejudices, superstitions and customs of the African
peoples. He was well aware from his Seychelles experience of the
assistance given to his medical treatment of Africans by his
sympathy with them and by his learning Swahili. Other remedies
suggested by the Commission's report were more free dispen-
saries, the free administration of quinine, the setting up of a
children's ward in the hospital, improved sanitation—better
wells, better surface drainage, the disposal of sewage, better
constituted houses, less overcrowding, and the oft-recurring plea
for the filling-in of the swamps. On this last point, even that
indefatigable battler MacGregor confessed that he had been discouraged by what he called 'deplorable delays': 'I do not blame
my predecessors for leaving these swamps alone'.[47]

In spite of his frustration he continued to think of further
possible remedies for death and disease, such as the teaching of
health in subsidized schools and the placing of some restrictions on the practice of untrained African doctors, of whom
there were some 400 in Lagos, and who he considered largely
contributed to the high mortality rate in the town. At this point
the Colonial Office approved his 'activity . . . in pushing forward
measures of all kinds for improving health . . . [which left]
nothing to be desired'.[48]

Following on this encouragement MacGregor planned a course
of lectures for all teacher trainees and also a widespread series of
public lectures by the Chief Medical Officer and other doctors,
which created great interest. One series in Lagos was reported to
have attracted 800 to 2,000 people.[49] Lectures were also given in
the hinterland, for example at Abeokuta, with the backing of the
Alake and his council.[50]

When MacGregor asked the Colonial Office to support him in improving the sanitation of the railway, Chamberlain remarked: 'I admit that I have not the least idea what is meant by the "sanitation" of a railway'. Nevertheless, he gave MacGregor both his support and approval.

> I have told all the Governors of the West Coast that I will approve of all reasonable expenditure which will save the lives of European officials from the effects of the climate. We have in Sir William MacGregor an unusually able and experienced governor and I am inclined to give him a free hand.[51]

On the recommendation of the Commission of Enquiry, MacGregor had a chemical analysis done on the wells of Lagos, which confirmed his earlier suspicions, for of 160 tested, only seven were found good, twenty-one were suspicious and the rest were definitely polluted. MacGregor urged rapid action to dig new wells, store water in tanks, and remove sewage into the sea. The Colonial Office praised these schemes because they were cheaper than other suggestions and so were compatible with the aim of economizing.[52] Unfortunately, progress with sanitation was hampered by MacGregor's clashes with Chadwick, and with each clash his natural obstinacy seemed to be strengthened.[53] All these disputes meant delays, and it was not until May 1902 that a type of well was finally agreed upon for Lagos. These disagreements with Chadwick were also significant as one part of a story of degenerating relationships between MacGregor and the Crown Agents. In January 1902 MacGregor asked if he could requisition medical supplies directly from wholesale houses—as he had done in New Guinea—because of delays by the Crown Agents in complying with previous orders. The Colonial Office refused but again tried to hurry up the Crown Agents. On every issue conflict could be expected. It was an unhealthy situation for the progress of Lagos when Minutes like 'I think the Crown Agents win this time' or 'a decided score for Crown Agents' could be written.[54]

MacGregor, at this stage, was well to the fore in British colonial malarial research and wanted to form a great malarial trust for Lagos, to represent the various bodies interested in the Colony. He also circularized his translations of papers by Professor Celli of Rome and Professor Koch of Berlin, whose researches had been carried out in German New Guinea. As in New Guinea, MacGregor insisted on the use of quinine and antifebrine, and in 1901 he published in the Gazette translations of a report by Dr Bludau of the Cameroons which gave his findings on the control of malarial fever by quinine.[55]

Dislike of racial prejudice as well as his medical convictions encouraged MacGregor in his refusal in July 1901 to accept Lord Onslow's London Malaria Committee's recommendation, that Europeans and natives should be separated as a way of guarding the former against the disease. He considered that the validity of Koch's theory on which segregation was recommended could be debated,[56] and that 'in a place like Lagos it would be most unwise to introduce any racial discrimination of that kind'.[57] Today MacGregor would be considered right on both sociological and practical grounds. Nevertheless, years after he had left Lagos MacGregor's refusal to adopt segregation was remembered against him, and in 1908 Antrobus wrote:

> The last Governor of Lagos, Sir William MacGregor, notwithstanding his scientific attainments, was slow to accept the mosquito theory about malaria; and although ultimately he accepted it and acted upon it in many respects with great vigour there was a curious streak of sentimentalism in him which made him object to the segregation of Europeans and natives.[58]

His concern for the sick African children was shared by some of the women of the colony, and he was able to form a Ladies League of both Europeans and Africans to attend the children who had fever and dysentery. MacGregor told the ladies that their efforts were backed by women in England, Scotland and eleswhere, giving the specific example of

> Mrs. Antrobus . . . the accomplished wife of the Colonial Office gentleman that principally has to do with Lagos business, . . . [she is] an Italian scholar, [who] is in the habit of translating Italian treatises on malaria into English for people that study these matters scientifically. The same lady also devotes much time to subjects connected with the nursing of the sick and such matters.[59]

The disagreements between Antrobus and MacGregor are given more significance when it is known that Antrobus, through his wife, had an understanding of the mosquito debate. Their disagreements, based on fundamentally different attitudes to the African people, were important in several Lagos questions, as were differences between MacGregor and others at the Colonial Office including the Under-Secretary, Sir Montagu Ommanney. MacGregor told Ross that '. . . So far the greatest obstacle is the Colonial Office. It is bad enough to have to

deal with malaria alone: but malaria entrenched behind Sir——
is impregnable'.[60]

In 1901 Ross visited Lagos and was full of praise both for the
work and character of MacGregor, of whom he said, 'of all the
men I have met I honour him perhaps the most'.[61] The contact
with such a man, who was capable of a true appraisal of his
medical abilities, may have caused MacGregor to dream of
returning to full-time medical practice, for he confided in Ross
that he had an ambition to be allowed by the Colonial Office to
give up his governorship and to be appointed as malarial commissioner for the British Empire. No such application exists,
however, in the official Lagos despatches. So it may simply have
been a passing thought induced by his insecurity, and the frustrations caused by an idea, however exaggerated, of the hostility
of the Colonial Office. His letter to Griffith in April 1901 suggests an almost pathological state:

> I am still alive in this land of the dead and dying. I spend very
> much of my time in playing at pitch and toss with the enemy, that
> is alas! last to be destroyed. I am to send you copies of the convinc-
> ing papers I have translated for the edification of our people from
> the Germans and Italians. You will see from them that they already
> represent two distinct schools, and you will gather from my message
> on the Estimates that I am using the practice of both. But could
> you imagine my being at every point thwarted by the Colonial
> Office. It is all the fault of the 'caposmalto' of that man Omman-
> ney. I do not think I can return here for another tour if I outlive
> this one . . . I have a horror of being buried in Lagos mud, the
> noisome remains of Negrodom.

At the end of this letter is a pathetic reminder of his personal
sacrifices: 'I find it more and more hard each year to turn my
back on my wife and children to wander into the wilderness'.[62]

As in each colony in which he served MacGregor followed a
strict policy of quarantine, and in this he came into conflict with
the Colonial Office again. Its policy was to adopt more flexible
rules such as those adopted at the 1897 Venice Convention, but
they could not prevail on MacGregor to agree, and finally
capitulated, Antrobus remarking, 'Sir William MacGregor's
time in Lagos is coming to an end soon'.[63]

Again, as he had in other colonies, MacGregor set about
recruiting doctors, and, reflecting his experience of inefficient
colleagues, he wished to choose these himself. He had accepted
in 1901 an offer by the steamship line, Elder Dempster, to carry
free *bona fide* medical students from Lagos to the Liverpool

School of Tropical Medicine.[64] In the same year he suggested that applications be made to Professors Reid of Aberdeen and Clark of Glasgow for Scottish doctors. Unfortunately, neither professor could find suitable candidates at the low salary offered.[65] In March 1902 in a confidential report to a committee set up to discuss the problem of finding medical staff for the West African colonies, he criticized what he felt to be the deliberate omission of candidates from the Scottish universities.

> The recommendations of the Committee as to the means of obtaining candidates are not laid on a broad basis. It is not long since I read in the Gazette Medicale de Paris that the Edinburgh University is the best school in Europe, yet the Committee pass it by. . . . I studied medicine myself under Lord Lister, Sir William Gairdner, and Sir George Macleod, at Glasgow University, yet the Committee ignore that great educational centre, alike with the University of Aberdeen.

Although some of this criticism might be discountenanced as reflecting his always strong national prejudices, there is much evidence of the reputation of the Scottish medical courses to support his allegations of English pride ignoring Scottish achievements. An even more important point in his report was that he gave greater emphasis to qualifications other than formal education:

> a second or third class officer that knows the people, their habits, their customs, their suspicions, their superstitions etc. is safer and more valuable than a first class man that does not possess this knowledge.

For much the same reasons he strongly supported the appointment of more indigenous doctors:

> it is clearly advisable to employ as many active medical officers as possible, that is wherever well educated, well trained, men can be obtained. The Committee very strangely seems to forget that the principal function of a medical officer is to attend native patients. It would be most unwise to cause political dissent in the population of a country like this simply to comply with and nourish the race prejudice of a mere handful of Europeans, the prejudice that exists in inverse ratio to liberal education.

He considered that indigenous doctors must be treated fairly, which he thought had not been the case in some of the African colonies—in Southern Nigeria, for example.

> I do not hesitate to say that so long as humanity is what it is, they will not succeed if they are, for example, kept on a separate roster, are made to live apart, and are excluded from military expeditions.

His deduction has a prophetic ring:

> it may be accepted as an axiom that where the native medical
> officer does not succeed, British administration will not get that
> hold on the population that you would wish.[66]

Much of MacGregor's second leave between 25 May and 31
December 1902 was devoted to the questions of health, con-
centrating, as ever, on malaria, and winning praise from the
Colonial Office for the keenness and energy with which he pursued the 'wily mosquito'.[67] He travelled to Italy visiting Florence
and Rome, and then in September with Ross to Egypt.[68] In
November he visited Holland to investigate the measures adopted there against malaria.

In Italy MacGregor discussed with Professor Celli and others
the anti-malaria measures which were so urgent in a country
which had about two million cases each year. He was impressed
by the use of wire gauze in doors, windows and chimneys at
Agro Romano, and as in Africa he showed his sympathy for the
sick children—this time near the Pontine Marshes:

> Some of the children living in unprotected huts presented a truly
> pitiful spectacle, wasted by malaria, and this up to two or three
> miles from the gates of Rome, poverty-stricken, helpless beings;
> dwelling within sight of St. Peter's, in huts in every way inferior
> to a tree-house in New Guinea or a mud house in a Lagos swamp.[69]

In Egypt MacGregor's main interest centred on discussions of
how to store water without breeding mosquitoes. He found that
water could be kept in great open cisterns for distribution without breeding them so long as the breeze from the desert agitated
the surface at regular intervals. He compared small shallow
garden cisterns with rather dirty water, undisturbed by wind,
which he found full of larvae.

His Dutch trip was to study malaria 'with special reference
to the effect of salt water in the canals' of Amsterdam in reducing its prevalence. Deaths from malaria had dropped considerably in this city, so MacGregor took the Lagos Director of
Works with him, as he believed it possible that a water supply
for Lagos could be obtained from deep wells like the ones in
Amsterdam. He realized, however, that only scientific experiment could determine the quality and quantity of the water.[70]

Before returning for what was to be his last year in Lagos,
MacGregor told medical students at Glasgow University that 'the
question whether malaria can be controlled or not, is practically
one of stagnation or progress to the West African colonies gener-

ally'.[71] Back in the colony his fight against malaria went on unabated, and he did have some success. But he was not satisfied with his achievement and with a melancholy that was becoming typical[72] he wrote to Griffith in February 1903:

> I am to celebrate this month the completion of thirty years in the service of the Sovereign. My experience of it is that it does not pay, I should not recommend it to young men in general now that the good appointments are generally given to outsiders. I should have been delighted had they given me Queensland.[73]

Nevertheless, the fight went on. He had brought back from leave a medical library, and lantern slides to help in his medical education campaign. He applied his Amsterdam water investigations to Lagos wells and asked in March 1903 for a bacteriologist and parasitologist to examine fully the waters of the wells.[74] In April an analysis of the water in four of the new model wells showed that they were very satisfactory. In August he submitted the results of the examination of the Apapa plain as a collecting ground for the water supply for the town of Lagos. Once a decent water supply was assured he hoped to improve the sewerage system of the town. As a result of his investigation of canals in Amsterdam he requested money for the formation of canals in Lagos town. One result of this was spectacular and effective— a canal cut through the island to drain the swamp once existing between the town and Ikoyi, a canal which still justifiably perpetuates his name.

Vaccination was another project on which he continued to work, and in this campaign he ran into opposition from the Colonial Office, which objected to the expense of his ten-year scheme which was to cost £33,000.[75] There were also objections from the uninformed public, both in Africa and also in England where a newspaper editorial referred to vaccination as 'a filthy practice'.[73] In order to carry out this campaign it was necessary to train more medical staff, and MacGregor went into the possibility of teaching Africans to do this work. His Principal Medical Officer disagreed with the idea, so MacGregor suggested that Dr Corney, who had worked with him on the Fijian scheme, and who had succeeded him there as Chief Medical Officer, should be consulted, as MacGregor felt he had left Fiji before he was 'able to form a fair estimate as to the success or non-success of the plan'.[77] Corney's report was inconclusive and stressed the problem of doctors who could not speak in the vernacular teaching students who hardly spoke English and the ingrained superstition of some Fijians about illness. He concluded by saying that much would depend on the 'intelligence, application and natural bent' of the Africans selected.[78]

Before a decision could be reached on this question an ironic urgency was given to all MacGregor's attempts to improve the health of Lagos when he almost died from a severe attack of malaria in September and October 1903. He left Ibadan on the morning of 22 September and was taken ill in the train. On arrival in Lagos he was taken to Government House, where he was attended by doctors and put under the care of the senior nurse from the hospital. His life was in danger during most of the next fortnight, at first from malaria fever and, after it had abated by the beginning of October, from a fresh complication, the 'intervention of fatigue'.[79] He was regarded as 'seriously ill' until 5 October when he began to improve and by 8 October he was able to telegraph reporting his recovery and asking the Colonial Office to tell his wife and family that he was out of danger, for his doctor now classed him as convalescent, adding that he need not leave Africa. By 14 October he took over the government again from Reeve who had acted as his deputy during the twenty-two days of his illness. Just after his illness he wrote to Griffith:

> I have been ill for some time sitting on the fence that divides life from death. I am convalescent, but have not been able to read 'The Inferno' [Griffith's translation that he had just received] yet. I wish I had strength and time to review it.

He turned to morbid introspection:

> This serious illness has I fear given me a new and regrettable idea when lying here at the point of death I began to think that if fairly treated by the Colonial Office I should not be here. I feel, now, that I have not had fair play . . . I suppose I must die in a swamp eventually.[80]

The Colonial Office was in a quandary about his illness, for on 24 September, just four days before they received the first telegram advising of his illness, they had written a despatch advising that his days in Lagos were over. Antrobus wrote on 13 November;

> I think that Sir William MacGregor does not contemplate returning [to Africa], but I am not sure, and it is necessary to get the point cleared up, as we want to get on with the arrangements for amal- gamating Lagos and Southern Nigeria. It is very undesirable that he should return both in his own and in the public interests; but,

when he finds that there is no chance of his getting a first class government, he may want to go back.[81]

Ommanney was even blunter on 21 December:

He has not been altogether a success at Lagos—and I doubt whether, if his health permits of further tropical service, it will be possible to offer him another government, certainly not a first class job.[82]

Further sections of the collision course which led MacGregor to this clash with the Colonial Office will be discussed in later chapters, but whatever was said of his faults few reproaches were ever made for his efforts to improve the health of the possession, and on this issue alone his governorship of Lagos deserves high praise. He managed to avoid the white man's grave and his efforts ensured better health for the colony. He received recognition for his efforts both from the Colonial Office, and from the Society for Tropical Medicine, which awarded him the Mary Kingsley Medal for his anti-malarial work.[83]

Ross had no doubt of MacGregor's ability in other than medical work, and it would seem only fair to conclude this chapter with his appreciation of his colleague.

Wise, grave, but humorous, bearded, thick-set, with wrinkled forehead and a high and somewhat conical bald head, his low voice and kindly manner filled all with trust in him. He drank no wine and did not smoke, but was no fanatic in these respects, and kept a hospitable table. Every night he read from his Greek Testament, and was also skilled in French and Italian, and knew something of many barbarous tongues. He was a mathematician, a practised surveyor, a lapidary, and a master of many arts, but always proud of his medical upbringing and of his nationality. Simply dignified, he did not allow his dignity to obscure his personality, and he had no trace of that meanest and most mischievous vice, jealousy. He was not a politician, but a genuine administrator careful of all the interests of the people entrusted to him—still more, a scientific administrator who added knowledge to his solicitude.[84]

II

Lagos : African Rights 1899-1904

Both the local papers have on many occasions roundly abused me, and I feel as great contempt for their praise, as I formerly despised their blame.

MacGregor had been very critical of British policy towards Africans before he reached Lagos, and in assessing his governorship it is essential to delineate the attitudes he adopted towards them, and to show how far his ideas clashed with Colonial Office opinions and with the views of other British governors. It is not easy to reach overall answers, for every British action was subject to the complicated earlier history of the colony and its hinterland, as well as to events beyond Lagos and even outside Africa.

Generally MacGregor began with humanitarian sympathy for all Africans, some of whom he thought were far more civilized than Fijians or Papuans. His attitudes, however, eventually differed between the Africans in Lagos and those in the surrounding states. In the town of Lagos his main dealings were with educated Africans whom he thought were completely detribalized, while in the surrounding partly-independent states, his closest contacts were with Yoruba chiefs, jealous of their centuries-old traditions. MacGregor tried to apply ideas developed in Fiji of ruling through native institutions, both in Lagos and in his negotiations with the heads of these inland states. In both cases his policies caused clashes: in Lagos with the educated Africans who felt that he was holding back the development of their individual independence, and in the states with Africans who were challenging the traditional rule of the chiefs. He also fell foul of the Colonial Office which was trying to increase British influence while leaving undefined the chiefs' position.

Aderibigbe analyses MacGregor's difficulties in the following way:

MacGregor was a governor whose administrative brilliance no one

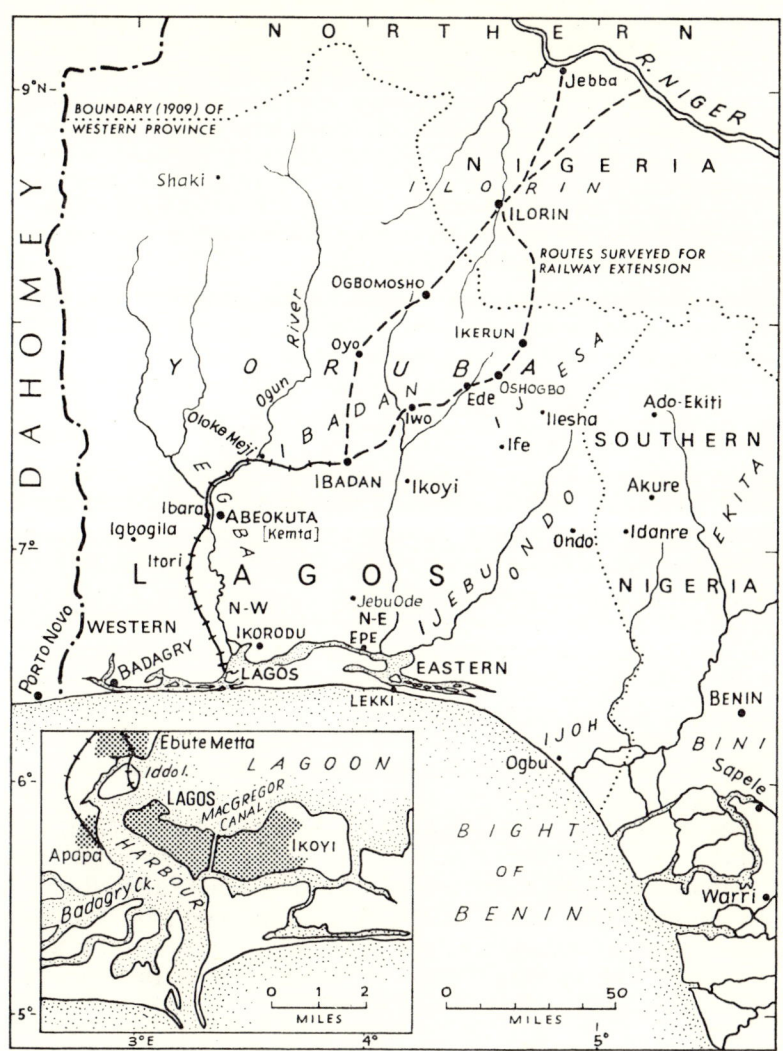

5 Lagos

could deny. It was largely owing to his endeavours in Lagos that the Colonial Office formally approved in principle, the policy 'of ruling as far as possible through the chiefs'. What is more remarkable was MacGregor's patient appreciation of the political arrangements, laws and customs of Yoruba people. For this he was personally admired by the leading educated Africans, whose prejudices he also tried to respect. Yet, the irony of the situation was that in the end MacGregor had to fall foul of these same educated Africans on the treaty rights of chiefs whose interests he had aspired to safeguard. . . .[1]

The vociferous attacks made on him by the journalists who wrote for the Lagos newspapers, the *Standard* and the *Record*, also contributed greatly to the lowering of his popularity.

The heterogeneous mixture in Lagos of a few Englishmen and many Africans was ruled by the pattern of institutions now so familiar to MacGregor, as they were common to most British Crown colonies. Below the governor, who represented the Crown, were Executive and Legislative Councils with appointed members and the usual British structure of government departments —but no Native Department. As all Africans in the colony were regarded as British subjects who had been delivered from tyrannical rule to the enjoyment of the blessings of the British rule of law, little consideration, apart from McCallum's experiments such as the little-used Native Advisory Board, had been devoted to any idea of giving the deposed chiefs any real power or even, as had been attempted in Fiji, of including them in the institutions of government. Africans, however, unlike the Papuans, had been given positions in the civil service. The Education Department, for instance, was headed by a Nigerian, Henry Carr, and all departments had a competitive system of entrance and promotion with no racial barriers. In MacGregor's time the civil service employed about ninety Europeans and about twenty Africans—exact numbers cannot now be ascertained as many of the latter had adopted European names, and as there was no racial separation in lists of employees.[2]

Because of the stress on the 'rule of law' the District Commissioners of the colony were legal officers of the Supreme Court, paid from the judicial department vote. As in British New Guinea, they were magistrates with limited powers in civil and criminal jurisdiction, with special functions under statute law as well as being coroners of their districts. But they could also be called upon for executive and other duties: each was issued with geological equipment; each had to keep a journal of 'everything of interest to the Government';[3] each was urged to suggest improvements, especially in the economic and social life of the community.

Commissioners controlled in 1899 the five districts of the colony: Central, based on Lagos; Western, based on Badagry; North-Western based on Ikorodu; North-Eastern, based on Epe; and the Eastern based on Lekki. They were assisted in their direct rule of these districts by African officers in the towns and by the Lagos constabulary. In the hinterland no standard form of British rule existed, there being in 1899 a Resident Commissioner at Ibadan, Travelling Commissioners at Jebu Ode, Ogbomosho and Shaki, and a Superintendent of Native Affairs at Abeokuta (whose main function was to gain co-operation from the Africans for the railway planned to pass through that town) besides detachments of the constabulary at other towns.[4] The practice of paying stipends to certain chiefs had developed haphazardly; in 1899 ninety-three in the colony and protectorate were receiving annual sums varying from £200 to £5. MacGregor supported continuing the scheme to increase the chief's 'influence and authority, . . . [and to] give the government a good claim on his co-operation'.[5]

At various times MacGregor stated what he considered to be the main aims of his policy. Health measures were always very close to his heart; but also high on his priority lists were agricultural improvement, the building of the railway into the hinterland, and the support of the principle of provincial government through the chiefs. Soon after his arrival at the end of May 1899 MacGregor had promised that he would rule in the interests of the Africans, and he hoped for their co-operation in carrying out his aims.

One way in which he sought this co-operation was by reforming the central administration to give more responsibility to Africans. He proposed, after only four months in the colony, that there should be an African assistant for the Colonial Secretary, naming Henry Carr as the best candidate. His reasoning emphasizes the priority he gave to Africans:

> . . . for some time the conviction has been steadily growing on my mind that this government is not sufficiently in touch with the native part of the population of the Colony and Protectorate, and that certain means are wanting to establish the organic connection between the government and natives that is absolutely necessary in matters of native administration if this is to be conducted

intelligently and on sound principles. . . . This can never become a white man's colony. It is and must remain as regards industrial development almost exclusively in the hands of the natives. They will continue to carry on its agriculture; to do its retail trade. By nature the natives are intensely conservative, and generations will elapse before they fully and completely adapt themselves to European ways and customs. I need not discuss the question whether it is desirable that they should do so. They cannot during the present generation be governed on purely European lines, and attempts to do so will only end in failure. A compromise between the system of European and native administration is indispensable; but that is not attainable working with a staff that hardly comes into direct contact with ordinary native life, modelled as this staff is on the European system.

MacGregor thought that the Native Advisory Board did not meet often enough, and then only to deal with unimportant matters. He suggested that it should be reconstituted under the Colonial Secretary's Department as a special department to deal with all native questions. He argued that 'the European staff in the Secretariat have only a very superficial acquaintance with natives, and know very little about their habits, customs, or ways of thought'. On this point he felt that a permanent African appointment would give the needed continuity of action 'which it is impossible to preserve at present with the endless changes of European officers'. He envisaged later developments after this initial step of appointing an African as Secretary:

> . . . That it will be found necessary to create a legally constituted council of chiefs, with native district councils, is very probable. That a Board for preparing native regulations would be found useful, is very likely.[6]

Within the Colonial Office Antrobus showed suspicion of educated Africans, for although he agreed that 'Sir William MacGregor is no doubt right in wishing to have a native as Assistant Colonial Secretary for Native Affairs' he felt that 'the difficulty is to find a native who can be thoroughly trusted'. Although Carr had been to England twice, at St Mark's College, Chelsea, Antrobus was still suspicious of him: 'I thought that in one or two small matters . . . he was not quite straightforward, but in manners and education he is unquestionably far above the average educated native'.[7] The appointment of Carr on probation as Assistant Secretary, which was financially provided for in the 1899 estimates, was seen by MacGregor as 'a first step towards the establishment of a better system of native government through the chiefs and old existent native authorities'.[8] In a private letter to Gordon (unfortunately the only one extant from this Lagos governorship) MacGregor was very frank about the defects of the system of rule he had inherited:

> Our administration is a curious one. We have no Native Department. Our District Officers are Commissioners not of the Governor but of the Supreme Court. They are all barristers and solicitors. There are ten of them, nine of them could not drive a nail. We have no native code, no machinery for passing native law. We have no native council. The Commissioners of the Supreme Court are supposed to administer justice. They do so by quoting cases from the law journals as authority for their decisions. We have of course no summary procedure ordinance; no penal code. In part of the protectorate native courts may sit, not subject to any revision. The English barrister may operate alongside! Over the great bulk of the protectorate our courts have absolutely no jurisdiction whatever.

> We have no European planters and are not likely to ever have any. We are opening some model farms to try to improve native cultivation and to introduce new products. Our agricultural future clearly depends on the native.[9]

MacGregor's lack of trust in the existing staff, especially in dealing with Africans, was made clear to the Colonial Office in October 1899. In asking for a staff replacement he argued that the colony needed men who had had experience in tropical countries, and in bush life, and who had dealt with natives. At that time he thought he had only one man who could

> . . . lay off or measure a plot of land, lay out a road, build a bridge, paint a house, or drive a nail. They have [not] with very rare exceptions any knowledge of planting, or farming; or any scientific knowledge of botany, geology, or mineralogy.[10]

The Colonial Office desultorily discussed the problem of finding fit and proper candidates before deciding that the present was hardly the time for 'organic changes' in West African administrative staff.[11]

MacGregor wanted active African representatives on the Legislative Council which, in 1899, consisted of the Governor and four official members, the Chief Justice, the Colonial Secretary, the Treasurer and the Queen's Advocate (Attorney-General)[12] to whom MacGregor wanted to add the Chief Medical Officer. There were also four unofficial members two of whom were Europeans, representing the mercantile community, and two Africans, each appointed by the governor for a term of five years. By 1901 Dr Strachan, the Chief Medical Officer, held a personal appointment in the Council, and there were five unofficial members, including three Africans.[13] The Council had become much more active, criticism of some of MacGregor's policies coming from the Africans, notably from two of his appointees, a barrister, Sapara Williams, and a doctor, Obadiah Johnson.[14]

As usual, MacGregor busied himself with social problems, such as the reformation and custody of criminal and neglected African children, many of whom were the children of ex-slaves.[15] He also worked with the new Secretary for Native Affairs on marriage legislation, for he felt that 'no girl should be forced to marry any man', but he well realized the difficulties in changing African customs.[16] He intervened in African affairs to choose the Oba of Lagos. Oyekan, the successor in 1885 to Docemo who had ceded Lagos to Britain in 1861, died in 1900 and three of the family disputed the right to become nominal head of all the chiefs in Lagos. Following a meeting with Africans at Government House MacGregor recommended Eleko, a son of Docemo, and reported support; for instance, the influential landowning white-cap chiefs, who had favoured another candidate, had agreed 'that the choice had been properly made and has met with general approval'.[17] The Lagos press, however, strongly disapproved, claiming that MacGregor's 'political blunder' had caused 'considerable dissatisfaction' for he had ignored the prerogative of the various chiefs to nominate and had not consulted them before the meeting, although admitting that 'rivalry and jealousy have all been laid aside . . . people are now unanimous in their support of the recognised head of the royal house'.[18] MacGregor denied that the nomination had any political significance, defending his method of choice and his right to intervene in the deadlock because the Oba was being paid a pension by the British government.

In 1901 MacGregor, who had become increasingly dissatisfied with the poor reception and misunderstanding of his aims, decided to set up a Lagos Institute partly for adult education and partly to promote his policies. Both purposes were to be aided by developing a library for the citizens of Lagos. Mac-Gregor handed over to this library from Government House sets of 'a few classic authors such as Dickens, Thackeray, Carlyle etc'. which he presumed were part of the 'furniture' at the

House, for he could not 'suppose that there can be a Governor without his own library'.[19] In furthering its purposes the Institute was intended to sponsor public lectures, and significantly he gave the first address in October 1901, which can be regarded as a belated inaugural review of his policy. In this address he gave as his three main aims a policy of railway extension, the support of provincial government by the chiefs, and health improvement. He also answered allegations, made by the educated Africans of Lagos, that he gave no consideration to African rights, by claiming that

> . . . it is really of very great importance to try and rouse in the minds of these people an intelligent interest in public affairs. It is very dangerous to proceed to introduce any administrative change in this place by means of legislation or otherwise unless people are patiently prepared for it beforehand. Their attitude has been simple obstruction to anything and everything proposed. This is the outcome of ignorance.[20]

MacGregor was right only in so far as educated Africans of Lagos were a narrow *élite* concerned in obstruction to avoid interference with their immediate vested interests.

In this address MacGregor also elaborated his support of provincial government through the chiefs, stating that

> Perhaps the most interesting and the most important question connected with administration at the present moment is that of provincial government. This is one of those crucial questions on which men's minds are very apt to differ.[21] My own personal views are that the government of the hereditary chiefs of the country should not only be retained, but should be steadily and consistently strengthened and developed. Reasons for this policy may be found in these facts. In the first place some form or degree of native rule exists now in each Province. Certain men and certain families have long exercised it. They are accustomed to it; the country is used to it. It suits the genius of all classes of these communities, and it is therefore better adapted to the economic and social development than any other form of rule.

MacGregor's views on African contribution to government are revealed in his Native Councils Ordinance.[22] The idea was to have a series of councils of Africans which would exercise a certain amount of delegated power. The main Central Council was to consist mainly of the chiefs in the colony of Lagos, though rulers from the hinterland were later to attend. It could be consulted by its president, the governor, 'at any time on any question affecting native interests'.[23] The influence on Mac-

Gregor's ideas of the Fijian meetings of chiefs can clearly be seen. MacGregor also pointed out that some of his predecessors in Lagos had realized the need for such councils. For instance McCallum had formed the Native Advisory Board in Lagos.

MacGregor had proposed introducing a Central Council in 1900, before he went on leave in June. An ordinance had been introduced into the Legislative Council during his leave by the Acting Governor, Denton, but not taken past the committee stage.[24] This was partly due to Denton's reluctance to push the idea of an African council, which he had not experienced and seemed to distrust. But it was mainly due to opposition from native members of the Legislative Council backed by many of the educated natives in Lagos led by the local press, the English West African newspapers and by the Aborigines' Protection Society.

The Africans in Lagos first argued that the suggested Central Council was not as representative as the existing Native Advisory Board. This had represented the chiefs, the educated natives, the Moslem community and the Brazilian repatriates whereas Mac-Gregor's council was to consist of the head of the Docemo family (Eleko), the white-cap chiefs, Yesufu Shitta Bey with other representatives of the Moslem community, and the chiefs of Badagry, Epe and Ebute Metta. On the new council there was not a single representative of the educated native community nor of the Brazilian repratriates 'who form a large and influential portion of the community'. MacGregor, according to the press, was trying to 'ignore and repress the educated native element'. It was persuasively argued that this element was vitally important in Lagos:

> . . . the position of the educated native is certainly a curious one. Taken himself or his forefathers from his native country, through the cupidity of the Europeans, forced by his teachers to adopt the dress and habits of the civilization which he was taught to understand was essential to his salvation, he must now be made to suffer for what he is in no way responsible for. A former generation deprived his forefathers of their liberty; the present would do more—deprive him of even a nationality![25]

The Aborigines' Protection Society agreed with the press that selections to the Central Council should be: 'representative of and acceptable to native opinion'.[26]

MacGregor answered the press and this Society by assuring them in his despatch of 7 February 1902 that the Central Native

Council was representative of and responsible to native opinion since

> . . . the white-cap chiefs; the Native Traders' Guild; the leading Mohammedans; the head of the house of Docemo; the Bales and Chiefs of some of the neighbouring towns, were all selected and appointed to the Council to the number of twenty-three, so far as I know without a single dissentient voice in the community.[27]

He answered the specific objections of the Aborigines' Protection Society in the same despatch. He professed to be hurt by their criticism, writing

> . . . it is a real grief to me to find a society, whose theoretical principles in regard to the treatment of native races seem to me what I have consistently practised during the whole of my official career, should be in conflict with myself.

After denying other specific charges of this Society he concluded:

> I, who know every large town and every great chief in this territory, and who have studied native institutions on the spot in every one of these great communities, . . . [regard the Ordinance as suitable for its objects]. Apparently the Society deprecates military expeditions. You are aware that I never had a soldier in British New Guinea during my ten years' administration of that great province. I have had no military expedition here. Yet the society would apparently represent that I am following a course that makes such expeditions necessary.

After the Central Native Council's first meeting, on 20 December 1901, MacGregor regarded its establishment as a success, particularly because the 'chiefs regard it as a high honour to be a member of it' and he felt that no doubt 'it was a step in the right direction'.[28] Whenever MacGregor was in Lagos it continued to meet regularly at night (because of the custom that certain chiefs could not come out in daylight). It was attended by rulers from the hinterland, notably in 1903 when the venerated Oni of Ife—the Yoruba ruler from whom 'the greatest Chiefs including the Alafin of Oyo, traced their descent'—unprecedentedly left his capital to attend a Lagos meeting where he sat at MacGregor's side, with his back to the rest of the assembly, his face concealed from them as custom demanded. Because of his 'ancient authority and power' the Oni, although destitute, had been invited by MacGregor to give advice in a dispute querying the right of the Elepe of Epe to wear a crown. The Oni's overruling of the Elepe's claim was accepted and his listing of the twenty-one rulers who were entitled to wear crowns was welcomed by MacGregor as an aid to the understanding of Yoruba customs and to the safeguarding of 'the rights, the position, dignity and authority of the leading chiefs of the country'.[29] The Council gave MacGregor so much useful advice (for instance, each member had described customs of African land ownership) that at the last meeting over which he presided he introduced rules for conducting its business and providing for meetings at least once a month,[30] because he was sure it should continue. The Colonial Office on its part questioned the value of the meetings and decided to leave it to MacGregor's successor to decide whether they should be continued.[31] In fact this Council, like so many of MacGregor's attempts to gain co-operation from Africans, was to fall into disuse after he left the colony.

The Native Councils Ordinance was MacGregor's main attempt to systematize his rule. By it he showed his concern for the difficult position of the chiefs both in Lagos and the hinterland because of the way their authority was constantly being questioned by the younger generation, especially by those who could read or write, or by those who had served as soldiers and labourers in the other colonies. As well he was concerned in the rough handling and contemptuous treatment which could be meted out with impunity to any chief in the interior by some District Commissioner or other European official. He wanted to maintain the control by the British government, and by himself as a representative of the Crown, over the chiefs, but he wanted their position in the hierarchy recognized. As a pragmatist and as an administrator concerned with finding a solution to an immediate problem he had no direct concern in the final target of British colonial policy. While it is valid to claim that he was propping up authorities whose rule had clearly been challenged, it is equally valid to claim that he gave far more weight to African rule than did the Colonial Office. It is likewise true that in so far as he hoped to rule through the traditional authorities and to recognize their institutions, he was ahead of his time.[32]

His proposal was that existing African councils, such as those in Abeokuta, Ibadan and Shaki would be given official recognition, while new Provincial Councils could be begun by the government after consultation with Africans in places where no council existed. Each council was to be responsible 'for the conduct of the administrative business of its own province', as well as having judicial functions. The European officer in charge of each district was to assist, where possible, at all the council's sittings, but the ruling chief of the area was to preside. Provincial Councils could appoint Town or Village Councils to assist their work.[33] Ironically the Colonial Office welcomed the proposals as undermining the independence of the provinces, believing that the acceptance by the councils of responsibility to the British government for the administration of their lands would aid 'the inevitable extension of British influence'.[34]

MacGregor realized that the power of the chiefs was being challenged within their own states and that it had been limited by such British actions as abolishing the slave trade, and modifying or abolishing the tolls: 'All these causes have eclipsed the authority of the hereditary chiefs, and that too at a time when their active intervention as rulers is more required and needed than it ever was before'. He believed their rule was preferable to control by other Africans and that it would not be static: 'The great chiefs are, with very few exceptions, aware that things are changing fast here, and that they must advance with them in spite of their conservatism'. MacGregor also wanted to prevent European officers from challenging the chiefs:

> The position of the chiefs was entirely undefined in any way. European officers have very frequently caused serious trouble by arbitrarily setting aside the authority of the chief, by intentionally ignoring him, or even by acting in direct opposition to his wishes, and that without any reference to Headquarters.[35]

He hoped that this Ordinance would reassert the authority of the chiefs. The Lagos press attacked these provisions for the hinterland which were felt to be

> . . . nothing less than a subversion of existing law and custom . . . the destruction of native organisations, and the substitution of hybrid organisations of the various provinces, of which the Central Native Council in Lagos, with the Governor as President, will be the ruling spirit and final arbiter.[36]

Another line of opposition by Africans in the Legislative Council was that although the working of the ordinance would be 'safe' in MacGregor's hands, it gave too much potential power to 'a military governor' or a young man who could use it 'to undermine, destroy and set aside the authority of the chiefs'.[37] MacGregor realized that the European members of the Council were not enthusiastic supporters for 'their feelings would be towards annexation of the entire territory, and the establishment of a complete administration on the European model'. One

attempt he made to surmount opposition was by the appointment of a Select Committee consisting of Johnson and Williams,
the African members who vehemently opposed the bill, together
with two European members:

> I was able to modify the language used so as to retain intact all
> the principles of the bill, and finally to have it moved and
> seconded in its latest stages by the opposing native members. In its
> present form it has therefore been passed by the unanimous con-
> sent of the Council, a conclusion that at first did not seem to be
> very probable.[38]

But the journalists of Lagos were not so easily placated, and
those who had initially welcomed MacGregor for his 'brilliant
record and . . . respectable history',[39] now lashed out at him for
his policy in the hinterland. After his first visits to Abeokuta,
Ibadan and the western districts in 1899 an editorial had apparently approved his ideas:

> A policy of slow and progressive evolution, as opposed to drastic
> changes; which will utilise and strengthen the influence of native
> rulers in promoting civil and political order, and which will give
> the widest latitude to the application of such native laws and the
> support of such native institutions that do not conflict with the
> dictates of justice and humanity. In this way, and in this way only,
> will be built up a great empire—a lasting empire, because founded
> upon the peace, the happiness and the contentment of the people
> —the outcome of native confidence and the justice, equity and
> humanity of British rule.[40]

But now an editorial expressed concern at what was regarded
as a contradiction between MacGregor's intention—which the
writer admitted was to establish the authority of the chiefs—and
the effect of the ordinance—which the writer felt would be to
divest the chiefs of whatever 'modicum of power' they had left.
The ordinance was seen as part of a vast British scheme 'to
entirely deprive the Rulers of the Hinterland of the right to the
government of their native States'.

The conclusion made the moral point: 'Can this be done in the
Hinterland of Lagos without breaking political faith, and violat-
ing every moral and religious obligation?'[41] The allegation of a
contradiction in MacGregor's aims was repeated in an editorial
of January 1902 which considered that 'in his public utterances
no more enlightened and statesmanlike views, no more humane,
just and equitable policy could be enunciated', but that his deeds
and actions were so different.[42]

Press criticism seems to date from an incident in 1899 when MacGregor censured the Bale of Igbogila for allegedly granting illegal timber concessions.[43] This criticism increased over the years, and the whole attitude of the press is confusing to follow. Although strongly advocating independent native rulers, it supported slow development especially in the town of Lagos. Thus when MacGregor expressed a hope that municipal government could begin there during his governorship an editorial advocated hastening as slowly as possible, for few leaders had developed in the brief thirty-eight years of the existence of the British colony. There was also the fear that 'the various tribal jealousies, want of union and general distrust of each other, would all prove almost insuperable difficulties in the way of successfully managing a municipality'. It was admitted, however, that the greatest objection was the fear of fresh taxation,[44] and at the end of 1899 a newspaper retrospect of the previous year's events was noncommital about MacGregor's seven months rule, allocating neither praise nor blame.[45]

On 28 February 1900 his policy was criticized as

> an eccentric irrelevant and unprogressive 'policy of drift'. Pronounced indifference and lack of consideration for and interest in the native is the heritage which the native gets for the volume of hope and confidence with which he became inspired in May last.[46]

On 6 and 13 March a columnist, 'Junius', also attacked MacGregor listing his various alleged failings and arguing that MacGregor was carrying out a 'deliberate steady action' against the 'interests of the native population'.[47]

So at the end of MacGregor's first tour of office in June 1900, judgements on his rule were generally hostile.[48] By the end of the year it was said that the appointment of MacGregor could be looked upon as 'a most unfortunate incident in the colony's history', in so far as he had 'not come up to the expectation he had aroused considering his ability to govern, by the enunciation of a wise statesmanlike policy in what may be considered his inaugural address'.[49] His alleged failure in economic policy for not checking 'wasteful and extravagant' expenditure was another target for further disapproval.[50]

The bitter criticism of MacGregor by the press was heightened by his decision to take steps to prevent the leakage of confidential information from government departments. In September 1900 he had reorganized the Colonial Secretary's Office particularly to aid secrecy. In the previous system, he told the Colonial Office, despatches

> . . . passed in some way or another through the hands of half of dozen clerks. And I very soon learned by experience that the contents of these despatches were made known to such people as had any curiosity in the matter. Opinions that I have expressed in my despatches to you, and recommendations that I have made, have appeared in the local press here long before the despatches in question reached your hands.[51]

'Junius' had indeed publicly warned MacGregor in March 1900:

> it is on the cards that you are extremely anxious to discover my personality and to detect the channels through which valuable information reaches me. For your especial benefit, allow me to quote that solemn annunciation; I am the sole depository of my own secret, and it shall perish with me.[52]

MacGregor eventually took action against the newspapers, submitting to the Colonial Office in January a measure based on a Trinidad Ordinance providing for proceedings against the editors for libel.[53] The bill said that newspapers had to enter into a bond with sureties for £500 as a guarantee against the costs of successful libel actions. In the Colonial Office the figure of £500 was thought by one clerk to be high, for even an amount of £200 in a similar ordinance was supposed to have killed the *News* published at Scarborough in Tobago. Ommanney was less sympathetic with the colonial press: 'I am not sure that a newspaper which would be killed by having to pay security for £500 has any title to exist'. No objection was made in London to the principle of introducing such an ordinance.[54] In fact the sum was, after protests in the Lagos Legislative Council which stressed the poverty of Lagos Africans, reduced to £250.

The African councillors bitterly resented this apparent attempt 'to kill public opinion' and their opposition represented considerable public outcry against this ordinance, including a petition dated 13 May 1903 signed by about 270 citizens. When the Ordinance was passed by a majority vote (7 to 3) in the Legislative Council on 8 June another petition was sent, on 20 June, directly to the Secretary of State.[55] MacGregor had defended the ordinance in the Legislative Council where he attacked the press for its ingenuity in discovering 'a sinister motive for anything and everything ever done by the Government'.[56] To balance this slant of the press he expanded the *Government Gazettes*. From January 1903 under the heading 'General News' he reported his dealings with Africans, whether meetings with chiefs or the Minutes of councils he attended, and published some of the proceedings of the Legislative Council including the debate on 8 June on the Newspaper Ordinance. He submitted this ordinance to London as 'a moderate [measure] . . . that can hardly fail to be useful' and the Colonial Office gave it general support: 'under no consideration would I alter the provisions of the ordinance . . . officials and respectable citizens would otherwise be at the mercy of these Yellow Journals'.[57] The ordinance was originally to come into force on 1 August but after further petitions MacGregor decided to wait until the Colonial Office considered these before introducing it. Eventually it was sanctioned, becoming law in October 1903.

The verdicts of the press when MacGregor left Lagos were, no doubt, toned down by the Newspaper Ordinance; but even so they were far from complimentary. He was accused of almost everything from the drafting and passing of objectionable ordinances to racial discrimination and the muzzling of the press—and even to devoting most of his time to astronomical research, and searching for minerals in the hinterland. Taking into account the vast amount of time he obviously spent on the governing and welfare of the colony, it is difficult to treat these accusations seriously.[58]

The critics regarded the Lagos Institute as one 'redeeming feature in the otherwise general neglect and indifference in educational matters';[59] and this reference to education[60] could have some justification. MacGregor was well aware of the importance of education, including the training of teachers and providing more secondary courses for Africans. He did not, however, place as much stress on educating Africans as he had in the case of Pacific islanders. Partly this reflected his distaste for the 'educated' Africans of Lagos. But, as in his other colonies, the main reason for his lack of achievement was the shortage of government finance.

He felt obliged because of the seriousness of the health problems of the colony to give priority to expenditure on meliorative measures in that field, and he knew that most education was being provided not by the government, but by the missions. On this point he was criticized for not looking more closely into the content of mission education. He did, however, make an observation of which some present-day educators could take note, in criticizing the unsuitability of certain textbooks:

English reading books are of the English type with the names of British boys, and with pictures of European birds, beasts and flowers, all of which is absurdly unsuitable for a native child of this country struggling to learn and understand something of the English language.[61]

And later: 'It is absurd to teach the youth of this place, who never more than half learn English, a useless smattering of Greek, Latin and French'.[62]

MacGregor had supported increases of £500 for education in the estimates for 1900, and again for 1901, but the Colonial Office was disappointed that he was not interested in a suggestion that teachers be trained at government expense at Foorah Bay College in Sierra Leone, in fact he had disapproved, arguing that the extra £500 'on education was now as great as can be met by the public funds of the colony',[63] and that there was no shortage of teachers in Lagos. He then maintained that it would be better to make the existing teachers more useful by giving them a course of lectures on elementary hygiene. In the same despatch, however, he agreed that there was a need for better technical education, and earlier he had supported a scheme for a secondary school for Lagos, Southern and Northern Nigeria. On his first leave MacGregor raised the question of finance for education at a conference with the Liverpool Chamber of Commerce and Sir Alfred Jones said that 'Liverpool would be very glad to give any sum that was needed', particularly for a Teachers' Training College.[64]

The strongest criticism can be levelled at MacGregor on the dilatory manner in which he dealt with the 1902 report on schools, and the appointment of a new Inspector of Schools. This position had been vacant since 1899, and in spite of promptings from the Colonial Office, no appointment was made until 1904, which was after MacGregor had left Lagos.[65]

It could be argued that MacGregor's great interest in health measures caused him to economize on education in Lagos: but the fact remains that he showed keen interest in education in other colonies such as Fiji and New Guinea, where he also had health problems. So the legitimate query presents itself—had his experience of the tutored Africans of Lagos, the journalists in particular, led him to prefer to leave most Africans uneducated? Had he grown to regard with suspicion the writers, the 'mission-educated young men who live in the villages interfering with the native councils and acting as correspondents for the mendacious native press'? If this were so, it would be understandable as a human reaction to frustrating circumstances; but it would be short-sighted as a policy, and should stand as a criticism of his governorship.

The great mass of criticism, however, could be regarded as an inevitable concomitant of this stage of colonialism: for whatever policies MacGregor as governor had introduced these would have been opposed, even by those of the well-educated Africans, like Johnson and Williams with whom he remained on good terms, because of resentment against any manifestation of non-African control. The clash, however, was made worse because MacGregor was not prepared to accept the fact that many Africans had reached a more sophisticated stage of development than the Fijians or the New Guineans. He dismissed the Lagos papers as ignorant, misguided and self-interested, and eventually felt 'as great contempt for their praise' as he had 'formerly despised their blame'.[66] In fact he did not suffer gladly those who differed from him—too often dismissing them as fools.

The venom in a retrospective comment leaves no doubt about the feelings of the Lagos press for their late Governor:

> Sir William was an indefatigable worker, possessed of unbounded energy and determination that would brook no opposition nor be discouraged by difficulties. Thwarted in one direction, he would introduce the same or a similar scheme again and again, and push it on to success or partial success rather than acknowledge himself defeated. It speaks much for his tact, ability and perseverance that of the several ordinances—objectionable as all, and violently opposed as most of them were—he did not fail to carry them through.[67]

S

12

Lagos : An Independent Hinterland 1899-1904

He is our father—he is the best Governor we have ever had.

MacGregor's actions won praise from the chiefs in the protectorate areas in the hinterland despite the disapproval of many educated Africans of Lagos. This praise depended on bonds of friendship and on his systematized rule about which Aderibigbe claims that 'during . . . [his] governorship the justification of indirect administration as a method of colonial rule reached a level of consistency and rationalization never before attained in Lagos and, perhaps, hardly surpassed ever since'.[1] The core of his systematized rule was the hierarchy of Native Councils. Before MacGregor departed he gave recognition in the provinces to nineteen central and twenty-five town councils.[2] These covered all areas of the hinterland and proved his attempts to maintain the authority of the chiefs. He tried to uphold a balance between traditional leaders, such as the crowned Yoruba Oba recognized by the Oni of Ife, and the structure of power existing after the nineteenth century wars. He realized the importance of the rulers of Abeokuta (a city with a population of 60,000 controlling 350,000 Egbas) and of Ibadan (a city of 250,000 with widespread influence), as well as the significance of such groupings as the 1903 Ijoh confederation of Bini towns.

He insisted, as he had done in Fiji and British New Guinea, on his supremacy as representative of the British Crown over the head chiefs. Hence his action when he first met Gbadebo, the leading chief of Abeokuta:

> The Alake was seated in an armchair; and did not rise to shake hands with me; but he stood up smartly when asked by me through the interpreter whether he was a legless man or a woman. I then shook hands with him.[3]

Despite this inauspicious beginning a close friendship was to develop which culminated in MacGregor taking the Alake to

England in 1904. The Oni of Ife had also become MacGregor's friend despite a similar first encounter when the Oni was rebuked for ignoring the governor's arrival in Ife.[4]

In spite of his dislike of ruling by force, MacGregor opposed, in 1899, any reduction of the troops serving in Lagos, which he said were wanted more as a police than as a military force, mainly in dealing with the interior:

> The hinterland is not even nominally under our control. The great centre of Abeokuta for example is regarded as an independent nation exercising sovereign rights of which they are extremely jealous. In their territory the government is only a tenant paying rent; and they jostle Europeans, and among them government officers on the streets of Abeokuta.[5]

MacGregor's attitude changed when he became convinced that he should rule through the chiefs. Subsequently he wanted troops to prop up the authority of leaders such as the Alake of Abeokuta. At this ruler's request he took 300 troops to Abeokuta to settle a disturbance of May 1901, when he promised future aid.[6] Troops were requested again in November 1903 to quell a revolt of about 5,000 Africans against the Abeokuta authorities. This rebellion was suppressed on the day it began with the arrival of MacGregor and the military, which caused Antrobus to write:

> Sir William MacGregor has always held strongly to the recognition of the independence of Abeokuta, and we are not bound to assist the Alake in any troubles with his subjects. It may not be a bad thing if he comes to look to us for support, this may lead to a more satisfactory treaty arrangement than the one at present in force . . . the Colonial Secretary of Lagos observed, in conversation with me a few weeks ago, that the end of the policy of recognizing the 'independence' of the Egba country (of which Abeokuta is the capital) i.e. of the chiefs, would be that the people would rise against them. There is no reason to be alarmed at any such rising, as the force in Lagos should be strong enough to deal with it—and apparently has been, and reinforcements could easily be obtained from Southern Nigeria. The misfortune is that this rising should have occurred before Sir William MacGregor's departure for I agree that advantage ought to be taken of the opportunity to get rid of the independence, which is only good for the chiefs and the educated Egbas who use them for their own purposes, while it is bad for the people generally and for the development of the country.[7]

which not only illustrates how MacGregor used troops to support the chiefs, but hints at more than an element of insincerity on the part of the Colonial Office in their treaty arrangements with these chiefs.

MacGregor's position about troops had been clarified in a November 1899 despatch in which he distinguished between police and military functions, and went on to argue that 'the more the Lagos battalion becomes strictly military the less useful a factor it must be in civil administration work here'. As in New Guinea he wanted a police and not a military force to aid his policy towards the inland states, which he saw as a kind of 'peaceful penetration'. He wanted men who were prepared to fight in the bush if necessary but who would also 'discharge most useful and important duties of administration, control and police'.[8] He had misgivings about the conversion of the Lagos Constabulary into a battalion of the new West African Frontier Force, and the subsequent use of troops from Lagos in military campaigns in the Gold Coast, Southern and Northern Nigeria. It was the distinction between MacGregor's peaceful extension of control in Yorubaland which succeeded in retaining the confidence and sympathy of the chiefs, in contrast particularly to Lugard's warlike expansion in Northern Nigeria, which justified MacGregor's defence of his peaceful policy as against what he called the dominant British policy of 'smash'.[9]

One of the elements of peaceful penetration is the rule of law. Soon after his arrival MacGregor was certain that his troops and police should be enforcing a better defined system of jurisdiction in the hinterland. He received further ammunition from a report from A. R. Pennington, the District Commissioner for the western district stationed at Badagry, who wrote:

> . . . the old authority of the chiefs and Bales has been practically taken away from them. For years we seem to have been breaking down the old order of things and have placed nothing in its place, or practically nothing. A great part of the district is in the colony of Lagos, and here of course English law is in force supported by a few constables or Hausas scattered here and there in the bush. The net result in the bush districts is chaos. You cannot administer the nicities [sic] of English law in the middle of West African jungle. What is wanted is a short and summary method of dealing with malefactors and disturbers of the peace.[10]

MacGregor was sure, after various visits of inspection, that British laws could be enforced in most parts of the protectorate. For instance by February 1900 he claimed that he could enforce throughout the protectorate a decree to the effect that after a certain date no child would be born into slavery.[11] The Colonial Office had far more doubts about whether this was possible. On 20 July 1900, however, a public notice[12] was circulated announcing the abolition of the legal status of slavery. Doubts about the applicability of Lagos Ordinances in the parts of the hinterland added since 1887 led to a review of earlier legislation. MacGregor tried to ensure power by a revised Order of his Legislative Council on 29 December 1900, but the Colonial Office did not think this adequate.[13] Consequently the British Order-in-Council of 29 December 1887 was replaced on 24 July 1901 and under these extended powers a new Foreign Jurisdiction Ordinance was enacted by Lagos in 1902.[14]

Every attempt he made to legislate aroused opposition. Thus a law for the arrest in the hinterland of prisoners who had escaped from Lagos, although introduced at the request of the chiefs, was attacked as 'an encroachment on . . . [their] independence'.[15] MacGregor believed that his system of provincial councils would aid the spread of British law, as well as the recognition of African customs, dreaming of the time when the 'usages of the country that should be maintained . . . [would] be codified and reduced to order'.[16] This remained a dream though he welcomed advances such as the ruling of the Jebu Ode Council that 'every child born in the district . . . since the British took possession . . . shall be deemed free-born',[17] and he boasted in 1904 that 'slavery as an institution is now in this territory in a state of decrepitude'.[18]

MacGregor failed to see eye to eye with the Colonial Office and the British Chambers of Commerce on many points in their dealings with the chiefs. One of the most contentious issues concerned their powers to levy tolls on goods sold in or passing through their territories. The African states were an expanding market, especially for cotton goods and spirits, while the export economy of the colony of Lagos depended chiefly on palm kernels and palm oil, supported by rubber, mahogany and ivory, and all these goods had to be brought from the interior to the port of Lagos. The building of railways seemed one way of avoiding transit tolls since the land for the railways had been ceded to Britain.

In June 1900 MacGregor suggested (after discussion with Lugard) a fixed policy for dealing with these tolls: no new tolls should be allowed; no increase should be allowed in existing rates of tolls; well-established tolls should, wherever possible, be commuted to some other form of tribute or payment. He could not see what justification the British government would have in removing long-established tolls, unless they reached the point of involving a breach of existing treaties 'by unduly and unreasonably interfering with trade'.[19] He did not think this was the case in 1900. The question of tolls was raised by the Liverpool Chamber of Commerce in September of that year, but it was not given great prominence, and the question remained quiescent until the end of 1902 when it became a leading issue. A Mr Grey, of Lagos Stores Limited, in September suggested diverting to Lagos through Northern Nigeria the caravan trade, the trade of the Hausas now going north to Tripoli. He believed that the 'exorbitant' tolls imposed by the Egbas, and said to be favoured by the Lagos government, were major obstacles to his plan. Grey praised Major Bower,[20] an ex-Resident Commissioner of Ibadan, because he had claimed to abolish all tolls in his area; but MacGregor maintained that the Egbas had the right to collect tolls and other taxes in their own territory and considered that 'they would most probably fight for their rights and in doing so they would have justice on their side'. He also believed that Major Bower had no power to abolish the tolls, and that he and Grey had not realized that

> . . . the Lagos government is bound by a network of treaties with the different chiefs of the countries. I am in no way responsible for these contracts, but I do deem it my duty to respect them as long as they exist.[21]

MacGregor pointed out that these tolls were practically the only revenue or source of income for the principal chiefs, and that it would need large-scale compensation to set aside these payments. He calculated that the Egbas probably received £10,000 a year from the tolls.

In March 1903, after a visit to Abeokuta, MacGregor was able to report that the Egba United Government had agreed to allow goods in transit to pass through free of tolls. He reiterated that it was neither wise nor even practicable to abolish tolls completely in Abeokuta and Ibadan as 'the chiefs have no other source of income . . . no other way of carrying on their rule'.[22] He did, however, after visiting Ibadan and Oyo, gain similar concessions from their rulers on goods in transit between Lagos and Northern Nigeria. This meant that there were now three roads free from tolls for goods in transit.[23]

Besides ending transit tolls MacGregor was able to gain assurances that domestic tolls on the imports and exports of the African towns would be collected regularly according to a fixed published scale (typical tolls[24] were 9d on a case of gin or 2s 6d on a bale of cloth imported; 3d on a bag of coffee or 1s on a horse exported). As well it was agreed that the rate of tolls imposed by Ibadan would not be made greater than for Abeokuta, and that no special exemptions would be granted either to Africans or Europeans. In Ibadan half the tolls collected were to be paid to the Bale and half kept for the public service. Mac-Gregor, as governor, approved all these new arrangements, and strongly opposed the European merchants' continued requests that these domestic tolls be abolished. Such action would, he thought, be 'highly impolitic and unjust' since the tolls were 'as deeply rooted in the institutions of the country as slavery, polygamy or circumcision'.[25] But again the Colonial Office, pressed by the merchants to abolish the remaining tolls, was influenced by considerations very different from those of Mac-Gregor. It believed the merchants' allegations that Ibadan's imposition of tolls on Europeans was a new move, while Antrobus wrote that

> . . . the policy of Sir William MacGregor (of which this was an incident) in laying stress upon the independence of Abeokuta and Ibadan, instead of paving the way for their being brought under control, constituted a grave danger . . . sooner or later the Egbas and Ibadans will have to be brought under our control, and it is better that they should be brought under it peacefully than that they should be encouraged in an attitude that will end in conflict.[26]

Such arguments led the Colonial Office to suspend the operation of MacGregor's revised toll system from the end of May. Assurances from MacGregor that the native members of the Legislative Council had given support to the system did nothing to impress the Colonial Office which expected such support for anything likely to 'exalt the native at the expense of the European'.[27] As well it had consulted Moor, the Governor of Southern Nigeria, who felt it was a 'very great mistake to support the chiefs in levying tolls' and who believed that an annual subsidy to the chiefs would be preferable, or, failing that, the collection of tolls by the Lagos government.[28]

The controversy continued unabated for over a month, whilst MacGregor bombarded the Colonial Office with a stream of telegrams. When the Colonial Office received a report[29] from the

British Resident at Ibadan which reinforced MacGregor's views of the strength of African indignation, they looked more closely at the three treaties of 1893 with the Egbas, Oyo and Ibadan. A clerk admitted that the treaties implied that these states could take whatever steps they thought fit for their internal administration, including levying of tolls, but he considered that MacGregor 'may have been unwise' in giving his formal approval to the new system, without first referring the question to the Secretary of State, since this action would strengthen 'the idea of independence which it is expedient not to emphasise, but the approval once given, it may be doubted whether it is not the greater unwisdom to revoke it'.[30] In comparing MacGregor's policy with that of McCallum, Antrobus wrote:

> If Sir H. McCallum had remained in Lagos he would probably have been prepared to risk a conflict for the purpose of bringing the Egbas and Ibadans under control. Sir William MacGregor, on the other hand, has been most anxious to avoid a conflict, but he has appreciated equally the importance of controlling the native authorities as far as possible and has endeavoured to obtain what he wanted by negotiation. It is unfortunate that his action should have the effect of confirming their independence, but in the circumstances I do not see how he could have acted otherwise. It would have been better, however, if he had given us and the Chambers of Commerce an opportunity of considering what he was doing before he actually committed himself[31]

which illustrates how differences between the Colonial Office and MacGregor were intensified by his methods.

The Colonial Office planned a conference in London for 18 June to meet with the Chambers of Commerce, and the results were telegraphed to MacGregor. The deputation from the Chambers of Commerce had again urged reconsideration, arguing that the collection of tolls by natives was 'liable to great abuse'; and that

> ... authority given for first time to natives to tax Europeans would make them arrogant and lead to abuse of their present qualified independence, ultimately tending to disturbance and war. If right once conceded it can never be withdrawn without a conflict.[32]

They urged that the tolls be replaced by paying the chiefs subsidies for municipal purposes. The deputation claimed that they would willingly pay for this purpose additional customs duties on spirits and even on cotton goods. Chamberlain concluded the telegram by telling MacGregor that British policy was close to that of the merchants:

. . . you are aware . . . that I entertain similar views and if not too
late I would urge strongly that you should consider whether with
your great influence with native chiefs you could not obtain
arrangement on these lines . . . subject to my concurrence.[33]

On 30 June MacGregor reported after addressing Council meetings at Abeokuta and Ibadan[34] that both had decidedly refused
the suggested subsidies, though they had agreed to certain concessions to meet some of the objections to the new system. Abeokuta promised to appoint a trained auditor; to publish annual
estimates of revenue and expenditure and the auditor's report;
not to increase tolls without the Colonial Office's sanction; to
allow all goods that were not the produce of Abeokuta to have
free transit on the railway through Abeokuta territory; and to
allow full drawback on goods re-exported. Ibadan promised the
same with an additional guarantee that tolls would not be collected twice on the same goods. Ibadan agreed to have a European inspector of tolls chosen by the government of Lagos.

MacGregor strongly urged the acceptance of these terms. Nine
members of the Legislative Council and the president of the local
Chamber of Commerce concurred.[35] The Colonial Office appreciated the fact that the clause requiring its sanction for the
increasing of tolls amounted to a repudiation of part of the
theoretical independence which the provinces enjoyed. But it
was also aware of the intense opposition that the concessions
would arouse among the British merchants, who suspected possibilities of great abuse in Abeokuta, where collections were to be
in African hands. The Colonial Office considered that the merchants' fears were exaggerated and that as MacGregor's arrangements could be regarded as a step towards 'bringing these so-
called independent states into the position of municipalities—
controlled by the central government, but yet to a large extent
managing their own affairs', Antrobus thought they could well be
sanctioned. Chamberlain agreed on 8 July, and MacGregor's
arrangements were affirmed,[36] but while the Colonial Office was
considering its decision African opinion had hardened. The
principal African merchants of Lagos on 2 July passed a resolution unanimously opposing a suggested imposition of additional
customs duties on spirits (to provide more general revenue to
pay subsidies to Abeokuta and Ibadan if the tolls were abolished)
'as calculated to greatly affect trade driving it . . . [to] neighbouring foreign territories', and they at the same time 'most emphatically . . . [condemned] abolition of tolls in the interior'.[37]

In Abeokuta resentment increased, particularly against the campaigns of the British merchants. On 8 July 100 African traders signed a petition protesting against the end of their tolls; on 9 July a mass meeting attended by over 10,000 adopted similar resolutions, which were supported on the same day by all principal native chiefs in the different towns of Abeokuta. The chiefs, traders and people of Abeokuta were thus unanimous against ending the tolls, and 'the pride of the Egbas . . . [had been] stirred up by the indiscreet and injudicious' campaign of the merchants which, MacGregor thought, 'had stirred up the racial question in a way that . . . [was] very offensive to the Egbas'.[38] As MacGregor held these views about the merchants' campaign he was not swayed by a personal appeal for his support telegraphed by Sir Arthur Jones on 16 July.[39]

The Colonial Office in retrospect appreciated MacGregor's negotiations with the Africans and his attempts to meet the objections of the merchants, commenting on his explanations:

> This is really a good and statesmanlike despatch, and supplies a strong argument in favour of the tolls . . . although we would have preferred to see the tolls abolished. I think that it is clear that Sir William MacGregor has done the best that could be done in the circumstances and that the Chambers of Commerce have either not understood or shut their eyes to the difficulties in the way of doing what they wanted.[40]

MacGregor had successfully persuaded the Colonial Office and had resisted efforts, especially by the merchants, to abolish the tolls. For the rest of his term of office his main concern was to ensure the efficient working of his agreements, and to limit transit and domestic tolls in other provinces; thus the acceptance by the Alafin of Oyo of subsidies in place of tolls in December 1903 meant that he was able to declare that there were now 'no tolls on the north [and east] between Ibadan and Northern Nigeria'.[41]

The issue of the tolls had led, besides the clash with the merchants, to the clearest example of the confrontation between MacGregor's genuine sympathy with the chiefs and his sincere desire to uphold African institutions maintaining financial powers, and the Colonial Office policy of only supporting Africans' interests which were compatible with British interests. MacGregor's humanitarian gestures of friendship with these African potentates were quite inexplicable to the Colonial Office.

The response of the chiefs to MacGregor's friendship can be gauged by the words of the Alafin of Oyo:

> I know you love me; I know you love my people and country; I am sure you will do what is just and right. I therefore leave the whole question [of tolls] in your hands.[42]

The implications of the friendly terms of this and other letters led to another significant clash between MacGregor and the Colonial Office. After MacGregor had visited Abeokuta in August 1903, to open a railway bridge, his actions and correspondence to the Alake led to criticism by both Antrobus and the Duke of Marlborough. The former wrote:

> I am afraid that Sir William MacGregor is making a mistake, which will cause trouble to his successors, in addressing and allowing himself to be addressed by the Alake as if they were equals. But it can't be helped now

while the latter generalized: 'amiability and dignity are not incompatible. The Governor while cultivating the former has done so somewhat at the expense of the latter'.[43] The assumptions that the Alake could not be the equal of a British governor, and that it was not dignified to observe the customs of an African chief, could well serve as a text to condemn much of British colonial policy. Earlier MacGregor had sent to London copies of the letters he had written to the Alake of Abeokuta and the Bale of Ibadan congratulating his 'good friends' on the sanctioning of the tolls, signed by him as 'your good friend'. These letters were published in the English *West African Mail,* and at first were praised in the Colonial Office as showing MacGregor's efforts to 'smooth the ruffled relations between the chiefs and the European traders'.[44] When, however, he sent the replies from these chiefs, the Colonial Office's attitude changed to one of censure because of the alleged extent of his subservience to these rulers. The opening of a letter written by the resident at Ibadan to the Colonial Secretary at Lagos using the phrase 'I am directed by the Bale and council' led to most censure. A Colonial Office clerk wrote:

> we have known for some time past that MacGregor's policy has been to exalt the native rulers of Abeokuta and Ibadan, and to treat them as friends and equals. He is said to have walked arm-in-arm with the Alake of Abeokuta along the Marina at Lagos, and it is even rumoured that he once held the royal umbrella over the Alake's head. This attitude of the Governor is one which must tend to make the native arrogant, and may lead to trouble in the

future. There has hitherto been nothing sufficiently definite to enable us to protest against his policy; but I think that we should now point out to the Governor that the Resident at Ibadan is not under the directions of the Bale and Council.[45]

The possible explanation of the censure of MacGregor's friendship with the chiefs could be that the Colonial Office considered these rulers were no longer acceptable to their subjects. This interpretation gains apparent support from the revolts in Abeokuta mentioned earlier especially that of 1903 which proved, Antrobus believed, that the 'people generally' were opposed to the Alake; but MacGregor's interpretation of the revolts differed. He thought they had arisen from disputes between the Alake and his Council and rival chiefs, in 1901 with the vanity of the Onitori of Itori, in 1903 with the leaders of part of the town of Abeokuta called Kemta.[46] Even if MacGregor's support of established structures, in maintaining the authority of the Alake and his Council, and of the chiefs of other areas, ignored objections to elements of despotic rule, it is clear that his attitude[47] was more straightforward than that of the Colonial Office, which paid lip service to the rule of the chiefs and recorded objections to their despotism mainly as a potential excuse for ending the independence of the provinces.

A significant difference of opinion had arisen between Mac-Gregor and the Colonial Office in 1901 after the Governor suggested that trivial legal cases in Lagos could be heard by two or more justices of the peace, rather than by a European stipendiary magistrate. MacGregor argued that

> Of still greater importance than . . . public convenience, would be the fact that a certain number of the native educated gentlement of Lagos would sit on the bench, and in this way learn to take a greater interest in the municipal life of the town, from which at present they remain almost apart.

Although a London lawyer thought this would be a valuable reform a Colonial Office clerk urged 'caution . . . as to trying cases by a bench of magistrates in which coloured "Lagos gentlemen" are in a majority'.[48]

A similar difference of opinion existed between MacGregor's policy and that of the Colonial Office towards the inland states, and this was highlighted in Abeokuta. MacGregor was determined to conclude a judicial treaty with this state to improve the procedure for mixed cases, that is, those involving Europeans in native courts.

He began his final negotiations on this subject in April 1903 asking the British government for copies of the laws of British New Guinea and of the capitulations for such mixed courts in any country where arrangements had been made for hearing mixed cases by mixed tribunals.[49] The Foreign Office thought MacGregor was confused since there were no cases of capitulations or mixed tribunals in a country which, like Abeokuta or Ibadan, had no foreign relations except with the British Government.[50] The Colonial Office's approach to the problem was to consider how much jurisdiction should be given up by the Egbas to British courts. Under existing agreements the Lagos government could arrest British subjects in any part of Abeokuta, while in addition Britons and other specified persons were subject to British law on the land granted for railways. Chamberlain made it clear that he would have preferred the Lagos courts to have exclusive jurisdiction, but since the Egbas 'would not give it',[51] alternatives were considered in order of preference, either a British judge with native assessors, or a native court with a British assessor.

MacGregor's views were not far removed from those of the Colonial Office. For instance, in a letter of 30 April he had told the Alake that for criminal and civil cases involving Europeans his courts were 'not sufficiently developed', and had suggested granting jurisdiction to the British Crown with the cases to be tried before the Lagos Chief Justice sitting at Abeokuta, with perhaps two Abeokuta assessors to assist. MacGregor pointed out that the Lagos Supreme Court 'is required and enabled by law to recognise and give effect to native law, whenever that is not repugnant to the requirements of British civilisation'.[52]

On 3 June 1903 the Alake and his Council offered to grant to the British king for a period of twenty years jurisdiction in Abeokuta in all criminal offences, or in civil cases for claims over £250. The Lagos Chief Justice was to sit with two native judges and two magistrates as assessors. Abeokuta wanted a treaty covering this grant, and MacGregor supported such a treaty, especially as he argued that it would create a precedent which 'before long will be accepted by every other province'.[53] He wanted the negotiations kept secret, fearing alarmist cries by the local press that such a treaty would be the beginning of annexation, so sacrificing the independence of Abeokuta and other states. There is no evidence that MacGregor visualized such a result. His efforts to improve jurisdiction seem genuine, and the

Alake's faith in him, as expressed in a letter, appears to be justified:

> I need scarcely assure you that I place absolute and entire dependence on your goodwill and have implicit and unwavering confidence in the sincere desire I know you have to consolidate my government and to maintain what is so dearest to my heart—the independence of my country and its internal adminstration.[54]

The Colonial Office considered the proposal carefully, reviewing precedents in other British colonies such as the Malay States, and being aware of possible opposition. For instance, the merchants would 'no doubt cry out against proposals invoking the submission of Europeans to courts composed partly of natives, just as they have objected to the levying of tolls by natives on Europeans'. Chamberlain was particularly concerned in the special position of Abeokuta as it was the only inland state whose independence had been formally recognized. Considering its independence this grant was formally a concession to Britain. Informally, however, the British government was most reluctant either to admit or to encourage Abeokuta's ideas of independence, and certainly did not wish the treaty to be used as a precedent:

> We have not formally recognized the independence of other provinces, and in them I did not think that we ought to be content with anything less than the scheme of courts in the Sierra Leone Protectorate where if a European was involved the case was heard before the British District Commissioner alone.[55]

Although the Colonial Office decided in August to accept the terms of the Abeokuta scheme, they asked for variations in September for reasons expressed by Antrobus: 'What we were afraid of was that the Governor would not get enough and that by making an agreement he would render it impossible to get more'.[56] MacGregor in December regretted that the original agreement had not been accepted especially as he claimed it had been

> ... brought about only by the exercise of a personal influence that is perhaps unique in this country; and that for some three years I have been trying to prepare them for entering into it. It is surely a very great advance on the present state of matters, which is, I respectfully submit, highly unsatisfactory.[57]

MacGregor criticized the suggested treaty, since the Colonial

Office's revisions reduced 'the jurisdiction of the native authorities over Europeans . . . to the lowest practicable minimum under existing circumstances'. The extent of jurisdiction ceded to British courts had been considerably increased. There were to be two courts. The superior court, the Lagos Supreme Court which could sit at Abeokuta, was to hear all cases dealing with murder or manslaughter, be the accused a native Egba, a European, or any other foreigner. This court was also to deal with civil claims over £50. Other cases were to be tried by the inferior court, a new Mixed Court which, unlike the superior had mixed judges, but the European president had to be there to provide a quorum. In cases involving more than £5 there was provision for an appeal to the superior court if the judges in the inferior court were not unanimous. Despite his objections MacGregor wanted to conclude an agreement, so on 15 December 1903, only four weeks before he left the colony, he asked the Colonial Office to approve the revised treaty, and this was done.

MacGregor indicated the difficulties in applying the precedent of the Abeokuta treaty, since it had been held that Lagos courts had 'no jurisdiction in for example Ibadan, Oyo, Ilesha, Ekiti, Ondo, Akure and Idanre. No jurisdiction has been established there by force; none has been ceded; and no jurisdiction has grown up by use or custom';[58] in addition all these provinces were

> . . . extremely jealous of their hereditary authority and quasi-independence to manage their own affairs. The holding of courts is regarded . . . as being an attribute of the chief which is inseparable from his dignity and the maintenance of his position and authority.[59]

An added difficulty was that court fees were in many cases the principal source of income for the chiefs, especially since the British government had ended the slave trade and had reduced the imposition of tolls.

MacGregor's concern began with the chiefs, whereas the Colonial Office saw other difficulties in applying the precedent of the Abeokuta treaty to other states. It would, for instance, never do

> to admit that Ibadan has any jurisdiction over Europeans to 'cede' to the King. The fact that the formal independence of Ibadan and the other places has never been recognized, as that of Abeokuta has unfortunately been, does constitute a real difference in the position; and as regards Ibadan and Oyo in particular, our position

is strengthened by the first clause of the treaty with Oyo which was confirmed by an agreement with Ibadan that any difference or dispute shall be referred to the governor of Lagos for the time being, and his decision shall be final and binding upon us all.

If a judicial treaty was to be made with Ibadan it should be imposed by Britain, rather than be granted by Ibadan. The subsequent treaty (after MacGregor left Lagos) was welcomed by the Colonial Office because of a statement in the preamble admitting that Ibadan was under British protection.[60] The Colonial Office was reiterating its reluctance to recognize the independence of these states, so that MacGregor's encouragement of them and of their chiefs was being increasingly deprecated in London. This was the background to MacGregor's invitation to the Alake of Abeokuta to come to England. The visit beginning in May 1904 was to re-stress the contrast between the policies of MacGregor and the Colonial Office.

The Alake set out from Lagos five months after MacGregor left Africa. In the meantime some of the emphases of MacGregor on the interests of the Africans had been reversed by Acting-Governor Moseley, who had used the impending visit as an opportunity to criticize these policies. Thus Moseley wrote to the Colonial Office on 26 April complaining that although the Alake intended to leave in eight days time he had given no official intimation of his visit; that Moseley had not been told what steps had been taken to carry on the Egba government during his absence; that Moseley had been told unofficially that £1,000 had been voted to pay for the expense of the visit which 'will presumably come out of revenue derived from tolls which we were lately led to believe was barely sufficient to carry on the ordinary work of government'. Moseley claimed that 'in view of the independent position of the Egba government I have not considered I had any right to interfere with the Alake's movements', but he was apprehensive of complications 'having regard to the commanding position which he [the Alake] has been allowed to assume in the Egba United Government'.[61]

Although one Colonial Office clerk said he did not 'quite like the tone of this despatch' Antrobus thought that 'there is ground for Mr. Moseley's apprehension and that Sir William MacGregor would have done better if he had discouraged the Alake from coming'.[62]

This suspicion, basically caused by the desire to avoid any acts tending to confirm the independence of Abeokuta, made the

Colonial Office constantly apprehensive while the Alake was in England. One hope that he would admit British control was expressed by a Colonial Office clerk: 'the Alake should be encouraged as much as possible to behave as though he and his people were under British protection. This appeared to be his inclination at present'.[63] MacGregor had suggested that King Edward VII should receive the Alake in audience, in order to strengthen the loyalty of the Alake to Great Britain, and a royal audience had to be hastily arranged 'as it does not seem advisable that he should stay long in England'.[64] Antrobus wrote:

> Sir William MacGregor is inclined to exaggerate both the good qualities and the importance of the Alake. But we cannot prevent the Alake from coming to England, and, if he comes, I do not think that there would be any objection to his seeing the King if His Majesty will receive him. We must, however, be careful not to let too much be made of him while he is in England.

The Secretary of State, Lyttleton, agreed that the audience would have a 'good effect' so this recommendation and MacGregor's despatch were passed on to the king who minuted 'I will gladly see the "Alake of Abeokuta" when he comes to England—in state in the Throne Room'. The audience was arranged for 30 May.[65]

MacGregor, in contrast to the Colonial Office, welcomed the visit which he thought would help in carrying on the policy he had tried to adopt in Africa. To his mind friendship with such an African ruler must aid British influence in Africa. In his attitudes signs can be seen both of the concept of indirect rule, as developed earlier by Gordon in Fiji and later applied by the changed administration of Lugard in Nigeria. The idea of partnership in anticipation of African independence can even be detected. Undoubtedly in this particular case his sympathies were far more with this African than were those of anyone at the Colonial Office.

The visit had been planned while MacGregor was still in Lagos, probably in one of their many private conversations— perhaps when he so shocked the Colonial Office by walking arm-in-arm with the Alake. The extent of MacGregor's promises was made clear by a letter written on 26 January which he received in England from an Egba prince, Ademola of Ake, telling him that the Alake hoped to leave on the first steamer in May 'but would be pleased to know . . . if you have succeeded to make all necessary arrangements to enable the Alake to see His Majesty the King as you had kindly promised, this being his chief aim

T

and desire'. The tone of this letter was both flattering and friendly—MacGregor was told, for instance, that 'I do not think that any Governor has succeeded to gain the confidence of the native as Your Excellency, and your name has already become a household talk in Abeokuta, and in most enlightened of the interior countries'.[66]

MacGregor did not pass this request on to the Colonial Office until 17 March, probably a month after he received the letter. He then wrote a ten-page memorandum[67] on the proposed visit, in which he highly praised the Alake both for his personal life which he considered to be temperate and active, and for his public life which showed his concern for his people. MacGregor stressed the importance of the visit as he pointed out that the Alake, the principal ruling chief of the Egbas, was 'by far the most powerful and influential, and at the same time the most enlightened chief and ruler in Yorubaland' who 'subject to His Majesty's guidance, rules his country in a spirit of sincere and loving loyalty'.

The visit was given considerable publicity both in the Lagos and English press. It was still a novelty, despite the visits for the 1897 jubilee and the 1902 coronation, for an African prince to arrive in England. The Alake and his suite reached Lagos on 2 May. The Alake was accompanied by his secretary, Adegloyega Edun (who had recently reverted from his non-African name Jacob Henry Samuel); Prince Ladapo Ademola, the Egba Government Agent, and his attendants Adegbite and Adeula. This party of five left on the boat *Nigeria* for Plymouth on 4 May. They were accompanied by R. B. Blaize who had been described as the richest native merchant in Lagos. By 25 May the party had reached England where the Alake stayed until 10 July, returning to Lagos by 29 July.

The royal audience was held on 30 May, a few days after the Alake's arrival, at Buckingham Palace. The *Daily Chronicle* reported that King Edward 'seemed to be slightly amused at first, but was evidently touched at the childish sincerity and loyalty of his vassal'. Large crowds watched in the Mall, where the Alake 'enthusiastically waved his handkerchief'.[68] The Alake was received at the Colonial Office on the morning of the royal audience, then on a later day he had an interview with the Duke of Marlborough and Ommanney and later still he discussed the affairs of Abeokuta with Antrobus, as chief of the West African Department. He visited the Royal Geographical Society, where

Sir Charles Markham escorted him, and he finished the day at the Alhambra Theatre watching a performance of 'High Jinks'.

His robes diverted London journalists, and detailed descriptions were given of what he wore to the Colonial Office, Buckingham Palace and other places. Thus after his visit to Madam Tussaud's a journalist wrote about the 'little procession of coal blackmen so radiantly attired that to look at them was to blink. The Alake was a blaze of gold': he wore a black silken gown with a heavy weight of golden thread, in fantastic designs, studded with golden roses, in whose petals rubies, emeralds and amethysts shimmered. The dress of the other Africans was scarcely less imposing, while his boys were said to follow behind with their eyes fixed on the Alake's face 'fearful lest some look or word of command should be missed'.[69] On 13 July Akigbaya Oluwole assured readers of the *Liverpool Echo*, who had been misled by an earlier report, that the Alake did not live in a thatched hut, nor did he wear a loin cloth in Africa.

> It is not becoming of any civilized nation to taunt another nation on its customs, for even we Africans have read your country's history, and have learnt that your former barbarity was not better than that of some of the most barbarous tribes of Africa.[70]

Generally, however, comments were sympathetic and the columnist 'On Dit' in Lagos felt sure that the most favourable impression would 'serve to correct any preconceived notions that may have existed about the savage and benighted condition of the inhabitants of the Hinterland of West Africa',[71] The *West African Mail* said that the Alake had received more space in the London newspapers in the past fortnight than any West African potentate before him. The paper doubted if the ultimate effect 'of this excessive hospitality is altogether happy' and hoped that the Alake's sense of proportion was not swamped, that he would return with 'his native simplicity, wherein lies the truest dignity, unimpaired'.[72]

The Alake's energetic programme made the most of his six weeks in Britain. After about a fortnight in London—which included his official duties and visits to the theatre, Madam Tussaud's, the Zoo, the Abbey, the Pavilion Theatre of Varieties, the Tower of London, the Mansion House, the Bank of England and the Bank of West Africa, and receptions by the African Society—he went on to the Royal Counties Agricultural Show at Guildford, then by train to Liverpool. There the local Chamber of Commerce entertained him, aided by the representatives of the steamship company, Elder Dempster and Co.

After visiting a cotton mill at Oldham in Lancashire he went north to Scotland, since MacGregor who had accompanied the Alake for most of his tour had insisted on this visit to his native land. MacGregor must have regretted his insistence when University students at Marischal College in Aberdeen were 'very demonstrative'; one placed a straw hat on the Alake's head; another tore his gorgeous robe. 'The Alake felt his dignity seriously insulted' reported MacGregor, indeed 'he had never seen him so annoyed and angry', for it was a great offence to tear his 'very sacred' robes.[73] The students apologized next day and, after investigations, six were fined £10, and a seventh £5. Obviously the people of Abeokuta would never have treated their chief in so undignified a manner, and if they had, their punishment would probably have been far more severe!

The Alake went out on a fish trawler from Aberdeen, and examined the fish market there. He also went to the granite quarries at Kenmay, his interest stemming from the granite base of Abeokuta. In Edinburgh he was met, peaceably, by African students, then went to St Giles Cathedral, Holyrood Palace and Edinburgh Castle. He returned to the south for a dinner given by the West African Society of the London Chamber of Commerce, and a banquet given by Blaize.

The visit ended with much formal, yet sincere, praise for MacGregor. Edun, the Alake's Secretary, claimed that MacGregor 'has made our country; we must have him back or everything will retrograde; even since he has been away the difference has begun to be apparent',[74] while the Alake praised him as 'our father—he is the best Governor we have ever had'[75] for he was 'absolutely just'. The editor of the *West African Mail* expanded on this theme:

> . . . this is a quality of the greatest power in any country peopled by coloured races, they have an intense perception of justice. Just the same feeling was expressed by the Papuans of New Guinea when Sir William held office there. Surely . . . it would be a short-sighted policy on the part of the Colonial Office, having found the right man and once put him in the right place, to replace him by an untried ruler.[76]

The Colonial Office took no notice of this praise, however, and MacGregor was appointed to the governorship of Newfoundland. On the eve of his departure, when speaking at a banquet given in his honour by Sir Alfred Jones, he was reported as saying that when speaking to coloured men he did not notice the fact, and always sought to recognize them as whites. And that he believed if people were to treat natives as equals, they would not lose anything by it.[77] This had certainly been his philosophy behind his dealings with the chiefs.

13

Lagos: Progress as a Colony 1899-1904

We shall have to tell MacGregor that this is a matter on which the Secretary of State has made up his mind

MacGregor's differences with the Colonial Office have already been described; but this was not the only section of the British government with which he clashed. He also pursued a running battle with the Crown Agents from London to Lagos and its hinterland.

The Crown Agents, middle men of the Colonial Office who supplied goods for the Crown colonies, were first criticized by MacGregor because of their delays in filling his requisitions for medical supplies, but more serious clashes stemmed from delays in obtaining equipment from these Agents for the railways, so by the time of his first leave—June to December 1900—he was openly hostile to the Crown Agents system. He complained that

> I believe at the present moment—and I have said so to the Secretary of State—I believe there would be men living who are now rotting in their graves if it [supply for the railways] had been taken out of the control of the Crown Agents . . . they send out new men with little or no experience who are absolutely free of any control of the colonial government.

His complaint made orally before the Manchester Chamber of Commerce was published in their annual report.[1]

In 1902 MacGregor's friend, E. D. Morel, gave the statement further publicity in his book *Affairs of West Africa*. Morel had been a clerk in the office of Sir Alfred Jones, but had given up shipping in favour of journalism, and had become the principal writer in the weekly newspaper, the *West African Mail*. This book, in which Morel supported MacGregor's attack on the Crown Agents, received considerable publicity, and the favourable reviews in the *Times Literary Supplement,* the London *Sun* and the *Daily Chronicle* all featured the criticism.[2]

The Crown Agents were, understandably, incensed with this public criticism, particularly Morel's but also MacGregor's. In fact, in some ways MacGregor's attack was more serious, for he was a government official. On 4 March 1903 the Crown Agents complained to the Colonial Office suggesting that he should be asked for an explanation and that efforts should be made to find out how Morel had received his information. The Crown Agents had been tempted to proceed for malicious libel, but had been advised by their solicitors that such action would be unwise against public officials. They consequently claimed to be treating the attacks with 'the contempt which they undoubtedly deserve'.[3]

In commenting on the Crown Agents' complaint one Colonial Office clerk professed to be at a loss to understand what MacGregor meant by his attack. Antrobus thought that MacGregor should be asked for explanations although 'he is now in a different frame of mind'. Ommanney was much more critical of both Morel and MacGregor. Morel should have no encouragements from the Colonial Office, while MacGregor, he thought, had 'frequently shown great want of judgment in his utterances and never more so than on this occasion'. Chamberlain decided that 'Sir William MacGregor should at once be called to account'. Morel, in his opinion, like so many journalists, had accepted false statements too readily, but he agreed that it was not in the interests of the public service to make an enemy of him. He expected that 'if he is a gentleman' he would give an apology.[4]

MacGregor in his reply of 8 August 1903 to a confidential despatch from the Colonial Office denied that he had intended any personal reflections on either the Crown Agents or the construction engineers, but that he had been concerned in criticizing the system. He defended the soundness of his opinions on this point, and virtually repeated his attack on the Crown Agents:

> In my humble judgment the system was unsound. The results were very unsatisfactory, and could hardly have been otherwise. Experience has converted that opinion into conviction in my mind.

> I recognize that my opinion may be entirely wrong on this point, but I do believe that there are men in their graves in this territory some of whom would, in all human probability, have been alive today had the medical branch of construction which the Crown Agents supervised been under the control of the governor and chief medical officer of the colony.[5]

While the Colonial Office was considering this despatch, news arrived telling of MacGregor's severe illness, and most officials expressed sympathy for the Governor, although all agreed that he had been indiscreet. But the matter was not dropped by Sir Edward Blake, the head of the Crown Agents. In June 1904[6] he suggested that the papers dealing with the subject should be shown to the Duke of Marlborough, as the case had been mentioned in the House of Lords. After MacGregor's return to England, Blake pursued the matter, saying that he would appreciate a public apology from MacGregor, who, he believed, 'has no doubt a bad conscience as well as a bad case'. Ommanney consequently on 20 August wrote to MacGregor:[7]

> . . . you will, I have no doubt, consider whether you cannot say a few words which will remove the impression created by the mischievous interpretations which Mr. Morel in his book has attached to your reference to the Crown Agents in connection with the Lagos Railway.

MacGregor replied that if the question of the railway extension did come up, 'or if any other opportunity presents itself, I shall remove any misconception which may have been created as to my personal opinion on the subject of the Crown Agents'.

If any apology was given at Manchester or Liverpool where he addressed the Chambers of Commerce, it was not given publicity, although the Lagos press reported that at Liverpool MacGregor had expressed the hope for continued railway development.[8] On 15 September, however, he sent to Sir William Shelford, the consulting engineer of the Crown Agents, a letter of appreciation for his services in connection with railway and bridge construction in Lagos, which Antrobus said was 'satisfactory'.[9] MacGregor had made some amends for his statements, but his excuses came too late to overcome the hostility of the Crown Agents, and this hostility contributed to the decision to keep him in the ranks of second-class governorships.[10]

Railway expansion from Lagos had contributed incidentally to this quarrel. MacGregor considered that the initial proposals in 1893 for a railway inland to Ibadan were made by a 'western syndicate' led by the Liverpool merchant, Sir Alfred Jones. British government support followed and in May 1894 the Colonial Office approved the survey from the coast to Ibadan, and also approved the ultimate extension of the railway to Ilorin and even to the Niger. Even if the first impetus came from merchants hoping for better and faster transport of goods, and for avoidance of African tolls, the railways were built by the British government using the Crown Agents.

The British government was concerned in tapping the trade of the interior and was also keenly conscious that every railway extension involved problems of imperial rivalry: France, Germany and Great Britain watched every mile built by the other powers with keen concern. The preliminary survey of the Lagos railway had been completed in May 1895, and building had commenced in December 1895. In March 1901 MacGregor opened for traffic the $123\frac{1}{2}$ miles from Iddo Island to Ibadan.

Besides the quarrel with the Crown Agents on health precautions in the building of this railway MacGregor was involved in disputes with those engaged both in planning and running it. Soon after his arrival in Lagos he had complained that the railway engineer at Abeokuta had been seeking political information from a government officer and so overstepping his authority. Antrobus felt that the quarrel had little foundation, and the Earl of Selborne regarded is as 'punctilious red tape run mad'. Antrobus pointed out also that 'there is always a certain amount of friction between the Crown Agents and the engineers on the one hand and the local governor on the other'.[11]

In February 1900 relations between MacGregor and the Crown Agents were again strained to breaking point. This time it was because the Agents, instead of sending a three-ton railway locomotive as ordered, had sent one weighing five and three quarter tons, thus necessitating the re-laying of line.[12] In this instance the Colonial Office supported MacGregor, and Chamberlain remarked, 'I regret to say that I am not at all satisfied as to this transaction, as at present advised I think the Crown Agents have been much too careless'.[13]

Part of the general dispute over the railway rested on paying for the line. The railway from Lagos was being financed from money borrowed by the Lagos government, and the first 123 miles had cost about £1 million, a considerable debt. As local Lagos government funds were always low, the Crown Agents were used to raise further loans in England. These loans were difficult to fill, and consequently there was anxiety in Lagos over funds.[14]

Another of the issues which led to contention was how far the railway was to run. The Colonial Office in 1894 had referred to Ilorin, and to the possibility of reaching the Niger. But in July 1899 it decided after discussion that this extension of the Lagos railway to the Niger was 'not the most pressing of railway schemes and would not justify the heavy addition of debt to the colony'.[15]

In March 1900 both the Liverpool and the Lagos Chambers of Commerce urged that the railway be extended over the Niger River into Northern Nigeria. The Lagos merchants wanted to divert trade from the traditional routes down the Niger River to its mouth, or across the Sahara by caravan to Tripoli, to the new railway and the port of Lagos. The Colonial Office had to reconcile conflicting advice from three of its colonial adminstrators: Lagos under MacGregor, Southern Nigeria under Moor and Northern Nigeria under Lugard, each of whom advocated railways in his respective area.

The Colonial Office, besides the need to balance rival colonial claims by considering overall British interests, was as ever influenced by questions of finance, which proved the determining factor at this time. After a conference held early in April 1900 between Shelford, the consulting engineer, Chamberlain, Antrobus and Herbert, it was decided not to approve further construction. One reason for this decision was that if the Niger trade were to be diverted to Lagos, the harbour would need to be improved at an estimated cost of £160,000, and it was by no means certain that the profit from the trade would be sufficient to warrant this.[16] MacGregor admitted that the Colony could not afford such harbour works, but felt that for imperial reasons Britain should tap the trade of the north before the French did so, as he had good reason to believe that they intended to build a railway through Algeria from the Mediterranean to the Niger.[17]

In March 1901 MacGregor officially opened the line from Lagos to Ibadan and he used this public occasion to stress how urgently he felt the line should be extended to the Niger. He included the defence of British territory and advantages to trade in his argument.[18] Later in the year he warned the Colonial Office of the urgent need for railway construction 'to protect our territory and commerce'.[19] But it was not an easy matter to divert trade from the traditional road and river routes, and it was estimated that the existing railway would have a deficit of £6,000 at the end of the first year.[20] Construction and operating faults combined with staffing difficulties added to the problems of running the railway. MacGregor recommended West Indian fitters and drivers, in the interests of economy,[21] but suggested European station masters who, he hoped, would not only control the stations, but also use their contacts with the merchants to get trade for the railway.[22]

There was African hostility to the railway among those interested in road and river trade, and those who resented any British interference. MacGregor discounted this criticism for he was sure that the railway was for the ultimate good of the populace. He was, however, sensitive to the fact that hostility existed among the Africans for he was aware that '. . . in any measure connected with social or political advance, the smallest incident may at any time and in the most unexpected manner create very serious commotion'.[23]

A certain Mr T. Harding, a missionary, at Ibadan, seemed to encourage the Africans in their disapproval of surveys for the railway. MacGregor felt that Harding's real concern was that the railway would increase the taxable value of mission land. This attitude so annoyed the Governor that he was moved to write

> . . . the incident is inseparable from the fact that it seems necessary to send abroad as missionaries men who are only half-educated, who not infrequently approach subjects that do not concern them in the spirit of conceit that is peculiar to that class of man when he is posted on the boundary line between civilization and barbarism.[24]

MacGregor was supported by English journals in his criticism of Harding, which induced Antrobus to write that articles in the *West African Mail* on 15 and 22 June read like a distorted account and that he would like to see the other side of the question for 'the editor . . . believes in Sir William MacGregor, considering for some reason or other that he is activated by motives entirely different from those of any other Governor in dealing with natives'.[25]

African opposition did not prevent continued extension of the railway, but construction was marred by quarrels between MacGregor and members of the technical staff, including Glasier, one of the engineers.[26] He also fell out with S. Smith who was in charge of the Abeokuta branch, and who, in his opinion, did not make sufficient use of the railway. MacGregor further considered Smith to be an 'inexperienced, conceited junior'; whose 'views with regard to anything except his own importance are extremely narrow'; he was 'ever ready to set the governor at defiance'. Colonial Office opinion was that MacGregor must be feeling the climate—at this time he had been in Lagos eleven months after his first leave—for this was 'one of several despatches written

about the same time in which Sir William MacGregor has differed from other authorities and expressed his opinion in terms
which seem unnecessarily strong'. Chamberlain, however, backed
MacGregor in the Smith case:

> It may be that the Governor was strained and his language is
> undoubtedly strong. But the charge is serious. The Governor is
> the Governor and no junior officer can be allowed to flout him nor
> ignore his advice. I must have the matter sifted.[27]

Later, however, the Crown Agents provided Smith's explanation
which contradicted MacGregor's attack, for Smith had used the
railway to transport all goods except barges, which were too large
to be carried by rail. Ommanney commented on this explanation: 'Sir William MacGregor should satisfy himself as to his
facts before making complaints couched in such strong terms' to
which Chamberlain now agreed: 'The Governor must be asked to
explain this when he comes. He has given a great deal of trouble
and apparently without the slightest reason. He may see this
minute'.[28] MacGregor's stocks at the Colonial Office fell as instances like these increased suspicion about the impartiality of
his judgement. The following incident gives a clear example of
MacGregor's lack of tact, particularly in writing despatches, and
of the Colonial Office's methods of dealing with this problem.

In November 1901 the Colonial Office sent out to MacGregor a
report by the consulting engineer, Shelford, about the extension
of the line beyond Ibadan to Ilorin. Shelford favoured the western route because it was shorter, 115 compared to 142 miles,
because there was less forest clearing required, and because there
would be fewer rivers to cross. MacGregor disagreed, having
walked in 1901 over both alternative routes. He favoured the
eastern route since the country was more fertile and the population denser, so that local traffic would be greater, although at this
time he thought there would be similar engineering problems on
both routes. MacGregor had received pressure from the inhabitants of the areas through which the railway might run. For
instance, on the eastern route the Owa of Ilesha favoured extending the line to his province. The Owa's arguments were based
on the large quantity of palm kernels which were thrown away
annually, and the number of nuts which were left on the trees.
He also stressed the value of rubber and mahogany trees that
could be used if only there were rapid communications to the
coast. In December 1901 MacGregor used the Owa's enthusiasm
for the railway as a favourable argument, especially as both he

and Governor Carter had promised the Owa that it would go to this province. MacGregor also raised engineering arguments against Shelford, claiming that on the eastern route the gradients were less severe, and that rock-cutting, less banking and fewer sharp curves would be required.[29]

The Colonial Office agreed that MacGregor's arguments must be given greater weight, and that the question should be referred back to Shelford. Chamberlain said:

> he writes as a man thoroughly knowing the country and I think we should have to take his advice . . . an old stager like Sir William Macgregor is likely to be right when a young railway engineer unaccustomed to the country may well make mistakes.[30]

Before referring the matter to Shelford the Colonial Office edited the despatch of its *'ipsissima verba'*; phrases which they felt were 'unnecessarily violent', for this despatch was yet another example of MacGregor's impatience with those who disagreed with him. For instance, he had written: 'It is hardly possible that the most unobservant man that ever traversed the two routes could share the opinion of the consulting engineer on this point' (changed to 'I am far from sharing . . .'), similarly the statement 'I am not able to account for the strange statements' was changed to 'I am not able to agree with', and 'that a serious mistake should be made by a specially selected party sent here at such great expense to this colony' was omitted; and 'I sincerely hope that you will not accept these reports as a solution to the problem' was likewise eliminated. In April 1902 Shelford, after considering Mac-Gregor's pruned despatch, agreed to recommend the eastern route.[31] The Crown Agents approved construction at least to Oshogbo—about halfway to Ilorin—at an estimated cost of about half a million pounds. The Crown Agents also supported the continuance of surveys in Southern and Northern Nigeria.

Besides the survey from Ibadan to Ilorin, the question of surveying the route from Ilorin to the Niger was considered by the Colonial Office. As Northern Nigeria had agreed to pay half the cost of survey from Ibadan to Ilorin, it was thought right that Lagos should pay half the cost from Ilorin on to the Niger. Mac-Gregor did not want to pay because of the parlous condition of Lagos finances and because he claimed that Lagos would not immediately benefit commercially. He thought that most ordinary merchandise came and went to Northern Nigeria along the River Niger and was not carried on men's heads to and from Ibadan. Antrobus was sure there was more existing trade between

Northern Nigeria and Lagos than MacGregor was prepared to admit, but he agreed that Lagos was not in a financial position to contribute. MacGregor admitted[32] that in the future the two colonies should be linked by a railway at which time Northern Nigeria should absorb Lagos. The railway would eventually successfully compete with river trade and would become the natural outlet, he maintained, for Northern Nigeria to the sea while Northern Nigeria was the natural complement of Lagos as its hinterland. Communications would be less difficult—even if the administrative union preceded the completion of further railway lines—than the problems he had faced in British New Guinea. The financial standing of both colonies was so precarious that further assistance from the British Treasury seemed likely to be necessary. The Colonial Office thought a case could be made for imperial financial aid, now agreeing with Mac-Gregor that 'vast imperial interests . . . [were] involved in a railway to the interior' especially when French activity was so marked—'when one reads of traders from Tunis, Morocco and Suakin [on the Red Sea] being even now at Ilorin one begins to realize what it really means'.[33] The Treasury agreed on 10 September to the proposed survey and the proposed division of costs between Northern Nigeria and Lagos, but did not think any extension should be begun until the finances of Northern Nigeria were in a much sounder condition.[34]

The expense of extending the railway was the only important factor delaying construction, for the British Government was by 1902 convinced of the imperial significance of this line. Thus Chamberlain wrote: 'I am, as always, most anxious to proceed with railway extension subject only to considerations of finance. . . .'[35]

When on leave in London MacGregor was asked for his views on the discussions, including this Minute by Chamberlain, and he reiterated the importance to Lagos of settling 'a general railway policy . . . as soon as possible'. He thought the ultimate objective of the Lagos railway should be Kano, if not Lake Chad, 300 miles farther east, but agreed that as other railways would be needed in other parts of Nigeria this extension must be considered in relation to other constructions. He listed three reasons why the railway was of value to Lagos—to defend its territory; to keep and develop its trade; and to maintain British prestige. French railway works were relevant to all these points for MacGregor claimed to have read 'much of what has been written in France on their African railways and other proposals'. These arguments were reinforced by other evidence available to the Colonial Office, for a map of West Africa summing up available information about railways constructed, under construction, authorized or proposed in the future, showed that all the ambitious schemes were French. The only British line shown as proposed was that from Ibadan to Jebba. MacGregor deduced from these plans that the British Lagos railway should be pushed on to the Niger before the French Dahomey railway tapped that river and diverted inland trade to the French coastal town of Porto Novo, and considered that the possibility of a French trans-Sahara line from Algeria to Lake Chad or to Timbuctoo on the Niger made rapid British extension even more important.

These grandiose plans could only be supported by British imperial aid, for if the extension of the Lagos railway was based only on Lagos' financial position—MacGregor had to agree this should not begin 'till the railway now open pays working expenses and something like £20,000 a year towards interest on capital borrowed. This will probably be the case a year and a half from now'. He thought that an extension to Oshogbo would eventually pay even if the railway went no farther,

> . . . provided that the trade were not diverted from Lagos by a line from Southern Nigeria to tap the Lagos railway and carry its produce away to Warri or Sapele, as appears to have been suggested by Sir R. Moor and Sir F. Lugard. It would be suicide on the part of Lagos to favour any such proposal.[36]

This was not MacGregor's final conclusion, for widening his viewpoint from that of Lagos concerns to general British interests, he could see the justification for these southern Nigerian lines if all of Nigeria—Lagos, Southern Nigeria and Northern Nigeria—were unified under one government.

From July 1902 until he left Lagos the effectiveness of MacGregor's advocacy of railway expansion was reduced by his personal quarrel with Glasier, now promoted to be general manager of the railway, and from the publicity given by Morel to his earlier criticisms of the Crown Agents. As the Colonial Office was also losing faith in him, particularly because of the clash about policies towards the hinterland states, MacGregor found it increasingly difficult to gain any support in London.

MacGregor had clashed with Glasier in 1901 and always had doubts about his competence, whereas both the consulting engineers and the Crown Agents backed Glasier. Personal discussions between these officials and MacGregor while he was on leave in 1902 did not lead to any agreement. And Ommanney, feeling that MacGregor had no specific charge to lay, was inclined to take the side of Glasier.[37]

In January 1903 MacGregor strongly disapproved Glasier's request that he should be recognized as having the power of appointing his own locum tenens. Symptomatic of attitudes in the Colonial Office were the Minutes by Antrobus: 'It is a preposterous claim for Mr Glasier to make; but he would hardly have made it if he had been serving under a governor who knew better how to manage men', and by Ommanney: 'another instance of a quite unnecessary wrangle between the Governor and the General Manager'.[38]

The same lines of criticism appeared in the Colonial Office when the appointment of an inspecting engineer was being considered. MacGregor had criticized the existing staff pointing out some of his difficulties. Antrobus commented that 'if the governor had common sense, he would get the remedy applied without having to give an order' and went on

> Sir William MacGregor's difficulties are of his own making. Other governors had no difficulty in getting the Chief Resident Engineer and the Consulting Engineers to listen to them, and in exercising the influence which they are entitled, and in fact bound, to exercise in regard both to construction and to open lines.

Ommanney agreed, writing:

> I cannot help thinking that Sir William MacGregor's methods must be at fault. Neither at Sierra Leone nor on the Gold Coast do the governors find it necessary to be constantly invoking the Secretary of State on small details connected with the railway.

Chamberlain also agreed: 'I suppose Sir William MacGregor with all his good qualities is a bad manager of men but he will not remain in Lagos for ever'.[39]

In the end it was Glasier who survived in Lagos despite his shortcomings, of which the Colonial Office were aware:

> . . . whatever Mr. Glasier's faults may be—in the way of bumptiousness, inkslinging or rubbing up the governor and his subordinates the wrong way—I do not think and I do not understand Mr. Shelford to imply, that the mismanagement of the locomotives is attributable to any direct neglect on his part.[40]

The last words on this tedious quarrel came on 9 February 1904 when a Minute recorded that

> Sir William MacGregor has now left Lagos. Mr. Glasier has clearly

taken to heart the lectures given to him at the Colonial Office, for during the six months he was with the Governor since his return to the colony their relations have been perfectly satisfactory and harmonious.[41]

Despite his quarrels with those constructing and running the railway, MacGregor consistently advocated its extension. His arguments seemed justified during the period he was in Lagos, while subsequent constructions supported his ideas. British prestige and influence might well have been increased if the Treasury had allowed more rapid building of the railways, and trade would have been facilitated by more rapid transport. After Nigeria was unified at the end of 1909, five years after Mac-Gregor left the colony, the Lagos railway reached Jebba on the Niger.

One of the main purposes of the Lagos railway was to tap the existing trade of the interior; but to make it an economic success it became necessary to improve existing products and establish new ones. Some 5,000 square miles of Lagos territory were covered by palms, and the colony's economic strength rested primarily on the export of palm oil and palm kernels. The promising rubber industry had collapsed in 1899 when seventy-five per cent of the colony's trees had died. Resolutions of native authorities had forbidden the collection of rubber before 1903. From his arrival MacGregor encouraged efforts to enforce these resolutions, and to preserve and utilize timber, systematizing in June 1900 the procedure for obtaining concessions of land and timber from Africans.[42] He debated with Kew Gardens whether the bass-fibre from the palm trees could be used as a source of income, and whether its removal would affect production of oil from the trees. Kew also investigated for him the possibility of shea butter (from the tree *Butyro Spernum Parkii*)[43] or kapok (from the silk of the cotton tree)[44] being developed commercially.

While MacGregor was on leave in London on 26 November 1900 the curator at Kew (Thiselton Dyer) presented a report about the possibilities of introducing new forms of agriculture in Lagos. Its pessimism was derived from the melancholy history of previous experiments in Lagos, which he considered had failed through 'ignorance and improvidence' added to the hopelessness of trying to preserve the forests and other resources of the Colony while using native authorities. Dyer went on to the general question of whether the existing methods of colonial

U

administration were suited to tropical Africa, and concluded that the net result may be summed up in the present case by the words: 'Liverpool has been enriched; Lagos has been impoverished'. He thought there may be some hope for planting enterprises if they were under European supervision, and suggested that Lagos needed some skilled Indian forest officers.[45] Two days after Dyer wrote this MacGregor had 'a prolonged conference' with him 'on various economic questions connected with the colony of Lagos'.[46] Dyer strongly supported MacGregor because of knowledge of his botanical work in Fiji and New Guinea, writing at this time, for instance, 'I can only wonder that a purely administrative measure of this kind [he was referring to the planting of the swamps with gum trees] should not be left to the discretion of so competent a governor as Sir William MacGregor'.[47] The immediate result of the conference with Dyer was MacGregor's request to the Colonial Office for authority to select a curator probably from India for a botanic station, which was to be amalgamated with the model farms already in existence.

On his return to Lagos after his first leave MacGregor gave serious consideration to developing and fostering economic industries. He introduced his Forestry Bill into the Legislative Council in September 1901, its purpose being to ensure the preservation of timber, rubber and other forest products, not only in Lagos but also in the hinterland. The Bill provided heavy penalties for any unauthorized use or destruction of the forest trees. There was great opposition to this Bill which was introduced at the same time as the Native Councils Bill, both being represented as interferences with the independence of the hinterland. MacGregor attempted to dismiss the 'malicious misrepresentations' of his aims by 'the ignorant and malevolent local press', educated natives and 'interested traders, who desire to exploit the forests without hindrance'.[48] The Colonial Office, however, agreed that the Bill was *ultra vires*[49] and MacGregor had to accept a revised Ordinance.[50] This proved, as he feared, 'quite inadequate to preserve the forests'[51] for it had no power over oil palms and gave him control only over other trees which were not privately owned. Only in the few forest reserves leased to the government could his new Forestry Department protect rubber and mahogany trees or begin replanting.

MacGregor had higher hopes of developing the export of cotton from Lagos. In July 1901 the steamship company of Elder

Dempster gave to the government ten tons of cotton seeds, eight tons of which had been 'widely distributed' in response to demands by chiefs and traders. Several specimens of cotton had been received by November 1901 and Elder Dempster was offering for the next three years very cheap freights, less than one farthing per pound, for carrying the cotton to England.[52]

By the time MacGregor reached England for his second leave, between May and December 1902, the future of cotton in Lagos had become the main concern of the Liverpool and Manchester Chambers of Commerce. MacGregor was convinced that cotton could be grown in Lagos both by Africans and Europeans, and that it should be encouraged to aid the unhealthy finances of the colony. Showing his typical enthusiastic interest in any question which he considered important, he undertook very thorough investigations into the prospects of cotton growing.

On 14 July 1902 he attended a conference of the Chambers of Commerce from Liverpool, Manchester and Oldham, which spent most of its time discussing cotton. MacGregor claimed that West Africans had 'grown, spun and woven cotton from time immemorial'[53] and he thought the cotton supply would be assured if action were taken simultaneously in all the West African colonies.

When he went with Ross to Italy and Egypt to investigate malaria he also devoted time to cotton-growing areas, and in November he submitted a report which he had prepared with the aid of Mr Fletcher, an assistant professor at the Gizeh School of Agriculture, Cairo. Their report covered climatic and soil conditions, the varieties of Egyptian cotton, methods of preparing the land—sowing, hoeing and digging, ways of collecting the cotton crop—ginning and baling, as well as considering the 'enemies' of cotton growers. Most points made were optimistic about the possibilities of cotton growing in Lagos, although MacGregor anticipated some difficulties. For instance, in the light soils, rotation of crops would probably be necessary; and the preparation of land might present difficulties for conservative African farmers for whom 'the plough would, it is to be feared, . . . [prove] a hopeless innovation in the Lagos territory'. On this point he felt that cotton could only be produced on a large scale for export if the Africans co-operated, using their own methods, which could, perhaps, be improved by lessons inculcated from above by influential leaders such as the Alake of Abeokuta or the Alafin of Oyo. As in other colonies which he had governed

MacGregor insisted that 'native lands cannot, and will not, be alienated to Europeans to grow cotton or anything else. This would be contrary to present native uses and customs. Land could, probably, be leased for a long term'. Cotton, MacGregor thought, should become the main feature of the model farms, and 'highly educated, specially trained men' should be appointed to aid the Africans in growing cotton, particularly around Iwo, Ede, Oshogbo and Ikerun.[54]

In 1902 Elder Dempster offered to transport cotton to England free of charge for two years, and MacGregor suggested that the Lagos railway should also carry it free. The Colonial Office agreed to this suggestion,[55] and when he returned to Lagos at the end of the year, MacGregor felt that he was ready to get the industry established. He enlisted the assistance of the British Cotton Growing Association, which, he hoped, would help in all aspects of the industry from supply to distribution. He planned to set up a steam-powered mill at Abeokuta, and seed was ordered from the Mississippi Valley for the hinterland. This seed was held up in America owing to floods, and MacGregor felt that the Colonial Office had been precipitate in sending out two cotton experts before the arrival of the seed. He was also disappointed that Mr Fletcher with whom he had worked in Cairo was not appointed to the position. He sent Mr Hoffmann, one of the experts, into the interior to select land and arrange for planting, processing and marketing the crop.[56]

Mr Hoffmann made a report in November 1903 after he had been in Lagos some eight months. In this report he claimed that a fair crop would be produced that year, for most plants had survived the serious drought, and he anticipated that by the end of the next year 20,000 acres would be planted, which could raise some £500,000 of cotton. MacGregor made no substantial comment but somewhat carpingly stated that 'Mr Hoffmann's report shows that he labours under considerable disadvantages as regards school education. He, however, gets on very peaceably and amicably with the natives by whom he is liked and trusted generally'.[57]

At this stage MacGregor seemed to become disillusioned about the prospects of the cotton industry. He reported at the end of December that he had inspected the cotton-ginning establishment near Ibara railway station, and that he was not happy with its site. He was also concerned about the price of cotton, pointing out that if it were not kept up to one penny a pound the

Africans would not grow it. He regretted that his recent severe illness had made it impossible for him to help the British Cotton Growing Association 'at a time when . . . [aid] was much needed'.[58]

The story of cotton, like so much in that last year of his governorship, continued on this pessimistic note. On 11 January 1904 he telegraphed seeking confirmation of reports that the British Cotton Growing Association contemplated not purchasing the cotton, pointing out that this would be 'highly prejudicial to the cotton industry',[59] for the farmers had been assured the Association would buy at one penny per pound.

The British Cotton Growing Association had expressed concern in December 1903 because of the scarcity of reports from Hoffmann—the Association had heard nothing since July—and also by rumours that the erection of the gins had been delayed, and that they were in an unsuitable place, that much of the cotton seed had not been distributed, and that MacGregor had not supervised Hoffmann's work. The Association concluded that 'MacGregor had not dealt fairly with them'. The Colonial Office accepted this criticism of MacGregor,[60] although it was rather harsh—considering his enthusiastic help, his querying of Hoffmann, and his severe illness.

Despite this final note of gloom and whatever the wisdom of launching a cotton growing experiment in Lagos, it seems a fair verdict that MacGregor had over all given substantial assistance from the time the Oldham Chamber and Elder Dempster had raised the question whether cotton could be grown economically. The enterprise had interesting parallels with the British New Guinea Syndicate affair: both came at the end of MacGregor's governorships, both could well have done far more for their respective colonies and MacGregor's reputation than they actually did. As it was, clearly the strictures of the British Cotton Growing Association helped to defeat his hopes for promotion to an important governorship.

Although MacGregor devoted so much of his time to the problems of cotton growing, he found time to encourage geological investigation, but the two hundred and five specimens sent from Lagos to Edinburgh University were found to be 'devoid of . . . valuable metal or metalliferous mineral'.[61] He founded the Lagos Agricultural Association in 1903 and encouraged agricultural shows.[62] Model farms also interested him, although after a tour of inspection, he echoed Dyer's pessimism of 1899.

A report by 'two native practical farmers', after a visit to model farms at Mamu and Oloke Meji in 1904, stated that of 384,000 rubber trees planted at the former only 50,000 survived; and that the sheep and cattle being reared at the latter were in a miserable condition.[63] Clearly no substitute for the economic staple palm oil and kernels had been found by MacGregor and the colony was not greatly aided financially by his efforts at diversification. In fact, the relative value of exports did not change significantly between 1899 and 1903, although the amounts and values of most exports increased.[64]

As in Fiji and British New Guinea MacGregor's work was always hampered by lack of finance, and he still had to work within the prevailing notion that the greater the surplus of revenue over expenditure the healthier the colony. The colony had received only limited loan funds, mainly for railway construction, although interest payments on these loans were a constant burden. For instance in 1902 a sum of £54,000 was allotted to charges on the public debt.[65]

Most revenue came from customs duties which were mainly— as much as ninety per cent in 1899—collected on trade spirits. Before MacGregor arrived controversy had developed as to the morality of financing government from liquor. Those opposed to excessive drinking, including church leaders such as Bishop Tugwell, wanted the duty to be increased in the hope of limiting consumption, but the result was paradoxically not a lessening of drinking but an increase in the relative dependence of the government on receipts from duties on spirits. After only four months in Lagos MacGregor deduced that further increases would have the same result: 'a duty of 10/- a gal. on spirits does not prevent hundreds, perhaps thousands, of men from getting drunk in Glasgow on any Saturday afternoon; a duty of fourteen shillings a gallon in British New Guinea does not in any way tend to make the drinking part of the community to any appreciable extent more temperate'.[66] He claimed that he would be pleased to raise the duty on spirits, only warning Chamberlain realistically that unless duties were simultaneously raised in the adjoining French colony of Dahomey the result would be frontier smuggling, which would be impossible to check adequately with his limited staff. As a total abstainer[67] MacGregor favoured total prohibition for Africans, arguing for instance that

   . . . any aboriginal people can and do understand total prohibition. It is far less easy for them to grasp or be guided by modified measures. The weak point in the liquor laws of Fiji lay, probably still lies, in the many exemptions made in favour of chiefs. The strong point in the liquor laws of British New Guinea is that they maintain absolute and unbending prohibition.[68]

Lagos, however, could not bear the expense of ending duties, and it was this realization of the need for finance which led to Mac-Gregor's continued support of high duties. He clashed publicly with Tugwell and Bishop Oluwole at the opening of the Lagos Institute when he suggested that the opponents of the liquor traffic would do more good by attacking malaria and other diseases.[69]

MacGregor's first estimates for Lagos, those for the financial year April 1900 to March 1901, were not optimistic, and although he hoped that receipts from the railway would relieve the financial situation by 1902, he knew that the immediate future would be difficult.[70] As it happened, the failure of the Egyptian cotton crop and the outbreak of the South African War caused such increases in the cost of imported goods that the position was even worse than he had anticipated. The only compensation MacGregor could gain from this unsatisfactory situation was that the Treasury was persuaded that Lagos 'cannot be expected to contribute anything to Northern Nigeria'.[71] This matter had been a bone of contention between Lugard and Mac-Gregor ever since Lugard began the administration of Northern Nigeria in January 1900. The British government had decided that Northern Nigeria should receive payments from Lagos, partly as compensation for the fact that customs duties were collected in Lagos on goods bound for Northern Nigeria. Another argument was that Lagos would benefit from Northern Nigeria's support of the West African Frontier Force, which would help to protect the colony. MacGregor felt that Lagos could not afford these payments (£15,000 had been suggested for 1900-1)[72] and certainly at this time he was proved correct.

Further differences arose between Lugard and MacGregor when Lugard advocated replacing import duties (except those on liquor, salt, guns and powder) by export duties on native produce. MacGregor was sure that this would do nothing but discourage exports and kill the embryonic industries that he was trying to foster.[73] Another change which he resisted was a suggestion by the merchants both in London and Lagos to abolish dues on goods held in bond before going on to other colonies. MacGregor was aware that in principle these transit dues were objectionable, but he needed the revenue, and as he had the support of his Legislative Council and other local opinion, the Colonial Office agreed to allow him to continue to collect these dues.[74]

In July 1901 in forwarding the customs report for 1900-1, MacGregor was still pessimistic about Lagos finances. He referred specifically to the decrease in trade of palm oil and kernel which he associated with the continued recruiting of men who would otherwise be assisting in the production of exports from Lagos for service in other territories. 'There is a constant drain of the best muscle of the country to Northern Nigeria, to Southern Nigeria, and to the Gold Coast. A great many of those that leave never return'.[75] MacGregor was more cheerful in October 1901 when the revenue figures were high: they were the highest quarterly amounts for the past five years, and indeed had only been exceeded once before in the quarter to June 1899. Ommanney hoped for even more improvement: 'If we can only develop a demand for imported goods at Abeokuta and Ibadan and in the neighbourhood of our Railway stations, these figures would soon tell a different tale'.[76]

The estimates for 1902-3 led to some hope: 'prepared with Sir William MacGregor's usual skill and care; . . . they show that he is making gallant efforts to steer the colony through the financial straits in which it has been involved by the large railway loans'.[77] In addition he hoped that his 1902 Ordinance controlling the exodus of labourers would aid production.[78]

In March 1902 MacGregor supported the raising of a loan of £207,300 to cover anticipated deficiencies for needed public works and to meet interest charges. Previous loans had raised over £1,000,000 by various ordinances. MacGregor now suggested that a loan be raised in London, for few of the traders in Lagos had considerable capital and 'it is not by any means desirable that the small amount of money they do possess should be locked up in inscribed stock in London'. He defended his financial policies since 1899 and was certain that the colony was now in a sound position, and was not living beyond its means. A Colonial Office clerk wrote that

> . . . it is unfortunate that he should have spent so much trouble over this defence, as it was quite unnecessary . . . I am sure that all of us here recognise that Sir William MacGregor had had to deal in Lagos with a period of exceptional financial stress, that he has been indefatigable in his efforts to save expenditure and that the

results he has achieved show that his efforts have been very successful.[79]

This loan ordinance was passed in April 1902.[80] Despite this
burden of loan money the improvement in financial figures for
the last quarter of 1902 was 'very reassuring'.[81] The aggregate
returns for 1902 were all records for Lagos, including an 'astonishing increase in exports, a rise of some 50% over 1901'.
One conclusion that the Colonial Office reached from these rising
figures was that Lagos must commence contributions to Northern
Nigeria.[82] MacGregor continued his opposition, so this became
yet another issue in 1903 on which there was a clash of policies
between him and the Colonial Office. Antrobus said flatly on 3
February:

> we shall have to tell him [MacGregor] when we write that this is a
> matter on which the Secretary of State has made up his mind and
> that he must support the Secretary of State instead of opposing
> him.[83]

Antrobus suggested in April a contribution by Lagos of £10,000,
adding that the 'Treasury would have serious grounds for complaint if we do not insist upon this'. Chamberlain wanted to
increase the sum using the same arguments as in 1900 that Lagos
gained by having the rest of the West African Frontier Force as
a reserve in case of need, and that trade through Lagos was
increased by British control of Northern Nigeria. MacGregor
had always denied the first point, arguing that he had never
wanted and had no intention of asking for more troops and that
contingents had been sent from Lagos to Northern Nigeria. His
arguments gained some support in the Colonial Office especially
because Lugard had 'stated very emphatically . . . that the military force [of Northern Nigeria] had become insufficient for its
needs' following the conquest of Kano and Sokoto and as 'it has
been decided that if Lagos is obliged to borrow troops from
Northern Nigeria, she will have to pay both the ordinary and
extraordinary expenses for employing them'. Chamberlain's
point about trade was again denied by MacGregor who was
consistent in believing that there was little gain to Lagos trade
from Northern Nigeria. Majority Colonial Office opinion backed
Chamberlain on both points, supporting the opinion that 'in
spite of MacGregor's stout maintenance to the contrary . . . Lagos
does derive commercial advantage from the maintenance of order
in Northern Nigeria and from the access of trade therefrom'.[84]
Eventually MacGregor was overruled and a sum of £20,000 was

decided upon as a fair contribution from Lagos for the year 1904-5, partly to cover arrears since 1900.

The last year MacGregor spent in Lagos was financially sound, the drop in agricultural exports was expected only to be temporary for it had been caused by the poor rainfall of 1902. MacGregor's innate caution, however, prevented his sanctioning any increase in expenditure and, when it became known that he was not to return to the Colony, applications for salary increases came in from all quarters. It was felt, however, that his temporary successor was a little too generous in this respect.[85]

Generally, apart from MacGregor's reluctance to saddle Lagos with expenditure for Northern Nigeria, he was in accord with the Colonial Office in financial matters. He had learnt bitter lessons of Treasury control from his years in Fiji and British New Guinea and his policy reflects this previous experience, as well as his characteristic interest in economy and his meticulous attention to detail which had become so developed, particularly during his Fijian Receiver-Generalship.

MacGregor obtained little satisfaction from his governorship of Lagos. His initial reluctance to go to West Africa had been confirmed by the shocking conditions of health he found there. His efforts to improve the situation especially by applying the results of his and other malarial research were frustrated by the resistance of ignorance. He had been separated from his family within a few months of his arrival and the reunions on his leave could not substitute for his lack of a home. He wrote sadly in November 1900 from London:

> . . . none of my people will go out again to Lagos. The children have gone today to Cheltenham College. I am becoming utterly tired of this vagabond sort of life. If you [Griffith] become Governor I think I must ask you to give me an appointment as Medical Officer in Queensland or British New Guinea. It is difficult to get ends to meet in Lagos, and the waste of one's life is terrible.[86]

His daughters had become almost strangers to him and even on leave he saw little of them, because of his travelling for health and cotton research. Thus he wrote in 1902 and 1903:

> . . . we spent two months in Italy, lest [sic] my family did, though I was generally away. The two girls did the *Inferno* and half the *Purgatorio* with Professor Falorsi, a man of great knowledge. They speak Italian quite fluently now, as easily as they speak French. The younger one is at Cheltenham College. The elder one is all music and painting.[87]

My wife and our elder daughter are in Lausanne. The younger is at Cheltenham. The girls can find their way very well over Europe now. Alas, I have not looked at Dante for months, I am always very busy on unproductive occupations here.[88]

So many of these 'unproductive occupations' led to clashes, with the 'educated' Africans in Lagos and with his colleagues, and most importantly with the Crown Agents and the Colonial Office. He found a certain amount of satisfaction in his personal friendships with the chiefs of the hinterland, but this, too, was lessened by the knowledge that the Colonial Office was not whole-heartedly behind his policies. The events of 1903 culminating in his near-fatal illness left an embittered man of fifty-seven who felt sure that he had been unfortunate. On the eve of his birth-day he wrote: 'this serious illness has I fear given me a new and regrettable idea . . . if fairly treated by the Colonial Office I should not be here. I feel, now, that I have not had fair play'.[89] Nine months later in July 1904, when he was told he was to go as governor to Newfoundland, he blamed the clash of policy with the Colonial Office for his failure to gain promotion:

I am not able to return to West Africa. I have given a new trend to government there, and I have met with great, almost virulent opposition to my policy. Lagos is the only British colony we pos-sess there that has had no war since I went out. I alone can travel without great military escorts to the most remote corner of the territory. West Africa is the arena for ribbons, and crosses, and medals. A man of peace is not wanted nor liked there. Those who at first opposed me bitterly, now ask the Colonial Office that my methods may be maintained. I had not shed a drop of blood in Africa. That is considered phenomenal but is it not a sad and woeful commentary on British rule, the policy of smash in West Africa is I fear an outcome of military imperialism. Why can we not adopt and practise elsewhere the peaceful imperial idea that you so successfully carried out in Australia? It grieves me now that all the little special knowledge and experience I possess should be utterly useless.[90]

However justified in the long run MacGregor's policies were, he cannot be absolved from blame for the personal clashes of his governorship. Arguments are never one-sided, and this embit-tered, obstinate Scotsman had helped to destroy his own chances of happiness and his opportunities to influence British policy. The lessons of the need for tolerance and understanding of the ideas of others had proved hard to acquire in his struggle for recognition from the valley of the Don through the Seychelles, Fiji and New Guinea to the swamps of Lagos.

14

Newfoundland: A Fossilised Colony? 1904-9

This place is fossilised . . . the worst is that I can do so very little to improve matters.

The five years spent by MacGregor in Newfoundland fulfilled many of his ambitions. At last, after twenty-one years of married life, he was able to live constantly with his family. His lifelong concern in health problems found added fulfilment, for he created opportunities to apply his medical training, not only among the neglected Innuit of Labrador but also on the main island of Newfoundland. His advice in most matters was respectfully listened to in London, and eventually influenced the policy of the United States towards the vital question of the fisheries of Newfoundland. He won his highest compliment from the British Ambassador in Washington, Viscount Bryce, who called him 'a model of what a Colonial Governor should be'.[1]

It would be expecting too much to think that he attained personal happiness. His bitterness, particularly following his Lagos days and his frustrated ambitions in British New Guinea, could not be soothed by such compensations. He still felt thwarted, pushed into a backwater when he would have preferred to be more in the mainstream of British colonial developments. He found in his visits to the Esquimaux in Labrador and to the few Indians surviving in Newfoundland, some opportunity to use his experience with people who could remind him of Fijians, Papuans and Africans. But most of his time was spent with Newfoundland politicians with whom he found little in common. In those years centring around his sixtieth birthday he lived almost a double life, on one hand his official duties in Newfoundland and on the other his constant unofficial efforts to achieve his ambition to return again to New Guinea and Australia.

This latter desire was no new feeling and had existed throughout his Lagos career.[2] In October 1903 it became definite that MacGregor would not be sent back to Lagos, while, as has been seen, well before this date the Colonial Office realized that a new post would have to be found for him. On his side MacGregor continued his agitation, mainly through Griffith, to get back to Australia,[3] and even after his appointment to Newfoundland was definite, wrote to him saying:

> But I still retain all my great desire to get to Queensland. Can you do anything to help me there when that place is next vacant? I should so dearly love to be installed there, that we might go over together to British New Guinea and the Solomons.

He wanted Griffith to let him know when the Governor of Queensland, Sir Herbert Chermside, was to leave. He presumed the Newfoundland appointment would be

> . . . banishment for me. I do not mind that, if I can only see some prospect of getting to Queensland or British New Guinea eventually. Had Barton remained Prime Minister I should have applied to him by cable for British New Guinea, which I should have preferred to anything else. That I suppose is now impossible.[4]

This theme of return occurs constantly in all his letters to Griffith until his Queensland appointment.[5]

But he had thoughts of other places as well as Queensland and New Guinea; he told Gordon in March 1905: 'I really do not know whether I can do any or much good here [Newfoundland]. I am often reminded from West Africa that all the great chiefs desire that I return to amalgamate the three provinces'.[6] It shows how unaware MacGregor was of Colonial Office opinion that he should have thought seriously of returning to West Africa; but in October 1906 he telegraphed the Colonial Office, following personal correspondence with its head, Lord Elgin, to say that he was willing to be considered for the appointment as high commissioner of Northern Nigeria. On this occasion Antrobus said flatly that even if he had recovered his health 'he is not the right man for Nigeria'.[7]

MacGregor had also taken some interest in New South Wales, Tasmania, Western Australia and Natal[8] when those governorships became vacant, but none of them came his way. In 1906 he was being seriously considered in Australia as Lieutenant-Governor of Papua, as it was felt by the Australian Prime Minister, Alfred Deakin, that a 'firm controlling hand'[9] was needed there at the time. Frank letters were exchanged between Deakin and MacGregor, who made his financial position clear in asking whether the salary could be raised from £1,250 to at least £2,750. But in July 1906 these negotiations were publicized and Mac-Gregor's chances declined in the face of nationalistic demands for the appointment of an Australian.[10] Although Deakin realized that he had little hope of appointing MacGregor, especially at an enhanced salary, he wrote encouragingly to him at the end of July: 'I feel so strongly the immense advantage to the possession to be gained by your return to its supreme control'. Deakin also told MacGregor that he was 'the only man of whom I know to whom we could have committed the fortunes of Papua with absolute confidence'.[11]

MacGregor believed that Deakin could overcome local opposition and their letters continued with MacGregor reducing his financial demands as his desire for his old command grew.[12] In May 1907, however, he told Griffith that Deakin

> has just informed me that he still desires I should take the governorship of Papua, but that there is little or no probability of his being able to put this through, as they are in a minority in the Senate, and there is a strong growing feeling that the Lieutenant-Governor should be an Australian.

MacGregor now despaired, saying that he saw no prospect of ever again holding office in Australia. He soon became bitter—he would ask Elgin again about New South Wales 'but the chances are that some Royal Engineer, or some Young Lord, may want it, and that I shall be told "the exigencies of the service require my presence in Newfoundland" '. He was, he felt, trying to do his duty to the best of his ability, but 'I can assure you it requires some sense of duty to do so when one suffers, as I frankly confess I do, from a sense and feeling of injustice'.[13]

It seemed a genuine plea when MacGregor asked Deakin if he could let him 'unite Papua and the Solomons . . . [and] organize them as a Dependency of the Commonwealth',[14] especially as he repeated the idea to Gordon[15] and to Griffith:

> Surely the time has come when the Solomons should be added to Papua. Of course I am personally known to thousands of Solomon Islanders whom I have treated in hospital, and I should be prepared to come any time after October to start an administration for that group.[16]

It should be noted, however, that at this time he was also pressing Elgin about the governorship of New South Wales.[17] These letters make it clear how much his tongue was in his cheek when he said in his reply to the Newfoundland parliament's farewell address: 'For nearly five years I have lived and thought as a Newfoundlander [and have had] no care [and] no interests outside of this colony while I have been its Governor'.[18] This yearning to leave Newfoundland and return to Australia or New Guinea did not necessarily conflict, however, with his devotion to his task as governor. Rather was the feeling like the stimulus of anticipated leave to servicemen, acting as a safety valve for inescapable frustrations.

MacGregor knew that his selection in 1904 for Newfoundland was intended to assist his recovery to health. He did not know that he could be considered for only a few places because of the Colonial Office's determination that he should not hold a 'first-class' governorship. There was pressure from Newfoundland in his favour when the governorship fell vacant. The retiring governor, Sir Cavendish Boyle, told the Colonial Office by a telegram on 10 March that his Premier, Sir Ralph Bond, when informed, 'in strict confidence that a change in this Governorship might take place, begged me as a personal favour to communicate . . . . that ministers would be grateful if Governor of Lagos MacGregor could be considered'.[19] Bond, in a refreshingly frank letter (which the Secretary of State, Alfred Lyttelton, said was 'in essence very satisfactory tho' expressed in the English of a superior bagman') had written:

> I have the pleasure and privilege of knowing him [MacGregor] and therefore have reason to believe that he would prove a worthy successor to your good self . . . in the past we have suffered from inaptness, if I may use the term, from the gentlemen appointed to represent the Crown here, and this fact must be my apology for presuming to ask you to move in the matter.[20]

MacGregor throughout his life owed much to the first impressions he made on others. He owed much to the aid in Scotland of his local minister, schoolteacher and doctor. He owed his Fijian beginnings to meeting Gordon in the Seychelles: he owed New Guinea to meeting Griffith; and now his meeting with Bond (presumably at the coronation of King Edward VII in 1902) was to influence his selection for Newfoundland.[21]

MacGregor was welcomed in Newfoundland. The *Evening Herald* had printed on 23 July 1904 a dramatized story of his rescues in Fiji of the 'Indians from the *Syria*', and this was repeated on the day he arrived, 26 September. The editor then wrote that there could be 'no better passport to the affections of our people than the heroic deed which we chronicle below, for nowhere is such a daring action better appreciated than among our hardy fisherfolk'.[22] An exaggerated version of his career followed. MacGregor appreciated this welcome, as well as other points about the capital city, St John's, especially the fact that his wife and his two daughters were with him.

> I hardly know myself in such a government as this is. First of all we have a comfortable, well-furnished, sufficiently-warmed house. Unfortunately it is too large for the salary, so extensive that it makes the number of servants far too great for £2,000 a year. I was surprised to learn from my predecessor that he, a single man, had to spend £700 a year out of his own pocket. I hope I may be able to do it cheaper than that, but I have not done so up to now.[23]

He pessimistically told Griffith in October 1904 'now for the first time in a service of nearly 32 years I cannot live on my pay, but shall be out of pocket as much as my predecessor, £700 a year as long as I stay here'.[24]

His health improved in his new environment.

> The climate is splendid. The air is pure, fresh and crisp. Our fogs begin in April and last, they say, till June. I love fog, being able to fancy myself at home in a good dense mist. We did not find the cold so disagreeable as the raw, damp weather of the English winter, though the thermometer was several times 10 or 20 degrees below zero. We have had the severest winter experienced here for 25 years. On the whole I have enjoyed it; and have been greatly benefited by the climate. It was, it seems, precisely what I required. I fear, however, that cold may lose its tonic effect on me next winter, should I be here then.[25]

Government House was a home with his family. His wife, for the first time in her life, filled for a considerable period her place as the first lady in a colony. She had never really settled to this position in her few months in Lagos, where the fear of malaria had been so strong. The French governor of St Pierre visited St John's in 1905 and reported that he was 'charmed and touched by the kindness and hospitality of Sir William and Lady MacGregor'.[26] This visit was followed by an official visit by MacGregor, accompanied by his family, to the French possession. His wife and daughters attended various functions—an official dinner and tea, a dance and a ball. At the ball and at the tea Viti played the violin and MacGregor's other daughter, Mary, the mandolin. A polite French journal said they played excellently. Other guests included a British naval Commodore Sir Alfred Paget and French naval captains, Kerillis and Santlire.[27]

The Governor's domestic happiness with his family was soon to be broken. Viti, soon after this visit to St Pierre, became engaged to Sir Alfred Paget and planned to leave Newfoundland for her marriage. MacGregor wrote to Gordon (in a letter which well shows his mixture of subservience, caution and practicality) asking him to give away the bride:

> It is only after much hesitation that I have decided to ask of you as the most highly esteemed friend I possess, to do me a very great kindness. It is this. Our elder daughter Viti, is to be married, probably in April next, to Commodore Sir Alfred Paget. It will be impossible for me, as far as can be seen at present, to leave this colony then. Viti will become a member of her husband's church, the Church of England, and the request I make with so much diffidence, is that you should honour us by performing the church ceremony of giving away the bride.
>
> I feel I am asking so much that I am really ashamed to make such a request. I think you can fully understand how highly we should all appreciate such an act of real kindness. But I am very much afraid you will prefer to be excused; and therefore I must, and do, ask you to not promise to comply if for any reason you would rather not do this; or if it would seriously inconvenience you.
>
> Viti is probably the first European of that name to be married; and it would be a coincidence were she given away by the first governor of Viti.
>
> There is a great disparity of age between the two; but the Commodore is a good man, and they have both set their heart on this marriage. In the meantime my wife has taken the two girls to have a course of Domestic Economy at the Edinburgh School. I hope you will forgive me for tendering such a request.[28]

After the wedding, in May 1906, he told Griffith that 'I am all alone here, and have been so for about six months'. He wrote about the engagement and his insistence on the course of Domestic Economy

> before she could undertake housekeeping. My wife took the two girls to Scotland accordingly and Viti was married on the 7th instant at London. I feel this very much, and fear I shall never be able to quite reconcile myself to this place again. Viti had been with me only twelve months; she had just finished her education, I had looked forward to some family life, of which I have had so little, and now our small circle is already broken into.[29]

MacGregor, besides pining to be in Australia, was temporarily as lonely a man as he had been in Lagos and New Guinea.

While his family were away Major Gibb and his wife helped

V

him entertain distinguished visitors. These absences were brief, and for most of his governorship MacGregor's wife and younger daughter were with him in St John's. Mary acted as his secretary in November 1907 and both fulfilled their social roles, particularly when MacGregor gave a garden party and concert in July 1906 for the Governor-General of Canada, Earl Grey. Newfoundland appreciated their efforts, thus a valedictory message in the *Daily News* said that Lady MacGregor's 'amiable personality' with 'her grace and hospitality has contributed very largely to the success of the social side of your tenure of office amongst us'.[30]

MacGregor's social role was more important in Newfoundland than in his previous governorships. Newfoundland, one of England's oldest possessions in America, had evolved as far as any colony of the British empire, and its responsible ministers were resentful of any unconstitutional interference by the governor. Yet MacGregor was to play a significant part, especially in the main problem of his fifty-seven months of office, that of the rights of Americans to fish in the colony's waters. This issue occupied most of his time with complicated diplomatic and political negotiations in which a growing rift developed between governor and prime minister, not to be resolved until Bond was defeated by Sir Edward Morris in 1909. MacGregor was also concerned and sometimes influential in other problems notably health, education, finance and the modernization of fishing methods.

His lifelong concern as a doctor in applied medicine made him acutely aware of what should be done to improve the health of Newfoundland. He wrote to Gordon eight months after he arrived: 'Sanitation is in a deplorable position. The death rate is very high for a good climate . . .'[31] At the end of his governorship in June 1909 the local newspapers praised his concern, sympathy and practical aid in combating the 'Great White Plague' (tuberculosis), where he had used his knowledge as a physician and a scientist.[32] He had also helped to found an Anti-Tuberculosis Society.

The health problems of the Micmac Indians on the mainland of Newfoundland and of the Innuit Esquimaux of Labrador, also interested MacGregor.[33] Labrador was controlled by Newfoundland, and the Governor paid his first visit there in August 1905. He blamed the decrease in the Innuit population to a high rate of infant mortality and the epidemics of European diseases. He was very critical of the fact that Esquimaux had been taken to

Chicago as 'an exhibition speculation' and on their return had brought typhoid fever to Labrador. Other introduced diseases also caused the Governor great concern.

> The fatality produced by these epidemics will be by no means surprising if it is borne in mind that these diseases are new to the race, and that medical treatment, nurses, medicines, and hospitals were not at hand to tend a stricken community, without resources, ignorant of medicines and sanitation. The Mission has only the one hospital, that just opened at Okak, but the Missionaries, male and female, have always done all within their power to relieve the sufferings of the natives, but in severe epidemics their utmost efforts can do but little. No man that has not witnessed the effects of epidemic disease in an aboriginal race can realise its horrors, as I found by very painful experience when measles destroyed 40,000 natives out of a total population of 150,000, in Fiji, in 1875.[34]

In May 1907 he wrote to his Prime Minister and to the Colonial Office in an endeavour to prevent Esquimaux being taken to the Jamestown Exposition. When later that year an outbreak of syphilis followed the return of some Esquimo recruits from an American exhibition, MacGregor was shocked by the apathy of the Bond government, and wrote to the Colonial Office deprecating the handing over of responsibility for native races from imperial to colonial hands.[35]

In 1908, when MacGregor again visited Labrador, he reported most favourably on the work of Dr S. K. Hutton of the Moravian Mission, and even more enthusiastically on the 'directing genius' of Dr Wilfred Grenfell[36] of the Royal Mission to Deep Sea Fishermen. The Roman Catholic Archbishop, Howley, and Sir Ralph Bond both felt that Grenfell exaggerated the role of the Mission and the hardships of the North. They also felt that enough was spent on health in Newfoundland.[37] This attitude caused MacGregor to attack the government on matters of health when forwarding the report of the Registrar-General for 1907. Despite the very high mortality from tuberculosis and cancer, he reported that 'the government has always appeared apathetic in this matter'. The Colonial Office appreciated his concern.[38]

In February 1908 MacGregor presided at a public meeting at St John's to organize a campaign against tuberculosis and there was considerable public interest.[39] Later in the year there was a meeting of school teachers under the auspices of the Society for the Prevention of Consumption in Newfoundland. But MacGregor was not enthusiastic as there was no proposal 'to provide a systematic course of teaching for the teachers, with correspond-

ing remuneration to those proved by examination to be competent to teach hygiene, such as would be suitable to local requirements'.[40]

After a long drawn out political crisis, involving a deadlocked
election in November 1908 and a further election in May 1909, a
new ministry under Sir Edward Morris took office in June 1909.
This ministry was far more in accord with MacGregor's ideas
than the long-lived Bond ministry, and some of his complaints of
previous years were to be met.[41] It must have given him satisfaction to know that soon after he left Newfoundland, in December
1909, the Morris ministry introduced legislation to prohibit
Esquimaux from going away from home to be on show at exhi-
bitions.

MacGregor was also critical of the backwardness of the education system in Newfoundland, telling Gordon soon after his arrival that if sanitation was 'deplorable', education was 'most
deplorable'. He went on to justify his charge and to show that he
was taking some action.

> The total population is about 225,000. Of these 76,000 are Roman
> Catholics; 73,500 Anglicans; and 62,000 Methodists. This cleavage
> divides the very bedrock of all social and administrative life in
> Newfoundland. Each of these sects has a special Superintendent of
> Education. In each village where there is a school each of these
> sects has a shanty in which theoretically their own children are
> taught by a miserably paid and poorly educated teacher.[42] Lately
> I certainly set many people a thinking. I was asked by the
> Methodists to be present at their Annual Missionary Meeting. I
> did not scruple to invite them to reconsider their proposal to send
> part of their funds to proselytise Roman Catholics at Quebec and
> to convert the Chinese, so long as there are in this colony no less
> than 72,000 [out of] 225,000 [32%] of people of readable age that
> cannot read the Bible. I put before them the case of Fiji, and con-
> trasted it with Newfoundland.

> I took advantage of presiding at the Annual Meeting of the
> British and Foreign Bible Society to return to this subject, telling
> them it is an excellent thing to distribute Bibles, but a better to
> read them, and to teach people to do so. It is my 'ceterum censeo
> Carthaginem delendamesse'. Yesterday I had a deputation of the
> Convention of Sunday School Teachers. I suggested they should
> through their schools organise Bible Readings for those that cannot
> read the Book.

MacGregor gave another illustration of the effect of the division of sects by referring to a meeting of the Rhodes scholarship

committee which consisted of two Roman Catholics, two Anglicans and two Methodists. This committee had to choose from four candidates, who included a representative of each of the three sects. 'If a log-roll has not been arranged, the election will be a sectarian combat. I am chairman. Thank goodness I am a Presbyterian!' MacGregor, however, had hopes that this division could be overcome:

> All this sectarian colouring is the work of the heads of the several churches: it is artificial: it is narrow and uncharitable. I am glad to say it is quite alien to the disposition of the people, who really possess no religious rancour.[43]

MacGregor made public his views on illiteracy by showing the limitations on Bond's intended increase in the education vote in 1905, and continued to use every 'opportunity of reminding people that in this Colony about one in four of the grown up population is not sufficiently well educated to be able to read the Bible'.[44]

On the question of education, like health, MacGregor was hampered by the limits of responsible government. The sectarian issue made it even more difficult for him to intervene openly, especially because of the close links between religion and politics. He soon became convinced of the influence of the Roman Catholic Archbishop, Howley, over the Prime Minister, Bond, though the latter was not a Roman Catholic, but a Methodist.[45] MacGregor stressed the relationship in reporting to the Colonial Office:

> It will doubtless have been brought to your notice that the opposition press constantly asseverate that the present Government is dependent on His Grace Archbishop Howley.[46]

MacGregor was not prepared, at that stage, to say how far the archbishop had influenced the 1904 elections—won so handsomely by Bond—but he became very aware of the link between Howley and Bond during his governorship, particularly in the long American fisheries dispute. Howley was to support Bond and to attack Britain's and MacGregor's policies openly in the press. Bond tried to maintain social equilibrium by distributing patronage equally among the three churches—thus the Executive Council always had three members from each church—but the influence of the Roman Catholics was the greatest. When MacGregor was in Queensland in 1912 he was asked by the Colonial Office whether there was any real objection to the appointment of a Roman Catholic as governor of Newfoundland. MacGregor replied 'there can be no reasonable objection, provided that the [governor] has character to maintain an independent position in his dealings with Archbishop Howley'.[47] Here, as in other colonies, he tried to remain unbiased by sectarian issues.

Throughout his governorship MacGregor maintained his concern in all educational problems, and in his letters to the Colonial Office continued to criticize Bond for his low expenditure on education. On his tours of inspection he always visited schools. He took the opportunity to do this in central Newfoundland, the west coastal area and Labrador, and everywhere he found people were anxious to have their children better educated.[48] MacGregor has reasonable hopes that the new parliament in 1909 would give more attention to education and less to the sectarian issue, for when Morris became Premier he promised to spend more on education.[49]

As ex-treasurer of Fiji MacGregor found much of interest in the finances of Newfoundland. The prolonged fishery crisis certainly had not helped the economic stability of the colony, which degenerated to a state that justified the Colonial Office's succinct comment in 1909: 'Newfoundland finance is admittedly and unquestionably rotten'.[50]

MacGregor had been well aware of the peculiarities of the colony's finances since his arrival. In January 1905 he suggested that the backward condition of the finances of the colony could be improved by the existence of a chamber of commerce which could 'direct public attention to such subjects'.[51] The Colonial Office was even more pessimistic, doubting if such a chamber would 'make any change'.[52] Soon after MacGregor's arrival he prepared a detailed report on the trade of Newfoundland,[53] and then began a similar historical survey of the finances. He told Gordon of two 'interesting' discoveries. The first concerned a loan of £550,000 floated for the colony in 1895 in London. MacGregor calculated from detailed figures that 'for each bond of £100, for which the colony received £94, it has on the average, paid about £13/10/- more than it received'. The second discovery concerned the coinage: the silver coins struck in the colony he decided had 'given a large profit to the Treasury' but there was no fund for redemption or renewal, and of course no Imperial responsibility. He was most concerned with the independence of the banks which furnished

. . . *no* returns. No-one knows what gold they have: what deposits they hold; or how many notes they issue; nor how much capital they employ. I think I have succeeded to some extent in opening the eyes of ministers to the dangers of all this. It does mean sooner or later a crash, if a little more care and prudence are not exercised.[54]

While preparing this report MacGregor asked the English mint to let him know how many coins had been struck for the colony so that he could form an estimate of this part of the colony's liability.[55]

MacGregor's financial report seems never to have been completed, and never to have been published, but he had collected enough information to be able to criticize all aspects of the colony's finances. Every report of the Auditor-General received his very keen scrutiny: for once in 1906 he was optimistic, as he thought the colony was temporarily financially sound. He suggested that a reserve fund was needed, especially as Newfoundland depended so much on one source of revenue—customs—and one industry—fishing. In 1908 he criticized the financial procedure, the preparation of the estimates and the way in which profits from the coinage were treated.[56]

The issues of the Reid contract and of the Harmsworth timber concession must have reminded MacGregor of the British New Guinea Syndicate's attempt to gain large concessions, or of the part played by Liverpool and Manchester capitalists in the development of Lagos. R. G. Reid in 1898 had tried to make a contract with the Newfoundland government which the British government had refused to entertain. The Reid Newfoundland Company had, however, considerable interests in the colony, especially in the railway and docks. Arbitration with Reid and negotiations for the purchase of the Newfoundland Company's interests by the government were still continuing after MacGregor's arrival.[57]

In 1904 Harmsworth, of the Anglo-Newfoundland Development Company, tried to obtain a concession to manufacture paper pulp from the forests of 2,500 acres of Newfoundland. MacGregor arrived in the middle of negotiations and in January 1905, before signing the agreement, drew Bond's attention to what was needed in the way of precision, to guard public rights and to avoid dispute with the lessees, particularly 'with regard to fishing and shooting within the leased area'.[58] A Bill passed the house of assembly on 5 May 1905, after which a petition was signed against the concession at a public meeting. MacGregor,

on the grounds of his limited powers as the governor of a colony
enjoying responsible government, refused to receive a deputation
from this meeting. The British government was then asked to
withhold Royal assent to the Bill. A dispute also developed
with the chairman of the meeting, who was 'engaged in commerce' in St John's. MacGregor regarded himself as bound by
the terms of Chamberlain's 1898 despatch on the Reid contract:
'Where no Imperial interests are involved, or unless the measure
was so radically vicious as to reflect discredit upon the Empire
of which Newfoundland forms a part, it would be improper for
Her Majesty's Government to intervene'.[59] The Colonial Office
agreed with MacGregor because it held that 'this is entirely
a local matter and no imperial interest of any kind is involved'
and because 'it is impossible . . . to judge whether the concessions
made . . . are greater than it was wise to make having regard to
the fact that it is desirable to bring capital into the colony to
develop its industries'.[60]

The exploitation of timber resources was to become a vital
part of Newfoundland's economy, but in MacGregor's years as
governor most attention had to be given to the economically
dominant fishing industry with its record of disputes with France
and, more particularly, with the United States.

Newfoundland's economic existence at this time depended on
fishing. In the long term the fishery share of the economy was, in
fact, declining. In 1891-95 it accounted for ninety per cent of
export earnings, in 1911-15 seventy-four per cent, in 1926-30
forty-six per cent. The contribution of forest products was increasing; in the same three periods this rose from less than one
to fifteen per cent and then to forty-one per cent. Mineral products provided an almost constant share of from nine to eleven
per cent. In 1904 about eighty per cent of Newfoundland's
export earnings came from cod (mainly dried), seal skins and
whale products.[61] MacGregor, after only four months in the
colony, with a concern to be expected more of the governor of a
crown colony than of a colony with responsible government, produced a detailed analysis of Newfoundland's trade figures. In
this he set out the amounts of exports and their prices for the
past century. His suggestion was that an inspector of fisheries
should be appointed to find new markets and extend present
ones.

MacGregor's main deduction from his survey was, however,
that 'the powerful aids of modern science' should be applied to

all aspects of the fishing industry, which had not advanced as in other countries.[62] He wrote to Griffith in private letters: 'this place is fossilised',[63] and again,

> The small amount of progress made here in four centuries seems exceedingly small to one that has seen much of Australia . . . Fish are cured just as they were under Henry VIII. People here do not trust in any scientific methods. We are moss-clad and pride ourselves on our decrepitude and call it honour.[64]

Besides his criticism of these traditional unscientific methods of the cod fishing, MacGregor was also critical of whaling and sealing, reporting that for the period July to September 1905, the whale fishery had not been a success. He commented that his 'observations seem to show that the fishing is carried on during the breeding season, and thus both cow and calf in utero, are destroyed at the same time. It is perfectly clear that such a fishery must speedily decline'.[65] Later, reporting on the period from October to December 1905, he was even more emphatic, writing that the whale fishery had been 'disastrous'.[66]

MacGregor could see arguments against too much modernization of the fishing industry, and argued in 1906 against the use of steam vessels for the Labrador cod fishery because of the fear that the fishery would fall into the hands of a few rich fishermen instead of the couple of thousand small vessels that were now working.[67] His basic sympathies, however, were with eventual modernization. He was aware that the French were taking strenuous measures to develop the cod industry on new lines, and he constantly sought to keep Newfoundland informed on new methods.[68] He investigated the methods of purse seine fishing in Norway,[69] the report of the Scottish Departmental Committee on whaling, and the proceedings of the Hull Conference of the National Sea Fisheries Protection Association.[70]

In accordance with MacGregor's suggestions, Newfoundland occupied herself with means of speeding the transport of fish to markets;[71] and, again backed by him, sought, particularly in the European arena, better trade arrangements for the export of her fish.[72] MacGregor also favoured efforts to persuade Britain to give preference to Newfoundland fish over European.[73] In 1909 the Morris Ministry satisfied some of his plans for modernization by bringing in more effective methods of searching for cod, and regulations covering the better classification and preparation of fish for export.[74]

There had been, then, some results to show from MacGregor's

campaign to end the fossilised state of the Newfoundland fisheries and to apply more modern scientific methods. Throughout his governorship, however, the main question in relation to fishing concerned the rights of other nations to use the Newfoundland fishing grounds. In the case of the United States of America the background of these disputes went back to the beginning of their independence.

15

Newfoundland: Fish and the United States 1904-9

It is a delicate task but Sir William MacGregor might manage it.

The fishing industry in Newfoundland at the date of Mac-Gregor's arrival was overshadowed by the unhappy negotiations with the United States of America. The story had begun in 1783 with a treaty between Britain (for Newfoundland and Canada) and the United States which gave the latter the right to take fish from all waters of British North America, but prohibited them from drying or curing fish on Newfoundland shores.[1] An Anglo-American Convention of 1818 conceded 'for ever' to Americans the rights to dry and cure fish in any of the unsettled[2] bays, harbours, creeks of the southern part of Newfoundland and all of Labrador, and the right to enter the bays and harbours of Newfoundland for shelter, to repair damages, to purchase wood and obtain water.

The Reciprocity Treaty of 1854 permitted certain Newfoundland products free entry into the United States, in return for 'the liberty' of Americans 'to take fish of every kind, except shell fish, on the sea coasts and shores, and in the bays, harbours and creeks' of areas including Newfoundland, Labrador and adjacent islands

> without being restricted to any distance from the shore, with permission to land upon the coasts and shores of those colonies . . . for drying their nets [and] curing their fish; provided [they did] not interfere with the rights of private property, or with British fishermen, in the peaceful use of any part of the said coast in their occupation for the same purpose.[3]

The clauses of this treaty were renewed in 1871 with provision for repudiation on two years notice by either party after ten years.[4]

Disputes followed concerning the comparative value of fishing rights, United States rights[5] to obtain bait in Newfoundland, and duties imposed by the United States on imports of cod-liver oil from Newfoundland. These differences led to the United States decision in 1883 to denounce the Washington Treaty of 1871, and the situation reverted to that in existence after the 1818 Convention.

Attempts were made in the following years to draw up a new treaty between Britain and the United States of America, but there were too many interests involved and the best that could be achieved was an uneasy peace based on a *modus vivendi* which was to continue until 1905. This allowed American ships to enter Newfoundland bays and harbours to purchase bait, but not to fish.[6] In 1901 Canada agreed to Newfoundland and the United States of America entering into separate negotiations, and it seemed that Bond would at last reach an agreement with John Hay, the United States Secretary of State. But the Bond-Hay Convention was not ratified owing to protests to the Senate by the New England fish merchants, who feared for their profits if the proposed agreement came into force.[7]

Into this situation MacGregor arrived as governor with meticulous instructions about the need for care in negotiations. As governor in a colony with responsible government, he had to balance his duty to his elected advisers with his position as representative of the British government. The British government had to balance responsibilities to its colonies (which were complicated since representations from Newfoundland often clashed with those from Canada) with its foreign policies, in endeavouring to maintain friendly relationships with the United States of America. In short, MacGregor was faced with his Prime Minister who was determined to protect the interests of the Newfoundland fishing industry, and the British government whose instructions were to avoid pushing the Americans too far. Throughout all the protracted negotiations that followed, MacGregor refused to be hastened by Bond's incessant pressure on him to try to force the Americans to sign the Bond-Hay Convention. For his diplomacy in this matter he won praise from the Colonial Office,[8] and from Earl Grey, the Governor-General of Canada.[9]

MacGregor soon realized how important his influence was to be:

> The Premier seems to leave nothing of importance to his colleagues . . . I am able to get him to adopt advice often by putting it in such a way that no one, especially his colleagues, know anything about it. He is, fortunately for such treatment, vain, and

fond of the open exercise of power. He enters into important contracts and engagements without submitting such undertakings to
his Attorney-General, or to his Treasurer, as the case may be. I am
not sure that I am not more frequently consulted than they are.
He abhors any suggestions made in a direct form.[10]

In the first fishing season[11] that MacGregor experienced,
Bond's main actions were the introduction of a Foreign Fishery
Vessels Act to prevent Americans buying or catching bait in the
waters of Newfoundland. Bond also argued that the rights granted to the Americans by the 1818 Convention should be restricted
to limited parts of the coast, and should not be exercised in 'the
whole of every bay from headland to headland'. As many of
Newfoundland's bays were large this would have excluded much
more sea than the rule that national waters extended three miles
from the shore.[12]

The general picture of the events of this first fishing season
can best be gained from MacGregor's succinct account in his
letter to Griffith:

My Prime Minister is ambitious and vindictive. He desires to have
a Treaty bearing his name the Bond-Hay Treaty to give a certain
amount of reciprocity in trade between this colony and the United
States. I extracted a reluctant consent from the Imperial Government to this treaty [on 25 October 1905[13]]. But the United States
Senate will not sanction it. Now Sir R. Bond desires to vex and
worry the Americans in order to compel them to adopt the Treaty.
The Americans have under the 1818 Convention very important
fishing rights on these coasts. We are passing laws amendments to
the Foreign Fishery Vessels Act[14] to make it a penal offence for our
own people to fish for, or to sell fish to, the Americans. The latter
used to catch few fish for themselves, but to load up by purchases
from our people. The Americans refuse (1) to recognise our local
laws passed subsequent to the 1818 Convention curtailing any
rights they thereby secured, even if these laws are for the preservation of the Fisheries, and (2) they refuse to enter at the Customs,
and to pay light dues. I had very great difficulty in keeping our
people from seizing American vessels last season. I see great danger
in their attempting to do so again this year should any of our
people engage to fish on an American vessel. We contend that only
inhabitants of the United States can fish on their vessels. Of course
I acted quite unconstitutionally last year in refusing to approve the
Minutes of the Executive Council [the reference is to a crisis at
the end of October][15] . . . when my Prime Minister desired to
proceed to extremities. It looked then as if we were fast drifting
into war with Germany [the Morocco crisis]. It would have been
sheer madness to quarrel with the United States at such a time, or

for that matter at any time. I took the risk of producing a political crisis here, though of 36 members of the House of Assembly 30 are Government. Had the Premier resigned, as he threatened to do for sometime, it would have been difficult to form a Government of any kind. It will not be so difficult this season if he pushes things to the extent of proceeding to seize American vessels. I shall certainly be no party to that. The United States, as you know, contend that all on board an American vessel are, ipso facto, American citizens; add to this their contention that any subject of a foreign power may at any time renounce his original nationality and claim American citizenship.[16]

MacGregor was not wholly out of sympathy with Bond, well realizing the provocativeness of some of the American actions. He criticized their 'flagrant and deliberate violations' of Newfoundland law[17] and their 'highly offensive' disregarding of the Sabbath observed 'universally' by Newfoundlanders.[18] The 1906 season followed a similar pattern with threats and recriminations following hard on each other, and MacGregor trying all the time to modify Bond's intransigent attitude, reminding him that 'this question seriously concerns the foreign relations of the Empire'.[19]

As agreement between Newfoundland and the United States seemed no nearer, for the Americans refused to accept Bond's amendments, Britain drew up a further *modus vivendi* which was signed on 6 October 1906. This gave the United States the right to use purse seine nets and to employ Newfoundlanders in the bait industry so overruling Bond's laws. Storms of protest ensued from the Newfoundland press and parliamentarians,[20] and MacGregor was hard put to it to persuade his ministers to respect the *modus vivendi,* and not to take action against United States ships. He was prepared to go beyond 'the functions of a constitutional governor . . . to proceed to any extremity, even to dismiss my Ministers, rather than give occasion to a war with America over a fishery of the value of £45,000 a year'.[21]

In the midst of all this bitterness it is interesting to note that MacGregor observed: 'the fishermen of the two nations manifest no disposition to quarrel with each other if they are left to themselves'.[22] But such was not the case in higher places, and in spite of MacGregor's efforts to dissuade him, Bond took out an action against two Newfoundland fishermen, Alexander Dubois and George Crane, for shipping herring on the United States vessel *Ralph Hall* on 12 November 1906. At the first legal level, before a stipendiary magistrate named Marsh,[23] the two fishermen were charged with violation of the Bait Act and were convicted. A penalty of $500, or three months imprisonment, was imposed on them. Bonds for the court of appeal were at once furnished.[24]

Soon after the successful prosecution of Crane and Dubois their solicitors, through MacGregor, asked the British government for support of their clients, who had acted in good faith relying on British policy. A clerk in the Colonial Office on 4 December predicted much of the subsequent action of the British government:

> I think that we ought to pay the fines, if the judgment of the stipendiary magistrate is upheld by the Supreme Court, and the lawyers' bill: also give the men something for the loss of a season's fishing. It would be ignoble of His Majesty's Government to leave the two unfortunate men to their fate. A liberal decision on the other hand would immensely strengthen the position of the Imperial Government with the local fishermen: a comparatively small sum is involved, if as now seems very probable no more prosecutions are to be set on foot.[25]

The Treasury agreed to this proposal, and the Colonial Office advised on 7 January that MacGregor should be informed since

> . . . the plan of not saying anything to the Governor about this until the result of the appeal is known may result in the men going to jail. Their friends may not be able to pay £200. Would it be possible to telegraph to the Governor personally and tell him to give his bond for the fines, if the sentence is upheld.[26]

MacGregor, on being informed, accepted the responsibility of passing on these conspiratorial payments.[27]

The Bond government knew of the request to the British government. Partly because it had been made, Bond said he was willing not to institute any further legal proceedings—so long as the British government arranged with the United States government that no more Newfoundland fishermen were employed on board American ships for the rest of the fishing season.[28] No formal arrangement was finalized between Britain and the United States, but local tensions eased. Bond's extreme action had succeeded to this extent although no final decision had been made about American rights.

MacGregor well realized the difficulties of his position, writing in December 1906 to Gordon:

> My position between my Ministers on one side, and His Majesty's Government on the other side, has been very much that of the iron between the hammer and the anvil. My Prime Minister has been bent in defying both Great Britain and the United States. The Secretary of State [Lord Elgin] has assumed that this government

would accept quietly whatever he found it necessary or desirable to arrange. His Majesty's Government found it imperative in the public interest to enter into an arrangement with the United States. My Ministers would not only not assist by advice or suggestion, but refused point blank to be bound by the arrangement. The Secretary of State required me to get my Ministers to comply; the latter insisted on my getting the Secretary of State to repudiate his own arrangement. Naturally this brought about that my position was uncomfortable, almost impossible. Eventually I got my Ministers to confine prosecutions to two test cases, instead of having 500. [MacGregor seems to exaggerate his influence with Bond.] The two were duly tried, sentences were imposed, an appeal was entered, and the cases will be brought before the Supreme Court on the 15th January when the fishery is over for the year. On the whole therefore I have got over the difficulty better, much better, than I at one time thought possible. Of course it is not possible that I can have pleased either Lord Elgin or my Ministers under such circumstances.[29]

MacGregor had pleased Elgin who entrusted him with the conspiratorial payments of advances to the lawyers, and the even more 'delicate task' of giving these Newfoundland lawyers advice from Britain.[30] The case eventually came before the Supreme Court in April, and the judgment of the magistrates was upheld on 6 May. Leave to appeal to the Privy Council was dismissed on 8 October and after further wrangling over lawyer's costs, the Colonial Office paid in January 1908 all the legal expenses and the fines imposed on Dubois and Crane.[31] It had taken fourteen months to reach the conclusion predicted in the Colonial Office within three weeks of the cause of action.

The delicate manoeuvres in which MacGregor was involved caused him to write an astute letter to Gordon:

It soon became clear to me that our present arrangements for regulating the relations between the Imperial and the Colonial Governments in matters that directly involve a foreign power are sadly defective. At one time I had thought I could not prevent the wholesale prosecution of American and of local fishermen, in spite of the *modus vivendi* signed by His Majesty's Government. There exists no machinery to compel this Government to accept or to carry out such an arrangement. The Secretary of State has under party government at Home extreme reluctance in asking Parliament to pass a special Act to compel obedience on the part of the Colony; and it suits party politics here that the Prime Minister assume the role of Bolivar, Tell etc. and save the Colony's rights etc.[32] It is very fine and grand on paper to leave these matters to

reason, moderation, loyalty, and to the logic that the whole is
greater than the part. But this does not work in practice. I feel
morally certain that if some general council, or some arrangement,
cannot be brought into existence by which a colony shall and must
accept agreements entered into by a foreign power and the Empire,
then dismemberment of the Empire must sooner or later come
about. It will come about the first time that a fanatical party man
assumes a similar attitude in Australia under such circumstances as
we have here now. A cognate position may arise at any time in that
part of the world with the Dutch, the Germans, or the French.

Should you not take up the question, say of the development of the
Colonial Conference into a body that might deal with all such
questions in such a way as to put on a colony the obligation of
obedience to the provisions of international agreements? I can
assure you from hard experience that something of the kind is a
necessity.[33]

He hoped that the 1907 Colonial Conference in London might
support such a change, writing to the Colonial Office just before
Bond left for this meeting:

If Colonial premiers had to answer to each other, as well as to His
Majesty's Government, for action that may disturb the foreign
relations of the Empire, they would not lightly enter on a policy
that they could not defend in a General Council of State. At the
present time there is no organ in the Empire of an executive
nature that can enforce compliance with such an arrangement as
the *modus vivendi* of last season as applicable to this Colony; and
for the action that renders that *modus vivendi* necessary the head
of this Ministry cannot be called to account. A certain latitude has
been conceded to Colonies in shaping their commercial relations
with foreign countries, and it is from this source that the present
American question has really arisen in this Colony. Greater latitude will doubtless be conceded in future in the same direction;
but if it is unattended with responsibility, it must eventually produce very grave results. At present a Governor possesses in such
affairs only the unknown quantity of moral power. And even that
influence has been much reduced by conferring on prime ministers
distinctions that overshadow those enjoyed by the majority of
Governors.[34]

On a more personal note he wrote to Griffith:

I have run great risks in restraining my ministers from proceeding
to arrest Americans, and to seize American ships. I have refused to
approve minutes of Council, and have acted unconstitutionally, to
preserve the peace. There I took the risk and responsibility spon-
taneously 'and saved His Majesty's Government from being pushed

W

to an extremity' as Lord Elgin has put it in a private letter to myself. Now I am made by the Secretary of State to engage counsel, in the utmost secrecy, to carry on an appeal in the Supreme Court here against the conviction of two test cases in which the men acted as permitted in express terms by the *modus vivendi*, but apparently contrary to the provisions of a local Act. It is a position of doubtful loyalty to my Ministers, and I hate it, but I cannot help myself, for I cannot on the other hand be disloyal to the King's home government.[35]

MacGregor's dilemma was not solved by the Colonial Conference which only served to intensify the differences between Newfoundland and Britain.[36] He thought, however, that his position would be made easier because of the political opposition to Bond beginning to appear in Newfoundland. On 22 July 1907 Morris, the Minister for Justice, resigned from the government, and in March of the following year he was to become Leader of the Opposition. MacGregor's sympathies were with Morris, whose elevation to be a King's Counsel of the English bar he had strongly recommended.[37]

A week before Morris's resignation MacGregor had written to Griffith that the American troubles were being intensified because 'of what the Premier feels on the subject individually. The country begins to see that; and he is now losing popular favour'. MacGregor went on to define what he thought to be the real question:

> We desire not preference with the United Kingdom, but to force the United States to grant us reciprocal trade: in other words, Sir R. Bond desires to turn what of our trade remains with the United Kingdom to the United States. People in England do not yet quite grasp this, but they will see it eventually.[38]

There is some merit in this interpretation of the issue, as Newfoundland trade was decreasing with the United Kingdom and increasing with the United States.[39] It would be idle, however, to deny that the surface issues involving Newfoundland patriotism, Bond's personal dignity and hostility to the United States fishermen had become vital to the complexities of the 'real question'. Economic determinism, as usual, would give an oversimplified interpretation.

It was in August 1907 agreed by all parties to submit the dispute to arbitration by the Hague Tribunal. Meanwhile, for the 1907 fishing a *modus vivendi* was drawn up by Sir Edward Grey on the lines of the previous season, except that purse seines were forbidden as was fishing on Sundays. This brought forth an indignant protest from Bond's ministers who thought it 'most humiliating that American Government view . . . has been accepted, whilst their views have been totally ignored'.[40] MacGregor faced constant pressure from Bond to urge the British Government not to introduce the *modus vivendi*, and equal pressure from London to persuade Bond to accept it.[41] Eventually the British Government itself under increasing pressure from the United States as the fishing season became more imminent, was forced to conclude a *modus vivendi*; and to issue an Order-in-Council in September 1907 overriding the Newfoundland Government's alternative suggestions;[42] and MacGregor wrote to Griffith that his Ministers 'changed route, but did not resign'.[43] He then continued:

> Sir R. Bond was articled to Sir W. Whiteway, but could not pass the examination. He therefore holds very decided opinions on legal questions. The present Minister of Justice is completely at the mercy of Bond, and thinks to order. They both contended [that] the *modus vivendi*, and the Order-in-Council, issued under 59 Geo. III c.38 [an 1819 Act empowering directives to ensure United States rights under the Convention of 1818] were illegal; and they refused to publish the order. I published it as Governor, having no doubt that it is lawful. They might very well have resigned. But they did not, because if they had gone to the country over an issue at variance with the Governor they would probably have been defeated.[44]

The Colonial Office had realized that the risk of resignation could be disregarded because of the growing political opposition, 'Sir R. Bond is too fond of office to give Sir E. Morris a chance of supplanting him',[45] and this opposition was reflected in St John's where the press was divided for and against Bond. On 7 November the pro-Bond *Evening Telegram,* commenting on past events, wrote that MacGregor's

> ardent desire to safeguard to the full extent of his influence and power what he considers to be Imperial interest will, we do not doubt, be properly appreciated at Home by the Secretary of State for the Colonies; just as the people of this Colony will appreciate the firm and determined effort of Premier Bond and his colleagues to resist by every constitutional means at their disposal every aggression in colonial autonomy, even though based on the subtle doctrine of 'Imperial and public expediency' which being interpreted in the light of the two Blue Books already published seems to be much the same as 'Yankee Bluff' spelt in more decorous and diplomatic language.

On the other hand the *Daily News* on 8 November opposed Bond's government for 'hang[ing] on like grim death' and praised MacGregor for showing 'that sound common sense, tact and courtesy which has characterised him throughout his public life'.[46]

The extent of 'colonial autonomy' mentioned in the *Evening Telegram* was taken up by MacGregor in a speech on 9 November. He agreed that 'the principle at the basis of Imperial authority was the recognition of the right of the people [of the colonies] to self-government', but, obviously for Bond's edification, stressed that 'autonomy meant the power to govern ourselves, but it did not mean the power to govern others'.[47] MacGregor believed Bond had overstepped the limits of autonomy in a different way by the appointment in February 1908 of J. M. Kent, who had led the government case against Crane and Dubois, as Minister for Justice. MacGregor objected partly because Kent was not an elected member of the legislature, but more importantly because he, as governor, had not been consulted. He was concerned because 'this is only one of many ways in which Sir R. Bond endeavours to establish an absolute autocracy, apart from all imperial control'. He eventually approved the appointment.[48] Another clash developed over recommendations for honours from the King. MacGregor argued that he should approve each name submitted, but realized that Bond's advocacy of colonial initiative was supported in other parts of the Empire, especially in Australia.[49]

In the meantime the terms of reference were being drawn up for the Hague Tribunal and in view of this MacGregor's ministers were 'most desirous of avoiding any action that would be likely to cause friction with the Government of the United States, or that would be prejudicial to the Colony's case before the Hague tribunal'.[50] In keeping with this feeling of maintaining peace, MacGregor was able to make a verbal agreement with Bond before the summer fishing began. This agreement provided that the arrangement of the previous year would be continued, provided the British government withdrew the *modus vivendi* and the Order-in-Council. MacGregor promised Bond to ask Great Britain to withdraw both these measures,[51] and he urged the Colonial Office to 'withdraw at least the Order-in-Council, which they all consider damaging to the Colony's case at the Hague'.[52]

On 2 July Bond asked, through MacGregor, for the revocation

of the Order-in-Council.[53] The Colonial Office agreed to make the concession especially as 'there seems little harm in repealing [it] for, after all, we can always re-enact it whenever we please'.[54] Sir Edward Grey, at the Foreign Office, and his advisers thought that the Order-in-Council should not be revoked, but the Colonial Office insisted.[55] On 29 September 1908, after further anxious pressure from Newfoundland, the revocation of the Order-in-Council was published in the colony.

MacGregor played a further role in the fishing crisis, that of mediator between Bond and the British Ambassador in the United States. When James Bryce's appointment was announced to this position in December 1906 MacGregor wondered whether

> to invite him to pay me a visit here on the way out. The only doubt I entertain as to the propriety of such a visit is that my Prime Minister desires to have in his own hands the direction of the proceedings, and does not wish the Ambassador at Washington to initiate or suggest anything. Unfortunately I have never met Mr. Bryce, and can thus form no opinion how far his temperament would be compatible with that of my Prime Minister.[56]

In fact MacGregor, rather than Bond, was to deal primarily with Bryce and they were to exchange frank opinions on the political and legal implications of the crisis.[57]

Their relationship was close by the time the terms of reference to the Hague tribunal were being settled. Bryce sent a telegram to MacGregor on 10 March 1908 urging 'prompt treatment'[58] by the Newfoundland government for Bryce feared further delays by the United States Senate. MacGregor had to press Bond carefully for he knew that any hint of outside interference would annoy Bond.[59] It is a tribute to MacGregor that the terms were settled and sent to the Hague in the same month. MacGregor told Griffith that the major part of his task in Newfoundland had been fulfilled, and that he felt he could now leave.[60] His idea that the fishing question was settled was prematurely optimistic. The terms of reference were disputed right up to his departure in June 1909. Further complications were the pecuniary claims made by the United States in September 1908. They wanted compensation for alleged wrongful acts against American ships on the treaty coast.[61] There was also keen debate on the appointment of arbitrators for the Hague. MacGregor tried unsuccessfully to induce Griffith, who had been Chief Justice of Australia since 1903, to act for Newfoundland.[62] In the discussions MacGregor showed a surprising knowledge of international lawyers and their writings. When Dr Heinrich Lammasch of Austria was suggested as the third arbitrator he warned that the British and United States arbitrators would cancel out each other, and 'the whole question thus [would be] left to Lammasch, who, of course is nurtured and moulded on Hefftler and Bluntschli to whom my people are complete strangers'. He urged Kent to study these writers, also lending his copy of a book by Calvo y Diaz who took a view unfavourable to Newfoundland's case.[63]

Before he left Newfoundland MacGregor was also to become involved in a political crisis of an unusual nature. An election was held on 20 November 1908, and the bitterly fought campaign between Bond and Morris—in which the question of the United States fishery rights was not made an open issue—resulted in a dramatic tie when both parties won eighteen seats in the lower house. One government seat was won by only one vote, but the subsequent recount did not break the tie.[64]

When the results were confirmed MacGregor faced a constitutional crisis: Should Bond or Morris be Prime Minister? Should Bond be given a dissolution and privilege of going to the polls as Prime Minister? Could Morris form a viable ministry? Morris urged MacGregor to call upon Bond to resign, as he had failed to secure a majority. MacGregor, however, decided not to ask for Bond's resignation, since Morris also had no majority. He asked the Colonial Office for guidance: 'though I fear that there is no real precedent to the present case'.[65] He was advised that until Morris could carry a vote of want of confidence there was no case for asking Bond to resign. The situation, however, increased MacGregor's powers as he was told by the Secretary of State: 'you must exercise your personal discretion in making appointments or agreeing to contracts because your Ministers cannot claim your full support inasmuch as they have no Parliamentary Majority'.[66] MacGregor had, in the meantime, determined 'to give no undue advantage to either party, but [to] try to keep the interests of the country as the first consideration'.[67]

Bond wanted to dissolve parliament and go to the people again, but MacGregor asked him to open parliament early in February. MacGregor had not decided what to do. He thought that Bond was in a stronger position than that in Canada in 1896, where Sir Charles Tupper had been unable to pass votes of supply even before he had been clearly defeated in a general election. As well the giving of greater scope to responsible ministers rather than intervening as governor was 'in harmony with the trend of constitutional government in the Dominions in recent years, a trend that has been strongly marked since I went to Australia in 1875, and which has made considerable progress since 1896'.[68] He hoped that the Government would be granted supply for a few months to obviate the necessity for a spring election. A large number of electors, including the sealers and bank fishermen, sailed in March; so if an election were held in April about one-eighth of the voters would be out of the country.[69]

MacGregor was concerned about the constitutional issues in the planned opening of the House in February. For instance, 'whether, and how, I can dissolve or prorogue a House that has no Speaker; a House, moreover, that I have not opened; and to which I have not communicated the purposes for which it was called together'. He thought an 1868 British precedent of the governor 'personally' opening the legislature without a governor's speech might be applicable, but that the appointment of a speaker would not solve the tie. The speaker, he considered, was entitled to an ordinary and a casting vote. If, however, a Bond follower was appointed Speaker Bond should cease to be Prime Minister for he would have a minority of members in his support. If an opposition member were appointed Speaker Bond would have a majority. MacGregor realized that no Morris supporter would want to accept this position, and he pointed out that although the resignation of a Speaker needed the acceptance of the governor, he could not see how a Speaker could be made to retain his office.[70]

A further problem was the appointment of officials by responsible ministers. On this point MacGregor said bluntly that he was not prepared to approve any such appointment when his ministers had no majority, unless reasons were given which he could use in reply to any new ministry which might want to cancel such an appointment.[71]

MacGregor's time in Newfoundland was to be extended because of this political crisis. In Queensland, where he had been appointed governor, he was expected in time for the jubilee celebrations (in June 1909, fifty years after separation from New South Wales) but it became clear early in 1909 that he would have to wait until this Newfoundland crisis was settled. By the end of March it had been decided that he could not reach Brisbane before the end of August. He was told that his successor in Newfoundland was to be Sir Ralph Williams.[72]

Bond manoeuvred to have the opening of parliament delayed,[73] and on 22 February he resigned. On 3 March MacGregor formally accepted Bond's resignation and appointed Morris as the new Prime Minister. The opening of parliament was again delayed but MacGregor said it would meet within a week. On 5 March, however, an indefinite postponement was announced. MacGregor wanted the House to meet early enough to allow time for Morris to attempt to govern and fail, so that the possibility of a coalition ministry could be explored. If this last failed, the House would at least have to meet to make arrangements for a general election.[74]

MacGregor would have preferred to have Morris as Prime Minister. He found Morris 'more reasonable, and less egoistic' than Bond who

> is a sort of *editione terrible* of Sir George Grey, and appears to be not unfamiliar with the philosophy of Herostratus. He speaks and writes in superlatives; and he has thus said many things to His Majesty's Government that might have been put differently.

MacGregor could not judge how long the Morris ministry would survive, but he feared a spring election, the results of which he could not foresee. 'I do not forget the 221 députés of Charles X in 1830, each returned for the same constituency: and history often repeats itself.'[75]

On 30 March the House met. After the formal swearing-in MacGregor instructed the House to elect a Speaker. Morris proposed Warren, who was defeated 18-17 (after he had not voted for himself). Bond then proposed Ellis, and the votes were tied at 18-all (Ellis voted for himself). MacGregor then prorogued the House to 6 April. A. Berriedale Keith said Bond had been 'silly' as he could have allowed Warren's election, then defeated Morris, and so have had a 'real victory'.[76]

After this meeting MacGregor reported that he now believed that a coalition was unlikely. He still intended to approach some other member to form a ministry, though he thought the possibility of anyone accepting was very remote. Morris was already advising dissolution, and he knew that Bond would ask that dissolution would be granted to him.[77]

Extremely bitter arguments followed as to who should be granted the dissolution. MacGregor consulted the Colonial Office where the majority opinion was that the dissolution should be granted to Morris. Keith was doubtful, but finally came round to the majority opinion.[78]

On 5 April MacGregor reported that he had attempted to procure a coalition government. He had decided not to see any member of the House of Assembly except his ministers, for he felt that to approach any follower of either Morris or Bond would seem an unwarrantable intrusion by the governor, who would be accused of attempting to break the deadlock by splitting the existing parties. MacGregor said he had gone 'as far as I deemed prudent in this small and excited community, controlled as it is by uncompromising party politics'. Keith was apt to be critical, writing that MacGregor's efforts seemed 'not very energetic', but other Colonial Office opinion was that he had done 'as much as he safely could'.[79]

Although MacGregor interviewed no member of either political party, those he consulted were declared opponents of Bond. He saw J. S. Winter and D. J. Greene, tried to see A. F. Goodridge (a former Newfoundland Premier) and interviewed Reid of the Newfoundland Company.[80] The pro-Bond *Evening Telegram* in St John's commented that 'the leaning of the Governor to the Reid-Morris outfit, long before the last general election, was plain to those who had eyes to see and ears to hear'.[81] This attack was made even stronger on 26 April when the same newspaper claimed that

> no unbiased man [after reading the correspondence between Bond and MacGregor] can arrive at any other conclusion than that the Governor from the very outset was determined 'by hook or by crook' to give the dissolution to the Reid-Morris combination. . . . The special pleadings, evasions and general crookedness that runs through his letters are not characteristic of that fair-mindedness that should direct the action of one who is responsible to the Crown for his discretionary exercise of the prerogative.[82]

The pro-Morris *Daily News,* on the other hand, said that MacGregor had 'displayed that impartiality and that interest for the welfare of the country which could only have been expected from him'.[83]

Eventually MacGregor, and Morris, decided on 8 April that there was no hope of a coalition and on 9 April MacGregor announced that he proposed to dissolve the House in preparation for a general election on 8 May. On the same day in April MacGregor formally accepted Morris's advice on the dissolution.[84]

The second election ended this long crisis. Morris won a majority of ten seats, assuring political stability in the future. MacGregor, partially because of the comments of Bond and the press now sought written aproval of his actions, especially of the granting of the dissolution to Morris. The Colonial Office prepared a dispatch of fulsome praise, going well beyond the formal requirements of solidarity between the British government and its overseas representatives. As has been shown from the Minutes written during the crisis, practically all Colonial Office opinion had been convinced that MacGregor had handled the crisis admirably. The dispatch read:

> Your action throughout the difficult political situation which was created in the Colony by the indecisive result of the last general election has met with my approval but I desire to place publicly on record my high appreciation of the manner in which you have handled a situation practically unprecedented in the history of responsible government in the Dominions.

> I may add that I consider your decision to grant a dissolution to Sir E. Morris—which has, I observe, been adversely criticised in a section of the Newfoundland press—to have been fully in accordance with the principles of responsible government.[85]

MacGregor now regarded his duties in Newfoundland as virtually completed, so he telegraphed London on 13 May asking when he could leave. He wished to open the new parliament in the first week of June and the Colonial Office decided he could leave 'as soon as agreeable to [himself] after the opening of parliament'.[86]

MacGregor was in Queensland when the fishing dispute with the United States eventually reached the Hague in 1910, but in many ways these proceedings, which lasted from 1 June to 8 August, were an anticlimax. Generally most of the questions were answered in Newfoundland's favour. The Court found that Newfoundland was legally competent to forbid its nationals to work on United States ships; that bays should be measured from a line drawn across the bay where it ceased to have a configuration of a bay; and that the three-mile exclusion limit should be applied in bays so defined as well as off the coastline; that the municipal law of Britain, as limited by the liberties granted to the United States by the 1818 Anglo-American Convention, was to apply; that the provisions of the 1906 *modus vivendi* as to ships reporting were valid; that United States ships could fish or trade but not both. Against Newfoundland it was decided to reject Bond's ideas of 1905 regarding the south coast of Newfoundland and parts of the western and southern coast. It was also decided that Newfoundland could not impose restrictions on the non-treaty coasts, but that United States ships should report to local authorities if they were on these coasts for more than forty hours.[87]

The crisis years were those of MacGregor's governorship when Bond was defying his governor, Britain and the United States. MacGregor succeeded as governor because he was not only able to curb Bond's excesses, but also to hold the confidence of the Colonial Office and of the British representatives in the United States. For a long period he was working well with Bond, walking a precarious tight-rope in his negotiations with him and the Colonial Office. Eventually he fell out with his Prime Minister, and was forced to turn to an alternative leader, Morris, but it is hard to visualize any governor being able to work with Bond, for Bond's refusal to compromise could well have led to an even more serious crisis with the United States, and to consequent condemnation of Newfoundland policy by Great Britain. Mac-Gregor had well deserved the praise bestowed on him by Keith: his 'service in Newfoundland was of great value to the Empire and deserves every commendation'.[88]

Certainly MacGregor could look back on his part in the various crises with satisfaction. His successes had almost completely dispelled official doubts about his ability as a governor, which had so clouded his last years in Lagos. By 1907 he was supported by the Colonial Office for elevation in the peerage,[89] and his next post was regarded by the Colonial Office as a promotion which he had well deserved.

16

Newfoundland: External Policies 1904-9

> One important duty in respect to the Esquimaux devolves on the
> Government of Newfoundland . . . to protect them in their rights
> to their own territory.

The long-drawn-out crisis with the United States had, however,
been exacerbated by a previously existing crisis with France.
MacGregor had arrived in Newfoundland just after a convention
had been signed on 8 April 1904 by the French and British
governments regulating the rights of French fishermen on the
Newfoundland coast between Cape St John and Cape Ray. This
convention did not finally solve all problems, but meant that
during MacGregor's governorship disputes never reached as
critical a stage as those with the United States. The convention
was part of the general improvement of British-French relationships that led to the *Entente Cordiale*. As Grey said in the House
of Commons in February 1907, the settlement was not 'of individual matters each on its merits, but the settlement of one
Imperial matter against another Imperial matter, the object of
the whole being to arrive at a good and friendly understanding
with the French Government'.[1]

Certain problems did arise out of the interpretation of individual matters in this convention, one being the limits to the
right of French fishermen to land on the shores of Newfoundland.[2] Bond and his ministry were afraid that unlimited access
would facilitate the smuggling of liquor into the country, and
MacGregor, at this time working closely with Bond, completely
supported his ministers. He told Gordon in a private letter on
31 March 1905:

> The really important part in practice is the framing and passing of
> the Regulations which are to determine the relations of the
> national fishermen. I have tried all I could to not have conceded to
> the French the right to land on our coast for any purpose, except

332

of course in stress of weather. The Colonial Office, I presume under pressure from the Foreign Office, are to let the French land to haul their seines. It will follow that they will water: that they will take firewood, then camp, then build shelters; and begin the old game over again.[3]

MacGregor agreed with those who believed that many of the French who wanted to land were not only fishermen but also smugglers:

It is the universal opinion here that the Colony of St Pierre has largely subsisted by smuggling goods into Newfoundland. The total exclusion of the French fishermen from this Island was looked upon here as an important and valuable aid in putting down the importation of contraband goods. So long as the French are allowed to land on and use the shore, the suppression of smuggling is impossible, no matter what expense and trouble may be incurred by this Government.[4]

MacGregor pointed out that the French could fish with seines without landing. He also supported his ministers' suggestions that a British consul should be appointed to St Pierre, particularly one who had a thorough knowledge of this illicit trade. A consul, C. S. Hampson, was appointed and he arrived in Newfoundland in May. The Foreign Office felt that it would be impossible to find a man who had knowledge of earlier smuggling, but hoped that Hampson, who had been vice-consul at Konieh,[5] would be free of 'preconceived ideas' and 'local prejudices'.[6]

In June 1904 relations with the French at St Pierre were strained by the decision of the Newfoundland Government to forbid the export of timber to them as a retaliation against infringements of the convention. This issue had led to one of the few criticisms from London of MacGregor as governor in Newfoundland because not only had he not kept the Colonial Office fully informed, but he also had not sent on colonial newspapers.[7] He apologized, explaining that he had not realized the full international significance of the issue.[8] During 1905 he played his part in endeavouring to improve relationships with the French by inviting the Governor of St Pierre and the naval officers to Government House at St John's; while later in the year he paid an official visit to St Pierre.[9] All was *fraternité*, and the press saw signs of the cementing of the *Entente Cordiale* 'so wisely promoted by King Edward and President Loubet'.[10] MacGregor welcomed the *Entente*, spoke of the historical links between France and Scotland and of his own friendly relations with the French, particularly in Africa. Remembering his warning to London from Lagos about French activity his ideas would seem to have changed as much as had British policy.

As a result of happier relations between the two countries, and on MacGregor's recommendations, both the Governor and the chief naval officer of St Pierre were granted an honorary C.M.G.[11]

The French government reciprocated by proposing to make MacGregor a Commander of the Legion of Honour. Foreign Office rules, however, prohibited a British governor from receiving such a French honour. The French government accepted the British regulation and substituted the gift of a Sèvres porcelain tea service. MacGregor was not so easily convinced and showed his resentment against the Colonial Office in a letter to Griffith. After bewailing that there seemed to him to be a 'dead set' in the Colonial Office against the older servants, he went on to this issue:

> Three times the King asked me personally to do all I could to get the French questions arranged, and to get this and the neighbouring Colonies on better terms. One result has been that the French Government wished to confer on me a higher grade of the Legion of Honour. His Majesty's Government have refused to allow it. Thus they not only give me no recognition themselves, but they prevent others from doing so![12]

He made the same complaints to London in a personal letter to Grey arguing that he should be allowed to accept the French decoration, and added in typically frank fashion, 'need hardly say that I should greatly prefer the Legion of Honour to a service that can be of little use to me'.[13] Elgin commented that MacGregor 'has the pertinacity of a Scotchman with which I am not ashamed to sympathise', but considered the case closed as the French Government had accepted the British ruling.[14]

As a sequel to MacGregor's friendship with the authorities at St Pierre the questions of timber exports and smuggling were settled. No other major problems arose, although there were rumours of St Pierre being ceded to the United States of America, of French freezing factories being erected on the treaty coast and of extensive trawling by the French on the banks.[15] It would seem, however, that the general peacefulness owed as much to the *Entente Cordiale* between the two home governments as to any efforts in Newfoundland, whether by the government or by the governor.

6 Newfoundland

MacGregor's interest in the more primitive parts of the colony, reminiscent of his work in British New Guinea, has already been shown by his concern in the health of the Esquimaux of Labrador and the survival of the Indians in Newfoundland. He was also determined to protect Esquimau territory which was partly threatened by a dispute over the boundary between Labrador and Canada.

MacGregor was so interested in the Esquimaux that he decided to make a visit to Labrador; this was also planned as a relief from his boredom and from his frustrations as a governor in a colony with responsible government.[16] He made this apparent in a private letter to Griffith:

> I shall meet with a country and a people new to me in many respects. I hope to learn something of botany, geology, mineralogy, esquimancy and missions. I am curious to see in practice the trading missions of the Moravians.[17]

On his visit between 30 July and 1 September 1905 he collected data on temperature at most of the Moravian mission stations; he made a considerable number of astronomical observations to determine exact geographical positions; he made 'a tolerably complete collection' of the botany of the Chidley Peninsula which he forwarded to Kew Gardens; he assembled many geological specimens;[18] and above all he was convinced of the value of the Moravian mission because '. . . the industrial advance of the native is highly creditable to the mission that trains and teaches'.[19] To Griffith he praised the 'Moravian combination of evangelisation and commerce',[20] reminiscent of some of the London Missionary Society experiments in the Eastern District of British New Guinea.

On his return from this visit MacGregor reported that Canada and Newfoundland should each appoint a commissioner to look into the boundary question. He, himself, favoured a coast-inland division; with Newfoundland controlling the Esquimaux on the east coast of Labrador, and Canada the Indians of the inland. If this division were adopted, he suggested that Canada should be given access to certain ports. The first problem was how much of the inland was needed for trapping and hunting by these people. Inland lived Indian tribes over whom the Canadian government could justly claim jurisdiction. The exact borderline, the frontier between these peoples, had not been agreed upon by Newfoundland and Canada. MacGregor, however, pointed out that a *de facto* boundary already existed:

For many generations there have been fierce disputes between the Esquimaux and Indians over these lands; but a condition of quiescence has been arrived at and bloodshed seems to occur no more over these quarrels. It would be a pity to disturb a settlement that seems to have been arrived at by natural processes.[21]

The Colonial Office, on the other hand, felt that Labrador naturally belonged to Canada for geographic reasons, and that Canada was in a better financial position to develop the country. It took no account of the welfare of the native inhabitants nor of the historical fact that the Moravian mission under the protection of Newfoundland had since 1765 accepted responsibility for the Esquimaux.[22]

MacGregor wrote exhaustive reports in reply to the Colonial Office, and on the financial issue he argued that the transfer of Labrador from Newfoundland to Canada might result in the bankruptcy of Newfoundland. He gave figures to show the interrelationship of their revenue—for instance, about one-third of the salt cod exported from Newfoundland was from Labrador. So long as Newfoundland was independent of Canada, his argument would have weight. MacGregor concluded by stating his firm conviction that Newfoundland should not join the Dominion for it was not

desirable in the broad interests of the Empire that direct control should be lost to the Imperial government over islands that occupy such strategic positions as that of Newfoundland. The loyalty of Newfoundland is deep and genuine. The people are proud of their direct dependence on the Crown and I am certain that the Imperial Government would always find it easier to deal with Newfoundland alone.[23]

The whole boundary issue became deadlocked; indeed, it was not until 1927 that the Privy Council finally decided the issue, and not until 1949 that Newfoundland became a part of Canada.[24] MacGregor, however, continued to involve himself in the matter, and in 1906 he and Earl Grey, the Governor-General of Canada, exchanged visits. MacGregor was amazed that Grey was the first Governor-General to visit Newfoundland which, he thought, had 'lived as isolated as a Papuan tribe, and it is consequently as suspicious'.[25] He hoped that the successful visit would facilitate better relations.[26] The two governors unofficially discussed the future relationships of Canada as well as the Labrador boundary problem.

A Colonial Office comment at this time admitted that the New-

x

foundland case was mainly good (apart from the claim for jurisdiction over the southern shore of Hudson Straits) but it should not be supported as 'in that event the entry of Newfoundland into the Dominion would be even less likely than it is even now'.[27]

In the same year MacGregor made a brief visit to l'Anse Sablon at the southernmost point of the disputed boundary. He had to admit that the inhabitants were predisposed to inclusion in the Dominion, mainly because they imported most of their food from Canada. He thought that the Newfoundland government should do more to aid the people of this area, suggesting the introduction of reindeer.[28] This was one of the recommendations MacGregor had made in his 1905 report, repeating the 1844 arguments of a Newfoundland member of parliament, and citing the successful introduction by the United States of reindeer into Alaska. With typical thoroughness he forwarded mosses and lichen, collected by two Moravian missionaries near Hopedale, to Kew Gardens for a report on their suitablity as food for reindeer. In May 1907 when Kew assured him that the lichen was the same as those growing in Norway, Sweden and Lapland, MacGregor expressed his confidence that there was every chance for an adequate supply of food for reindeer.[29] Subsequently reindeer were successfully introduced.[30]

In April 1907 MacGregor submitted a memorandum on the Labrador boundary question, which he hoped would be raised by either Bond or by Laurier, for Canada, at the Colonial Conference in London. He reiterated that

the dispute should be settled amicably between the two governments, in such a way as to save expense and disappointment; and so as to secure a workable boundary, favourable to the development of that part of North America, whether Canadian or Newfoundland.

MacGregor's views, however, did show one important change in so far as he now stressed that

eventually Newfoundland must form part of the Dominion though there is little probability of that at present, the union would no doubt be brought about sooner and with greater certainty were the Dominion inclined to be generous in settling this question.[31]

MacGregor's main dilemma in Labrador at this time arose from an application for a timber concession. This might, as he repeatedly advocated, help to develop Labrador. He realized, however, that such development could clash with other ends he desired. He wanted to preserve scarce resources, and he did not know if there was enough timber for despite his requests no survey had been made of the forests. More importantly a concession would clash with the rights of the Esquimaux, since the 'proposed grant lies in what is perhaps the most important part of the country now occupied by the settlements of the remnant of the Esquimaux race not yet extinguished . . . [and it] would probably lead ultimately to the closing of the Moravian station and Esquimaux settlement at Hopedale'.[32] He told Bond that as governor in a colony enjoying responsible government he would feel bound to approve their granting of a concession 'whatever may be . . . [his] personal view as to the wisdom of the course'.[33] But his dilemma remained and he referred final approval to the British government. In 1908 MacGregor after his second extensive tour of Labrador wrote:

> One important duty in respect to the Esquimaux devolves on the Government of Newfoundland, . . . that is, to protect them in their rights to their own territory. They are in danger from the concession seeker; and they are threatened by division through the action of Canadian Officers in the settlement of the Labrador Boundary.

He now argued that 'on the matter of concessions there clearly can be no compromise between right and wrong', and advocated that no timber concessions should be granted where the destruction of forests would interfere with the timber and fuel supplies of the Esquimaux, or where they would cause a decrease in game, which provided food and clothing for these people. He also believed that it would be immoral and unjust to grant concessions which would interfere with the Moravian Mission working with the Esquimaux in the area north of Cape Harrison.[34] On this journey he had revisited the Moravian mission stations on the coast again making many astronomical observations,[35] and also went inland. He went up Hamilton Inlet to the mouth of the Hamilton River and saw some of the bases of the Hudson's Bay Company. In this area MacGregor realized that Canada had done more than Newfoundland, and that it must be given credit for its efforts:

> Near the mouth of the Kennemou I saw one or two large log buildings that had been erected there two years ago by some of the men that have been sent by the Dominion Government to examine that part of the country . . . They gave the settlers here, . . . to understand that the south side of the Hamilton River, and of the Hamilton Inlet, is under the jurisdiction of Canada. They took stock of

what was being done by the Pulp and Lumber Company. These Canadian officers . . . expressed themselves to the settlers as much pleased with the district, which they considered of value. It is believed that a survey of the country was made by Canada as far as the Muskrat Falls. There can be no doubt that Canada has given much more attention to the district than Newfoundland has done, and consequently must be much better informed as to its condition and its worth.[36]

This report was written after MacGregor left Newfoundland, and it is interesting to note how his opinions had changed about Canada's claims to Labrador, just as he had come to realize the probability of Newfoundland's being incorporated into the Dominion of Canada.

In his four years as governor, neither Canada nor Newfoundland had done much to aid either of his main aims—which could be so incompatible—the development of Labrador and the protection of the Esquimaux. His concern for the Esquimaux, so typical of his approach to primitive peoples, cannot be doubted. This concern is obvious throughout his detailed reports on the boundary question, and in his two long reports on his visits to Labrador. It is apparent that at the end of his term of office MacGregor's attitude was that as long as the primitive people were protected, he was not vitally concerned whether Canada or Newfoundland controlled the area, nor whether it was developed at all by outsiders.

Wherever he served, MacGregor's concern for the primitive people of the land shone like a bright light out of a morass of administrative bickering. So it was fitting that his last despatch to the Colonial Office as Governor of Newfoundland[37] should have forwarded his reports on his visits to the Esquimaux.

17

Queensland: Limited Responsibility 1909-14

It would be very convenient . . . if they would abolish the State
Governor on or soon after 15 February 1913 . . . as at that date I
should finish forty years actual service.

MacGregor had been longing to return to Australia for years
despite occasional misgivings about his financial position there.
He retained his interest in New Guinea, he had Australian
friends, notably Griffith and Mackellar. In addition he found
much in Australia that did approach his ideals. His attitude is
suggested by a comment to Griffith soon after he returned to
London after his five years in Queensland:

> Perhaps it is natural that in a new country like Australia the
> human intellect should be more sensitive than it is in the artificial
> life of this country. Taking the people all round, in England and
> in Australia, I am decidedly disposed to say that the Australian,
> though perhaps not the more learned, is at the same time the
> better educated and understands better the natural history of
> man.[1]

In almost every issue, MacGregor in Queensland accepted the
limitations of a responsible governor in a colony now keenly conscious of its legal and conventional rights as a part of the recently
formed Australian federation. Yet this acceptance did not imply
tacit agreement with the policies of the Queensland governments
nor any lessening of his scientific curiosity. MacGregor examined
Queensland's problems in detail as if he had to decide policy and
was not reluctant to express disagreement. In particular he
showed concern with his government's policy towards Aboriginals and its limited support of scientific research. As Chancellor
of the new Queensland University MacGregor took an independent line which led to some disputes with his ministers.

Queensland would be MacGregor's last colonial charge. He
was sixty-three when he arrived, and he was recuperating from a

serious illness. Either literally or metaphorically he was not anticipating climbing any more mountains. The strain of ener-getic rule in New Guinea had aged him; malaria in Lagos had nearly killed him; his recovery in the climate of Newfoundland had been delayed by the incessant tension of the fishery dispute and then by another nearly fatal illness in Scotland.

The fishery dispute and constitutional crisis in Newfoundland had prevented MacGregor from being in Queensland for its celebrations in mid-1909 of fifty years of colonial independence. He finally left St John's on 23 June, planning to leave Eng-land for Queensland on 28 August. He went back to the Don Valley, visiting his relations and staying for part of the time in Strathdon. While at the Newe Arms Hotel in this area he was 'struck down with a serious illness' which an Aberdeen doctor diagnosed as 'biliary colic with jaundice', urging an immediate operation to remove one or more 'biliary calculi'.

MacGregor wrote on 7 August, the day he was to be moved to Aberdeen for the operation, expressing his 'deepest regret' for the inconvenience that his infirmities would cause the colonial service. He was sure, 'assuming the operation to succeed', that he would not be able to sail for Queensland by 28 August. He asked if his departure could be deferred for a month. If, 'in the interests of the service' it could not be, he would 'though with the greatest regret' place his resignation in the hands of the Colonial Office.[2] MacGregor's devotion to the Colonial Office, which he had served so long, was so strong that his formal expressions can be taken literally: he was unquestionably almost as concerned in the effect on Britain's colonial service as in the danger to his own life. The Colonial Office had no hesitation in expressing their own sympathy and were sure, subject only to confirmation from Australia, that there would be no objection to a month's delay.[3]

The operation on MacGregor was successful and his slow recovery began. He was still very troubled by his sense of duty, and this was little dispelled by reassurances from the Colonial Office. His wife's letter to the Colonial Office written on 29 August makes his concern clear:

> From the nature of his illness and the very severe operation he has undergone his complete recovery must take time, but the doctor assures me that he is quite satisfied with his condition, and feels confident that now the cause of his illness is removed that he will have better health than he has had for some years past . . .
>
> My husband has suffered from great depression for the last two

weeks, which I fear may be caused by the enforced delay in leaving for Queensland. The three doctors in attendance and myself had much difficulty in inducing him to undergo the operation on account of the delay it would necessitate, and it was only after four days of intense agony that our earnest persuasions prevailed, and when it was represented that another delay might cost him his life that he at last submitted to have the operation performed. My husband was so anxious to take up his duties at the earliest possible date, that he pleaded that he could not further postpone his departure.[4]

Mary MacGregor wanted reassurance that the end of October would not be too late for her husband to leave for Queensland. The Colonial Office agreed, as far as they were concerned, but they decided not to telegraph to Queensland for ten days or so,[5] presumably fearing that there might be pressure in Queensland either to obtain a local appointee, or to suggest that the delay was too long.

There was an underlying reason for MacGregor's concern. He probably knew that in the Colonial Office misgivings existed about any delay. Earlier Minutes suggest a concern at leaving Queensland without a British governor and under the control of a Queensland administrator, owing to a political crisis involving Lord Chelmsford, the previous governor.[6] The Colonial Office must also have been aware of anti-federal and anti-imperial views held by many Queenslanders.

The crisis which Lord Chelmsford had faced was related to party politics. This period, both in the Commonwealth and in most of the State governments, can be seen, in retrospect, as one in which there was evolution towards the major parties of subsequent decades—Labour and non-Labour, the latter combining elements from the factions and parties previously designated as Liberals, Conservatives, Free-Traders and Protectionists. The picture was, however, far less clear-cut to contemporaries, especially in Queensland prior to the 1907 'fusion' of the groups opposing emergent Labour. The difficulty of separating the factions can be illustrated by considering some of the views of their leaders. William Kidston, the Premier, had been an iron moulder, but later in the central coastal town of Rockhampton he ran a bookselling and stationery shop. In 1891 he had been sympathetic to the cause of the strikers, although always urging use of the ballot box as a better way to redress labour troubles. After his 1896 entry into politics, he concentrated on attempts to improve the social and material conditions of the working class.

He was open to strong attacks from Labour members, particularly after he accepted leadership over politicians who had opposed workers in the strike period. Labour, however, was prepared to support him, rather than Robert Philp, as Premier. Philp, like Kidston, was a Scotsman. He came to Queensland as a child, and was the founder of Burns Philp, the trading and shipping firm. Philp was more conservative than Kidston and Labour opposed him even more strongly. David Bowman, a forty-nine-year-old bootmaker, had been a Labour Party organizer for years and had taken part in the 1891 shearers' strike. He could be said to represent the left wing of the party, whereas the alternative leader of the Labour Party, William Lennon, a fifty-seven-year-old Irish-born ex-bank manager of Townsville, stood for the right wing.

The two non-Labour parties became known as the Philpites and the Kidstonites. In the elections of May 1907 the Philpites had a small majority over Kidston, but the latter became Premier with the support of Labour. A disturbed session followed, and after another election in 1908 Kidston again became Premier, as before with the support of Labour. At the time of the election campaign, Lord Chelmsford was attacked for obtaining appropriations for the continuance of the government by signing the necessary warrants without the counter-signature of his Attorney-General. There was also trouble over a sentence in the governor's proposed opening speech to which Chelmsford objected. The governor was quite openly criticized, and early in 1909 he left Queensland, the administration being taken over by Morgan, an ex-politician.

In the meantime, the Philpites had fused with the Kidstonites against Labour, but owing to some switching of allegiance among individual members, the government was not strong. So after a close vote on a vital issue in August 1909, Kidston asked Morgan for a dissolution. This was the crisis that coincided with MacGregor's illness.[7]

Morgan decided to grant the dissolution on condition that Supply was obtained first. The Colonial Office decided that his decision could be justified and that the Secretary of State should give no official opinion. Inside the office an interesting comparison was drawn with the Newfoundland crisis in which MacGregor had refused dissolution to Bond. The argument used was that Morgan, as MacGregor had done, should have first tried to see if the Opposition could form a government.[8] Right or wrong as his action may have been, Morgan's hope for a distribution of parties capable of 'supplying a stable government'[9] was fulfilled, and Kidston had a majority of forty-one to thirty-one in the new parliament.

In the meantime, MacGregor was regaining his strength; on 20 September he was up and about, and in mid-October he sailed for Australia in the *Orsova*.[10] Before he left he saw Gordon for the last time. Both men, one seventy-nine and the other sixty-three, realized that this could well be their final meeting and MacGregor openly expressed his sorrow:

> Your remark at parting has saddened me. To part from one's oldest and best friend must always be painful. In this instance it is especially so. I owe to you my official education and training through which any little good I have done in this world has been accomplished. You therefore occupy in my thoughts and feelings a place apart. I trust we may be both spared to meet again.[11]

There was a stable government during MacGregor's period in so far as non-Labour leaders remained in power: Kidston to February 1911, and then Denham throughout the rest of Mac-Gregor's governorship.[12] These leaders, however, faced growing opposition from the Labour Party. The neglect, especially by Denham, of union interests helped to precipitate a general strike in Brisbane in 1912.[13] MacGregor, never an advocate of direct industrial action, fully agreed with the moves of his premier during the strike, and with the consequent swing of his ministers towards an even more extreme conservatism and anti-socialism. Most of MacGregor's despatches during the strike were impersonal reports of events. But looking back on it he expressed his views very clearly. He referred to 'the revolutionary strike' and commented that

> the political consequences of the lawless proceedings of those directing or participating in that disturbance have been the opposite of what was apparently intended . . . The heavy losses thus caused to importers and exporters; to farmers and manufacturers; to traders, great and small; and the great inconvenience and hardship inflicted on all householders by the closing of shops and by the tabu put on all social and industrial intercourse, produced a deep and lasting impression on the minds of the people, which was intensified by seeing the leader of the Opposition, Mr. David Bowman, at the head of the processions formed to intimidate the Capital. The feeling thus produced by local events was further exaggerated by the reports, apparently well founded, of the material aid and sympathetic encouragement given to the revolutionary

leaders that sat in the Trades Hall in Brisbane, under the red flag, by the Prime Minister of the Commonwealth. The refusal of the Federal Government to give to Queensland the support of the military when established authority was in extremis was also highly resented by many.

MacGregor granted a dissolution to his ministers soon after the strike because he agreed with the premier that the issue was whether 'order or anarchy was to prevail in the state'.[14] Denham won the subsequent election on 27 April 1912 by forty-seven seats to twenty-four, so MacGregor's opinions as to the reactions of the majority to the strike may seem justified. But, as MacGregor himself admitted, at no other election had so many actual votes been cast for the Labour Party.[15] It seems a fair criticism that MacGregor, an old man of sixty-six at the time of the strike, was unable to adapt himself to change. Indeed his impatience with what he called 'labour agitators' and 'socialism' was to increase in the last seven years of his life.

He had been scathing in his comments about the 1911 strike on the sugar fields, organized by the Amalgamated Workers' Association. He reported that 'many acts of lawlessness and violence were perpetrated, but on the whole the police arrangements were remarkably well devised and ably carried out'.[16] MacGregor's criticisms of the Queensland labour movement were applied to all Australia:

> he would be a bold man that would open any new industry in Australia as long as the present labour domination lasts. The profits derived from the pastoral centres, and from dairying, are so great that they can survive the attacks made on them; but that could not last in new hands. We cannot engage a servant for more than a week, and must accept a week's notice from anyone of those in one's service. Our servants get what they choose to ask for; and if they are not allowed to do as they like, they are off. The labour agitator and Union organiser is everywhere.[17]

Certainly MacGregor's prejudices against socialism were confirmed by his experience in Queensland. Thus after he had returned to Scotland he claimed that it was decadent and 'honeycombed with socialism'.[18] He reverted to the same theme in February 1919, five months before his death:

> This country is entering an acute decadence. Impossible terms are demanded by miners; police striking; corrupting and pauperising allowances and pay to people that were employees on munitions at ridiculously high wages, and now *will not work*.[19]

A combination of motives besides that of conservatism associated with age may be deduced behind MacGregor's attitudes. As an agricultural labourer who had been able to rise from the proletariat by his own work, he was hardly disposed to any sympathy for a city working class that, to him, denied the importance of hard work. As well, overtones of his long life as part of the establishment must have influenced his views.

As Governor of Queensland, MacGregor retained the confidence of his ministers who throughout his term of office were non-Labour. Further, as most of his hostility to Labour was hidden in secret and confidential despatches, the Opposition had no official reason to doubt his impartiality. There is no reason to doubt that he would have acted constitutionally had the Labour Party won the 1912 election.

Indeed between the 1912 election and his departure he became increasingly aware of Labour's political gains, with which he even showed some sympathy, mainly because of the relative quality of the party leaders.[20]

He could also be fair to some Labour policies, for instance on Papua. While he was in Queensland he maintained a keen interest in Papua, now recovering from the schisms which culminated in the Royal Commission of 1906, and governed by Australia with Hubert Murray in charge. In its dealings with Papua, MacGregor was prepared to concede that the Australian Labour Party had shown some wisdom. Thus he wrote to Gordon in November 1911:

> The recent disorders you have had in England seem to have been copied from us. We conceal our labour troubles as far as possible. I am very sure the Federal Labour Ministers have great difficulty in controlling even to some extent their caucus, which rules Australia. They are not without some good points. An agitation was got up recently to show that the white man was being victimised to the native in Papua. A few months ago a number of the Labour Members of the Federal Parliament visited the dependency. They came to me before they went for suggestions as to what they should study. I willingly compiled. The other day the Minister charged with Papuan affairs replied in the House of Representatives that under all circumstances the Labour Government would give the first place to the interests of the natives. I am very certain that Mr Deakin would never have had the firmness to give such an answer. From what I have seen of the Labour Federal Government they are fair and just where their own interests are not concerned.[21]

A test of the fairness of the Federal and State labour parties was their attitude to British governors.

MacGregor's public reticence about government policy is partly explained by powerful attacks both on the existence of State governors and on the appointment of men from the British Isles to these jobs, attacks that would certainly have increased if MacGregor had advocated policies contrary to the advice of his responsible Ministers. These attacks were supported outside Australia. MacGregor knew that Sir Charles Lucas of the Colonial Office was in favour of the abolition of State governors. Lucas wanted 'to concentrate all power in the Governor-General, and probably to get rid of State governors. In that case it would be well to have an experienced administrator as Governor-General'.[22] Inside Australia imported State governors—and indeed anything connected with England—had often been criticized. From his contacts with Australians MacGregor in 1910 was aware of part of the historical background of this feeling. He said specifically that 'some twenty-five or thirty years [ago] the idea of local Governors was favoured by for example, a considerable section of the people of South Australia'.[23] Most historians agree that anti-English feelings throughout Australia reached levels in the 1880s, for instance in republican moves, which were not attained again in the years up to the First World War.[24] MacGregor was probably correct in believing that the movement in Queensland against British governors was a minority one and that the majority 'prefer to leave matters as they are . . . and treat [the Governor] as the personal representative of the King, towards whom they invariably . . . manifest sincere and genuine loyalty'.[25]

MacGregor sincerely believed that State governors appointed by the sovereign could do more to unite the Commonwealth, and to bind the Commonwealth to the Empire, than any Australian governor could ever do. He pointed out that, taking into account his age and term of service, his opinion in this matter must obviously be unbiased by personal aspiration.[26] In a letter to Gordon in 1911 he wrote:

> Personally it would be very convenient for me if they [the Federal Labour government] would abolish the State Governor on or soon after 15 February 1913, if I am still here then, as at that date I should finish forty years actual service, and would be glad to return to Europe then.[27]

MacGregor believed that the Federal Labour Party wanted not

only to abolish the State governors but also to swamp the State governments,[28] and knew that the former aim was shared by the Labour Party in Queensland.[29] This is well borne out by sentiments expressed by Labour members in parliamentary debates at the time. No one attacked MacGregor personally, and indeed MacGregor must have been flattered by the references to him. He might even be accused of devoting so much of one despatch[30] to the debates to ensure that encomiums about him should be read in London. He was described by V. B. J. Lesina as 'one of the best men who had come out here' who 'deserved the highest commendation and admiration for the great work he had done'; as 'an excellent officer and an able man all round'. This sort of compliment was paid to him from all sides and finally Kidston put his seal on this fulsome support saying,

> It was a very poor kind of democracy to grumble at getting a man of the people like Sir William MacGregor, who had made his own way and who had risen by merit, just as much as any member of the House [and who came to Queensland as] an experienced administrator perfectly free from prejudice for one party or the other, and was likely to act as fairly and friendly with honourable members opposite as with the Government.[31]

The debates on State governors became less frequent, and in the last two years of MacGregor's term of office no such debates took place. Some evidence of the weakened position of the Governor could be seen, however, in the fact that Kidston was forced to give up plans for building a grand new Government House. In fact, Fernberg, the temporary house[32] to which MacGregor moved in 1910 remains as Government House today.

Any waning in the importance of State governors was involved in the more important issue recognized by MacGregor as 'the Sovereign State versus the Commonwealth'.[33] MacGregor clashed with Baron Denman, the Governor-General who asked to see all his despatches to the Colonial Office.[34] But on most of these controversies, such as presentations of Imperial honours,[35] and appointments of consuls,[36] MacGregor remained as neutral as possible.[37]

MacGregor criticized his Ministers' comparative lack of attention to Commonwealth-State relations.[38] He was not completely against the extension of Commonwealth powers, regretting in 1911 that

> nothing has so far come of proposals for a conference of State Premiers to consider among other things the devolution of some of

the administrative duties of the States to the Commonwealth, a direction in which Queensland is, at least under its present Government, disposed to move slowly and cautiously.[39]

He also expressed disappointment that although 'much has been said elsewhere on the subject of a uniform Railway guage [sic] for Australia' construction of Queensland's lines had continued unabated, using the narrow gauge (3' 6") which had no chance of being adopted throughout the Commonwealth.[40]

The ambitious extensions of the Queensland railway system had MacGregor's enthusiastic support. He was sure that

> there must come around again in the course of time bad seasons similar to those of half a score of years ago but if this does occur, the results would not be nearly so serious once these railway systems are completed and stock can be shifted from one district to another.[41]

His confidence in Queensland's future made him certain that the State could repay any loan for railway extension without 'deranging her present fiscal system, even taking into account the loss sustained by this State by recent federal fiscal legislation'.[42]

Queensland usually resented any extension of Commonwealth activities so there was no enthusiasm for the formation of the Commonwealth Bank, and much opposition to the Commonwealth Savings Bank.[43] MacGregor felt that the Commonwealth Savings Bank proved to have a stimulating rather than a harmful effect on the State Savings Bank,[44] but he made one comment that suggests his views on proposed transfers of functions from the State to the Commonwealth Bank: 'If the awkwardness of having two authorities, Federal and State, under the same roof, is a reason . . . it is strange that it was not noticed during the preceding ten years of Federation'.[45]

MacGregor was critical of Fisher's Commonwealth Government for not granting aid to Queensland during the 1912 strike. He believed that 'the means now at the disposal of the State Government for the maintenance, or re-establishment, of order are insufficient'[46] so approved of the Queensland Industrial Peace Act, which was set up to hear disputes in the early stages 'before they became acute, or so wide spread as to be cognisable by the Commonwealth Arbitration Court'.[47] The Governor's unsympathetic attitude towards strikes can be judged from his comment in September 1913:

> Labour difficulties of a capricious nature are of frequent occurrence in railway construction. At one time the men will strike because

they are not doing task or contract work; then in a short time the same men will strike unless task or contract work is immediately abolished. It really looks at times as if they struck merely to have a holiday.[48]

When the Fisher Labour Government tried unsuccessfully to increase Commonwealth power by referenda in 1913, MacGregor remained neutral.[49] His interest must have been greatly aroused, however, by one of the main issues for Queensland in its relationship with the Commonwealth—the future of the sugar industry. MacGregor made himself thoroughly acquainted with this matter, even though the decisions were not his to make. His was a very informed interest, based on his practical knowledge of sugar-growing in the Seychelles and Fiji. After Federation the Commonwealth had forbidden the growers to import any more Kanaka labourers for the fields. As a result of this loss of cheap labour, it had been found necessary to have a Commonwealth excise on sugar, and to provide a bounty to the Queensland sugar-growers. With the expansion of the sugar industry this system became unsatisfactory to Queensland.[50] Negotiations, which more than once were halted by deadlocks, continued between the Commonwealth and Queensland governments from 1912 until after MacGregor left in 1914. These negotiations involved Queensland's restrictions on the employment of all aliens[51] in the sugar fields, and Commonwealth legislation to protect the Australian industry by a high tariff.

The sugar industry was a good example of a political question vital to Queensland in which MacGregor rarely intervened, despite his intense personal interest in the issues involved, not least the alien workers. When imperial interests were involved he did play a part but, unlike in Newfoundland, no major issues arose in which he and his ministers disagreed. An example of a passing clash concerned a Land Bill of 1911, which restricted leases to aliens. MacGregor returned the Bill to parliament asking for the addition of a clause to save treaty rights. When this addition was refused he told his Premier that he would not give his assent to it without instructions from the British Colonial Secretary. After some delay the British government pointed out that the Bill was in conflict with an 1884 treaty with Italy, whereupon Mac-Gregor's suggestion was adopted:

some of the Members of the Assembly were disposed to call in question the course I had adopted, but when it was shown to be regular, a new clause was at once added, and I then assented.[52]

Other than in a few cases of reservation of Bills, MacGregor did not intervene in his Ministers' policies, his criticisms remaining personal. Though such comments (in private letters, despatches and secret quarterly reports) are comparatively rare, some hints suggest how difficult it must have been for MacGregor to contain himself.[53]

Policy towards Aboriginals was one issue on which MacGregor's personal opinion varied greatly from that of the Queensland government. Before MacGregor left London his discussion at the Colonial Office considered the general problem of rights to native lands in colonies. Lucas had referred to the latest speech of the governor of Fiji on this question, and MacGregor commented:

> His Excellency talks always of 'waste lands'. I pointed out that there are 'waste', in the sense of unused, lands, of two entirely different categories: lands that are not used and are not owned; that these are very properly classed as Crown Lands: and unused lands that have been recognized as the property of aborigine owners, though perhaps not in actual occupation. I insisted that these cannot be sold or leased by the Government, not even leased, without a composition with the natives. I explained to him [Lucas] that the chiefs did not own the tribal possessions, could not alienate them, and would not dare try to do so. I informed him that the above were the principles on which I legislated in New Guinea; and I insisted on his admission of the soundness of these principles. As a matter of fact he did not appear conversant with the question. I drew his attention to the recent article in the *Daily Mail*, which argued that the Congo Chiefs could not make over the lands to the King or Kingdom of Belgium, because the lands were communal property.

A related question discussed was that of Australian attitudes to native peoples. MacGregor concluded that 'none of the Colonial Office chiefs desire to see any of the Pacific islands transferred to the Commonwealth government'.[54] MacGregor, himself, was not critical of Australia's administration of Papua; but he became doubtful of Queensland's activities in the Torres Strait islands.

Detailed reports after his visit to these islands show MacGregor's continuing concern for the welfare of indigenous people. He felt that some of the teachers were to be commended, and considered that 'one very pleasing feature of the schools at Thursday Island is the way that white, brown, yellow and black children blend without the least appearance of race or colour prejudice'. But, as in Lagos, he complained that the 'schools also suffer from the common defect of having English reading books, prepared for children under surroundings widely different from the ambient of children in Torres Straits'.

MacGregor's horror of disease was still with him, and he was appalled by the scourge of dysentery in these islands which had to his

certain knowledge, extending over an experience of a quarter of a century in this part of the world, done more to depopulate the Pacific than all other diseases put together. We have just seen that it is still lethal in Papua and in the Islands of the Torres Straits.

He suggested training island women as nurses at the Thursday Island hospital, and sending men to the school he had begun in Fiji for native medical practitioners.[55]

MacGregor gave praise where he could honestly do so; and in his correspondence with the Colonial Office, he was guarded in his criticism of the treatment of the islanders of Torres Strait and the Aboriginals of Queensland.

True to form, MacGregor travelled widely throughout the length and breadth of Queensland. In 1912 he visited the government Aboriginal Station at Barambah. He wrote to Gordon about this visit, and in this private letter it is easy to see his lack of sympathy with the traditional attitudes of white people towards the Aboriginals.

There are nearly 400 permanent residents there. They have a reserve of 7,000 acres of which perhaps 50 to 60 acres may be fit for cultivation. The rest is indifferent pasture, but with some good pools of water. Yet even that piece of poor land is begrudged to the natives, and deputations have waited on the Minister urging him to throw it open to selection! The staff is not of a high class. The school, roofed with iron, has space for 42 children, and from 70 to 80 are squeezed into it. There is one teacher, the young daughter of the superintendent. She has no chance to do good work, and is, like all connected with the settlement, discouraged. The settlement is made to supply a good deal of labour to settlers far and near. The huts are wretched and the rations equally so, a pint of flour a day. There are many fine young men among them. They have a bullock team, a few old horses, a herd of goats and over 200 cattle. There is a soup kitchen for the utterly infirm. But the general impression left on my mind is not pleasant. The tone of the place leaves much to be desired.[56]

As in Newfoundland MacGregor felt constrained to refrain from publicly criticizing his ministers; and it was not until his

Y

fifteenth quarterly report to the Colonial Office that he commented on the treatment of the Aboriginals. This report was dated 18 December 1913, and could well have been triggered off by the fact that in July 1913 a commission from South Australia had investigated Queensland's treatment of her Aboriginals, and both this commission and the Queensland Home Secretary (J. G. Appel) had praised Queensland's actions, particularly on the government station at Barambah. The other government station, Taroom, was said to be not yet quite in working order. MacGregor's comment was that 'my own personal observations on the stations of Barambah and Taroom have led me to regard them in a light much less favourable'.[57] He set out his reasons in a long special report[58] in which his own feelings were made abundantly clear. He dismissed the earliest period in a damning sentence: 'It appears that up to 1897 the protection of aborigines was left to the police, who relieved distress by distributing blankets and rations'.

MacGregor went on to state that the humane intentions of the 'professed policy of the aborigine department' set up by the 1897 Act were not being carried out in fact. He illustrated this by giving his views on the government stations at Barambah and Taroom, previously expressed in his private letter to Gordon. These views were amplified, and he included a comment which threw doubt on the Superintendent's skill with the livestock at Barambah:

> I was informed that some time prior to my visit the herd had suffered rather severely from 'foot rot', but there was no veterinary verification of the presence of the bacillus necrophorus or of any allied parasite. Indeed no one connected with the settlement seemed to have any knowledge of this disease; and I was not previously aware that it existed in Queensland.

The Governor's observant eye also fell disapprovingly on the daily distribution of rations to the Aboriginals.

> A member of each family attends with a small bag into which is put a pound of flour for each member of the family. That is the ordinary ration for twenty-four hours. Occasionally molasses is added. The flour is given out by a native whose lower extremities are atrophied, so that his locomotion is 'on all fours'. He has his favourites, if one may judge by his distribution of flour. The adult male natives complain that the double ration issued on Saturday is not sufficient, and that they have always to go to work on Monday morning on an empty stomach.

He added, probably sarcastically, 'this is of course caused by the improvidence of the natives themselves'. He regarded the lock (venereal disease) hospital as most unimpressive:

> The inmates were only two women. The building consists of galvanized iron, with a cement floor. The inmates were outside under blankets they had spread on branches so as to escape the heat of the building and the rays of the sun.

He thought the huts were poorly built and equipped containing 'not a single clock or sewing machine and no soap, articles present in nearly all houses of the Esquimaux on Labrador'. He found several Aboriginals,

> some of them at a considerable distance from the settlement, and old and helpless, or ill, sheltered under two or three sheets of galvanized iron; or below a blanket stretched out over a few boughs; or under a few pieces of bark and blanket.

He listed some of the complaints he had heard:

> On returning from work with Europeans they have only one day's rest before beginning to work for nothing on the settlement; when they want money out of their wages they can have only what the superintendent chooses to give them; they have to pay for the wood they cut on the settlement and carry it to their own houses.

MacGregor's second visit to Barambah had been an unscheduled one in August 1913, when he found 'no change in the conduct or condition of the settlement'. He hinted that a report by the Chief Protector in 1910 may have been misleading, and he tried to persuade the Queensland government to take action after his visits. He told the Home Secretary that 'it would be very desirable to place a Moravian in charge of Barambah' and the Minister agreed, but nothing was done until January 1914 when the Chief Protector tendered his resignation 'in consequence of malversation which he has been obliged to acknowledge'.

MacGregor had on 13 October 1912 visited the other settlement, Taroom, which had been begun some two years previously. In his opinion there were reasons for concern there: prickly pear was spreading; of the 190 Aboriginals only one—working for a European—had grown anything, a 'few ill-developed cabbages'.

He was concerned that at Taroom religious instruction was even more infrequent than at Barambah. A Christian Brother came from Charleville to hold a service once in three months and pending this visit those desiring to marry were given by the superintendent temporary permission to cohabit. There was no school, though MacGregor claimed that an educated Aboriginal living at the settlement 'was disposed to open a school to teach the children at least the alphabet'. The sick received no medical care; there was no nurse; most suffered from ophthalmia—spread by the myriads of house flies; 'the Superintendent had no medicine chest; no preserved milk, no arrowroot, no lotion to dress wounds with, no eye lotion for ophthalmia'. Again MacGregor resorted to irony, 'but he has some disinfectant'.

Although the rations were 'at least on paper, liberal' these general conditions were apalling, and MacGregor said 'every able-bodied man on the settlement appeared to have only one wish; to get away from the place. They wish to work for the European settlers'.

As ever, MacGregor tried to do justice to those responsible, and made it clear that the government provided satisfactory financial support. He said later that the present Home Secretary, Appel, was anxious 'to do all that is possible for the natives' and that he had commenced 'much good work' but he went on 'it is only too manifest that the staff is not animated with the same just, conscientious and humane feelings as is the Minister'.

Besides visiting these two government settlements MacGregor investigated Aboriginal living conditions wherever he travelled. He had found some in

> native camps; always near to some town or station in the central, but more commonly in the western districts. In a few places there are, as at Roma, Normanton, Boulia, etc., permanent camps. But many of the inmates of these wander about often over a large area of country. Numbers of them travel about with their smaller camps from place to place, camping where there is water, often not far from a station. They keep large numbers of dogs, for wallaby hunting, and the dogs and their owners become troublesome to the nearest stations, when, in at least some cases, they are driven off by poisoning their dogs.

> In the permanent camps, as at Normanton, they build small huts of the zinc linings of cases and scraps of galvanized iron. They do menial work for the whites such as providing firewood, scrubbing, etc.

> The most remarkable fact in connection with all the camps I have seen is the paucity of children. At the Normanton camp, for example, there were only three or four children with some three score of adults. This is very regrettable for several reasons, but more especially because it will become much more difficult to work the north-western stations when there are no more natives to assist.

On many stations there are native stockriders who are very profi-ficient. Some of those I met informed me they received £1 a week, and are 'found', and well treated. But, speaking generally, the condition of the women and their few children is wretched in the extreme.

MacGregor, drawing on his long experience of the treatment of primitive races, had no illusions about the failure of Aborigi-nal policy in Queensland. His conclusions to his report were reminiscent of the convictions of a quarter of a century earlier when the fitness of Queensland to control British New Guinea had been so strongly criticized by Gordon and MacGregor.

In the vicinity of towns they manage to obtain a certain amount of alcohol, or opium if there were Chinese in the district. Dirt, rags, venereal disease, hunger and exposure are hurrying the native race to extinction, and, so far, it would not appear that there is to be any survival of the fittest in this race any more than in the case of the aboriginal Tasmanian, or Beothic of Newfoundland.

Unless some success attend the stations under the management of the several churches another fifty years will extinguish the native race in Queensland.

MacGregor's views have, up to the present, been unnoticed by those studying Aboriginal policy in Queensland[59] and it is diffi-cult to judge whether he had any influence on the government. In 1913 a parliamentary debate on the Aboriginals included some criticism of government policy, one member reading a let-ter from a full-blood which attacked the bad points in the Aboriginal Protection Act. Most of the speeches in this debate, however, were complacent,[60] reflecting attitudes which Mac-Gregor had found dominant in the Department rather than the exceptional view taken by its responsible Minister, Appel. Mac-Gregor's personal concern cannot be doubted—his reluctance to intervene publicly showed awareness of his lack of power as governor.

His sensibility to this lack of power is also evident in his atti-tude to public health. He visited hospitals and ambulance stations wherever he went; approved the treatment of ophthal-mia in Western Queensland; praised the quality of the district hospitals but deplored their lack of funds and the shortage of nurses.[61] But in all these matters he took no active part. In opening the Institute of Tropical Medicine at Townsville his review of 'the policy of reserving tropical Australia as a home of a purely white race' stressed the needs for research and showed his awareness of recent debates.[62]

Impending old age had done nothing to dull MacGregor's inquiring mind, as was also shown by his great interest in the battle to rid Queensland of the prickly pear *(opuntia)*. He had botanical arguments with Lewis Harcourt, the British Secretary of State for the Colonies, about the possibilities of evolving a spineless cactus.[63] He critically assessed the experiments of the pathologist in the government laboratory at Dulacca. His interest was also aroused by the experiments of a Mr Roberts who was working on a theory that he could kill the leaves of prickly pear with the vapour of terchloride of arsenic, then burn the roots and plough them in thus enriching the soil with their notable quantity of potash.[64] The battle must have reminded MacGregor of his campaign against coffee leaf disease in Fiji.

His inquiring mind also led the Governor to investigate the possibility of increasing the number of angora goats in Queensland. He also thought that more ostriches should be kept as 'up to now these birds have not suffered from the intestinal parasites and bacterial diseases to which they are subject in Africa'.[65] The failure of experiments in coffee and rubber growing were, he felt, due to the fact that the interest and resources of the State were concentrated on sugar and fruit growing.[66] The proposal to protect the Queensland banana by heavy import duties brought forth an interesting comment from MacGregor:

> There can be no doubt that the banana grown in Fiji and carried to Australia is, as a dessert fruit, superior to the Queensland banana. The latter is not so carefully cultivated as is the Fiji banana. The additional duty will probably be imposed against the Fiji product, cultivated chiefly by coloured labour; and if this is so, then the banana is not likely to be more carefully cultivated in Queensland than is the case now. The result will therefore be: an inferior banana at a higher price. This result is of course far from being a solitary instance of its kind. Such things are here inevitable, and their influence extends far in the social and political life of Australia.[67]

MacGregor was always critical when his investigations led him to find any disregard for the scientific approach.

> The Agricultural College [at Gatton] and the State Farm are said by the department to continue to perform good work. Satisfactory results, it is claimed, have also been obtained from a subsidiary system, in which expert officers of the Department give advice and instruction on private farms . . . There is, however, a decided want of skilled direction in agricultural experiment in this State. The Department of Agriculture and Stock naturally represents things as

being highly creditable to those concerned. This is more owing to want of knowledge than to any other cause; and at present the want of necessary acquaintance with the subject on modern scientific lines is not recognised.

MacGregor cited two cases in point where modern scientific knowledge was lacking. The first was an outbreak of Irish blight in the potatoes of the Darling Downs when no one could advise the farmers what to do. The second concerned blowflies:

This Government possesses no Entomologist competent to deal in any way with [this] Pest. Two men have been sent to report on it, but they have not had an opportunity of acquiring the general principles of the science of entomology.

The question of Gatton came up again when MacGregor was shocked to know that

cattle on the Gatton College Farm were found recently . . . so affected by tuberculosis that a number of them had to be destroyed . . . there are many diseases in Stock the nature of which is not established, and no-one investigates them.

His general conclusion about the scientific backwardness of Queensland was damning, in its effect counterbalancing the evidence he had found of other development in the state:

No scientific experiments worth mentioning are being prosecuted here, none on strict scientific methods; and unfortunately, the Premier does not recognise the necessity for the establishment of a Faculty of Agriculture in the University which when complete so as to cover the Pastoral, the Horticultural and the farming industries would cost the small sum of about £3,000 annually.[68]

MacGregor had referred in 1912 to the need for a Chair of Agriculture at the university. An ex-Queensland squatter, Mr Robert Christison, who then lived in Burvall Park in Louth in Lincolnshire, had in 1910 donated £1,000 for such a Chair, and the public had donated a further £1,400 as a testimonial to Robert Philp which he had given to the university for a scholarship in Agriculture.[69] In 1913 after Christison had donated a further £1,000 and public collections amounted to £2,828 13s 6d MacGregor prepared for the University Senate 'an exhaustive and lucid memorandum' in favour of a Faculty of Agriculture. Although this was tabled in both Houses, and a Senate deputation headed by MacGregor waited on the Premier, no action was taken by the Government.[70]

The lack of foresight on the part of the government regarding forests and irrigation also worried MacGregor considerably. He

felt that some of the finest timbers in the world were being ruth-
lessly destroyed without any plans at all for reforestation.[71] The
total indifference of the government to irrigation caused the
Governor to write to the Colonial Office about

> The extremely important subject of Irrigation, on which manifestly
> the future of Queensland must ultimately depend if this country is
> ever to be occupied and cultivated intensively. I have been calling
> attention to the great subject of irrigation at district shows, and
> many thoughtful agriculturalists begin to think on this question,
> and to see something of its importance bearing on the future.[72]

The theme of criticism of unscientific conservatism became
constant in his despatches to the Colonial Office, lasting till his
final report when he reverted to the backwardness of the Department of Agriculture and Stock.[73] To consider these well-founded
criticisms is to understand the restraint that MacGregor must
have been under to deny himself the right to make public statements on these questions. His reticence on Aboriginal policy
was yet another example of his determination to adhere to the
position of a Governor in a colony which enjoyed responsible
government.

18

Queensland: The Problems of Education 1909-14

Doing away with a very suitable Government House, and exposing a young university to the risk of failure.

A matter that occupied much of MacGregor's attention was the launching of the new University of Queensland of which he became the first Chancellor in March 1910, within four months of his arrival in Queensland. His acceptance was dated a month before the gazettal of the twenty members of the first University Senate on 14 April, and before the meeting of 22 April at which one account claims that MacGregor was 'elected' as Chancellor.[1] The Secretary of State for the Colonies feared MacGregor's duties as Governor-in-Council might conflict with those as Chancellor and member of the University Senate; but left the decision to MacGregor's discretion.[2] MacGregor after twenty months of acting in both capacities had realized the difficulties, and had advised that his successor should not be asked to be Chancellor.[3] MacGregor was, until the 1966 appointment of Sir Alan Mansfield, the only State governor to be Chancellor of the University of Queensland.

MacGregor's appointment was not expected. The most likely appointee seemed to be the Director of Education, R. H. Roe, who became the Vice-Chancellor. The disagreements that developed between MacGregor and Roe may have been partly motivated by Roe's disappointment. Roe, a fellow of Balliol College, Oxford, who had been headmaster of Brisbane Grammar School since 1876, had considerable support in Brisbane where he had played an important role in founding the university. Griffith and Kidston were also considered for the position.[4]

One of the first decisions needed about the university concerned its site and buildings. MacGregor from his arrival disagreed with the proposal to use Government House and its grounds at the end of George Street in the city. He claimed that his objections were not based on any personal distaste at having to be moved and to live in temporary quarters, but that he considered the site was too small and the buildings unsuitable for the university.[5] The total building space was only eight acres for the university and technical college together. This, MacGregor pointed out, was 'only about equal to the floor space of the new Technical College of Glasgow'.[6]

Despite MacGregor's objections the university was opened on 14 March 1911 with some eighty students. Most of the Senate agreed with MacGregor about the unsuitability of the site, and it was decided to ask the Government to reserve land elsewhere.[7] Within five months the Chancellor could report

> . . . complete unanimity among the members of the Senate on this representation at its last meeting, but Mr. Reginald Roe, Director of Education, and Vice-Chancellor, was not present and he may be of a different opinion . . .[8]

The removal of the university was soon supported by the citizens of Brisbane, and by many of the cabinet ministers who had been unaware of the amount of land required. By 1912 there were one hundred and fifty internal students and sixteen external students enrolled; and the academic staff consisted of four professors, a director of external studies and sixteen lecturers. Before the end of the year it was obvious that the accommodation was quite inadequate. A Permanent University Site Committee was set up consisting of prominent professional men, clergymen and other citizens. On 18 November 1912 a deputation from this committee waited on the University Senate and urged an attempt to secure a site in Victoria Park, adjoining Brisbane Grammar School and the new site for Government House. MacGregor reiterated his criticism of the earlier decision:

> Dr. Kidston, who was responsible for the vain efforts to convert the former Government House into a University Building, now admits that it was a profound mistake. It was unfortunately a blunder that is very difficult, in some ways impossible, to repair. It did away with a very suitable Government House, and exposed a young University to the risk of failure.[9]

MacGregor continued to fight for room for his students who, by 1913, were spilling over into the wool-classing rooms of the technical college.[10] In his final year as Governor, the Brisbane City Council agreed to transfer to the university an area of one hundred and seventy acres at Victoria Park and MacGregor was able to say that 'the wise and patriotic action of the Mayor and

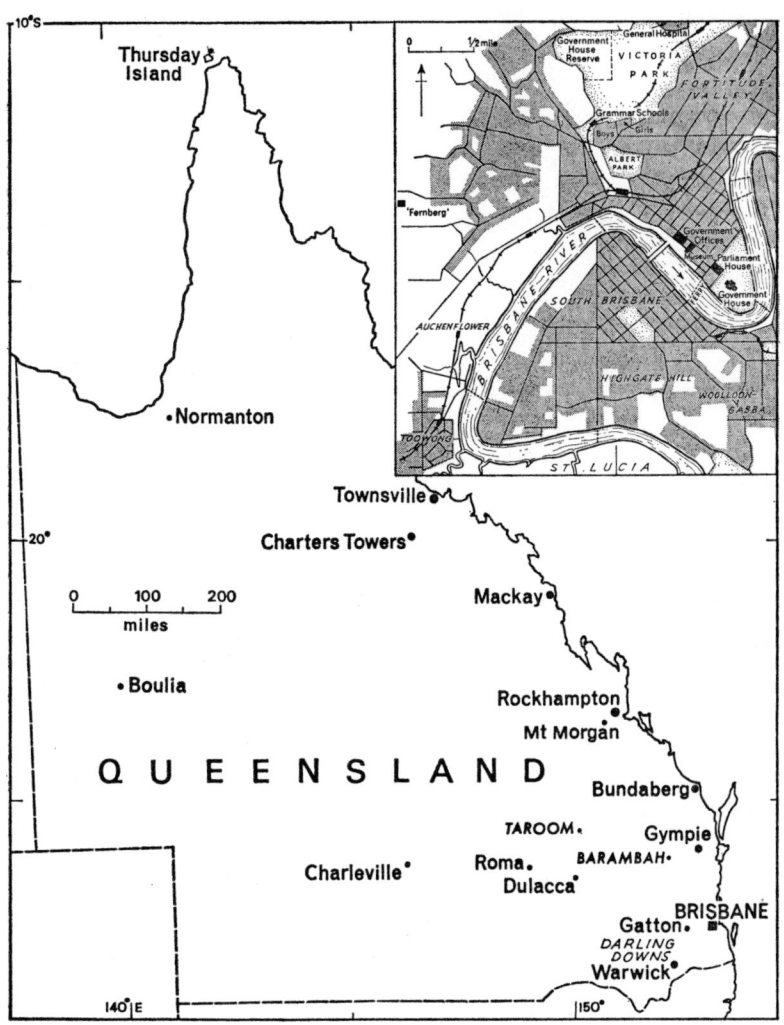

7 Queensland

Council' had given the university 'an almost ideal site', and that 'the acquisition of the Victoria Park ensures a brilliant future for the University of Queensland'.[11] Unfortunately MacGregor's predictions proved too optimistic: the First World War and then arguments for other sites prevented the use of the Victoria Park site. It was not until after the Second World War that the University of Queensland began using a site at St Lucia, purchased for the purpose by Dr and Miss Mayne of Auchenflower in 1926, and some departments were still using old Government House more than fifty years after MacGregor left Queensland.

Far more important to MacGregor than this question of a site were those concerning the academic standards of the university. A contemporary, J. D. Story, who was to have an important relationship with the university for over fifty years, gave evidence of how vital was the influence of MacGregor in these formative years of the university. Lacking at first any professorial Board, the University Senate was far more important than it was to be later in both major and minor matters. A Board of Faculties was established in March 1911, with both the Chancellor and Vice-Chancellor as members. On this Board and on the Senate, both because he was the governor and because of his strong character, MacGregor had considerable influence in every discussion. Story's impression was of an iron hand in a velvet glove, that he seemed to counsel rather than to direct, but that in fact his counsel was almost invariably followed.[12]

There is evidence of this in a clash of opinions which he had with Roe, and which is best described in his own words in a letter to Gordon:

> I was well aware that there would be persistent efforts to set up an inferior standard to meet the demands of all those that declared for 'a people's university' accessible 'to the poor boy'. I took the position that we should have an open door, but a standard not inferior to the sister universities. Matters came to a crisis in fixing the matriculation examinations for next year. The head of the utilitarians is the Vice-Chancellor, an Oxford man. The professors asked for Greek or Latin in the Arts matriculation; for French and German for Science and Engineering. They finally agreed to accept French *or* German. But the Vice-Chancellor wrote a cunning memorandum, excellently adapted to a public appeal, against any language requirement, except English, in candidates for Engineering and Science; as Director-General of Education he also showed that many teachers desirous of attaining a degree in Arts would be debarred by the matriculation, and that it must be reduced to

admit them, on the grounds that they had enjoyed no opportunity of education on a High School standard. I presented a counter memorandum to show that a school that adopted the Vice-Chancellor's standard had no right to call itself a University; that our students would not be recognized by other universities here or elsewhere, nor by the Institutes of Chemistry and Engineering; and I plainly informed the Government and the Senate that, if we did not adopt the standard that would command respect, I would at once tender my resignation as Chancellor. The result was that the Vice-Chancellor was left with one follower. In my memorandum I stated I was prepared to vote for an option in Arts matriculation between Latin, Greek, French and German. But the great majority of the Senate seemed to favour Latin or Greek for the B.A. matriculation, and I did not put the question to the vote. But the Senate will have to amend that before long . . .[13]

Roe's ideas were 'unshaken' by his defeat on the Senate and in parliament.[14] In the 1911 Report on Public Instruction he argued that his matriculation standards 'would very widely extend the university's sphere of action and also allow innovation and progress in our educational ideas'. He wanted to open the university doors 'as widely as possible', to remove 'all barriers which do not appear absolutely necessary' and 'to quicken university life itself by the admission of varied types of character and unstereotyped forms of thought'.[15]

MacGregor had asserted to the Secretary of State that he would resign as Chancellor if the decision on this issue of restrictive entrance requirements were reversed. His observation that

> . . . it is a question that can be very easily and readily used by any person that desires to obtain the favour of the masses that are not well acquainted with the nature of University education . . . [16]

was very apposite to Queensland of the time. This was made clear by the public protests at the high failure rate in the 1912 university examinations.[17] MacGregor calculated that the rate was 'about the same as at any other University' and he went on

> I have repeatedly warned my colleagues on the Senate that if a fair standard of pass proficiency were established by the Professors and Examiners, there would be many complaints, and probably some public agitation for a reduced standard. This was anticipated as a result of numerous political speeches that to many people would seem to mean that the University degree or diploma would be made easily accessible.

He was gratified to feel that the majority of the Senate was on his side in favour of 'an indisputable University Standard, which there is good reason to believe will be fully maintained'.[18]

Another constant in attitudes within Queensland to its university was the belief that one of its most important functions was to train school teachers. MacGregor was aware of this belief and attributed part of the opposition to Latin to 'a desire to let a large number of old school teachers have a University degree without a corresponding knowledge or education'. He was convinced that his advocacy of restrictive matriculation would ensure a high standard of education and that 'there is no likelihood that any further efforts will be made to degrade the standard'.[19] Although MacGregor's advocacy of the intrinsic value of language study can be validly criticized, his defence of standards against teacher training was needed. Unfortunately his optimism that pressure to degrade standards would end was not borne out during the following fifty years.

Besides these two major questions of site and standards, MacGregor was involved and interested in most university problems. MacGregor's opinion was influential in the choice of the first professors, and in deciding which Chairs should be filled first. Classics, Chemistry and Physics (with Mathematics) were the first three choices, soon followed by Engineering.[20] He supported plans for introducing Faculties of Agriculture and Medicine.[21] MacGregor played an important part in the day-to-day running of the university and the selection of all academic staff.[22] He also approved and encouraged the foundation of residential colleges.[23] The appreciation of the students for his interest in the university was recorded in their panegyrics when he left Queensland in 1914.[24]

MacGregor's interest in education extended beyond the university to schools,[25] and when J. W. Blair reorganized the education system in 1914 MacGregor believed it to be 'an advance on anything that has been hitherto tried in this State'. But he had some doubts about Blair's plan of beginning specialization at the age of eight or even of ten:

This seems to be a matter that requires much consideration. The syllabus of the primary schools is already overloaded by the addition of such things as agriculture, horticulture, geology, nature study, etc. and an unquestionable result is that children of fourteen do not read, or spell well; do not know arithmetic, geography and history as well as children of twelve knew these subjects when I attended a parish school in Scotland. There is a danger here of superficiality, of a want of thoroughness.[26]

The question of State support for Roman Catholic Schools concerned MacGregor, who corresponded with the Roman Catholic Archbishop Duhig, and it would be fascinating to know whether they discussed this contentious subject. In 1911 Mac-Gregor praised the planned introduction of free State secondary schools—to be called High Schools and anticipated that the State would also 'take charge of the existing Grammar Schools [the earliest of which had begun teaching in the 1860s] and institute free education in them also'.[27] He admitted this had not yet been adopted as government policy and, although he repeated this forecast in 1912, no successful move was made in the next fifty years towards this end. When the first High Schools were opened in 1912 in Gympie, Warwick and Bundaberg—soon to be followed by Charters Towers, Mt Morgan, Mackay and the Lockyer district—he turned his attention to the problem of staffing these schools. He hoped that university graduates would be found for them and he hoped for higher pay for these teachers, as 'not a few men with high qualifications leave the department, because other spheres of work bring better remuneration'.[28] In 1912 he was glad to report small increases in salary, and plans for a superannuation scheme for teachers. He felt 'public opinion', which he thought was beginning to understand the value of education, would support these educational changes. Such opinion, he considered, would support the enforcement of compulsory attendance at schools introduced in 1912 and the raising of the minimum leaving age from twelve to fourteen years as from 1 July of the same year. As well, the attendance at continuance schools of youths from fourteen to seventeen should, he thought, be enforced by the same State Act.

All educational improvements were obviously, for MacGregor, worth supporting. For instance he praised experiments such as the use of a motor car to take itinerant teachers to remote parts of the outback.[29] Questions of the health of school children combined MacGregor's interest in education and in medicine. He was shocked by a 1911 report saying that 31.71 per cent were so physically defective as to affect their educational progress, and that ninety-seven per cent had diseased teeth.[30] Another report disturbed him in 1913 because it showed 'an alarming frequency of ankylostomiasis [hook worm] and of dental caries. There is reason to believe that filariasis is also common, but figures for that are not as yet forthcoming'.[31] MacGregor encouraged all measures to improve the health of pupils, whether by better school hygiene, by regular medical and dental inspection, or by a campaign against ophthalmia spread by the house fly.

As in Lagos any measure which fostered adult education, whether the formation of a historical society, or the establishment of a school of mines, or the improvement of a museum, won MacGregor's approval. He supported the foundation of the Historical Society of Queensland by the staff of the University of Queensland, and agreed with its objectives of collecting and publishing historical documents 'particular attention being paid to Queensland, New Guinea, and to the adjacent Pacific Islands', and of encouraging 'the inspection, indexing, and calendaring of public records and registers, and the identification and marking of places of historical interest, and their preservation for posterity'.[32] He gave active encouragement to this and similar societies. He was president of the Royal Geographical Society of Queensland and 'frequently delivered lectures of high scientific value before this and kindred bodies'.[33] He criticized the school of mines at Charters Towers with its 'somewhat irksome and monotonous' lectures and its lack of an engineering laboratory.[34] He praised the more prominent part that the Queensland Museum was playing as an educational influence through its series of public lectures and by its publications.[35] While governor of British New Guinea he had sent many artefacts to this museum. A tribute, written just after his death, by implication stressed the important interrelationship between MacGregor's scientific collecting in New Guinea and his reception as a scientific expert in Queensland. In the Queensland Museum, the writer said, was

> . . . the most magnificent collection of Papuan ethnological specimens ever collected or ever likely to be collected. The value is estimated at £20,000—if we are to meanly value it in money. In the Museum in Sydney is a grand collection of those gorgeous Papuan birds which rival all else in the world, not even excepting Brazil, in the glory and eccentric beauty of their plumage. In the botanical department in Melbourne is the collection of Papuan flora over which the late Baron Von Mueller was wildly enthusiastic. And Australia is exclusively indebted to Sir William MacGregor for all these priceless collections.[36]

William MacGregor was probably as content as he could ever have been in Queensland. His governorship was, for him, peaceful with none of the emergencies or crises that had been so marked in Newfoundland, Lagos, British New Guinea and Fiji.

He accepted the limitations of responsible government though he retained independent opinions. His contentment was increased because his family was with him in Brisbane most of the time. The occasional absences of his wife and younger daughter, Bobs, were short compared with those he had endured in his early governorships. He enjoyed travelling throughout Queensland, often accompanied by Lady MacGregor; these were journeys of relaxation in contrast to his arduous patrols in New Guinea.

MacGregor found most satisfaction in his influential work with the Queensland University. His inaugural address had set out what he hoped could be achieved in its first fifty years[37] and he was pleased with its early progress. One formal occasion which particularly pleased him was the conferring of degrees in the Brisbane Exhibition Hall on 30 August 1912, when honorary degrees were conferred on James Bryce and Samuel Griffith. MacGregor's relationship with both these men was partly responsible for their acceptances of the invitations from the university. Griffith had, of course, a long relationship with Queensland and with its university movement in the nineteenth century, but he had since become more important as Chief Justice of Australia. James Bryce was known personally only to MacGregor in Queensland, and it was flattering for the University that this famous British Ambassador in Washington and distinguished scholar agreed to accept its accolade.

Both men received honorary doctorates of laws in an impressive ceremony. MacGregor's speech was well received, according to a flattering review in the contemporary university magazine.

The Chancellor is accustomed to say the right thing when the theme is academic; but here he was peculiarly happy. For he had personal acquaintanceship with Sir Samuel Griffith on which to build; they had met in New Guinea on furlough, and it is the tradition that there the Chancellor introduced Sir Samuel to the language in which the Divina Commedia is written. The achievements and personality of the other guest made inspiring themes, for they are a universal topic in the gossip of Politics and Literature. Sir William MacGregor took full value from the wealth of his dual theme—speaking of Sir Samuel in a way which personal intimacy alone made possible [it is worth interpolating that MacGregor had written to Griffith saying he would speak impersonally][38] and of Mr. Bryce as one must speak who has followed the story of contemporary international politics, and of the historical writing which his own day has produced. His Excellency's remarks, when they did not bear upon the careers of the men whom the

Z1

University was delighting to honour, were comments upon the University itself. He referred to the high standard fixed in the work—which, however hard it may hit some of us in November, every student rejoices at, and recognises as an honourable necessity.[39]

MacGregor undoubtedly used this formal opportunity to impress his view of standards. Likewise Bryce was probably primed by him to take as one of his themes a plea for the study of ancient history and of the classics. MacGregor would almost certainly have agreed with Bryce's argument that

> . . . to be able to enjoy the literature of Greece and Rome provides an invaluable stimulus to knowledge and the cultivation of literary taste as well as an assistance in the practical work of life.[40]

MacGregor's pleasure in conferring these honorary degrees was in contrast with his feelings when the ex-premier William Kidston received an honorary doctorate of laws at the opening ceremony of the university on 1 June 1911. The decision had been made by the Senate in MacGregor's absence, and on hearing of it he remarked, 'I would have refused to do the Chancellor's part only that I learnt that the Senate's decision was already known outside . . .'[41]

Before MacGregor left Queensland the local government proposed making a farewell presentation to his family for services to the state, but the Colonial Office disapproved on the grounds of precedent.[42] The university, however, recognized their Chancellor's work by the presentation of an honorary doctorate of laws. At the ceremony Griffith, in outlining MacGregor's colonial record, said that he thought

> . . . there was never better work done in the history of the British Empire in respect of subject races than Sir William MacGregor's ten years of administration [in British New Guinea]—never before had the interests of the governed been so entirely the object of the government.

Griffith went on to consider MacGregor's efforts in the 'worse climate of Lagos . . . [where] by his scientific knowledge and other administration, he transformed the nature of the mosquito-ridden country', and in Newfoundland where he 'saved a situation that threatened serious complications' and 'successfully dealt with some of the most difficult constitutional problems that had ever occurred in the colonial administration of the Empire'.[43]

Another honour for MacGregor was the decision to make a public appeal for £35,000 to found a Chair named after him in

8 MacGregor visiting the Aboriginals at Barambah, Queensland

9 MacGregor with a local family in the Beenleigh area, Queensland

10 MacGregor in his robes as Chancellor of the University of
Queensland

either agriculture or medicine. A good deal had already been donated towards a Faculty of Agriculture, so this was probably one reason why MacGregor chose Medicine. Unfortunately only £3,050 had been collected by the time he left Queensland.[44] But it was fitting that when the Faculty of Medicine was opened in 1936, there was incorporated in it the Sir William MacGregor School of Physiology.

MacGregor hoped to leave Queensland before his five-year term ended in December, as he was afraid that his health would not stand up to the sudden change from the heat of Brisbane to the cold of a Scottish winter. He therefore wrote to the Colonial Office, pointing out to the Secretary of State that he had had no absences from the State since his arrival in 1909. As he understood the practice was to grant State Governors a month's leave each year he now requested four months leave, so that he could leave Brisbane early in August.

He continued in a way that is reminiscent of his first letter to the Colonial Office in 1872, suggesting how little his long service had affected some of his basic Scottish ideas.

> I hope it may not be thought I am too exigent in asking that I might be allowed the half-pay of my office during the four months, and the usual return passage money to England (£800). Indeed without this last I should not care to accept the leave asked for . . . I may be pardoned if in this connection I state that the low figure of my different salaries as a representative of the Crown for more than a quarter of a century is probably a record. I may add that the cost of living has greatly advanced in Brisbane since my arrival here.[45]

The Colonial Office agreed to release him early,[46] and in July the Governor and his family sailed for Scotland. It seems sad, that at the end of forty-two years service with the Colonial Office, and after what were probably five of the happiest years of his career, that his letters still had a querulous tone.

19

Retirement: 1914-19

I have found how Scotland is honeycombed with socialism.

MacGregor left Brisbane on 16 July for Sydney, then went on to Melbourne to join the *Marathon* which left Australia on 25 July 1914. He told a reporter in Sydney that he hoped to return to Australia:

> The winters of Great Britain are likely to be rather too severe for me, and, of course, I cannot forget that my two greatest friends, Sir Samuel Griffith and Sir Charles Mackellar, live in Australia. Furthermore, I have been mostly associated with Australia and its history, and directly have served Queensland for fifteen years and New South Wales and Victoria ten each.[1]

To these reasons, adequate in themselves, was soon to be added his disappointment in living in Scotland, especially in wartime. Britain was at war with Germany ten days after he left the Australian coast, and MacGregor was to find every task, including his planned purchase of a home for his family, made more difficult by the state of the war. He was not to find happiness in his retirement. In many ways Australia was the closest he had to a home as was shown so clearly by his failure to adapt himself to living in Scotland. Many colonial governors, after the long years of their chosen exile from their homeland, have found themselves at variance with the society of their origin, since the patterns of change of their characters have rarely conformed to those in their homeland. Likewise, and this was especially so in the case of MacGregor, the experience of societies varying so much in attainments and standards must almost inevitably breed a critical attitude towards all institutions. In this sense MacGregor, once he had left his medical career in Scotland, was never able to identify himself completely with any society, and even his nostalgic desire to return to his birthplace was to turn sour.

Practically the whole of his retirement was spent in a country at war, for he died only eight months after the Armistice. Apart from the obvious distresses of war, MacGregor was concerned with ideological problems. While his loyalty to England was unquestionable and while he distrusted German overseas expansion he maintained his admiration for aspects of German culture, so that to him the war was partly a tragic waste. He was also disturbed by the extent of Labour influence, it proving a bitter blow to find, in his words, Scotland 'honeycombed with socialism'.[2] The resultant accentuation of differences between classes notably in the later years of the war did not inspire him with confidence in the future of Britain, including Australia. In addition the war diverted attention from British imperial responsibility for the future of primitive peoples, particularly in the Pacific. For most of the war years nothing was done for them, although MacGregor may have been consoled by some glimmerings of hope, during the last few months of life, that the peace settlements might lead to improvements.

Partly because of all these frustrations, and because of his indifferent health, his domestic life was not altogether happy. His wife tried as much as she could to console him; but he received less comfort from their two daughters. Mary was increasingly alienated by differing interests and eventually left Scotland, while Viti was separated from him by her marriage. Then in June 1918 both she and her husband died. His first family was completely lost to him, bitter letters surviving to show how far apart they were. He found some compensation in his long-enduring friendships such as with Griffith, but missed others, particularly Gordon who had died in 1912, and the picture that emerges is basically that of a lonely man, embittered both by what he regarded as insufficient use of his knowledge and experience by the Colonial Office, and by the tragic frustration of his hope of a peaceful home life.

MacGregor offered his services as a doctor to the Australian High Commissioner or to the British Government being 'willing to undertake any position however subordinate'. When it was pointed out that he was too old for military service he volunteered to rejoin the Colonial Service to release a younger man who could join the forces.[3] His offers were not accepted and he had to be content with voluntary positions on various war associations, including a position in London as chairman of the executive committee of the Queen Alexandra Field Force Fund. This position was arranged by the Colonial Office, and the object of the fund was to provide comforts for the troops. When he resigned to return to Scotland[4] MacGregor handed this post over to his friend Henry Fenwick Reeve.[5]

While he was temporarily living in London the Colonial Office recommended that he be appointed to the Privy Council. He was granted an audience with King George V[6] and told Griffith:

> I had a long talk with the King lately, and was much impressed by the clearness of his views, and with his intense hatred of the Germans.[7] His Majesty assured me that the worst atrocities of the Germans cannot be printed, and are not made public. When I said to the King that England's unreadiness is due to the fact that Englishmen do not read the continental press, he replied 'They cannot'. The King spoke with great appreciation of the splendid efforts of Australia in the war, and of the Scottish highlands . . .[8]

MacGregor was consulted by the Colonial Office on some official questions. He, for instance, translated for Lewis Harcourt an article from *La Nuova Antologia* of November 1914, in which Karl Helferrich, then chief of the Deutsche Bank (and later finance minister of Germany), proposed the capture of Italy. MacGregor commented that if ever an indemnity were claimed, Helferrich would regret writing this article, since he gave such a high figure—over £2 billion—for the annual income of Germany.[9] MacGregor's reading of the European press and periodicals persuaded him well before 1912 that war was likely to come with Germany. He had written to Gordon in that year:

> You did not share my apprehensions of Germany. Time only strengthens my misgivings. Indeed the German press is brutally frank in its detestation of England, and states in plain language that England is *the* enemy: and that they are going to take something worth having from somebody. The papers I get strongly urge that we should be invited to show regard for Germany by robbing our old ally, Portugal. English people do not, I fancy, often read the German press. That is advantageous, for the language of most German papers is very insulting to England. I cannot but believe that Germany means mischief. Certainly they give us more than fair warning.[10]

Before leaving Queensland MacGregor had expressed the wish to retire to Scotland; but at that time he felt he should await the final draft of the Land Act that was before the Commons.

> It appears to me to become within measureable distance of our 'Free Selection' in Queensland; that it would put the landlord at the mercy of the tenant, and make the latter dominus. I see that

they also proposed that the trout fishing should belong to each farmer! Now a place with some fishing is what I specially desire for my wife and myself. I must therefore wait a little.[11]

He was now to find that other changes made Donside unacceptable. For he rapidly realized how much out of touch he was with both the area and with his kin. His parents were both dead, his brothers had not moved from Scotland apart from the trip to America on his money, his sisters were domesticated in the area. Surviving relatives remember Sir William at this time as a distant figure, a 'great man' either revered or jealously despised by his less endowed relatives.[12] It is hard for any governor to step from Government House to any other society. It proved impossible for MacGregor to revert to Aberdeen and Donside.

When he realized that he could not settle in his native area he looked elsewhere, and it was almost symbolic that he chose the border country, neither the valley of the Don nor London. He soon wrote triumphantly:

> I have purchased a place called Chapel-on-Leader, six miles from Melrose. It contains 1,326 acres, of which some 1,050 acres are in three farms, let at the wonderfully low rate of 11/6 an acre. The house belonged, I understand, to the monks of St. John's, who made the garden, and planted a lot of the trees. It was probably connected with Melrose Abbey. It has a ghost and an underground passage; and the treasure of the fraternity has never been found. The garden is an exceptionally fine one, even for Scotland. We shall have entry on 28th May. The district is a pleasant residential one. Our nearest neighbour will be Lord Reay, the chief of the Clan Mackay.[13]

After MacGregor's death this beautiful estate was valued at £24,800. MacGregor by 1914 was a wealthy man, able to arrange finance for the purchase of this estate, receiving a regular pension from the Colonial Office of £1,300 a year: as ex-governor of Queensland, ex-chief medical officer and registrar-general of Fiji, and as ex-assistant government medical officer of the Seychelles. His main investments had been in Government of Newfoundland debenture bonds and Canadian bonds. He held Newfoundland bonds which had a value at his death of some £22,500, and Canadian bonds which had a value at his death of £9,500. Counting other minor assets his property at death was valued at over £60,000.[14] His complaints in Queensland in 1914 that he required an £800 travel allowance seem exaggerated, for even if much of his money was tied up in bonds he must at least have

given a substantial deposit for Chapel-on-Leader. His justifications for complaining would be his realization, in his usual
careful approach to finance, that he would need ready cash to
obtain a house, as well as his understandable desire after what
he regarded as forty-two underpaid years to extract every possible penny from the Treasury. His elevation to the status of a
man of property was relevant to his lack of sympathy with the
working class in Scotland.

It could be hoped that MacGregor would find happiness at
Chapel-on-Leader. At last he had financial security, and a
beautiful estate, with a house dating back in parts to the eleventh
century,[15] set in one of the loveliest parts of Scotland. It is not
surprising that he developed a great curiosity about border
history. His house, he discovered, had been the rest-house used
by the monks of Jedburgh in travelling to and from Edinburgh.
When he attended a three-hour lecture on 'the Story of Earlston'
he already knew enough to suggest to the speaker 'apposite ad-
ditions' and to advise the lecturer, the Reverend W. S. Crockett
of the local Presbyterian kirk, to have his address printed.
Crockett later recorded that Sir William developed 'a Borderer's
passion for the locality'. Crockett saw MacGregor in these years
as having

> many hobbies—gardening, botany, geology, scientific research,
> mechanics, classical literature, languages . . . statistics, and, greatest
> of all, a study of the Greek Testament. His interleaved copy of the
> Expositor's edition in eight volumes was a marvel of penmanship
> and exegetical exactness. His copies of Virgil, Homer and Dante
> were similarly interleaved with the comments of a profound
> scholar. Every volume in his library seemed to bear evidence of
> critical handling. He filled his shelves with favourite authors—
> books which covered the whole field of Colonial history as well as
> the rich record of his native land. He was seen at his best amongst
> his books, and though he was apt to become discursive, even
> tedious at times, the true bookman, at all events, heard him out
> patiently and reverently, remembering the reality of the man and
> his inherent greatness from every point of view.

The portrait intimates that MacGregor, always long-winded,
could be boring and he must have found few bookmen willing to
listen. Crockett, indeed, suggests this loneliness: 'He died before
his actual greatness had been discovered by fellow-dwellers of
the romantic Leader valley'.[16] Contributing to his loneliness was
MacGregor's realization of a lack of sympathy with many of his
countrymen. In a letter to Griffith written about a year after his

return his disgust in what was to him a decadent Scotland became uppermost.

> We are all exercised over the Budget and conscription. The incidence of taxation here is such that the worker all but escapes everything save on luxuries, as the customs house barely touches him; but the upper and middle classes will in a great many instances be impoverished. Conscription for the army, and for industry, is terribly needed. The selfishness, the want of patriotism, the ignorance of Germans, the dishonesty, of working men in this country is to any one that does not see it all simply incredible. I had no idea of the decadence we have already reached. I am sorry, now that I have found how Scotland is honeycombed with socialism, that I bought this place.[17]

A year later, after Asquith had been replaced as Prime Minister by Lloyd George (from whose energy and wisdom MacGregor expected that 'new life' would be put into British affairs) MacGregor showed how unhappy he was in Scotland:

> I have been very greatly surprised by the wonderful changes in this country during my 42 years of absence. Socialistic ideas have permeated the people here to an extent that is astounding. The fact that combines of labour of most kinds intentionally limit output is a most serious matter for the future of the United Kingdom. When this war is over there will certainly be a determined effort on the part of our present enemies to beat us in the markets of the world. The patriotism of the German is not known, not understood here. Our workmen combine here to restrain production; in Germany they are united to increase it, and their Government, being the owners of the Railways etc. lend the exporters substantial assistance. Then the burden of tax is more even than here. With us the working man pays nothing in customs except on what one can do without whilst the Income and other taxes, if maintained after the war as now, must send capital out of the United Kingdom. You would not believe the degree to which the working classes have become luxurious. One of our maids refused to eat local butter and demanded Danish. Now, when the Government is urging economy in sugar we are not able to induce our house servants to abandon Tea at 7 a.m. before they begin to prepare breakfast. They insist on Tea and accompanying garnishings five times a day. Last year I had four gardeners, and we had to buy potatoes in October. They ate practically all they grew! We do need a tonic, and we are, I fear, to receive it, for the war is far from being over yet *we could win*. Let us hope in a new ministry.[18]

MacGregor began to doubt the efficacy of the British system

of democratic government in time of war. He had been very impressed by the system of compulsory training which had been introduced by Fisher into Australia in 1911,[19] and he took a keen interest in the bitter conscription campaign there in 1917. He bewailed the fact that conscription was 'not carried out rigorously' in Britain, and in writing to Griffith suggested a drastic remedy:

> I am beginning to think that the blessed Democracy has not the same chance in a great war that an autocracy possesses. We want a Dictator; and it would be well to have less talk and more work.[20]

He did not, however, advocate such a government in time of peace. The farthest he went was to support peace-time universal military training, though he considered in 1918 that

> no government dare touch the subject in this country. Everyone is oblivious of the facts that such training was formerly obligatory in both England and Scotland, when it was less necessary than now.[21]

MacGregor's pessimism about the future, reflecting his age and his insecurity, was growing.

> What, it seems to me, is most wanted in this country is a change of mental attitude . . . the great aim of the vast majority is a more easy life and more amusement. If we were to win in the field of Mars, we should, unless there is a great change psychologically, be utterly beaten by the Germans and Americans to say nothing of the Japanese, in the field of commerce. Our people now talk in hundreds of millions; 250,000 new cottages are to be built; wages are to be increased; holidays are to be multiplied etc. etc. No one asks whence the money is to come. Even the Secretary for Scotland said the other day that we must so beat the Germans that this shall be the last war. The Secretary manifestly is not acquainted with the natural history of man.[22]

He wrote to Griffith in the same vein in February 1919:

> This country is entering an acute decadence. Impossible terms are demanded by miners; police striking; corrupting and pauperising allowances and pay to people that were employees on munitions at ridiculously high wages, and now *will not work*. There are tens of thousands of unemployed, and we cannot obtain a servant![23]

Just as MacGregor, despite his age and pessimism, was still deeply interested in the future of Britain and his life there, so was he always involved in the future of the Pacific. He was consulted from time to time by the Colonial Office during those five years, he kept in touch with others concerned in the area, and in the last year of his life he publicized his views at several meetings.

His interest is shown from a 1916 discussion with Australia's High Commissioner:

> I found that Mr. Fisher has very pronounced views on the future settlement of the Pacific. He concurred with me yesterday that the Pacific Islands without the native population would not be of much value and that therefore the preservation of the native races is, or should be, our first care. I am afraid the Japanese question will be the most difficult and most serious one. The phosphate islands will be of very great importance when peace comes round again.[24]

This was during the visit of the Australian Prime Minister, 'Billy' Hughes, to England, and it is clear from MacGregor's comments that he would have been, had he lived, a strong supporter of Hughes' subsequent strong stand against the Japanese and against Woodrow Wilson.[25] He praised Hughes who had

> for the moment put all other Australians into the shade. Sir G. Reid is completely eclipsed, and people see that his pleasant and bubbling after-meal speeches contained none of the solid matter they find in the pregnant utterances of Mr. Hughes who is undoubtedly the man of the hour in this country.[26]

MacGregor was not as impressed by Wilson:

> I have always been a little afraid of the prolixity of President Wilson. Nobody doubts his sincerity and lofty purpose, but it is clear that he is an idealist, and it is also manifest that he is in a commanding position. It is to be hoped that he is sound on the Pacific.[27]

MacGregor's deep concern for the people of New Guinea is evident in a letter to Griffith asking him to use his influence with the Governor-General to:

> impress on him that they adopt in the new native possessions the measures you and I worked out for British New Guinea on Land; Liquor and Opium; and the ultra simple Native Regulations by which we established individual criminal responsibility and punishment (instead of the vicarious, tribal responsibility and punishments of the Germans next door). And, if possible, the allotment of fixed areas for the different missionary bodies. You are sure to be called upon for much advice on the Pacific Question. Its settlement will greatly influence the future of Australia. There is no man living in the Pacific now that knows the political position there as well as you do.[28]

In 1918 MacGregor spoke on the Pacific to the Royal Colonial Institute, to the Royal Scottish Geographical Society and to the

Chambers of Commerce at Glasgow, Aberdeen and Edinburgh.[29] His ideas were made explicit in these addresses which outlined the history of European penetration into the Pacific, its tragic effects on the islanders, and future problems. He thought that the post-war settlement would be difficult 'by reason of the magnitude and diversity of interests involved',[30] particularly as the declared policy of the *Entente* was that small nations would be heard. Exclusive of Germany, he thought that thirteen states, nine western and four eastern, would have to be consulted. His account of the 1883 New Guinea annexation included a strong criticism of Granville as Foreign Secretary for denying, in a despatch of 7 February 1885, that he had been told of Bismarck's statement of 5 May 1884 which admitted Germany's interest in the island.[31]

Throughout his addresses MacGregor made it quite clear that his sympathies since 1883 had been veering away from Great Britain and towards Australia. He contended that the islands of the Western Pacific, south of the equator, with the exception of American Samoa and French New Caledonia, would eventually 'come under the dominions of Australia and New Zealand'.[32] He considered that Australia would be capable of taking this responsibility for the native people in spite of her trouble in dealing with her Aboriginals. Without contradicting his criticism of 1912,[33] he was prepared to admit the unusual circumstances surrounding these people—their nomadic wanderings in a vast continent and the strangeness of some Aboriginal manners and customs. He implied that Australia's attitude to the Pacific Islanders when living outside Australia was different, and that she was aware of the fact that the greatest assets of the islands were the islanders.[34] MacGregor explained his change of opinion also in the light of her administration in Papua, which in his view showed that Australia 'knows how to govern the islands' especially under the 'remarkably wise, strong and capable Lieutenant-Governor . . . Mr. Murray'. The Australian Commonwealth, he considered, by continuing Murray's service and by supporting his administration, had

> adhered to the features of government formerly established with only such changes as time and circumstances have rendered necessary and advisable. No doubt the system followed in Papua would be applied generally to the other islands by the Commonwealth.

He made it clear that he considered Australia had men at home who would oppose any idea of despoiling or enslaving the Papuans. Among these he listed Griffith, who drew up the laws for Papua, and also Barton, Hughes, Cook, Forrest and Deakin.[35] As far as administrators in the field were concerned, he believed that Australia and New Zealand

> . . . now possess a large number of officers better acquainted with the islands and with their inhabitants than could be provided by any other Power, even by the Imperial Government itself. The basis upon which native administration has been carried out under the British flag in the Pacific can be studied by anyone in the case of Fiji and Papua, and especially is the administration in the latter of importance in this respect, because since 1906, Papua has been a dependency, and its administration has been under the direct control of the Federal Government. There is, therefore, before the world a practical example of the kind of administration that it may be safely assumed would be extended under the Federal Government, and under New Zealand to the other Islands of the South-West Pacific.[36]

In these addresses MacGregor forecast a rather exaggerated future for trade across the Pacific Ocean, which he thought would eventually assume a volume greater than that of the Atlantic. He envisaged government support for firms such as Burns Philp to enable them to open up trade with the islands. He mentioned in particular the islands of Nauru and Angaur whose resources, he felt, were hardly touched.[37]

In August 1918 the proofs of a proposed memorandum by a Foreign Office Committee on the Pacific were sent to MacGregor for revision. He thought the most optimistic aspect of the draft was the unanimity of both the Imperial Government and the Australian representatives to keep Germany out of the Pacific.[38] Perhaps up to his death a year later he was able to retain his optimistic view of the future of the Pacific. Despite the almost complete neglect of the islands and their people for five years he could hope for an Australasian Pacific created by the bluster of Hughes, nurtured by the knowledge of Griffith, and ruled sympathetically by men like Murray in the pattern that MacGregor himself had set.

In 1919 MacGregor gave an interview[39] in which he repeated his hope for the elimination of Germany from the Pacific. He opposed condominiums generally, believing in particular that the existing union in the New Hebrides was unfair both to the natives and to the 'civilising, colonising genius of modern

France and of the British Empire'. He was even less sympathetic with the suggested Mandate system since

> . . . a Mandate from any source that would interfere with the bases or practice of administration of the nation or people entrusted with the government of these islands would, in my humble opinion, be worse than the most objectionable form of condominium that we had yet experienced.

Drawing on his practice of twenty-six years as a colonial governor[40] he had 'no hesitation in saying that the best form of government may be neutralised by divided authority'. His thoughts must have gone back to the British New Guinea Syndicate or to the Crown Agents and Colonial Office in Lagos, or perhaps to the limits on his powers as governor in Newfoundland or Queensland.

In the same interview MacGregor's opinion on the future of Japan in the Pacific led to a prophetic view of Australia's role:

> Personally, I should like to see Japan firm in the possession of the islands which she now occupies extending south to the Equator.

> Some writers have pointed out that there would be danger to Australia by having Japan such a near neighbour. Personally, I do not share that view. It can only be favourable to the virile character of the manhood of Australia if the idea is entertained that Japan will be a dangerous neighbour, for it will make them keep themselves in training, not only to meet Japan, if necessary, but to meet any aggressor whoever he may be. It will prevent Australia from suffering the decadence that undermined Rome.

At this time MacGregor wrote an article on health problems in the Pacific area.[41] His concern was particularly drawn towards diseases brought in by the white people. He specifically mentioned the Fijian measles epidemic, venereal disease and dysentery. The problem was not only historical, but was of immediate concern because of 'the great mortality reported . . . in some of the Pacific islands from the world-wide epidemic of influenza'. He believed that effective quarantine could check such epidemics, and that Australia could be entrusted to enforce strict measures for 'safeguards were established on a firm and scientific basis many years ago, chiefly on the initiative of the Hon. Sir Charles Mackellar'. But he admitted that 'the strictest quarantine may fail, in any case there remains the great and serious question of the diseases already domesticated in the islands, which . . . will before long reduce the inhabitants of many of the islands to the verge of extinction'. As it was unlikely that any administration could afford to provide enough doctors to control these diseases he suggested that every Christian missionary and teacher, 'white or coloured, man or woman' should be given a course of medical instruction.[42] He pointed out that this would be nothing new in missionary work:

> Indeed it would only be following the practice of the Founder of our religion, as told to us in each one of the synoptic gospels. The first Christian mission sent out had a double purpose: to preach the approach of the Kingdom, and to cure all infirmities. We know that long before the advent of Christianity, medicine was a sacred art, intimately associated with religion. And we are shown, as for example in Harnack's *Verbreitung Des Christentums*,[43] that the Fathers of the primitive church studied and practised medicine.

MacGregor had told his friend William Forbes-Sempill that he, himself, had thought of becoming a missionary when he was a young man, but that this ambition had been sublimated by his medical work. In his years at Chapel-on-Leader he discussed his beliefs with the Presbyterian minister who thought he had a 'childlike faith in God and the cardinal doctrines of Christianity'.[44] But his beliefs were more complex than this for he was tolerant towards all Christian denominations,[45] as well as towards Eastern faiths and primitive religions. Yet his views differed from those of the realist who sees Christianity as an important influence for good whether in the Pacific Islands or in many developed societies. There is enough evidence[46] to conclude that MacGregor believed in the risen Christ, and to suggest that he died in the hope of a happier eternity.

During the last years of his life the cold weather of Scotland caused Sir William and Lady MacGregor to long for the Queensland sunshine, but he enjoyed reasonable health at Chapel-on-Leader.[47] The health of his friends, however, was of great concern to him, and he made diagnoses and suggested lines of treatment whenever Griffith mentioned an illness. Research still interested him, and he included in a letter a detailed opinion on the curative qualities of the pawpaw.[48] In an article written in August 1918 MacGregor combined his enthusiasm for research with a healthy respect for German methods.

> We have . . . a certain number of men who are working hard to improve methods and devise new means of improving quite a number of industrial and economic branches. Today I visited some of those that are working at glass, pottery and several minerals. They are, however, teachers, and their lectures interrupt and inter-

fere sadly with their research work. Our manufacturers do not yet employ their own chemists, and keep them at research work, in the way the German does. And until that is done we can never compete with them successfully. The Dye undertaking has for this reason turned out a failure, as shown by Professor Armstrong, a very competent man, in the *Times* of this morning. No one seemed to know until after the war had been some time in operation, and stocks became exhausted, how greatly we had become dependent on Germany. Because the great majority of our younger men are in the army or at war work at home, we have very few men capable of doing the research work necessary; and the bulk of the older men have to keep lectures going and have not much time for experiment.[49]

In his public life MacGregor must have had some satisfaction during his retirement, and he certainly retained his interest in affairs of state. But his private life gave him little pleasure. It is doubtful whether it would have been in MacGregor's nature to see out his life in halcyon days, and the exigencies of running a great estate in war time made it impossible. There were continual difficulties in finding staff, and by 1918 he had only one domestic servant indoors; and outdoors one keeper who had returned wounded having lost part of his jaw and of his right shoulder.[50]

Added to the practical difficulties of running Chapel-on-Leader was the fact that this beautiful place, which MacGregor had pictured as a centre for his family, was so often empty. War-time commitments meant that he and Mary, his unmarried daughter, were often away from Scotland. Mary was working in 1915 and 1916 in the King George V Hospital in London, where she met many Australian wounded troops of whom MacGregor said

They have immensely raised the status of Australians in this country, where their splendid fighting qualities are fully appreciated. The nurses say that the Australian wounded are so polite and courteous, and are always cheerful and contented, just the reverse of the English. Of course they are of higher social status, and far better educated than the vast majority of English soldiers.[51]

His elder daughter, Viti, who had married Lord Paget, was also working is hospitals; in 1915 at the English hospital at Nevers in France, and in 1916 in Paris. Her husband, then an admiral, was commanding what MacGregor described as 'the mine-sweeping flotilla on the east coast, a very hazardous post'.[52] In 1917 the Pagets' daughter, Honor, MacGregor's only granddaughter, was at school at Malvern, far from Scotland. She spent some of her holidays at Chapel-on-Leader, but neither of Mac-Gregor's daughters paid regular visits.

The year 1918 brought great tragedy to the family. It began with the death of a fifteen-year-old grand-nephew on active service in the Navy.[53] Shortly after came the death of Admiral Paget from a heart attack; and on 13 September followed the greatest personal loss that MacGregor was to suffer—the death of his daughter Viti. He was quite overcome and became dangerously ill, but his health was forgotten in his sadness for Viti. He remembered her as *'a very affectionate daughter'*, a woman of great charm, an excellent musician on the piano and the violin, a talented artist, a good German and Italian scholar, and a perfect mistress of French. He found some consolation in having her daughter, Honor, at Chapel-on-Leader for her Christmas holidays, especially as she promised 'to be nearly as pretty as her mother'.[54] Later, however, he said that although Honor was affectionate she lacked the talents of her mother 'who was of finer fibre than the Paget family'.[55] When he received a letter of sympathy from Griffith he repeated his praise of his daughter, adding that 'I find that she kept her diary as I did mine, in German, French and Italian on successive days . . . and as well written as I could have done it'. He admitted that Viti's death had been a tremendous blow to him and that 'much, very much, of the sunshine has gone out of my life with her'. He concluded that he was thinking of selling Chapel-on-Leader partly because 'a chief purpose in buying was to have Viti and Honor here in summers. Now that has vanished'.[56]

The praise of Viti, by implication, makes it clear that Mary was not his favoured daughter. Those who knew Mary tell how confined she felt in the enormous house in the north, and how she resented its austere atmosphere. Her own life had known sadness; she had become engaged to a naval A.D.C. who was killed on active service. For some time before her father died Mary was living in London far away from him both in distance and in spirit.[57]

If William MacGregor had little contact with Mary, he had far less with the children of his first marriage, James and Helen. The melancholy history of the breakdown of his relationships with these children added to the total picture of William's unhappiness. When he was in New Guinea William had received poor reports of James from Glasgow University and there is no evidence of any improvement in their relationship during the years that followed. Just before Sir William left Queensland he paid, through an intermediary, the fares and travel expenses for James, his wife and family from England to Australia. It does not seem fanciful to interpret this payment as a father ensuring that he would be nowhere in the vicinity of his first-born son.[58]

William's relationship with his daughter Helen had also worsened in the last years of his life. Helen had lived with him in Port Moresby, but had never gone out to Lagos. In 1902 she had married a Mr Hahn and William gave her £1,200. Some time before 1916 Helen had remarried, becoming Mrs Faden. In August that year William paid £858 19s 2d for an annuity of £50 to Helen. His letter to her makes their relationship abundantly and tragically clear:

> I have sent you today by the Swiss Bankverein £20. I am arranging for you an annuity of £50 (fifty pounds). This will be paid to you quarterly, £12/10/-. It will be from the Colonial Mutual Life Assurance Society which has a London office. This will be paid to you however long you live, and will not be dependent on my life. It will cease with your life. You will not be able to touch it, and can only receive the sum due each quarter. The first will be payable three months after the 19th of this month. It embarrasses me to pay this sum. Understand now that we have finished; and under no circumstances can you, or will you, ever receive another penny from me. You have had already, without this, more than any of your sisters, and have certainly deserved it less. My death will bring you absolutely nothing material.

Despite this letter William purchased for Helen on 14 February 1918 £1,000 five per cent National War Bonds, but no love was associated with this purchase any more than with the annuity.[59]

It is easy to imagine the bitter state of mind in which Mac-Gregor set about drawing up his will in October 1918. At the same time he wrote, 'the death of our dear Viti, 13th September produced such depression that it brought on a very acute attack of that exceedingly painful disease "shingles" '. His stomach and his liver were then affected as he described in detail: 'for several days not a particle of bile entered the intestine and all was absorbed into the blood, a danger that completely overshadowed the "shingles" '.[60] His will was drawn up by the factor of Chapel-on-Leader, D. G. Stalker, who with William Sempill was made his trustee and executor. It was signed in London at William's lodging on 12 October, during his illness, one of the witnesses being a trained nurse. This will, which was to become one of the

11 MacGregor with Bryce and Griffith

12 Chapel-on-Leader, bought by MacGregor for his retirement

13 The tombstone at Towie, Aberdeenshire

14 A detail of the inscription

issues in a law case not ended until the year 1935, left to his wife, during her widowhood, a liferent of the estate of Chapel-on-Leader and the furnishings of that house, and also a liferent of the residue of his moveable estate, as well as a small legacy of £300 for mournings for herself and household. After her death his property was to be divided between his daughter, Mary, and his granddaughter, Honor. Mary was to take one half of the residue of his moveable estate, the other half to go to Honor when she reached twenty-five on 18 June 1932. Honor was favoured in so far as she was also to take Chapel-on-Leader and its furnishings, again when she reached twenty-five. Honor's issue were also given priority over Mary; only if Honor died without issue before she reached twenty-five would Mary have taken over Honor's moveable and real property. These bequests were drawn up very deliberately by William; the provisions of his will[61] tally with the sentiments which he expressed to Sempill, who is on record as saying 'I was a close friend of Sir William MacGregor and he, as a matter of fact, informed me in broad outline of his testamentary intentions and of the relations that existed between him and his family generally'.[62] Mary was undoubtedly hurt by the favouring of Honor. During the law suit Sempill said that 'she seemed to be not anxious to go back to times when memories were very sad to her' and whenever he touched on 'the question of her father and his Will she asked me very clearly and definitely not to remind her of those times and not to discuss those matters'.[63]

MacGregor was also determined to leave only the barest legal minimum to the children of his first marriage. The will reads:

> To my son James Rob MacGregor and to my daughter Mrs. Helen Hahn such sum as represents the amount of legitim which they each can claim in terms of the law of moveable estate in Scotland, but under deduction of all sums which I have already paid to them or on their account respectively and which are properly deductable from their shares of legitim.[64]

MacGregor's death was sudden. On 1 July 1919 he was operated on in Aberdeen, but did not recover. Two days later, at five past three in the afternoon he died. The official cause was 'intestinal adhesions and gall stones',[65] but the psychological strains of his last years must have diminished his desire to recover. William had provided in his will that his 'remains shall be cremated and the ashes interred with the remains of my parents in the cemetery of Towie, Aberdeenshire'. One of the few present at the interment wrote:

On a beautiful July afternoon, in presence of his widow, his daughter, other relations, a representative of the Queensland Government, and a few intimate friends, the last simple and solemn funeral rites of the Church of Scotland were performed by his old college class-fellow, the Reverend Alexander Jack, minister of Towie, and by the Reverend William Watt, minister of Strathdon, nephew of and successor to the late Reverend John Watt, who had encouraged and befriended him in his early days.[66]

So another circle had been completed, but it is significant that only after death had William returned to the Don Valley.

His wife Mary did not long survive William. She drew up a will on 23 August which showed her clear preference for her daughter over her granddaughter and perhaps her belief that William's settlement had been unjust. Mary was left 'the whole Estate heritable and moveable, real and personal of whatever nature or wherever situated'. Honor was to be given 'an article of jewellery' to be chosen by Mary or by her executor.[67] Less than three months after William's death, on 8 October, his widow had a 'slight paralytic stroke' from which she never fully recovered. From mid-November there was no hope of recovery, as she had cerebral haemorrhage, and on 4 December angina pectoris ended her life.[68] Her daughter came to Chapel-on-Leader to accept on 11 December the office of executrix, then hastened back to London from the house she so disliked.[69]

As has been stated, there were sixteen years of litigation before MacGregor's estate was wound up. James MacGregor came back from Australia to get what he could, and both he and his sister Helen used the intricacies of the Scottish law of inheritance to obtain substantial amounts.[70] In the final judgment, again in opposition to MacGregor's wishes, the inheritance of his granddaughter, Honor, was reduced in favour of her aunt, Mary MacGregor.[71]

This long and often bitter legal dispute was of a piece with MacGregor's life. Here domestic faction, plus a family life exacerbated by the strains put on it by his colonial career, came to a last unpleasant head. The discord in part mirrored and in part paralleled the frustrations of MacGregor's life and career. He would probably have not thought it too fanciful to see a resemblance between the alternatives available in Scottish testamentary law and the changes in policy adopted by the Colonial Office.

What should be stressed is how many of MacGregor's policies were not overthrown, and how many of his ideas are still strikingly relevant. Some of his bequests cannot be overturned: his care for the liberated Africans in the Seychelles; his medical scheme in Fiji; his protection of the Papuans; his respect for the African rulers in Lagos; his part in the prevention of a clash between the United States and Great Britain in Newfoundland; his respect for university standards in Queensland. Above all, his insistence on a scientific approach, and on careful research into every problem, provides a legacy which has a relevance far beyond colonial administration, and far beyond the confines of his day.

His value was appreciated during his lifetime by his friends, four of whom were left legacies in his will.[72] One of these was Sir Charles Mackellar, whose assessment of his character is still apposite:

> He was a great block of rough, unhewn granite, but recognized to be of sterling character and possessed of excellent, indeed unusual, ability, although I am sure no one could have predicted then that he would rise to the great position he ultimately occupied in the service of his country. As iron sharpeneth iron, so his intercourse with all sorts of men in so many parts of the Empire, hewed and polished his roughness of manner, until he became the polite and courteous man of later life. But even that did not remove all the angles. He maintained to the last an independent reticence and a stubborn opinionativeness, which were the result no doubt of a life which had fought its own way through a hard fight to a position of great eminence. I am sure, if there had been a Carnegie Trust in his day, and all his fees had been paid for him, he would never have been the Governor of Newfoundland and Queensland. To bear loneliness and poverty in youth and to despise them and struggle on in spite of them, is to get an original impetus, which no obstacles in after years can wholly withstand. To the man who has conquered such initial difficulties, anything seems to be possible.[73]

AA

Notes

CHAPTER 1

1 This clan history was intensively investigated by a John MacGregor who was interviewed by Sir William MacGregor on 26 February 1918. *Modern McGregor Genealogical Notes*, vol. 184, box 15, part X; another John MacGregor of London has recently researched this history. Letter to author, 19 September 1965.

2 See F. W. Robinson, 'University Antiquities III. The Banner of the First Chancellor of the University of Queensland', *Galmahra* (Queensland University) Third Term, 1932, pp. 7-8.

3 Information from relations particularly Mrs Muirden and Mrs McHardy, nieces of Sir William MacGregor.

4 She was born on 6 December 1822, daughter of William and Anne (nee Riddel) Smith of Pitprone in Leochel-Cushnie parish. Information from relations and 1841-51-61-71 Scottish Census Returns, General Registry Office, Edinburgh.

5 About 1909-10 William reputedly sent each of his three brothers $300 for emigration. One other verified gift was to his niece, Mrs Warren, for her education. Information from relations.

6 Asked in 1895 whether he came from Aberdeen William replied, 'In a sense, yes. But I must tell you I was sixteen before I ever saw the Granite City.' 'The Future of New Guinea', *Newspaper Cuttings*, vol. 52, Mitchell Library.

7 See W. Watt, *Aberdeen and Banff*, ch. XIII; and S. Mechie, *The Church and Scottish Social Development 1780-1870*, London, 1960.

8 Some of his known habitations were in Tarland parish in 1844 where Ann was born; at the croft Hillockhead in Towie parish from 1846-8 where William and Christian were born; at a cottage in Clashnewnie on a farm called Old Mains in Towie parish in 1851; some time later at a croft called Howmuir; in 1855 in Leochel-Cushnie parish where Catherine was born; from 1857-60 in Strathdon parish where Gordon and John were born probably at the croft Claverhouse.

9 *Records of Parochial Board of Strathdon*, 1845-92.

10 Mrs M. Blacklaw, daughter of William's brother, John.

11 H. Scott, *Fasti Ecclesiae Scoticanae. The Succession of Ministers in the Parish Church of Scotland from the Reformation to the Present Times*, Vol. 6, *Synods of Aberdeen and Moray*, Edinburgh, 1926, p. 139.

12 William attended several schools, including Tillyduke and Cushnie. Kennedy taught at Tillyduke school, and after 1860 was Inspector and Collector for the Strathdon Parochial Board which was granting relief to William's father. See also R. W. Reid, 'Sir William MacGregor', *The Aberdeen University Review*, VII, no. 19, November 1919, p. 2.

13 Robb and William later married sisters, and William's first son was christened James Robb McGregor. Extract from Entry in Register of Births (dated 27 January 1869), General Registry Office, Edinburgh.

14 Reid, *op. cit.*, p. 2 and W. S. Crockett 'A Notable Scot. The late Sir William MacGregor' reprinted from the *Border Magazine* (Scotland) in *The Scottish Australasian*, XI, 130, 30 October 1920, p. 7662.

15 'A Distinguished F.P. [Former Pupil]', *The Grammar School [Aberdeen] Magazine*, N.S., vol. 1, 1894-5, pp. 213-14.

16 'Sir William MacGregor. An Appreciation', *Sydney Morning Herald*, 16 July 1914.

17 MacGregor to Colonial Office [C.O.], 16 December 1872, C.O. 167/549, on 12461.

18 T. Watt, *Aberdeen Grammar School. Roll of Pupils 1795-1919*, Aberdeen, 1923, errs in giving 1865 as his date of entry. The *Public Catalogue* of the school gives the correct date. Details supplied by the headmaster, Reverend John Skinner, letter to author 16 November 1960.

19 His results in this grading exam surprised his friend (G. W. Beattie) who had tested him just before entry. Beattie thought he would probably be enrolled in the second, and might scrape into the higher third class. 'A Distinguished F.P.', *op. cit.*, p. 214.

20 Merit certificate in 1866; 4th Prize in Latin in October 1866; 5th Prize in Latin and 3rd Prize in Greek in October 1867.

21 'A Distinguished F.P.', *op. cit.*, pp. 214-15.

22 Details of subjects (English, Latin, Greek, Arithmetic and Euclid) and marks are given in *Aberdeen University Calendar* 1867-8, pp. 8-9.

23 'Sir William MacGregor. An Appreciation', *op. cit.*

24 University of Aberdeen records consulted by J. Hargreaves, History Department, King's College.

25 Extract of Entry in a Register of Marriages, dated 4 October 1868, General Registry Office, Edinburgh. Their son, James, was born on 27 January 1869. Birth extract, n. 13 above.

26 *Prospectus of Medical School, Anderson's University, Glasgow* (n.d.). *Calendar of Anderson's University, Glasgow, for the year 1871-72*, Glasgow, 1871.

27 He was one of 320 medical students in 1871. J. Christie, *The Medical Institutes of Glasgow. A Handbook*, Glasgow, 1888.

28 In 1872 he was one of 216 medical students, *Aberdeen University Calendar*, 1867-72; Professor J. Struthers, 'The Progress of the Medical School', in P. J. Anderson, *Aurora Borealis Academica, Aberdeen University Appreciations*, Aberdeen, 1899, p. 213.

29 His *Graduate Schedule*, Aberdeen University, gives details of his courses and lectures each year. The famous Lister taught him surgery at Glasgow; while typically of other teachers Professor Struthers who taught him Anatomy at Aberdeen urged his students to investigate for themselves 'dissect, analyze, observe, verify, systematize from the actualities. And to the scalpel he added the microscope . . . To this exciting objectivity in method, Struthers applied the living ideas of Darwin. . . . In his teaching, he brought the two into synthesis', W. L. Mackenzie, 'The Professor of Anatomy, 1863-1889', in P. J. Anderson, *op. cit.*, p. 241.

30 A British 1858 Medical Act set up a Council for registering all doctors in the United Kingdom, while the 1858 Scottish Universities Act provided that from 1860 medical degrees required four university years of professional study. J. D. Comrie, *History of Scottish Medicine to 1860*, Research Studies in Medical History no. 4, 1927.

31 In 1870 he topped Botany with 92.6% and a first-class certificate; and was third in Zoology with 78% (second-class); in 1871 he gained firsts in Practice of Medicine and Materia Medica (88%); *Examination Roll for Materia Medica*, Session 1870-71, Glasgow University; *Glasgow University Calendar* 1871-2; his results and methods were later exaggerated: 'he practically committed to memory the entire text book of anatomy, the result being that he took the first position in every subject except medical history in which he was second'. 'A Distinguished F.P.', *op. cit.*, p. 215.

32 'Sir William MacGregor. An Appreciation', *op. cit.*

33 Probably an exaggerated story of his Aberdeen thesis, see below n. 35. *ibid.*

34 For instance at Glasgow Infirmary he had been House Surgeon in

1870-1, and House Physician in 1871; at Glasgow Lock Hospital House Surgeon in 1871; at Glasgow Skin Dispensary he was clerk in 1870-1; at Aberdeen Asylum he was House Physician in 1872.

35 His 'Series of illustrations of pathological histology . . . was considered deserving of high commendation', *Minutes of the Medical Faculty*, Aberdeen University, 1872.

36 Professor Macrobin to O. C. Waterfield, 3 October 1872, with Waterfield to Meade, 8 October 1872, C.O. 167/549/10707.

37 His two Diplomas were granted conjointly after an examination (for university medical graduates) by a Board representing the Faculty and College, so giving students by one test 'at less expense, a double qualification in Medicine and Surgery'. The fees for the examination were £10, and for the diplomas £16. As MacGregor's university medical course cost him about £45—if he paid fees (he probably lost his bursary after changing to Medicine)—the total fees for his medical qualifications were some £71. *Glasgow University Calendar*, 1870-1, p. 13; *Medical Register*, 1873, p. 315.

38 The famous meeting between Livingstone, who had also attended Anderson's University, and Stanley was in November 1871.

39 A. G. L. Shaw, 'A Revision of the Meaning of Imperialism', in *Australian Journal of Politics and History*, vol. VII, no. 2, November 1961, p. 202.

40 Gordon wrote to the C.O. on 16 October 1871, C.O. 167/536/11337.

41 Gordon wrote to the schoolmaster, O.C. Waterfield, of East Sheen in mid-1872; the latter wrote to Dr Hooker of Glasgow who spoke to Dickie before writing to the C.O. on 30 September 1872, C.O. 167/549/9753.

42 Reid, *op. cit.*, p. 3, repeated by F.P.S. on MacGregor in the *Dictionary of National Biography*, and by W. S. Crockett, op. cit., 7662.

43 Information from relatives, and Mechie, *op. cit.*, ch. 8, pp. 129 and 133.

44 MacGregor to and from C.O., 19 October, 28 October, 4 November, 7 November, 19 November, 17 and 27 December 1872, C.O. 167/549/10450, 10956, 11490, 12461, 12706.

45 Minute of E. H. Wingfield, 4 October 1870, C.O. 429/1.

46 Arguments based on MacGregor's experience and review of patronage volumes (C.O. 429). For specific examples and references see R. B. Joyce, 'Sir William MacGregor: Colonial Governor', *Historical Studies Australia and New Zealand*, vol. 11, no. 41, pp. 18-31.

CHAPTER 2

1 Port Louis, the administrative centre of this Indian Ocean island, is situated at 20°10′S., 57°32′E.

2 Gordon to Gladstone, 3 May 1871, Gladstone Papers, vol. 235, 44320.

3 Gordon to Wood, Easter Day 1872, Stanmore Papers, vol. 38, 49326 and see J. K. Chapman, *The Career of Arthur Hamilton Gordon*, Toronto, 1964, p. 106.

4 K. L. Gillion, *Fiji's Indian Migrants, a History to the End of Indenture in 1920*, Melbourne, 1962, p. 13.

5 Gordon to Gladstone, 31 December 1872, Gladstone Papers, vol. 235, 44320.

6 Gordon to Gladstone, 26 July 1874, *ibid.*

7 Their approximate position is 4°S., 55°E.

8 Gordon to Gladstone, 31 December 1872, Gladstone Papers, vol. 235, 44320.

9 Gordon to Kimberley, 7 March 1871, draft despatch no. 6, Gordon MSS. Indian Ocean Correspondence Books, Rhodes House, Oxford.

10 Reference to C.O. despatch, 24 November 1870, *loc. cit.*

11 16 October 1871, *ibid,* and C.O. 167/536 on 11337.

12 Franklyn to Col. Sec., Mauritius, 2 March 1873, Mauritius Archives, vol. TA69.

13 MacGregor's description, in Mauritius Archives, quoted in letter from Archivist to author.

14 MacGregor to Chief Civil Commissioner, Seychelles, two letters, 24 February 1873, Mauritius Archives, vol. TA69.

15 Ordinance 13 of 8 December 1873, Mauritius *Government Gazette* no. 212 of 1873, p. 548.

16 Order-in-Council of 26 January 1874, to take effect 1 May 1874, four days after MacGregor had moved to Mauritius. The delay was partly because of lack of funds. Mauritius *Government Gazette* no. 23 of 1874, 11 April 1874; C.O. to Gordon 30 January 1874, Mauritius Archives, vol. TA69.

17 MacGregor to Franklyn, 27 February 1873, Mauritius Archives, vol. TA69.

18 Newton to C.O., 1 April 1873, Mauritius Archives, vol. SD119, and Minutes on this despatch C.O. 167/552/4405. Reply Kimberley to Acting-Administrator, 23 May 1873, Mauritius Archives, vol. SA108.

19 The same Stanley who 'found' Livingstone. Chapman, *op. cit.,* p. 116.

20 Regulations of 27 December 1872 enclosed in Newton to C.O., 1 April 1873, C.O. 167/552/4405.

21 MacGregor to Franklyn, 27 August 1873, Mauritius Archives, vol. TA69.

22 'On the last occasion of his [MacGregor] making a tour of inspection he was prostrated with sickness, and laid up at Govt. House for more than a week', Minute on above, 22 September 1873, *ibid.*

23 Gordon to C.O., 8 November 1873, Mauritius Archives, vol. SD121.

24 Gordon's diary, [November 1873], Mauritius, 11, 323 cited by Chapman, *op. cit.,* p. 116.

25 See Franklyn's Annual Report on the Seychelles Islands for 1873, Mauritius Archives.

26 Chapman, *op. cit.,* p. 117.

27 He sailed with his wife and daughter on 27 April, reaching Mauritius on 21 May. Passenger List 1874, Mauritius Archives Series Z2D.

28 Came 'to oblige the Governor', MacGregor's letter to Sir Charles Farquhar Shand, Chief Judge Mauritius Supreme Court, 18 November 1874; and a clerk's Minute, 2 February 1875, Mauritius Archives, vol. TA71.

29 Havelock to Col. Sec. Mauritius, 9 January 1875, Mauritius Archives, vol. TA71.

30 Reid to Acting Col. Sec. Mauritius, 10 October 1874, Mauritius Archives, vol. RA2199.

31 He left Mauritius on 9 December, reaching the Seychelles on 17 December 1874, Passenger List 1874, Mauritius Archives, Series Z2D.

CHAPTER 3

1 The reasons for the annexation are discussed in E. Drus, 'The Colonial Office and the Annexation of Fiji', *Transactions of the Royal Historical Society* 4th series, XXXII, 1950; J. D. Legge, *Britain in Fiji 1858-1880,* London, 1958; W. P. Morrell, *Britain in the Pacific Islands,* Oxford, 1960; J. M. Ward, *British Policy in the South Pacific,* Sydney, 1948.

2 Carnarvon to Robinson, 16 January 1875, C.O. 83/5.

3 Carnarvon to Gordon, 23 October 1874, Stanmore Papers, vol. 1, 49199.

4 Herbert to Gordon, 19 December 1874, *ibid.*

5 When the Fijian Legislative Council debated in 1885 reducing the gover-

nor's salary to save expenditure Herbert, as in 1874, doubted that it would be wise to reduce because 'Fiji is a great banishment and requires a strong Governor'. See below Chap. IV, p. 54, and Minute by Herbert, 25 September 1885 on C.O. 83/41/16728.

6 Gordon to Gladstone, 29 December 1874, Gladstone Papers, vol. 235, 44320.

7 Gladstone to Gordon, 31 December 1874, *ibid.*

8 As 'Sanitary Warden of Port Louis', MacGregor to Gordon, 17 May 1884, Stanmore Papers.

9 They reached Sydney via Aden in June where MacGregor discussed policy with Gordon. MacGregor travelled to Fiji from 8-20 June in the *Barracouta;* his wife and daughter from 16 June—2 July in the *Meteor;* Gordon from 14-24 June in the *Pearl, Fiji Times,* 23 and 26 June and 3 July 1875.

10 *Fiji Government Gazette,* 26 June 1875, no. 21, p. 65.

11 MacGregor to Col. Sec. Fiji, 5 February 1876, on Gordon to C.O., 7 April 1877, C.O. 83/13/6284.

12 The 1881 Census listed:

Natives	114,635
Natives on estates	520
Natives on coastal vessels	480
Europeans	2,293
Half-castes	753
Indian coolies	442
Polynesian indentured immigrants	5,352
Non-European immigrants	156
	124,631

13 To Col. Sec. Fiji, 27 October, C.S.O. (Inwards) 87/2851.

14 MacGregor to Col. Sec. Fiji, 30 August 1887, on C.S.O. (Inwards) 87/2039 of 17 July 1887.

15 Des Voeux to C.O., 26 September 1884, C.O. 83/38/19966.

16 Using figures cited by Blyth which differ slightly from those in the 1881 Census. Blyth's report in Mitchell to C.O., 23 September 1887, C.O. 83/46/22879.

17 W. H. Mercer on Mitchell to C.O., *loc. cit.* For recent discussion of reasons for decline, N. McArthur, *Island Populations of the Pacific,* Canberra, 1967.

18 'The Chief Medical Officer, Dr. McGregor has been untiring in his endeavour to discover what, and where, the checks [on population growth] are, and to apply the necessary remedies.' James Harding, *Fiji Times,* 11 January 1888.

19 MacGregor to Col. Sec. Fiji, 21 September 1875, C.S.O. (Inwards) 75/50.

20 MacGregor to Col. Sec., 24 December 1875, on Gordon to C.O., 27 December 1875, C.O. 83/7/2638.

21 MacGregor report in *Fiji Times,* 16 September 1876 in Gordon to C.O., 26 September 1876, C.O. 83/10/13344.

22 Undated memo on C.S.O. (Inwards) 77/1093 of 17 August 1877.

23 *loc. cit.* He had published in 1876 *Parasitic Skin Disease* in Fiji, and in 1877 *New Form of Parasitic Disease.*

24 MacGregor to Col. Sec Fiji, 5 February 1876, with Gordon to C.O., 7 April 1877, C.O. 83/13/6284.

25 MacGregor to Col. Sec. Fiji, 3 September 1878, C.S.O. (Inwards) 78/1241.

26 Malcolm, 31 May 1877, on C.O. 83/13/6284.

27 Des Voeux to C.O., 4 October 1878, C.O. 83/17/16505.

28 21 June 1881, on C.O. 83/25/7144.

29 The name given by Gordon to the 1876 campaign to control Fijian uprisings in central Viti Levu. See the two published volumes of letters to and from members of his staff. *Story of a Little War, Letters and Notes written during the disturbances in the Highlands (known as the 'Devil Country') of Viti Levu, Fiji, 1876*, Edinburgh, 1879.

30 See n. 21 above.

31 MacGregor saw the waning of the epidemic by September 1875. MacGregor to Col. Sec., Fiji, 8 and 7 September 1875, C.S.O. (Inwards) 75/16 and 18.

32 MacGregor to Col. Sec. Fiji, 7 June 1880, C.S.O. (Inwards) 80/1003.

33 MacGregor to Gordon, 12 December 1881, Stanmore Papers.

34 He quarantined Gordon on an official visit to Fiji in September 1881. MacGregor to Col. Sec. Fiji, 30 September 1881, C.S.O. (Inwards) 81/1749; see also Gordon to Lady Gordon, 21 September 1881, Stanmore Papers, vol. 27, 49225.

35 September 1879, on C.O. 83/19/13971.

36 MacGregor to Col. Sec. Fiji, 3 December 1878, C.S.O. (Inwards) 78/1739.

37 *ibid.*, 19 January 1879, C.S.O. (Inwards) 79/99.

38 Thurston, 19 September 1884, on C.S.O. (Inwards) 84/1517 of 15 July 1884.

39 Contagious Disease Ordinance 9/1880.

40 14 January 1881, on C.O. 83/25/5539.

41 Missionary and Fijian opinions and C.O. comments on des Voeux to C.O., 3 December 1881, C.O. 83/27/3105.

42 Des Voeux to C.O., 18 September 1882, C.O. 83/30/19972.

43 The C.O. made the Fijian ordinance an exception to their general objection partly because of the allegations at pp. 66-7 of a book published in 1886, H. H. Romilly's *The Western Pacific and New Guinea*, that islanders could be 'exterminated' by 'the seeds of disease hitherto unknown among' them. Discussion on Mitchell to C.O., 13 January 1887, C.O. 83/45/4754.

44 Copy of entry in *Register of Death*, no. 1987, Registrar-General, Fiji; *Fiji Times*, 10 February 1877.

45 'Helen MacGregor is still here and Mrs. Des Voeux deserves credit for her kindness to her', Gordon to Lady Gordon, 1 October 1881, Stanmore Papers, vol. 27, 49225.

46 J. B. Thurston wrote when his wife broke her arm: 'sent for Macgregor who has been in constant attendance and most assiduous ever since' and later, 'Macgregor who [sic] kindnesses and attention has been very great seems rather proud of his case'. Letters to Gordon 25 November 1880, and 23 December 1880, Stanmore Papers, vol. VI, 49204.

When Mrs des Voeux was in 'great danger' for two days after her confinement 'nothing but MacGregor's skill and attention saved her'. Gordon to Lady Gordon, 2 July 1882, Stanmore Papers, vol. 27, 49225.

47 Written on his return from leave in 1883, *Suva Times*, 4 August 1883.

48 *Fiji Times*, 6 June 1888.

49 *Fiji Times*, 15 March 1884.

50 MacGregor memo, 10 November 1879, 79/148 and MacGregor to Col. Sec. Fiji, 15 September 1883, both filed with C.S.O. (Inwards) 83/2555.

51 J. B. Thurston minute, 28 November, Mitchell minute, 30 November, on MacGregor to Col. Sec. Fiji, 26 October 1887, C.S.O. (Inwards) 87/2811.

52 MacGregor Minute, 29 November, *loc. cit.*; MacGregor to Gordon, 17 July 1887; Stanmore Papers.

53 MacGregor in W.H.R. Rivers ed., *Essays on the Depopulation of Melanesia*, Cambridge, 1922, pp. 80-3.

54 Des Voeux to C.O., 24 July 1884, C.O. 83/37/15803.

55 See for example his Minute, 27 May 1885, on Dr Blyth to Col. Sec. Fiji, 6 May 1885, C.S.O. (Inwards) 85/1438.

56 For dispute see MacGregor to Col. Sec. Fiji, 27 March 1876, C.S.O. (Inwards) 514/76; Dr Mayo to Col. Sec. Fiji, 4 October 1876, C.S.O. (Inwards) 1399/76; Gordon, 24 April 1877, on C.S.O. (Inwards) 505/77; Captain Saunders to Col. Sec. Fiji, 8 August 1877, C.S.O. (Inwards) 77/1034; MacGregor memo on 1102 filed with 77/1034.

57 Gordon memo on MacGregor to Col. Sec. Fiji, 5 August 1875, C.S.O. (Inwards) 572/75.

58 MacGregor to Col. Sec. Fiji, 16 September 1875, C.S.O. (Inwards) 75/56.

59 MacGregor claimed £1 10s a day for replacing Dr Mayo at Kadavu as a special case, distinct from leaving 'Levuka on any service as Chief Medical Officer'. MacGregor to Col. Sec. Fiji, 17 March 1876, C.S.O. (Inwards) 76/456.

60 28 September and 1 November 1886 on C. H. H. Irvine to Col. Sec. Fiji, 9 September 1886, C.S.O. (Inwards) 86/2514.

61 10 October 1884 and 7 January 1885, on Rewa Sugar Co. to Col. Sec. Fiji, 23 September 1884, C.S.O. (Inwards) 84/2035.

62 Des Voeux' Minute, 29 August 1884, on C.S.O. out-letter 84/1542.

63 Reply by MacGregor to Col. Sec. Fiji, 19 September 1884, C.S.O. (Inwards) 84/2010.

64 Corney's tariff had differential rates for Europeans, Indians and half-castes. Charges for a visit were respectively 7s 6d—10s 6d; 2s 6d—5s. 29 October 1884. MacGregor's Minute, 18 December 1884, on *ibid.*

65 A fellow official, W. Seed, told Gordon on 31 March 1879 that MacGregor wanted to go back to Mauritius as C.M.O., vol. XL; MacGregor told Gordon on 10 June 1881 that he had declined more than one offer to leave Fiji, Stanmore Papers.

66 MacGregor obtained periodicals: 'ever since I have been in the colony I have subscribed to the principal medical papers of Europe . . . procured at great expense'. MacGregor to Col. Sec. Fiji, 18 June 1886, C.S.O. (Inwards) 86/1418.

67 MacGregor to Gordon, 12 December 1881, Stanmore Papers.

68 27 April 1882, on C.O. 83/29/11504.

69 MacGregor to C.O., 29 January 1883, C.O. 83/35/1896.

70 Des Voeux to C.O., 27 June, and G. V. Fiddes memo, 4 October 1883, C.O. 83/33/16432.

71 MacGregor to Gordon, 7 May 1884, Stanmore Papers.

72 Des Voeux to C.O., 26 July, memos by G. V. Fiddes (cf. n. 70 above), 23 September and Herbert, 21 October 1884, C.O. 83/37/15807.

73 MacGregor to Gordon, 3 February 1887 (see also 17 July 1887), Stanmore Papers.

74 *Fiji Times*, 15 August 1888.

CHAPTER 4

1 Seed feared that MacGregor was trying to replace him permanently. Seed to Gordon, 20 December 1879, Stanmore Papers, vol. XL, 49238.

2 Details of offices extracted from *Fiji Royal Gazette* 1875-88.

3 Thurston, who had been in Fiji since the 1860s, impressed Gordon who appointed him as Colonial Secretary in 1878. From then on when in the colony he was always MacGregor's superior officer as Colonial Secretary, Acting Administrator and eventually from 1886 as Governor. D. Scarr is writing his biography, see his 'John Bates Thurston, Commodore J. G. Goodenough, and rampant Anglo-Saxons in Fiji', *Historical Studies, Australia and New Zealand*, vol. XI, 43, pp. 361-82.

4 Gordon to C.O., 27 September 1876, C.O. 83/10/13355.

5 Although MacGregor was still officially Chief Medical Officer, in fact Dr Corney was acting in this position. See pp. oo-oo for an explanation of the cut in salaries. MacGregor often discussed his pay in writing to Gordon, e.g. 3 February, 21 June, 17 July 1887, Stanmore Papers.

6 Given the smallness of the staff no formal definition is possible of the limits of the 'business' of a Receiver-General or Treasurer in Fiji. Mac-Gregor was consulted on the financial aspects of every major policy decision, as well as having to decide minor issues such as whether Government accounts should be transferred to another bank or how to save on improving wharves. It was a C.O. clerk who suggested that this remark by MacGregor, made about other colonies, could be applied to Fiji, while another clerk commented on 'the somewhat amusing appreciation by Dr McGregor of his own and the Governor's financial skill', 14 February 1882, with MacGregor's memo (n.d.), on des Voeux to C.O., 18 July 1881, C.O. 83/26/16149.

7 MacGregor (with Gordon) visited Tonga for a week in November 1879, and described his report on its finances as 'crude and undigested'. Yet Gordon recommended the King to adopt its practical suggestions, 14 February 1880, on Gordon to F.O., 29 March 1880, F.O. 58/168.

8 The Cakobau government owed money (c. £87,000) to various debtors, including this New Zealand Bank (n. 18 below) and government officials such as G. A. Woods, who while upholding various offices, including that of 'Premier' between 1871 and 1874 needed to account for expenditure of some £9,000. Legge, *Britain in Fiji 1858-1880*, pp. 270-1.

9 Ordinance 16/1881. Des Voeux to C.O., 6 August 1881, C.O. 83/27/18404.

10 See n. 8 above; 25 May 1881 on G. A. Woods to Col. Sec. Fiji, 19 May 1881, C.S.O. (Inwards) 81/895.

11 The writer claimed that MacGregor disagreed with much of Fijian policy, but that as a loyal civil servant he had submitted to 'galling restrictions [at] the dicta of men, over whom he towers, in all mental qualities, at least a head and shoulders'. *Fiji Times*, editorial, 4 February 1888.

12 MacGregor to Col. Sec. Fiji, 15 September 1887, C.S.O. (Inwards) 81/1659.

13 MacGregor to Col. Sec. Fiji, 21 November 1881, C.S.O. (Inwards) 81/2128.

14 Carnarvon memo, 28 March on Gordon to C.O., 14 January 1877, C.O. 83/13/2615.

15 J. D. Legge, *op. cit.*, p. 168.

16 J. D. Legge, *op. cit.*, pp. 270-9, compare J. K. Chapman, *Arthur Hamilton Gordon*, pp. 179-81.

17 Ordinance 17/1880. Minutes by W. C. Sargeant, 9 February 1882; Gladstone cited from *Hansard*, vol. 162, pp. 261ff.; C.O. draft reply; MacGregor's memorandum; E. Wingfield, 23 November 1881, all on des Voeux to C.O., 18 July 1881, C.O. 83/26/16149.

18 This Bank was concerned in paying the debts of Cakobau's government. This outstanding amount was only part of the Bank's total claims which in 1878 aggregated £61,743 19s 10d, MacGregor to Col. Sec. Fiji, C.S.O. (Inwards) 78/565. See MacGregor, 21 March 1882 and minute by F. Fuller, 5 June 1883, on des Voeux to C.O., 14 April 1883, C.O. 83/32/9270.

19 Bramston (n.d.); F. Fuller re MacGregor and des Voeux 8 August, on des Voeux to C.O., 15 May 1882, C.O. 83/30/13147.

20 MacGregor to C.O., 19 March 1885 (despatch 48), C.O. 83/40/8255.

21 G. V. Fiddes, memo 13 May, on MacGregor's report to C.O., 19 March 1885 (despatch 49), C.O. 83/40/8256.

22 Des Voeux, minute (n.d.); G. V. Fiddes 25 and 26 June; F. Fuller 26 June; J. Bramston 26 June all on MacGregor to C.O., 17 April 1885, C.O. 83/40/10250.

23 MacGregor to C.O., 11 May 1885, C.O. 83/40/11660.

24 Thurston to C.O., 16 February 1886, C.O. 83/43/6197; and MacGregor to N.Z., 15 April 1886 in Thurston to C.O., 17 May 1886, C.O. 83/43/11592.

25 G. V. Fiddes, 20 July 1886, on Thurston to C.O. 18 May 1886, C.O. 83/43/11600.

26 The Crown Agents were the commercial and financial agents in England for all the Crown Colonies. They were instructed and supervised by the Colonial Office, which also fixed their charges. *C.O. List.*

27 R. Meade, 14 October 1886, on 83/43/11600.

28 G. V. Fiddes, 29 October, on Treasury to C.O., 26 October 1886, C.O. 83/44/19275.

29 Thurston to C.O., 21 October 1886, C.O. 83/44/22832.

30 See R. G. W. Herbert, Minute, 6 February 1887 on Report in Thurston to C.O., 29 November 1886, C.O. 83/44/849.

31 Draft C.O. reply (n.d.), on Thurston to C.O., 22 December 1886, C.O. 83/44/2738.

32 Mitchell to C.O., 17 January 1887, C.O. 83/45/4757.

33 J. Anderson, 13 May 1887, on Mitchell to C.O., 18 March 1887, C.O. 83/45/8288.

34 6 February 1887 on Mitchell to C.O., telegram (n.d.), January 1887, C.O. 83/45/1576.

35 MacGregor's 66-page report of 31 May 1887 in Mitchell to C.O., 2 June 1887, C.O. 83/46/14741.

36 Mitchell to C.O., 7 July 1887, C.O. 83/46/18918.

37 Mitchell to C.O., 7 November 1887, C.O. 83/47/49.

38 For Blyth see Chapter 3, p. 26, Anson Chapter 5, p. 78; Thomson Chapter 8, pp. 150-1. Colonists' petition in Mitchell to C.O., 13 December 1887, C.O. 83/47/2547.

39 J. Anderson, 13 May, on Treasury to C.O., 5 May 1887, C.O. 83/47/8813.

40 Draft dated 7 September 1887, on Treasury to C.O., 26 August 1887, C.O. 83/47/17305.

41 See Minutes on Mitchell to C.O. (n.d.), December 1887, C.O. 83/47/25332.

42 Thurston to C.O., 9 March 1888, C.O. 83/48/8362.

43 E. Wingfield, 21 June; R. Meade, 14 August 1888, on Thurston to C.O., 10 March 1888, C.O. 83/48/8361.

44 Treasury to C.O., 2 March 1888, C.O. 83/49/4232.

45 Fiddes, 2 July, Herbert, 4 August 1887 (Meade on 2 August reiterated the phrase 'the coat must be cut according to the cloth', which he had used ten years earlier on 23 August 1877 on Gordon to C.O., 9 May 1877, C.O. 83/13), all on Thurston to C.O., 9 April 1887, C.O. 83/45/10708.

46 See MacGregor to Gordon, 1 January 1888, Stanmore Papers.

47 Gordon to C.O., 16 February 1876, C.O. 83/9/3635.

48 See discussion by W. P. Morrell, *Britain in the Pacific Islands,* p. 374.

49 Gordon to C.O., 16 February 1876, C.O. 83/9/3635.

50 G. K. Roth, *Fijian Way of Life,* Melbourne, 1953, p. 46, cited by Morrell, *op. cit.,* p. 376.

51 Morrell, *op. cit.,* p. 375.

52 J. K. Chapman, *op. cit.,* p. 172.

53 23 September 1886 on Captain David Robbie to Col. Sec. Fiji (n.d.), C.S.O. (Inwards) 86/2015.

54 Gordon to C.O., 24 March 1878, C.O. 83/16/7110. See also his 18 March 1879 address on 'Native Taxation in Fiji' in *Royal Colonial Institute, Proceedings,* vol. V, 1878-9, pp. 192-4.

55 Wilkinson to Gordon, Stanmore Papers, 49208 cited in Legge, *op. cit.,* p. 244, n. 2 and Gordon 'Native Taxation in Fiji', *op. cit.,* p. 188.

56 29 January 1884, on G. Bayley to Col. Sec. Fiji, 3 January 1884, C.S.O. (Inwards) 84/218.

57 MacGregor to Col. Sec. Fiji, 5 August 1884, C.S.O. (Inwards) 84/1654.

58 Blyth to Col. Sec. Fiji, 2 December 1884, C.S.O. (Inwards) 84/2715.

59 J. B. Thurston, 10 December 1884 on C.S.O. (Inwards) 84/2818. See below Chapter 5, n. 41.

60 MacGregor, 19 May 1884 on C.S.O. (Inwards) 85/1283.

61 MacGregor to Gordon, 1 January 1888, Stanmore Papers.

62 Mitchell, 17 February, Thurston, 16 February, on MacGregor to Col. Sec. Fiji, 11 February 1887, C.S.O. (Inwards) 87/315.

63 MacGregor to Col. Sec. Fiji, 9 February 1887, C.S.O. (Inwards) 87/312.

64 Wilson to MacGregor, 18 August 1887, C.S.O. (Inwards) 87/2010.

65 MacGregor to Col. Sec. Fiji, 8 August, 1887 C.S.O. (Inwards) 87/1795.

66 MacGregor, 17 October and Mitchell, 17 October, both on Wilson to MacGregor, 7 October 1887, C.S.O. (Inwards) 87/2642.

67 MacGregor, 13 November, Emberson, 15 November 1887, both on C.S.O. (Inwards) 87/3060.

68 Legge, *op. cit.* p. 237.

69 MacGregor to Gordon, 30 March 1879, Stanmore Papers, the earliest surviving letter of their long correspondence. Gordon to keep informed of Fijian development while on leave (June 1878-September 1879) asked various people in Fiji to write to him.

70 MacGregor to Gordon, 18 April 1881, Stanmore Papers.

71 MacGregor to Gordon, 10 June 1881. Stanmore Papers.

72 18 July 1882, in des Voeux to C.O., 22 August 1882, C.O. 83/30/18288.

73 G. V. Fiddes, 27 October; J. Bramston, 1 December and F. Fuller (n.d.), on *ibid.*

74 Thurston to C.O., 28 April 1884, C.O. 83/36/10368.

75 MacGregor to Gordon, 11 June 1884, Stanmore Papers.

76 Chisholm, chief clerk in the Audit branch, was paid £75 as Accountant for Native Taxes. MacGregor to Gordon, 21 July 1884, Stanmore Papers.

77 R. G. W. Herbert, 13 November and Derby, 14 November on des Voeux to C.O., 25 August 1884, C.O. 83/37/18125.

78 R. G. W. Herbert, 21 August, E. Ashley, 24 August, on G. Anderson, 8 August 1884 to C.O., C.O. 83/39/13517. See Chapter 5 below. J. Bramston feared extra expense if natives were governed 'individually' instead of 'tribally', Minute, 3 April 1885, C.O. 83/40/4324.

79 MacGregor to Gordon, 29 April 1885, Stanmore Papers.

80 F. Fuller, 11 June 1886, on Thurston to C.O., 15 April 1886, C.O. 83/43/9673.

81 MacGregor to Gordon, 17 July 1887, Stanmore Papers.

CHAPTER 5

1 Speech of 2 September 1875, cited in Morrell, *Britain in the Pacific Islands,* p. 381.

2 Ordinance XV of 1876 and X of 1877 controlled the recruiting of Fijian labour and were intended to limit 'migratory habits among the native population'. Gordon to Carnarvon, 12 March 1877, C.O. 83/11, cited in Legge, *Britain in Fiji 1858-1880,* p. 258.

3 K. L. Gillion, *Fiji's Indian Migrants,* p. 15.

4 MacGregor to Col. Sec. Fiji, 31 July 1878, C.S.O. (Inwards) 78/1065.

5 MacGregor to Col. Sec., 26 May 1879, C.S.O., (Inwards) 79/1235.

6 *ibid.,* 30 July 1879. C.S.O. (Inwards) 79/1309.

7 Morrell, *op. cit.,* pp. 382-3.

8 MacGregor had urged compulsory vaccination in 1875. By 1876 Dr Mayo was investigating how many had been vaccinated and inducing others to be vaccinated. MacGregor drafted an ordinance in 1876, which was passed as

number 4 of 1877. Mayo to Col. Sec. Fiji, 4 October 1876, C.S.O. (Inwards) 76/1399. MacGregor to Col. Sec. Fiji, 14 September 1875 and 27 October 1876, C.S.O. (Inwards) 75/61 and 76/1634.

9 MacGregor wrote in 1876 a 20-page report on a quarantine site and in 1877 urged the need of 'speedily preparing the quarantine station'. Mac-Gregor to Col. Sec. Fiji, 24 April 1876, C.S.O. (Inwards) 76/636. MacGregor to Col Sec. Fiji, 3 March 1877, C.S.O. (Inwards) 77/251.

10 MacGregor to Col. Sec. Fiji, 23 August 1879, C.S.O. (Inwards) 79/1446.

11 The second Indian migrant ship arrived in June 1882 by which time the capital had been moved on the advice of MacGregor and others, because of the unhealthiness of Levuka, to Suva. MacGregor and Pratt, Report, 27 November 1875, in Gordon to C.O., 25 January 1876, C.O. 83/9/4603.

12 MacGregor to Col. Sec. Fiji, 5 January 1880 and 19 May 1882, C.S.O. (Inwards) 80/18 and 82/1241.

13 MacGregor to Col. Sec., 16 August 1879, C.S.O. (Inwards) 79/1413.

14 MacGregor to Col. Sec. Fiji, 30 August 1879, C.S.O. (Inwards) 79/1475.

15 Thurston to C.O., 30 April 1888, C.O. 83/48/8362.

16 MacGregor to Col. Sec. Fiji, 16 June, Thurston's memo, 22 June 1882, C.S.O. (Inwards) 82/1482.

17 29 September 1883, on C.S.O. (Inwards) 83/2445.

18 3 July 1887, on C.S.O. (Inwards) 87/1357.

19 Report on Polynesian Immigration for 1884, Thurston to C.O., 31 December 1886, C.O. 83/44/3717.

20 MacGregor, 17 November and Thurston, 19 November, memos, on 15 November 1883, C.S.O. (Inwards) 83/3280.

21 Fiji Times, 9 June 1888.

22 Carew to Col. Sec. Fiji, 2 November 1887, C.S.O. (Inwards) 87/2523.

23 For descriptions see C.S.O. (Inwards) 84/1040, 1060, 1143, 1343.

24 MacGregor to Gordon, 11 June 1884, Stanmore Papers.

25 Sec. Royal Humane Society of Australasia to Col. Sec. Fiji, C.S.O. (Inwards) 85/1096.

26 Fiji Times, 21 May 1884.

27 Aberdeen Grammar School Magazine, N.S. vol. 23, October 1919, p. 14. This account with variations acquired a wide circulation. See, e.g. The Evening Herald, St John's, Newfoundland, 23 July 1904, on the eve of Mac-Gregor's arrival there.

28 Ordinance XXIV of 1877, Legge, op. cit., pp. 262-3.

29 Ordinance XI of 1877, Legge, op. cit., pp. 263-4.

30 Legge, op. cit., p. 266.

31 Many died of dysentery after reaching Levuka Hospital, despite Mac-Gregor's efforts to save them. MacGregor to Col. Sec. Fiji, 14 January 1880, C.S.O. (Inwards) 80/75.

32 Report of 13 September 1880 with Gordon to C.O., 13 September 1880, C.O. 83/23/17597. See also MacGregor's 1879 suggestions to Col. Sec. Fiji, 1 May 1879, C.S.O. (Inwards) 79/763, attached with 79/814 to 79/1818.

33 MacGregor to Col. Sec. Fiji, 13 July 1880, C.S.O. (Inwards) 80/1295.

34 Herbert (n.d.), on Gordon to C.O., 13 September 1880 (forwarding Mac-Gregor's despatch of 13 July 1880), C.O. 83/23/17597.

35 Ordinance XV of 1881. MacGregor to Col. Sec. Fiji, 12 April 1881, C.S.O. (Inwards) 81/667, and MacGregor to Col. Sec. Fiji, 13 July 1881, in des Voeux to C.O., 18 July 1881, C.O. 83/26/16148.

36 Corney to MacGregor, Annual (for 1881) Report of Local Authority for Viti Levu, in MacGregor to Col. Sec. Fiji, 20 May 1882, C.S.O. (Inwards) 82/1276.

37 MacGregor to Col. Sec. Fiji, 16 June 1882, C.S.O. (Inwards) 82/1482.

38 MacGregor to Gordon, 29 April 1885, Stanmore Papers.

39 R. Robertson to Col. Sec. Fiji, 9 August 1886, C.S.O. (Inwards) 86/1689.

40 Ordinance IX of 1886; Thurston to C.O., 22 December 1886, C.O.

83/44/2738; Wilkinson 7 March 1886 with Thurston to C.O., 17 May 1886, C.O. 83/43/11594.

41 See Chapter 4, p. 60, Thurston, *ibid.* In 1884 MacGregor thought that 50 to 60 Fijians idling in Levuka and Suva 'without permission of their chiefs . . . ought to be sent back to their provinces'. By 1886 he was not as condemnatory of the continuing drift of Fijians to the towns: 'I should think it very desirable that each province should have a house for itself in Suva'. In 1887 the Council of Chiefs resolved to register Fijians living in Levuka and Suva. MacGregor, 10 December 1884 and 23 November 1886, on C.S.O. (Inwards) 84/2715 and 86/2174, and Resolution 5 in Mitchell to C.O., 1 June 1887, C.O. 83/46/14738.

42 11 February 1888, on C.S.O. (Inwards) 88/277 filed with 88/685.

43 J. Anderson, 13 June 1888, on Thurston to C.O., 6 April 1888, C.O. 83/48/10509.

44 Gillion, *op. cit.,* pp. 86-7.

45 Copies of Reports of 26 July, 24 September (62 pages) and 29 October (24 pages) 1879 and map, are enclosed in Gordon to C.O., 29 March 1879, C.O. 83/22/7858.

46 Gordon to C.O., 8 October 1879, C.O. 83/20/19462.

47 MacGregor to Gordon, 22 February 1880, Stanmore Papers.

48 MacGregor, 29 March, with Gordon to C.O., 29 March 1880, C.O. 83/22/7858.

49 Kew Gardens to C.O., 8 June 1880, C.O. 83/24/8724.

50 MacGregor by 1884 owned 9 blocks, totalling about 193 acres, des Voeux to C.O., 19 November 1884, C.O. 83/38/853.

51 MacGregor to Gordon, 9 October 1880, 3 March 1882 and 9 October 1883, Stanmore Papers.

52 Gillion, *op. cit.,* p. 87.

53 MacGregor to Gordon, 21 January 1886, Stanmore Papers.

54 MacGregor to Gordon, 17 July 1887, Stanmore Papers.

55 Gordon to Carnarvon, 26 September 1876, Stanmore Papers, quoted in Morrell, *op. cit.,* p. 370.

56 Gordon to Carnarvon, 30 October 1875, quoted in Morrell, *op. cit.,* p. 372, and see Legge, *op. cit.,* pp. 210, 226-7.

57 MacGregor to Gordon, 25 February 1882, Stanmore Papers.

58 'The system cannot therefore be changed. Its greatest danger would be from a man that devoted to native government a less amount of personal supervision than its founder calculated on and than the system requires', MacGregor to Gordon, 23 July 1886, Stanmore Papers.

59 MacGregor to Gordon, 23 February 1884, Stanmore Papers.

60 'There are good grounds for believing that many arbitrary acts are now carried out by chiefs that never would have been expected had you remained here', MacGregor to Gordon, 3 March 1882, Stanmore Papers.

61 MacGregor to Gordon, 21 July 1884, Stanmore Papers.

62 *loc. cit.*

63 MacGregor to Gordon, 1 January 1888, Stanmore Papers.

64 Deposition of Zephania (variant spellings include Zephanaia, Sefenaiya and Sefania), 1 March 1887, in Mitchell to C.O., 12 March 1887, C.O. 83/45/8286.

65 MacGregor, 10 July and Thurston, 13 July 1886 on Blyth (Native Commissioner) to Col. Sec. Fiji, 7 July 1886, C.S.O. (Inwards) 86/1480, filed with 87/2860.

66 Langham's letter, 28 September 1886, in Aborigines' Protection Society to C.O., 20 November 1886, C.O. 83/44/21123.

67 MacGregor, 2 March 1887, on Mitchell to C.O., 12 March 1887, C.O. 83/45/8286.

68 Mitchell to C.O., 1 June 1887, C.O. 83/46/14738.

69 Aborigines' Protection Society to C.O., 6 September 1887, C.O. 83/47/18163.

70 Thurston to C.O., 11 April 1888, C.O. 84/48/10515.

71 MacGregor, 2 November 1887 on Col. Sec. Fiji, 31 October 1887, C.S.O. (Inwards) 87/2846.

72 MacGregor to Gordon, 21 June 1887, Stanmore Papers.

73 Langham to Chapman, 22 September 1875, Letters 1862-79, Methodist Overseas Mission [M.O.M.] 103.

74 Langham to H. Worrall, 15 March 1887, M.O.M. 295.

75 Langham to Worrall, 30 December 1886, M.O.M. 295; see also Chapman, op. cit., pp. 197-8.

76 Fison to Chapman, 15 July 1878, M.O.M. 104.

77 F. P. Winter, the Attorney-General, who later became MacGregor's Chief Judicial Officer in British New Guinea, MacGregor to Gordon, 1 January 1888, Stanmore Papers.

78 MacGregor, 15 November 1887, on Mitchell to C.O., 16 November 1887, C.O. 83/47/674.

79 Knutsford, 5 June 1888, on Thurston to C.O., 11 April 1888, C.O. 83/48/10515.

80 Thurston to C.O., 30 August 1888, C.O. 83/49/20632.

81 Both cases referred to in Queenslander, 26 March 1887, then explained by Fielding Clarke to C.O., 8 December 1887, C.O. 83/47/24763.

82 Mitchell to C.O., 1 June 1887, C.O. 83/46/14738.

83 MacGregor, 16 and 17 January 1888, on Col. Sec. (Inwards) 88/132.

84 Fiji Times, 19 July 1882.

85 Mary was about eleven years younger than William. Hints of the courtship come from letters, Seed to Gordon, 8 January 1879, vol. 40, 49238; Gordon to Lady Gordon (n.d.) 1879 and 2 July 1882, vol. 27, 49225, Stanmore Papers.

86 See his commendation of the Mechanics Institutes' libraries (the Levuka branch had in 1880 more than 2,000 volumes); although he opened the 1885 Council of Chiefs with an address in Fijian he asked in 1885 for an official letter to be translated lacking the 'time to spell it through', Fiji Times, 19 July 1882; 8 May 1885 on C.S.O. (Inwards) 85/1120.

87 MacGregor, 14 August 1886, on Rev. J. D. Jory to Col. Sec. (Fiji), C.S.O. (Inwards) 86/639.

88 MacGregor to Gordon, 11 April 1882, Stanmore Papers.

89 'In about 40 years the civilisation of the heathen has been completed. In the records of antiquity I know of nothing that can be compared with that . . . amongst the more modern misions. . . . As far as I know, none surpass and very few equal it'. His views help to explain his isolation from his more secular government colleagues and planters: 'we live amongst a people so recently converted to Christianity that we are, to some extent, all preachers. If we take to playing croquet, lawn tennis or whist on Sundays; if we drink ourselves drunk on any day in the week, we wickedly neutralize the work of the Mission to the extent of our several spheres'. MacGregor's 'sermon' at Jubilee meeting, October 1885, Newspaper Cuttings re M.O.M., 1880-6, IV, 124, pp. 78-84.

90 Journal of Rev. Arthur J. Webb, 31 July 1881.

91 They were married by Rev. W. W. Lindsay. Copy of Entry in Register of Marriages, Suva, Fiji.

92 Both born on 28 September; Alpina in 1884 and Mary in 1886 (their mother's age is recorded as 27 on both birth certificates). Copies of Entries in Register of Births, Suva, Fiji.

93 'It is a good indication as to the state of matters here that I have to send them—wife and three children—without a servant of any kind'. MacGregor to Stanmore, 21 June 1887, Stanmore Papers.

94 MacGregor to Gordon, 5 November 1881, Stanmore Papers.

95 Copy of Letters Patent of 1884, Lyon Office, Edinburgh (copied by John MacGregor of London).
96 See MacGregor to Gordon, 7 May 1884 and 22 July 1885, Stanmore Papers.
97 MacGregor to Griffith, 4 March 1887, Griffith Papers.
98 MacGregor to Gordon, 3 February 1887, Stanmore Papers. E. Newton was Colonial Secretary in Mauritius.

CHAPTER 6

1 Morrell, *Britain in the Pacific Islands*, p. 422.
2 Scarr, *Fragments of Empire*, pp. 125-36.
3 MacGregor to Gordon, 21 January 1884, Stanmore Papers.
4 9 October 1884, on des Voeux to C.O., 26 July 1884, C.O. 83/37/15807.
5 Morrell, *op. cit.*, p. 257.
6 A C.O. comment was 'something was necessary to please Queensland'; on Romilly to C.O., 5 January 1887, C.O. 422/3/216; as well Romilly's heavy drinking was suspect (MacGregor referred to his 'ill health . . . the product of his own excesses'), MacGregor to Gordon, 21 January 1886, Stanmore Papers.
7 Morrell, *op. cit.*, p. 404; telegram, 9 January 1886, C.O. to Musgrave, Governor of Queensland, C.O. 808/68; Thurston recollecting his telegram in 1887 said the subsequent appointment of Douglas 'was quite agreeable' to him; Thurston to C.O. 1 October 1887, C.O. 83/47/19857.
8 MacGregor to Gordon, 29 April 1885, Stanmore Papers.
9 MacGregor to Gordon, 21 January 1886, Stanmore Papers.
10 See Minutes on telegram, Thurston to C.O., December 1885, C.O. 83/42/160 and Minutes with Thurston's instructions to MacGregor, 2 January 1886, on Thurston to C.O., 15 January 1886, C.O. 83/43/4357.
11 An attempt, he wrote, to give the Councillors 'the right turn to their view of the future government'; Speech, 3 February 1886, *Federal Council of Australasia Debates*, Hobart Session 1886, pp. 136-7; letter to Gordon, 1 March 1886, Stanmore Papers.
12 MacGregor to Gordon, *ibid.*
13 Stout was New Zealand's Premier whom he had interviewed for Griffith; J. W. Agnew was Tasmania's Premier from 1886-87; Sir John Robertson was Premier of New South Wales from 1885-86; Gordon and Mackellar were, of course, his close friends.
14 MacGregor to Griffith, 28 May 1886, Griffith Papers.
15 MacGregor to Gordon, 5 June 1886, Stanmore Papers.
16 He feared the rivalry of 'men with powerful influence at command', MacGregor to Gordon, 29 August 1886, Stanmore Papers.
17 MacGregor to Griffith, 17 September 1886, Griffith Papers.
18 Berry was Victoria's Agent-General in London. MacGregor to Griffith, 4 March 1887, Griffith Papers; see also MacGregor to Gordon, 3 February 1887, Stanmore Papers.
19 MacGregor to Gordon, 17 July 1887, Stanmore Papers; see also MacGregor to Griffith, 6 July 1887, Griffith Papers.
20 Minutes of Proceedings on 28 April and 6 May at 1887 Colonial Conference, C.O. 422/3/9629.
21 F. Fuller 14 May, H. T. Holland 12 May, R. G. W. Herbert 15 May on Griffith to C.O., 12 May 1887, C.O. 422/3/9257.
22 C.O. to Mitchell for MacGregor, telegram 11 July 1887, C.O. 806/76.
23 Mitchell to C.O., telegram 15 August 1887, C.O. 808/76.
24 Thurston, the Chief Secretary of the Cakobau Government, was replaced by A. Havelock when Gordon arrived, but became Colonial Secretary in 1878. Thurston to C.O., 1 October 1887, C.O. 83/47/19857.
25 MacGregor to Gordon, 1 January 1888, Stanmore Papers.

26 The Attorney-General hoped that MacGregor's new life would give 'scope for the exercise of those bright and manly qualities, that unflagging energy, and varied knowledge which you have hitherto so conspicuously displayed', while Thurston expressed gratification at MacGregor's 'promotion'. *Fiji Times*, 6 June 1888.

27 Thurston to C.O., 7 June 1888, C.O. 83/48/14875.

28 Herbert, 19 June 1888, on Thurston to C.O., 18 June 1888, C.O. 83/48/12059.

29 Musgrave objected to the form of government in 1887, his despatch to C.O., 20 October 1887, C.O. 808/76/24563; see also Musgrave to C.O., despatch 31 March and telegram, 10 April 1888, C.O. 808/76/6959.

30 MacGregor to Gordon, 5 June 1886, Stanmore Papers.

31 Western Australia contributed the small amount of £161 16s 9d each year for ten years. See letters Patent and Instructions, 8 June 1888, *British New Guinea Government Gazette*, 1888.

32 C.O. to MacGregor, 20 June 1888 (also C.O. to Musgrave, 20 June 1888), C.O. 808/76/9449.

33 MacGregor to Gordon, 25 December 1888, Stanmore Papers.

34 Palmer was described as McIlwraith's 'old friend and colleague', J. Anderson, 4 March 1889, on Palmer to C.O., 17 January 1889, C.O. 422/5/4440.

35 Yet in 1883 a C.O. view was that Queensland under supervision could be trusted: 'in dealing with so large a native population, the colony will probably be more careful than it has been at home, for the sake of its own future, to study moderation and prudence, and to listen to any directions which may be given by Her Majesty's Government', W. H. Mercer, 15 May 1883, on Aborigines' Protection Society to C.O., 14 May 1883. C.O. 234/43/8739.

36 MacGregor's attitude was revealed when an ex-Government Agent for Queensland and sub-lieutenant in the Queensland Navy applied for a position in the Fijian police: 'it may be doubted that a man with a Queensland "knowledge of blacks" would be a desirable policeman here', 29 November 1886. W. H. Keays-Young Chapman to Col. Sec. (Fiji), 29 October 1886, C.S.O. (Inwards) 86/2236.

37 D. Dignan, Kanaka Political Struggle, unpublished B.A. thesis, 1949, University of Queensland; J. P. C. Sheppard, The Pacific Islanders in Queensland, 1863-1883, unpublished B.A. (Hons.) thesis, 1966, University of Queensland.

38 Gordon to Gladstone, 20 April 1883, Gladstone Papers 44321; Aborigines' Prot. Soc. to C.O., 14 May 1883, C.O. 234/43/8739, Maclay and Chalmers joint letter to C.O., 1 June 1883, C.O. 234/43/14706.

39 MacGregor 'British New Guinea: Administration' read on 28 February 1895. *Proceedings of the Royal Colonial Institute*, XXVI, 1894-95, pp. 195-6.

40 15 August 1888, *Queensland Parliamentary Debates*, vol. LV, p. 27.

41 The Governor reported 'some desire' by the Queensland Government 'during the past two years', Norman to C.O., 13 August 1894, C.O. 422/9/16864.

42 'British New Guinea: Administration', *op. cit.*, p. 196.

43 MacGregor to Gordon, 25 December 1888, Stanmore Papers.

44 MacGregor to Griffith, 29 August 1888, Griffith Papers.

45 MacGregor to Griffith, 21 December 1888, Griffith Papers.

46 MacGregor to Gordon, 25 December 1888, Stanmore Papers.

47 Norman to C.O., 2 September 1889, and 25 January 1890, C.O. 422/5/20232 and 808/86/4613.

48 See Norman to C.O., 25 January 1890, C.O. 808/86/4612; and MacGregor to Gordon, 20 June 1890, Stanmore Papers.

49 He had also been Governor of Jamaica (1883-88) and on a mission to Egypt; see Sir Henry Wylie Norman (1826-1904) *D.N.B.*

50 R. D. Morehead was Queensland's Premier from 30 November 1888 to 12 August 1890; Lord Augustus Loftus born in 1817, after his ambassadorial career at European capitals was Governor of New South Wales in his sixties from 1879-85; Honorius, Roman Emperor in the West from 395-423 A.D., retired to Ravenna during the invasions of the Goths, who captured Rome in 410, and 'devoted himself to keeping chickens', M. Hadas, *A History of Rome*, London, 1958, p. 180; Louis XVI (1764-93) was 'an acknowledged master' in 'the craft of locksmithing', S. K. Padover, *The Life and Death of Louis XVI*, New York, 1963.

51 See MacGregor to Norman (marked 'private'), 29 October 1889, in Norman to C.O., 26 June 1890, C.O. 422/5/15120.

52 MacGregor to Gordon, 30 October 1889, Stanmore Papers.

53 Ordinance IX of 1889, *British New Guinea Gazette*, 23 November 1889.

54 MacGregor to Gordon, 20 April 1890, Stanmore Papers.

55 *loc. cit.*

56 For these and other examples see MacGregor to Gordon, 5 September and 13 October 1890, 21 May 1891, and 24 March 1892, Stanmore Papers.

57 According to MacGregor, Morehead wanted to obtain a Cabinet decision backing MacGregor against Norman; but MacGregor had persuaded Morehead to leave it as a private matter. MacGregor to Gordon, 13 October 1890, and C.O. comments, 3 July 1890, on Norman to C.O., 21 May 1890, C.O. 422/5/12546.

58 MacGregor to Gordon, 5 September 1890, Stanmore Papers.

59 Lilley, a liberal, who had been in the Queensland parliament from 1860 to 1874 when he resigned to become an acting judge of the Supreme Court, was Chief Justice in 1892, and as such clashed with McIlwraith in 1893. See C. A. Bernays, *Queensland Politics during Sixty Years, 1859-1919*, Brisbane, *c.* 1920, pp. 12-13.

60 MacGregor to Gordon, 24 March 1892, Stanmore Papers.

61 MacGregor to Griffith, 9 November 1893, Griffith Papers.

62 MacGregor to Norman, 22 November 1893, in Norman to C.O., 14 December 1893, C.O. 422/8/1260.

63 MacGregor to Norman, 15 February 1894, on Norman to C.O., 14 April 1894, C.O. 422/9/8281.

64 C.O. Minutes (May 1894), on Norman to C.O., 5 April 1894, C.O. 422/9/8282.

65 MacGregor to Norman, 5 March 1894, *ibid.*

66 MacGregor to Griffith, 16 February 1894, Griffith Papers.

67 25 October 1891, MacGregor's Diary.

68 F. Fuller, 22 June 1894, on Norman (telegram) to C.O., 22 June 1894, C.O. 422/9/10831.

69 Ripon was the Secretary of State for the Colonies from 17 August 1892 to 27 June 1895; MacGregor to Griffith, 2 December 1902, 19 October 1903, 2 December 1904, 2 May 1907, Griffith Papers; see also MacGregor to Gordon, 31 March 1905, Stanmore Papers.

70 W. H. Mercer, 22 January 1894, on Norman to C.O., 14 December 1893, C.O. 422/8/1260.

71 'Your confidential despatch February 10. McGregor agrees as to retaining appointment and goes on leave'. Norman to C.O., telegram, 22 June 1894, C.O. 422/9/10831.

72 F. Fuller hoped the decision had 'not been taken too hastily', 22 June 1894, on Norman to C.O., 22 June 1894, *ibid.*

73 F. Fuller, 14 May 1894, on Norman to C.O., 5 April 1894, C.O. 422/9/8281.

74 F. Fuller and R. Meade Minutes (n.d.), on Norman to C.O., 5 April 1894, *ibid.*

75 MacGregor to Griffith, 16 May 1894, Griffith Papers.

76 Griffith Minute, 30 November 1892, on Norman to C.O., 7 December 1892, C.O. 422/7/851.
77 Conditions prescribed in MacGregor to Norman, 16 May 1894, on Norman to C.O., 22 June 1894, C.O. 422/9/13322 and MacGregor to Griffith, 16 May 1894, Griffith Papers.
78 They were separated for twenty-six months to August 1889, after the family left Fiji in June 1887; Mary was in Australia in May 1891, March 1893 and July 1894, dates from references in letters to Griffith, Gordon and his diary.
79 February 1891, MacGregor's Diary. He had noted earlier: 'this is my only son! But my determination is taken. He can pursue his own path', 26 December 1890, MacGregor's Diary.
80 MacGregor to Griffith, 16 May 1894, Griffith Papers.
81 G. V. Fiddes, 24 January 1893, on Norman to C.O., 13 December 1892, C.O. 422/7/1149.
82 J. Bramston, 2 August 1894, on Norman to C.O., 22 June 1894, C.O. 422/9/13322.
83 Norman to C.O., 3 July 1894, C.O. 422/9/14222.

CHAPTER 7

1 For detailed figures, see *British New Guinea Annual Reports,* 1888-98.
2 F. R. Round, 23 March 1896, on printed statements of revenue and expenditure for 1894-95, forwarded in Palmer to C.O., 31 January 1896, C.O. 422/10/5657.
3 Made up of original cost £12,352; voyage out £1,120; repairs and alterations £960; steam launch £700: a total of £15,132. Figures in C.O. to Treasury, 6 January 1890, C.O. 808/86/22255; Queensland figures differed slightly totalling £15,121 3s 7d, Norman to C.O., 2 November 1891, C.O. 422/6/23967.
4 'The Queensland government would be in too great fear of the white working man'. R. G. W. Herbert, 17 March 1890, on communications between MacGregor and Morehead, in Norman to C.O., 29 January 1890, C.O. 422/5/4863.
5 J. Anderson, 2 October 1889, on MacGregor to C.O., 15 August 1889, C.O. 422/5/19446.
6 F. R. Round, 23 December 1891, on Treasury to C.O., 22 December 1891, C.O. 422/6/24618.
7 G. V. Fiddes, 30 August 1893, on Norman to C.O., 20 July 1893, C.O. 422/8/14738.
8 R. G. W. Herbert, 4 October 1889, on MacGregor to C.O., 15 August 1889, C.O. 422/5/19446.
9 J. Anderson, 14 November 1890, on Norman to C.O., 1 October 1890, C.O. 422/5/22147.
10 On Norman to C.O., 30 October 1891, C.O. 422/6/23504.
11 MacGregor and Griffith, on Norman to C.O., 4 April and 4 November 1892, C.O. 422/7/9778 and 23803. In 1889 (to gain police) and later in 1895 and 1897 (for administrative convenience) amalgamation was also abortively discussed, Scarr, *Fragments of Empire,* pp. 259-62.
12 'The Colonies had hoped that the Imperial Grant-in-Aid of New Guinea would be £100,000, the amount advanced to start the Government of Fiji.' R. G. W. Herbert, 22 March 1889, on Treasury to C.O., 18 March 1889, C.O. 422/5/5663.
13 F. R. Round, 2 April 1890, on Norman to C.O., 28 February 1890, C.O. 422/5/6809.

14 Correspondence in C.O. 422/11-13 analysed in R. B. Joyce, 'The British New Guinea Syndicate Affair', *Journal [Royal] Queensland Historical Society*, V, 1, 1953, pp. 771-93.

15 J. Anderson, 11 August 1898, on Lamington to C.O., telegram, 11 August 1898, C.O. 422/12/18045. A year earlier the same clerk had described its backers as 'a first class list of guinea pigs and company promoters', 17 August 1897, on Lowles to C.O., C.O. 422/11/17772.

16 Theodore Bevan, an explorer and trader, wrote in the Melbourne *Age* on 21 May 1898; Louis Becke, journalist and novelist, in the London *Daily Chronicle* and *Pall Mall Gazette:* C. Kennedy, stockbroker (representing a rival syndicate from Liverpool) exerted pressure in Sydney; Burns Philp was almost certainly opposed; see Vine to C.O., 16 July 1898, C.O. 422/13/16092.

17 For instance, an article denounced the 'Great Papuan Grab', hoping that the Queensland Government would bring pressure on 'the infuriated Scotch understrapper who runs British Papua'. 'Plain English', (Sydney) *Bulletin*, 21 May 1898.

18 Conference of premiers of contributing colonies, Melbourne, 24 January 1898. Sir John Forrest from Western Australia (see Ch. 6, n. 31) was also present, Lamington to C.O., 18 June 1898, C.O. 422/12/16595.

19 'a serious business which we owe . . . chiefly to Mr. B's offended dignity', J. Chamberlain, 25 August 1898, on Lamington to C.O., 23 August 1898, C.O. 422/12/19058.

20 Byrnes had died on 28 September 1898. MacGregor (from Lausanne, Switzerland) to Griffith, 27 December 1898, Griffith Papers.

21 Nelson had told MacGregor at the Melbourne conference of January 1898; 'You are safe for 3 years, and that is something', but this verbal guarantee of continuing government support had been given grudgingly and might well have been renounced without the publicity. In fact, the interregnum period to 1906 was to prove even move frustrating for Papua.

22 MacGregor to Griffith, 9 April 1896, Griffith Papers.

23 Quoted in F. M. Synge, *Albert Maclaren, A Pioneer Missionary in New Guinea*, London, 1908, p. 69.

24 Referring to either of two famous Gallic leaders; see *Oxford Classical Dictionary*. MacGregor to Gordon, 25 December 1888, Stanmore Papers.

25 MacGregor to Gordon, 20 April 1890, Stanmore Papers.

26 MacGregor to Gordon, 5 September 1890, Stanmore Papers.

27 MacGregor's diary, 27 June 1891. The reference (given in letter n. 28) is to a party during Douglas's period led by H. O. Forbes. Minister said he was directed to bring heads for photographing and identifying. MacGregor commented: 'these wonderful instructions . . . kept by Nicolas . . . were kept in suspension over the heads of Douglas and Forbes'.

28 MacGregor to Gordon, 25 December 1888, Stanmore Papers.

29 The following account is taken mainly from his letter to Gordon, *op. cit.* The case is also described in J. P. Thomson, *British New Guinea*, London, 1892, pp. 33-41; despatch MacGregor to C.O., 22 December 1888, in C.O. 422/4/2968; and *Annual Report* for 1888-89, pp. 22-8.

30 L. P. Mair, *Australia in New Guinea*, London, 1948, p. 24 and *passim;* and Lewis Lett, *Sir Hubert Murray of Papua*, Sydney, 1949, p. 125.

31 Morrell, *Britain in the Pacific Islands*, p. 414.

32 'During an attack upon an enemy stronghold Dr. MacGregor, who was a capital marksman, shot one of the enemy in the thigh at a distance of some 600 yards'. He later amputated his victim's leg. R. W. Reid, 'Sir William MacGregor', *op. cit.*, p. 4.

33 In the Fijian war MacGregor had urged that 'mercy should be largely exercised in dealing with the unfortunate opponents of the Government'. MacGregor to Gordon, 16 July 1876, *Story of a Little War*, vol. II, pp. 171-2.

34 Winter argued that 'the question of example should not be considered'.

But MacGregor was supported by the third member of the Executive Council, B. A. Hely, who wanted the execution carried out as an example to others. Executive Council Minutes, 19 January 1889, C.O. 436/1.

35 C.O. opinion backed MacGregor rather than Winter: 'MacGregor's bold proceedings are very remarkable from the fear which he evidently caused among the natives . . . a severe lesson at first may save more lives hereafter—and I hope the influence he has gained among them will not be lost. If he tries and hangs the murderers on the spot it will have a great effect'. J. Bramston, 14 February 1889, on MacGregor to C.O., 22 December 1888, C.O. 422/4/2968.

36 MacGregor to Gordon, 6 February 1889, Stanmore Papers.

37 The three cases were those of Tamana, sentenced to death for the murder of William Bakem (both Hely and Winter supported execution); Viviga for murdering Albert Kickbusch (both Hely and Winter recommended commutation); and Roko for murdering Neil Anderson (Hely for death, Winter for commutation). MacGregor recorded his reasons on 28 January 1891 for disregarding the advice of his Executive Councillors in the case of Viviga. Minutes of Executive Council, meetings of 23 January and 7 February, C.O. 436/1.

38 MacGregor to Gordon, 21 May 1891, Stanmore Papers.

39 In the Executive Council the day before this letter to Griffith he had announced his decision to hang two Papuans, Geberisisila and Guduamere, but to commute six other death sentences. Six of these, including the two executed, were sentenced for murdering George Hunter, a government agent at Rigo. In these cases MacGregor was more merciful than his advisers, (Winter, T. H. Richards and F. E. P. Lawes) who had unanimously recommended executing two of those he spared. Executive Council Minutes, 31 October 1890 and 12 November 1890, C.O. 436/1, and MacGregor to Palmer, 1 November 1890, in Palmer to C.O., 17 December 1890, C.O. 422/5/1838.

40 MacGregor to Griffith, 13 November 1890, Griffith Papers.

41 MacGregor to Gordon, 6 February 1889, Stanmore Papers.

42 The two 'tribes' or villages of Merani and Isimari. This expedition in search of the murderers of Rochefort and James McTier is described in Thomson, *British New Guinea*, pp. 42-7.

43 MacGregor to Gordon, 30 October 1889, Stanmore Papers.

44 MacGregor to Gordon, 14 November 1889, Stanmore Papers.

45 Examples in Mekeo district (Inawaia, Inawabui etc.), see MacGregor's Diary, 8, 10 and 15 September 1891, and despatch, 2 October 1891 to Norman, in Norman to C.O., 25 November 1891, C.O. 422/6/279.

46 MacGregor to Griffith, 5 February 1897, Griffith Papers. Later in 1897 he applied his principles following the murder of one of his officers, J. Green, in the northern Mambare area.

47 Here, as in other places, MacGregor's handwriting is not clear.

48 MacGregor's Diary, 25 March 1892.

49 MacGregor to Gordon, 24 March 1892, Stanmore Papers.

50 MacGregor's Diary, 25 March 1892.

51 Governor Phillip to E. Nepean (Home Department), 12 February 1790, *Historical Records of Australia*, series 1, vol. 1, p. 148.

52 MacGregor to Musgrave, 14 August 1888, on Musgrave to C.O., 27 August 1888, C.O. 808/76.

53 'British New Guinea: Administration', 28 February 1895, *Proceedings of the Royal Colonial Institute, op. cit.*, p. 220.

54 In 1897 he suggested the middle of the Gira River as the German boundary after investigations dating back to 1893, see MacGregor to Griffith, 9 November 1893, Griffith Papers and MacGregor in Lamington to C.O., 21 October 1897, C.O. 422/11/26119. In 1892 MacGregor suggested exchanging 280 square miles (whereby Britain would gain the area bounded

by the Fly River west of 141°). Agreement was reached in 1893 after investigation and a conference, but was not legally ratified until the signing of a Convention between Holland and Britain on 16 May 1895 and a British Order-in-Council on 8 February 1896. F.O. to C.O., 21 May 1895, C.O. 422/10/9238; 4 July 1896, *British New Guinea Government Gazette.*

55 MacGregor to Norman, 23 March 1893, on Norman to C.O., 3 September 1894, C.O. 422/9/18062.

56 MacGregor to Griffith, 29 June 1896, Griffith Papers.

57 Griffith and Douglas (as Resident Commissioner at Thursday Island) in 1893 had made proposals for a new boundary; these, with MacGregor's, are shown on a map in Chief Secretary (Queensland) to Norman, 31 August 1894, on Norman to C.O., 3 September 1894, C.O. 422/9/18062. For fuller discussion, see van der Veur, *Search for New Guinea's Boundaries from Torres Strait to the Pacific,* Canberra [c. 1966], and *Documents and Correspondence on New Guinea's Boundaries,* Canberra, 1966.

58 MacGregor to Gordon, 20 April 1890, Stanmore Papers.

59 See MacGregor's Diary, 5 June 1889; cited in G. Souter, *New Guinea: The Last Unknown,* Sydney, 1963, p. 66. The journey which lasted from 20 April to 25 June is also described in Thomson, *op. cit.,* pp. 88-113.

60 MacGregor to Gordon, 21 May 1891, Stanmore Papers.

61 *loc. cit.*

62 'So far I have done next to nothing. I have barely taken the first step on the road', MacGregor to Gordon, 21 October 1890, Stanmore Papers.

63 MacGregor at Melbourne Conference of Premiers of contributing Australian colonies, 24 January 1898, on Lamington to C.O., 18 June 1898, C.O. 422/12/16595.

64 J. Strachan, *Explorations and Adventures in New Guinea,* London, 1888, pp. 131-4.

65 MacGregor to C.O., 19 March 1890, in Norman to C.O., 15 April 1890, C.O. 422/5/9861.

66 J. Chalmers's Journal, February 1890, L.M.S. records.

67 F. Fuller, 5 December 1891, on Norman to C.O., 27 October 1891, C.O. 422/6/23498.

68 MacGregor to Gordon, 21 May 1891, Stanmore Papers.

69 MacGregor to Norman, 12 October 1891, on Norman to C.O., 27 October 1891, C.O. 422/6/23498.

70 From exchange between M. van Genness, and M. van Dedein, in First Chamber of Dutch parliament. Report by Rumbold in F.O. to C.O., 9 February 1893, C.O. 422/8/2430.

71 Hely's Monthly Report for December 1892, Western Division Reports, and Hely to MacGregor, 28 April 1893, Daru Station Reports, File 7.

72 British New Guinea *Annual Report,* for 1895-96.

73 MacGregor to Lamington, 5 June 1896, in Lamington to C.O., 6 August 1896, C.O. 422/10/19166.

74 J. Chalmers to L.M.S. Board, 27 June 1896, L.M.S. Records, Box 7, Folder 3, Packet C.

75 MacGregor to Lamington, 3 June 1898, in Lamington to C.O., 13 August 1898, C.O. 422/12/21122.

76 MacGregor to Gordon, 20 June 1890, Stanmore Papers.

77 The colonial policy of Ferdinand V and Isabella I of Castile (1474-1504) has other supporters: 'The Hispanization of these islands [the Canaries] was rapid; and it was carried out with the same feeling of equality as between the natives (in this case the *Guanches*) and the Spaniards, and with the same earnest desire for complete mutual understanding culturally and judicially, which . . . was to characterize the normal official conduct of Spaniards in the colonization of the Americas', R. Altamira, *A History of Spain,* New York, 1949, p. 273.

78 MacGregor to Gordon, 21 May 1891, Stanmore Papers.
79 MacGregor to Griffith, 14 July 1904, Griffith Papers.
80 'The New Guinea Company [between 1885 and 1899] established a viable economy but its native policy was incompetent and oppressive', P. Lawrence, *Road Belong Cargo*, Melbourne, 1964, p. 36. A contemporary German wrote that MacGregor's colonial administration was a veritable model, Hans Blum, *Neu Guinea etc.*, Berlin, 1900, p. 41.

CHAPTER 8

1 See Instructions, Clause XII. Other exceptions were listed: material prejudice if consulted, if too unimportant or too urgent (Clause X). The Administrator had a casting vote in the Legislative Council (Clause XIX). 8 June 1888, *Instructions*.
2 This vote by W. H. Gors, the local manager of Burns Philp, was on 12 September 1898 after MacGregor had left New Guinea. Minutes of the Legislative Council 1888-1909, C.O. 436/2.
3 R. B. Joyce (ed), A.C.V. Melbourne, *Early Constitutional Development in Australia 1788-1856*, St Lucia, 1963, pp. 128ff.
4 MacGregor to Gordon, 29 April 1885, Stanmore Papers.
5 *ibid.*, 20 April 1890.
6 Details of changes in boundaries are given in *British New Guinea Government Gazettes*.
7 B. Hely's 1889-90 Annual Report, Hely to Gov. Sec., 8 August 1890, Eastern Division Reports.
8 Hely's Journal, 25 August 1893, Daru Station Reports.
9 A typical day's entry is that of Thursday 3 June 1897, Central Division Reports.
10 A visit to Goruoni and Galirupu inland of Galoma, Lawes' Monthly Report for July 1892, *ibid.*
11 A. M. Campbell's Journal, 17 October 1897, South-Eastern Division Reports.
12 'The difficulty is that the natives fight, and fight well, and I have no force to oppose to them except my staff and such odd officers as I can scratch together', MacGregor to Griffith, 21 December 1888, Griffith Papers.
13 MacGregor to Gordon, 20 June 1890.
14 MacGregor to Palmer, 7 December 1895, on Palmer to C.O., 20 January 1896, C.O. 422/10/4527. For appointments generally see *British New Guinea Government Gazettes*.
15 MacGregor Minute (while in England), November 1894, on Norman to C.O., 28 September 1894, C.O. 422/9/19306.
16 See particularly C.O. Minutes on Mrs Glubb (mother of G. Wriford, Commandant of Police in B.N.G.) to C.O., 12 February 1892, C.O. 422/7/2944.
17 W. L. Allardyce was 'clerk and interpreter' in the Fijian colonial service in the 1880s; E. O. B. Heffernan a stipendiary magistrate also in Fiji. 'Woodruff' is not named under Seychelles in *C.O. List* for 1873-75; MacGregor to Gordon, 18 January 1889, Stanmore Papers.
18 *ibid.*, 18 January 1889.
19 J. Meredith, a master mariner and first officer of the *Merrie England*, acted as magistrate in the Eastern Division. He had served the Fijian government for six years. MacGregor to C.O., 24 December 1893, C.O. 422/8/4280. A. M. Campbell was appointed in 1896 as magistrate for the S.E. Division. Aged over thirty he had some years experience in the Fijian

customs department, then in Tonga. Lamington to C.O., 27 May 1896, C.O. 422/10/14224.

20 MacGregor memo, 14 August 1888, in Musgrave to C.O., 27 August 1888, C.O. 808/76.

21 MacGregor to Gordon, 20 June 1890, Stanmore Papers.

22 'Lord Knutsford half promises a C.M.G. to Winter in a private note', MacGregor's Diary, 6 August 1891.

23 MacGregor to Gordon, 24 March 1892, Stanmore Papers.

24 J. B. Thurston, 15 February 1887, in Mitchell to C.O., 16 February 1887, C.O. 83/45/6424.

25 Archbishop of York to C.O., 29 November 1887, C.O. 83/47/24350.

26 *Sarasara* is a Fijian verb meaning 'to see' or 'to survey'; MacGregor to Gordon, 6 February 1889, Stanmore Papers.

27 MacGregor claimed that Hely and Campbell took a month to do three days work in building part of a prison at Samarai, Diary, 9 December 1890; Campbell's defence was that he 'cut down one tree only and that the houses he burned were only garden houses', MacGregor's Diary, 11 June 1891.

28 MacGregor to Palmer, 7 December 1895, on Palmer to C.O., 20 January 1896, C.O. 422/10/4527.

29 MacGregor to Gordon, 18 January 1889, Stanmore Papers.

30 *ibid.*, 20 June 1890; Musgrave wrote in 1890: 'most of the bad characteristics of a savage are found in the Papuan. They are cowardly, selfish, thievish, untruthful, treacherous, grasping, bloodthirsty, and morbidly superstitious'. *British New Guinea. An Abstract of Statistical Notes, Etc. Prepared for the Use of Publishers of Almanacs, Directories etc. for the year 1891*, Brisbane, 1890. MacGregor to Norman, 25 May 1892, in Norman to C.O., 16 June 1892, C.O. 422/7/15010.

31 MacGregor's Diary, 23 February 1891.

32 MacGregor's support was charitable, for Musgrave, an alcoholic, 'was in bad health, and . . . never was able to perform his work'. He had left his family in Sydney and lived with the MacGregors from December 1909 to about June 1911. MacGregor to Lady Musgrave, 17 February 1912, Musgrave Papers; see also MacGregor to Prime Minister A. Fisher, 2 September 1911, Dept of External Affairs, 11/18058 (an attempt to gain Commonwealth aid for Musgrave); and Mary MacGregor to Lady Musgrave, 10[?] and 16 June 1912, Musgrave Papers.

33 MacGregor to Gordon, 18 January 1889, Stanmore Papers.

34 MacGregor to Griffith, 13 November 1890, Griffith Papers.

35 MacGregor's Diary, 11 January 1891.

36 MacGregor to Gordon, 18 January 1889, Stanmore Papers.

37 Hely's Journal, 7 April 1893, Western Division Reports.

38 Hely's Journal, 22 April 1893, *ibid.*

39 Hely's Journal, 7 December 1892, *ibid.*

40 Edelfelt, primarily a commercial agent of Burns Philp, worked for the Protectorate from 1886. He was moved during 1886 from Motu Motu to Port Moresby and then to Samarai. MacGregor to C.O., 18 October 1888, C.O. 422/4/1055.

41 MacGregor to Gordon, 18 January 1889, Stanmore Papers.

42 MacGregor to Norman, 25 July 1889, C.O. 808/86/18340.

43 MacGregor to Gordon, 18 January 1889, Stanmore Papers.

44 MacGregor to Norman, 25 July 1889, C.O. 808/86/18340.

45 MacGregor to Gordon, 20 June 1890, Stanmore Papers.

46 *ibid.*, 18 January and 14 November 1889.

47 28 February 1895, 'British New Guinea: Administration' *Proceedings of the Royal Colonial Institute, op cit.*, p. 226. Lawes died from an 'internal ailment' in August 1894. MacGregor to Norman, 20 August 1894, in Norman to C.O., 21 August 1894, C.O. 422/9/17201. MacGregor recorded in 1891

that Lawes was back 'but I should judge from the way his hand shakes that he has had a good "burst" in Cooktown'. MacGregor's Diary, 27 February 1891.

48 MacGregor employed Denis Gleeson as head gaoler from 5 September 1888 until his suicide on 26 July 1893. The prisoners played an important part in MacGregor's aim 'to raise and educate' Papuans, see below p. 195. MacGregor to Norman, 9 November 1893, on Norman to C.O., 13 December, 1893, C.O. 422/8/1256.

49 MacGregor to Griffith, 5 February 1897, Griffith Papers.

50 Kowald's English spelling was not always accurate, Kowald to Mac-Gregor, 31 March 1891, Mekeo Station Reports.

51 Kowald's Monthly Report, 30 April 1891, ibid.

52 MacGregor note, 24 November 1893, on Kowald's Monthly Report, 31 July, and also 31 May 1893, ibid.

53 Kowald's Journal, 15 November 1893, ibid.

54 Priests of the Roman Catholic Church. The Sacred Heart Mission (Notre Dame du Sacré-Coeur) had its headquarters on Yule Island in the Mekeo district.

55 Kowald's Journal, 31 July 1895, Mekeo Station Reports.

56 Kowald's Monthly Report, 31 March 1893, ibid.

57 Several returns have survived for various districts; see Station Reports.

58 MacGregor, 3 May 1892, on Kowald to MacGregor, 20 February 1892, Mekeo Station Reports.

59 Kowald to Musgrave, 18 October 1893, ibid.

60 Kowald to MacGregor, 15 March 1895, ibid.

61 MacGregor to Norman, 10 October 1895, on Palmer to C.O., 13 December 1895, C.O. 422/10/1997.

62 MacGregor to Griffith, 26 April 1897, Griffith Papers.

63 M. H. Moreton, however, served beyond MacGregor's term of office, notably as Resident Magistrate of the Eastern Division (1895-1902); although A. C. English was 'illiterate . . . utterly uneducated' MacGregor had recruited him in 1889 because he had 'the tact and patience for native work', MacGregor to Gordon, 18 January 1889, Stanmore Papers.

64 MacGregor to Griffith, 29 March 1897, Griffith Papers.

65 MacGregor to Griffith, 26 April 1897, Griffith Papers. Butterworth's manners also disconcerted MacGregor; as his dinner guest Butterworth proved 'rather boisterous' in the presence of Mrs MacGregor, even exclaiming 'upon my soul'. MacGregor's Diary, 5 May 1892.

66 MacGregor's Diary, 24 December 1890; MacGregor to Gordon, 20 June 1890, Stanmore Papers; MacGregor's Diary, 11 June 1891.

67 MacGregor to Griffith, 31 March 1893, Griffith Papers; earlier MacGregor had reported Hatton-Richards getting 'fever about twice a week', MacGregor to Gordon, 20 April 1890, Stanmore Papers.

68 Transactions of the Royal Geographical Society of Australasia, part II, vol. VIII, March 1891, p. 45.

69 C. A. W. Monckton, Some Experiences of a Resident Magistrate, p.9.

70 J. T. Arundel in discussion on T. H. Hatton-Richards' paper 'British New Guinea', Proceedings of the Royal Colonial Institute, XXIV, 1892-93, p. 310.

71 MacGregor to Gordon, 6 February 1889, Stanmore Papers.

72 ibid., 20 June 1890.

73 Report on Protectorate, 1884-85, G. S. Fort (private secretary to Scratchley) to Governor Loch (of Victoria), 12 April 1886, in Loch to C.O., 14 April 1886, C.O. 808/68.

74 MacGregor to Gordon, 25 December 1888, Stanmore Papers.

75 A. Gordon, Records of Private and Public Life 1875-80, Edinburgh 1897-1910, III, p. 220.

76 Report on Protectorate, 2 December 1885 to 31 December 1886, J. Douglas to C.O., 16 January 1887, C.O. 808/70.

77 Fairfax to Admiralty, 1 January 1888, in Admiralty to C.O., 11 February 1888, C.O. 422/4/3098. After British New Guinea became a Crown Colony Fairfax doubted 'whether the Western Pacific Act can apply in any way . . . or whether any act of war on the part of Her Majesty's ships, excepting only so far as necessary to protect life and property would be legally permitted'. Winter considered that naval officers could act in certain cases on their responsibility in the colony. Winter's memo, 29 June 1889, on Fairfax to MacGregor, 27 April 1889, External Territories, Records of Administration, Correspondence Bundle 6, Section 2, 1889, Letter 4.

78 F. Fuller, 15 February 1888, on Fairfax to Admiralty, 1 January 1888, *op. cit.*

79 MacGregor to Norman, 20 May 1890, on Norman to C.O., 20 June 1890, C.O. 422/5/14777.

80 MacGregor to Gordon, 14 November 1889, Stanmore Papers.

81 G. Wriford, who had police experience in Africa, stayed in charge for almost two years (1 October 1890-31 August 1892). MacGregor, however, was 'not at all satisfied with Wriford's work' (Diary, 28 September 1891) giving one specific example at Koiari: 'all the natives fled from them and seemed to be very suspicious and in great terror of the police, looking after their pigs and clearing out of the villages. I suggest that Mr Wriford's visit there did a great deal of harm last time'. (Diary, 8 June 1892). Wriford resigned because of illness. Mrs Glubb (his mother) to C.O., 12 February, 18 October and 14 November 1892. C.O. 422/7/2944, 20649, 22219.

82 MacGregor to Thurston, 20 May 1890, enclosed with Thurston to C.O., 25 August 1890, C.O. 808/86/20159.

83 Thurston to MacGregor, 5 August 1890, External Territories, Records of Administration, Correspondence Bundle 6, Section 4, 1890, Letter 9.

84 Ordinance I of 1890; Griffith, 6 October 1890, with Norman to C.O., 8 October 1890, C.O. 808/86/22335.

85 J. Anderson, 2 August 1890, on Norman to C.O., 20 June 1890, C.O. 422/5/14777.

86 The regular pay, usually in trade, was another inducement; Constables began at 10s a month rising to £1 (£6 to £12 a year), sergeants from £1 10s to £1 13s 4d (£18 to £20 a year). British New Guinea, *Annual Report*, 1897-98, p. 44.

87 Section 20, Ordinance I of 1890.

88 MacGregor to Armit, 16 June 1894, Cloudy Bay Reports.

89 23 December 1893, on Moreton's Report of 22 December 1893, *ibid.*

90 Moreton made arrests at Aru on 4 December, and went on to Vea on 5 December, 5 December 1893, *ibid.*

91 For instance see reference to three Papuans (of Maipua and Orokolo) who ran away, in Butterworth's Journal, 23 June 1895, Native Constabulary Papers.

92 Minute, Hatton-Richards, 29 April 1892, *ibid.*

93 Patrol in Cloudy Bay area after a Papuan attack on Magaubo village, Armit to Gov. Sec., 3 July 1894, Cloudy Bay Reports.

94 On T. Anderson to W. H. Gors, 8 July 1894, *ibid.*

95 20 December 1892, both on Wriford to Gov. Sec., 18 December 1892, Native Constabulary Papers.

96 Evidence of Doni, Minutes of Inquiry by Monckton re Charges of Misconduct of constabulary at Goodenough Island in November 1897, 2 January 1898, *ibid.*

97 Circular, 20 October 1902, signed A. Musgrave, reading 'Sir William MacGregor laid it down . . .', External Territories Miscellaneous Correspondence, Unofficial Correspondence, 12.

98 British New Guinea, *Annual Report*, 1897-98, p. 44.

99 MacGregor to Norman, 2 November 1892, in Norman to C.O., 27 January 1893, C.O. 422/8/3633.

100 Kowald to MacGregor, 31 March 1891, Mekeo Station Reports.

101 Some were paid more, £2 or £3 to more important chiefs. Thus Mainopanau of Veifa as 'Head Chief Mekeo District' was paid £3 in 1898. Monthly Return to 30 June, Village Constables, Mekeo Station Reports.

102 Native Regulation 1/1892, *British New Guinea Government Gazette*, 31 December 1892.

103 British New Guinea, *Annual Report*, 1897-98, p. 45.

104 Regulation 1/1895, explained in Winter to Norman, 13 December 1894, in Norman to C.O., 9 May 1895, C.O. 422/10/10543.

105 'British New Guinea; Administration'; 28 February 1895, *Proceedings of the Royal Colonial Institute, op. cit.,* p. 222.

106 L. Mair, *Native Policies in Africa,* London, 1936, p. 15. J. Legge, *Australian Colonial Policy,* Sydney, 1956, pp. 73-4. J. Legge, *Britain in Fiji,* London, 1958, pp. 166-8.

107 MacGregor to Norman, 31 August 1889, in Norman to C.O., 23 September 1889, C.O. 808/86/21676.

108 MacGregor gives an outline history citing Verguet's *Histoire de la Premiere Mission Catholique au Vicariat de Mélanésie,* in MacGregor to Norman, 16 September 1890, in Norman to C.O., 30 September 1890, C.O. 808/86/22146.

109 Chalmers' 1884 Report to London Sec. L.M.S.

110 Lawes to London Sec. L.M.S., 20 November 1886, L.M.S. Correspondence.

111 He was referring to both English missionaries and South Sea Island teachers. *ibid.,* 5 April 1886, L.M.S. Correspondence.

112 MacGregor to Gordon, 20 April 1890, Stanmore Papers

113 MacGregor to Griffith, 21 December 1888, Griffith Papers.

114 MacGregor's Preface to Synge, *op. cit.,* p. xiii.

115 MacGregor to Gordon, 25 December 1888, Stanmore Papers; and MacGregor to Griffith, 21 December 1888, Griffith Papers.

116 MacGregor to Gordon, 18 January 1889, Stanmore Papers.

117 MacGregor to London Sec. L.M.S., 25 August 1889, L.M.S. Correspondence.

118 MacGregor to Gordon, 6 February 1889, Stanmore Papers.

119 MacGregor's Minute, n.d., on Hely's Journal, 5 October 1893, Western Division Reports.

120 Hely to Gov. Sec., 25 February 1894, Western Division Reports.

121 Butterworth's Journal, 7 and 10 March 1895, Native Constabulary Papers.

122 MacGregor, 11 August 1895, on Butterworth's Special Report for 2-10 August 1895, Native Constabulary Papers.

123 Another issue was the relative powers of governor and government of Queensland. Musgrave had not consulted his government when he gave his approval.

124 MacGregor to Griffith, 21 December 1888, Griffith Papers.

125 *ibid.,* 19 March 1889.

126 Ordinance VI of 1888 applied Queensland rates of custom duties; these were lowered by Ordinances VIII of 1888 and III of 1889. For MacGregor's further efforts to aid missionaries see MacGregor to Norman, 3 October 1890 on Norman to C.O., 16 October 1890, C.O. 808/86/22912.

127 An industrial settlement was established at Matadona (see below p. 179), R. Wardlaw Thompson to MacGregor, 25 May 1897. External Territories, Correspondence 1897, Mission, Bundle 6, File 15.

128 Statistics from British New Guinea, *Annual Report,* 1897-98, pp. 48-50.

129 The Roman Catholics were not at this meeting despite later suggestions (e.g. by MacGregor in his Introduction to Synge, *op. cit.,* p. xii). See Lawes'

letter written on the day of the conference, 17 June 1890, W. G. Lawes to London Sec. L.M.S., L.M.S. Correspondence.

130 Bishop de Boismenu to Deakin, 13 March 1908, Yule Island Mission Records.

131 'A man that has either no weakness, no defect, or is the most cunning man I have ever met in concealing it. . . . Dr. Brown is the most limpid, the most pellucid man of my acquaintance', MacGregor to C. B. Fletcher, n.d. [c. 1917] cited as motto to C. B. Fletcher, *The Black Knight of the Pacific*, Sydney, 1944, Foreword and p. 94.

132 MacGregor's Preface to Synge, *op. cit.*, p. ix.

133 MacGregor to Gordon, 20 June 1890, Stanmore Papers.

134 MacGregor to Gordon, 5 September 1890, Stanmore Papers.

135 André Dupeyrat, *Papousie, Histoire de la Mission*, Paris, 1935.

136 MacGregor's Diary, 21 and 13 June 1891.

137 Statistics from British New Guinea, *Annual Report*, 1897-98, p. 52. MacGregor told George Brown during a visit to Dobu in July 1897 of the 'entirely different appearance and expression' of the local people. Rev. W. E. Bromilow, *Twenty Years Among Primitive Papuans*, pp. 222-4.

138 Cited in Synge, *op. cit.*, p. 163.

139 MacGregor to Bishop of Melbourne, n.d. [1897] and also draft, 26 April 1897, External Territories, Mission Correspondence, Correspondence Bundle No. 6, File 15.

140 MacGregor to Norman, 25 March 1890, in Norman to C.O., 21 June 1890, C.O. 422/5/15117.

141 MacGregor's Introduction to Synge, *op. cit.*, p. xiii.

142 MacGregor's Diary, 8 September 1891.

143 M. André Navarre, *Notes et Journal*, 7 February 1889, typed copy S.H. Mission records, pp. 16-18.

144 *op. cit.*, pp. 39-40.

145 Quoted in André Dupeyrat, *op. cit.*, p. 196.

146 Navarre, *op. cit.*, p. 127.

147 MacGregor to Griffith, 21 December 1893, Griffith Papers.

148 MacGregor to Navarre, 3 February 1897, External Territories, Mission Correspondence, Correspondence Bundle No. 6, File 15.

149 For example, in 1896 as an L.M.S. site at Vanamai was vacant, land there was granted to the S.H.M., 6 November 1896, *Minutes of Executive Council*, C.O. 436/1; H.M. Dauncey to London Sec. L.M.S., 8 and 14 May 1896, L.M.S. Records.

150 MacGregor to Lamington, 13 July 1896, on Lamington to C.O., 7 October 1896, C.O. 422/10/23769.

151 Vaughan to C.O., 18 December 1896, C.O. 422/10/25985; MacGregor to Lamington, 20 July 1897, on Lamington to C.O., 28 September 1897, C.O. 422/11/24123.

152 MacGregor to Bridge, 12 July and 13 September 1897, draft copies, External Territories, Miscellaneous Correspondence, Correspondence Bundle 6, File 14.

153 He also feared that Mohammedanism might reach the colony, *Proceedings of the Royal Colonial Institute*, XXX, 1898-99, p. 248.

154 From letter quoted in *Brisbane Church Chronicle*, December 1898.

155 Dupeyrat, *op. cit.*, p. 256.

156 Statistics from British New Guinea, *Annual Report*, 1897-98, pp. 48-56, and Synge, *op. cit.*, Appendix II.

157 MacGregor, 14 July 1898, in Dogura Mission Log Book, 26 May 1898-30 September 1900.

158 MacGregor approved the planning of Lawes' training college at Vatorata: 'It is well built, is imposing, and will be healthy and comfortable'. MacGregor to London Sec. L.M.S., 18 July 1895, L.M.S. Records.

159 Revs C. H. Abel and F. W. Walker planned this scheme which had

MacGregor's 'hearty approbation'. After disputes about the compatability of his scheme with mission work Walker left the L.M.S. on 30 June 1896 but continued training Papuans to avoid 'the idleness of heathenism', Walker to London Sec. L.M.S., 13 July 1896, L.M.S. Records.

160 MacGregor to Thompson, 16 July 1897, External Territories, Correspondence 1897, Missions, Bundle 6, File 15.

161 MacGregor gave support to the use of 'police Motu' and 'pidgin English' as unifying languages. J. Anderson, 17 November 1897; Earl of Selborne, 1 January 1898; and J. Chamberlain, 4 January 1898, on Lamington to C.O., 24 September 1897, C.O. 422/11/24113.

CHAPTER 9

1 *Federal Council of Australasia Debates*, p. 139.

2 MacGregor to Norman, 23 March 1893, on Norman to C.O., 3 September 1894, C.O. 422/9/18062.

3 *Annual Report, British New Guinea*, 1893-94, p. 65.

4 It is remotely conceivable that MacGregor could have endeavoured to introduce British ideas into Papuan society and so have ruled through unwritten principles, resembling the conventions of common law. MacGregor, however, preferred to rule with the assistance of written regulations.

5 C.O. to MacGregor, 20 June 1888, C.O. 808/76/9449.

6 Musgrave to MacGregor, 16 August 1888, on Musgrave to C.O., 27 August 1888, C.O. 808/76/19437.

7 MacGregor to Musgrave, 14 August 1888, *loc. cit.*

8 Palmer to C.O., 26 February 1891, C.O. 422/6/7129.

9 Ordinance IX of 1889, *British New Guinea Government Gazette*, 23 November 1889.

10 Regulation IX of 1890, and Regulation I of 1893, *British New Guinea Government Gazette*, 15 November 1890 and 16 December 1893.

11 MacGregor to Griffith, 19 March 1889, Griffith Papers.

12 MacGregor to C.O., 12 January 1889, C.O. 808/76/5930.

13 MacGregor to Norman, 31 August 1889, on Norman to C.O., 23 September 1889, C.O. 808/86/21676.

14 The arresting and charging of over forty Papuans each year was no mean achievement, considering the shortage of staff and finance, although the numbers were low in proportion to the total number of killings in the controlled areas. For analyses of criminal cases based on figures in *Annual Reports* see R. B. Joyce, The Administration of British New Guinea 1888-1902, unpublished Cambridge M.Litt. thesis 1953, Appendixes, pp. xxxi-xxxvi.

15 MacGregor to Palmer, 13 December 1890, on Palmer to C.O., 13 January 1891, C.O. 422/6/3893.

16 See Ch. 7 above; MacGregor's Minute, 28 January 1891, on Executive Council Minutes of 23 January, C.O. 436/1.

17 Regulation IV of 1891, *British New Guinea Government Gazette*, 25 August 1891; both in Fiji and the Seychelles adultery was punishable; see his note urging its enforcement, 5 May 1892, on Lawes' Journal, 31 March 1892, Port Moresby Station Reports; Hely, in the Western Division, also emphasized that adultery was punishable by imprisonment, Journal, 6 April 1893, Daru Station Reports; see also Minutes on Norman to C.O., 3 December 1891, C.O. 422/6/612.

18 Regulation II of 1893, *British New Guinea Government Gazette*, 16 December 1893; MacGregor referred to English laws, 9 Geo. II, c. 5, Geo. IV, c. 83, and 24-5 Vict., c. 96; Fijian to suppress the 'Diau ni Kau'; and West

Indies measures against the 'Obeah' man, MacGregor to Norman, 11 May 1891, on Norman to C.O., 30 January 1894, C.O. 422/9/4282.

[19] For criticism see R. Fortune, *Sorcerers of Dobu*, London, 1932, Appendix.

[20] A Milne Bay case was reported by F. W. Walker to London Sec. L.M.S., Report for 1893, L.M.S. Records; and a Saguane case, worship of Kina (the great snake idol), by Chalmers to London Sec. L.M.S., Annual Report for 1896, L.M.S. Records. See recent interpretative studies, P. Lawrence, *Road Belong Cargo*, Melbourne, 1964; K.O.L. Burridge, *Mambu (A Melanesian Millenium)*, London, 1960; and P. M. Worsley, *The Trumpet Shall Sound (A Study of 'Cargo' Cults in Melanesia)*, London, 1957.

[21] For a critical appraisal of the so-called 'Shepstone policy' introduced in Natal in the 1840s whereby the Zulus were to be protected on their Reserves and separated from Europeans, see E. H. Brookes and N. Hurwitz, *The Native Reserves of Natal*, Cape Town, 1957, Ch. 1.

[22] MacGregor to Lamington, 9 July 1897, on Lamington to C.O., 25 September 1897; C.O. Minutes by C. A. Harris, 25 November; J. Anderson, 1 December 1897; J. Chamberlain, 18 January 1898; and draft reply, C.O. 422/11/24114.

[23] Regulation I of 1894, *British New Guinea Government Gazette*, 17 February 1894; MacGregor to Norman, 25 November 1893, in Norman to C.O., 26 March 1894, C.O. 422/9/7848.

[24] Regulation III of 1895, *British New Guinea Government Gazette*, 20 November 1895.

[25] Regulation I of 1897, *ibid.*, 3 February 1897.

[26] Regulation XIII of 1890, British New Guinea, *Annual Report* 1891-92, pp. 22-3; MacGregor to Norman, 18 April 1890, in Norman to C.O., 15 July 1890, C.O. 422/5/16729.

[27] MacGregor's Diary, 8 June 1891.

[28] Some Notes on Disease in British New Guinea:, Inter-colonial Medical Congress of Australasia, 2nd Session 1889, pp. 46-8.

[29] 'Sanitary' section, 'British New Guinea: Administration', 28 February 1895, *Proceedings of the Royal Colonial Institute, op. cit.*, pp. 204-11.

[30] In fairness to MacGregor note that in a later review of sanitary problems he listed as safeguards against fever 'total abstinence and the never-failing use of a muslin mosquito net at night'. British New Guinea, *Annual Report*, 1897-98, p. 59.

[31] 'Sanitary' section, 'British New Guinea: Administration', 28 February 1895, *Proceedings of the Royal Colonial Institute, op. cit.*, pp. 204-11.

[32] Campbell's Journal, 3 January 1898, South Eastern Division Reports.

[33] Blayney's Journal, 19 and 20 December 1897, Port Moresby Station Reports.

[34] Ordinances No. X, of 1898, 'For the Better Preservation of the Health of the Public'—providing for vaccination and that infected districts could be declared, and No. XI of 1898, 'To provide for Public Hospitals'. *British New Guinea Government Gazette*, 10 September 1898.

[35] J. Anderson, 28 December, and H. B. Lucas, 29 December, on Lamington to C.O., 31 October 1898, C.O. 422/12/29143.

[36] Ordinance V of 1889, amended by Ordinance VI of 1890, *British New Guinea Government Gazette*, 28 September 1889 and 15 November 1890. After an address by MacGregor, Gordon commented that he had been trying to persuade the British Colonial Office that 'in a certain type of civilisation' people had different attitudes to prisons and punishment; *Proceedings of the Royal Colonial Institute*, XXX, 1898-99, p. 256.

[37] Prison Rules, Schedule B, Ordinance V, 1889.

[38] British New Guinea, *Annual Report*, 1897-98, p. 47.

[39] MacGregor to Lamington, 12 September 1897, in Lamington to C.O., 28 October 1897, C.O. 422/11/26120.

40 British New Guinea, *Annual Report*, 1897-98, p. 47.

41 C.O. to MacGregor, 20 June 1888, C.O. 808/76/9449.

42 Correspondence presented to 1883 Intercolonial Convention, Sydney, *British Parliamentary Papers*, 1884, vol. LV, pp. 487-713.

43 Suggestion in either *Colonies and India* or the *European Mail*, Mac-Gregor to Gordon, 21 October 1890, Stanmore Papers.

44 British New Guinea, *Annual Report*, 1888-89, p. 40.

45 MacGregor to Griffith, 11 March 1891, Griffith Papers.

46 Regulation II of 1894, *British New Guinea Government Gazette*, 17 February 1894.

47 MacGregor to Norman, 25 November 1893, in Norman to C.O., 26 March 1894, C.O. 422/9/7848.

48 MacGregor's three despatches, in Norman to C.O., 3 November 1891, C.O. 422/6/23968; Kew Gardens to C.O., 6 April and 31 December 1891, C.O. 422/6/7009 and 44. An 1895 law protected 'all plants from the sap of which india-rubber or guttapercha can be made', Regulation IV of 1895, *British New Guinea Government Gazette*, 20 November 1895.

49 Regulation VII of 1892, *British New Guinea Government Gazette*, 29 September 1892.

50 British New Guinea *Annual Reports* give production figures. For coal prospects see MacGregor's, 'British New Guinea: Administration', 28 February 1895, *Proceedings of the Royal Colonial Institute, op. cit.*, p. 202.

51 T. Bevan, *Toil, Travel and Discovery in British New Guinea*, London, 1890, p. 147.

52 See above, Ch. 6, p. 108.

53 In 1892 MacGregor supported the District Committee of the London Missionary Society when it passed a resolution condemning any revival of the labour traffic. MacGregor to C.O., 27 September 1892, C.O. 422/7/22924; the C.O. recognized MacGregor's role, see W. H. Mercer, 6 February 1895, on Norman to C.O., 13 August 1894, C.O. 422/9/16864; and in 1898 when Byrnes, the Premier of Queensland, was reported as 'going round abusing the Imperial Government to his planter friends, and would no doubt wish to be able to offer them cheap "niggers" from New Guinea'. J. Anderson, 4 August 1898, Minute on Lamington to C.O., 21 June 1898, C.O. 422/12/17291.

54 MacGregor to Griffith, 11 March 1891, Griffith Papers.

55 Ordinance II of 1892, ss. 23-4, *British New Guinea Government Gazette*, 4 June 1892.

56 Griffith's suggestions, and Norman's opposition, are in Norman to C.O., 4 April 1892, C.O. 422/7/9778. MacGregor revived the plan for the Solomons in a six-page despatch to Norman, 22 August 1894, in Norman to C.O., 27 August 1894, C.O. 422/9/17807.

57 See above, Ch. 7, p. 137.

58 Ordinance II of 1892, s. 25, *British New Guinea Government Gazette*, 4 June 1892.

59 Ordinance III of 1893, *op. cit.*, 16 December 1893.

60 Ordinance II of 1898, *op. cit.*, 13 August 1898.

61 Ordinance III of 1888, *op. cit.*, 12 September 1888.

62 British New Guinea, *Annual Report*, 1888-89, p. 13.

63 Proclamations under Natives Removal Prohibition Ordinance III of 1888, *British New Guinea Government Gazette*, 22 March 1889.

64 Ordinances III of 1891; IV of 1894 and IV of 1897, *British New Guinea Government Gazette*, 28 February 1891, 1 September 1894 and 28 January 1897.

65 MacGregor to Norman, 2 November 1891, in Norman to C.O., 14 June 1892, C.O. 422/7/15007.

66 Ordinance II of 1892, *British New Guinea Government Gazette*, 4 June 1892.

67 Mair, *Australia in New Guinea*, p. 112.

68 MacGregor to Norman, 23 March 1893, on Norman to C.O., 3 September 1894, C.O. 422/9/18062.

69 Ordinance II of 1893, *British New Guinea Government Gazette*, 16 December 1893; MacGregor to Norman, 20 April 1893, on Norman to C.O., 1 February 1894; C.O. memo by J. Anderson, 19 March 1894, C.O. 422/9/4284.

70 Ordinance III of 1893, *British New Guinea Government Gazette*, 16 December 1893.

71 Ordinance II of 1897, *op. cit.*, 28 January 1897.

72 Ordinance VIII of 1897, *op. cit.*, 23 November 1897.

73 British New Guinea, *Annual Report*, 1897-98, p. 11.

74 *op. cit.*, p. 78.

75 Sent to the press by the Colonial Office, MacGregor to Lamington, 18 January 1897, in Lamington to C.O., 26 February 1897, C.O. 422/11/7118.

76 British New Guinea, *Annual Report*, 1888-89, MacGregor re Sudest (p. 18); Hely re Saganai (p. 56).

77 See MacGregor to Lamington, [28 July] 1896, in Lamington to C.O., 14 October 1896, C.O. 422/10/24027.

78 British New Guinea, *Annual Report*, 1895-96, p. 21.

79 This particular reference to the Yodda field in 1900 is applicable to these northern gold-fields generally British New Guinea, *Annual Report*, 1900-1, p. XXX.

80 British New Guinea, *Annual Report*, 1896-97, p. 20.

81 MacGregor to Lamington, 28 April 1897, on Lamington to C.O., 14 May 1897, C.O. 422/11/13287.

82 See above Ch. 7, pp. 123-6.

83 Case of A. H. Kissack cited in W. D. Pitcairn, *Two Years Among the Savages of New Guinea*, London, 1891, p. 232; 27 February 1891, Minutes of Executive Council, C.O. 436/1.

84 Ordinance II of 1888, *British New Guinea Government Gazette*, 12 September 1888.

85 Ordinance VIII of 1889, *op. cit.*, 23 November 1889.

86 Ordinance XI of 1889, *loc. cit.*

87 Ordinance X of 1889, *loc. cit.*

88 Ordinance VII of 1890, *op. cit.*, 15 November 1890.

89 British New Guinea, *Annual Report*, 1890-91, p. 35.

90 Interview with MacGregor, *Brisbane Telegraph*, 16 October 1891.

91 MacGregor to Norman, [c. December 1892], in Norman to C.O., 20 July 1893, C.O. 422/8/14739.

92 About fifty miles upstream on the Lakekamu River; on the same trip he found on the Baïlala River 'much unoccupied land fit for tropical agriculture'; and on the Tauri River a 'considerable area of good land available for European settlement'. British New Guinea, *Annual Report*, 1892-93, pp. 25-6.

93 'Land suitable for growing sugar-cane on a large scale could certainly be had at several places'. He spoke also in favour of large-scale development and capital investment in other products. Review of 'Potential Capabilities' in MacGregor's address 'British New Guinea', Journal of the *Manchester Geographical Society*, vol. X, nos. 10-12, October-December 1894, pp. 281-5. He also reviewed the prospects of tropical products in his address 'British New Guinea: Administration' 28 February 1895, *Proceedings of the Royal Colonial Institute*, *op. cit.*, pp. 200-4.

94 MacGregor gave details (without naming the companies) in his despatch to Lamington, 4 October 1898, in Lamington to C.O., 14 October 1898, C.O. 422/12/26130.

95 British New Guinea, *Annual Report*, 1895-96, p. 47.

96 Based on Minutes of Executive Council, C.O. 436/1.

97 MacGregor to Lamington, 4 October 1898, in Lamington to C.O., 14 October 1898, C.O. 422/12/26130.

98 MacGregor had been knighted (K.C.M.G.) in 1889. C.O. 447/51/9385. J. Bramston included MacGregor's name in a list of recommendations at the time of Queen Victoria's Jubilee in 1897. His award to the 'Civil Division of the Third Class, or Companion' of the Order was gazetted on 14 March 1898, *London Gazette Extraordinary*, p. 1685; C.O. 448/4/13837.

99 J. Anderson, 24 February 1899, on Lamington to C.O. (enclosing MacGregor's British New Guinea, *Annual Report*, 1898-99), 24 December 1898, C.O. 422/13/2354.

100 See above, p. 95, by Morrell, *Britain in the Pacific Islands*, p. 422.

101 MacGregor to Griffith, 9 April 1896, Griffith Papers.

102 See above, pp. 138-9, MacGregor at Melbourne Conference of Premiers of contributing Australian colonies, 24 January 1898, in Lamington to C.O., 18 June 1898, C.O. 422/12/16595.

103 Gordon to Havelock, 18 February 1895, vol. 49207, Stanmore Papers.

104 The Public Orator of St John's College, Dr Sandys, delivered a speech in Latin at the Cambridge ceremony describing MacGregor as a '*vir insignis . . . medicinae doctor, . . . scientiarum complurium non modo fautor et adiutor, sed etiam ipse auctor atque investigator indefessus. Praesidis nostri auxilio, Anthropologiae, Geographiae, Geologiae, aliis denique scientiis nova lux affulsit*'. Cited in 'A Distinguished F.P.', *Aberdeen Grammar School Magazine*, N.S., 1, 1894-95, p. 216.

105 MacGregor to Gordon, 21 May 1891, Stanmore Papers; see also *ibid.*, 20 April 1890; and MacGregor's Diary, 14 March 1891.

106 MacGregor to Gordon, 21 May 1891, Stanmore Papers.

107 MacGregor to Griffith, 19 March 1889, Griffith Papers.

108 MacGregor to Gordon, 21 May 1891, Stanmore Papers. From his diary on 17 May he was 'at home all day, doing something at Italian, and various points in Literature', and on 19-21 May, 'doing a little Italian'.

109 MacGregor to Gordon, 21 May 1891, Stanmore Papers.

110 MacGregor to Griffith, 9 August 1894, Griffith Papers.

111 *ibid.*, 9 April 1896.

112 *ibid.*, 27 December 1898.

113 *Nouvelle Revue* had been published in Paris monthly from 1 October 1879; *Revue des Deux Mondes* had been published in Paris since 1831. In 1888 each issue, dated the 1st and 15th of every month, had 240 pages; MacGregor to Griffith, 19 March 1889, Griffith Papers.

114 On 23 September 1891, he records reading an article on St Francis of Assisi in this journal, MacGregor's Diary.

115 *Deutsche Rundschau* had been published monthly in Stuttgart from 1874; MacGregor to Gordon, 20 April 1890, Stanmore Papers.

116 MacGregor to Gordon, n.d. [*c*. Aug. 1889], Stanmore Papers.

117 While travelling in New Guinea, see *In Savage Isles and Settled Lands*, London, 1892, p. 155, cited Morrell, *op. cit.*, p. 412.

118 Count Friedrich F. von Beust, *Aus drei Viertel—Jahrhunderten. Erinnerungen und Aufzeichnungen*, 2 Bde, Stuttgart, 1887; Von Ernst II, Herzog von Sachsen—Coburg—Gotha, *Aus meinem Leben und aus meiner Zeit*, 3 Bde, Berlin, 1887-89 (reviewed by G. Valbert, *Revue des Deux Mondes*, 1 December 1888-90, pp. 683-94). These periodicals sometimes substantially reduced MacGregor's isolation, thus the delay in receiving this issue was only seven weeks (his letter to Gordon of 18 January acknowledges receipt 'to-day' of 'yours of 23 November'). Delays were far longer if he was absent from Port Moresby, or if shipping services were not in harmony with posting dates; thus the same letter acknowledges Gordon's letter of 3 October, received 'about 10 days ago', a delay of 14 weeks. MacGregor to Gordon, 18 January 1889, Stanmore Papers.

119 'My bookseller sent me Duke Ernst's *Memoirs,* also Beust's, in German. Yours I shall return first chance'. MacGregor to Gordon, 30 October 1889, Stanmore Papers.

120 Gordon's *The Earl of Aberdeen* was published in London in 1893. Probably the books referred to were: Sir Spencer Walpole, *The Life of Lord John Russell,* 2 vols, London, 1889; Lecky, *History of England in the Eighteenth Century,* 8 vols, London, 1878-90; William Pierson, *Preussische Geschichte,* Berlin, 1875; Otto Bismarck, *Gedanken und Erinnerungen,* Stuttgart, 1898; Gustav Freytag, (ed. H. Hager), *Der Staat Friedrich des Grossen,* London 1886; Jules Michelet, *Histoire de la Revolution Francaise,* 9 vols, Paris, 1883-87, *ibid.,* 5 September 1890.

121 Probably these books were: C. C. A. Dehaisnes, *Dupleix Notes biographiques et historiques,* Lille, 1888; N. D. Fustel de Coulanges, *Histoire des institutions politiques de l'ancienne France,* 6 vols, Paris, 1888-92; Bernhard von Kugler, *Kaiser Wilhelm und seine Zeit,* Munchen, 1888, *ibid.,* 20 April 1890 and 30 October 1889.

122 Presumably Walpole's *Russell* (see n. 120), and von Ernst's *Memoirs* (see n. 118), *ibid.,* 21 October 1890.

123 *ibid.,* 18 January 1889.

124 *ibid.,* 13 October 1890.

125 *ibid.,* 21 October 1890.

126 *ibid.,* 21 May 1891.

CHAPTER 10

1 J. R. Dickson (Premier of Queensland), telegram, to G. H. Reid (Premier of New South Wales) and Sir George Turner (Premier of Victoria), 22 April 1899, copy in Griffith Papers.

2 MacGregor to Griffith, 14 July 1904, Griffith Papers.

3 A good recent history is Robert S. Smith, *Kingdoms of the Yoruba,* London, 1969.

4 The treaty is printed as Appendix C to Sir Alan Burns, *History of Nigeria,* London, 1955, p. 123.

5 Both figures are contemporary estimates. The 1901 Census recorded 41,847 in the colony of Lagos. MacGregor to C.O., 20 November 1901, C.O. 147/157/45565.

6 I. F. Nicholson, *The Administration of Nigeria 1900 to 1906,* Oxford, 1969, pp. 51-2. Some of 'the incongrous elements that make up the heterogenous mass' are discussed in *Lagos Standard,* 29 November 1899, editorial.

7 MacGregor, Minute, 17 March 1904, on Moseley to C.O., 26 April 1904, C.O. 147/170/17489.

8 See A. A. B. Aderibigbe, Expansion of the Lagos Protectorate, Ph.D. thesis, London University, 1959, pp. 165-6. My account uses much of his analysis of the period 1863 to 1900.

9 The Egba United Government's 'independence' was to last to 1914. The Treaty is printed as Appendix M, Burns, *op. cit.,* pp. 332-3. For effect of 1893 Ibadan treaty, see B. Awe in P. C. Lloyd *et al.* (edd.), *The City of Ibadan,* London, 1967, p. 25.

10 Aderibigbe, *op. cit.,* pp. 320-2.

11 J. A. O. Payne, *Table of Principal Events in Yoruba History,* Lagos, 1893; J. O. George, *Historical Notes on the Yoruba Country and Its Tribes,* Baden, n.d. [1897]; Rev. S. Johnson, The History of the Yorubas, Lagos (original draft completed 1897).

12 Aderibigbe, *op. cit.,* p. 334.

13 *Colonial Office List*, 1900, p. 133. The Order is in Denton to C.O., 4 April 1899, C.O. 147/142/10655.
14 MacGregor to Griffith, 27 December 1898, Griffith Papers. He told Griffith in 1903 that he had been offered Western Australia but had refused because of the low pay. MacGregor to Griffith, 19 October 1903, Griffith Papers.
15 Chamberlain's 1898 committee which had discussed the buying out of the Royal Niger Company had considered the future of Nigeria.
16 MacGregor to Griffith, 16 May 1899, Griffith Papers.
17 Dickson (Premier Queensland) suggested to other premiers that the governors of Queensland, New South Wales and Victoria should protest. See his telegram to Reid (New South Wales) and Turner (Victoria), 22 April 1899, copy in Griffith Papers.
18 *Lagos Standard*, 1 February 1899.
19 Mary Kingsley, *West African Studies* (3rd ed.), London, 1964, p. 264.
20 *op. cit.*, p. 281. Dr John E. Flint's Introduction to this third edition critically assessed Mary Kingsley's ideas, see especially pp. lxi-lxv.
21 17 of 239 Europeans died in 1899, 22 of 251 in 1900. Medical statistics for 1899-1903 are consolidated in Blue Book, 1903, MacGregor to C.O., 4 August 1904, C.O. 147/173/27547.
22 MacGregor to Griffith, 16 May 1899, Griffith Papers.
23 *ibid.*, 25 December 1899.
24 MacGregor to Gordon, 18 February 1900, Stanmore Papers.
25 MacGregor to C.O., 23 June 1899, C.O. 147/143/22805.
26 MacGregor to Gordon, 18 February 1900, Stanmore Papers.
27 J. Chamberlain, Minute, 3 September 1899, on MacGregor to C.O., 23 June 1899, C.O. 147/143/22805.
28 MacGregor to C.O., 9 November 1899, C.O. 147/145/33659.
29 MacGregor to Gordon, 18 February 1900, Stanmore Papers.
30 MacGregor to C.O., 3 July 1899, C.O. 147/143/19506.
31 P. H. Ezechiel, Minute, 29 January 1900, on MacGregor to C.O., 22 December 1899, C.O. 147/145/2829.
32 MacGregor to C.O., 13 July 1899, C.O. 147/143/20968.
33 *ibid.*, 19 September 1899, C.O. 147/144/28237.
34 *ibid.*, 11 December 1899, C.O. 147/145/2763.
35 R. L. Antrobus, Minute, 25 October 1899, on MacGregor to C.O., 28 August 1899, C.O. 147/144/25894.
36 MacGregor to C.O., 22 December 1899, C.O. 147/145/2830.
37 Written just before going to London on leave, *ibid.*, 30 June 1900, C.O. 147/149/23538.
38 Printed report of proceedings at Constitutional Club, London, 26 September 1900, pp. 18-23 in *ibid.*, 24 November 1900, C.O. 147/153/38828.
39 It has been claimed that Chamberlain's support of tropical medicine 'was his greatest service to humanity', Julian Amery, *Joseph Chamberlain*, London, 1957, vol. IV, p. 228. See also Robert V. Kubicek, *The Administration of Imperialism: Joseph Chamberlain at the Colonial Office*, Durham, 1969, ch. 7, pp. 141-53.
40 MacGregor to Gordon, 18 February 1900, Stanmore Papers. For a sympathetic study of MacGregor's campaign against malaria attributed to his 'vibrant energy and humanitarian zeal', see Raymond E. Dumett, 'The Campaign against Malaria and the Expansion of Scientific Medical and Sanitary Services in British West Africa, 1898-1910', *African Historical Studies*, 1968, 1, 2, pp. 181-5.
41 R. Ross, *Memoirs*, London, 1923, p. 379.
42 MacGregor to Griffith, 10 November 1900, Griffith Papers.
43 *op. cit., loc. cit.*
44 *op. cit., loc. cit.*
45 *op. cit.*, 4 February 1901, Griffith Papers.

46 Report in MacGregor to C.O., 20 April 1901, C.O. 147/155/16769.

47 MacGregor to C.O., 20 April 1901, *loc. cit.*

48 P. H. Ezechiel, Minute, 18 May 1901, on *loc. cit.* MacGregor reported local support for untrained doctors, for example by Right Rev. Bishop Johnson.

49 MacGregor to C.O., 28 June 1901, C.O. 147/155/25062.

50 *ibid.*, 26 June and 7 December 1901, C.O. 147/155/25055 and 147/158/282.

51 J. Chamberlain, Minute, 12 February 1901, on MacGregor to C.O., 12 January 1901, C.O. 147/154/4312.

52 MacGregor to C.O., 4 and 11 February 1901, C.O. 147/154/7739 and 8218.

53 F. A. Butler, Minutes, 22 and 24 June 1901, and W. B. Hamilton, Minute, 25 June 1901, on Crown Agents to C.O., 19 and 20 June 1901, C.O. 147/158/21050 and 21301.

54 See below Ch. 13 p. 278; P. H. Ezechiel, Minute, 14 April 1902 and C. Strachey, Minute, 15 April 1902, on Crown Agents to C.O., 10 April 1902, C.O. 147/163/14057.

55 He sent multi-copies of these reports to the C.O. for distribution to other colonies. MacGregor to C.O., 22 February and 20 May 1901, C.O. 147/154/10103 and C.O. 147/155/19875.

56 Koch argued that African children under five were the principal reservoirs of the malarial parasites. MacGregor to C.O., 8 July 1901, C.O. 147/155/26685, and see Dumett, *op. cit.*, pp. 171-2 and 184, and Kubicek, *op. cit.*, p. 152.

57 MacGregor's lecture at Glasgow University, 28 November 1902, C.O. Medical Pamphlets No. 30, P11203.

58 R. L. Antrobus, Minute, 22 January 1908, on Egerton to Elgin, 27 December 1907, Southern Nigerian volume, reference acknowledged with gratitude to Mrs M. Bull, see Nicholson, *op. cit.*, pp. 77-8.

59 Ross reports a champagne luncheon to raise funds for this League on 2 August 1901, *op. cit.*, p. 446; MacGregor to C.O., 23 February 1901, C.O. 147/154/10104.

60 Ommanney is probably the omitted name from the letter to Griffith quoted below (reference in note 61). Letter, MacGregor to Ross, quoted by Ross, *op. cit.*, p. 458. See Nicholson, *op. cit.*, p. 63, n.1.

61 Ross, *op. cit.*, p. 445.

62 MacGregor to Griffith, 13 April 1901, Griffith Papers. Chamberlain was not in favour of a central sanitary authority for British West Africa, Dumett, *op. cit.*, p. 166.

63 R. L. Antrobus, Minute, 5 September 1902, on Local Government Board to C.O., 1 January 1902, C.O. 147/164/150. See also MacGregor to C.O., 28 January 1901 and 6 August 1901, C.O. 147/154/6162 and 147/156/30574; *Encyclopaedia Britannica* (11th ed.), pp. 710-11.

64 MacGregor to C.O., 26 June 1901, C.O. 147/155/25055.

65 *ibid.*, telegram, 21 September 1901, C.O. 147/157/33211.

66 MacGregor to C.O., 10 March 1902, C.O. 147/160/14569.

67 P. H. Ezechiel, Minute, 20 November 1902, and R. L. Antrobus, Minute, 3 December 1902, on *ibid.*, 22 October 1902, C.O. 147/164/46224.

68 MacGregor received from Edinburgh University an honorary LL.D. on 26 July 1902. He met Ross, who was also being honoured, and arranged to accompany him to Egypt. Ross, *op. cit.*, p. 469; see also MacGregor to Griffith, 2 December 1902, Griffith Papers.

69 MacGregor to C.O., 22 October 1902, C.O. 147/164/46224.

70 MacGregor's Report of a Visit to Amsterdam, 10-14 November 1902, C.O. Misc. Pamphlets No. 10.

71 MacGregor's lecture at Glasgow University, 28 November 1902, *op. cit.*

72 Yet he wrote to Ross cheerfully: 'malaria has lost its terrors for us in

Lagos'. Reported by Ross in 'Malaria in India and the Colonies', *Proceedings of the Royal Colonial Institute*, XXXV, 1903-4, p. 13.

73 MacGregor to Griffith, 5 February 1903, Griffith Papers. His longing for the governorship of Queensland goes back to his New Guinea years.

74 MacGregor to C.O., 4 March 1903, C.O. 147/165/11051. He also wanted two of his doctors to study tropical medicine on their leave, under Ross at the Liverpool School.

75 See Minutes on MacGregor to C.O., 24 November 1903, C.O. 147/167/44867.

76 The *Midland Herald*, 2 January 1904, cited in *Lagos Standard*, 27 January 1904.

77 MacGregor to C.O., 12 August 1903, C.O. 147/166/33244.

78 Corney to C.O., 5 December 1903, C.O. 147/168/44003.

79 Reeve to C.O., telegram, 2 October 1903, C.O. 147/167/36480.

80 MacGregor to Griffith, 19 October 1903, Griffith Papers.

81 R. L. Antrobus, Minute, 13 November 1903, on MacGregor to C.O., 17 October 1903, C.O. 147/167/40871.

82 M. F. Ommanney, Minute, 21 December 1903, on MacGregor to C.O., telegram, 19 December 1903, C.O. 147/167/45581.

83 Yet no mention of his achievement was made by Lugard or his wife, who tended to denigrate unhealthy Lagos: see Flora Shaw [Lugard], 18 March 1904, 'Nigeria', *Journal of the Royal Society of Arts*, 1904, vol. lii, cited in Nicholson, *op. cit.*, pp. 157-65.

84 Ross, *op. cit.*, p. 445.

CHAPTER 11

1 A. A. B. Aderibigbe, Expansion of the Lagos Protectorate, 1863-1900, Ph.D. thesis, London University, p. 351. He cites E. Baillaud, *La Politique Indigène de l'Angleterre en Afrique Occidentale*, Paris, 1912, p. 181.

2 The names are in the annual *Colonial Office List*.

3 *Lagos Official Handbook* 1897-98, cited by Nicholson, *The Administration of Nigeria 1900 to 1906*, p. 53.

4 The *Colonial Office List*, 1899-1904, shows changes in these officers.

5 MacGregor to C.O., 7 October 1899, C.O. 147/144/358.

6 *ibid.*, 20 September 1899, C.O. 147/144/29066.

7 R. L. Antrobus, Minute, 8 December 1899, on *ibid.*

8 MacGregor to C.O., 9 November 1899, C.O., 147/145/33659.

9 MacGregor to Gordon, 18 February 1900, Stanmore Papers.

10 MacGregor to C.O., 19 October 1899, C.O. 147/145/32932. He also wrote privately to Chamberlain criticizing the intemperance of three of his Lagos staff, 11 August 1899, cited Kubicek, *The Administration of Imperialism: Joseph Chamberlain at the Colonial Office*, p. 46, n. 12.

11 Lord Ampthill, Minute, 26 February 1900, and other minutes by W. H. Mercer, 9 December 1899, R. L. Antrobus, 20 February, H. B. Cox, 26 February and E. Wingfield, 27 February 1900, on *ibid.*

12 This office was vacant in 1899, and changed title in 1901.

13 Minutes of the Legislative Council, 2 September 1901, C.O. 149/6.

14 Johnson's appointment was criticized in the Colonial Office on his past record, but MacGregor insisted on both appointments. The Yoruba historian, O. Payne, was a provisional member in 1900-1. See MacGregor to C.O., 1 and 7 February, 26 May and 14 August 1901, C.O. 147/154/7766 and 8221; 147/155/21500 and 147/156/31589.

15 Ordinance No. 7 of 1899 set a precedent for West Africa. R. G. W.

Herbert, Minute, 10 February 1900, on MacGregor to C.O., 27 December 1899, C.O. 147/145/2834.

16 After discussion he left marriage and burial proposals to be considered by future native councils, MacGregor to C.O., 24 November 1899 (2), C.O. 147/145/35583 and 35584.

17 MacGregor to C.O., 23 February 1901, C.O. 147/154/10106.

18 Lagos Standard, 27 February 1901, and 1 January 1902.

19 MacGregor to C.O., 7 November 1901, C.O. 147/157/43183.

20 ibid., loc. cit.

21 Although I have found no direct reference MacGregor could have had in mind such attempts as those of Henry Venn of the Anglican Church Missionary Society, and his followers, to encourage an African middle class against the chiefs. See J. F. A. Ajayi, 'Henry Venn and the Policy of Development', Journal of the Historical Society of Nigeria, December 1959, I, 4, pp. 331-42.

22 Ordinance No. 15 of 1901.

23 MacGregor to C.O., 11 November 1901, C.O. 147/157/45594.

24 Legislative Council Minutes 16 and 23 July and 7 September 1900, C.O. 149/6.

25 Lagos Standard, 15 January 1902.

26 Letter, Aborigines' Protection Society to C.O., 27 November 1901, (discussed in editorial, Lagos Standard, 22 January 1902), C.O. 147/159/42018.

27 MacGregor to C.O., 7 February 1902, C.O. 147/160/8920.

28 ibid., 16 May 1902, C.O. 147/161/23840.

29 The list of rulers and details of discussions are in Minutes of Central Native Council, 24 February 1903, Lagos Government Gazette, 28 February 1903, pp. 165-170, C.O. 150/11.

30 See Minutes of Central Native Council passim, especially 2 February 1903 (land); 8 December 1903 (rules); C.O. 150/10 and 11.

31 P. H. Ezechiel, Minute, 30 October 1903, on MacGregor to C.O., 28 July 1903, C.O. 147/166/30630.

32 This was a form of 'indirect' rule, and preceded Lugard's classic experiments later in Nigeria. For a discussion which recognizes MacGregor's importance see Oboro Ikeme, 'Reconsidering Indirect Rule: The Nigerian Example', Journal of the Historical Society of Nigeria, December 1968, IV, 3, pp. 424-38.

33 Besides MacGregor's despatch of 11 November 1901 to the C.O., his speech in the Legislative Council on 24 September 1901 explains his intentions, C.O. 149/6.

34 R. L. Antrobus, Minute, 7 February 1902, on MacGregor to C.O., 11 November 1901, C.O. 147/157/45594.

35 MacGregor to C.O., ibid.

36 Lagos Standard, 25 September 1901, editorial.

37 Opposition speeches by Johnson, Williams and the third African member, C. J. George, 24 September 1901, C.O. 149/6.

38 MacGregor to C.O., 11 November 1901, C.O. 147/157/45594.

39 Lagos Standard, 1 February 1899, editorial.

40 ibid., 10 October 1899, editorial.

41 The criticism could be validly applied to the Colonial Office (see above, n. 34). ibid., 9 October 1901, editorial.

42 ibid., 22 January 1902, editorial.

43 For MacGregor's efforts to preserve the forests see Ch. 13 below. He suspected that the Bale was senile before his death on 19 October. MacGregor to C.O., 10 October 1899, C.O. 147/144/31612; Lagos Standard, 11 October 1899, correspondence; 18 October 1899, editorial; 1 November 1899, news.

44 Lagos Standard, 29 November 1899, editorial.

45 ibid., 27 December 1899 and 3 January 1900, retrospect.

46 ibid., 28 February 1900, correspondence.

47 *ibid.*, 6 and 13 March 1900, 'Junius'.

48 *ibid.*, 27 June 1900, 'Junius'; 4 July 1900, 'On Dit'.

49 His reply in May 1899 to a delegation on the liquor trade when he had promised steady actions after deliberations in the interests of the native people.

50 *Lagos Standard*, 26 December 1900, retrospect.

51 MacGregor to C.O., 4 September 1901, C.O. 147/156/34717.

52 *Lagos Standard*, 14 March 1900, 'Junius'.

53 The question of the origin of this Ordinance was raised in the Legislative Council. Although MacGregor attributed it to the Colonial Office, it probably arose from discussions in London in 1902. MacGregor referred to a Colonial Office confidential despatch of 20 August 1902 discussing Southern Nigeria, where the administrator Sir Ralph Moor decided not to allow a free press because of the extreme views of the Lagos papers. See J. C. Anene, *Southern Nigeria in Transition*, Cambridge, 1966.

54 F. A. Butler, Minute, 10 February 1902, and M. F. Ommanney, Minute, 8 March 1902, on MacGregor to C.O., 4 January 1902, C.O. 147/160/4229.

55 Petition enclosed in MacGregor to C.O., 5 July 1903, C.O. 147/166/28304.

56 Johnson, Williams and George opposed the Ordinance, Legislative Council Minutes, 11 January 1903, 4 June 1903 (includes MacGregor's defence), 8 June 1903, C.O. 149/6.

57 Duke of Marlborough, Minute, 11 August 1903, on MacGregor to C.O., 5 July 1903, C.O. 147/166/28304.

58 MacGregor's astronomical observations, fixing the position of towns, and the results of his minerals searches were publicized in the *Government Gazettes*. The dismissals of Africans from the public service were, said MacGregor, an economy measure.

59 *Lagos Standard*, 27 July 1904, editorial.

60 Earl of Selborne, Minute, n.d., on MacGregor to C.O., 4 December 1899, C.O. 147/145/177. Partly because of their clash over the liquor question (see Ch. 13 below) MacGregor's relationships with the Anglican Church Missionary Society were not as close as with missionaries in his previous colonies. His support of the chiefs also differed from most mission views. See n. 21 above, and n. 25, Ch. 13, and compare Fiji, Ch. 5.

61 After visiting a Moslem school at Epe, MacGregor to C.O., 9 August 1899, C.O. 147/143/25872.

62 *ibid.*, 2 January 1904, C.O. 147/169/2570.

63 *ibid.*, 9 November 1900, C.O. 147/153/36862.

64 *ibid.*, 24 November 1900, C.O. 147/153/38828.

65 See Minutes on *ibid.*, 22 July 1903, C.O. 147/166/30521.

66 *ibid.*, 7 December 1901, C.O. 147/160/419. See his attempts to belittle the editors and to find financial reasons for their opposition, *ibid.*, 10 February 1902, C.O. 147/159/8921.

67 Editorial, *Lagos Standard*, 27 July 1904.

CHAPTER 12

1 Aderibigbe, Expansion of the Lagos Protectorate, 1863-1900, Ph.D. thesis, London University, p. 343.

2 Councils listed in the *Lagos Government Gazettes*, from 7 December 1901 to 9 January 1904.

3 MacGregor to C.O., 3 July 1899, C.O. 147/143/19533.

4 *ibid.*, 19 June 1900, C.O. 147/149/23470.

5 *ibid.*, 9 October 1899, C.O. 147/144/31645.

6 *ibid.*, 26 May 1901, C.O. 147/155/21501.

7 R. L. Antrobus, Minute, 23 November 1903, on MacGregor to C.O., telegram, 21 November 1903, C.O. 147/167/42509.

8 MacGregor to C.O., 20 November 1899, C.O. 147/145/32933.

9 MacGregor to Griffith, 14 July 1904, Griffith Papers.

10 A. R. Pennington, Report, in MacGregor to C.O., 28 October 1899, C.O. 147/145/32841.

11 MacGregor to C.O., 10 February 1900, C.O. 147/148/8590.

12 See *ibid.*, 17 August 1900, C.O. 147/150/27076.

13 Minutes on *ibid.*, 20 March 1901, C.O. 147/154/13651.

14 Ordinance 1/1902. Powers were based on the British Foreign Jurisdiction Acts of 1843 and 1890.

15 Ordinance 11/1901, MacGregor to C.O., 6 November 1901, C.O. 147/157/43182.

16 MacGregor to C.O., 11 November 1901, C.O. 147/157/45594.

17 Rules of Jebu Ode Council, 12 August 1902, *Lagos Government Gazette,* 4 July 1903.

18 Blue Book for 1903, MacGregor to C.O., 4 August 1904, C.O. 147/173/27547.

19 MacGregor to C.O., 17 June 1900, C.O. 147/149/23530.

20 Minutes by Bower and Lugard, and correspondence between Grey and the Lagos government, on Lagos Stores Limited to C.O., 26 September 1902, C.O. 147/164/43069.

21 MacGregor to C.O., 9 December 1902, C.O. 147/164/50795.

22 *ibid.*, 10 March 1903, C.O. 147/165/11934.

23 *ibid.*, 21 March 1903, C.O. 147/165/13755.

24 From Ibadan 1903 tolls, *Lagos Government Gazette,* 25 April 1903.

25 MacGregor to C.O., 21 March 1903, C.O. 147/165/13755.

26 R. L. Antrobus, Minute, 28 May 1903, on Liverpool Chamber of Commerce to C.O., 26 May 1903, C.O. 147/168/19530.

27 H. A. Butler, Minute, 10 June 1903, on MacGregor to C.O., telegram, 9 June 1903, C.O. 147/166/21187.

28 R. L. Antrobus reported an interview with Moor 'last night' in Minute, 6 June 1903, on MacGregor to C.O., 4 June 1903, C.O. 147/166/20569.

29 In MacGregor to C.O., 14 June 1903, C.O. 147/166/21891.

30 H. A. Butler, Minute, 15 June 1903, on *ibid.*

31 R. L. Antrobus, Minute, 16 June 1903, on *ibid.*

32 Deputation from Liverpool and Manchester Chambers of Commerce to C.O., 18 June 1903, on MacGregor to C.O., telegram, 17 June 1903, C.O. 147/166/22221.

33 J. Chamberlain, draft telegram, sent 18 June 1903, on *ibid.*

34 MacGregor had supported the Africans' view that the existence of provincial governments was at stake and reiterated his policy: 'I believe the Chiefs are capable of governing the country better than any other person could. I wish to see your authority maintained'. Speech at Ibadan Council, 26 June 1903, *Lagos Government Gazette,* 18 July 1903.

35 MacGregor to C.O., telegram, 30 June 1903, C.O. 147/166/24279.

36 P. H. Ezechiel, Minute, 3 July 1903; R. L. Antrobus, Minute, 7 July 1903; J. Chamberlain, Minute, 8 July 1903, on *ibid.*

37 MacGregor to C.O., telegram, 2 July 1903, C.O. 147/166/24614. Missionary opinion also supported MacGregor, see *ibid.*, 25 July 1903, C.O. 147/166/30816.

38 *ibid.*, 13 July 1903, C.O. 147/166/28880.

39 See *ibid.*, telegram, 23 July 1903, C.O. 147/166/27433; see also Liverpool Chamber of Commerce to C.O., 17 July 1903, C.O. 147/168/26596 enclosing a frank letter from John Holt to his fellow merchant, Jones, 16 July 1903, explaining his reluctance to support African rights if these interfered with trade.

40 R. L. Antrobus, Minute, 13 August 1903, on MacGregor to C.O., 7 July 1903, C.O. 147/166/27998.

41 MacGregor to C.O., 30 December 1903, C.O. 147/167/2703. See also *ibid.*, 31 October 1903, C.O. 147/167/43100 and *ibid.*, 17 November 1903, C.O. 147/167/44101.

42 *ibid.*, 30 December 1903, C.O. 147/167/2703.

43 R. L. Antrobus, Minute, 24 September 1903; Marlborough, Minute, 25 September 1903, *ibid.*, 29 August 1903, C.O. 147/166/35029.

44 P. H. Ezechiel, Minute, 15 September 1903, on *ibid.*, 10 August 1903, C.O. 147/166/32454.

45 Captain Elgee to Col. Sec. Lagos; and P. H. Ezechiel, Minute, 8 October 1903, on *ibid.*, 14 August 1903, C.O. 147/166/33245. MacGregor subsequently explained that 'directed' in Elgee's letter was a slip of the pen for 'requested', *ibid.*, 17 November 1903, C.O. 147/167/44101.

46 R. L. Antrobus, Minute, 23 November 1903, on *ibid.*, telegram, 21 November 1903. C.O. 147/167/42509; MacGregor's views of the 1901 revolt, *ibid.*, 26 May 1901, C.O. 147/155/21501; and of the 1903 revolt, *ibid.*, 23 November 1903, C.O. 147/167/44862.

47 MacGregor knew that his choice of rule by the chiefs was being challenged, but he thought this form of rule preferable to any other alternative. He supported the Alake because he believed he was 'enlightened and progressive' and was critical of Ibadan as the Bale was 'old and feeble' and the Council held not 'a single enlightened man, not a man of the new school'. *ibid.*, 10 March 1903, C.O. 147/165/11934, and *ibid.*, 21 March 1903, C.O. 147/165/13755.

48 T. S. Risley (lawyer), Minute, 13 May 1901; H. B. Cox, Minute, 13 May 1901; on *ibid.*, 23 February 1901, C.O. 147/154/10113.

49 *ibid.*, 25 April 1903, C.O. 147/165/18249.

50 C. Strachey, reporting consulting head of the Treaty Department at the Foreign Office and Mr Farrell, Minute, 29 May 1903, on *ibid.*

51 J. Chamberlain, Minute, 15 June 1903, and other Minutes on *ibid.*

52 MacGregor to Alake, 30 April 1903, in *ibid.*, 30 April 1903, C.O. 147/165/19469.

53 MacGregor to C.O., 9 June 1903, C.O. 147/166/24042.

54 Alake to MacGregor, 3 June 1903, in MacGregor to C.O., *loc. cit.*

55 R. L. Antrobus (re merchants and Sierra Leone scheme), Minute, 27 July 1903; J. Chamberlain, Minute, 30 July 1903, on *ibid.*

56 R. L. Antrobus, Note, n.d., on *ibid.*, 15 December 1903, C.O. 147/167/498.

57 MacGregor to C.O., *loc. cit.*

58 *ibid.*

59 P. H. Ezechiel, Minute, 16 January 1904, on *ibid.*

60 Agreements were signed with Ibadan on 8 August 1904; Oyo 16 August 1904 and Ife 23 September 1904; C.O. 148/3.

61 Moseley to C.O., 26 April 1904, C.O. 147/170/17489.

62 C. Strachey, Minute, 18 May 1904; R. L. Antrobus, Minute, 19 May 1904, on *ibid.*

63 C. Strachey, Minute, 26 March 1904, on MacGregor to C.O., 17 March 1904, C.O. 147/173/10674.

64 B. H. Howard, Minute, 20 May 1904, on Moseley to C.O., 26 April 1904, C.O. 147/170/17489.

65 R. L. Antrobus, Minute, 26 March 1904; B. H. Howard, reported Lyttleton, in undated Minute; King Edward VII, undated Minute; on MacGregor to C.O., 17 March 1904, C.O. 147/173/10674.

66 Ademola of Ake to MacGregor, 26 January 1904, in *ibid.*

67 MacGregor, Memorandum, 17 March 1904, on Moseley to C.O., 26 April 1904, C.O. 147/170/17489.

68 *Daily Chronicle*, quoted in *Lagos Standard*, 22 June 1904.

69 *Daily Mail*, quoted in *ibid.*, 15 June 1904.

70 *Liverpool Echo*, 13 July 1904, quoted in *ibid.*, 24 August 1904.
71 *Lagos Standard*, 22 June 1904.
72 *West African Mail*, quoted in *ibid.*, 20 July 1904.
73 *Lagos Standard*, 13 July 1904.
74 News, Notes and Comment, *ibid., loc. cit.*
75 *Morning Post*, quoted in *ibid.*, 27 July 1904.
76 *West African Mail*, quoted in *ibid.*, 13 July 1904.
77 *Lagos Standard*, 12 October 1904, News, Notes and Comments. This theme was further discussed in *ibid.*, 9 November 1904.

CHAPTER 13

1 9th Annual Report of the Chamber for 1900, quoted in Crown Agents to C.O., 4 March 1903, C.O. 147/168/8585.
2 Review, *Times Literary Supplement*, 19 December 1902; *Sun*, 18 December 1902; H. H. Johnston review, *Daily Chronicle*, 9 December 1902, in *ibid.*
3 Crown Agents to C.O., *loc. cit.*
4 F. A. Butler, Minute, 6 March 1903; R. L. Antrobus, Minute, 16 March 1903; M. F. Ommanney, Minute, 21 March 1903; J. Chamberlain, Minute, n.d., on *ibid.*
5 MacGregor to C.O., 8 August 1903, C.O., 147/166/31878.
6 E. Blake, Minute, 2 June 1904, with *ibid.*
7 E. Blake, Minute, 17 August 1904; M. F. Ommanney to MacGregor, 20 August 1904, and MacGregor to Ommanney, 22 August 1904, with *ibid.*
8 *Lagos Standard*, 12 October 1904, News, Notes and Comment.
9 R. L. Antrobus, Minute, 20 September 1904, on MacGregor to Shelford, 15 September 1904, C.O. 147/173/32317.
10 Blake's hostility persisted; see his Minutes of 3 and 31 May 1906, on MacGregor to C.O., 30 March 1906, C.O. 194/262/13316. For an analysis of other criticisms of the Crown Agents, and subsequent reforms after 1909, see Kubicek. *The Administration of Imperialism: Joseph Chamberlain at the Colonial Office*, pp. 62-5.
11 The issue was the location of the bridge over the Ogun River. R. L. Antrobus, Minute, 25 October 1899; Selborne (Parliamentary Under-Secretary), Minute, 25 October 1899; on MacGregor to C.O., 4 September 1899, C.O. 147/144/25907.
12 MacGregor to C.O., 21 February 1900, C.O. 147/148/8486.
13 R. L. Antrobus, Minute, 22 July 1900; J. Chamberlain, Minute, n.d., on Crown Agents to C.O., 9 May 1900, C.O. 147/152/14525.
14 For example, MacGregor to C.O., 14 June 1900, C.O. 147/149/18824. For the Crown Agents' difficulties in raising loans and their use in June 1900 of £792,500 provided by the British Treasury for Lagos railways under the Colonial Loans Act of 1899 see Kubicek, *op. cit.*, pp. 84-5.
15 E. Wingfield, 22 July, and J. Chamberlain, 24 July 1899, on Crown Agents to C.O., 20 June 1899, C.O. 147/146/15785.
16 R. G. W. Herbert, 3 April 1900, on Liverpool Chamber of Commerce to C.O., 21 March 1900, C.O. 147/153/9149.
17 MacGregor to C.O., 9 August 1901, C.O. 147/153/26132.
18 *ibid.*, 23 March 1901, C.O. 147/154/14911.
19 *ibid.*, 9 April 1901, C.O. 147/155/16755.
20 *ibid.*, 22 July 1901, C.O. 147/156/28492.
21 *ibid.*, 27 March 1903, and 12 December 1903, C.O. 147/165/14596 and C.O. 147/167/486.
22 *ibid.*, telegram, 25 October 1901, C.O. 147/157/37421, and *ibid.*, 6 January 1902, C.O. 147/160/4052.

23 *ibid.*, 21 May 1901, C.O. 147/155/21380. He opposed land grant railways because it was 'contrary to native law and usage . . . to alienate land in perpetuity', *ibid.*, 4 March 1903, C.O. 147/165/13757.

24 *ibid.*, 26 May 1901, C.O. 147/155/21499.

25 R. L. Antrobus, Minute, 27 June 1901, on *ibid., loc. cit.* Although Harding admitted he was partly trying to protect mission property he claimed to be protecting Ibadan people against the chiefs, especially the Bashorun. His claim that the Bashorun appropriated proceeds from land increased MacGregor's anger. The Executive Committee of the C.M.S. supported Harding. See letters of 29 May and 24 July, C.M.S. correspondence.

26 MacGregor to C.O., telegram, 28 May 1901, C.O. 147/155/18449.

27 R. L. Antrobus, Minute, 19 February 1902; J. Chamberlain, Minute, 20 February 1902; on *ibid.*, 20 November 1901, C.O. 147/157/45564.

28 M. F. Ommanney, Minute, 24 April 1902; J. Chamberlain, Minute, 25 April 1902, on Crown Agents to C.O., 17 April 1902, C.O. 147/163/15038.

29 MacGregor to C.O., 23 December 1901, and 9 July 1901, C.O. 147/158/2481 and C.O. 147/155/28473.

30 J. Chamberlain, Minute, 20 February 1902 on *ibid.*, 23 December 1901, C.O. 147/158/2481.

31 Crown Agents to C.O., 26 April 1902, C.O. 147/163/16292.

32 R. L. Antrobus, Minute, 27 October 1901, on MacGregor to C.O., 23 April 1901, C.O. 147/155/18278.

33 W. B. Hamilton, Minute, 17 August 1901, on Crown Agents to C.O., 29 July 1901, C.O. 147/158/26276.

34 Treasury to C.O., 10 September 1901, C.O. 147/159/31776.

35 J. Chamberlain, Minute, 25 June 1902, on Crown Agents to C.O., 26 April 1902, C.O. 147/163/16292.

36 MacGregor, Minute, 30 August 1902 and railway map, on *ibid.*

37 M. F. Ommanney, Minute, 30 July 1902, on Crown Agents to C.O., 26 July 1902, C.O. 147/163/30692.

38 R. L. Antrobus, Minute, 2 May 1903; M. F. Ommanney, Minute, 4 May 1903; on MacGregor to C.O., 26 January 1903, C.O. 147/165/6378; see also minutes on *ibid.*, 29 January 1903, C.O. 147/165/8280.

39 R. L. Antrobus, Minute, 2 May 1903; M. F. Ommanney, Minute, 6 May 1903; J. Chamberlain, Minute, 7 May 1903; on *ibid.*, 8 March 1903, C.O. 147/165/11926.

40 P. H. Ezechiel, Minute, 27 August 1903, on Crown Agents to C.O., 21 July 1903, C.O. 147/168/27101.

41 P. H. Ezechiel, Minute, 9 February 1904, on *ibid.*, 21 July 1903, C.O. 147/168/27103.

42 MacGregor to C.O., 22 June 1900, C.O. 147/149/23472.

43 Kew Gardens to C.O., 23 August 1900, C.O. 147/153/27707.

44 *ibid.*, 6 September 1900, C.O. 147/153/29319.

45 *ibid.*, 26 November 1900, C.O. 147/153/38865.

46 Conference on 28 November 1900, *ibid.*, 4 December 1900, C.O. 147/153/39690.

47 *ibid.*, 26 November 1900, C.O. 147/153/38866.

48 MacGregor to C.O., 2 October 1901, C.O. 147/157/37175. Reasons for its introduction in MacGregor's speech in Legislative Council, 2 September, considered 24 September and referred to Select Committee 12 December 1901, L. C. Minutes, C.O. 149/6; Lagos *Standard* 4, 11, 18 Sept. 1901.

49 Minutes, on MacGregor to C.O., 2 October 1901, C.O. 147/157/37175.

50 The Legislative Council Select Committee amended the Bill, and it was accepted on 23 May 1902. Johnson still opposed it, *L.C. Minutes*, C.O. 149/6; *Lagos Standard*, 28 May 1902, editorial.

51 Blue Book for 1903, p. 26, MacGregor to C.O., 4 August 1904, C.O. 147/173/27547. He had been prepared to control African rights to forests because he regarded their preservation as vital to the economy of the

Africans. Moor introduced in December 1901, in Southern Nigeria, rules similar to MacGregor's original proposals.

52 MacGregor to C.O., 1 November 1901, C.O. 147/157/41251.

53 *ibid.*, 31 July 1902, C.O. 147/164/31494.

54 *ibid.*, 10 November 1902, C.O. 147/164/47665.

55 M. F. Ommanney, Minute, 14 January 1903, on *ibid.*, 12 December 1902, C.O. 147/164/51591.

56 MacGregor to C.O., 24 March 1903, 27 March 1903 and 16 April 1903, C.O. 147/165/11057, 14597 and 17271.

57 Hoffmann's report, in *ibid.*, 30 November 1903, C.O. 147/167/45508.

58 MacGregor to C.O., 28 December 1903, C.O. 147/167/2562.

59 *ibid.*, telegram, 11 January 1904, C.O. 147/169/1308.

60 R. L. Antrobus, Minute, 10 December 1903, on British Cotton Growing Association to C.O., 5 December 1903, C.O. 147/168/43893.

61 Geikie report, 4 July, 1903, on MacGregor to C.O., 5 May 1903, C.O. 147/166/19431.

62 MacGregor to C.O., 30 November 1903, C.O. 147/167/45507.

63 Report, in Moseley to C.O., 7 March 1904, C.O. 147/170/11251; commented on by MacGregor to C.O., 28 June 1904, C.O. 147/173/22908.

64 MacGregor prepared tables comparing exports for the five years. Palm kernels and oil in successive years made up 72%, 78%, 90%, 91% and 85% of total exports. Mahogany came next, then rubber despite its decline after 1899. Blue Book for 1903, pp. 20-33, MacGregor to C.O., 4 August 1904, C.O. 147/173/27547.

65 See MacGregor to C.O., telegram, 6 January 1902, and E. Blake, Minute, 8 January 1902, C.O. 147/160/822. For railway loan of £792,500 see n. 14 above.

66 MacGregor to C.O., 15 September 1899, C.O. 147/144/27419.

67 'I am myself of conviction and practice a total abstainer'. A statement that is not reconciled with his New Guinea drinking of brandy, unless it was medicinal! *ibid.*, 21 September 1901, C.O. 147/157/35737.

68 *ibid.*, 4 October 1899, C.O. 147/144/31608.

69 MacGregor's paper, 16 October 1901, and discussion by Bishops Tugwell and Oluwole, in MacGregor to C.O., 7 November 1901, C.O. 147/157/43183.

70 MacGregor to C.O., 4 December 1899; 9 December 1899 (telegram) and 4 January 1900, C.O. 147/145/33659; 34397 and 147/148/2838.

71 Reported in P. H. Ezechiel, Minute, 15 February 1901, on *ibid.*, 28 January 1901, C.O. 147/154/3633.

72 J. Chamberlain, Minute, 24 October 1899, on *ibid.*, 22 September 1899, C.O. 147/144/28240.

73 MacGregor to C.O., 28 February 1900, enclosing Lugard to MacGregor, 30 January 1900, C.O. 147/148/10476.

74 Holt to Jones, Jones to C.O., and Minutes on MacGregor to C.O., 25 November 1901, C.O. 147/157/291, and *ibid.*, 23 May 1902, C.O. 147/161/23833.

75 MacGregor to C.O., 17 July 1901, C.O. 147/156/28484.

76 M. F. Ommanney, Minute, 18 October 1901, on *ibid.*, C.O. 147/157/36255.

77 P. H. Ezechiel, Minute, 21 April 1902, on *ibid.*, 8 March 1902, C.O. 147/160/12707.

78 Ordinance 3 of 1902, *ibid.*, 3 February 1902, C.O. 147/160/4774.

79 P. H. Ezechiel, Minute, 7 May 1902, on *ibid.*, 21 March 1902, C.O. 147/160/16549.

80 MacGregor to C.O., telegram, 23 April 1902, C.O. 147/161/15712.

81 P. H. Ezechiel, Minute, 22 January 1903, on *ibid.*, telegram, 13 January 1903, C.O. 147/165/1783.

82 See, for example, C. Strachey, Minute, 2 February 1903, on *ibid.*, *loc. cit.*

83 R. L. Antrobus, Minute, 3 February 1903, on *ibid.*
84 R. L. Antrobus, 1st Minute, 26 April 1903, and 2nd Minute (citing Lugard), 16 May 1903; J. Chamberlain, Minute, 1 May 1903; P. H. Ezechiel, Minute (last two quotations), 9 May 1903, on *ibid.*, 4 March 1903, C.O. 147/165/11051.
85 P. H. Ezechiel, Minute, 4 May 1904, on Moseley to C.O., 17 March 1904, C.O. 147/170/12726.
86 MacGregor to Griffith, 10 November 1900, Griffith Papers.
87 *ibid.*, 2 December 1902.
88 *ibid.*, 5 February 1903.
89 *ibid.*, 19 October 1903.
90 *ibid.*, 14 July 1904.

CHAPTER 14

1 Preface to C. B. Fletcher, *The New Pacific*, London, 1917, p. xv.
2 See MacGregor to Griffith, 10 November 1900, 13 April 1901, 2 December 1902 and 5 February 1903, Griffith Papers.
3 *ibid.*, 19 October 1903.
4 Chermside's term ended in October 1904. Sir Edmund Barton was Commonwealth Prime Minister 1901-3.
5 *ibid.*, 10 October, 27 October, 7 November, 2 December 1904 and 7 October 1905.
6 MacGregor to Gordon, 31 March 1905, Stanmore Papers.
7 R. L. Antrobus, Minute, 3 October 1906, on MacGregor to C.O.; telegram, 2 October 1906, C.O. 194/263/36427. Elgin was Secretary of State for the Colonies, 1905-8.
8 New South Wales, MacGregor to Griffith, 12 May 1906; Tasmania, *ibid.*, 14 July 1904; Western Australia, *ibid.*, 19 October 1903; Natal, *ibid.*, 12 May 1906, where he hoped 'to have a trial of the Zulus. I am not able to believe that the Zulu is an unmanageable animal. In any case I should like to be able to put the matter to the test'.
9 The phrase was Deakin's. See J. A. La Nauze, *Alfred Deakin*, Melbourne, 1965, vol. 2, p. 461.
10 See Commonwealth of Australia, *Parliamentary Debates*, XXXII, pp. 1289-2624.
11 No appointment could be made until the Royal Commission demanded by the administrator, F. R. Barton, had reported. Deakin to MacGregor, 31 July 1906, Deakin Papers.
12 See MacGregor to Deakin, 9 August and 10 September 1906, Deakin Papers.
13 MacGregor to Griffith, 2 May 1907, Griffith Papers.
14 MacGregor was reviving plans he had formulated while in New Guinea. MacGregor to Deakin, 4 May 1907, Deakin Papers.
15 MacGregor to Gordon, 27 July 1907, Stanmore Papers.
16 MacGregor to Griffith, 15 July 1907, Griffith Papers.
17 See also following letters, MacGregor to Griffith, 21 May and 9 November 1908 and 25 March 1909, Griffith Papers, and MacGregor to Gordon, 23 June 1908, Stanmore Papers. He was finally offered, and he accepted, Queensland on 21 January 1909, telegram, C.O. 418/77/3050.
18 Speech enclosed in MacGregor to C.O., 18 June 1909, C.O. 194/276/21923.
19 Boyle to C.O., telegram, 10 March 1904, C.O. 194/254/8805.
20 Bond to Boyle, 10 March 1904 (Minute of Lyttelton, 28 March), in Boyle to C.O., 25 March 1904, C.O. 194/254/10711.

21 The Colonial Office carefully considered the claims of MacGregor and Sir C. C. Knollys for Newfoundland and Tasmania. There seems no evidence for MacGregor's suspicions that 'social and political, sometimes religious' influences were given more weight than personal qualifications, and that 'One has to pull petticoats. A lady told me I was appointed to Newfoundland just one week before I had any intimation of this from the Colonial Office'. MacGregor to Griffith, 14 July 1904, Griffith Papers.

22 See above, Ch. 5, pp. 72-3; the *Evening Herald*, 23 July and 26 September 1904.

23 MacGregor to Gordon, 31 March 1905, Stanmore Papers.

24 MacGregor to Griffith, 10 October 1904, Griffith Papers.

25 MacGregor to Gordon, 31 March 1905, Stanmore Papers.

26 Consul Hamson to Foreign Office, 28 July 1905, on Foreign Office to C.O., 6 September 1905, C.O. 194/260/31964.

27 Visit 22-5 September 1905. Report in *Journel Officiel des Iles Saint-Pierre et Miquelon*, in MacGregor to C.O., 19 October 1905, C.O. 194/257/39446.

28 MacGregor to Gordon, 30 November 1905, Stanmore Papers.

29 MacGregor to Griffith, 12 May 1906, Griffith Papers.

30 *Daily News*, 22 June 1909.

31 MacGregor to Gordon, 31 March 1905, Stanmore Papers.

32 *Daily News*, 22 June 1909.

33 MacGregor's report of his 1908 visit to the Micmac Indians and their settlement at the Bay d'Espoir, Newfoundland, was printed for parliament (as Cmd. 4197). H. F. Butler commented 'MacGregor is very good at this sort of thing. The visit was I am sure dear to his heart'. MacGregor to C.O., 8 July 1908, C.O. 194/273/25922.

34 Epidemics included influenza, measles, typhoid fever and whooping cough. Reports of Sir W. MacGregor's Official Visits to Labrador, 1905 Report, Section 32.

35 MacGregor to C.O., 9 May and 4 October 1907, C.O. 194/268/17885, and 269/37072.

36 MacGregor's efforts with primitive peoples can be compared with those of Grenfell, one of the most famous of medical missionaries. See his *Labrador Doctor*, 3rd ed., New York, 1921, and, *et al.*, *Labrador: the Country and the People*, new ed., New York, 1910. Report of Sir W. MacGregor's Official Visits to Labrador, 1905 Report, Sections 24 and 32.

37 St. John's *Daily News* in December 1906, published Howley's strictures on Grenfell; see MacGregor to C.O., 22 January 1906, C.O. 194/262/4456; Bond's comments in letter to MacGregor, *ibid.*, 23 March 1906, C.O. 194/262/12855.

38 MacGregor to C.O., 1 June 1908, C.O. 194/273/21297.

39 *ibid.*, 13 April 1908, C.O. 194/272/14662.

40 *ibid.*, 11 November 1908, C.O. 194/273/42905.

41 Governor's Opening Speech, 1 June 1909, in MacGregor to C.O., 7 June 1909, C.O. 194/276/20376.

42 MacGregor made the same point more succinctly to Griffith: 'Education is very backward. The explanation is that the schools are all denominational', 13 July 1905, Griffith Papers.

43 MacGregor to Gordon, 31 March 1905, Stanmore Papers.

44 Governor's Speech at Opening of Legislature, comments on programme in MacGregor to C.O., 1 April 1905, C.O. 194/256/13616.

45 'It seems he is greatly under the influence, many say the control, of the Roman Catholic Archbishop, though he is himself a Methodist'. MacGregor to Gordon, 31 March 1905, Stanmore Papers.

46 MacGregor to C.O., 18 February 1905, C.O. 194/256/8061.

47 *ibid.*, 10 July 1912, Queensland Govt. 68, p. 659.

48 See, for instance, MacGregor to C.O., 18 July 1907, C.O. 194/268/26813.

49 MacGregor's work for education was formally, at least, recognized in a valedictory parliamentary address: 'your work in the cause of education and charity, the active identification of yourself with all the philanthropic and moral organisations, have made your name a household word'. Address enclosed in MacGregor to C.O., 18 June 1909, C.O. 194/276/21923. MacGregor's Opening Speech, 1 June 1909, in MacGregor to C.O., 7 June 1909, C.O. 194/276/20376.

50 MacGregor in his despatch of 9 June 1909 criticized his government's budget on several grounds: the public debt was $22 million; the government did not know how much land had been alienated, leased or remained as Crown lands; there was unsoundness in the practice of treating profits on bronze and silver coins as revenue. A. B. Keith, Minute, 19 June 1909, on above, C.O. 194/276/20378.

51 MacGregor to C.O., 14 January 1905, C.O. 194/256/2741.

52 A. Fiddian, 30 January 1905, on *ibid.*

53 'Report on the Foreign Trade and Commerce of Newfoundland', in MacGregor to C.O., 31 January 1905, C.O. 194/256/7146 (printed May 1905, Cmd. 2480). See comments on MacGregor's 'wisdom' by St John Chadwick, *Newfoundland: Island into Province,* Cambridge, 1967, p. 117.

54 MacGregor to Gordon, 31 March 1905, Stanmore Papers.

55 MacGregor to C.O., 2 March 1905, C.O. 194/256/8805.

56 *ibid.,* 19 April 1906 and 22 February 1908, C.O. 194/262/16156 and 272/8100.

57 See *ibid.,* 15 March 1905, C.O. 194/256/8387.

58 *ibid.,* 19 May 1905, C.O. 194/256/18540.

59 Quoted by the chairman, J. Barron, with MacGregor to C.O., 13 June 1905, C.O. 194/257/21654.

60 H. B. Cox, 25 November, and H. W. Just, 24 November 1905, on MacGregor to C.O., Act. 10 of 1905, C.O. 194/257/36857.

61 For economic development, see R. A. Mackay (ed.), *Newfoundland: Economic, Diplomatic and Strategic Studies,* Toronto, 1946, Part I, and St John Chadwick, *op. cit.,* Ch. 9.

62 MacGregor to C.O., 31 January 1905, C.O. 194/256/7146.

63 He continued 'I fear there are very many things in practice here that would shock you. The worst is that I can do so very little to improve matters'. MacGregor to Griffith, 10 October 1904, Griffith Papers.

64 *ibid.,* 13 July 1905; See also MacGregor to Gordon, 31 March 1905, Stanmore Papers.

65 MacGregor to C.O., 20 October 1905, C.O. 194/257/39597.

66 *ibid.,* 22 January 1906, C.O. 194/262/4456.

67 *ibid.,* 9 April 1906, C.O. 194/262/14399.

68 See *ibid.,* 10 March 1907, C.O. 194/267/10757.

69 *ibid.,* 24 February 1907, C.O. 194/267/8690.

70 Board of Agriculture to C.O., 5 February 1907, C.O. 194/270/4632; See also for attempts to develop the herring industry, MacGregor to C.O., 14 January 1908, C.O. 194/272/2966.

71 For improvement of transport to the West Indies, see MacGregor to C.O., 5 March 1908, C.O. 194/272/10484, and *ibid.,* 24 January 1908, C.O. 194/272/3997.

72 For instance, to Greece and Portugal; see MacGregor to C.O., 15 July 1905, C.O. 194/257/24724, and *ibid.,* 11 December 1908, C.O. 194/273/47758.

73 MacGregor to C.O., 27 April 1907, C.O. 194/268/17616.

74 MacGregor's Opening Speech, 1 June 1909, in MacGregor to C.O., 7 June 1909, C.O. 194/276/20376.

CHAPTER 15

1 Professor A. M. Fraser has published a careful review of the negotiations between Newfoundland and the United States of America from 1783 to 1910. His four chapters (78 pages) include the crisis period of MacGregor's 1904-9 governorship. The present account emphasizes highlights necessary to understand the dispute, and in particular MacGregor's contributions. R. A. Mackay (ed.), *Newfoundland: Economic, Diplomatic and Strategic Studies*, Toronto, 1946, pp. 333-410. The dispute has been analysed from the Colonial Office viewpoint by R. Hyam, *Elgin and Churchill at the Colonial Office 1905-1908*, London, 1968, pp. 289-303.

2 A proviso read that once the area had been 'settled', agreement was needed with the owners of the land. Bond objected to this proviso, *op. cit.*, p. 335.

3 Article I, applicable specifically to Newfoundland by Article VI, *op. cit.*, p. 338.

4 The Treaty of Washington of 1871, *op. cit.*, p. 342.

5 In 1878 U.S.A. paid, under protest, $5½ million, including $1 million for Newfoundland, to Britain, *op. cit.*, pp. 344-7.

6 *op. cit.*, pp. 356-8.

7 The interests of these fishermen were threatened by the proposed free entry of Newfoundland fish into U.S. markets, *op. cit.*, pp. 385-6.

8 See, for instance, Minutes by C. T. Davis, 8 November, M. F. Ommanney, 8 November, and A. Lyttelton, 9 November 1905, on MacGregor to C.O., 24 October 1905, C.O. 194/257/39600.

9 MacGregor to Griffith, 12 May 1906, Griffith Papers.

10 MacGregor to Gordon, 31 March 1905, Stanmore Papers.

11 The season especially over the deep-sea banks was brief because of the severe winter. Most cod were caught between early March and early May, with a peak period of some 12 days. Few were caught between May and October, after which open navigation was usually impossible. Cod were caught in traps or by use of other fish—herring, caplin or squid—as bait.

12 Fraser in Mackay, *op. cit.*, p. 387; MacGregor to C.O., 13 April 1905, C.O. 194/256/14468.

13 C.O. to MacGregor, telegram, 25 October 1905, copy in Law Office to C.O., 24 October 1905, C.O. 194/261/37898.

14 Proposed amendments outlined in MacGregor to C.O., telegram, 7 April 1906, C.O. 194/262/12394.

15 See MacGregor to C.O., telegrams, 28 and 30 October 1905, C.O. 194/257/38632 and 38654.

16 MacGregor to Griffith, 12 May 1906, Griffith Papers.

17 See MacGregor to C.O., 4 December 1905, 21 November 1905 and 20 February 1906, C.O. 194/258/44302; also 42760 and 262/8401.

18 *ibid.*, 7 January 1906, C.O. 194/262/1677.

19 *ibid.*, 20 August 1906, C.O. 194/263/32365.

20 See, for instance, *Evening Telegram*, 8 October 1906, in MacGregor to C.O., 9 October 1906, C.O. 194/263/38583, and ministerial protests in *ibid.*, 12 October 1906, C.O. 194/263/37760.

21 MacGregor to Griffith, 10 September 1906, Griffith Papers.

22 MacGregor to C.O., 3 November 1906, C.O. 194/263/42042.

23 For his views on the ignorance of Marsh see MacGregor to C.O., 29 October 1906, C.O. 194/263/42038.

24 A contemporary comment was:

> The Story of the Famous Trial
> As it appeared to the Onlookers
> The Sentence 'Read' by the Magistrate
> The whole Savouring of Comic Opera.

For outline of the case see MacGregor to C.O., 20 November 1906, C.O. 194/264/44614.

25 C. T. Davis, Minute, 4 December 1906, on MacGregor to C.O., 22 November 1906, C.O. 194/264/44616.

26 C. T. Davis, Minute, 7 January 1907, on Treasury to C.O., 20 December 1906, C.O. 194/266/46882.

27 MacGregor paid the lawyers from his private account in cash; MacGregor to C.O., 22 January 1907, C.O. 194/267/4769. The Colonial Office reimbursed him from the savings from the year's vote for Newfoundland; C. T. Davis, Minute, 11 February 1907, on MacGregor to C.O., 1 February 1907, C.O. 194/267/5310. MacGregor promised that the men would not go to gaol; MacGregor to C.O., 12 January 1907, C.O. 194/267/1762.

28 Bond's Minute, in MacGregor to C.O., telegram, 23 November 1906, C.O. 194/264/43340.

29 MacGregor to Gordon, 27 December 1906, Stanmore Papers.

30 'It is a delicate task, but Sir William MacGregor might manage it', Minute, 5 February 1907, on MacGregor to C.O., 12 January 1907, C.O. 194/267/2717.

31 Details of costs in *ibid.*, 24 January 1908, C.O. 194/272/4026.

32 Simon Bolivar (1783-1830) 'the Liberator of South America' from Spanish rule and William Tell (died *c.* 1350) who was reputed to have saved Switzerland from Austrian control.

33 MacGregor to Gordon, 27 December 1906, Stanmore Papers.

34 MacGregor to C.O., 2 April 1907, C.O. 194/268/12978. Similar ideas were being canvassed by Lyttelton in England and Deakin in Australia. St John Chadwick also considers MacGregor's remedy 'worthy today [1967] of being reproduced in full' as it 'makes interesting reading not only in relation to the between-the-wars efforts of Australia to promote a centralized Dominions Secretariat for the co-ordination of Dominion foreign policy: but also in respect of the post-war "Entrustments" to Southern Rhodesia and the Central African Federation. It could still well be studied with profit by those now engaged in schemes for the "free association" of the remaining small colonial territories with Britain', *op. cit.*, pp. 119-21. The position in 1907 of the long-involved debate on imperial organization and subsequent developments are fully analysed by J. E. Kendle, *The Colonial and Imperial Conferences 1887-1911*, 1967, esp. ch. IV-V, pp. 55-106.

35 MacGregor to Griffith, 2 May 1907, Griffith Papers.

36 See notes of interview Elgin, Grey and Bond, Colonial, 11 May 1907, C.O. 194/270/33388 and interview Elgin and Bond, 17 May 1907 and later private correspondence with Bond, *ibid.*, June 1907, C.O. 194/270/21846. Despite some progress, especially at the second interview, Bond proved irreconcilable after his return to Newfoundland; Hyam, *op. cit.*, p. 296.

37 MacGregor to C.O., 24 May 1907, C.O. 194/268/20110.

38 MacGregor to Griffith, 15 July 1907, Griffith Papers.

39 Quinquennial averages, especially for imports, suggest these trends:

	1901-5	1906-10
% Exports to:		
United Kingdom	20.4	12.8
U.S.A.	12.8	9.8
% Imports from:		
United Kingdom	27.0	23.8
U.S.A.	30.8	35.6

Mackay, *op. cit.*, Appendix A, 6 and 13.

40 MacGregor to C.O., telegram, 14 August 1907, C.O. 194/269/29216.

41 See, for instance, C.O. draft telegram, with *ibid.*, telegram, 2 August

1907, C.O. 194/269/27595, and discussion by Bond's Executive Council on MacGregor's Minute of 13 August 1907, in *ibid.*, 17 August 1907, C.O. 194/269/30818.

42 Dated 6 and 9 September; on 2 September Keith noted that as King Edward VII was in Europe, a special Council might have to be arranged in Vienna on 7 September to sign the Order. On 3 September Elgin suggested waiting till the King returned to England on 8 or 9 September—the last opportunity before mid-October as the King was going to Scotland. Minutes on *ibid.*, 30 August 1907, C.O. 194/269/31268. For Bond's protests in September see, for instance, *ibid.*, 2 September 1907, C.O. 194/269/32931; telegram, 3 September 1907, C.O. 194/269/31702, and telegram, 8 September 1907, C.O. 194/269/32292.

43 MacGregor attributed the change to one of his Minutes to Bond, probably that of 12 September 1907, in *ibid.*, 12 September 1907, C.O. 194/269/34493.

44 MacGregor to Griffith, 19 November 1907, Griffith Papers. MacGregor also asked Griffith whether he could 'constitutionally object' to any disloyal statements written by Bond into the Governor's Speech from the Throne. Griffith assured him he could, *ibid.*, 25 March 1908.

45 A. B. Keith, Minute, 2 September 1907, on MacGregor to C.O., telegram, 1 September 1907, C.O. 194/269/31453.

46 *Evening Telegram*, 7 November, *Daily News*, 8 November 1907, in MacGregor to C.O., 8 November 1907, C.O. 194/270/40638.

47 Speech in *ibid.*, 13 January 1908, C.O. 194/272/3064.

48 After citing references to J. Morley, *Life of Gladstone*, London, 1903, 1, p. 288 (Gladstone, from December 1845 to July 1846 was colonial secretary in Peel's reconstituted Ministry without a seat in parliament. Morley said this would 'in our own day . . . be regarded [as] a political anomaly, too dark to be tolerated') and to A. Gordon, *Sydney Herbert: A Memoir*, London, 1906, 1, p. 61 (the same incident which, said Gordon, would 'probably never again find a parallel in English history'). Both books show that Peel's resignation, and reacceptance of office, followed close consultation with Queen Victoria. In the C.O. Keith thought Bond's appointment of a non-party minister was justified, but agreed with MacGregor's concern at non-consultation, Keith, 2 March 1908, on *ibid.*, 10 February 1908, C.O. 194/272/6865.

49 *ibid., loc. cit.*

50 MacGregor to C.O., 13 April 1908, C.O. 194/272/14664.

51 MacGregor to Gordon, 23 June 1908, Stanmore Papers.

52 MacGregor to Lucas, personal, 18 May 1908, C.O. 194/273/19214.

53 MacGregor to C.O., telegram, 2 July 1908, C.O. 194/273/23971.

54 J. Seely, Under-Secretary, Minute, 6 July 1908; F. J. S. Hopwood had doubts about repeal but thought, whimsically, 'it is pleasant to placate Bond if we can', n.d., on *ibid.*

55 C. P. Lucas, reporting Grey's opposition, wrote 'I am very loth not to press [revocation] with all deference; it will leave the Colony with a sore head if we do not do it'; Minute, 29 July 1908, on Foreign Office to C.O., 27 July 1908, C.O. 194/274/27462.

56 MacGregor to Gordon, 27 December 1906, Stanmore Papers.

57 See Bryce Papers. For MacGregor's invitation to Bryce to be honoured by Queensland University, see Ch. 18, pp. 369-70.

58 Bryce to MacGregor, 10 March 1908, in MacGregor to C.O., 14 March 1908, C.O. 194/272/11454.

59 MacGregor to Bryce, 21 March 1908, copy with MacGregor to Lucas, private, 21 March 1908, C.O. 194/272/12214.

60 MacGregor to Griffith, 25 March 1908, Griffith Papers.

61 U.S.A. claimed $37,533.16 from Newfoundland as compensation. Shea (Deputy-Governor) to C.O., 4 September 1908, C.O. 194/273/33661. Fraser in Mackay, *op. cit.*, p. 409.

62 MacGregor to Griffith, 21 May 1908, Griffith Papers.

63 See Heinrich Lammasch, *Die Fortbildung des Völkerrechts durch die Haager Konferenz*, Stuttgart, 1900; August Wilhelm Heffter, *Das Europäische Völkerrecht der Gegenwart*, Berlin 1844; Johann Kasper Bluntschli, *Lehre vom modernen Staat*, 3 Bde., Stuttgart, 1875-6; and probably Carlos F. V. Calvo y Diaz's, *Derecho internacional teorico y practico de Europa y America*, 2 vols, Paris 1868 (or its French translation, Paris, 1870). MacGregor thought Drago (a suggested arbitrator) would follow Calvo's views. Luis Maria Drago had published *Les Emprunts d'état et leurs Rapports avec la Politique Internationale*, Paris, 1907. MacGregor to Gordon, 23 June 1908, Stanmore Papers; MacGregor to Griffith, 9 November 1908, Griffith Papers; and MacGregor to Bryce, 9 March 1909, Bryce Papers.

64 Results analysed in MacGregor to C.O., 25 November 1908, C.O. 194/273/44477.

65 MacGregor to C.O., 13 November 1908, C.O. 194/273/41772.

66 Earl of Crewe, Minute, 16 November 1908, on *ibid.*

67 MacGregor to C.O., telegram, 13 November 1908, C.O. 194/273/42907.

68 The clerk, A. Berriedale Keith, later became an academic constitutional expert; author of, amongst other books, *Responsible Government in the Dominions*, 3 vols, Oxford, 1912, which contains several references to Newfoundland in these years. He describes Tupper's experience as 'the classical case' of the relationship between a governor and a defeated ministry, claiming that 'the beneficial results of the whole affair' were the actions of the Newfoundland government in this crisis. Keith, *op. cit.*, 1, pp. 213-20.

69 Also some electors would be disenfranchized as the ice did not melt in some areas till May, MacGregor to C.O., 24 December 1908, C.O. 194/273/889.

70 MacGregor to C.O., 7 January 1909, C.O. 194/275/2119.

71 Debate with Bond reported in MacGregor to C.O., 21 January 1909, C.O. 194/275/3848; See Keith, *op. cit.*, 1, p. 220.

72 C.O. Minutes on MacGregor to C.O., telegram, 31 March 1909, C.O. 194/275/11284; see also *ibid.*, telegrams, 4 and 13 May 1909, C.O. 194/276/15141 and 16202.

73 See, for instance, *ibid.*, 18 January 1908, C.O. 194/275/3395.

74 *ibid.*, 5 and 6 March 1909, C.O. 194/275/10309 and 10310.

75 The 'redoubtable' George Grey often clashed with the C.O. while Governor of the Cape (1854-61) and of New Zealand (1845-53 and 1861-68); see J. Rutherford, *Sir George Grey*, London, 1961; Herostratus, to make his name immortal, burnt the famous temple near Ephesus; Charles X and his Prime Minister, Prince Jules de Polignac, who ignored such signs of opposition, were overthrown in the 1830 French Revolution; see E. Bourgeois, *History of Modern France 1815-1913*, Cambridge, 1919, 1, pp. 107-10.

76 Keith's Minute, 21 April 1909, on MacGregor to C.O., 31 March 1909, C.O. 194/275/13495; See Keith, *op. cit.*, 1, p. 211.

77 MacGregor to C.O., 1 and 2 April 1909, C.O. 194/275/13504 and 13506.

78 See, particularly, Minute, 1 April 1909, on MacGregor to C.O., telegram, 31 March 1909, C.O. 194/275/11285 and Keith, Minute, 5 April 1909, together with the C.O. draft reply favouring Morris, 5 April 1909, on *ibid.*, telegram, 4 April 1909, C.O. 194/276/11720. Keith agreed with the majority in 1912, *op. cit.*, 1, p. 210.

79 Keith, Minute, 21 April 1909, and H. W. Just, Minute, 23 April 1909, on MacGregor to C.O., 5 April 1909, C.O. 194/276/13509.

80 *ibid.*, 12 April 1909, C.O. 194/276/14138.

81 *Evening Telegram*, 10 April 1909 on *ibid.*

82 *Evening Telegram*, 26 April 1909, in MacGregor to C.O., 27 April 1909, C.O. 194/276/15559.

83 *Daily News*, 27 April 1909, in *ibid.*

[84] See MacGregor to C.O., telegram, 9 April 1909, C.O. 194/276/12402.

[85] Draft, 14 May 1909, on MacGregor to C.O., telegram, 12 May 1909, C.O. 194/276/16114; see Keith, *op. cit.*, 1, p. 210.

[86] Draft with MacGregor to C.O., telegram, 13 May 1909, C.O. 194/276/16202.

[87] Fraser in Mackay, *op. cit.*, pp. 400-9. The pecuniary claims of the U.S.A. were settled much later, in November 1925, again generally in Newfoundland's favour, *op. cit.*, p. 410.

[88] Keith, Minute, 7 July 1909, on MacGregor (from Ivanhoe Hotel, London) to C.O., 5 July 1909, C.O. 194/279/22498; see also Bryce's praise, cited above, Ch. 14, note 1.

[89] He received his G.C.M.G. (Grand Cross of the Order of St Michael and St George) in 1907. He thanked Gordon for supporting his nomination, MacGregor to Gordon, 27 July 1907, Stanmore Papers. His desire to wear his decorations is shown by his concern when his Collar arrived in a damaged state, MacGregor to Ommanney, 15 August 1907, C.O. 447/79/30880.

CHAPTER 16

[1] Draft on House of Commons file, 26 February 1906, C.O. 194/266/6994.

[2] See, for instance, discussion by M. F. Ommanney, 10 January 1905, on MacGregor to C.O., telegram, 4 January 1905, C.O. 194/256/284.

[3] MacGregor to Gordon, 31 March 1905, Stanmore Papers.

[4] MacGregor to C.O., 7 January 1905, C.O. 194/256/1899.

[5] Konieh (or Konya) was a province in southern central Turkey. Its main city of the same name (the ancient Konium) is at 37° 50′N, 32° 25′E.

[6] Foreign Office to C.O., 25 February 1905, C.O. 194/259/6447.

[7] C. T. Davis, 15 July 1905, on MacGregor to C.O., 21 June 1905, C.O. 194/257/23523.

[8] MacGregor to C.O., 16 September 1905, C.O. 194/257/35086.

[9] MacGregor to C.O., 30 July and 19 October 1905, C.O. 194/257/29687 and 39446.

[10] *Evening Telegram,* 27 September 1905; and see also *Free Press,* 3 October 1905, in MacGregor to C.O., 19 October 1905, C.O. 194/257/39446.

[11] See MacGregor to C.O., 19 October 1905, C.O. 194/257/39488 and *ibid.*, 16 March 1906, C.O. 194/262/12387.

[12] MacGregor to Griffith, 2 May 1907, Griffith Papers.

[13] MacGregor to Grey (Personal), 15 August 1907, in Foreign Office to C.O., 19 September 1907, C.O. 194/271/33440.

[14] Elgin to Lucas, 5 September 1907, in *ibid.*

[15] See MacGregor to C.O., 12 January and 26 March 1906, C.O. 194/262/3108 and 12901; *ibid.*, 9 July and 24 September 1906, C.O. 194/263/26921 and 37635; and *ibid.*, 2 April 1907, C.O. 194/268/12955.

[16] See his despatch written eight months after reaching St John's, MacGregor to C.O., 16 May 1905, C.O. 194/256/18539.

[17] MacGregor to Griffith, 13 July 1905, Griffith Papers.

[18] Reports of Sir W. MacGregor's Official Visits to Labrador, 1905 Report, Section 68.

[19] *ibid.*, Section 48.

[20] MacGregor to Griffith, 7 October 1905, Griffith Papers.

[21] MacGregor to C.O., 18 September 1905, C.O. 194/257/35083.

[22] C.O. Minutes on *ibid.*, MacGregor had included as appendices to his Report the original invitation and offer of protection to the Mission by the governor of Newfoundland, Appendices C and D.

23 MacGregor to C.O., 8 June 1906, C.O. 194/262/22158. See C.O. Minutes on this despatch and on *ibid.*, 14 May 1906, C.O. 194/262/19010.

24 St John Chadwick, *Newfoundland: Island into Province*, Cambridge, 1967, Ch. 11, pp. 132-53; and Ch. 17, pp. 203-25.

25 MacGregor to Griffith, 18 August 1906, Griffith Papers.

26 MacGregor to C.O., 15 August 1906, C.O. 194/263/32362.

27 C. T. Davis, 1 September 1906, on MacGregor to C.O., 15 August 1906, C.O. 194/263/32363.

28 Visit from 12 to 16 July 1906, MacGregor to C.O., 27 August 1906, C.O. 194/263/33725.

29 *Kew Bulletin* report, enclosed in MacGregor to C.O., 2 May 1907, C.O. 194/268/17617.

30 See MacGregor to C.O., 9 July 1908, C.O. 194/273/25923.

31 MacGregor to C.O., 2 April 1907, C.O. 194/268/12980.

32 MacGregor to C.O., 25 May 1907, C.O. 194/268/20061.

33 MacGregor's Minute to Bond, 23 April, in *ibid.*

34 54° 56'N. 58° 0'W., recognized as the southern limit of the Moravian mission field; see Reports of Sir W. MacGregor's Official Visits to Labrador, 1908 Report, Section 31.

35 He sailed in the *Strathcona* with Dr Grenfell who assisted his hydrographic and other scientific work; see 1908 Report and J. K. Kerr, *Wilfred Grenfell—His Life and Work*, 1959, p. 169.

36 Reports of Sir W. MacGregor's Official Visits to Labrador, 1908 Report, Section 13.

37 MacGregor to C.O., 18 October 1909, C.O. 194/279/34460.

CHAPTER 17

1 MacGregor to Griffith, 26 February 1915, Griffith Papers.

2 MacGregor to C.O., 7 August 1909, C.O. 418/77/26591.

3 Draft reply, 12 August 1909, on *ibid.*

4 Lady MacGregor to C.O., 29 August 1909, filed with Morgan to C.O., telegram, 19 August 1909, C.O. 418/72/27781.

5 Earl of Crewe, Minute, 30 August 1909, on *ibid.*

6 See A. B. Keith, Minute, 11 February 1909, and H. W. Just, Minute, 25 March 1909, on Dudley to C.O., telegram, 11 February 1909, C.O. 418/70/5099.

7 A contemporary view of the 1907-10 political scene was given to MacGregor by J. Gilligan, 'The Present Position of Political Parties in Queensland' 7 April 1910, Appendix to Governor's Quarterly Report to 31 March 1910, 28 April 1910, GOV. 68, pp. 346ff, C.O. 418/81/17161.

8 H. E. Dale, Minute, 8 October 1909, on Morgan to C.O., 28 August 1909, C.O. 418/72/32589.

9 Morgan to C.O., 28 August 1909, GOV. 68, pp. 314-16, C.O. 418/72/32589.

10 He was to sail on the 15th, but on the 16th was still in London. He had reached the Great Australian Bight by 22 November; see MacGregor to Johnson, 20 September 1909, filed with Morgan to C.O., 19 August 1909, C.O. 418/72/27781; and MacGregor to C.O., 16 September 1909, on Treasury to C.O., 28 July 1909, C.O. 194/279/25358.

11 MacGregor to Gordon, 16 October 1909, Stanmore Papers.

12 W. H. Barnes was Acting-Premier from 18 December 1913 until mid-1914, while Denham visited England. Denham, after MacGregor left Queensland, was defeated by Labour in the election of 22 May 1915.

13 The events of the strike are outlined by A. A. Morrison, 'The Brisbane

General Strike of 1912', *Historical Studies Australia and New Zealand*, IV, 14, May 1950, pp. 125-44.

14 MacGregor to C.O., 1 June 1912, GOV. 68, pp. 639-41, C.O. 418/102/21244. Compare his impersonal report, MacGregor to Denham, 2 February 1912, GOV. 68, p. 582.

15 Governor's Quarterly Report, to 30 June 1912, 7 September 1912, GOV. 68, p. 669, C.O. 418/102/32330.

16 *ibid.*, to 30 September 1911, 24 October 1911, GOV. 68, pp. 543-4, C.O. 418/91/39012.

17 MacGregor to Gordon, 19 January 1912, Stanmore Papers. He made the same point to the C.O.; see Governor's Quarterly Report, to 31 December 1911, 26 March 1912, GOV. 68, p. 618, C.O. 418/102/13908.

18 MacGregor to Griffith, 24 September 1915, Griffith Papers.

19 *ibid.*, 19 February 1919, Griffith Papers.

20 See his praise of T. J. Ryan and E. G. Theodore in comparison with his depreciation of Denham and Barnes, Governor's Quarterly Report to 30 September 1913, 18 December 1913, GOV. 68, p. 850, C.O. 418/114/3134; Governor's Quarterly Report to 31 March 1914, 12 June 1914, GOV. 68; pp. 938-9, C.O. 418/125/26451.

21 MacGregor to Gordon, 24 November 1911, Stanmore Papers.

22 *ibid.*, 16 October 1909, Stanmore Papers.

23 Governor's Quarterly Report, to 30 September 1910, 18 November 1910, GOV. 68, p. 405, C.O. 418/81/39458.

24 See C. Grimshaw, 'Australian Nationalism and the Imperial Connection 1900-1914', *Australian Journal of Politics and History*, III, 2, May 1958, pp. 161-82; Ailsa G. Thomson, 'The Early History of the Bulletin', *Historical Studies Australia and New Zealand*, VI, 22, May 1954, pp. 121-34.

25 MacGregor thought that the governor should be treated as the personal representative of the King. He deprecated attempts to boost the celebration of Empire Day rather than the King's birthday. His hopes that Empire Day would cease being celebrated were not fulfilled. See K. S. Inglis, 'Australia Day', *Historical Studies Australia and New Zealand*, XIII, 49, October 1967, p. 20. MacGregor to C.O., 11 June 1913, GOV. 68, pp. 790-1.

26 Governor's Quarterly Report, to 30 September 1910, 18 November 1910, GOV. 68, p. 405, C.O. 418/81/39458.

27 MacGregor to Gordon, 20 March 1911, Stanmore Papers.

28 See *ibid.*, 20 March 1911, Stanmore Papers.

29 Clause 1 of the General Programme advocated the 'abolition of the position of State Governor', as well as curtailing the power of the High Court, and abolishing the Senate, adopted at Convention of Labour Party, March 1907.

30 Fifteen out of twenty-two pages of his Governor's Quarterly Report, to 30 September 1910, 18 November 1910, GOV. 68, C.O. 418/81/39458.

31 V. B. J. Lesina, 20 September 1910, *Queensland Parliamentary Debates*, CV, pp. 1012-3; W. Kidston, 20 September 1910, *ibid.*, p. 1015. See also similar tributes from members of all parties, by W. Lennon, I. Nevitt, J. O'Sullivan, J. M. Hunter, B. Fahey, A. J. Carter, W. H. Campbell and R. Philp.

32 See MacGregor to Gordon, 19 January 1912, Stanmore Papers; Governor's Quarterly Report, to 31 December 1912, 17 February 1913, GOV. 68, p. 735, C.O. 418/114/9969; *ibid.*, to 31 March 1914, 12 June 1914, GOV. 68, p. 960, C.O. 418/125/26451.

33 His phrase in MacGregor to Denman, 22 December 1911, GOV. 68, pp. 569-70.

34 MacGregor to Gordon, 24 November 1911, Stanmore Papers.

35 For details of a dispute whether the Governor-General or State Governor should present them, see MacGregor to Denman, 22 December 1911 and 11 January 1912, GOV. 68, p. 569 and pp. 574-5.

36 MacGregor to C.O., 30 May 1913, GOV. 68, p. 788.

37 He told Gordon he was 'personally all but indifferent in the matter'; MacGregor to Gordon, 19 January 1912, Stanmore Papers. He had been warned in London by the C.O. of the clash between Lord Dudley (Governor-General 1908-11) and some State governors, notably Sir Gerald Strickland (Tasmania 1904-9; Western Australia 1909-13); *ibid.*, 16 October 1909.

38 Governor's Quarterly Report, to 31 March 1910, 28 April 1910, GOV. 68, p. 348, C.O. 418/81/17161.

39. *ibid.*, to 30 September 1911, 24 October 1911, GOV. 68, p. 534, C.O. 418/91/39012.

40 *ibid.*, to 30 June 1913, 1 September 1913, GOV. 68, p. 804, C.O. 418/114/34706.

41 He was particularly impressed by the plans for a new western line from Tobermory to Camooweal, *ibid.*, to 31 December 1910, 20 February 1911, GOV. 68, p. 452, C.O. 418/91/10009.

42 *ibid.*, pp. 451-2.

43 *ibid.*, to 31 December 1911, 26 March 1912, GOV. 68, p. 614, C.O. 418/102/13908.

44 *ibid.*, to 30 September 1912, 23 November 1912, GOV. 68, p. 710, C.O. 418/102/41384.

45 *ibid.*, to 31 March 1913, 19 April 1913, GOV. 68, p. 770, C.O. 418/114/17643.

46 MacGregor to C.O., 24 February 1912, GOV. 68, p. 603, C.O. 418/102/9851.

47 Governor's Quarterly Report, to 31 December 1912, 17 February 1913, GOV. 68, p. 731, C.O. 418/114/9969.

48 *ibid.*, to 30 June 1913, 1 September 1913, GOV. 68, p. 804, C.O. 418/114/34706.

49 *ibid.*, to 31 December 1912, 17 February 1913, GOV. 68, p. 736, C.O. 418/114/9969.

50 See *ibid.*, to 30 June 1912, 7 September 1912, GOV. 68, p. 671, C.O. 418/102/32330.

51 Japanese and Indians as well as Kanakas were exempt if they had been resident in Queensland for ten years. See *ibid.*, to 31 March 1914, 12 June 1914, GOV. 68, pp. 946 ff, C.O. 418/125/26451.

52 MacGregor to Gordon, 19 January 1912, Stanmore Papers. Other treaty rights were later found to be involved, MacGregor to C.O., 19 December 1912, C.O. 418/102/3373.

53 See, for instance, his criticism of Brisbane's water and sewerage arrangements; Governor's Quarterly Report, to 31 March 1910, 28 April 1910, GOV. 68, p. 347, C.O. 418/81/17161.

54 The Governor of Fiji was Sir Everard im Thurn; MacGregor to Gordon, 16 October 1909, Stanmore Papers.

55 He visited the islands for three weeks in 1911, MacGregor to C.O., 20 July 1911, PRE/A, 530, 10468/16, cited at pp. 15, 22, 24.

56 MacGregor to Gordon, 19 January 1912, Stanmore Papers.

57 Governor's Quarterly Report, to 30 September 1913, 18 December 1913, GOV. 68, p.850, C.O. 418/114/3134.

58 The report was illustrated with photographs. MacGregor to C.O., 23 January 1914, GOV. 68, cited below between pp. 868-82, C.O. 418/125/7631.

59 One thesis centred on government policy does not include his criticisms because it was written before Queensland records were available in the State Archives. It has, however, no mention of the resignation of the superintendent at Barambah. B. Lockley. Queensland's Native Policy, 1897-1939, unpublished B.A. (Honours) thesis, University of Queensland, 1957.

60 Supply debate, motion that £25,347 be granted for 'Relief of Aboriginals'. Letter read by W. N. Gillies, *Queensland Parliamentary Debates,* 1913, CXV, pp. 1627-40.

[61] See, for instance, Governor's Quarterly Report, to 30 June 1910, 22 August 1910, GOV. 68, p. 390-1, C.O. 418/81/29638.

[62] Newspaper reports of his Speech, in MacGregor to C.O., 7 July 1913, C.O. 418/114/27779.

[63] See, for instance, Harcourt's Minutes of 16 August and 28 November 1911 on *ibid.*, 30 June 1911, C.O. 418/91/25929; of 10 April 1913 on *ibid.*, 3 March 1913, GOV. 68, p. 758, C.O. 418/114/11621, and of 19 February 1914 on *ibid.*, 5 January 1914, C.O. 418/125/5714.

[64] See Governor's Quarterly Report, to 30 June 1912, 7 September 1912, GOV. 68, p. 694, C.O. 418/102/32330, and *ibid.*, to 30 June 1913, 1 September 1913, GOV. 68, p. 806, C.O. 418/114/34706.

[65] *ibid.*, to 31 December 1912, 17 February 1913, GOV. 68, pp. 747-8, C.O. 418/114/9969.

[66] *ibid.*, to 30 June 1913, 1 September 1913, GOV. 68, p. 807, C.O. 418/114/34706.

[67] *ibid.*, to 30 September 1911, 24 October 1911, GOV. 68, p. 546, C.O. 418/91/39012.

[68] *ibid.*, to 30 June 1913, 1 September 1913, GOV. 68, pp. 809-11, C.O. 418/114/34706. Criticisms repeated in *ibid.*, to 30 September 1913, 18 December 1913, GOV. 68, p. 857, C.O. 418/114/3134, and *ibid.*, to 31 March 1914, 12 June 1914, GOV. 68, p. 943, C.O. 418/125/26451.

[69] *ibid.*, to 30 June 1912, 7 September 1912, GOV. 68, p. 680, C.O. 418/102/32330.

[70] 'It was found that the Government was . . . unable to assist', *Queensland Parliamentary Papers*, 1913, 1, 1606. The memorandum (enclosed in MacGregor to C.O., 2 March 1914, C.O. 418/125/12477) included a plea for the establishment by the Commonwealth of a 'Great National Research Institute' of pure science as in Germany, the United States of America and the Punjab.

[71] See Governor's Quarterly Report, to 31 December 1913, 21 March 1914, GOV. 68, p. 918, C.O. 418/125/15352.

[72] *ibid.*, to 31 March 1914, 12 June 1914, GOV. 68, p. 899, C.O. 418/125/26451.

[73] *ibid.*, p. 944.

CHAPTER 18

[1] Professor J. L. Michie, 'Organisation of the Queensland University', *The University of Queensland 1910-1935*, Brisbane, 1935, p. 3.

[2] C.O. to MacGregor, n.d., in Musgrave to Chief Sec. (Q'ld), 5 April 1910, Despatches 1905-14, GOV. 68, p. 343.

[3] MacGregor to Gordon, 24 November 1911, Stanmore Papers.

[4] See tributes to Roe and Kidston by Chelmsford to C.O., 25 February 1909, GOV. 68, p. 290; suggestion of Griffith by MacGregor to Griffith, 24 December 1909, Griffith Papers; and outline of contributions of Roe and Griffith in 'The University Movement in Queensland 1870-1910', *The University of Queensland 1910-1935*, pp. 1-2.

[5] Government House, designed by the Government Architect, was built during 1860-2 and had been occupied by every Queensland Governor; Governor's Quarterly Report, to 31 March 1910, 28 April 1910, GOV. 68, p. 347, C.O. 418/81/17161.

[6] MacGregor moved from Government House in July 1910; Governor's Quarterly Report, to September 1911, 24 October 1911, GOV. 68, p. 555, C.O. 418/91/39012.

7 In 1902 an area of 60 acres in Victoria Park near the city had been vested in the Secretary for Public Instruction as a site for a University. An area of 600 acres, St Lucia estate in the suburb of Toowong, was proposed to the first Senate. W. M. L'Estrange, 'The University in its Setting', *The University of Queensland 1910-1935*, pp. 23-4.

8 MacGregor believed that Roe was responsible for the choice of Government House for the University; Governor's Quarterly Report, to June 1911, 18 August 1911, GOV. 68, pp. 520-1, C.O. 418/91/31287.

9 *ibid.*, to December 1912, 17 February 1913, GOV. 68, p. 740, C.O. 418/114/9969.

10 *ibid.*, to March 1913, 19 April 1913, GOV. 68, p. 774, C.O. 418/114/17643.

11 The transfer added 110 acres to the 60 acres acquired in 1902 (n. 4 above); *ibid.*, to March 1914, 12 June 1914, GOV. 68, pp. 959-60, C.O. 418/125/26451.

12 Personal interview with J. D. Story in 1961. Story, who died in 1966, was on the University Senate from 1910 until 1963. He was Vice-Chancellor from 1938 to 1960.

13 MacGregor to Gordon, Stanmore Papers, 19 January 1912. He had earlier complained to Gordon that 'it is very difficult to get people to understand how French and German have become absolutely necessary for all engaged in scientific work of any kind', *ibid.*, 24 November 1911.

14 Roe's one supporter on the Senate, A. H. Barlow, carried the fight to parliament where in the Legislative Council he read Roe's memorandum and argued that 'We want a practical teaching University which will be accessible to the poorest child in the State'. A. H. Barlow, 14 December 1911, *Queensland Parliamentary Debates*, 1911-12, LX, pp. 2941-4. In reply another Senator, A. J. Thynne, used MacGregor's arguments without citing his name. No action was taken by parliament. A. J. Thynne, 18 December 1911, *op. cit.*, pp. 3000-10.

15 Secretary for Public Instruction, 36th Report for 1911, p. 35.

16 Governor's Quarterly Report, to December 1911, 26 March 1912, GOV. 68, p. 625, C.O. 418/102/13908.

17 49.35% of 77 day students passed; lower percentage of evening and external students.

18 Governor's Quarterly Report, to December 1912, 17 February 1913, GOV. 68, p. 738, C.O. 418/114/9969.

19 *ibid.*, p. 739.

20 Professor J. L. Michie (Classics); Professor B. D. Steele (Chemistry); Professor H. J. Priestley (Mathematics and Physics) and Professor A. J. Gibson (Engineering) were all appointed in 1910. No other professors were appointed until 1919, when Philosophy, Biology and Geology (in all of which teaching had begun in 1911) were raised in status and Physics separated from Mathematics. Modern Language and Literature, Philosophy and Social Studies, all begun in 1911, were the only other subjects taught.

21 See above Ch. 17, p. 359, and below, p. 371.

22 See Governor's Quarterly Report, to December 1911, 26 March 1912, GOV. 68, p. 625, C.O. 418/102/13908.

23 Emmanuel (Presbyterian), St John's (Anglican) and King's (Methodist). Funds were collected from 18 April 1913 for Women's (undenominational); Governor's Quarterly Report, to June 1913, 1 September 1913, GOV. 68, p. 811, C.O. 418/114/34706.

24 For instance, *Queensland University Magazine*, August 1914, p. 62.

25 He discussed language teaching in secondary schools and examination systems; see Governor's Quarterly Report, to December 1912, 17 February 1913, GOV. 68, p. 739, C.O. 418/114/9969.

26 Blair was Minister of Public Instruction; *ibid.*, to March 1914, 12 June 1914, GOV. 68, pp. 957-9, C.O. 418/125/26451.

27 *ibid.*, to December 1911, 26 March 1912, GOV. 68, p. 623, C.O. 418/102/13908.

28 *ibid.*, to March 1912, 1 June 1912, GOV. 68, p. 654, C.O. 418/102/21244.

29 *ibid.*, to June 1912, 7 September 1912, GOV. 68, p. 684, C.O. 418/102/32330.

30 *ibid.*, to December 1911, 26 March 1912, GOV. 68, p. 622, C.O. 418/102/13908.

31 *ibid.*, to June 1913, 1 September 1913, GOV. 68, p. 812, C.O. 418/114/34706.

32 *ibid.*, p. 813.

33 Brisbane *Mail*, 5 September 1919; see also tribute to his scholarship by C. A. Bernays, 'Queensland Governors, Sir W. MacGregor', Brisbane *Courier*, November-December 1922, January 1923.

34 Governor's Quarterly Report, to December 1913, 21 March 1914, GOV. 68, p. 915, C.O. 418/125/15352.

35 *ibid.*, to December 1912, 17 February 1913, GOV. 68, p. 741, C.O. 418/114/9969.

36 A. Meston, Brisbane *Mail*, 12 July 1919.

37 See a copy of his Speech, delivered only a few days after arriving in Brisbane, in MacGregor to C.O., 11 December 1909, C.O. 418/72/1768.

38 MacGregor to Griffith, 2 August 1912, Griffith Papers.

39 *Queensland University Magazine*, 1, 4, October 1912, p. 117.

40 Bryce's publications include: *Studies in History and Jurisprudence*, Oxford, 1901; *The Relations of the Advanced and the Backward Races of Mankind*, Oxford, 1902; *The Ancient Roman Empire and the British Empire in India*, London, 1914; and *The American Commonwealth*, New York, 1916-17.

41 MacGregor to Griffith, 24 May 1911, Griffith Papers. MacGregor's speech at this function repeated his views on the standards and future of the University, Secretary for Public Instruction, 36th Report for 1911, p. 125.

42 MacGregor to C.O., 26 June 1914, GOV. 68, p. 967, C.O. Minutes on *ibid.*, 8 June 1914, C.O. 418/125/20977.

43 'Sir William MacGregor: An Appreciation', *Sydney Morning Herald*, 16 July 1914.

44 Details of public meetings and other fund-raising methods, enclosed in MacGregor to C.O., 14 July 1914, C.O. 418/125/32159. See also *Queensland University Magazine*, August 1914, p. 62, and *The University of Queensland 1910-1935*, App. B, p. 56.

45 MacGregor to C.O., 3 April 1914, GOV. 68, pp. 969-70, C.O. 418/125/17002.

46 C.O. Minutes on *ibid.*, telegram, 5 June 1914, C.O. 418/125/20428.

CHAPTER 19

1 *Sydney Mail*, 22 July 1914. MacGregor's calculations stem from his 10 years in New Guinea when it was controlled by Queensland, New South Wales and Victoria, and his 5 years in Queensland.

2 MacGregor to Griffith, 24 September 1915, Griffith Papers.

3 MacGregor's offers are so reported by R. W. Reid, 'Sir William MacGregor', *Aberdeen University Review*, VII, p. 12. F. P. Sprent, *D.N.B.*, and W. S. Crockett, 'A Notable Scot' etc., *The Scottish Australasian*, XI, p. 7663. follow Reid's account.

4 'I have to go home at once as my men are nearly all ordered to join the colours', MacGregor to Griffith, 17 March 1916, Griffith Papers.

5 Correspondence with Reeve has not been located. MacGregor remembered Reeve in his will. Reeve 'served in Newfoundland. There, as also in Lagos, and in Fiji, he worked with Sir William MacGregor, with whom he formed one of the most valued friendships of his life'. Sir Alfred Sharpe, Introduction to H. F. Reeve, *The Black Republic*, London, 1923, p. 14.

6 He became a Privy Councillor in 1915. It is argued above (Introduction p. xi) that MacGregor's reports of his interviews with King Edward VII and George V have an air of self-enhancement. This attitude can also be discerned in a letter from MacGregor to Gordon in 1911: 'I had much conversation with His present Majesty when at Balmoral just before [in October 1909] I came out here [Queensland] and I was much impressed by the intellectual development of the Prince during the five years that had elapsed between then and the last time I had the honour to dine with him [at Balmoral on 10 September 1904]. He has felt most keenly the calumny of the pretended early marriage; and he privately sent me thanks for the steps I took in that matter here. One of our newspapers was a principal sinner in publishing the libel. After the trial our three principal papers, including the peccant one, had leading articles on the case, quite in the right tone, and I sent copies of them to Mr. Wallington, private secretary to His Majesty. He is of course an old friend of mine, and hence communicated with me on the subject. [The utterer of this criminal libel about George V's alleged marriage to 'a lady in Malta' was sentenced on 1 February 1911, *D.N.B.*]
The King, when I saw him last, told me that the Arch-duke Franz Ferdinand was a very good friend of his. I hope it may last, for it would be, probably of much importance'.
[The friendship did not 'last' beyond 28 June 1914]. MacGregor to Gordon, 20 March 1911, Stanmore Papers.

7 MacGregor, like so many others in wartime, came to share this hatred of Britain's enemies, despite his earlier admiration for Germany. He wrote of 'their arrogance, their abuse of hospitality, their unscrupulous espionage, their intrigues in creating strife and ill-feeling, and their strange vein of brutality'. W. S. Crockett, reporting MacGregor's 'own words', *op. cit.*, p. 7663.

8 MacGregor to Griffith, 26 February 1915, Griffith Papers.

9 *ibid.*

10 Gordon, who died on 30 January, did not receive this letter written in Brisbane on 19 January. MacGregor to Gordon, 19 January 1912, Stanmore Papers.

11 *loc. cit.*

12 Personal interviews with Mrs Muirden, Mrs McHardy, Mrs Warren and Mrs Archbold.

13 MacGregor to Griffith, 26 February 1915, Griffith Papers.

14 £60,612 17s 6d. Account of Charge and Discharge, Sir William MacGregor's Trust, 4 June 1921, Stalker and Thomson, Solicitors, Galashiels.

15 MacGregor to Griffith, 24 September 1915, Griffith Papers.

16 W. S. Crockett, *op. cit.*, pp. 7661 and 7664.

17 MacGregor to Griffith, 24 September 1915, Griffith Papers.

18 *ibid.*, 9 December 1916.

19 MacGregor said he had discussed universal training with King George V, and he urged Fisher when he came to Britain in 1915 as Australian High Commissioner to give the King 'a second dose of it'; *ibid.*, 17 March 1916.

20 *ibid.*, 3 December 1917.

21 *ibid.*, 31 August 1918.

22 *ibid.*, 30 May 1918.

23 *ibid.*, 19 February 1919.

24 *ibid.*, 17 March 1916.

25 At the Versailles peace conference between January and June 1919 Hughes, Australia's Prime Minister, clashed vigorously with Wilson, Ameri-

ca's President, about the control of Pacific islands; and Hughes opposed the Japanese there and subsequently. E. Scott, *Australia During the War (Official History of Australia in the War of 1914-18*, XI), Sydney, 1936, Book 14, Ch. XXII, pp. 739-811.

26 George Reid was Australia's High Commissioner from 1909 (he reached London in February 1910) to January 1916 when he was succeeded by Fisher. MacGregor to Griffith, 17 March 1916, Griffith Papers.

27 *ibid.,* 31 December 1918.

28 This was written after Australia's occupation of German New Guinea. MacGregor corresponded with Sir R. C. M. Ferguson, Governor-General from 18 May 1914 to 6 October 1920, *ibid.,* 17 March 1916.

29 For details of published papers see Bibliography.

30 MacGregor 'The Pacific and its Political Settlement', *United Empire, Journal of the Royal Colonial Institute*, March 1918, IX, New Series, 3, p. 103.

31 For discussion of their negotiations see Marjorie Jacobs, 'Bismarck and the Annexation of New Guinea' *Historical Studies Australia and New Zealand,* 5, 17, November 1951, p. 25; MacGregor, *op. cit.,* p. 107.

32 His argument is reminiscent of Australia's bold declaration in 1883 of a Monroe Doctrine over the Pacific islands, *op. cit.,* p. 108.

33 See Ch. 17 above. He admitted that 'thirty or more years ago' he would not have trusted New Guinea and its surrounding islands to Australian control, *op. cit., loc. cit.*

34 If for no other reason than that any other races entering the islands would be 'less docile and desirable subjects'. MacGregor admitted that the white Australia policy meant that there was no place in Australia for Pacific islanders. *op. cit.,* pp. 108-9.

35 *op. cit.,* p. 109.

36 Interview with MacGregor, published after his death. 'Rule in the Pacific', Sydney *Sun,* 13 July 1919.

37 For instance, 'The Pacific and its Political Settlement', *op. cit.,* pp. 109-110.

38 MacGregor to Griffith, 31 December 1918, Griffith Papers.

39 'Rule in the Pacific', Sydney *Sun,* 13 July 1919.

40 Dating from 1893, the date of his change of title from Administrator to Lieutenant-Governor of British New Guinea.

41 'Disease and its Treatment', in *Essays on the Depopulation of Melanesia,* W. H. R. Rivers (ed.), Cambridge, 1922, cited below pp. 78-83.

42 He referred to the training of students, from the Fijian Methodist Missionary colleges, which he had begun in 1885, and the offer of the Queensland School of Tropical Medicine, which he had opened in June 1913, to give missionaries medical instruction.

43 Probably Adolf von Hernack's, *Die Mission und Ausbreitung des Christentums in den ersten drei Jahrhunderten*, Leipzig, 1902.

44 W. S. Crockett, *op. cit.,* p. 7664.

45 Despite his inherited Presbyterian prejudices against Roman Catholics.

46 From personal interviews with Lord Sempill, Mrs Muirden and Mrs Warren, and his letters to Gordon, 19 January 1912, Stanmore Papers, and Griffith, 26 February 1915 and 3 December 1917, Griffith Papers.

47 MacGregor to Griffith, 3 December 1917 and 31 December 1918, Griffith Papers.

48 He discussed its use as a vermifuge, as exeptic and its influence in disintegrating animal tissue; as well as the occurrence of fruit on male trees and the changing of plants from males to females; *ibid.,* 1 January 1917.

49 *ibid.,* 31 August 1918.

50 *ibid.,* 30 May 1918.

51 *ibid.,* 24 September 1915.

52 *ibid., loc. cit.*

53 *ibid.,* 30 May 1918.

54 Paget died on 17 June; *ibid.*, 31 December 1918.

55 Honor was in her 12th year having been born in 1907 'on Waterloo Day [18 June] at which her great-grandfather, the first Marquis of Anglesey, was in command of the Cavalry but it appears, preferred to fight with his own hand instead of commanding'; *ibid.*, 19 February 1919.

56 *ibid., loc. cit.*

57 From personal interviews with relatives and Lord Sempill.

58 Sempill remembers MacGregor's opinion that James was a 'bad lot'. Interview with Lord Sempill. MacGregor paid small amounts to James, £15 from Newfoundland; £115 for the fares to Australia; £50 to his wife in Sydney and £10 for James' entrance fee to the Society of Engineers in Sydney. From information (including citations from 'Memorandum Book' left by MacGregor) in *Memorial* for the Trustees of the late Sir William MacGregor, prepared for opinion and advice of Counsel, June 1921, by Stalker and Thomson, Solicitors, Galashiels, pp. 5-7.

59 From information, including letter of 11 July 1916, cited in *ibid.*, pp. 4-5.

60 MacGregor to Griffith, 31 December 1918, Griffith Papers.

61 Trust Desposition and Settlement by Sir William MacGregor, dated 12 October 1919, extracted by Scottish Record Office.

62 Examination of Sempill in *Proof* before Lord Moncrieff, Stalker, Pursuer *v.* Sempill *et anor.* (Trustees and Executors of MacGregor), Defenders, 28 May 1935, p. 83.

63 *ibid.*, pp. 85 and 88.

64 By Scottish law the three surviving legitimate children were each entitled to an equal share ($\frac{1}{3}$) of $\frac{1}{3}$ of their father's moveable estate.

65 'Intestinal adhesions and gall stones several months. Operation 1st July 1919, followed by shock as certified by John Marnoch'; Entry in Register of Deaths, extracted by General Registry Office, Edinburgh.

66 Reid, *op. cit.*, p. 13.

67 If Mary predeceased her mother the estate was not to go to Honor, but to a niece, Mrs A. Dennis of Suva, Fiji. Supplement by Lady Mary MacGregor, dated 23 August 1919, extracted by Scottish Records Office.

68 'Cerebral Haemorrhage 21 days Angina Pectoris 1 day'; entry in Register of Deaths, extracted by General Registry Office, Edinburgh.

69 It was soon sold, negotiations having begun before Lady MacGregor died. *Proof*, 28 May 1935, *op. cit.*, p. 5.

70 'The gross moveable estate amounted to some £35,000 and the net moveable estate available in fixing the amount of *jus relictae* was £30,738/10/7.' Each of the three children was entitled to about £3,400, less gifts before death. In 1920 James received £2,000 and Helen £678, but not until 23 June 1924 were their claims finally discharged. *Account of Charge and Discharge*, Sir William MacGregor's Trust, 3 July 1919 to 3 June 1921, Stalker and Thomson, Solicitors, Galashiels; *Amended Closed Record*, 12 June 1934, in case Mary MacGregor against Sempill *et anor.*

71 The case depended on whether Mary, as heir of her mother, could choose her legal rights (*jus relictae*, $\frac{1}{3}$ of moveable estate, and *terce*, $\frac{1}{3}$ of rents of land) or had to accept the provisions of her father's will: Mary chose the former and her right to do so was upheld in the judgment of Lord Moncrieff. *Closed Record*, 12 June 1934, and Opinion of Lord Moncrieff, 29 June 1934, in *Appendix to Reclaiming Note . . .* , 19 October 1934, MacGregor against Sempill *et ors.*

72 Griffith, Mackellar, Reeve (see p. 374 above) and J. P. Marnoch, Professor of Surgery at the University of Aberdeen, who certified MacGregor's death. Obituary of Marnoch has no mention of friendship with MacGregor, *Aberdeen University Review*, 23, 1935-6, pp. 97 ff. MacGregor also left a gift to a relation of Sir William des Voeux under whose governorship of Fiji (1880-85) he had served. Finally MacGregor left his ethnological and ornitho-

logical collections at Chapel-on-Leader to Aberdeen University, and his Banner of the Order of St Michael and St George to Queensland University.

[73] Almost certainly by Mackellar, said to have been written by 'an eminent surgeon who knew him well from his student days and onwards'; quoted by R. W. Reid, *op. cit.*, p. 14.

Bibliography

SCOTLAND—PRIMARY

Correspondence and interviews with relatives of Sir William MacGregor
Mrs M. Muirden (niece)
Miss A. C. McHardy (niece)
Mrs M. B. Warren (niece)
Mr John McGregor (distant connection—descended from William's
    grandfather's brother)
Mrs Blacklaw (niece)
Mrs A. Archibald (grand-niece)
Mrs E. Yule (great-grand-niece)
Mrs A. C. Bremner (nephew's wife)
Mrs A. Patterson (grand-niece)
Mrs D. F. Patterson (grand-niece)
Miss A. C. Taylor (daughter of second cousin)
Seventh Marquis of Anglesey (Sir Alfred Paget married William's
    second daughter)

Correspondence and interviews with acquaintances of the MacGregors
Baron Sempill (friend of Sir William and executor of his will)
Mrs L. Forsyth
Mr and Mrs McPherson
Dr A. A. Cormack (historian, present at Sir William's funeral)
Mrs M. Dickson
Mrs F. Fettes
Mr Alexander MacGregor
Mr J. F. MacGregor
Miss M. Mackay

Manuscript:
John MacGregor Collection, bequeathed to H.M. General Registry
    Office, Edinburgh

Official Records:
Colonial Office Files, Patronage, C.O. 429/1, 2, 3, 4, 17, 18, 23; Honours
    C.O. 448/1B, 2, 3, 4, 6; Order of St Michael and St George C.O.
    447/37, 50, 51, 78, 79, Public Records Office, London
Colonial Appointments, Printed for Colonial Office, July 1898, Miscel-
    laneous Pamphlet No. 96, *ibid.*
Census Records (Parishes of Strathdon, Towie and Leochnel-Cushnie)
    of 6 June 1841, 30 March 1851, 30 March 1861, 30 March 1871
held at *General Registry Office, Edinburgh*
        Extract from Entry in a Register of Marriages, 4 October 1868,
        William and Mary McGregor, *ibid.*

Extract from Entry in a Register of Births, 27 January 1869 James Robb McGregor, *ibid.*

Valuation Roll of the County of Aberdeen for year ending Whitsunday 1860

Valuation Roll of the County of Aberdeen for year ending Whitsunday 1865, *ibid.*

Valuation Roll of the County of West Aberdeenshire for year ending Whitsunday 1887, *ibid.*

Aberdeen Directory 1865-66, 1866-67, 1867-68, 1872-73, Aberdeen Public Library

Records of Parochial Board of the Parish of Strathdon, 16 September 1845–19 March 1892 Department of Education, County Hall, Aberdeen

Records of Towie School Board, 24 March 1873–2 April 1906, *ibid.*

Aberdeen Grammar School Records, held at the school

Public Catalogue of the Aberdeen Grammar School, November 1864 to February 1884

Prospectus of the Aberdeen Grammar School 1866-67

University Records:

William MacGregor, *Medical (Graduate) Schedule,* University of Aberdeen

Aberdeen University Calendar, 1867-68

Records of Arts Faculty, 1867-68, University of Aberdeen

Minutes of Medical Faculty, 1872-74, University of Aberdeen

Prospectus of Medical School, Anderson's University, Glasgow (n.d. *c.* 1855)

Calendar of Anderson's University, Glasgow for the year 1871-72 (Glasgow, 1871)

Glasgow University Calendar, 1870-71, 1871-72

Examination Roll (Materia Medica) 1870-71, Glasgow University

Medical Records:

Medical Register 1873 (printed and published under the direction of the General Council of Medical Education and Registration of the United Kingdom)

Catalogue of Specimens deposited by Sir William MacGregor, Anthropological Museum, Marischal College, University of Aberdeen, 1899-1909, (Aberdeen, 1912)

Aberdeen Royal Lunatic Asylum Medical Reports, 1871, 1873, 1875

Newspapers:

The *Aberdeen Journal,* weekly, at selected dates (1847, 1898, 1900, 1902, 1904, 1909, 1919)

SCOTLAND—SECONDARY

Articles:

'Universities of Edinburgh, Glasgow, Aberdeen and St Andrews. Regulations for the degree in Medicine', *British Medical Journal,* 1868/2, p. 279

'Education of Medical Students', *Lancet,* 1869/2, pp. 361 ff.

'A Distinguished F.P. [Former Pupil] Sir William MacGregor, K.C.M.G., M.D., D. Sc., Ll.D.', *Aberdeen Grammar School Magazine*, N.S., 1, 1894-95, pp. 213-16

'Notable Men and Women of Aberdeenshire', *Scottish Notes and Queries*, XI, 4, October 1897, p. 52

'Sir William MacGregor. An Appreciation', *Sydney Morning Herald*, 16 July 1914

Personalia, *Aberdeen University Review*, 11, 1914-15, pp. 180-1

J. D. Comrie, *History of Scottish Medicine to 1860*, Research Studies in Medical History, 4 (1927)

A. G. L. Shaw, 'A Revision of the Meaning of Imperialism', *Australian Journal of Politics and History*, VII, 2, November 1961, pp. 198-213

R. Sanderson Taylor, 'Scots We Know. Sir William MacGregor', *The Scottish Australasian*, 11, 2, 1 January 1911, pp. 5-7

Books:

The Roll of the Graduates of the University of Aberdeen 1860-1900

Anderson, P. J., *Aurora Borealis Academica: Aberdeen University Appreciations* (1860-1889), Aberdeen, 1889

J. Brown, *The Life of a Scottish Probationer*, Glasgow, 1908

Burke's Peerage 1904, p. 1875

J. Christie, *The Medical Institutions of Glasgow. A Handbook*, Glasgow, 1888

A. Geckie, *Scottish Reminiscences*, Glasgow, 1908

S. Mechie, *The Church and Scottish Social Development 1780-1870*, London, 1960

H. Scott, *Fasti Ecclesiae Scoticanae. The Succession of Ministers in the Church of Scotland from the Reformation*, 6, Synods of Aberdeen and of Moray, Edinburgh, 1926

T. Watt, *Aberdeen Grammar School Roll of Pupils 1795-1919*, Aberdeen, 1923

W. Watt, *A History of Aberdeen and Banff* (The County Histories of Scotland), Edinburgh, 1900

MAURITIUS AND SEYCHELLES—PRIMARY

Government Records:

Colonial Office Files, Public Records Office, London

Mauritius—C.O. 167 Original Correspondence,
Secretary of State, vols 536-7
> 541
> 549-50
> 552-3
> 555-8
> 570

C.O. 171 Original Correspondence,
Secretary of State, vols 45-6

Archives Department, Mauritius

(a) Despatches of Governor of Mauritius to Colonial Office, 1872-5 (Series SD—selected data from vols SD119, 121, 124 only)

(b) Despatches of Colonial Office to Governor of Mauritius, 1872-5 (Series SA—selected data from vols SA107, 108, 109, 111, 112 only)

(c) Letters of Chief Civil Commissioner of Seychelles to Colonial Secretary, Mauritius, 1873-5 (Series TA—selected data from vols TA69, 71 only)

(d) Letters of Chief Medical Officer, Mauritius, to Colonial Secretary, Mauritius, 1874 (Series RA—selected data from vol. RA2199 only)

(e) Annual reports of Chief Civil Commissioner on Seychelles 1873-5 (printed) (selected data only)

(f) Ordinances, Proclamations and Government Notices, 1873-5 (printed) (selected data only)

(g) Passenger Lists 1874 (Series Z2D—selected data only)

(h) Civil Status Records (birth certificate of Helen McGregor) 1874

(i) Government Gazettes and Local Newspapers 1873-5 (printed) (selected data only)

(The archival records were searched by the Archivist to fulfil specific lines of inquiry.)

Letters of Correspondence:

Gordon Correspondence Books—Mauritius, 1871-3 (MSS. Indian Ocean 21 February 1871—16 January 1873, 2 vols, Rhodes House Library, Oxford

MAURITIUS AND SEYCHELLES—SECONDARY

Chapman, J. K., *The Career of Arthur Hamilton Gordon*, Toronto, 1964

Gillion, K. L., *Fiji's Indian Migrants*, Melbourne, 1962

FIJI—PRIMARY

Government Records:

Colonial Secretary, Fiji, Inwards Correspondence, C.S.O. 75/531-88/1192 (1875-88), Archives Fiji and the Western Pacific High Commission, Suva, Fiji

Colonial Office Files, Public Records Office, London
  Fiji—C.O. 83 Original Correspondence, Secretary of State, vols 6-48 (1875-88)

Fiji—F.O. 58 Original Correspondence, Secretary of State, vols 163-5 (1879) and 168-9 (1880)

Pacific—C.O. 225 Original Correspondence, Secretary of State, vols 1-6 (1878-80)

Despatches from United States Consuls in Lauthala (1844-90) National Archives, Washington, D.C., U.S.A.

Fiji Government (Royal) Gazette, selected dates

Colonial Office Lists, selected dates

Fiji Papers, Q.336.988 PAI, Mitchell Library, Sydney

EE

Newspapers:

Suva, Fiji, (1875-88)
   Fiji Observer and West Pacific Advertiser   Colindale, London
   Suva Times   "
Levuka, Fiji (1875-88)   "
   Fiji Argus   "
   Fiji Gazette   "
   Fiji Times   "
   Fijian Weekly News and Planter's Journal   "
   Polynesian Gazette   "

Fiji, Newspaper Cutting Book, $\dfrac{988 \cdot 8}{F}$, Mitchell Library, Sydney

Other:

Proceedings Provincial Council, Kadavu, 4-23 May 1885—Fiji Histori-
   cal Records   Q354·988/F Mitchell Library
Fiji—uncatalogued MSS. Set 125   "   "
Journal of Rev. Arthur J. Webb, B.573   "   "
Diary of G. H. W. Markham, 1876-8, B.221 "   "
Fiji Miscellaneous Papers, A.472   "   "
Diary of Rev. T. Williams, 1885, B.490   "   "
McGregor, Birth, Death and Marriage Certificates, Registrar-
   Generals Office, Suva, Fiji
W. McGregor, Letters Patent of Coat of Arms 1884, Lyon Office,
   Edinburgh

Letters/Correspondence:

W. F. Parr to Sir T. F. Buxton, 20 May 1885 in Anti-Slavery Papers,
   Gurney, Buxton, C. 109/95 MSS. B.E. S18. Rhodes House, Oxford
Methodist Overseas Missions Archives, 1875-88, Mitchell Library

Articles:

McGregor, W., *Parasitic Skin Disease in Fiji,* Levuka (?), 1876
————, *New Form of Paralytic Disease,* Levuka (?) , 1877
Gordon, A., 'Native Taxation in Fiji', *Proceedings of Royal Colonial
   Institute,* Vol. X, 1878-79, pp. 173-99
Australian Medical Gazette, Vol. 4, October 1884–September 1885 (in-
   cludes opening speech of Dr MacGregor at Annual Meeting of
   Chiefs)
Trotter, C., 'Fiji', *Blackwoods Magazine,* 143, 1888

FIJI—SECONDARY

Articles:

Drus, E., 'The Colonial Office and the Annexation of Fiji', *Transac-
   tions of the Royal Historical Society,* 4th series, XXXII, 1950
————, 'The Foundations of the Crown Colony System in Fiji', Uni-
   versity of London, Institute of Commonwealth Studies, November
   1960, MRC/60/3
Peacock, Alan T., 'Economic Problems of a Multi-Racial Society—the
   Fiji Case', University of London, Institute of Commonwealth
   Studies, November 1960, MRC/60/4

Books:

The Colony of Fiji, 1880, By the Committee to Promote the Representation of the Colony at the Melbourne International Exhibition, December 1880, Mitchell Library

Benians, E. A., 'The Western Pacific, 1788-1885' Ch. XII, *Cambridge History of the British Empire,* VII, Pt 1, Australia

Chapman, J. K., *The Career of Arthur Hamilton Gordon,* Toronto, 1964

Gillion, K. L., *Fiji's Indian Migrants, Melbourne,* 1962

Gordon, A., *Records of Private and Public Life 1875-80,* Edinburgh, 1897-1910

————, *Story of a Little War, Letters and Notes written during the disturbances in the Highlands (known as the 'Devil Country') of Viti Levu, Fiji, 1876,* Edinburgh, 1879

Legge, J. D., *Britain in Fiji 1858-1880,* London, 1958

McArthur, N., *Island Populations of the Pacific,* Canberra, 1967

Morrell, W. P., *Britain in the Pacific Islands,* Oxford, 1960

Rivers, W. H. R., *Essays on the Depopulation of Melanesia,* Cambridge, 1922

Romilly, H. H., *The Western Pacific and New Guinea,* 2nd ed., London, 1887

Ross, C. Stuart, *Fiji and the Western Pacific,* Geelong, 1909

Roth, G. K., *Fijian Way of Life,* Melbourne, 1953

Des Voeux, G. W., *My Colonial Service,* London, 1903

Ward, J. M., *British Policy in the South Pacific, 1768-1893,* Sydney, 1948

NEW GUINEA—primary

Government:

Colonial Office Files, Public Records Office, London

British New Guinea	C.O. 422 Original Correspondence, Secretary of State, vols 1-15 (1884-1900)
Queensland	C.O. 234 Original Correspondence, Secretary of State, vols 43-4 (1883-4)
British New Guinea	C.O. 436 Minutes of Executive and Legislative Councils and Annual Reports, Secretary of State, vols 1-4 (1888-1906)
British New Guinea	C.O. 453 Government Gazettes, Secretary of State, vols 1-2 (1888-1906)
British New Guinea	C.O. 200 Ordinances, Secretary of State, vols 1-2 (1888-1906)
British New Guinea	C.O. 808 Miscellaneous Confidential Prints, Secretary of State, vols 45, 52, 60, 61, 62, 68, 69, 70, 76, 83, 86 (1882-90)
British New Guinea	C.O. 418 Original Correspondence, Secretary of State, vols 14 and 19 (1901-2)

(a) *Inventories,* Australian National Library, Canberra

J. A. Miles and A. T. Dix Inventory of Records of the Papuan (previously British New Guinea) Administration 1885-1942 Selected Records referred to in Inventory Calendar of Correspondence of Administration of British New Guinea, 1885-1898

Selected Correspondence referred to in Calendar

(b) *British New Guinea Administration Files*, Australian National Library, Canberra

Station Reports
1 Mekeo 1890-1902
2 Samarai 1889-1903
3 Tamata, Bogi and Papangi 1898-1902
4 Nivani 1896-1900
5 Rigo 1899-1902
6 Port Moresby 1892-1901
7 Cloudy Bay 1893-4
8 Daru 1900-2
9 Cape Nelson 1900-2

(c) Native Constabulary, Reports, Journals and Correspondence, 1893-1907
(d) Private Secretary, Letters, 1899-1905
(e) Government Secretary, Miscellaneous Records and Correspondence
(f) Oath Book 1888-1904
(g) Native Regulation Board, Minutes, 1890-1907
(h) Lieutenant-Governor's Office, Papers of his office
(i) Lands, Mines, Surveys, etc., Records, 1889-1902
(j) Register of Instruments of Attestation, 1892-1907, CP399, Series 6
(k) Register of Surveys, 1888-1902, CP399, Series 8
(l) Miscellaneous Correspondence, Papua, 1887-1906
(m) Bundle of Telegrams, 1899-1906
(n) Dept of External Affairs, 1911, Musgrave files (12632, 14610, 15553, 18058 and 18182)

British New Guinea Annual Reports, mainly in Blue Books [B.B.], British Parliamentary Papers
(a) November 1884—December 1885, Fort's Report (in Gov. Loch (Vic.) to C.O., 14 April 1886, C.O. 808/68)
(b) January 1886—December 1886, Douglas' (in Douglas to C.O., 16 January 1887, C.O. 808/70 and B.B. 1887, LV-1)
(c) January 1887–December 1887 Douglas' B.B. 1888, LXXII-591
(d) January 1888–September 1888 " B.B. 1889, LIV-423
(e) September 1888–June 1889 McGregor B.B. 1890, LVIII-675
(f) July 1889–June 1890 " B.B. 1890-1, LV-297
(g) " 1890– " 1891 " B.B. 1892, LV-571
(h) " 1891– " 1892 " B.B. 1893-4, LX-83
(i) " 1892– " 1893 " B.B. 1895, LXIX-411
(j) " 1893– " 1894 " B.B. 1895, LXIX-411
(k) " 1894– " 1895 " B.B. 1896, LVII-195
(l) " 1895– " 1896 " B.B. 1897, LIX-119
(m) " 1896– " 1897 " B.B. 1899, LXII-209
(n) " 1897–September 1898 " B.B. 1899, LXII-257

Queensland Parliamentary Debates, 1883-98, XXXIX-LXXX
Commonwealth of Australia Parliamentary Debates, 1906, vol. XXXII
Federal Council of Australasia Debates, Hobart Session, 1886

Mission Records:

London Missionary Society, Livingstone House, London
  L.M.S. Register of Missionaries, Deputations, Etc. 1796-1923
  L.M.S. Reports (1883-1901)
        Journals (1890-1901)
  and
        Correspondence (Boxes 4-8 1886-1900)
Church of England, Library, Dogura, T.P.N.G.
  Newspaper Cuttings 1885 ff.
  Log Book, Dogura, 26 May 1898-30 September 1900
  School Log, Dogura, 13 June 1898-22 December 1899
  Miscellaneous Correspondence, Bishop David Hand's office, Dogura
  (1898 ff.)
Roman Catholic, Sacred Heart Mission, Yule Island, T.P.N.G.
  File 'A List of a Few Documents on the question of "Spheres of
  Influence" '
  M. Andre Navarre, Notes et Journal (copy)
Wesleyan, Methodist Overseas Mission, Mitchell Library, Sydney (see
  Fiji bibliography)

Newspapers:

New Guinea—Newspaper Cutting Book, vol. 52, Mitchell Library

Articles:

H. O. Forbes, 'British New Guinea as a Colony', *Blackwoods Edinburgh
  Magazine,* July 1892
T. Hatton-Richards, 'British New Guinea' in *Proceedings of the Royal
  Colonial Institute,* XXIV, 1892-93, pp. 289-314
————, 'Travels with the Hon. Sir William McGregor KCMG, Ad-
  ministrator of British New Guinea', 26 September 1890, *Transac-
  tions of the Royal Geographical Society of Australasia,* Pt 11, VIII,
  March 1891
R. B. Joyce, 'The British New Guinea Syndicate Affair', *Journal of the
  [Royal] Queensland Historical Society,* V, 1, 1953, pp. 771-93
MacGregor, W., 'Record of Observations on Sir William MacGregor's
  Highland Plants from New Guinea 1889', *Royal Society of Vic-
  torian, Transactions etc.,* N.S., 1, pt 2, 1888
————, *Handbook of Information for Intending Settlers in British
  New Guinea,* Brisbane, 1892
————, 'British New Guinea' in *Journal of Manchester Geographical
  Society,* X, October–December 1894, pp. 271-85, Mitchell Library
————, 'British New Guinea: Administration' 28 February 1895, in
  Proceedings of the Royal Colonial Institute, XXVI, 1894-5, pp. 193-
  239
————, *British New Guinea, London,* 1897
————, 'British New Guinea' 28 March 1899 in *Proceedings of the
  Royal Colonial Institute,* XXX, 1898-99, pp. 238-70
————, Introduction to Frances M. Synge, *Albert Maclaren,* London-
  1908
————, Introduction to J. H. P. Murray, *Papua or British New
  Guinea,* London, 1912

———, Preface to C. B. Fletcher, *The Problem of the Pacific*, Sydney,
  1919

Other:

W. McGregor, Field Note Book, Exploration of Owen Stanley Range
  2-23 June 1889, B. 838a, Mitchell Library
———, Diary, 4 vols, Australian National Library
        14 November 1890–14 April 1891
        5 April 1891–31 August 1891
        1 September 1891–8 December 1891
        29 February 1892–28 August 1892
Newspaper Cuttings, Vols 52, 117, 118, Mitchell Library
Intercolonial Medical Congress of Australia, 2nd Session, 1889
(includes W. McGregor 'Some Notes on Disease in British New
Guinea'), $\frac{610 \cdot 6}{A}$, Mitchell Library
Musgrave Papers B, 1603, W. MacGregor to Lady Musgrave 17.2.1912;
        Lady MacGregor to Lady Musgrave 10.6.1912 and 16.6.1912,
                                            Mitchell Library

NEW GUINEA—SECONDARY

Theses:

D. Dignan, Kanaka Political Struggle, unpublished B.A. thesis, University of Queensland, 1949
R. B. Joyce, The Administration of British New Guinea (1888-1902),
  unpublished M. Litt. thesis, Cambridge, 1953 (see bibliography)
B. Scott, The Governorship of Sir Anthony Musgrave 1883-1888, unpublished B.A. (Hons.) thesis, University of Queensland, 1954
J. P. C. Sheppard, The Pacific Islanders in Queensland, 1863-1883, unpublished B.A. (Hons.) thesis, University of Queensland, 1966

Books:

Abel, C. W., *Savage Life in New Guinea*, London, n.d. [1901]
Brown, G., *Pioneer Missionary and Explorer*, London, 1908
Bromilow, W. E., *Twenty Years Among Primitive Papuans*, London,
  1929
Burridge, K. O. L., *Mambu*, London, 1960
Chalmers, J., *Pioneer Life and Work in New Guinea 1877-94*, London,
  1895
Dupeyrat, A., *Papouasie. Histoire de la Mission*, Paris, 1934
Fletcher, C., *The Black Knight of the Pacific*, Sydney, 1944
———, *The New Pacific*, London, 1917
Fortune, R., *Sorcerers of Dobu*, London, 1932
Joyce, R. B. (ed.), A.C.V. Melbourne, *Early Constitutional Develop-
  ment in Australia 1788-1856*, St Lucia, 1963
King, Copland, *A History of the New Guinea Mission,* Sydney, n.d.
  [1899?]
Kinloch Cooke, C. (ed.), *Australian Defences and New Guinea (1878-
  91)*, London, 1887
La Nauze, J. A., *Alfred Deakin*, 2 vols, Melbourne, 1965
Lawrence, P., *Road Belong Cargo*, Melbourne, 1964

Legge, J. D., *Australian Colonial Policy*, Sydney, 1956
Lennox, C., *James Chalmers of New Guinea*, London, 1902
Lett, Lewis, *The Papuan Achievement*, Melbourne, 1944
————, *Sir Hubert Murray of Papua*, Sydney, 1949
————, *Papua*, Melbourne, 1944
Mair, L. P., *Australia in New Guinea*, London, 1948
————, *Native Policies in Africa*, London, 1936
Monckton, C. A. W., *Some Experiences of a New Guinea Resident Magistrate*, London, 1920
Morrell, W. P., *Britain in the Pacific Islands*, Oxford, 1960
Musgrave, A., *British New Guinea, An Abstract of Statistical Notes, Etc. Prepared for the use of Publishers of Almanacs, Directions etc. for the year 1891*, Brisbane, 1890
Pascoe, C. F., *Two Hundred Years of the S.P.G.*, 1701-1900
Parnaby, O. W., *Britain and the Labour Trade in the Southwest Pacific*, Durham, 1964
Pitcairn, W. D., *Two Years Among the Savages of New Guinea*, London, 1891
Robson, J. W., *James Chalmers, Missionary and Explorer*, London, 1933
Romilly, H. H., *The Western Pacific and New Guinea*, London, 1887
————, *From my Verandah in New Guinea*, London, 1889
Scarr, D., *Fragments of Empire*, Canberra, 1967
Souter, G., *New Guinea: The Last Unknown*, Sydney, 1963
Strachan, J., *Explorations and Adventures in New Guinea*, London, 1888
Synge, F. M. (introduction by Sir William MacGregor), *Albert Maclaren, A Pioneer Missionary in New Guinea*, London, 1908
Thomson, J. P., *British New Guinea*, London, 1892
Van der Veur, *Search for New Guinea's Boundaries from Torres Strait to the Pacific*, Canberra, (*c.* 1966)
————, *Documents and Correspondence on New Guinea's Boundaries*, Canberra, 1966
White, Gilbert, *A Pioneer of Papua*, London, 1929
Worsley, P. M., *The Trumpet Shall Sound*, London, 1957

LAGOS—PRIMARY

Colonial Office:

Colonial Office Files, Public Records Office, London
Lagos, C.O. 147, Original Correspondence
Secretary of State, vols 142-73 (1899-1904)
Lagos, C.O. 148, Acts, vols 2-3 (1886-1905)
Lagos, C.O. 149, Minutes of Executive and Legislative Councils, Annual Reports, vols 2-7 (1886-1906)
Lagos, C.O. 150, Government Gazettes, vols 9-11 (1899-1904)
Medical Pamphlets, Nos 30, 31, 32, 33, 34, 36, Colonial Office Library, London
Africa Pamphlets, vol. 1
Miscellaneous Pamphlets, no. 10

Newspapers:

Lagos Standard, selected dates, 1899-1904   Colindale, London
Lagos Weekly Record, selected dates, 1899   "
West African Mail, selected dates, 1903-4   "
Edinburgh Review, vol. 229, 1919   "

Correspondence:

William MacGregor—Joseph Chamberlain Correspondence, Birmingham University; See references in Kubicek, Robert V., *The Administration of Imperialism: Joseph Chamberlain at the Colonial Office*, Durham, 1969

Articles:

Lugard, Lady (Shaw, Flora), 'West African Negroland', *Proceedings of the Royal Colonial Institute*, XXXV, June 1904, pp. 300-25
————, 'Nigeria', *Journal of the Royal Society of Arts*, vol. LII, 1904
Ross, R., 'Malaria in India and the Colonies', *Proceedings of the Royal Colonial Institute*, XXXV, 1903-4, pp. 7-26

LAGOS—SECONDARY

Books:

Amery, Julian, *Life of Joseph Chamberlain*, 4, London, 1951
Anene, J. C., *Southern Nigeria in Transition*, 1885-1906, Cambridge, 1966
Ayendele, E. A., *The Missionary Impact on Modern Nigeria*, London, 1966
Baillaud, E., *La Politique Indigène de l'Angleterre en Afrique Occidentale*, Paris, 1912
Burns, A., *History of Nigeria*, London, 1955
Burton, R., *Wanderings in West Africa*, London, 1863
Garvin, J. L. *Life of Joseph Chamberlain*, 1-3, London, 1932
George, J. O., *Historical Notes on the Yoruba Country and its Tribes*, Baden, n.d. [1897]
Hailey, Lord, *Native Administration in the British African Territories*, London, 1951
Johnson, Rev. S., *The History of the Yorubas*, Lagos (1897 original draft)
Kingsley, Mary, *West African Studies*, 3rd ed., London, 1964
Kubicek, Robert V., *The Administration of Imperialism: Joseph Chamberlain at the Colonial Office*, Durham, 1969
Lloyd, P. C., Mabogunje, A. L., and Awe, B., eds, *The City of Ibadan*, London, 1967
Lugard, Sir F., *The Dual Mandate*, London, 1922
Nicholson, I. F., *The Administration of Nigeria 1900-1906*, Oxford, 1969
Payne, J. A. O., *Table of Principal Events in Yoruba History*, Lagos, 1893
Perham, M., *Lugard, The Years of Adventure*, London, 1956
————, *Lugard, The Years of Authority*, London, 1960
Ross, R., *Memoirs*, London, 1923
Shaw, F., *A Tropical Dependency*, London, 1905
Smith, R. S., *Kingdoms of the Yoruba*, London, 1969

Articles:

Ajayi, J. F. A., 'Henry Venn and the policy of Development', *Journal of the Historical Society of Nigeria*, 1, 4, December 1959

Bidbaku, V.S.O., 'Historical Sketch of Egba Traditional Authorities', *Africa*, 22, 1952

Dumett, Raymond E., 'The Campaign against Malaria and the Expansion of Scientific Medical and Sanitary Services in British West Africa 1898-1910', *African Historical Studies*, 1968, 1, 2, pp. 181-5

Ikeme, O., 'Reconsidering Indirect Rule. The Nigerian Example', *Journal of the Historical Society of Nigeria*, IV, 3, December 1968

Thesis:

Aderibigbe, A. A. B., Expansion of the Lagos Protectorate, 1863-1900, Ph.D. thesis, London University, 1959

NEWFOUNDLAND—PRIMARY

Government:

Colonial Office Files, Public Records Office, London
Newfoundland—C.O. 194 Original Correspondence,
Secretary of State, vols 254-79 (1904-9)
Order of St Michael and St George, C.O. 447 Honours,
vol. 79 (1907)
Commonwealth of Australia Parliamentary Debates,
vol. XXXII, 1906

Letters/Correspondence:

William MacGregor—James Bryce Correspondence,
4 April 1908–26 February 1909,
MSS. U.S.A. 28,
Bodleian Library, Oxford
William MacGregor—Alfred Deakin Correspondence,
Deakin draft to MacGregor, 31 July 1906
MacGregor to Deakin, 9 August 1906; 10 September 1906;
26 March 1907; 4 May 1907
(in Deakin's papers, consulted when in the possession of Professor J. A. La Nauze, subsequently deposited in Australian National Library, Canberra)
William MacGregor—Lord Elgin Correspondence, Broomhall, Dunfermline, 1905-8; see references in Hyam, R., *Elgin and Churchill at the Colonial Office*, London, 1968

Newspapers:

St John's, Newfoundland

Daily News,	Selected dates	Colindale, London
Evening Herald,	" "	"
Evening Telegram,	" "	"
Free Press,	" "	"

Other:

MacGregor, W., Reports of *Official Visits to Labrador, 1905 and 1908*, Copy, University of Queensland

*Report by the Governor on a visit to the Micmac In-
dians at Bay d'Espoir*, Cd. 4197, London, 1908
*Report on the Foreign Trade and Commerce of New-
foundland*, Cd. 2480, London, 1905
*Report on the Foreign Trade and Commerce of New-
foundland 1905-6*, (not printed)
*Report on the trade and commerce of Newfoundland
for the four years ending with 30 June 1906* (not
printed)

NEWFOUNDLAND—SECONDARY

Books:

Chadwick, St John, *Newfoundland, Island into Province*, Cambridge,
1967
Grenfell, W. T., *A Labrador Doctor—The Autobiography of Wilfred
Thomason Grenfell*, New York, 3rd ed., 1921
————, *Labrador: The Country and the People*, new ed., New York,
1910
Hyam, R., *Elgin and Churchill at the Colonial Office*, London, 1968
Keith, A. B., *Responsible Government in the Dominions*, 3 vols, Oxford,
1912
Kendle, J. E., *The Colonial and Imperial Conferences 1887-1911*, Lon-
don, 1967
Kerr, J. Lennox, *Wilfred Grenfell—His Life and Work*, Rhodes House,
1959
Mackay, R. A. (ed.), *Newfoundland: Economic, Diplomatic and Stra-
tegic Studies*, Toronto, 1946

QUEENSLAND—PRIMARY

Government:

Colonial Office Files
Australia, C.O. 418, Original Correspondence,
Secretary of State, vols 70, 72, 77, 81, 91, 102, 114, 125
(1909-14)
Queensland State Archives
Governor's Secret and Confidential Outward Despatches to
Secretary of State, 1905-14, GOV. 68
MacGregor to Colonial Office, visit to Torres Strait islands,
20 July 1911, PRE/A 530, 10468/16
Queensland Parliamentary Debates
CIV-CXIX, 1909-14
Commonwealth Parliamentary Debates
XVIII-LXXV, 1904-14
Queensland Parliamentary Papers
1909-14
Secretary for Public Instruction,
Annual Reports, 34-39, 1909-14

Newspapers:

Brisbane, Queensland (selected dates 1909-14)
Courier—Public Library, Brisbane

Daily Mail—Public Library, Brisbane
Brisbane *Courier*, C. A. Bernays, 'The Governors of Queensland', November 1922–January 1923, Mitchell Library

University:

Queensland University Magazine
    1911-14, Queensland University Library
Galmahra
    1909-14
Letter Book of the Queensland University Union, to 1925
Students Representative Council Minutes, 1911-18

Articles:

Grimshaw, C., 'Australian Nationalism and the Imperial Connection', *Australian Journal of Politics and History*, III, 11, May 1958, pp. 161-82
Inglis, K. S., 'Australia Day', *Historical Studies of Australia and New Zealand*, XIII, 49, October 1967, pp. 20-41
Morrison, A. A., 'The Brisbane General Strike of 1912', *Historical Studies Australia and New Zealand*, IV, 14, May 1950, pp. 125-44
Thomson, Ailsa G., 'The Early History of the Bulletin', *Historical Studies of Australia and New Zealand*, VI, 22, May 1954, pp. 121-34

Theses:

Crook, D. P., Queensland Politics from 1900 to 1915, unpublished B.A. thesis, University of Queensland, 1957
Dalton, J. B., The Queensland Labour Movement, 1889-1915, unpublished B.A. (Hons.) thesis, University of Queensland, 1962
Lockley, B., Queensland's Native Policy, 1897-1939, unpublished B.A. (Hons.) thesis, University of Queensland, 1957

Other:

Convention of Labour Party, Queensland, March 1907
Interview with J. D. Story, 1961

QUEENSLAND—SECONDARY

Books:

The University of Queensland 1910-1935, Brisbane, 1935
Bernays, C. A., *Queensland Politics during Sixty Years 1859-1919*, Brisbane, c. 1920
Joyce, R. B. (ed.), Melbourne A.C.V. 'Constitutional Development in Queensland' in *Early Constitutional Development in Australia*, St Lucia, 1963, pp. 443-93
Moore, R. W., *The History of the Townsville Grammar School*, n.p. [Brisbane], 1959
Murphy, D., Joyce, R. B., Hughes, C. (eds), *Prelude to Power* (A history of the Labour Party in Queensland 1880-1915), Brisbane, 1970

RETIREMENT AND OVERALL—PRIMARY

Correspondence:

Stanmore Papers

58 letters from William MacGregor to Arthur Gordon are in vol. 5, MSS, 49,203. They cover the period 30 March 1879 to 19 January 1912 (with long gaps from 24 March 1892 to 18 February 1900 and 18 February 1900 to 31 March 1905).

Other volumes of the Stanmore papers were consulted, especially for MacGregor's Fijian years. The records are catalogued as follows:

MSS. 49199-49223, I-XXV, special
49224-49232, XXVI-XXXIV, family
49233-49242, XXXV-XLIV, general
49243-49252, XLV-LIV, letter-books
49253-49269, LV-LXXI, journals and diaries
49270-49272, LXXII-LXXIV, literary
49273-49285, LXXV-LXXXVII, miscellaneous
British Museum, London

Griffith Correspondence

82 letters from William MacGregor to Samuel Walker Griffith are in Dixson ADD. vol. 449 (26 February 1886–4 March 1887), 450 (6 July 1887–11 March 1891), 451 (10 May 1891–9 August 1894), 452 (9 April 1896–25 December 1899), 453 (10 November 1900–19 October 1903) and in Mitchell vol. 6 uncatalogued MSS. Set 363 (14 July 1904–19 February 1919).

Other volumes of the Griffith papers were consulted, e.g. Dixson 454 concerns MacGregor and Queensland University, and 428 Diary has many references to MacGregor.

Set 363 includes:

Diaries etc. 1854-1919
Family letters 1851-1915
Letters to his wife 1873-1916
General correspondence 1886-1920
Letters from Ferguson 1914-20
Memos, Articles and Addresses 1887-1919
Literary 1862-1920
Dante 1879-1917
Business Papers 1878, 1889-1919
Dixson and Mitchell Libraries, Sydney

Parkes Correspondence, with J. B. Thurston
Mitchell Library

Gladstone Papers (letters to Gordon, CCXXXV-VI, 44320-1),
British Museum

Government Sources:

Colonial Office List, 1872-1919

Legal Papers:

Entry in Register of Deaths
William MacGregor, General Registry Office, Edinburgh

Entry in Register of Deaths
  Mary MacGregor, General Registry Office, Edinburgh
Trust Disposition and Settlement of Sir William MacGregor,
  23 July 1919, General Register House, Edinburgh
Settlement of Lady Mary MacGregor
  13 December 1919, General Register House, Edinburgh
Legal Papers:
  Sir William MacGregor's Trust, 1919-21; valuation 30 April 1936,
    Articles stored July 1937
  Case Mary MacGregor against William Francis Forbes-Sempill
    et anor., et. ors., 1933-5
    Stalker and Thomson, Solicitors, Galashiels
    (now in possession of author)

Articles and Essays:

'Sir William MacGregor. An Appreciation', *Sydney Morning Herald,*
  16 July 1914
Sydney Mail, 22 July 1914
'Rule in the Pacific', *Sun,* Sydney, 13 July 1919
W. MacGregor, 'The Pacific and its Political Settlement', *United Em-
  pire Journal of the Royal Colonial Institute,* March 1918, ix, N.S., 3
F. W. Robinson, 'University Antiquities 111. The Banner of the First
  Chancellor of the University of Queensland', *Galmahra* (Queens-
  land University), Third Term, 1932, pp. 7-8
R. Sanderson Taylor, 'Scots We Know. Sir William MacGregor', *Scot-
  tish Australasian,* 11, 2, 1 January 1911, pp. 5-7

Obituaries:

Scotsman, 4 July 1919
Brisbane Mail, 5 September 1919
'The Right Hon. Sir William MacGregor', *Aberdeen Grammar School
  Magazine,* N.S., 23, October 1919, pp. 13-16
W. S. Crockett, 'A Notable Scot. The Late Sir William MacGregor (A
  Pro-Consul for Britain)', *Border Magazine* (Scotland) reprinted in
  The Scottish Australasian, XI ,130, 30 October 1920, pp. 7661-4
A. Meston, *Brisbane Mail,* 12 July 1919
R. W. Reid, 'Sir William MacGregor', *Aberdeen University Review,*
  VII, 19, November 1919, 1-14
George Woolnough, *Daily Mail, Brisbane,* 19 July 1919

RETIREMENT AND OVERALL—SECONDARY

Articles:

M. Jacobs, 'Bismarck and the Annexation of New Guinea', *Historical
  Studies Australia and New Zealand,* 5, 17, November 1951
R. B. Joyce, 'Sir William MacGregor: A Colonial Governor', *Historical
  Studies Australia and New Zealand,* 11, 41, November 1963

Books:

Chapman, J. K., *The Career of Arthur Hamilton Gordon,* Toronto,
  1964
Morrell, W. P., *Britain in the Pacific Islands,* Oxford, 1960

Reeve, H. F., *The Black Republic,* London, 1923

Rivers, W. H. R. (ed.), *Essays on the Depopulation of Melanesia,* Cambridge, 1922

Scott, E., *Australia During the War* (Official History of Australia in the War of 1914-18, XI), Sydney, 1936

Index

Abel, Reverend C. H., 415
Abeokuta, 222, 231, 243, 250, 252, 258-9, 262-3, 265-74, 276, 281, 283, 292, 296;
Alake of, 231, 258-9, 267-70, 272-6, 291, 428
Aberdeen, Lord, *see* Gordon, George Hamilton
Aberdeen, 2, 9-10, 342, 375, 387, 390; Chamber of Commerce, 380; Geographical Society, 215; Grammar School, 6-7; Museum, 129; Royal Lunatic Asylum, 9; Shire, 3; University, x-xi, xiii, 4, 7-10, 215, 229, 235, 276, 448-9
Abernethy, John, 30
Abioma, 132
Aboriginals (Australian), xii, 107, 341, 352-7, 380, 404, 442; 1897 Queensland Aboriginals Protection Act, 354, 357; Queensland policy, 352-7, 404
Aborigines' Protection Society, 52, 87, 107, 222, 248-9
Adegbite, 274
Adelaide and New Guinea Rubber Planting Syndicate, 213
Ademola, Ladapo, 273-4
Aden, 394
Aderibigbe, Dr A. A. B., 222, 240, 242, 421
Adeula, 274
Africa, *see also* Lagos, Nigeria, ix, 94, 106, 121, 141-3, 219-99, 301, 334, 358, 413; Central African Federation, 436
Africans, *see also* Lagos, Bini, Hausa, Ijebu, Egba, Yoruba, xiii, 14, 223, 225, 233, 240, 242, 244, 252, 263, 283, 289, 300; 'black Englishmen', 221; customs, 220, 240; doctors, 231; 'educated' (individualism), xiii, 220, 222, 240, 242, 244, 247-8, 250, 255-9, 266, 290, 299; 'liberated', 12-13, 17-20, 389
Agnew, J. W., 99, 403
Agriculture, *see also* Products, 56-66; Fiji, 78-80; New Guinea, 196-9; Lagos, 293-4, 298; Australia, 346, 353,

355; Queensland, 358-60, 366, 371, 374; New Zealand, 50
Aird River, 134
Ake, 273
Akitoye, Oba of Lagos, 220
Akure, 271
Alaska, 338
Albert Medal, 73
Alford, 6
Algeria, 282, 287
Alice Meade, 156
Allardyce, W. L., 150, 410
Amalgamated Workers' Association, Queensland, 346
Amsterdam, 236-7
Anasa, 91
Anderson, J., 53, 190
Anderson, Neil, 408
Anderson, T., 203
Anderson's University, Glasgow, x, 8
Angaur, 381
Anglo-Newfoundland Development Company, 311-12
Ansell, Captain, *see also* Law, New Guinea, 129-30
Anson, H., 53, 78, 80
Antrobus, Sir Reginald, 228, 233-4, 238, 244, 259, 264-5, 267, 270, 274, 279, 281-3, 285, 288, 297, 301, 427; wife, 233
Apapa plain, 237
Appel, J. G., 354-7
Arabian slave dhows, 14
Aristocracy, *see* Class
Armit, W. E., 156, 163, 413
Aru, 413
Armstrong, Professor, 384
Asquith, H. H., 377
Aroma, 166
Atlantic Ocean, 381
Auckland, 49, 102
Australia, xii, 23, 36-7, 41, 46, 48, 50-1, 67, 81, 95, 97, 100-1, 104-6, 114, 119, 121, 123-5, 138, 143, 145, 149, 151, 174-7, 197, 200, 205, 214, 216, 224, 300-2, 324, 327, 341-2, 346, 348, 352, 368, 372-4, 378-82, 384, 446-8; anti-British feelings, 348; Colonial policy, 149-50, 380-1; Depression, 105, 212; Federal Council

467

(1886), 97-9, 102; Federation, 105, 341, 349-51; foreign policy, 106, 108, 299, 381-2; governors, 348; Senate abolition, 441; strikes (1890s), 105, 205, 343-4
Australian Steam Navigation Company, 49

Ba (and Yasawas) province, 59, 81; Roko of, 83, 85
Badagry, 243, 248, 260
Baden-Powell, B. D. S., 216
Baiaa, 135
Bailala River, 419
Bakem, William, 408
Bamu River, 138
Banks, Savings (Fiji), xii, 45-6; Newfoundland, 310-11; Commonwealth (Australian), 350; Swiss, 386
Barambah, 353-5, 442
Barlow, A. H., 444
Barnes, W. H., 440-1
Barracouta, 394
Bartle Bay, 207
Barton, Edmund, 301, 381, 432
Barton, F. R., 432
Bau, 28, 60, 85
Beattie, G. W., 391
Beche-de-mer, 57, 59-61, 128, 199, 202, 206
Bechuanaland, 182
Becke, Louis, 407
Bega, 60
Belfast, 229
Belgium, 352
Beothic, 357
Berkeley, Henry Spencer, 89
Berlin, 36, 232
Berry, Graham, 100, 403
Berry, John, 44
Bevan, Theodore, 407
Bini, 220, 258
Bismarck, Otto, 217, 380
Bituvatu, 85-7
Blackwood, Captain, 138
Blair, J. W., 366, 444
Blaize, R. B., 274, 276
Blake, Sir Edward, 280, 429
Blayney, Dr J. A., 147, 191, 194
Bludau, Dr, 233
Bluntschli, J. K., 326, 438
Blyth, J., 26, 53, 59, 86-7
Boi, Iveri, 91
Boigu Island, 137, 140
Bond, Sir Ralph, 303, 306-11, 316-31, 332, 338-9, 344, 435-7
Boulia, 356
Bower, Major, 262

Bowman, David, 344-5
Boyle, Sir Cavendish, 303
Bramston, J., 47, 420
Brazil, 220, 248, 368
Bridge, Admiral, 177
Brisbane, 105, 108-10, 125, 129, 157, 183, 224, 345-6, 361-2, 369, 371-2, 442; Auchenflower (suburb), 364; City Council, 362; Exhibition Hall, 369; General Strike (1912), 345-6; Government House, 224, 349, 361-2, 364; Grammar School, 361-2; St Lucia (suburb), 364, 444; Toowong (suburb), 444; Victoria Park, 362, 364, 444
Britain, *see also* Scotland, Indirect rule, Imperialism, names of rulers and politicians;
  as country, 23, 73, 100, 102, 117, 218, 221, 224, 233, 259, 272-6, 291, 304, 322, 341-2, 347-8, 371-2, 374, 377-9, 384, 386, 436;
Colonialism:
  Colonial appointments, 11, 13, 42, 149-50, 224-5, 237, 392, 403, 433;
  Colonial conferences (1887), ix, 101-2, 104-5, 121; *(1897 Jubilee),* 124-5, 274; *(1902),* ix, 274, 303; *(1907),* ix, 321-2, 338, 436;
  Colonial co-operation, 320-1, 324, 337, 348, 351, 436;
  Colonial Institute, Royal, 107-8, 154, 166, 215, 379;
  Colonial policy, ix, xi, xiii-xiv, 13-14, 17, 23, 29, 41, 64-8, 75, 81, 90, 94-6, 100-5, 108, 110, 113, 118-26, 141-3, 160, 162, 176-7, 180, 182, 185, 188-90, 194-6, 213-14, 219-24, 228, 231, 236, 238, 240, 242, 245, 250-3, 256-7, 261-73, 280, 282, 285, 288-90, 296-7, 299-301, 303, 307, 310-12, 316, 319-26, 328, 330-1, 333, 337, 339, 343-4, 348, 351-2, 370, 374, 380-1, 388, 417, 424-6, 435;
  Colonial Office (other mentions), xii, 6, 10-11, 16, 20, 22, 33, 36-8, 49, 87, 97-9, 115-17, 139, 145, 148-52, 172, 218, 225, 227, 229-30, 232-4, 239, 244, 254-5, 260, 274-6, 278-9, 281, 283-4, 286-7, 292-3, 329, 334, 340, 342, 349, 353-4, 360-1, 371, 373, 375, 382;
  Colonial financial policy, 41, 44-

8, 50-6, 75, 120-2, 215, 228, 237, 294, 298, 313;
Treasury (other mentions), 119, 227, 286, 289, 295, 297, 310, 319, 376, 429;
Colonial service, 9, 11, 23, 33, 36-9, 42, 149-52, 334, 342, 373;
Crown Agents, 46, 51, 55, 227-8, 232, 278-81, 287, 299, 381, 398, 429;
Royal Society, 230;
Establishment, English, xi, xiii, 11, 94, 197, 225, 235, 302, 347;
Government, xi, 373, 377;
House of Commons, 332, 374;
House of Lords, 280;
Monarchy, xi, 273-4, 374, 437, 441, 446
British Honduras, 94
British New Guinea, see New Guinea
British New Guinea Syndicate, 105, 123-6, 205, 209, 211, 213, 293, 381, 407
Bromilow, Reverend W. E., 172, 174, 203
Brown, Reverend George, 173-4, 415
Bruce, Victor Alexander (9th Earl of Elgin), 301-2, 319-20, 334, 432, 435-7
Bryce, Viscount James, 300, 325, 369-70, 437, 445
Bua, 81; Roko of, 84
Bundaberg High School, 367
Buni, 134
Bure, Buli, 86
Burns Philp, 106, 145, 212, 344, 381, 407, 410-11
Butler, H. F., 433
Butterworth, A. W., 157, 161, 171-2, 412
Byrnes, T. J., 123, 125, 407, 418

Cakaudrove, 60, 81
Cakobau (Thakombau), 28, 39, 46, 58, 81, 397
Cairo, 291
Calcutta, 72
Cambridge University, 18, 215, 229
Cameron, J. B., 134-5, 157-8
Cameroons, 221, 233
Camooweal, 442
Campbell, A. M., 150, 410-11
Campbell, W. H., 441
Campbell, W. T., 151, 411
Canada, 315-16, 326, 336-40, 375
Candle-nuts, see Products
Cannibalism, 81
Carew, W. S., 57, 72
'Cargo cult', see under Papuans
FF

Carnarvon, Lord, see Herbert, Henry Howard Molyneux
Carnegie Trust, 389
Carr, Henry, 242-4
Carter, A. J., 441
Carter, Sir G. T., 221-2, 225, 285
Celli, Professor, 230, 232, 236
Ceylon, 25, 68, 80, 94, 96-7, 99-101, 112
Chad, Lake, 286-7
Chads Bay, 129, 132, 152
Chadwick, Osbert, 228, 232
Chadwick, St John, 434, 436
Chalmers, Reverend James, 107, 139-40, 168, 170-1, 417
Chamberlain, Joseph, xiv, 177, 180, 190, 223-4, 227, 229-30, 232, 264-5, 269-70, 279, 281-2, 284-6, 288, 294, 297, 312, 422-4
Chapel-on-Leader, x, 375-7, 383-8, 448
Chapman, J. K., 58
Charles X, of France, 328, 438
Charters Towers, High School, 367; School of Mines, 368
Chelmsford, Lord, 343-4, 443
Cheltenham, 298-9
Chermside, Sir Herbert, 301, 432
Chicago, xii, 307
Chidley Peninsula, 336
China, 229
Chinese, 145, 308, 357
Chisholm, D. J., 65, 399
Christison, Robert, 359
Churches, Christian, see also Mac-Gregor, William, Christian belief, x, 7, 142, 189-90, 221, 226, 305-433;
missionaries, 67, 106, 126-8, 139-40, 144, 147-8, 160, 167-80, 186, 189, 199-201, 203, 209, 211, 379, 414, 447;
Scotland, 3-4, 93, 303, 309, 376, 388;
Seychelles, 19;
Fiji, 23, 31, 41, 57, 82, 85, 98, 402;
Wesleyan missionaries, 27, 29, 32, 85-9, 92-3, 173;
New Guinea:
Anglican missionaries, 128, 167, 173-5, 179-80;
London Missionary Society, 126-7, 139-40, 147, 151, 167-80, 194, 200, 336, 415-18;
Methodist missionaries, 167, 170-1, 173-5, 179-80, 203;
Roman Catholic missionaries, 128, 155-6, 167-8, 173-80, 191, 200, 412, 414-15;
Lagos:
missionaries (Church Missionary

Society), 220, 223-3, 255, 283, 294, 425-6, 430;
Newfoundland, 307-10, 433;
  British and Foreign Bible Society, 308;
  Labrador:
    missionaries, 307, 336;
    Moravians, 307, 336-9, 439-40;
    Royal Mission to Deep Sea Fishermen, 307;
  Queensland, 362, 367, 444;
    missions to *Aboriginals*, 357;
    Moravians, 355;
    Roman Catholics, 355;
  Pacific, missionaries, 383, 447
Civilization (as British goal of colonial policy), xii-xiii, 45, 80-1, 91, 106, 120, 129, 141-3, 155, 166-7, 178, 181-2, 184, 193, 195, 204, 218, 225, 248, 269, 275, 283, 402, 417
Clark, Professor, 235
Clarke Medals, 73
Clarke, miner, 208
Class *see also* heading 'power of chiefs' under Fiji and Lagos, barriers, divisions, 3, 4, 373, 376; aristocracy (upper), x, xiii, 4, 12-13, 377; (middle), 4, 98, 377, 425; working (lower), x, 1-4, 13, 45, 107, 121, 343, 347, 364-5, 373, 376-7
Claverhouse 2, 390
Cloudy Bay, 133-4, 146, 163, 413
Coal, *see* Minerals
Cocks, Captain, 92-3
Cocks, Mary Jane, *see* MacGregor, Mary Jane
Coffee, *see* Products
Colo, 27
Colonialism, *see* Britain, colonial heading; names of imperial countries and colonies; Paternalism; Humanitarianism; Civilization; Imperialism; Indirect rule
Colonial Mutual Life Assurance Society, 386
Colonial Sugar Refining Company, 48-9, 80
Congo, 352
Conservatism, 343, 345, 360
Cook, Joseph, 381
Copra, *see* Products
Corney, Dr, 32-3, 35, 76, 237-8, 397
Cotton, *see* Products
Crane, George, 318-20, 322, 324
Creoles, 13, 18
Crockett, Reverend W. S., 376, 383
Crown Agents, *see* under Britain

Curieuse, 16

Dahomey, 287, 294
D'Albertis, 137
Dante, *see* Literary references
Daphne, 74
Darling, R., Governor, 145
Darling Downs, 359
Daru, 140, 146, 212
Dauan Island, 137, 200
Deakin, Alfred, 301-2, 347, 381, 436
Dedele, 203
Delena, 156
Denham, Digby, 345, 440-1
Denman, Baron, 349
Denmark, 377
Dennis, Mrs A., 448
Denton, George C., 223, 248
D'Entrecasteaux islands, 173
Derby, Earl of, *see* Stanley, Edward Henry
d'Espoir, Bay, 433
des Voeux, Mrs, 30, 395
  34-7, 40, 43, 47-8, 50, 56, 63-4, 78, 83, 94, 197, 448
des Voeux, Mrs. 30, 395
Diaz, Calvo y, 326, 438
Dickie, Professor, 10, 392
Dickson, J. R., 125, 421-2
Dido, H.M.S., 28
Dilke, Sir Charles, 59
Diseases:
  dysentery, 25, 30-1, 68, 77, 192-4, 233, 353, 382, 400;
  leprosy, 16, 191-2;
  malaria, xiii, 13, 68, 97, 114-15, 148, 151, 158, 191-5, 219, 225-7, 229-34, 236-9, 291, 295, 298, 342, 370, 417, 422-4;
  measles, 26-8, 50, 192-3, 307, 382, 433;
  ophthalmia, 31, 192, 356-7, 368;
  ringworm (Tokelau), 26;
  skin, 26, 191-3, 195, 394;
  smallpox, 27-8, 47, 68-9, 192, 194-5;
  tuberculosis, 193, 306-7;
  venereal, *Fiji*, 27-30; *Pacific*, 28-9, 382; *New Guinea*, 192-3; *Labrador*, 307; *Queensland*, 355, 357;
  whooping cough, 192-3, 433;
  other, 31, 50, 68, 94, 77, 191-3, 229, 307, 367-8, 381, 433
Disraeli, Benjamin, 23
Dobu, 172, 174, 203, 415
Docemo, Oba of Lagos, 220, 246, 248-9
Doni, 413
Donside, 2, 7, 9, 299, 342, 375, 388

Douglas, John, 97-9, 153, 160, 168-9, 196, 403, 407, 409
Drago, L. M., 438
Drakiniwai, 85-6
Drekiti, Roko, 85
Dubois, Alexander, 318-20, 322, 324
Dudley, Earl of, see Ward, William Humble
Duhig, Archbishop, 367
Dulacca, 358
Dupeyrat, Father André, 174, 178
Dyer, Sir William T. Thiselton, 289-90
Dysentery, see Diseases

Earlston, 376
Ebute Metta, 248
Ede, 292
Edelfelt, E. G., 153, 411
Edinburgh, 9, 94, 117, 276, 305, 376; University, x, 229, 235, 276, 293; Chamber of Commerce, 280
Education, see also MacGregor, William, colonial career, Education; Universities, x, xi, 1, 3-4, 57, 178-80, 195, 200, 204-5, 221, 228, 242, 246, 255, 292, 303, 305, 307, 341, 352-3, 356, 361-2, 364-71, 384, 412, 433-4
Edun, Adegloyega, 274, 276
Edward VII, King of England, xi, 273-4, 303, 333-4, 437, 446
Egba, 222-3, 258-9, 262-4, 266, 269, 271-2, 274, 421
Egypt, 236, 291, 295
Ekiti, 271
Ela, 212
Elder Dempster, 229, 234, 276, 290-3
Eleko, Oba of Lagos, 246, 248-9
Elgee, Captain, 428
Elgin, Lord, see Bruce, Victor Alexander
Ellis, M. H. A. Newfoundland, 328
Emberson, Horace G. C., 61
Enauta, 148
English, A. C., 157, 163, 412
Epe, 243, 248, 426; Elepe of, 249
Erskine, Commander, 196
Esquimaux, xii, xiv, 300, 306-8, 332, 336-7, 339-40, 355
Europeans, 25, 30, 34, 40-1, 71, 83, 114, 118, 122-3, 127, 134, 138, 147-8, 159, 164-5, 167, 169, 181, 187, 192, 196, 199, 201, 208-10, 212-13, 220-2, 231-3, 235, 242, 244-5, 248, 250-2, 263-4, 268-71, 282, 290-1, 299, 313, 348, 355-6, 374, 380

Explorers, see also MacGregor, William, colonial career, exploration, 126, 208

Faden, Mr, see MacGregor, Helen
Fahey, B., 441
Fairfax, Rear-Admiral, 160, 413
Falkland Island, 94
Falorsi, Professor, 298
Fellows, Reverend, 171
Ferdinand V and Isabella I of Castile, 142, 409
Ferdinand, Franz Arch-duke, 446
Ferguson, R. C. M., 447
Fergusson Island, 129, 207
Fernberg, 349
Fiddes, G. V., 55
Fiji, see also subject headings (pp. 22-94) under MacGregor, William, colonial career; Churches, Christian; Labour; Law, ix, xii-xiv, 12-13, 20-99, 102-3, 106, 114, 122, 130, 142-3, 145, 149-50, 158-62, 167, 173, 187, 192, 194-7, 199, 202, 219-20, 224, 228, 237, 256, 258, 273, 295, 298-9, 303, 307-8, 352-3, 368, 375, 381, 389, 416-17, 442, 446, 448; economy:
    trade, 48-9; development, 78-80; population, 25-8, 394; Native Debts Commission, 39; Savings Bank, 45-6;
government:
    Legislative Council, 50, 57; cadet scheme, 150-1;
    native Councils, 28, 57, 81-2, 91, 401;
    power of chiefs, 28-9, 32, 41, 57, 60, 65-6, 80-92, 126, 248, 295
Fijians, xii, 24-5, 27-31, 40-1, 44, 238, 240, 257, 300;
customs, 81, 86;
growth of individualism, 41, 81-2, 84, 88, 90-2, 399;
Firearms, 104-5, 182, 295
Fisher, Andrew, 350-1, 378-9, 446-7
Fishing, see also Beche-de-mer, Pearl-shell,
    New Guinea, 120, 197, 199-200, 206-7, 209;
    Newfoundland, xii, 300, 306, 309-27, 330-4, 337, 342, 370, 434-5, 437, 439;
    Scotland, 375
Fison, Reverend Lorimer, 88-9, 92
Fletcher, Asst Professor, 291-2
Florence, 230, 236
Fly River, xiv, 134, 136-8

Foorah Bay College, 256
Forbes, H. O., 407
Forbes-Sempill, William Francis (19th Lord, 10th Baronet, Sempill), 383, 386-7, 448
Forests, see Timber
Forrest, John, 381, 407
Fowler, J., 72-3
France, ix, 12-14, 18, 167, 220-1, 223, 281-2, 286-7, 294, 304, 312-13, 332-4, 380-1, 384
Franklyn, Captain W. H., 16-17
Fraser, Professor A. M., 435
Free trade, see New South Wales, 48, 52
Fruit, see Products
Fuller, Commissioner, 223
Fuller, F., 101

Gairdner, Sir William, 235
Galirupu, 410
Galoma, 410
Gatton Agricultural College, 358-9
Gauria, 153
Gbadebo, Alake of Abeokuta, 231, 258-9, 267-70, 272-6, 291, 428
Geberisisila, 408
Geddes, Sir William, 216
Genii, 153
Geographical Societies;
  Royal British, 107, 138, 274;
  Royal Scottish, 379;
  Royal Victoria, 138;
  Manchester, 215;
  Aberdeen, 215;
  Queensland, 368
George V, King of England, xi, 374, 446; Hospital, London, 384
George, C. J., 425-6
George, J. O., 222, 421
Germany, ix, 36, 41, 51, 105, 141-2, 174, 220-1, 223, 232-4, 317, 372-4, 377-8, 380, 383, 443, 446;
  German New Guinea Company, 143, 410;
  German New Guinea, 137, 194, 232, 379, 408, 447
Gibb, Major, 305
Gibson, Professor A. J., 444
Gilbert islands, 67
Gillion, K. L., 68, 80
Gira River, 206, 208, 408
Gladstone, W. E., 24, 27, 45, 215, 437
Glasgow, 294; Chamber of Commerce, 380;
  Technical College, 362;
  University, x, xiii, 7-9, 88, 117-18, 169, 235-6, 385, 391-2

Glasier, F. Bedford, 283, 285, 287-9
Gleeson, Denis, 154, 412
Goats, angora, 358
Gold, New Guinea, 106, 120, 126, 128, 133, 137-8, 146-8, 199, 205-8;
  Africa (metaphorical), 142
Gold Coast, 220-1, 260, 288, 296
Goodenough Island, 164, 413;
  Bay, 208
Goodridge, A. F., 329
Gordon, Arthur (Lord Stanmore), xi-xiii, 9-10, 12-14, 16-20, 22-4, 26, 33, 38, 40-2, 44, 47, 56-62, 66-8, 72-3, 78-84, 88, 92-4, 96, 98-101, 103, 106-7, 111-12, 126, 132, 135, 137-8, 141-2, 150, 195, 214-18, 227, 230, 273, 301-3, 305-6, 319-20, 332, 345, 347-8, 353-4, 357, 373-4, 403, 417, 420, 439, 446
Gordon, George Hamilton (4th Earl of Aberdeen), 18, 217
Gordon, Rachel, 30
Goruoni, 410
Government, see names of colonies
Governors, see names of colonies, individuals, and Australian States
Granville, see Leveson-Gower, Granville George
Granville, 212
Grassi, Dr, 230
Great Amalgam Estate, 78
Greece, see also Languages, Greek, 129, 434
Green, John, 157, 164, 208
Greene, D. J., 329
Grenfell, Dr Wilfred, 307, 433, 440
Grey, Mr, 262
Grey, Albert Henry George (4th Earl Grey), 306, 316, 337
Grey, Sir Edward, 322, 325, 332, 334, 436
Grey, Sir George, 328, 438
Griffith, Samuel Walker, xiii, 98-103, 106-9, 113-18, 137, 143, 161-2, 169, 172, 176, 182-3, 197, 199-200, 215-16, 224-5, 234, 237-8, 298, 301-2, 304, 313, 317, 321-3, 325, 334, 336, 341, 361, 369-70, 372-4, 376, 378-9, 381, 383, 385, 409, 437, 443, 448
Guduamere, 408
Guise, R. E., 203
Guadalcanal, 161
Guildford, 275
Gulf of Papua, 138, 211
Gume, 153
Gympie High School, 367

Hackett, Sir William, 82
Hahn, Mr, *see also* MacGregor, Helen, 386
Hall Sound, 156, 212
Hamilton Inlet, 339; River, 339
Hampson, C. S., 333
Harcourt, Lewis, 358, 374
Harding, T., 283, 430
Harmsworth concession, 311-12
Harrison, Cape, 339
Hatton-Richards, T., 158, 408, 412
Hausa, 220, 260, 262
Havelock, A., 403
Hay, John, 316
Heffernan, E. O. B., 150, 410
Hefftler, A. W., 326, 438
Helferrich, Karl, 374
Hely, B., 140, 147, 152-3, 157, 171, 408, 411, 416
Henley Villa, 16
Herbert, Henry Howard Molyneux (4th Earl of Carnarvon), 23-4, 44, 56
Herbert, R. G. W., 23, 28, 37, 52, 55-6, 65, 94, 96-7, 101-3, 282, 394
Hillockhead, croft, 390
Historical references, xiv, 18, 111, 142, 159-60, 216-17, 246, 328, 376, 405, 409, 420-1, 438
Hobart, 98
Hoffmann, Mr, 292-3
Holland, 57, 59, 65, 137, 139-40, 236, 408-9
Holland, Sir Henry Thurston (1st Viscount Knutsford), 55, 90, 101, 127-8, 411
Holt, John, 427
Honorius, Roman Emperor, 111, 405
Honours:
  MacGregor, William, *C.M.G. (1881)*, 93-4; *K.C.M.G. (1889)*, 420; *G.C.M.G. (1907)*, 331, 439; *English arms*, 7th illustration; *Scottish arms (1884)*, 94, 403; *C.B.*, 214, 420; *P.C.*, 374, 446; *French offer of Legion of Honour*, 334; *Ll.D. (Aberdeen)*, 215; *D.Sc. (Cambridge)*, 215, 420; *Ll.D. (Queensland)*, 370; *School of Physiology (Queensland)*, 371;
  Bryce, James, *Ll.D. (Queensland)*, 369;
  Griffith, Samuel, *Ll.D. (Queensland)*, 369;
  Kidston, William, *Ll.D. (Queensland)*, 370; Ross, Ronald, 423; Winter, F. J., *C.M.G.*, 150, 411;

Australian, 324, 349, 441; Newfoundland, 324; St Pierre, 334
Hooker, Dr, 392
Hooker, Sir Joseph, 79
Hopedale, 339
Hopeful, 170
Howley, Archbishop, 307, 309-10, 433
Hudson's Bay Company, 339
Hudson Straits, 338
Hughes, W. M., 379, 381, 446-7
Hula, 203
Hull, Conference of the National Sea Fisheries Protection Association, 313
Humanitarianism, 14, 67-8, 75, 106-7, 142, 186, 190, 195, 197
Hunter, George, 153-4, 186, 408
Hunter, J. M., 441
Hunter, Robert, 153
Huss, John, 132
Hutton, Dr S. K., 307

Ibadan, 221-3, 228, 238, 243, 250, 252, 258, 262-5, 269, 271-2, 280-5, 296, 421, 427-8, 430; Bale of, 263, 267-8, 428; Bashorun of, 430
Ibara, 292
Idanre, 271
Iddo Island, 220, 281
Ife, 428; Oni of, 249, 258-9
Igbogila, Bale of, 253, 425
Ijebu, 222
Ijoh, 258
Ikerun, 292
Ikorodu, 243
Ikoyi, 228, 237
Ilesha, 271; Owa of, 284-5
Ilorin, 280-1, 284-6
Immigration, 39, 47, 54, 56
Imperialism:
  Australian, 108, 299, 381-2;
  British, ix-xii, 9, 12-13, 23, 106, 141-3, 177-8, 216, 219-21, 223, 252, 260, 281-2, 286-7, 299, 315-18, 323, 331-4, 372-4, 377-8, 381, 389, 446;
  French, 12-13, 177-8, 220-1, 223, 281-2, 286-7, 332-4;
  German, ix, 141-2, 220-1, 223, 281, 317, 372-4, 377-8, 381;
  Japanese, 382;
  United States, 315-18, 323, 331, 389;
  Entente Cordiale, 332-3, 380;
  Berlin Conference (1884-5), 221;
  Empire Day, 441
im Thurn, Sir Everard, 442

Inawa, 155
Inawabui, 408
Inawaia, 408
Inawi, 155
India, *see also* Labour, imported: *Indians in Fiji*, 13, 70-3, 90, 109, 111, 113, 229, 443;
Office, 55;
spices, 70
Indian Ocean, 14
Indians, xii, 13, 25, 41, 290, 303;
Tamils, 68;
in Labrador, 336-7;
in Newfoundland, 300, 306, 336, 433;
in Queensland, 442
Indirect rule:
Fiji, 81-3;
New Guinea, 166-7;
Lagos, 222, 240, 242, 244-5, 247, 250, 258, 273, 425;
Nigeria, 425
Innuit, 300, 306
Irrigation, Queensland, 359-60
Isimari, 408
Issi, 134
Italy, *see also* Languages, Italian, 137, 167, 230, 232-4, 236, 291, 298, 351, 374
Itori, Onitori of, 268
Iwo, 292

Jack, Reverend Alexander, 388
Jamaica, 198
Jamestown, 307
Japanese, 378-9, 382, 442, 447
Java, 57, 59, 65
Jebba, 287, 289
Jebu Ode, 243, 261, 427
Jedburgh, 376
Joannet Island, 207
'Johnny', 135
Johnson, Dr Obadiah, 246, 252, 257, 424-6, 430
Johnson, Reverend Samuel, 222, 421, 423
Jones, Sir Alfred, 229-30, 256, 266, 277, 280, 427

Kabadi, 157
Kadavu, 31-2, 62, 81, 396
Kanakas, *see* Labour, imported: *Kanakas in Queensland*
Kano, 286, 297
Kasava, 78
Keith A,. Berriedale, 328-9, 437-8
Kemta, Abeokuta, 268

Kenmay, 276
Kennedy, C., 407
Kennedy, Sir C. M., 123
Kennedy, James, 4, 6
Kennedy, R. J., 148, 171
Kennemou River, 339
Kent, J. M., 324, 326
Kerepunu, 194
Kerillis, Captain, 304
Kew Gardens, 79, 198, 289-90, 336, 338
Kickbusch, Albert, 186, 408
Kidston, William, 343-5, 349, 361-2, 370, 441, 443
Kikori, 134
Kimberley, Lord, *see* Wodehouse, John
King, Reverend Copland, 174, 194
Kingsley, Mary, 225, 422;
medal, 239
Kingsmill islands, 67
Kiriwina, 171, 174
Knollys, Sir C. C., 433
Knollys, Captain L. F., 27
Knowhead, 3
Knutsford, Lord, *see* Holland, Henry Thurston
Koch, Professor, 232-3, 423
Koiari, 413
Konieh, 333, 439
Kowald, Charles, 154-7, 165
Labour:
Australian, 105, 121, 125, 205, 347;
Party, 343, 347-8, 350-1;
English, 347;
Fijian, 56-8, 64-5, 67-8, 77, 81, 358, 399;
Lagos, 296;
New Guinea, 108, 125, 162, 167, 179, 195-6, 199-205, 418;
Queensland, 358, 406; *Brisbane strike (1912)*, 345-6, 350, 440-1; *sugar strike (1911)*, 346; *Party*, 343-51, 440-1;
West African, 250;
Imported: *Africans in Seychelles*, 14, 21;
aliens in Queensland, 351, 442;
Kanakas in Queensland, 67, 97-8, 107-8, 122, 170, 192, 199-200, 351, 418, 442;
Indians in Fiji, 21, 27, 41, 46-8, 51, 54-6, 67-73, 76-8, 80, 199, 394, 400;
Pacific Islanders in Fiji, 27-8, 34, 41, 46-8, 67-8, 70-1, 73-8, 80, 192, 199, 394

Labrador, xii, xiv, 300, 306, 310, 313, 315, 336-40, 355, 433
La Digue, 16
Lagos, *see also* subject headings (pp. 219-99) under MacGregor, William, colonial career; Labour; Churches, Christian; Law; Africans, ix, xii-xiii, 142-3, 219-301, 303-5, 331, 334, 342, 368, 370, 381, 386, 389, 446;
economy:
  Chamber of Commerce, 265, 282;
  development, 220, 243-4;
  finance, 253, 281-2, 285-7, 291, 294-8;
government:
  Central Native Council, 247-51, 425;
  chiefs', xii, 219, 223, 240, 242-3, 246-52, 258-77, 291, 299, 389, 426-8;
  constabulary, 243, 260;
  Executive Council, 242;
  form, 220, 242-6, 252;
  hinterland states, 220-2, 243, 245, 250-2, 258-77, 287, 290;
  Legislative Council, 242, 245-6, 248, 251-2, 254-5, 261, 263, 265, 290, 296, 425-6, 430;
  Native Advisory Board, 223, 242, 244, 248;
  Native Councils Ordinance, 247-52, 290;
  Provincial Councils, 250-1, 258, 261;
  Institute, 246-7, 255, 295;
  Stores Limited, 262;
  trade routes, 221-2, 261-6, 282-3, 285-7
Laird (Principal Glasgow University), 118
Laissez-faire, xii, 46
Lakekamu River, 419
Lala, Ratu, 83
Lamb, Charles, 8
Lamington, Baron, 124
Lammasch, Dr Heinrich, 326, 438
Lancashire, 220, 276
Land:
  Fijian, 45, 58, 352;
  New Guinea, 104, 107, 120, 123-5, 136, 143-4, 160, 167, 172-3, 176-7, 184, 196-7, 201, 208-13, 352, 379, 415, 419;
  Lagos, 246, 250, 261, 269, 283, 289, 292, 430;
  Newfoundland, 434-5;
  Labrador, 332, 336-40;
  Queensland, 351, 353, 374;

Britain, 374-5;
Crown Lands Ordinance of 1890, 210
Langham, Reverend Frederick, 86-9, 92
Languages, *see also* Literary references, xii, 444;
  Africa, 231;
  Creole French, 18;
  English, 7, 178, 256, 364;
  Fijian, 92, 150-1, 237, 239, 402;
  French, 167, 178, 215-17, 235, 239, 256, 298, 364-5, 385, 420, 444;
  German, 215-17, 230, 364-5, 373, 385, 420-1, 444;
  Greek, xiii, 4, 7, 18, 215, 239, 256, 364-5, 370, 376;
  Italian, xiii, 98, 215-16, 230, 232-4, 238-9, 369, 385, 420;
  Latin, 4, 7, 18, 215, 256, 298, 364-6, 370, 376;
  Motu, 151, 154, 416;
  New Guinea, 152, 154, 157, 169, 201-2, 239;
  'Pidgin English', 416;
  Swahili, 18, 231, 239;
  Tongan, 151
l'Anse Sablon, 338
Lapland, 338
Latin, *see* Languages
Lau, 81, 85
Laurier, Sir Wilfred, 338
Lausanne, 214, 216, 299
Law, *see also* Murder, Sorcery, Theft, 42, 81, 83, 98, 141-3, 150, 213, 416;
  Seychelles, 17;
  Fiji, 74, 82, 87-90;
  New Guinea, 91, 104-5, 111-12, 120, 123, 127-30, 132-4, 137, 139, 144, 148-53, 155, 158, 160, 162, 164-6, 170, 179-91, 194-6, 199, 202-5, 207-8, 379, 407-8, 412-13, 416-17;
  Lagos, 221-4, 227, 242, 245-6, 254-5, 260-1, 264, 268-72, 279, 427;
  Newfoundland, 317-20, 322-5, 330-1, 435-6;
  Queensland, 216, 346, 350, 354;
  Scotland, 387-8;
  Australian, 325, 350, 369, 441;
  Italian, 215;
  international, 322, 324-6, 330-1, 438
Lawes, F. E., 147, 154, 408, 411-12
Lawes, Reverend William G., 147, 168-9, 172, 414-15
Leader River, 376
Leeward islands, 54
Legge, J., 44, 61
Le Hunte, George, 158, 224

Lekki, 243
Lennon, William, 344, 441
Leonidas, 68-70
Leochnel-Cushnie parish, 390
Leprosy, *see* Diseases
Lesina, V. B. J., 349, 441
Lett, Lewis, 130
Leveson-Gower, Granville George (9th Earl Granville), 380
Levuka, 24, 27-8, 31, 33-5, 51, 60, 62, 69, 72, 396, 400;
  Chamber of Commerce, 48;
  Hospital, 75;
  Wesleyan church, 93
Lilley, Sir Charles, 113, 405
Liquor, intoxicating, 105, 182, 261, 263, 265, 294-5, 332-4, 357, 379, 417, 424, 426, 431
Lister, Lord (Sir Joseph), 229, 235, 391
Literary references, *see also* Historical references; Languages, Brennus, 127, 407; Carlyle, 246; Dante, 98, 215-16, 238, 299, 369, 376; Dickens, 246; Dido, 132; Goethe, 216; Herostratus, 328, 438; Homer, 4, 7; *Iliad*, 215; Livy, 4; Portia, 43; Schiller, 216; Thackeray, 246
Liverpool, 226, 275-6, 280, 290, 311, 407;
  Chamber of Commerce, 222, 256, 262, 275-6, 280, 282, 291, 427;
  School of Tropical Medicine, 229-30, 234-5, 424
Livingstone, David, 9, 168, 392
Lloyd George, David, 377
Loans:
  Fiji, 47-8, 50-2, 55, 70;
  New Guinea, 406;
  Lagos, 281, 294, 296-7, 429;
  Newfoundland, 310
Lobb, E. C., 203
Lockley, B., 442
Lockyer District High School, 367
Loftus, Lord Augustus, 111, 405
Lomaiviti, 81;
  Roko, 85
London, xi, 18, 27-8, 47, 65, 96-7, 101, 104-5, 107, 110, 116-17, 125, 183, 211, 217, 224, 233, 254-5, 274-6, 278, 287, 295-6, 300, 305, 310, 323, 330, 334, 341, 349, 352, 373-5, 384-6, 388, 426;
  Exhibition (1851), ix;
  Missionary Society, *see* under Churches, Christian
Loubet, Emile, 333
Louis XVI, of France, 111, 405

Louisiades, 146, 148, 173, 199, 206-7
Louth, Lincolnshire, 359
Lowles, J., 123
Lucas, Sir Charles, 348, 352
Lugard, Sir Frederick, 260-1, 273, 282, 287, 295, 297, 424-5
Luki, 85
Ly-ee-moon, 33
Lyttelton, Alfred, 273, 303, 436

Mabudauan, 146
McCallum, Sir H. E., 221, 223, 225, 242, 264
Macarthurs, planters in Fiji, 76
McFarlane, Dr Samuel, 168
McGregor, Agnes (*née* Smith), 2
MacGregor,, Alpina Viti, xiv, 93, 117, 214, 298-9, 304-5, 373, 384-5, 402
McGregor, Ann, 3, 390
McGregor, Catherine, 3, 390
McGregor, Christian, 390
MacGregor clan, 1
MacGregor, George, 3
McGregor, Gordon, 390
MacGregor, Helen, xiv, 16, 24, 30, 93, 117, 214, 373, 385-8, 394-5, 448
MacGregor, James, xiv, 9, 12, 93, 117-18, 214, 373, 385-8, 391, 406, 448
McGregor, John (Snr), ix, x, 1, 2, 3, 6, 22, 390
McGregor, John (Jnr), x, 3, 390
McGregor, Mary (*née* Thomson), 7, 18, 22, 24, 30, 394
MacGregor, Mary (Bobs), 93, 117, 214, 226, 298-9, 304-5, 369, 373, 384-5, 387-8, 402, 448
MacGregor, Mary Jane (*née* Cocks), 92-3, 117, 298-9, 304-5, 342-3, 369, 373, 383, 387-8, 402, 406, 412, 448
MacGregor, William, *see also* names of his colonies; Honours; Languages; agricultural labourer, x, 2-4, 6-7, 12, 347;
  colonial career, ix-xiii, 1, 9-11;
    education, 12, 17, 19, 31-2, 139, 178-80, 195, 246, 255-7, 306, 308-10, 352-3, 356, 361-2, 364-71, 433-4;
    exploration, xiv, 106, 115, 121, 135-9, 141, 145, 208, 342;
    finance, xii-xiii, 12, 19, 22, 26-7, 34-6, 39-66, 76-7, 80, 95, 120, 129, 140, 143, 178-9, 195, 211-13, 215, 219, 228-9, 232, 255, 281, 291, 294-8, 306, 310-12, 322, 337, 397, 431, 434;
    health, xii, 12-14, 16, 20-2, 24-38,

42-3, 56, 68-71, 74-9, 115, 128,
191-5, 202, 219, 225-39, 243, 247,
255-6, 278-9, 281, 295, 298, 300,
306-8, 353, 355-7, 367-8, 382-3,
389, 395, 399-400, 417, 422-4,
447;
leave, (1882-3) 36, 39-40, 92-3, 96;
(1888) 103; (1894-5) 95, 106,
114, 116, 118-19, 214; (1898-9)
224; (1900) 230, 283, 298;
(1902) 236, 291, 298; (1904) 272,
276, 298; (1909) 303, 342; (1914)
371, 375-6;
science, 26, 35-6, 78-9, 198-9, 207,
227-8, 233, 237, 242-3, 245, 255,
290, 293, 306, 312-14, 336, 338,
341, 354, 358-60, 368, 370;
financial (private) situation, xi, 10-
11, 16-17, 33-8, 40, 42, 79, 94, 103,
117-18, 224, 301-2, 304, 341, 371,
375-6, 422, 446, 448;
medical (private) career, ix-xi, xiii-
xiv, 1, 3-4, 6-12, 22, 32-40, 42,
93-4, 98, 103, 114, 219, 227, 229-
30, 234, 239, 298, 300, 372-3, 396,
449;
personal life:
birth, ix, x, 1; marriages (1st), xiv,
7, 9-10, 12, 18, 20, 22, 24, 30, 92
(2nd), xiv, 22, 92-3, 115, 117, 214,
224, 226, 234, 238, 298-300, 304-6,
369, 372-3, 375, 406, 412; parent,
xiv, 9, 12, 16, 24, 93, 115, 117-18,
214, 224, 226, 234, 298, 300, 304-6,
369, 372-3, 384-8, 448; grand-
father, 384-5; death, ix, 387-8,
448; relatives, 1-4, 375; friends,
xiii, 4, 6, 11, 18-19, 22, 98, 100,
216-18, 230, 234, 239, 258-9, 266-7,
270, 274, 299, 341, 345, 372, 383,
389, 391, 446; appearance, xiv,
130, 158, 239; health, 10, 17, 36,
80, 94, 114-15, 128, 130, 139, 158,
191, 194, 214, 226, 230, 234, 238-
9, 280, 293-4, 298-9, 301, 303-4,
341-5, 371-3, 383, 386-7, 393;
character, xii-xiv, 1-4, 6-7, 9, 12,
17, 19, 20-2, 24, 33-4, 37-8, 40,
42-3, 70-3, 76, 83, 92-6, 98, 100,
102, 107, 111, 113-14, 116-18, 123,
126, 128-30, 132-3, 138-43, 149,
154, 156, 158-9, 163, 169, 186, 203,
213-15, 217-18, 231-5, 237-40, 242,
257, 266, 277, 283-4, 288, 299-300,
303-4, 307, 334, 336, 340, 342-3,
347, 352-7, 368, 370, 372-3, 375-6,
378-9, 385-9, 422, 431, 433, 448-9;
Christian belief, 92-3, 174-5, 177-

8, 309, 383, 402, 447; reading, xiii,
2, 4, 7, 18, 92, 98, 215-18, 246-7,
299, 326, 376, 396, 402, 420-1
McIlwraith, T., 97-8, 103, 105-9, 113,
172, 199, 404-5
Mackay High School, 367
Mackay, Donald James (11th Baron
Reay of Carolside, Earlston), 375
Mackellar, Charles, xiii, 37, 98-100,
341, 372, 382, 389, 403, 448-9
Maclaren, Reverend Albert, 173-4
Macleod, Sir George, 235
McNeill, D. A., 161
Macrobin, Professor, 8
McTier, James, 408
Macuata, 66, 81
Magaubo, 413
Mahé, 14, 16
Mainopanau, 414
Maipua, 413
Mair, Dr L., 130, 166, 203-4
Mairu, 189
Maitasiri, see Tai Levu
Maiva, 155
Maize, 57
Malaria, see Diseases
Malaya, 162, 223, 270
Malayata, 161
Malvern, 385
Mambare, 146, 157, 174, 208, 408
Mamu, 294
Manchester, 311;
Chamber of Commerce, 222, 278,
280, 291, 427;
Geographical Society, 215
Manila, Tom, 156
Mansfield, Sir Alan, 361
Manson, Dr Patrick, 229
Manu Manu, 168
Marathon, 372
Marika, Ratu, 84-5
Marists, see Churches, Christian, New
Guinea: Roman Catholic mission-
aries
Markham, Sir Charles, 275
Marlborough, Duke of, 267, 274, 280
Marnoch, Professor John P., xiii, 448
Marsh, Magistrate, 318, 435
Matadona, 179, 414
Maudsley, A., 39
Mauritius, 12-21, 22-4, 94
Mayne, Dr and Miss, 364
Mayo, Dr, 32-3, 399
Meade, Sir Robert, 117
Measles, see Diseases
Medicine, see also MacGregor, Wil-
liam, health headings; Diseases, x,
8, 25, 34-7, 42, 80, 169, 221, 228-39,

303, 353, 355-7, 366-7, 371, 382-3, 422-3;
Australasia, *Intercolonial Congress*, 192;
England, *doctors' earnings*, 35;
Fiji, 32, 35;
Central Medical School, Suva, xii, 31-2, 237-8, 353, 389;
Scotland, *doctors*, 25, 235;
Tropical, *Schools of, Liverpool and London*, 228-30, 234-5;
Society for, England, 239;
Institute of, Townsville, 357, 447
Mediterranean, 282
Mekeo, 146, 154-7, 175-6, 412, 414
Melanesia, 167
Melbourne, 49, 97, 372;
botanical department, 368
Melrose, 375
Merani, 408
Merauke River, 140
Meredith, J., 150, 410
Merrie England, 112-13, 117-19, 121-2, 126, 157, 161, 406
Meteor, 394
Michie, Professor J. L., 444
Micmac, 306, 433
Mikluho Maclay, Baron, 107
Military:
Australia, 97, 346, 378, 382;
universal training, 378;
Britain,
universal training, 377-8, 446;
Fiji, 92;
India, 111;
Lagos, 259-60, 282, 286, 297, 299;
New Guinea, 106, 133, 162;
Sudan, *Fijian volunteers*, 94;
West Africa, 143, 235, 249-51, 299;
Frontier Force, 260, 295, 297
Milne Bay, 129, 132, 152, 417
Minerals, *see also* Gold
New Guinea (coal), 199, 418;
Lagos, 293, 426;
Newfoundland, 312;
Labrador, 336;
Scotland, 346, 378, 383;
Queensland, 368
Minister, Nicholas, 129, 407
Misima, 147, 206-7
Missionaries, *see* Churches, Christian
Mississippi, 292
Mitchell, Sir Charles, 22, 30, 32, 40, 52-4, 56, 60-1, 87-8, 90-1, 102
Mohammedanism, 248-9, 415, 426
Moloney, Sir C. A., 221-2, 225
Monckton, C. A. W., 158, 164, 413
Money, J. W. B., 57

Moor, Sir Ralph, 263, 282, 287, 426-7, 431
Moravian Mission, *see* Churches, Christian, Labrador
Morehead, B. D., 111, 113, 172
Morel, E. D., 278-80, 287
Moreton, M. H., 157, 163, 208, 412-13
Morgan, Arthur, 344-5
Morocco, 286, 317
Morrell, W. P., 58, 69-70, 130
Morris, Sir Edward, 306, 308, 310, 313, 322-3, 326-31
Moseley, C. H. Harley, 272
Motu, *see* Languages
Motu Motu, 153, 411
Mt Morgan High School, 367
Mt Victoria, 138
Mueller, Baron von, 368
Murder, 81, 126-7, 161, 166, 184-7, 207-8, 271, 416;
Ansell, 129, 132-3, 186;
Bakem, 408;
Clarke, 208;
Green, 157, 164, 208, 408;
Hunter, 153, 186, 408;
Kickbusch, 186, 408;
Murray, Hubert, 347, 380-1
Museums, Aberdeen, 129;
Queensland, 129, 368
Musgrave, A., Governor, 104-7, 112, 182, 414
Musgrave, Anthony (Jnr), 144, 151-2, 154, 169-70, 411
Muskrat Falls, 340

Nadroga, 66, 81, 85
Namata, 61, 85
Namosi, 61, 81, 85
Nasilai Reef, 72
Natal, 190, 301
Native peoples, *see also* Aboriginals (Australian), Africans, Creoles, Esquimaux, Fijians, Indians, Papuans, Polynesians, ix, xii, xiii, 13, 24, 50, 95, 98, 100, 105
Nauru, 381
Nausori, 80
Navarre, Louis André, 167-8, 175-6
Navuloa, 31, 93
Navy, Royal (British), 127, 160
Neimani, 85
Nelson, Sir Hugh, 117, 123-5, 407
Nevers, 384
Nevitt, I., 441
New Britain, 108, 173
New Brunswick, 18
New Caledonia, 67, 380
New England, 316

Newfoundland, *see also* subject headings under MacGregor, William, colonial career; Fishing: Labrador; Law; Churches, Christian, ix, xii, 276, 299-340, 353, 357, 368, 370, 389, 433, 435-6, 438, 446, 448; economy, 312;
  Bonds, 375; finances, 310-12;
  government, 302-3, 308-9, 316-18, 323, 334:
    crisis (*1908-9*), 326-30, 342, 344, 438;
    Executive Council, 309, 317, 321; *House of Assembly*, 311, 318, 327-9;
    responsible, 306, 309, 312, 316, 323-4, 326-30, 339, 382
New Guinea *see also* subject headings (pp. 95-218) under MacGregor, William, colonial career; Labour; Churches, Christian; Gold; Papuans; Law, ix, xiii-xiv, 23, 38, 40, 56, 95-220, 224, 230, 232, 236, 249, 256, 258, 269, 276, 286, 294-5, 298-302, 305, 336, 341-2, 347, 352-3, 357, 368-70, 380-1, 385, 431, 445; boundaries, 137, 200, 408-9; economy:
    communications, 147, 153, 156, 162, 191, 204;
    development, 106, 136, 196-9, 201, 205;
    finances, 95, 110, 120-5;
  government, 104-6, 109-10, 118-19, 124-5, 144-6, 148, 165-7;
    Armed constabulary, 128, 148, 157, 159-64, 166, 185, 196, 204, 260, 413;
    Executive Council, 132, 144-5, 183, 186, 201, 207, 209, 212, 407-8;
    Legislative Council, 144-5, 410;
    Native Regulation Board, 183;
    officers, 145-59, 242;
    patrols, 126, 128, 130, 134-5, 140-1, 155-6, 161-3, 186, 191, 197, 205, 207-8, 215, 369;
    village constables, 148, 164-6, 196, 204, 414;
  Protectorate (1884-8), 96-7, 127, 129, 139, 153, 160, 168-9, 196-7, 210, 407, 411;
  Royal Commission (1906), 347, 432
New Hebrides, 29, 67, 122, 160, 200, 381
New South Wales, 37, 301-2;
  Fiji, financial relations, 49, 52;
  free trade policy, 48;

New Guinea, relations with, 104, 116, 119, 123-5, 172, 372, 445
Newton, E., 94
New Zealand, 40, 46, 50, 52, 99, 380-1, 438;
  annexation of Fiji, 50, 52;
  reciprocity with Fiji, 42, 48-50;
  Bank, 42, 45-7, 397
Niger River, 280-2, 285, 287, 289
Nigeria, 274
Nigeria, Northern, 256, 260, 262, 266, 273, 282, 285-7, 289, 295-8, 301, 422
Nigeria, Southern, 235, 238, 256, 260, 263, 273, 282, 285, 287, 289, 296, 422, 426-7, 431
Nivani, 146
Norman, Sir Henry, 95, 105-6, 109-18, 122, 127-8, 200, 404
Normanby Island, 207
Normanton, 356
Norway, 313, 338
Nukulau, 70

Ogbomosho, 243
Ogun River, 429
Okak, 307
Oldham, 276;
  Chamber of Commerce, 291, 293
Oloke Meji, 294
Oluwole, Akigbaya, 275
Oluwole, Bishop, 295
Ommanney, Sir Montagu, 233-4, 239, 254, 274, 279-80, 284, 288, 423
Ondo, 271
Onslow, William Hillier, 4th Earl of, 233
Ophthalmia, *see* Diseases
Opium, 105, 182, 357, 379
Orokolo, 413
Orsova, 345
Oshogbo, 285, 287, 292
Ostriches, 358
O'Sullivan, J., 441
Owen Stanley Range, xiv, 38, 136
Oxford University, 361, 364
Oyekan, Oba of Lagos, 246
Oyo, 222-3, 262, 264, 271-2, 428;
  Alafin of, 221, 249, 266-7, 291

Pacific, Ocean and islands, 23, 25, 28, 31-2, 75, 168, 174, 193, 224, 352-3, 368, 373, 378-83, 447;
  phosphate islands, 379;
  Western Pacific High Commission, 96-7, 186, 200
Paget, Sir Alfred, 304-5, 373, 384-5, 448
Paget, Honor, 384-5, 387-8, 448

Palm (oil and kernels), *see* Products
Palmer, Arthur, 106-7, 112, 404
Palmer, William Waldegrave (2nd Earl of Selborne), 281
Pannaet Island (or Panaieti), 129, 174
Papua, *see* New Guinea
Papuans *see also* New Guinea; Land;
    Law, xiii, 98, 106, 120, 123, 126-7, 130, 132, 134-5, 138, 141, 144-7, 149, 154, 157, 160, 162-3, 166-7, 173, 181-3, 186-7, 195, 196-213, 240, 257, 276, 300, 337, 412;
    cargo cult, 188, 417;
    customs, 126-8, 152-3, 166, 181-5, 187-9, 193-4;
    growth individualism, 126, 129, 136, 181, 186, 188, 203-4, 379;
    lack of chiefs, 159-60, 165
Paris, 235
Parkes, Henry, 48
Pastoral industries, 346, 350, 353-4, 356-7, 359
Paternalism:
    Fiji, 84-5;
    New Guinea, 120, 130, 141, 143, 167
Patronage, 11, 42, 101, 392, 403, 433
Payne, J. A. Otonda, 222, 421, 424
Pearl-shell, 199, 206
Pearl, 394
Pearse, Reverend A., 194
Peel, Sir Robert (2nd Baronet), 437
Pender, John, 94
Peni, Ratu, 85
Pennington, A. R., 260
Peps, Dr Parker, 30
Phillip, Governor Arthur, 135
Philp, Robert, 344, 359, 441
Pita, 91
Pitprone, 390
Planters:
    Seychelles and Mauritius, 12-14, 17-18;
    Fiji, 20-1, 23-4, 30, 40-1, 46-9, 51, 58, 64, 67-8, 71, 74-81, 84-5;
    New Guinea, 106, 126, 187, 196-9, 201-5, 207, 209-10, 212;
    Lagos, 244-5;
    Queensland, 98, 107-8, 119, 418
Plymouth, 274
Police, New Guinea, 139
Polignac, Prince Jules de, 438
Polynesia and Polynesians, 25, 29, 41, 70-1, 77, 192, 197;
    rations, 75-6
Port Moresby, 96, 104, 110, 128, 130, 134, 144-7, 156-7, 159, 163, 168, 171, 173, 197-8, 209, 212, 386, 411, 420
Porto Novo, 287

Portugal, 374, 434
Poukama, 212
Poverty, xi, 2, 3, 6, 8, 10-11, 17;
    Fiji, 61; Lagos, 231, 254;
    Queensland, 444
Praslin, 14, 16
Press:
    Australian, 95, 105-6, 124-5, 145, 172, 206, 407;
    British, 206, 230, 237, 248, 274-5, 279, 283;
        Daily Chronicle, 274, 278;
        Daily Mail, 352;
        Liverpool Echo, 275;
        London *Sun*, 278;
        Times Literary Supplement, 278;
        The Times, 384;
        West African Mail, 267, 275-6, 278, 283;
    Fijian, 30, 38, 43, 72-3;
        ..*Fiji Times*, 38, 48;
    Lagos, 221, 240, 246, 248, 251-7, 269, 274-5, 280, 290, 426;
        Record, 242;
        Standard, 224, 242;
    Newfoundland, 309, 318, 323, 330, 333, 433;
        St John's *Evening Herald*, 303-4;
        Daily News, 306, 324, 329;
        Evening Telegram, 323-4, 329;
    Southern Nigeria, 426;
    St Pierre, 304
Prickly pear (*opuntia*), 358
Priestley, Professor, H. J., 444
Privy Council, 374
Products, agricultural:
    candle-nuts, 57;
    coffee, 40-1, 78-9, 198, 209, 211, 263, 358;
    copra, 40-1, 47-8, 50, 57, 60, 79, 84, 151, 158, 171, 184, 197-9, 201, 204, 206;
    cotton, 57, 220, 261, 263-4, 289-93, 295, 298;
    fruit, 40, 49, 61, 129, 198, 358-9;
    palm (oil and kernels), 220, 261, 284, 289-90, 294, 296, 431;
    rice, 70;
    rubber, 123, 198, 213, 261, 284, 289-90, 294, 358, 418, 431;
    sandalwood, 85, 155, 199, 206;
    sugar, 12, 40-1, 47-51, 56, 61, 79-80, 98, 107, 125, 129, 199, 211, 351, 358, 419;
    taro, 129;
    timber, 148, 199, 253, 261, 284, 289, 311-12, 333-4, 338-9, 359-60, 425,

431 (Lagos Forestry Ordinance, 290, 430-1);
tobacco, 57, 60, 199, 207;
yams, 129
Protection, *see* Victoria
Public works:
Fiji, 47, 51, 58;
Lagos, 226-7, 229-32, 236-7, 282;
Newfoundland, 311
Punjab, 443

Quarantine, 382;
Australian, 37, 382;
Fiji, 27-8, 35, 47, 50, 68-9, 72, 400;
Lagos, 234;
Venice Convention (1897), 234
Quebec, 308
Queen Alexandra Field Force Fund, 373-4
Queensland, *see also* subject headings (pp. 341-71) under MacGregor, William, colonial career; Labour: Law; Churches, Christian; Aboriginals; Sugar, ix, xii-xiv, 49, 51, 67, 97-9, 102-3, 107-8, 128, 162, 199-200, 208, 216, 237, 298, 301, 309, 327, 330, 341-72, 374-5, 386, 388-9, 404, 406, 409, 412, 424, 445;
economy, *agricultural policy*, 358-60;
government,
crisis (1908), 343-4;
governors, 348-9, 441;
'Irish element', 172;
New Guinea, relations with, 95, 102, 104-26, 137, 144, 149-50, 172, 175-7, 180, 182-5, 191, 199-200, 206, 213-14, 404;
parties, 343-7, 349, 440;
relations Commonwealth, 343, 346, 348-51;
responsible, 341, 348, 351-4, 360, 369, 382;
Government House, 349, 443-4;
Historical Society, 368;
Museum, 129, 368;
University, 341, 359, 361-2, 364-71, 388-9, 437, 443-5, 449
Racial attitudes, 70-2, 76, 113, 121, 141, 145, 151, 154, 159, 161-2, 181-2, 185, 198, 212, 218, 233-6, 242, 244, 249, 255, 263-4, 266-8, 275-6, 283, 307, 347, 352-3, 357, 370, 379-80, 404, 406, 409, 411, 417, 432, 447
Ra province, 59, 66, 81
Railways:
Australia, 350;
French Africa, 282, 286-7;

Germany, 377;
Lagos, 223, 226, 231-2, 243, 247, 261, 265, 269, 278-89, 292, 294-6, 429-30;
Newfoundland, 311;
Queensland, 350, 442
Ralph Hall, 318
Raratonga, 139
Ray, Cape, 332
Reay, Lord, *see* Mackay, Donald James
Receiver-General (or Treasurer) *see* MacGregor, William, colonial career; finance
Red Sea, 286
Reeve-Tucker, W. R., 238
Reeve, Henry Fenwick, xiii, 374, 446, 448
Reid, Dr, 20
Reid, G. H., 123-4, 379, 421-2, 447
Reid, Professor, 235
Reid, R. G., 311, 329
Reindeer, 338
Responsible government, ix;
Newfoundland, 306, 309, 312, 316, 323-4, 326-30, 339, 382;
Queensland, 341, 348, 351-4, 360, 369, 382
Rewa River, 78; district, 34, 81, 85
Rhodesia, Southern, 436
Richards, T. Hatton, *see* Hatton-Richards, T.
Rigo, 146, 153, 163
Ripon, Lord, 114, 116, 176, 405
Robb, Dr, 4, 6, 390
Roberts, Oliver Cromwell, 358
Robertson, Sir John, 99, 403
Robinson, Sir Hercules, 58, 82
Rochefort, Mr, 408
Rockhampton, 343
Roe, R. H., 361-2, 364-5, 443-4
Roko, 408
Roma, 356
Rome, 230, 232, 236;
Agro Romano, 236;
Pontine Marshes, 236;
St Peter's, 236
Romilly, H. H., 97, 403
Ross, Captain, 135
Ross, Ronald, xiii, 229-30, 233-4, 236, 239, 291, 423-4
Rossel Island, 128, 207
Roth, G. K., 58
Royal Mission to Deep Sea Fishermen, *see* Churches, Christian, Labrador
Rubber, *see* Products
Russia, 84

Ryan, T. J., 441

Saganai, 207
Saguane, 417
Sahara Desert, 282, 287
Saibai Island, 137, 140
St Aignan Island, 129, 206-7
St Andrews (university), x
St John, Cape, 332
St John's, 304, 307, 312, 323, 329, 333, 342
St Joseph district, 128, 176
St Mark's College, 244
St Pierre, 304-5, 333-4
Saivo, Buli, 60
Sacred Heart Society, *see* Churches, Christian, New Guinea, *Roman Catholic missionaries*
Samarai, 130, 132, 146, 152-3, 212, 411
Samoa, 67, 76, 139, 173, 380
Sandalwood, *see* Products
Santlire, Captain, 304
Sapele, 287
Sawakasa, 85
Scarborough, 254
Scotland, ix-xi, xiii, 1-12, 18, 25, 36-7, 94, 147, 230, 233, 239, 276, 299, 303-5, 313, 334, 342, 344, 346, 366, 371-8, 383-5, 387, 437;
    comparisons with England, x, 1, 3-4, 11, 235, 334;
    Scotland Departmental Committee on Whaling, 313
Scratchley, P. H., 97, 160
Sealing, *see* Fishing
Sedu, Corporal, 164
Seed, William, 39, 396
Selbourne, Earl J., *see* Palmer, William Waldegrave
Seligmann, 143
Sempill, Lord, *see* Forbes-Sempill, William Francis
Service, J., 49
Seychelles, *see also* sub headings (pp. 12-21) under MacGregor, William, colonial career; Labour, ix, 9, 12-21, 22, 24, 68, 76, 78, 103, 130, 149-50, 192, 199, 231, 299, 303, 375, 389, 416
Shaki, 243, 250
Shelford, Sir William, 280, 282, 284-5, 288
Shepstone family, 190, 417
Shipping:
    with Fiji, 47, 102;
    within Fiji, 59;
    with and within New Guinea, 104, 110, 118, 121, 126, 134-5, 137, 148, 152, 155-6, 172, 197, 201-4, 420;
    with Lagos, 224, 226, 234, 278, 290-1;
    with Newfoundland, 313;
    Australian, 106, 145, 212, 344;
    French, 178;
    German, 51
Siai, 164
Siai, 172
Sierra Leone, 220, 256, 270, 288
Simpson, William, 208
Skin diseases (yaws, tinea, scrub itch), *see* Diseases
Slavery, 13, 14, 17-18, 59, 220, 246, 251, 261, 263, 271
Smallpox, *see* Diseases
Smith, Robert Murray, 98
Smith, S., 283-4
Socialism, 345-6, 372-3, 377
Society for the Prevention of Consumption in Newfoundland, 307
Sokoto, 297
Solomon islands, 29, 67, 122, 134, 161-2, 200, 301-2, 406, 418
Sorcery, 152-3, 166, 168, 184-5, 187-8, 416-17
South Africa, 295, 438
South Australia, 348, 354
Spaniards, 142, 409
Spirits, *see* Liquor, intoxicating
Stalker, D. G., 386
Stanley, 74
Stanley, Edward Henry (15th Earl of Derby), 65
Stanley, H. M., 17, 392-3
Stanmore, Lord, *see* Gordon, Arthur
Steele, Professor B. D., 444
Stone-wigg, Reverend Canon, 175
Story, J. D., 364, 444
Stout, Sir Robert, 99, 403
Strachan, Dr, 230, 246
Strachan, John, 139
Strathcona, 440
Strathdon, 342, 388
Suakin, 286
Sudan, 94
Sudest Island, 206-7
Sugar, *see* Products
Strickland, Sir Gerald, 442
Suva, *see also* Medicine, *Central Medical School*, xii, 25, 31, 34-5, 47, 59, 70-1, 77, 92, 94, 96, 400, 448;
    Hospital, 71;
    Powder Magazine, 43;
Swahili, 18
Sweden, 338

Switzerland, 214, 216, 224, 386
Sydney, 28, 48-9, 57, 99, 103, 211, 372, 394, 407, 448; Museum, 368
Syria, 72-3, 303
Tai Levu (and Maitasiri), 61, 65, 81, 85
Tamana, 408
Tamata Creek, 208
Tarland Parish, 390
Taroom, 354-6
Tasmania, 48-9, 99, 301, 433, 442; Tasmanians, 357
Tauko (Fisherman) Island, 197
Tauputa, 129
Tauri River, 419
Taxation:
　direct
　　British, 377;
　　Fiji, xiii, 41, 53-4, 58, 80, 399; produce, 56-66, 84;
　　Germany, 377;
　　Lagos, 253, 283; tolls, 251, 261-6, 270-2, 281;
　　Mauritius, 13;
　customs dues
　　Britain, 377;
　　Fiji, 42-3, 49;
　　Lagos, 265, 294-6;
　　Newfoundland, 311, 316-17, 322;
　　New Guinea, 120, 154, 172, 175, 206, 294, 414;
　　Queensland, 351, 358
Ternate, 139
Theft, 132, 155-6, 165, 172, 184-5, 187
Theodore, E. G., 441
Thiselton Dyer, see Dyer, Thiselton
Thompson, R. W., 172-3
Thomson, B. H. (son of Archbishop of York), 53, 150-1
Thomson, Mary, see McGregor, Mary
Thursday Island, 97, 156, 158, 200, 352-3
Thurston, John Bates, 22, 35-7, 40, 43, 50-2, 54-7, 60, 63-5, 70-1, 77, 83-4, 86-8, 90, 92, 96-9, 101-3, 151, 158, 161, 395-6, 403
Thynne, A. J., 444
Tillyduke, 6, 30
Timber, see Products
Timbuctoo, 287
Tobacco, see Products
Tobermory, 442
Tokelau islands, 67
'Tom', 134
Tonga, 42, 397, 411; language, 151
Toorak, 77
Torrens system, 209

Torres Strait, 200; islanders, 143, 352-3, 442
Towie, 4, 387-8
Townsville, 344, 357, 447
Trade (and traders):
　in Labrador, 336-7;
　in Lagos, 220-3, 229, 244-5, 262-7, 270, 274, 280, 282, 286-7, 289-90, 295-7, 311, 427;
　in Newfoundland, 310, 312, 315, 322, 436;
　in New Guinea, 126, 128-9, 145, 147, 155, 168, 186, 199, 209, 212;
　American, 378;
　Australian, 23, 48-9, 58;
　British, 378;
　Fijian, 49-50, 53;
　German, 377-8;
　Japanese, 378;
　Pacific, 381;
　Queensland, 345
Trepang, see Beche-de-mer
Trinidad, 18, 254
Tripoli, 262, 282
Tubetube, 124
Tugeri tribe, 139-40
Tugwell, Bishop, 294-5
Tunis, 286
Tupper, Sir Charles, 326, 438
Turkey, 439
Turner, Sir George, 123-4, 421-2

United Empire Trade League, 123
United Kingdom, see Britain
United States of America, ix, 2, 217, 292, 300, 307, 312, 314, 315-26, 330-1, 338, 375, 378, 380, 389, 435-6, 439, 443
Universities, see also Aberdeen, Anderson's, Cambridge, Edinburgh, Glasgow, Oxford, Queensland, St Andrews, x, 25, 36, 364-5

Vaccination:
　Fiji, 27-8, 35, 70, 75, 228, 399-400;
　New Guinea, 194-5, 417;
　Lagos, 228, 237-8
Vanamai, 415
Vanua Levu, 32
Vatorata, 415
Vaughan, Cardinal, 177
Vea, 413
Veifa, 414
Venereal disease, see Diseases
Venice, 234
Venn, Henry, 425
Verjus, Reverend Stanislas Henry, 168, 175-6

Victoria:
  Fiji, *annexation of*, 53
    reciprocity with, 42, 48-52, 94;
  New Guinea:
    protection policy, 48;
    relations with, 172, 372, 445;
  Tasmania, *reciprocity with*, 49
Victoria, Queen, 124-5, 274, 437
Vine, Sir Somers, 123
Viti Levu, 27, 30-1, 40, 76, 81
Viviga, 408
Vogel, Sir Julius, 50

Wai, Totini, 132-3
Waimanu River, 78
Walker, F. W., 415-17
Wallington, Mr, 446
War, *see also* Military:
  Fiji *'little war'*, 27, 30-1, 40, 130,
    395, 407;
  First World, 348, 364, 372-4, 377-8,
    384, 445-7;
  Lagos, 143, 221-2, 258, 264;
  Labrador, 337;
  New Guinea, 126-7, 129-30, 133-4,
    139-41, 166, 168, 185, 203, 208,
    213, 410, 413;
  South African (Boer), 295;
  Southern Nigeria, 235;
  Sudan, 94;
  U.S.A. crisis, 318
Ward, William Humble (2nd Earl of
  Dudley), 442
Warren, W. R., 328
Warri, 287
Warrior Island, 137
Waterfield, O. C., 392
Warwick High School, 367
Washington, 300, 369
Watt, Reverend John, 4, 6-7, 388
Watt, Reverend William, 388
Wedau, 179
Welfare, 26, 52, 54, 58, 106, 255,
  337, 352
Wentworth, W. C., 145
Wereweri (Mullens Harbour), 191
Western Australia, 301, 404, 407, 422,
  442

West Indies, 114, 187, 198, 230, 282,
  417, 434
Whaling, *see* Fishing
Whitehall, *see* Britain, *Colonial
  policy* and *Colonial Office*
Whiteway, Sir W., 323
Whooping cough, *see* Diseases
Wilkinson, D., 57, 59, 77
Williams, Sir Ralph, 327
Williams, Sapara, 246, 252, 257, 425-6
Wilson, Woodrow, 379, 446-7
Wingfield, E., 55
Winter, F. J., 89-90, 130, 132, 144,
  150, 181-2, 407-8, 413
Winter, J. S., 329
Wodehouse, John (1st Earl of Kim-
  berley), 11, 27
Women, *see also* Diseases, venereal:
  adultery, 184, 187, 215, 416;
  agricultural labour, 204;
  College, *University of Queensland*,
    444;
  marriage, 81, 105, 188-90, 246, 425;
  polygamy, 26, 263;
  status, 26;
  New Guinea, 164, 185-6;
  Lagos, *Ladies League*, 233, 423;
  Queensland, *Aboriginals*, 355, 357
Woodlark Island, 167, 186, 203, 206-7
Woodruff, Mr, 150, 410
Woods, G.A., 42-3, 397
Working-class, *see* Class
Wriford, G., 161, 164, 413

Xenophobia, xii

Yanuca Lailai, and Yanuca Levu, 69-
  70
Yasawas, *see* Ba
Yesufu Shitta Bey, 248
Yoruba, 220, 222-3, 240, 242, 250, 258,
  260
Yule Island, 156, 168, 175, 177, 412
Yule Range, 138

Zanzibar, 14
Zephania, 85-92
Zululand, 182, 190, 417, 432